# The History of the Fourteenth Battalion A.I.F.

LIEUT.-GEN. SIR JOHN MONASH, G.C.M.G., K.C.B., V.D.

# The History of the Fourteenth Battalion, A.I.F.

Being the Story of the Vicissitudes of an Australian Unit during the Great War.

By

NEWTON WANLISS

with a Foreword by
LIEUTENANT-GENERAL SIR JOHN MONASH.

The Naval & Military Press Ltd

Published by
**The Naval & Military Press Ltd**
5 Riverside, Brambleside, Bellbrook
Industrial Estate, Uckfield, East Sussex,
TN22 1QQ England
Tel: +44 (0) 1825 749494
Fax: +44 (0) 1825 765701
www.naval-military-press.com
www.military-genealogy.com
www.militarymaproom.com

*In reprinting in facsimile from the original, any imperfections are inevitably reproduced and the quality may fall short of modern type and cartographic standards.*

DEDICATED

to

THE MEMORY OF OUR FALLEN COMRADES

*"Nor shall your glory be forgot  
While Fame her record keeps."*

# CONTENTS

|  | Page |
|---|---|
| Foreword | ix. |
| Author's Preface | xii. |

### 1914.

| Chapters. |  | Page |
|---|---|---|
| I. | The Outbreak of War and Formation of the Battalion (June 30 to December 17) | 1 |
| II. | Personnel and Voyage to Egypt (December 18 to January 31) | 7 |

### 1915.

| III. | Egypt (January 31 to April 24) | 12 |
|---|---|---|
| IV. | The Baptism of Blood (April 25 to April 30) | 18 |
| V. | Steele's Post and Pope's Hill (April 27 to April 29) | 29 |
| VI. | Early Days on the Peninsula (May 1 to May 18) | 33 |
| VII. | The Great Turkish Assault and the First Australian V.C. (May 19) | 41 |
| VIII. | Last Days on Courtney's Post (May 20 to May 31) | 46 |
| IX. | Reserve Gully (June 1 to August 6) | 50 |
| X. | Battle of Abdel-Rahman Bair (August 7-8) | 54 |
| XI. | Miscellaneous Duties (August 9 to August 13) | 65 |
| XII. | Attacks on Hill 60 (August 20 to September 2) | 68 |
| XIII. | Durrant's Post and the Evacuation (September 3 to December 31) | 75 |
| XIV. | Sidelights on the Peninsula | 85 |

### 1916.

| XV. | The Birth of the 4th Division (January 1 to May 31) | 92 |
|---|---|---|
| XVI. | Arrival in France (June 1 to June 10) | 101 |

## Contents.

| | | |
|---|---|---|
| XVII. | Initial Days in France (June 11 to June 30) | 107 |
| XVIII. | First Trench Raid of the 4th Division (July 2-3) | 111 |
| XIX. | The German Counter-Raid (July 3) | 125 |
| XX. | An Interlude (July 4 to August 5) | 130 |
| XXI. | Pozieres Ridge (August 6 to August 16) | 134 |
| XXII. | Mouquet Farm (August 17 to August 31) | 151 |
| XXIII. | Care and Distribution of the Wounded | 158 |
| XXIV. | Flanders, and Return to the Somme (September 1 to December 14) | 162 |
| XXV. | A New Regime (December 15 to December 31) | 170 |

### 1917.

| | | |
|---|---|---|
| XXVI. | Stormy Trench (January 1 to February 7) | 174 |
| XXVII. | Preparation and Training (February 8 to April 8) | 181 |
| XXVIII. | The Battle of Bullecourt (April 9 to April 11) | 188 |
| XXIX. | Recuperation (April 12 to May 29) | 213 |
| XXX. | Messines (May 30 to June 26) | 218 |
| XXXI. | Ploegsteert and Gapaard (June 27 to August 31) | 225 |
| XXXII. | The Battle of Polygon Wood (September 1 to September 30) | 233 |
| XXXIII. | Passchendaele (October 1 to November 15) | 249 |
| XXXIV. | The Last War Winter (November 16 to February 28) | 256 |

### 1918.

| | | |
|---|---|---|
| XXXV. | Huburterne (March 1 to April 24) | 263 |
| XXXVI. | Villers-Bretonneux (April 25 to May 26) | 274 |
| XXXVII. | The Holocaust at Allonville (May 27 to May 31) | 284 |
| XXXVIII. | The Battalion's Second Raid, and Other Matters (June 1 to June 25) | 292 |
| XXXIX. | The Battle of Hamel (June 26 to July 30) | 302 |
| XL. | The Battle of Amiens (July 31 to August 20) | 314 |
| XLI. | The Battle of the Hindenburg Outpost Line (August 21 to November 11) | 335 |
| XLII. | Reflections and Conclusion | 352 |

Contents. vii.

## APPENDICES.

(A)—The Battalion's Roll of Honour .............. 357
(B)—Decorations and Other Honours ........... 386
(C)—A.I.F. and Fourth Brigade Casualties ......... 391
(D)—British Empire War Statistics ............. 392
(E)—Some A.I.F. Statistics ................... 393
(F)—Fourteenth Battalion Battle Honours ......... 394
(G)—List of Brothers Killed in the Fourteenth Battalion 395
(H)—List of Fourteenth Battalion Details ......... 396
(I) —Fourteenth Battalion, A.M.F. ............... 397
(J) —Rations in France .................... 398

## MAPS.

1.—Broadmeadows ....................... 5
2.—Quinn's Post .......................... 28
    (Drawn from a sketch supplied by Capt. R. W. Jones, M.C., M.M.)
3.—Courtney's and Adjoining Posts ........... 34
4.—Capt. Jacka's V.C. Exploit ............... 43
    (Adapted from maps in Australian Official War History, Vol. II.)
5.—The Battle of Abdel-Rahman Bair .......... 56
    (Published by permission from a model made by Mr. Justice Ferguson.)
6.—Locality Map of the Gallipoli Peninsula ....... 77
7.—Locality Map of Egypt .................. 93
8.—Battalion's Route through the Mediterranean Sea . 102
9.—Battalion's Route through France ........... 106
10.—Batttalion Trench Raid of July 2-3, 1916 ...... 122
    (Drawn from a sketch supplied by Capt. Fred. Anderson, M.M.)
11.—The Battle of Pozieres Ridge .............. 136
12.—The Battle of Bullecourt ................ 190
13.—The Battle of Messines ................. 217
14.—The Battle of Polygon Wood ............. 237
15.—The Battle of Amiens .................. 316
16.—The Battle of the Hindenburg Outpost Line .... 338

viii.                    *Contents.*

## PHOTOGRAPHS.

### PERSONS.

| | | |
|---|---|---|
| 1.—Lieutenant-General Sir John Monash, G.C.M.G., K.C.B., V.D. ................ | | Frontispiece |
| 2.—Lieut.-Colonel R. E. Courtney ...... | facing page | xiv. |
| 3.—Lieut. Colonel C. M. M. Dare ...... | ,, | 32 |
| 4.—Lieut.-Colonel J. H. Peck ........ | ,, | 32 |
| 5.—Lieut.-Colonel H. A. Crowther, D.S.O. | ,, | 32 |
| 6.—Chaplain-Captain Andrew Gillison, M.I.D. ........................ | ,, | 130 |
| 7.—Capt. Albert Jacka ............ | ,, | 96 |
| 8.—Capt. Harold B. Wanliss ........ | ,, | 96 |
| 9.—Capt. Reginald W. Jones ........ | ,, | 96 |
| 10.—Sgt. W. H. Boyes ............. | ,, | 130 |
| 11.—Sgt. C. J. Clarke ............. | ,, | 130 |

### PLACES.

| | | |
|---|---|---|
| 12.—Ribemont-sur-Ancre ............ (Supplied by Pte. J. H. Gifford.) | ,, | 194 |
| 13.—Men of Fourteenth Battalion studying a Raised Plan of Messines ........ | ,, | 226 |
| 14.—Deconinck Farm (Messines) ...... | ,, | 194 |
| 15.—Fourteenth Battalion Men at China Wall .................... | ,, | 290 |
| 16.—Fourteenth Battalion Men under Cover of Two Captured Shelters at Battle of Polygon Wood ............... | ,, | 322 |
| 17.—"Smart Set" Concert Party in Barn at Allonville .................. | ,, | 322 |
| Index ........................... | | 401 |

### ERRATA.

On page 28, 4th line, under map of Quinn's Post, the name "Thompdon" should read "Thompson."

# FOREWORD

By LIEUTENANT-GENERAL SIR JOHN MONASH.

UPON the outbreak of the Great War, the Commonwealth Government offered, as Australia's contribution to the Imperial Armies, one Division and one Light Horse Brigade, fully equipped for war. That was thought to be the largest fighting force that Australian resources could maintain in the field for a war of even short duration. None would then have believed that the ultimate performance of this young nation would grow to more than five times its initial undertaking, and for a war lasting for more than four years. But the rush to the colors was so prompt, so widespread and so enthusiastic, that the Government speedily took the decision that at least one additional Infantry Brigade and one additional Light Horse Brigade could be furnished at once, from the man-power which became available.

Thus was born the 4th Australian Infantry Brigade. It fell to my lot to be accorded the honor and the responsibility of organising and training this Brigade, and of leading it for the first two years of the War. In its composition, the 4th Brigade had the unique distinction, among all the fifteen Infantry Brigades ultimately put into the field, of being the only All-Australian unit in the Australian Imperial Force. For its four Battalions were raised, and regularly recruited throughout the whole period of the War, from all of the six States of the Commonwealth. The 15th Battalion came from Queensland and Tasmania, the 16th from South and West Australia, the 13th wholly from New South Wales, and the 14th wholly from Victoria.

The 4th Brigade, unconscious of its great destiny, entered upon methodical war training, first at Broadmeadows, in Victoria, and, later, on the sands of Egypt. Although not privileged to sail with the first convoy of Australian troops, it aspired to rank as an equal beside its three senior Infantry Brigades in all that the fortune of war might bring. It was not disappointed. By intense concentration upon the work of war training, the Brigade was deemed fit to participate in that great adventure of the Gallipoli landing. In the hectic days that followed the landing, the 4th Brigade held the key position on the Peninsula, and valiantly defended it against many imperious assaults. It led the advance to Sari Bair of August, 1915, and it had the distinction of being the only Australian Brigade which gained extensive ground during the Dardanelles campaign. Its subsequent services—in the defence of the Canal zone in Egypt; on the Sinai desert; in its successful occupation and active defence of the Armentieres sector in France in the first battle of the Somme; at Pozieres; at Bullecourt; at the operations of Messines and of Passchendaele: at the defence of Hebuterne; in the great victories of Hamel, Amiens and Hargicourt—are one long record of glorious and successful endeavor. No other Infantry Brigade of the A.I.F. dare challenge the reputation of the 4th for its first rank soldierly prowess and performance, or for its brilliant record of battle honors.

The 14th Battalion, which helped to compose this wonderful fighting force, numbered originally a thousand of the very flower of the youth of the City of Melbourne. It counted in its ranks many public school men of fine morale and physique, and was officered by splendid men of high character and capacity. It was subsequently maintained, during four years of war, by reinforcements drawn from the areas of its first enlistment, to the number of several times its original complement. It bore, throughout its history, its full share of the labors, the hardships, the sacrifices, the fighting record and the honors which made up the story of the 4th Brigade.

It is right and proper that the tale of this famous Battalion should be written for posterity. The tradition which it did so much to create will surely be an inspiration to the youth of Australia in all the days to come. To set himself the task of becoming the historian of this Battalion has been the opportunity of one who has given, as his sacrifice to the cause of King and Country, a gallant and dearly beloved son who was an ornament to the office which he held, and an example to all whom he led.

This book is therefore not merely a tribute to the memory of a gallant soldier who fell in battle, and of the comrades who shared his fortunes, but, as a contribution to an illustrious page in the history of Australia, is also a labor of devoted service to her people.

It will also, for other reasons, lay claim to the interest and admiration of every reader. In its completeness, in its accuracy, in the painstaking researches which went to its making, in its scholarly diction and its vivid portrayal, it is unrivalled by any other war book of its kind.

The Author, although fated not to be a participant in the happenings of which he has written, has brought to his task a capacity for historical research, for the handling of extensive documentary material, with discrimination and judgment, and for lucid exposition in graceful periods, which have rarely been equalled in the literature of the Great War.

It is small wonder that I should esteem it a special privilege to have been accorded the opportunity of commending to the reader this volume, its high purpose, and the arresting story which it unfolds.

—JOHN MONASH, Lieut.-General.

# PREFACE

THE Author, though not a member of the 14th Battalion, was appointed by the Committee of the Association of that Battalion to undertake the compilation of this history, for the obvious reason that there was not anyone connected with the unit who had the time available for the task. The lack of knowledge on the writer's part, both of the terrain which was the scene of the Battalion's activities and of the personnel of the unit, had to be supplemented by much personal effort, as well as by a most voluminous correspondence. All official and private diaries obtainable, bearing either directly or indirectly on the story of the Battalion, have been perused, and further information has been gathered from both the written experiences of ex-combatants, and personal conversations with them. Every effort has been made and much time spent to obtain accuracy, whilst all evidence has been carefully weighed and sifted. The Author, however, is not responsible for occasional and unavoidable official or other errors which he has not had the means or opportunity of checking.

Whilst primarily the history of a unit, this record is indirectly a tribute to the A.I.F., of which that unit was but a component part. It has been written with an outlook on the future. As the centuries pass, there will arise a great craving in Australia for exact and positive information as to her participation in the World War, and the marvellous deeds performed therein by her virile sons. Posterity, accordingly, has a right to expect that the stories of the various units comprising the A.I.F. should be written with an essential completeness of detail at a time when facts are obtainable—this point of view appears to have been largely overlooked. In addition, it is also a debt that Australia owes to the A.I.F. that its individual exploits should be accurately and fully recorded. These considerations coincide with the earnest desire of the writer that future generations of his countrymen should look to the deeds of the A.I.F. for inspiration—that the patriotism, the heroism, and the virile manhood which inspired the Anzacs should permeate their descendants for all time, and that the

## Preface. xiii.

latter should endeavor to build up, on solid foundations, a nation worthy of the men who died and suffered so willingly and so freely for it. These reasons are accordingly an excuse for the fullness of detail with which this work has been written, and, if its production helps to further those ideals, it will have accomplished its purpose. It can be emphatically stated that its object has not been to glorify war, the abomination and futility of which are too obvious to require more than a passing reference.

This book could not have been written without the co-operation and the assistance of others, and the author finds it difficult to adequately express his gratitude for the unselfish aid willingly and gratuitously given by many generous and able collaborators. The Author is deeply indebted to Lieut.-General Sir John Monash, whose library, records, and papers were unreservedly placed at his disposal, and who wrote the Foreword which opens this history; to Mr. C. E. W. Bean, the Australian official historian of the war, who spared neither time nor trouble, and lent notes and maps, besides advising, suggesting, and also revising some of the proofs; to Mr. A. W. Bazley, who revised the roll of honor and supplied many details about the Battalion dead; to Mr. Chas. Barrett, organiser of these unit histories, who revised the first nine chapters of this work; to Mr. Alan S. Murray, who has been responsible for the making of all the maps; to Major J. L. Treloar, Messrs. A. G. Pretty and H. O. McAllan (of the Australian War Memorial); to Capt. W. Mackintosh and Pte. E. L. Darcy (of Base Records); and to my wife, who typed the majority of the chapters.

For details of the Gallipoli campaign, I am indebted for information (among others) to the following combatants:—To Capt. H. G. Loughran (R.M.O.) and Cpl. Chas. Smith (author of the poem "Withdrawn" in the 13th chapter), who both wrote a full detailed account of their experiences throughout the whole campaign; to Captains F. H. Wright, D. R. Macdermid, H. N. Boyle, and Reg. Jones (who, inter alia, prepared the draft of the sketch-map of Quinn's Post, in Chapter IV.), all of whom gave accounts of engagements in which they participated; to Lieuts. L. Luscombe and Les. Bain, Sgt. T. A. Smith and Pte. D. H. Fraser, who gave details of the August. 1915, fighting; also to Lt.-Col. C. M. M. Dare, for the use of his diary dealing with the whole campaign.

For details of the various campaigns in France, the writer is indebted (among others) to the following members of the unit for the use of their diaries:—Lt.-Col. C. M. M. Dare,

Chaplains J. L. Cope and F. W. Rolland, the late Capt. H. B. Wanliss, Lieut. E. J. Rule (an invaluable diary), Lieut. W. P. Boland, Sgt. Les. Guppy, Sgt. W. Groves, the late Cpl. J. J. Moriarty, Cpl. W. H. Rutherford, Ptes. J. H. Gifford, H. A. Middleton, and Cpl. Chas. Smith for his excellent and detailed written account of his experiences in France. The following have also been of material assistance. mostly in the form of literary contributions of their experiences, some having given details of various engagements; L/Cpl. A. J. A'Court, Capt. F. Anderson, Pte. J. Anderton, Lieut. Les. Bain, Capt. W. R. M. Beamond, Lieut. N. J. Bear, Cpl. E. E. Bishop, Sgt. J. C. Blair, Lieut. F. H. Boyes, Sgt. W. H. Boyes, Sgt. J. A. Brotchie, Lieut. A. R. Bruford, Pte. A. Cameron, Lieut. E. R. Chubb, Sgt. C. J. Clarke, Cpl. J. H. Clements, Lieut.-Col. H. A. Crowther, Pte. Geo. Curnick, Pte. J. T. Dadsey, C.S.M. A. C. Dalitz, Lieut. S. d'Arengo, Lieut. G. F. Davies, Pte. Alan Downie, Sgt. David Drummond, Pte. L. C. Dunphy, Pte. W. H. Ericson, L/Cpl. H. C. Finger, Major W. M. A. Fletcher, Pte. D. H. Fraser, Lieut. J. Garcia, Lieut. Cyril George, Pte. J. T. Gifford, Lieut. O. C. D. Gower, Cpl. J. Grieves, Lieut. T. H. Griffith, Sgt. L. Guppy, Sgt. Raymond Hare, Capt. R. E. Hayes, Lieut. A. T. Harvey, Lieut. E. P. Hill, Pte. R. J. Hyatt, 2nd-Lieut. F. G. Hyett, Capt. A. Jacka, Lieut. H. B. Jackson, Major C. M. Johnston, Capt. Reg. Jones, Pte. E. L. Kohls, Pte. V. Lacon, Lieut. F. T. Larter, Pte. H. Lee, Capt. D. R. Macdermid, Pte. J. W. Malseed, Sgt. C. H. Mayer, Sgt. Allan McDonald, Pte. F. G. Miller, Capt. J. A. Mitchell, Sgt. D. Mortimer, L/Cpl. Percy Muir, Lieut. A. J. Naylor, the late Lieut.-Col. J. H. Peck, Sgt. A. Rich, Sgt. T. A. Rose, Cpl. W. H. Rutherford, Lieut. R. E. Sanders, Sgt. H R. Scott, Sgt. L. Shelton, Pte. A. A. Stevens, Capt. Hugh Trumble, Major. W. R. Wadsworth, Lieut. G. F. Wilson, Cpl. L. Webb, and Capt. R. C. Winn. The Author also is under special obligation to Mr. C. E. W. Bean, for permission to use maps appearing in his official history; to Lieut.-Col. J. M. A. Durrant (15th Battalion); to Capt. David Dunworth, of the 15th Battalion, who wrote an account of his experiences at Bullecourt; to Lieut. A. R. Bruford, who organised meetings of ex-14th Battalion combatants at his house; and to Cpl. Chas. Smith, who typed some of the chapters, as well as the roll of honor, and who is solely responsible for the excellent index which completes this work. Regret is expressed for any whose names have been inadvertently omitted.

N. W.

18th January, 1929.

Lieut.-Col. R. E. Courtney, C. B.

# The History of the 14th Battalion

## CHAPTER I.

### THE OUTBREAK OF WAR AND FORMATION OF THE BATTALION.

#### 1914—June 30 to December 17.

On the 30th day of June, 1914, the Australian press published a European cablegram describing the the brutal assassination by a fanatic called Prinzip of the heir to the throne of the Austrian-Hungarian Empire, the Archduke Francis Ferdinand, at Serajevo, in Bosnia. The average Australian is essentially politically self-centred, and beyond the levelling of some expletives upon the assassin—for assassination is absolutely foreign to the Australian character—but cursory notice was taken of the incident throughout the Commonwealth. That incident, however, occurring in such a distant land, and apparently so unconnected with Australia or its politics, was to have a tremendous influence upon its history, for out of it arose the series of political events which culminated in the greatest war in history.

*Assassination of Austrian Archduke.*

It is not necessary to describe the political moves that brought on the war, but within less than six weeks of the assassination a state of war existed between the great Central European Empires of Germany and Austria-Hungary on the one side and Great Britain, France, Russia, Servia, Montenegro and Belgium on the other. History will probably ultimately throw the blame for the origin of the war upon the ambition of the German Kaiser, whose obsession to pose as a great world conqueror is evident to all who have closely studied his character. Saturated in militarism, intoxicated by the

*Outbreak of War.*

*The Kaiser.*

remembrance of the glories and successes of the German armies under his grandfather, the war for which he had dreamt and planned for a quarter of a century was probably inevitable from the moment that he ascended the throne, and its outbreak merely a matter of time.

**His Character.** The Kaiser was a man of varied abilities, but, unfortunately, of unstable and neurotic temperament. His attainments were brilliant rather than solid, and he approached great political questions from the standpoint of the theorist rather than from that of a business man, his foreign policy in particular being indicative of meddlesomeness rather than foresight. His judgment, too, was blurred by an excessively sanguine temperament. He was determined to exploit the patriotism, blood and industry of his people in order to place himself on the highest political pinnacle ever attained by mortal man; and, soaked in the optimism of the gambler, he was prepared to risk his throne and the future of his country for the chance of success in the dazzling dream of a world empire which he had conjured up.

**Australia Participates in War.** The news of the participation of the British Empire in the war roused the people of the Australian Commonwealth like a political galvanic shock. Australia was far from the scene of hostilities and not under any political obligation to enter the conflict at all, but there was no hesitation on the part either of the people or the government as to their course of action. Their course was clear; the whole community was throbbing with patriotism, and the government of the mother country was offered Australian troops for service abroad. On the acceptance of the offer recruiting began without delay.

**Recruiting.** Alone of the English-speaking communities the Commonwealth had adopted compulsory military training, and although its adoption had been less than four years in operation a substantial number of youths had, at the outbreak of war, some knowledge of the elements of military life.*

---

*There was not a large proportion of trainees among the original members of the 14th Battalion, but many of them joined the battalion later as reinforcements. The compulsory training system also had its effects on the A.I.F. in (a) previous training of officers; (b) the provision of a supply of guns, equipment, rifles, clothing, etc., available and up-to-date; and (c) the machinery under the compulsory training system was quickly adapted to raising and organising the A.I.F.

The depots were soon crowded with recruits, and the first contingent of about 20,000 men, consisting of a complete division and a brigade of light horse, was soon raised. As it was realised that the war was to be waged on a gigantic scale, the Commonwealth authorities notified the British Government that a further body of troops (including an additional infantry brigade) would be despatched. This brigade was known later as the 4th Brigade. It was a composite brigade, the various battalions being raised in different States, the 13th in New South Wales, the 14th in Victoria, the 15th in Queensland and Tasmania, and the 16th in Western and South Australia. This history deals with the story of the 14th Battalion, the Victorian unit of the 4th Infantry Brigade of the A.I.F. The brigadier selected to command the new brigade was a Victorian citizen soldier, Colonel John Monash, V.D., the greatest and most capable soldier who ever commanded an Australian infantry brigade. Colonel Monash chose Lieutenant-Colonel R. E. Courtney, V.D., as C.O. of the 14th Battalion. Colonel Courtney was another citizen soldier who had devoted much time to soldiering before the war. His appointment to the 14th was dated September 19, 1914, and he immediately set about forming his battalion staff. On September 21 Major H. M. Young, V.D., was appointed quartermaster, and Captain C. M. M. Dare adjutant. Two ex-British non-commissioned officers, now members of the Australian Instructional Staff, were respectively appointed regimental sergeant-major and regimental quartermaster-sergeant.

*4th Brigade.*

*14th Battalion.*

*Col. Courtney.*

A temporary battalion headquarters was established at No. 178 Collins Street, Melbourne, and during the last few days of September the staff met daily at the new headquarters, making active preparations for the enrolment of 1000 men to form the personnel of the new battalion. Officers† were selected from those who had volunteered for active service, and, on October 1, camp lines were laid for the new battalion at the training depot at Broadmeadows, at that time a scene of tremendous activity, and the officers chosen as company commanders selected 1070 men from among those they had been training in the depots. Men were organised into

*Selection of Officers.*

*Camp at Broadmeadows.*

---

†Most of the original 14th Battalion officers (except the four Duntroon graduates who joined in November, 1914) had been officers in A.M.F. units before the war.

companies, half-companies and sections, and acting N.C.O.'s were appointed. October 1, 1914 was virtually the birthday of the new battalion—the day when it became a live unit.

**Fine Type of Men Chosen.** The men chosen were in the main a very fine stamp, for, owing to the large number of recruits in the depots, the officers of the 4th Brigade had a wide choice and could, and did, pick the cream of the recruits, with the result that the 4th Brigade contained a body of men whose physique was rarely equalled even in the A.I.F.

The advantages of compulsory training was now making itself felt, and the foresight of those politicians who had initiated the measure was being rewarded.

**Training.** During the month of October training began in earnest. Little bodies of men clad in blue suits of dungarees and white linen hats were busy learning squad and company drill under their officers, whilst attention was given to route marching, field training, skirmishing, signalling, first aid, physical drill and rifle practice at the butts at Williamstown. Classes of instruction for non-commissioned officers were formed, and an examination took place at the completion of the class, after which the first substantive promotions were made.

After rifles, equipment and clothing had been issued (including the famous felt hats afterwards so well known in France) the men began to feel like soldiers. Colonel Courtney had few equals in Australia at training a battalion and his efforts now produced very good results, especially as all ranks were so keen to learn. On October 20 proceedings were varied by a 20-mile march to Melbourne and back, the eight companies marching through the city with fixed bayonets, cheered by a large and enthusiastic crowd. It was evident that the recruits had made great progress in their short period of training.

On the following day a very successful battalion sports was held. F Company won the presentation cup mainly owing to the fine performances of Private W. Isbel, of Ararat.

About the middle of October the 1st Division, which had been raised, armed and equipped in a remarkably short space of time left Australia for the front, and the 14th Battalion moved up into the 2nd Brigade camping ground, and a few days subsequently was joined by its sister battalions, the 13th, 15th and 16th from their respective States, the intention being that the units of the brigade should concentrate in Melbourne for brigade training prior to embarkation abroad. The battalion field training days became more frequent and much strenuous marching was undertaken.

A pleasant interlude to the training took place on Sunday, December 13, when the citizens of St. Kilda presented the battalion with regimental and King's colours.
**Presentation** The ceremony entailed a battalion entrain-
**of Colours.** ment from Broadmeadows to the St. Kilda railway station and a march to the St. Kilda Cricket Ground, where the men were entertained by the citizens at lunch. A march was then made to the esplanade where all formed up in line to receive the Governor-General (Sir Ronald Munro Ferguson. After the colours had been uncased and consecrated by the regimental chaplain (Padre Gillison) they were presented by the Governor-General to Lieutenants W. H. Hamilton and B. Combes. At the conclusion of the ceremony the battalion marched back to the city. The colours were subsequently placed in St. George's Presbyterian Church, St. Kilda, for safe keeping.

The time for embarkation was now rapidly approaching. Much keenness had been shown among all ranks, and there had been many individual applications from men in the depot to join the battalion during the weeks prior to embarkation. The camp life had not been unpleasant. The work had been hard but it had become interesting. Food was wholesome and plentiful, and Melbourne was accessible to those who had leave. On Sundays and holidays the public swarmed out in thousands to the camp to see their soldier relatives.

Old friendships were renewed and new ones formed, and many sweethearts made tender promises one to another. The continuous training too was having its effect upon the personnel of the 4th Brigade, which, hardened by exercise and its confidence strengthened by discipline, was by this time as fine a body of men as ever left Australia.

**Brigade Marches Through Melbourne.** On December 17 the brigade, in marching order, marched through the streets of Melbourne, setting out from Broadmeadows at 7 a.m. All traffic was stopped in Melbourne for the occasion and the roadway was fenced off by barriers. The city was crowded; everyone knew that the brigade was on the eve of embarkation, and the public turned out in thousands to give it a farewell. The Governor-General and State Governor took their stand at the saluting base near Parliament House and watched the march past. Each battalion was preceded by its pioneers and followed by its transport waggons. Preceded by Colonel Monash and his staff, company after company of the various battalions (the 13th leading) swept through the streets "their gleaming bayonets forming a sparkling crest to the khaki river." The scene was stirring and impressive to a degree. The men marched magnificently and their bearing was that of veterans. The spectators felt proud of the brigade and were convinced that the honour of Australia was safe in its hands. "The troops are magnificent," said the Governor-General. "Nothing could have been finer." The march was a fitting finale to months of training, and an augury of the war record of the brigade.‡

---

‡Full accounts of this march appear in the "Argus" and "Age" of December 18, 1914.

## CHAPTER II.

### PERSONNEL AND VOYAGE TO EGYPT.

#### 1914-1915—December 18 to January 31.

Preparations for Embarkation.
The five days subsequent to the march through the city were devoted to preparations for embarkation; sea kit bags were issued, rifles labelled, transport vehicles embarked and every preparation made to enable the battalion to depart at short notice. Before dealing with the voyage it will be necessary to glance at the personnel of the battalion. Immediately prior to embarkation the officers were as follow:—

#### REGIMENTAL STAFF.

Commissioned Officers of Battalion.
Lieut.-Col. R. E. Courtney, V.D. (commanding); Major J. Adams (second in command); Capt. C. M. M. Dare (adjutant); Capt. G. H. Loughran (medical officer); Major H. M. Young, V.D. (quartermaster); Capt. A. Gillison (chaplain).

#### COMPANIES.

A Company—Major R. Rankine, Lieut. J. G. T. Hanby, 2nd-Lieut. K. G. W. Crabbe. B Company—Capt. W. R. Hoggart, Lieut. H. N. Boyle, 2nd-Lieut. H. R. Harris. C Company—Capt. T. H. Steel, 2nd-Lieut. W. E. Groome, 2nd-Lieut. V. C. Cumberland. D Company—Capt. C. E. Connelly, Lieut. W. H. Hamilton, 2nd-Lieut. D. L. K. Richardson. E Company—Capt. F. H. Wright, 2nd-Lieut. C. L. Giles, 2nd-Lieut. A. R. Cox. F Company—Capt. W. C. N. Baldock, Lieut. B. Combes, 2nd-Lieut. L. E. Ball. G Company—Lieut. C. R. Hutton, Lieut. A. H. Curwen-Walker, 2nd-Lieut. R. Warren. H Company—Lieut. A. Henry, 2nd-Lieut. R. W. Graham, 2nd-Lieut. O. C. W. Fuhrmann. Machine Gun Section—Lieut. J. B. Rutland. Transport Officer—Lieut. C. R. M. Cox. Signalling Officer—Lieut. G. H. Clark.

Lieuts. Boyle, Hamilton, Combes and Curwen-Walker had been trained at the Royal Military College, Duntroon.*

---

*The normal course at Duntroon is for four years, but for the war period this term was reduced and the above officers were allowed to graduate in time to join the 14th Battalion in November, 1914.

Lieut. A. R. Cox was the only original officer who served practically right through the war with the battalion. Major Rankine subsequently became C.O. of the 39th Battalion, and Lieuts. Giles and Hutton joined the same unit. Capt. Dare ultimately became for a time C.O., and Lieut. Fuhrmann second in command of the 14th Battalion. Capts. Hoggart, Connelly and Gillison and Lieuts. Crabbe, Harris, Groom, Hamilton, Curwen-Walker, Warren and Rutland were killed or died of wounds during operations on the Peninsula, which took a heavy toll of the battalion's manhood. The original battalion officer ranged from excellent to indifferent, for in every battalion, both among officers and other ranks, there is a handful which is temperamentally unsuited for soldiering and is quickly found out by the dangers and hardships of such a war. The battalion at this time was formed on the old eight company basis. Subsequently, in Egypt, all battalions in the A.I.F. were organised on a four company basis. The N.C.O.'s and privates of the battalion were almost all natives or residents of Victoria, the latter comprising a sprinkling of settlers from other States and immigrants from Great Britain who had settled in Australia before the war.

Many of the battalion's original members were killed or crippled by wounds. Some during the war were transferred to other units—the 4th Field Ambulance, 4th Machine Gun Company, 4th Pioneers or the 46th Battalion, when that unit was formed in Egypt. The following original N.C.O.'s and privates obtained commissions during the war, in the 14th, the commissions being granted in the localities hereunder named:—

**Original N.C.O.'s and Privates who Obtained Commissions.**

Gallipoli Peninsula—A. R. Blainey, N. G. Booth, F. H. Dadson,† S. M. Hansen,† F. L. Laloe, R. E. Sanders, J. H. M. Matthews,† D. R. Macdermid, V. J. G. Couttie, F. Duffield,† K. Curlewis,† J. Quirke. Egypt—Frederick C. W. Symonds, W. G. Laver, J. B. Roderick, N. Wilson, Reg. W. Jones, Albert Jacka. France (to the Battle of Bullecourt, April 11, 1917)—W. R. M.

---

†Killed in action or died of wounds:—
Lieut. F. H. Dadson killed in action April 11, 1917 (Bullecourt).
Capt. S. M. Hansen, M.C., died of wounds February 7, 1917 (Stormy Trench). Lieut. J. H. M. Matthews killed in action August 8, 1915. 2nd-Lieut. Duffield killed in action August 21, 1915. Lieut. K. Curlewis killed in action August 8, 1915. Lieut. H. W. Thompson, M.C., died of wounds August 9, 1918 (Morcourt).
2nd-Lieut. A. J. Harris died of wounds April 12, 1917 (Bullecourt).
Lieut. N. A. Kent died of wounds April 12, 1917 (Bullecourt).
2nd-Lieut. V. G. Garner killed in action August 8, 1917 (Gapaard).

## The History of the 14th Battalion.

Beamond, J. Millis, Harold Thompson,† H. Loughhead, Fred. Anderson, Norman Harris, A. J. Harris,‡ Clarendon Hyde, Gustav Landsberg (interpreter), Norman Kent,† France (after the Battle of Bullecourt)—D. H. G. Hawkins, G. T. Trewheela, Alf. King, Lou Garcia, H. J. Schutz, E. P. Hill, E. R. Chubb, V. G. Garner,† S. de'Arengo, F. H. Boyes, R. J. Garcia, F. T. Larter, C. Thompson, Norman Bear, Leslie Bain, G. L. Huse, S. Booley, T. W. Cleland, Rodger Scanlon.

It was the old originals‡ who laid the foundations of the battalion's history, who founded its traditions, and who figure largely on its roll of honour. As was inevitable, some of them of course were failures, but the great majority did their duty under conditions of unparalleled hardship and danger, and set a high standard of conduct and proficiency for future reinforcements.

**Battalion Embarks on the "Ulysses."** On Tuesday, December 22, the whole battalion entrained at Broadmeadows for Port Melbourne and marched down the Town Pier—a pier down which thousands of brave men marched never to return—and embarked on board the transport "Ulysses" (15,000 tons). In addition to the 14th, the 13th battalion and the 4th Brigade Headquarters were also aboard the "Ulysses," which was the flagship of the convoy, and which left the pier, to which the public had been admitted, about 7 p.m. All were in great spirits and the departure of the boat was an inspiring spectacle, last farewells to friends being waved, and the battalion band which had been formed at Broadmeadows playing inspiriting airs, including "Tipperary," "Australia Will Be There" and the 14th Battalion regimental march, that famous southern folk-song "The Swannee River." The transport moved down the bay and anchored, and next morning passed through the Heads, skirted the forest-clad Otway coast and finally turned her bow west. All fell in daily for ship's inspection at 10 a.m., a most ceremonial parade, each deck being inspected in turn by a procession of officers headed by a bugler. On December 27 occurred the first of the innumerable inoculations; the authorities seemed determined that those whom the Turks or Germans spared would not succumb to the microbes.

On December 28 the "Ulysses" reached King George's

---

†Killed in action or died of wounds.

‡Approximately about twenty-five per cent. of the originals lost their lives during the war in the service of the battalion. Some transferred to and lost their lives in other units.

Sound, the chosen rendezvous of the convoy. Leave ashore was not granted. Advantage was taken here, prior to finally leaving Australia, to have a last cleaning up of the battalion, and eighteen men were discharged from its ranks, one-half as medically unfit, and the other half for disobedience of orders re inoculation. The discharged personnel was landed at King George's Sound on December 30.

On the last day of the year the convoy of nineteen transports steamed out from Albany in single file, and when outside the harbour formed up in three lines, the "Ulysses" as flagship leading in the centre, the "Ceramic" the port and the "Themistocles" the starboard division. The convoy carried both Australian and New Zealand troops, the Australian convoy consisting of sixteen vessels carrying 318 officers and 10,030 men, and the New Zealand convoy three vessels carrying 66 officers and 1962 men.§ There were 74 officers and 2005 men on the "Ulysses" alone. Cape Leeuwin was passed on New Year's Day (1915) and that was the last view of the Australian coast, a coast which many were fated never to see again. The majestic convoy now headed for Colombo, and nearing the tropics the weather became warmer. Training on board commenced in earnest, and the vessel was darkened at night as a precautionary measure against possible raiders. The only escort that the convoy had was the Australian submarine A.E.2. which was afterwards lost in the Dardanelles. Speculation during the voyage was of course rife as to the brigade's destination.

On January 13th, 1915, at 8 a.m., Colombo was reached and the "Ulysses was tied up to buoys in the inner harbour.

**Colombo Reached.**
The morning was beautiful and the tropical foliage and white houses made an enticing background. Scantily clad natives immediately surrounded the transport in their small boats and a brisk trade was done in fruit and other goods, which are hauled aboard on baskets attached to a long cord. Leave was very sparingly granted, but the temptation to visit Ceylon proved too much for some adventurous spirits who, on the approach of darkness, slipped into native boats and got ashore. It was more difficult to return undetected and as a result of this nocturnal flitting three corporals were reduced to the ranks. When the "Ulysses" left Colombo at 8 a.m. on January 13 several men were still missing but they

§These figures were furnished by respective O.'s C. troops to the brigade-major of the 4th Infantry Brigade as representing personnel actually aboad, with the exception of ship's officers and crew.

followed subsequently in other vessels. A twelve hours' stay was made at Aden, the next port of call, and, shortly after, the Red Sea was entered and the heat greatly increased.

On January 28 anchor was cast off Suez, and for the first time the propinquity of hostilities was realised. Information came to hand that Turkish snipers were firing at passing vessels, and a barricade of flour bags was built on the bridge to protect the wheel house from bullets. On the 29th the "Ulysses" steamed slowly up the canal at the head of the convoy. The novel surroundings proved of great interest, for comparatively few of those on the transports had ever been outside Australia before. Warships were anchored in the canal and there were troops everywhere along the banks. Anchor was cast for the night in Lake Timsah, and next morning the journey was continued to Port Said. Here coal and water were taken aboard, and much interest was caused watching the vessel being coaled by native coolies, very scantily clad, who ran up the narrow gangway, tipped their baskets of coal into the hold, and ran down another plank for a further supply. Alexandria, on the Mediterranean coast, was reached on the morning of January 31. The long sea journey was now over. The battalion went ashore for a short route march through the town, and had its first experience of the insanitary conditions of the East, the smells of the slum quarters being quite sufficient to make dinner a very light meal. Disembarkation took place that evening about 8 p.m. Once more ashore all looked forward with pleasure to the excitement and novelty to be found in Egypt, that strange, fascinating and interesting land, on which fate and the fortune of war had thrown them.

*Suez.*

**Disembarkation at Alexandria.**

## CHAPTER III.

### EGYPT.

#### 1915—February 1 to April 24.

The right half of the battalion departed from Alexandria by train on the evening of January 31, followed by the left half on the next morning, and the transport some days later. The destination was the new camping ground known as the Aerodrome Camp, on the fringe of the desert and just outside Heliopolis, a southern suburb of Cairo. Australian money had now been changed for Egyptian coinage, and "wet canteens" were permitted, two marquees being erected, one to be utilised as a coffee stall and the other for the sale of beer and soft drinks.

*Departure from Alexandria.*

*Arrival at Heliopolis.*

On arrival at the new quarters the first step taken was the reorganisation of the battalion on a four or double company system. This new organisation was adopted in all Australian infantry units.* This reform was given effect to, as far as the 14th was concerned, on February 4, and henceforth A and E Companies formed A Company—O.C., Major Rankine;† second in command, Capt. F. H. Wright. B and F Companies formed B Company—O.C., Capt. Baldock; second in command, Capt. W. R. Hoggart. C and G Companies formed C Company—O.C., Major Steel; second in command, Capt. Hutton. D and H Companies formed D Company—O.C., Capt. Connelly; second in command, Capt. A. Henry.

*Adoption of the Four Company System.*

The ten weeks during which the battalion remained in Egypt was a period of strenuous and gruelling marches on the desert sand, varied by company and field training, and divisional exercises, the object being to harden the men and prepare them for the strenuous campaign ahead, and also to train the staffs in handling their units. The 4th Brigade

*Strenuous Training.*

---

*The double company organisation was adopted to bring the A.I.F. units into line with the organisation of the British Army which had adopted this system some time previously. The half-companies were called platoons, four of which went to the company.

†Vide Chapter 11.

now became portion of the newly formed New Zealand and Australian Division, under the command of Major-General Sir Alexander Godley. The first few days were devoted to platoon and company training in the newly formed double companies. Subsequently the training became more strenuous, and, among other marches, the participation of the battalion in a divisional attack on a ridge beyond No. 2 Tower on the Cairo-Suez Road will not readily be forgotten by the participants. It lasted about twelve hours and the distance covered was about twenty-two miles, but no one fell out, and it was the first time the men took part in a combined operation.

These desert marches through the sand were very exhausting, and the heavy tramping together with the additional weight of the equipment tried the men's pluck and stamina to the utmost, but the fear of ridicule of their comrades stimulated the weary to the required effort and it became a point of honour not to fall out. Few who took part in these battalion desert marches will forget No. 3 Tower, as the marches in its neighbourhood became more numerous than popular. Rifle practice was not neglected, and every man was put through a test on the Abassieh rifle range.

On March 23 the whole of the New Zealand and Australian Division formed up in the desert for inspection by the High Commissioner of Egypt. After the inspection the division, at war strength, marched past the saluting base.

Meanwhile, during these months of training, the Australians had become acquainted with Egypt. There was much around them to excite their interest. The customs, habits and dress of the natives always provided food for observation. They viewed monuments that were old and venerable in the time of Moses. Many of the scenes they looked on had behind them scores of centuries of history. Some, too, of the great world conquerors—Alexander the Great, Julius Cæsar and Napoleon, among others—had campaigned on Egyptian soil. Cairo, the greatest and most populous city in Africa, was close by and connected with Heliopolis by an electric tram service which was taxed to the full to take the Australians to and fro. There were sights in that famous city akin to those described in the Arabian Nights upwards of one thousand years ago. Australians filled the cafes, and spent their money as prodigally as they afterwards shed their blood. The many bushmen in the battalion were keen to notice the primitive methods of agriculture, and the fact that the natives did not live on their

*Egypt Excites Interest of Australians.*

allotments, but clustered in villages and went out to their work daily like city men going into business. The Anzac attitude towards the natives was one of good humoured contempt. Their labour, however, was utilised, and all the sanitary work about the camps was performed by them.

Keen as was the interest of the Australians in their surroundings, they themselves excited universal interest among the polyglot population of Cairo. Their physique became the talk of the Mediterranean, and their bearing and independence of character excited the admiration and jealousy of others less favoured. Thoughtful strangers‡ were quick to realise their potential military value.

**Australians Excite Interest in Egypt.**

During the sojourn in Egypt it was decided that all the Australian units should wear distinctive colours. Colours were always duplicated and worn contiguously. One (the lower) represented the brigade, whilst the upper represented the battalion in that brigade. The colours were worn on both arms, and the initiated at one glance could tell immediately the unit and brigade of the wearer. The 4th Brigade colour (chosen by Col. Monash) was dark navy blue, and the 14th colour gold. All members of the 14th wore accordingly small horizontal stripes of gold and dark navy blue, representing respectively the battalion and the brigade. The 13th colours were light blue,§ the 15th brown and the 16th white, all worn of course over the brigade colours.

**A.I.F. Units Adopt Distinctive Colours.**

It was during the stay in Egypt that death took its first toll of the battalion's manhood. No. 1212, Private Hooke,‖ a machine gunner, died of illness on March 7. Two other deaths occurred about this time in the battalion from the same cause; No. 1292, Private J. W. McDougall, of D Company,

**First Death in Battalion.**

---

‡H. W. Nevinson:—"The Dardanelles Campaign," page 72, states: "A finer set of men than the Anzacs after their three months' training on the desert sands could hardly be found in any country . . . they walked the earth with careless and daredevil self confidence." The more poetic Masefield states in his "Gallipoli," page 19: "They were the finest body of young men ever brought together in modern times. For physical beauty and nobility of bearing they surpassed any men I have ever seen."

§Light blue was chosen by the 13th Battalion senior officers, as it was the New South Wales sporting colour, and it identified the Battalion with that State. Lieut.-Col. Durrant, C.M.G., D.S.O. (then adjutant of the Battalion), was responsible for this selection.

‖Private John Clement Hooke (No. 1212), labourer, of Leongatha, V. Son of Mr. John Hooke, of Croydon, England.

died on March 26, and No. 1258, Sergeant Sutcliffe¶, also a machine gunner, on March 30.

**Preparations for Departure.** During the early part of April preparations were made for embarkation, and on April 6 a divisional parade by ships was held. All the troops having to travel by any one ship met together, everything was carefully checked and preparations for the great adventure were now complete. The time for leaving Egypt was rapidly drawing nigh. The government of the Turkish Empire had fallen into the hands of a gang of unscrupulous adventurers on whose vanity the political leaders of Germany adroitly played, with the result that Turkey threw in her lot with the central powers. A

**Expedition Formed to Attack Dardanelles.** Franco-British military and naval expedition had been planned for the purpose of forcing the Dardanelles and capturing Constantinople, and the Australian Division and the New Zealand and Australian Division were included in the troops to be employed for that purpose. Prior to leaving Egypt 2nd-Lieut. Fuhrmann became transport officer of the battalion, vice 2nd-Lieut. C. R. M. Cox who was transferred to D Company.

On April 11 tents were struck, kits packed and half of the battalion, followed later by the remaining moiety, marched from Heliopolis to Helmia railway station and entrained there, to the music of bands and the cheers of crowds of envious light horsemen, who were still remaining in Egypt but eager to get nearer the firing line. Alexandria was reached before daybreak. Under the plan of operations the island of Lemnos, situated about 40 miles from the mouth of the Dardanelles, was to be the rendezvous of the British Expeditionary Force. The transport allotted for the conveyance of the 14th Battalion and Brigade Headquarters to Lemnos was the s.s. "Seang Choon," a Rangoon trader of about 5000 tons—a dirty boat full of cockroaches, fleas and rats. On April 13 the "Seang Choon" left Alexandria for Lemnos, the regimental transport being taken on board the s.s. "California."

**Battalion Leaves Heliopolis.**

**Arrival at Lemnos.** The initial weather was beautiful, but the transport struck heavy seas next day with the result that sea-sickness prostrated a large number of the men. About noon on April 15 the island of Lemnos was reached and the "Seang Choon" anchored in the commodious harbour of Mudros. The

---

¶ Sergeant Alfred Sutcliffe (No. 1258), gunsmith, of Mildura, V.

grass and verdant surroundings were a pleasant contrast to the sand and desolation of Egypt. The scene in the harbour was striking; it was crammed with craft of every description —British, French and Russian battleships, torpedo boats, repair ships, mine layers, balloon and hydroplane ships, mine sweepers of all sizes and transports crowded with troops. Even at night there was much to excite interest, including the twinkling lights from every class of vessel, signals flashing in Morse code and rows of green lights indicating hospital ships.

The transports were tied together in twos and threes. The "Seang Choon" lay alongside the transport "Itonus" containing New Zealanders. Some irritation was caused among the latter, who were being fed on bully beef and biscuits, when they ascertained that the boys of the 14th had been regaling on fresh bread and meat from the refrigerator. The few days spent at Mudros were occupied getting everything into fighting trim, practising ascending and descending rope ladders in full marching order and rowing about the harbour in the ship's boats. The unexpected arrival and distribution of an Australian mail on April 20 caused some excitement. On the same day Capt. Henry and four other ranks were evacuated to the stationary hospital at Lemnos.

On the evening of April 22 detailed orders of the operations for landing on the Peninsula were received. The expedition was commanded by General Sir Ian Hamilton, a British officer of wide experience. The Anzac Divisions* were placed under the command of Lieut.-General Birdwood. The plan was to attack near Cape Helles, at the entrance to the Dardanelles, with the 29th Division, a splendid body of British regulars, and simultaneously to hurl the Australian and New Zealand forces ashore near Gabe Tepe. Meanwhile, feints were to be made at Bulair and Kum Kale, in Asia, to distract the attention of the Turks and prevent reinforcements being sent to the vital points attacked. The theory of the attack was that the army was to open a road for the fleet to enter the Dardanelles, and force its way to Constantinople. The locality where the great attack was to be made was rich in historical associations, some of which extended back hundreds of years before the Christian era.

*Operation Orders Received for Attack on Peninsula.*

---

*The Anzac corps was composed of the Australian Division and the New Zealand and Australian Division.

## The History of the 14th Battalion. 17

**Stupendous Difficulties to be Faced.**

The attack planned for the Antipodean forces was one of the toughest military propositions ever presented to an untried volunteer army, and one that might well have tested the mettle of the most seasoned veterans. The difficulties were so stupendous that the attempt was almost courting disaster. They were expected to land from open boats, in the semi-dusk of morning, on an unknown and almost impregnable coast, easily defended, and within less than 150 miles of the enemy's capital, whence unlimited reserves of men and material could be drawn. The coast was manned by hostile forces of excellent quality and unknown strength, well supplied with artillery, who were perfectly aware of the proposed attack and possessed every advantage of local knowledge and artificial assistance that foresight or skill might have improvised.

**Fourth Brigade the Reserve Brigade.**

The Australian attack was to be initiated by the 1st Australian Division. The 4th was to be the reserve brigade, and the 14th the reserve battalion of that brigade, C Company, 14th, being the reserve company of the battalion.

**Optimism of Australians.**

In spite of the desperate character of the enterprise the Australians were full of their characteristic optimism. The possibility of failure was not even entertained. Bets at short odds were freely made by the members of the 14th Battalion officers' mess that they would be in Constantinople within three days of the landing, whilst the more cautious who were only prepared to bet on being there within a week could obtain almost any odds they wished to lay.

The Australian attack took place just before dawn on April 25. It thrilled the world with its daring and brilliancy, but the "Seang Choon" did not leave Mudros Harbour till breakfast time on that date, so that the 14th was unable to participate in the glories and perils of that great assault.

A great sensation was caused on board the transport about midnight of the 24th when a Lance-Corporal, who was afterwards killed near Pozières in France, threw himself overboard. Swimming strongly he was rescued by a boat which put out after him. "The silly blighter might just as well have waited until tomorrow, and chance earning a V.C., if he wants to lose his blanky life," was the general comment, but, as the man concerned stoutly asserted that he knew nothing until he found himself in the water, his explanation was accepted.

## CHAPTER IV.

### THE BAPTISM OF BLOOD.

#### 1915—April 25 to April 30.

 Immediately after the transport left Mudros for the Peninsula a church parade was held on board (the last before the troops went into action), a most impressive service being conducted by Chaplain Gillison. As the vessel approached the entrance to the Straits those on board were presented with a panoramic view of a modern, up-to-date naval bombardment. About mid-day the roar of the guns became more distinct and later, as the transport approached the entrance to the Dardanelles, the terrific naval bombardment of the coast and the heroic tragedy of the landing of the 29th Division were witnessed from the deck. The whole Peninsula was like an inferno. Columns of earth and dust, apparently hundreds of feet in height, were caused by the shelling, while vast clouds of smoke threw a shade over the lurid scene, which reminded many who saw it of a great bush fire, whilst the unearthly din provided a true devil's orchestra.

*Naval Bombardment Witnessed.*

 The scene put all in great heart, but many thought that nothing living could exist under this awful pounding, and that their task would be simply that of burying dead Turks. Whilst this unparalleled drama was being enacted, and all the officers were crowding spellbound on the bridge, imperturbable "Aussies" filled the decks of the transport, intent on card playing, and utterly indifferent to, and apparently oblivious of, the extraordinary events taking place in the vicinity.[1]

 As the transport approached Gaba Tepe two hospital ships, crowded with wounded, passed on their way to Egypt. About 5 p.m. the vessel anchored beside many other transports, and lighters full of wounded, towed by naval pinnaces, began to appear, seeking for some vessel to which to transfer their pathetic human freight; the official arrangements for the disposal of casualties were inadequate. The heroism of these

*Hospital Ships Appear.*

---

[1] The Brigadier, Col. Monash, particularly noted this, and called the attention of other officers to it.

wounded men, many of whom were beyond hope of recovery, was marvellous. Orders were now received that the 14th Battalion was not to land until next day, but that the decks were to be cleared to make room for the wounded. The few hospital ships available were soon overcrowded, and, in spite of the lack of accommodation on the "Seang Choon," the wounded continued to arrive on board until, by daylight, several hundred had been accommodated. The 14th boys worked hard and unceasingly getting the wounded on board. Few had any sleep that night, whilst Capt. Loughran (the R.M.O.), Chaplain Gillison and the stretcher bearers worked to the limit of endurance dressing wounds and endeavouring to alleviate suffering; amputations and operations were carried on all night. The ship resembled a shambles and the decks were saturated with blood. The less severely wounded were plied with questions concerning the fight, and the 14th men heard the story of the landing, of the heavy losses before the 1st Division got ashore, of the brilliant charge under rifle and machine gun fire and of the seizing of the heights above the beach.

*Wounded Accommodated on the "Seang Choon."*

*14th Men Work All Night Assisting the Wounded.*

A beach party, consisting of 2nd reinforcements to the 14th that had come from Egypt in another vessel, was ashore early on the 25th; these men were actually the first members of the battalion to land on the Peninsula. Meanwhile, late in the afternoon of the 25th, Col. Courtney instructed Capt. Wright to take two platoons of A Company ashore. Capt. Wright chose No. 2 Platoon (Lieut. Crabbe) and No. 3 Platoon (Lieut. A. R. Cox) and the two platoons, comprising about 100 men, were transhipped into a heavy lighter, and, after a long wait, were towed ashore in the dusk by a launch in charge of a midshipman. Each man carried three days' rations, a bundle of firewood and one hundred extra rounds of ammunition. The scene ashore was almost indescribable; dead and wounded men (some of the wreckage of the day's fighting) were lying all over the beach, and masses of equipment were piled up everywhere. Sailors from the landing parties were trying to straighten things up.

*2nd Reinforcements First Ashore.*

*Platoons Nos. 2 and 3 Land.*

Capt. Wright reported to Major-General Godley, the divisional commander, who deputed an officer to take his detachment along the beach to the north, and he was instructed to dig in, and not to retire under any circumstances as there was not anything between his men and Divisional Headquarters. The two platoons remained in that position, with only a couple of slight casualties, until after 8 a.m. on April 27, when they rejoined the remainder of the battalion on the march to Shrapnel Gully. Meanwhile the lack of Australian artillery ashore (for some inscrutable reason the artillery had not been allowed to land) had created a rather serious position, and for a brief period during the night there was danger of a re-embarkation of the remnants of the 1st Division. Fortunately, however, that crisis passed.

The remainder of the battalion, together with Brigade Headquarters, on the morning of April 26 landed under shrapnel fire which, fortunately, mostly fell too high or too wide, though Sgt. W. P. Murphy, of D Company, was shot through the heart. He was a resident of the Warracknabeal district, an immigrant from Great Britain and an old Imperial soldier. He achieved the melancholy distinction of being the first member of the 14th Battalion to be killed in action. The battalion (less Platoons 2 and 3) remained all day on the beach as a reserve, near the northern point of Anzac Cove at Ari Burnu, and close to where the wireless station was afterwards erected. There was shrapnel fire in the vicinity during the day, but it was too high and did little damage. The time was utilised by the men in collecting the arms, equipment and packs, which were strewn all over the beach, and in the water where they had been thrown off on the previous day by the men of the 1st Division on landing as they advanced on their whirlwind assault. The battalion bivouacked under the cliffs during the night.

*Remainder of Battalion Lands.*
*Sgt. Murphy Killed.*

It is necessary now to give a brief description of the position at Anzac in order that future operations may be understood. The position captured by the Australians on April 25 and permanently held consisted of a mass of scrubby ridges rising almost sheer from the sea, and containing about 300 acres, roughly triangular in shape, with the sea as a base. The apex of the triangle, and the key of the whole Anzac position, consisted of a series of so-called posts, eg., Pope's Hill, Quinn's Post, Courtney's Post and Steele's Post. These knolls facing the Turkish positions were, in some cases, commanded by high ground in the rear of the enemy's lines, but they were important for they were situated at the head of a gully flanked by high cliffs (known as Shrapnel Gully)

*Position at Anzac.*

## The History of the 14th Battalion. 21

which bisected the whole Anzac position. The posts (except Courtney's and Steele's) were disconnected and separated by branches of the gully out of which they rose precipitously. The 4th Brigade became the guardian of these posts, and held them for weeks against continuous attacks. Some of the best blood of Australia was shed in their defence.

**Battalion Marches up Shrapnel Gully.** The 1st Division, which had been fighting continuously for two days, was now in a state of complete exhaustion, and urgently in need of reinforcements. On the morning of April 27 Capt. Baldock, O.C. of B Company, was evacuated sick. About 8.15 a.m. on that date the battalion received orders to march up Shrapnel Gully (Nos. 2 and 3 Platoons having been instructed to rejoin the main body), and, taking such cover as was available, the advance was made under an intermittent shrapnel fire. Wounded men met on their way to the dressing station did not hesitate to state how badly reinforcements were needed at the front. Many dead bodies were passed, and also little clusters of wounded men under the shelter of cliffs and being attended to by doctors. Men with only a few hours to live would ask for cigarettes as our boys passed them. After the advance had been made some distance up the gully orders were given to throw off packs. This was done but few men ever saw their packs or personal belongings again. During this advance Major Adams, the battalion's second in command, was wounded in the leg and had to be taken to the beach. As the battalion approached the head of the gully it was broken up into detachments and sent in to reinforce the various strong posts there on which the Turks were then pressing. The whole of A Company, with portions of other companies, under Major Rankine, reinforced the garrison at Quinn's. Later in the day Major Steel,* with the whole of C and portion of D Company, took charge of Steele's Post,* whilst Lieut. Boyle with No. 8 Platoon joined Col. Pope in the defence of Pope's Hill.

### QUINN'S POST.

It will be advisable in the first place to deal with the defence of Quinn's Post. It was shortly before mid-day that Lieut. Hanby, with No. 1 Platoon, followed shortly by the residue allotted to the post, advanced to that famous position the defence of which, during the ensuing months, forms one of the most thrilling stories of the Peninsula.

---

*Although named after Major H. Steel, 14th Battalion, this post was officially designated "Steele's Post."—Official History of A.I.F., Vol. I., p. 285.

## The Baptism of Blood.

**Description of Quinn's Post.**

As approached from the gully in the rear, it rose abruptly and precipitously to a height of about 150 feet, but the surrounding country was rugged and hilly and the summit was commanded by some higher ground in the vicinity. The summit was crescent shaped with one arm pointing to the gully between Quinn's and Pope's, known as Bloody Angle, whilst the surface of the hill was not level but saucer shaped, with the result that the right flank of the position was dangerously open to the fire of snipers located in the high and difficult ground in the front of Pope's. The steep and slippery slopes facing the gully made difficult climbing for men who had already undergone a gruelling march in the heat, and all arrived exhausted at the summit. Many dead and wounded men were passed during the ascent.

**Critical Position at Front.**

At the summit conditions were found to be critical. A handful of men from different A.I.F. battalions, under a lance-corporal, exhausted and fought to a standstill, were slowly retiring before the Turks who were pressing them strongly. A few rounds of rapid fire from the new-comers drove the pursuing Turks to cover and the party on the hill joined up with the 14th in the defence of the post. An attempt was immediately made to consolidate the position. Few pickaxes and shovels were available, most of them having been left with the packs in the gully, but, with the aid of entrenching tools, rough head cover was improvised and some kind of protection obtained. During these operations at Quinn's Battalion Headquarters was at the foot of Courtney's Post; Major Rankine's dugout was at the back of Quinn's, whilst Capt. Wright was in charge of the actual firing line and was also responsible for the distribution of stores, water and ammunition. Bodies of troops could be seen moving about in the scrub opposite, but they were supposed to be detachments of our men. The chaotic fighting of the two previous days had left everything in confusion and it was difficult to obtain reliable information. Many false messages, too, some inspired by the enemy, came through to Quinn's, one being an order to retire, of which, however, no notice was taken. This lack of knowledge of facts added greatly to the strain imposed on those responsible for the safety of the post. The men had not

## The History of the 14th Battalion. 23

**Death of Capt. Hoggart.** been long in position, and desultory firing was occurring, when Capt. Hoggart,² now O.C. of B Company, in an endeavour to clarify the situation and ascertain the movements of the Turks, rose on his knees, fieldglasses in hand, and was immediately killed—shot through the head. He was the first officer of the 14th Battalion killed in the war. He united personal bravery with consideration for the comfort and well-being of his men. Prior to the war he had been a master in the Melbourne Grammar School.³

**Turkish Machine Gun Opens. Slaughter in A Company.** Immediately after Hoggart's death a Turkish machine gun, from the right rear (between Courtney's and Quinn's) at close quarters, opened a terrible burst of enfilade fire which blew out a large number of A Company on the right centre of Quinn's, and strewed the hill with dead and writhing men. The senior subaltern, Lieut. Hanby,⁴ was dangerously wounded in the arm and chest, Capt. Wright's rifle⁵ was shot to pieces and he was knocked down with the concussion, whilst a large number of other ranks were killed or mortally wounded. Among them were many excellent N.C.O.'s, including Cpls. Butterworth,⁶ Bowen,⁷ Thompson,⁸ Young,⁹ Macoboy,¹⁰ Chisholm,¹¹ Burton¹² and Doyle.¹³ Several privates shared the same fate, including

---

²Information supplied by Major (then 2nd-Lieut.) A. R. Cox who was beside Hoggart at the time of his death. The story universally circulated that he died endeavouring to locate the machine gun is incorrect. He was killed just before the machine gun opened fire.

³Capt. W. R. Hoggart, O.C. of B Company, born Buangor, Victoria, August 22, 1876. Killed in action April 27, 1915.

⁴Lieut. J. G. T. Hanby, clerk, of Brighton, Victoria.

⁵It is not usual for officers to carry rifles in action, but prior to landing on the Peninsula the junior officers were equipped precisely the same as the men (including rifles). This did not occur later in the Peninsula or in France.

⁶Corporal James Butterworth, A Company (1 Platoon), farm hand, England. Killed in action April 27, 1915.

⁷Corporal James Bowen, A Company (1 Platoon), tuckpointer, Kensington, Victoria. Died of wounds April 29, 1915.

⁸Lance-Corporal J. W. Thompson, A Company, wood merchant, Carlton, Victoria. Killed in action April 27, 1915.

⁹Lance-Corporal R. E. Young, A Company, labourer, Fitzroy, Victoria. Died of Wounds April 29, 1915.

¹⁰Corporal M. F. Macoboy, A Company (4 Platoon), motor mechanic, Bendigo, Victoria. Killed in action April 27, 1915.

¹¹Corporal C. Chisholm, A Company, merchant, England. Killed in action April 27, 1915.

¹²Corporal R. H. Burton, D Company, saddler, Richmond, Victoria. Killed in action April 27, 1915.

¹³Lance-Corporal W. J. Doyle, D Company, jeweller, Richmond, Victoria. Killed in action April 27, 1915.

W. Cohen (Major Rankine's batman), D. Wren, C. Gist, C. G. Greenham and R. B. Earll. Private S. McDermott was mortally wounded and his brother, Sgt. C. McDermott,[14] was shot dead beside him. The wounded—a large number—included Sgt. Reynolds (of No. 3 Platoon) whose jaw was shattered, and Cpl. Garner. There were some marvellous escapes; Sgt. Raymond Jones (No. 1 Platoon) had his haversack shot to pieces on his back but escaped unhurt, whilst Private C. H. Coleman received no fewer than six superficial bullet wounds. This unexpected and murderous attack at short range shook the survivors and some of the men on the extreme right started to creep back from the head cover they had formed. Matters were made much worse by a rumour, which found credence among many, that they were being fired on in error by their own machine guns.[15] The critical situation, however, was faced by the officers and the cooler heads among other ranks, and the men were steadied. One who helped materially in the crisis by example and forceful language was a stretcher bearer of the 13th Battalion. Some of the men, thinking that they had been victims of a tragic mistake, put their caps on their rifles and called out that they were Australians; the majority, however, finally convinced that the enemy was responsible for the carnage, settled down in grim earnest to pour in a hail of fire on the masked batteries on their front.

**Battalion's Mascot "Gunner."** That was the first experience that the battalion had of the effect of machine gun fire—that scythe of the modern battlefield—which was to take a heavy toll of its ranks before the termination of the war. Among the combatants on the hill at this time was the battalion mascot, a fox terrier named "Gunner,"[16] which had become attached to the battalion at Broadmeadows, had been smuggled aboard the "Ulysses" at Port Melbourne and ultimately found its way into the firing line. "Gunner" barked furiously when the bullets scattered dust, and his antics under fire doubtless provided a comic

---

[14]Sergeant C. McDermott, B Company, packer, Albert Park, Victoria. Killed in action April 27, 1915. (Real Christian name Frank, but enlisted under the name of Christopher). His father was an old Imperial soldier.

[15]This incident formed the theme of innumerable arguments among the survivors of the battalion. Many are still convinced that the slaughter was mistakenly caused by our own guns.

[16]"The Illustrated London News" (a famous London periodical) of June 5, 1915, has a full page illustration of the defence of Quinn's, showing the 14th men holding up their caps and "Gunner" in the foreground barking amid the bullets.

element which distracted attention from the seriousness of the position. But as the men were risking their lives to keep their mascot out of danger "Gunner" had to be sent back to Egypt.

The wounding of Lieut. Hanby led to a fine display of that spirit of comradeship which is one of the Australian's finest mental assets. When he had been lying under fire for some time Privates A. T. Cook,[17] E. J. McMaster,[18] A. J. Rennie[19] and another,[20] all belonging to his company, rushed out and carried him on an overcoat down the hill, two of them being wounded whilst engaged in this gallant rescue. After his treatment by the R.M.O. it was considered that the wounded officer's only hope of recovery lay in getting him off immediately to a hospital ship. Cpl. Hudson[21] and Private Cook volunteered to carry him down to the beach, though the route was infested by snipers; their self-imposed and dangerous task was carried out successfully, though Cook's hat was shot off his head en route. Hanby survived his injuries.

As the afternoon wore on, things became a little quieter; the cover was improved and some semblance of a line of trenches made. There was considerable difficulty in disposing of the wounded, and no attempt could be made to collect the dead. During the night the Turks made two determined attacks on Quinn's amid terrific noise; their bugles were blown and they shouted and called on "Allah." Both attacks were repulsed. Many ruses were practised by the Turks, or their German coadjutors, during the first few days on the Peninsula, such as calling out "officer wanted here," "stretcher bearer wanted," "ammunition wanted," in very good English, to confuse our men. Immediately after calling out the enemy would pour in a heavy fire. No notice subsequently was taken of these ruses, but at first they added to the confusion on Quinn's of raw troops fighting in an unknown country, raked at all angles by machine guns and snipers, shivering through cold and wet nights, with little shelter, and without overcoats or blankets, but sparsely supplied with food and water and with little cover for wounded and dying. Men

---

[17]Private A. T. C. Cook, A Company, steward, Fitzroy, Victoria.

[18]Corporal E. J. McMaster, A Company, railway porter, Ovens Vale, Victoria.

[19]Private A. J. Rennie, A Company, railway porter, Longwood, Victoria.

[20]Name of this man is unknown.

[21]Corporal J. B. Hudson, C Company, student, Garden Vale, Victoria. (Vide also chapter XIV., "Medical Personnel.")

less staunch might easily have succumbed to the dangers and difficulties surrounding them; that they did not was due to their own inherent manhood and the confidence now begotten of discipline and training.

Wednesday morning (April 28) was ushered in by Turkish snipers, who had secured favourable positions during the night and were intent on making themselves disagreeable. Many, including Signaller Holmes, Q.M.S. Alston, his assistant Robinson, young Bugler Trevan and some New Zealand engineers (who had come to Quinn's to see whether they could assist in the defence of the post by improvising barbed wire entanglements) fell victims to these snipers who were firing, as it became known later, from a depression to the left of Quinn's, and who had the right flank of the position under fire. Those on the left, including Company Headquarters, were immune, but during the whole of the day most of the stores, ammunition and water supply were under fire. After Q.M.S. Alston fell Sgt. D. R. Macdermid took over his duties, getting the stores, water and ammunition in order. Efforts were made to locate these snipers, and shortly after mid-day Cpl. Reg. Jones, at considerable personal risk, located them and endeavoured subsequently, assisted by Private Verswywelt ("Belgian Joe") to put them out of action, but was unable to do so effectually owing to the activities of snipers just ahead of Pope's Hill.

*Turkish Snipers Open Fire.*

An attempt was made during this evening to collect the dead, and L.-Cpl. Bronson was placed in charge of a burial party. Whilst the large grave was being dug an attack threatened the post from the Bloody Angle and the grave had to be prepared as a firing trench. Fortunately, our artillery obtained the range up Shrapnel Gully and the attack did not materialise. Chaplain Gillison subsequently came up and read the burial service, and 39 men (including some New Zealand engineers) were buried in a common grave. Decent burial was also given to two Turks. There was rain during the night of April 28, and, as neither overcoats nor waterproof sheets were available, the men had to shiver through the night. It had been impossible during the day to make a connected trench line owing to snipers, but in the evening Lieut. Crabbe organised a determined attempt and the work was successfully accomplished before daylight. A sap run out to the left of the position gave a fire command over the depression utilised by the snipers on the previous day, and they were driven out, some being killed and others wounded. It was now fairly safe to move about Quinn's.

## The History of the 14th Battalion. 27

During the first few days pandemonium reigned both day and night. The firing was continuous and all night the Turks blew their bugles and shouted, and our own men, too, were making plenty of noise calling out for water, ammunition or stretcher bearers. This shouting was stopped and messages had to be sent in an orderly and proper manner. All ranks were now showing signs of exhaustion.

**Relief.** About noon on April 30 the C.O. and adjutant came up to state that relief would be effected during the afternoon. Towards evening Capt. Corser, of the 15th Battalion, took over the position from the shattered survivors of the garrison, which had lost about thirty per cent. of its numbers in defending the position.

**Capt. Wright Wounded.** The survivors retired and spent the night at Courtney's Post. Just after the relief Capt. Wright,[22] who remained behind to hand over the position, received concussion of the brain from an exploding shell and was incapacitated from further service with the battalion.

The battalion had opened its war record by holding for seventy-six hours, under most adverse conditions, with only a portion of its personnel, one of the keys of Anzac, and, though its casualties had been heavy, it acquitted itself well. Its excellent work was recognised by the authorities and Major Rankine, who was O.C. of the post, received the D.S.O.; this was one of the very first decorations granted on the Peninsula. Much of the credit of the successful defence must be given to those young officers, Capt. Wright and Lieuts. A. R. Cox and Crabbe, who showed throughout energy and a complete disregard of their own safety. Other subalterns also did good work. Among the other ranks reference must be made to Sgt. Dadson, who was prominent in many ways, and whose South African war experience was of considerable value. Bugler Lyons, Sgt. Mahoney and some others showed coolness and intrepidity. It was noteworthy that some of the best men in the trenches were those who had given most trouble during the period of training. The rough initial experience proved invaluable and the survivors, drawn together by the bond of common suffering and danger, acquired confidence, experience and war cunning. Already, at this early stage, it was becoming evident that the war was to be a subalterns' war, and that success would depend largely upon the courage, skill and initiative of the junior officers. The senior battalion officers prepared the plans or gave in-

---

[22]Capt. Ferdinand Henry Wright, A Company, insurance manager, Malvern, Victoria. Born South Yarra, Victoria, on September 29, 1888.

structions, but during the actual fighting their duties lay largely in the rear, receiving and transmitting reports to the brigade. The varying phases arising out of the actual fighting had to be dealt with promptly by the junior officers and N.C.O.'s on the spot. Indeed, one of the outstanding features of the war, among all combatant nationalities, was the fearful carnage among subalterns.

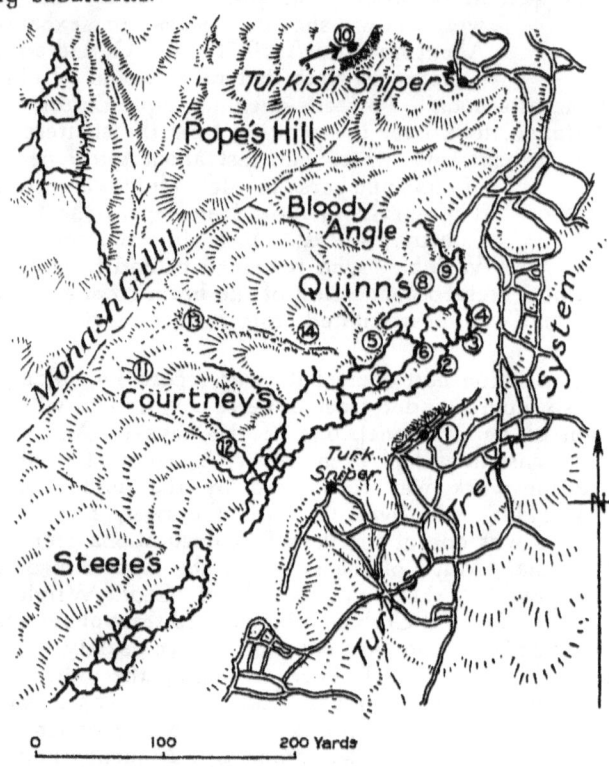

QUINN'S POST

1. Turkish Machine Gun.
2. Captain Hoggart.
3. Cohen, Lt. Crabbe, and Anderson.
4. Thompdon, Butterworth, and Bowen.
5. Rations were issued here.
6. Where Captain Wright and Signaller Holmes stood when the latter was wounded.
7. New Zealand Engineers sapping here were wounded.
8. Company Headquarters—Major Rankine.
9. Turkish Snipers wrought havoc from here on our right.
10. Turkish Sniper, whose fire commanded Monash Gully, but who could not sight Quinn's Post, except at one or two isolated points.
11. Loughran—M.O.'s Dressing Station, exposed to fire from (10).
12. McDermaid's place for issue of rations.
13. Point on track down from Quinn's, exposed to fire from sniper at (10).
14. Large grave where 39 were buried on Wednesday, April 28th, 1915.

# CHAPTER V.

### STEELE'S POST AND POPE'S HILL.

#### 1915—April 27 to April 29.

**C Company Reinforces Steele's Post.**

C and D Companies had followed the leading companies up Shrapnel Gully on April 27. Portion of D had joined with A and B and fought at Quinn's Post, but the residue of D, together with C, on reaching the brigade area at the head of the gully, remained and awaited orders at the foot of the hills. Very severe fighting appeared to be taking place on the cliffs above, and scores of wounded men were carried past. Late in the afternoon orders were received to reinforce the right of Quinn's Post, the flank of which was in the air. It was now about 5 p.m. and the reserves moved up the steep ascent later known as Steele's Post. The post was then in possession of a very mixed body of officers and men of different battalions, disorganised and badly shaken by the rough experience that they had undergone. The trenches were little better than gutters, the garrison not having had any opportunity to dig in properly. Major Steel, being senior officer on the spot, set to work immediately to organise the defence. The newcomers found themselves in an exposed position, in broad daylight and in full view of the enemy, who seemed well entrenched. The ground, fortunately, was rough, and there was a fair amount of cover from the searching rifle and machine gun fire which had proved so deadly at Quinn's. The battalion machine gun section was sent up later to hold a position on the left, and found fairly well covered places. Several small feints by the enemy were, apparently, broken up by our machine gun fire. Capt. Connelly (O.C. of D Company) going forward to reconnoitre for a proposed bayonet charge, was accidentally wounded by one of our men on his return. There was pandemonium after dark, for the Turks kept up a tremendous fusilade all night and made constant small attacks but did not push them home, though several of their dead were left between the lines. The battalion machine guns were busy firing into the darkness in case the enemy's attacks should become serious.

The night was cold, and, as all overcoats and blankets had been left in the gully, there was great discomfort. Some attempt was made in the darkness to improve the trenches. During the night some of the Turks had crept into the broken ground near the left of the position, and attempting, in daylight, to retire across the open, furnished excellent targets; our men took heavy toll.

The Turks used a good hand throwing bomb, about the size of a cricket ball, which were a source of annoyance to our men, who later on retaliated with an improvised fuse-burning grenade made by the field engineers out of empty jam tins filled with explosives.

About mid-day on April 29 C Company was relieved by the Royal Naval Division, and went down into the gully for a rest. The casualties had been light. The snipers by this time had been cleared from the hills in the rear and it was possible to move about more freely on the slopes of the hills behind the trenches.

C Company Relieved.

### POPE'S HILL.

When the battalion advanced up Shrapnel Gully on April 27 Lieut. H. N. Boyle, O.C. of No. 8 Platoon, B Company received orders to report with his platoon to the 16th Battalion, commanded by Lieut.-Col. Pope, and then occupying Pope's Hill. Col. Pope ordered him to move to the extreme left of the 16th's position and support Major Margolin's[1] company of that battalion. He accordingly led the platoon along the gully in the rear of Pope's Hill and brought up the men in small parties, reaching the trenches without any loss. As the 16th Battalion men on this post had been continuously on duty for two days the 8th Platoon reinforced them at once, and were shown how to hold the line. The platoon remained there until April 29 when it received orders to return to its own battalion. The front line trench here was at that time very narrow and about four feet in depth. The immediate front of the position was covered with low scrub which hid the enemy. The first casualties soon occurred as fire was being received from every side— front, flanks and rear. The men improved the trenches that day, but during the night they were kept alert and anxious by the sound of the Turkish bugles along the front. Good

No. 8 Platoon Reinforces Pope's Hill.

---

[1] Major Margolin, D.S.O. Afterwards C.O. of the 14th Battalion, during June, July and August, 1917.

## The History of the 14th Battalion. 31

work was done by Cpl. Johnson[2] with his section. During the two days occupation at Pope's Hill the platoon (about 45 men) suffered heavy casualties, among the killed being Cpls. H. McLaren[3] and J. A. Harding,[4] and Ptes. D. Lee, L. Hyde H. Honeychurch, A. Elmslie, R. Cowan, E. Partridge and G. C. English.

**Arduous Work of the R.M.O. and Stretcher Bearers.**

During the fighting which has been described the battalion R.M.O. and his personnel worked unceasingly, and their labour was not lightened by the extremely precipitous nature of the country over which the stretcher bearers had to carry the wounded, nor was their comfort added to by the continual explosion of shells and the attention of snipers. On April 27 the dressing station had been located in Monash Valley at almost the identical spot where Major-General Bridges, shortly afterwards was mortally wounded. It was a very dangerous spot, and several wounded men lying there were wounded a second time. Next day a move was made further up the valley and nearer to the line on Courtney's Post, a much safer spot, though if anyone was sniped in the vicinity—this frequently happened—the R.M.O. and the stretcher bearers had to go to his assistance no matter to what unit the injured man belonged, with the result that cases were attended to on Courtney's, Steele's, Quinn's and even on Walker's Ridge. Medical organisation, or indeed any organisation, during the first few chaotic days was hardly possible; everything had to be improvised on the spot, when even the essentials of proper organisation were often lacking. The April casualties of the battalion (as set out in its official diary) were one officer and forty-three other ranks killed, three officers and a hundred and two other ranks wounded, and thirty-nine other ranks missing (mostly on Quinn's Post on April 27). The Australians had met in the Turk an enemy as brave as

**April Casualties of the Battalion.**

---

[2]Cpl. John Frederick Johnson (8th Platoon), labourer, West Richmond, Victoria. Killed in action May 29, 1915.

[3]Cpl. Hector McLaren (8th Platoon), blacksmith, Moe, Victoria. Killed in action April 27, 1915.

[4]Cpl. J. A. Harding (8th Platoon), labourer, Dubbo, N.S.W. Killed in action April 27, 1915.

**Flower of the Turkish Army Encountered.** themselves, and, at this early stage of the war, more cunning at sniping and ruses, though the Turks of course had the double advantage of fighting in their own country and of having many veterans in their ranks; those on the Peninsula were the flower of the Ottoman Army; they had been specially trained by German officers and were well equipped.

Lieut.-Col. J. H. Peck, C.M.G., D.S.O.

Lieut.-Col. H. A. Crowther, D.S.O.

Lieut.-Col. C. M. M. Dare, D.S.O., V.D.

## CHAPTER VI.

### EARLY DAYS ON THE PENINSULA.

#### 1915—May 1 to May 18.

The arrival of some battalions of the Royal Naval Division, sent to Anzac as reinforcements, enabled the hard-fought and mingled Australian units to be temporarily withdrawn, sorted out and reorganised. The units of the 4th Brigade were henceforth disposed of as follows:—The 13th, 15th and 16th Battalions collectively were to hold and be responsible for Pope's Hill and Quinn's Post, one battalion being on each post, and the third in reserve in Monash Gully. They were to relieve one another in rotation.

The 14th, on the other hand, was to hold Courtney's Post continuously, the routine being one half of the battalion (i.e., two companies) in the trenches and the other half in reserve. The trenches were held for forty-eight hours; reliefs were always sent in at 9 a.m., when the two companies relieved would retire to the reserve trenches. It will be noted that the other three battalions of the brigade thus had to work in conjunction with one another, whilst the 14th had a job quite alone. Brigade Headquarters at this time was at the foot of Courtney's Post, just behind the 14th, and at this early stage of the brigade's history the casualties in the 14th had been considerably less than those in any of the other three battalions. Though all this was purely accidental it caused some jealousy among the other units of the brigade, least pronounced in the 13th (which had travelled across the seas with the 14th in the "Ulysses"), and gave rise to the erroneous impression that the 14th was receiving preferential treatment. This feeling died away (though not altogether) in France, where all four battalions worked together and came to know each other better. Rumours drifted to Australia at the time and caused a bad feeling

*Defence of Courtney's Post Assigned to the 14th.*

*Jealousy Aroused in Other Units.*

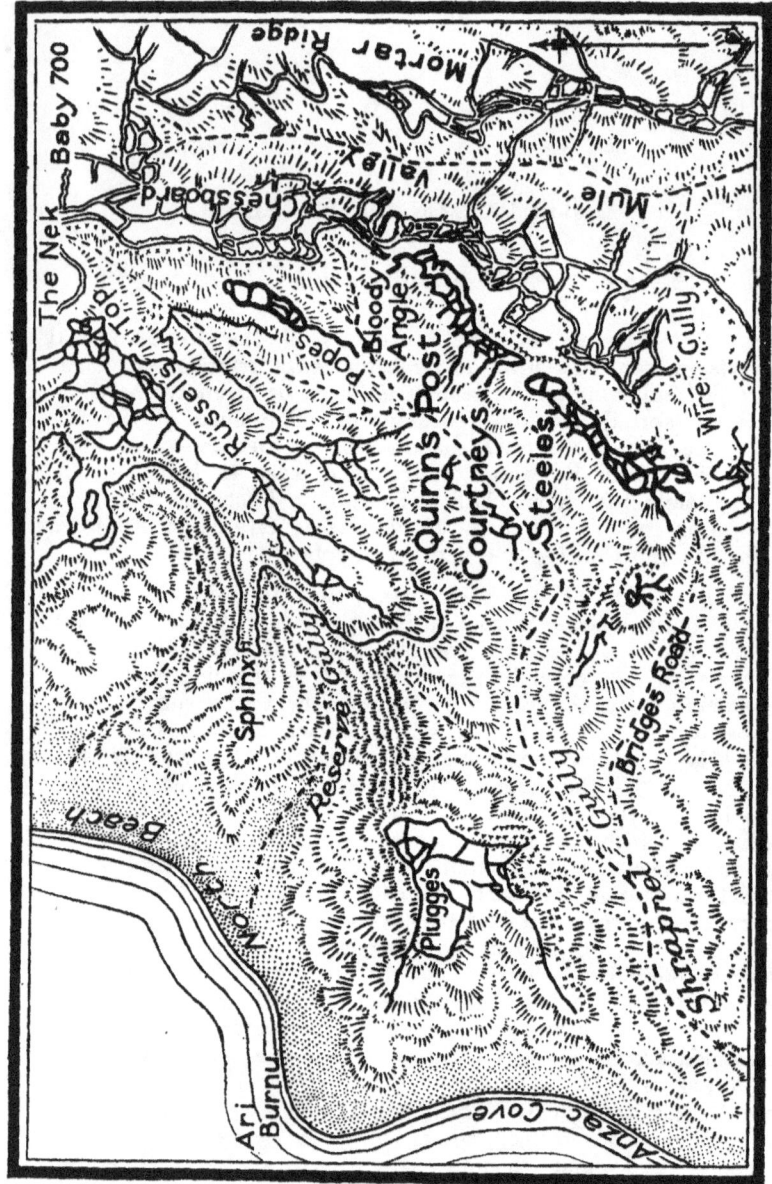

COURTNEY'S AND ADJOINING POSTS

## The History of the 14th Battalion.

towards the 14th to arise in the minds of many outsiders who were, and are, ignorant of the origin of the prejudice. The author has deemed it necessary to make a passing reference to the matter.

It has been related that C Company was relieved on April 29 by the Royal Naval Division, but on the 30th, about 2 p.m. (after a very short spell), it was again sent into the trenches at Courtney's to relieve the naval men, who moved further to the right. On the same afternoon, first at 4 p.m. and again at about 9.30 p.m., the naval division was heavily attacked, portion of the attack on each occasion coming against our right. A Company (which usually worked in conjunction with C) was sent up to support, but the latter repulsed the attack without assistance. During these attacks Lieut. Hutton was shot through both legs, and Lieut. Warren, a very keen officer, through the lung. Ptes. Dods and Rackstraw (both sniped) and Bugler Sheldon were killed and a large number of other ranks wounded. Several of our men were killed by snipers during the first few days because, after firing, they kept their heads exposed to see the result of their shots. The Turkish trenches, too, were sand-bagged, and afforded better cover for their occupants at this stage than did ours, where heads were exposed to the sky line when raised above the papapet.

*Losses from Enemy Snipers.*

A mysterious rider on a white horse occasionally was observed about this time, shortly after daybreak, riding across a small gap distant but visible from Courtney's, and several efforts were made to bring him down. He ceased to be seen but may not have been shot. Some thought that he was a Turkish general, but possibly he was a far less exalted personage.

*Enemy Rider on White Horse.*

Another heavy attack was launched by the enemy against our position at 5 a.m. on May 1 and pressed with great determination. The Turks were mown down in scores by machine guns and rifle fire and retired. The attack was renewed but was again repulsed. Great numbers of the enemy were shot down in these attacks, in one of which a Turkish (or German) officer reached our parapet, struck with his sword at one of the machine gunners and fell dead, riddled with bullets. No man's land was covered with dead bodies. Our losses were infinitesimal on this day compared with those

**Death of Lieuts. Rutland and Curwen-Walker.** of the Turks, but nevertheless some valuable lives were lost, including those of Lieut. J. B. Rutland[1] (the machine gun officer), Lieut. Curwen-Walker[2] (mortally wounded), Sgts. Kewley[3] and Barratt,[4] L.-Cpls. Bazen[5] and Neal,[6] and Ptes. Rooney, Fraser, Gorman, Richards, Jordan, Tippett, Allen, Delaney, Currie and Hislop. Lieut. Rutland was removing the parapet in front of his gun when he was shot through the head and killed instantly. He had done excellent and valuable work during the few days that he was in action, and his machine guns had broken up several Turkish attacks. Lieut. Curwen-Walker was fighting on the left of the position when he was mortally wounded in the stomach; no stretcher was available and he was carried away on a waterproof coat. He died on board ship on May 3. He was a native of Ballarat and a Duntroon graduate; a man who had won a reputation for coolness and bravery.

On May 2 the New Zealand and Australian Division made a vigorous and determined attempt to clear the Turks off the high ground which dominated Monash Valley. New Zealand and 4th Brigade troops took part in the operation. It was the first of many assaults made by the 4th Brigade during the war. The 13th and 16th Battalions took a prominent part and suffered heavily, but, with the exception of B Company, the 14th was not represented in the attack. Just at dusk a heavy bombardment was opened by the navy upon Baby 700, and the 16th seized a ridge connecting Quinn's with the Chessboard,[7] whilst the 13th seized a slope opposite to the position captured by the 16th, and on the other side of the valley.

**First Assault by 4th Brigade.**

---

[1]Lieut. John Bishop Rutland, machine gun officer, Canterbury, Victoria. Born April 12, 1894 at Camberwell, Victoria. Killed in action May 1, 1915. Capt. Jacka, V.C., who was an eye-witness, wrote an account of Rutland's death in the Melbourne "Herald" newspaper of April 24, 1926.

[2]Lieut. Arthur Herbert Curwen-Walker, Duntroon graduate, Ballarat, Victoria. Born at Ballarat. Educated at Ballarat College and Ballarat High School. Died of wounds May 3, 1915.

[3]Sgt. F. H. Kewley, C Company, draper, Ballarat East. Born February 16, 1895. Killed in action May 1, 1915.

[4]Sgt. T. L. Barratt, C Company, bootmaker, Bendigo. Killed in action May 1, 1915.

[5]L.-Cpl. R. C. Bazen, C Company, fitter. Killed in action May 1, 1915.

[6]L.-Cpl. F. M. Neal, C Company, school teacher, Tara, Queensland. Killed in action May 1, 1915.

[7]The Chessboard faced Pope's Hill.

## The History of the 14th Battalion.

About 9 p.m. B Company, which was then in reserve, received orders to stand by and be in readiness when required to move out and support the 16th Battalion.

**B Company, 14th, Participates.** The four platoons of the company moved out about 10 p.m., and after a strenuous tramp in the dark over holes and bushes reported to Lieut.-Col. Pope of the 16th with the result that Platoons Nos. 5, 6 and 7, under Lieuts. Ball, Combes and Harris respectively, were detached to the right to support the 16th, whilst No. 8 (Lieut. Boyle) was ordered to move to the left and assist the 13th. No. 7 Platoon was sent forward into a trench which was short-handed, whilst Platoons 5 and 6 remained as reserves at the head of the gully, just below the ridge on which the 16th Battalion trenches were situated. Here they remained all night, but shortly after daylight shells from our own guns in the rear began bursting over the 16th position. Three shells bursting over Platoons 5 and 6 caused about twenty casualties; Lieut. Combes,[8] the senior subaltern of B Company, was wounded. Some companies of marines arrived about daybreak and were thrown in as reinforcements, but the attack went to pieces during the morning as the Turks fought desperately and their positions were strong.

**Assault Unsuccessful.**

The 16th, which had put up a great fight during the night and suffered upwards of three hundred casualties, gradually retired during the forenoon. This retirement brought back Platoons 5, 6 and 7 with it.

Meanwhile, Lieut. Boyle, with No. 8 Platoon (numbering about twenty-five men[9]), had moved to the left and reported at 13th Battalion Headquarters, whose C.O. (Lieut.-Col. Burnage) instructed the platoon to stand by in the rear and dig in. Shallow holes were dug, just sufficient to give cover to a man lying down. When it became light on May 3 Boyle posted Pte. Larsen to keep a lookout towards the right flank, and, later, when the Turks commenced digging a new trench in front of Quinn's Post, the platoon was enabled to interrupt the work and inflict casualties on them. As no means of communication existed with the 16th Battalion on the right Pte. J. T. Straughair[10] volunteered to go down the valley on the rear and find out where the left of the 16th rested. He found that its withdrawal had been ordered and returned with this information. Meanwhile, fire was coming from both flanks and it was dangerous to move. Owing to the heavy fire on

---

[8]Lieut. Bertrand Combes, Duntroon graduate, Moonee Ponds, Victoria.
[9]It numbered 45 men on April 27, 1915.
[10]Pte. J. T. Straughair, No. 464, B Company, clerk, Bendigo, Victoria.

the rear slopes of the ridge the task of carrying ammunition up to the line was risky, and excellent work was done by Ptes. Lawson[11] and Sayer[12] in traversing dangerous ground; the former was dangerously wounded. In the evening orders were received to retire as a general retirement was to take place.

In the short period during which these captured positions were held by us there was not any Turkish sniping down Monash Valley; next day, however, it recommenced. At daylight on the 3rd the battalion R.M.O. (Capt. Loughran), L.-Cpl. Michie, Chaplain Gillison and the stretcher bearers made their way up the ravine to the left of Dead Man's Ridge. It was full of wounded, mostly Royal Naval Division and 13th men, and all the stretcher bearers soon had burdens. The R.M.O., Michie and Gillison then pushed on alone to the top of the plateau and discovered No. 8 Platoon on the right of Dead Man's Ridge. Numerous wounded were bandaged here until the dressings ran out, when the party returned to Courtney's.

B Company was the only portion of the 14th that was engaged in this disastrous struggle. The battalion casualties during May 2 to 3 were officially set out as twelve other ranks killed, and one officer (Lieut. Combes) and thirty other ranks wounded.

**Casualties in B Company.**

The killed included the following :L.-Cpl. W. H. O'Bree,[13] Ptes J. McNab, E. H. Spencer, H. J. Feetam, W. A. Brown, H. W. A. Baker, C. Thewlis, A. Abernethy, R. M. Thornton, N. S. Layton, W. H. C. Leeson and H. A. Mew. Among those wounded on May 2 was No. 612, Pte. H. J. Mullen,[14] of Terrick South, Victoria, and of No. 3 Platoon, who was invalided to England and died at Birmingham on May 19, 1915. He was the first member of the A.I.F. to be buried in England during the war. The High Commissioner for the Commonwealth, Sir George Reid, sent a beautiful wreath, and also sent Lieut.-Col. Tunbridge to represent him at the funeral.

---

[11]Pte. R. C. Lawson, No. 231, B Company, labourer, Mildura, Victoria.

[12]Pte. Percival James Sayer, No. 1215, B Company, carpenter, Bendigo, Victoria.

[13]L.-Cpl. William Henry O'Bree, No. 632, labourer, Orange, N.S.W. Killed in action May 2, 1915.

[14]Pte. Hugh James Mullen, No. 612, A Company, farmer, Terrick South, Victoria. Born at Terrick South January 14, 1892. Died of wounds at Birmingham on May 19, 1915. (Vide "Birmingham News" of May 29, 1915; also Melbourne "Argus" of July 28, 1915.)

The 4th Brigade had now been in the firing line for more than a week, and during that time had lost about two-thirds of its officers and upwards of one half of its men. The casualties of the 14th had been the lightest in the brigade.

On May 3 the unit's strength was reported as fifteen officers and six hundred and twenty other ranks.[15] The difficulties of the task facing the expedition were beginning to be appreciated, but optimism still prevailed. After the heavy fighting from April 27 to May 3 ensued a period of comparative calm, with few casualties (except from snipers), till the great Turkish attack on May 19. Although the enemy in some of his numerous attacks upon Courtney's had reached our parapet, he had not at any time been in our trenches. Lieut. Q. R. Smith,[16] of the 2nd reinforcements, was mortally wounded by a shell on May 2 when lying in a dugout beside L.-Cpl. Albert Jacka, who was uninjured.

*Death of Lieut. Quinton Smith.*

During the early days on the Peninsula Turkish snipers, by their daring and skill, had caused serious losses in our ranks. Sniping had never formed part of the battalion training, but it was taken in hand seriously by some of the more daring spirits about a week after the landing. The brigade assault of May 2 to 3, though unsuccessful, disturbed the Turkish positions and caused the enemy to send reinforcements to that locality. This enabled our men to do some excellent shooting, and gradually they wore the Turkish snipers down. C.S.M. Quirk, L.-Sgt Mahoney and Cpls. Lewis, Howard, Reg. Jones and others took an active part in this work. On May 17 Jones was severely wounded on the left shoulder by a sniper who was lying in wait in the scrub close to our lines. A few minutes later Mahoney[17] was killed by the same man. Mahoney was one of the bravest men in the battalion, and had particularly distinguished himself in the defence of Quinn's.

*Battalion Snipers.*

*L.-Sgt. Mahoney Killed.*

On May 6 the battalion received a welcome addition, its third reinforcements, whilst 'the third echelon, consisting

---

[15] The battalion strength on April 26, 1915, was set out as 28 officers and 900 other ranks.

[16] Lieut. Quinton R. Smith, 2nd Reinforcements, clerk, Essendon, Victoria. Died of wounds May 3, 1915.

[17] L.-Sgt. James Anthony Mahoney, No. 95,. A Company, labourer, Hawthorn, Victoria. Killed in action May 17, 1915.

**3rd Reinforcements Arrive.** of sixty-two men who had been left on board the "Seang Choon," arrived under Lieut. G. Cooper. The 15th Battalion made a night attack on May 9, and our trenches gave covering fire which caused many casualties among the Turkish supports. Major Steel[18] was invalided on May 11 and was unable to return to the battalion.

On the following day a splendid body of men, the Australian Light Horsemen (who had volunteered to serve as infantry), arrived from Egypt and took over from the 13th, 15th and 16th Battalions, allowing these war-worn and depleted units to enjoy a spell. The 14th, however, remained in the line. Periscopes and bombs were now available in much larger quantities, and proved to be of inestimable value. An advance was made from Quinn's Post on May 15, our trenches assisting with covering fire while our machine guns opened on the good target offered by the Turkish supports, and did considerable damage. Major-General Bridges, commanding the Australian Division, was mortally wounded by a sniper on this day in Monash Valley, not far from Courtney's Post.

Communication trenches by this time had been sapped forward, both to Quinn's, where a listening sap was put out, and to General Walker's position on the right, Sgt. Stewart Hansen taking an active part in the latter work. There was great activity in sapping and improving the trenches during this period, and both officers and men now had definite hours of duty in the trenches and resting. The carriage of water and ammunition from the beach to the front in those early days, involving as it did strenuous journeys over steep and rough roads, often under a broiling sun and frequently under the fire of snipers, tried to the utmost the strength, temper and nerve of those engaged in it. Valuable transport assistance was sometimes rendered by mules, a large number of which had been imported from Egypt. Several of these useful animals fell victims to the Turkish snipers. The fighting men had, on the Peninsula, one satisfaction. The men belonging to the non-combatant branches of the service, e.g., supply, ordinance, etc., here had to take a much greater share of the risks than they did after 1915.

---

[18]Lieut.-Col. T. H. Steel, O.B.E., merchant, Malvern, Victoria. Born Horsham, Victoria, November 19, 1878.

## CHAPTER VII.

### THE GREAT TURKISH ASSAULT AND THE FIRST AUSTRALIAN V.C.

#### 1915—May 19.

After a series of intermittent attacks on isolated posts, carried on now for more than three weeks, the Turks had decided on making one tremendous effort to break through the Australian lines and drive their occupants into the sea. Enver Pasha, who was largely responsible for dragging Turkey into the war, is credited with the conception of this idea. New Turkish batteries were erected and reinforcements hurried up from Constantinople. About dusk on May 18 a seventy-five came into action in an emplacement about six hundreds yards from Courtney's, and, opening fire, knocked our parapet about. No casualties resulted.

Information was received during the evening, as the result of aeroplane reconnaisance, that the Turks were massing preparatory to an attack, and everyone stood to arms. The communication trenches were filled with troops. Major Rankine was in command of the post, battalion headquarters being lower down the hill. B Company was in the line, D in support, and A and C in reserve. Fire was opened in defence by the supporting battleships and field guns. About midnight a heavy fire was opened on our trenches from rifles and machine-guns, while the massive "football" bombs were hurled over; it lasted for about half an hour. The noise was terrific, and the air was full of lead; many men were partially deaf for days afterwards. About 3.30 a.m. a general Turkish infantry attack was launched, and extended right along the Australian line.

**Great Turkish Attack Launched.** The Turks came on in thousands, shouting "Allah! Allah!" Our men would spring on to the fire steps, fire rapidly into the semi-darkness in front, and then disappear and reload. The firing was so furious, it is stated, that the woodwork of some rifles became almost too hot to be held. The

14th men probably at no other time during the war had so many human targets at close range, and in the breaking dawn they took full advantage of the opportunity. The battalion machine-guns tore great gaps in the enemy's ranks. Occasionally one of our men would fall, for the carnage was not completely one-sided, but his place was immediately taken by one of the many who were waiting for a chance to get into the front trenches. The Turks fought gallantly, but melted away under the torrent of lead that was poured against them, both frontally and enfilade. It was sheer butchery. No troops in the world could have successfully faced the fire. Shortly after daylight the Turks commenced to retire to their trenches, and as they went our rifles and machine-guns caused great slaughter in their ranks.

*Its Repulse.*

Just about daybreak, when the Turkish attack was at its height, Lieut. Boyle, who had gone to see whether the ammunition supply was in order. was informed that the Turks had broken into one of our trenches. Going past the corner of a trench to investigate, he was shot through the ear by a Turk at close quarters and stunned. He saw that there were not any supports in the trench immediately behind, and got them in. Lieut. Crabbe then took over from him, and Boyle was later wounded by shrapnel. Lieut. Hamilton[1] attempted to dislodge the Turks by advancing along the direct communication trench, but was shot dead.

*Turks Break into Trench.*

*Lieut. Hamilton Killed.*

Meanwhile, a brilliant piece of work by L.-Cpl. Albert Jacka[2] (D Company), of Wedderburn (Vic.) resulted in his winning the first Victoria Cross awarded to an Australian during the war. Hearing that the Turks were in our trenches, Jacka, with characteristic promptitude, and acting on his own initiative, set out to investigate. An attempted approach along the direct communication trench proving impracticable, as it was under Turkish fire, he, with true tactical intuition, made a flank movement, and secured a position behind a traverse in a fire trench, which blocked any

*L.-Cpl. Albert Jacka Wins First Australian V.C.*

---

[1] Lieut. W. H. Hamilton, Ballarat. Born May 24, 1894, at Natimuk, Victoria. Educated at Urquhart Street State School, Ballarat; Perth Boys' Hill School, Western Australia, and at Royal Military College, Duntroon. Killed in action May 19, 1915.

[2] Capt. Albert Jacka, V.C., M.C. and Bar.

attempted Turkish advance. Here he remained alone for several minutes, holding the Turks back until the arrival of Lieut. Crabbe, who took charge of operations. Jacka then volunteered to lead a bayonet charge to clear out the Turks, if ten others would follow him. Four[3] agreed to do so (three of them Bendigo men). Jacka then rushed the trench, but finding himself alone, among a number of Turks, and apparently unsupported, had to beat a retreat. What had

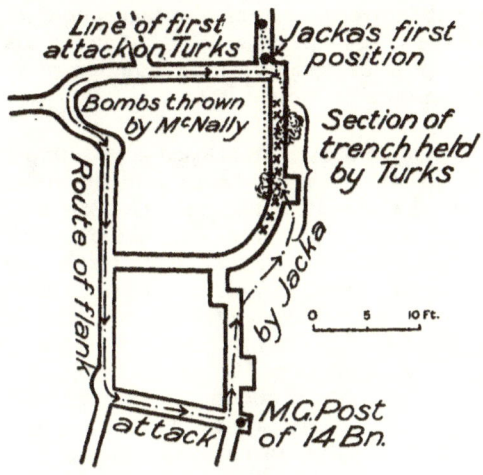

Portion of trench system
Courtney's Post

JACKA'S V.C. (May 19)

actually happened was that Howard and Bickley, following him, had been wounded and put out of action.

This direct frontal attack having failed, some discussion arose, and it was decided to endeavour to shift the Turks with bombs. Only two bombs were available, however, and both

---

[3]The four volunteers for the bayonet charge were:—L.-Cpl. Stephen d'Arango, No. 49, A Company, driver, Bendigo, born Bendigo, December 26, 1894; L.-Cpl. William Donald Howard, No. 73, A Company, driller, Bendigo, born Bendigo, May 13, 1891; Pte. Francis Edward Poliness, No. 114, A Company, metal polisher, Bendigo, born Geelong, December 18, 1893; Pte. Joseph Bickley, No. 533, D Company, grocer's assistant, Hastings, Victoria.

were thrown by Pte. McNally[4], the first being a failure. The second bomb, bursting on the parapet, raised a cloud of smoke and dust, under cover of which Jacka ran the whole length of the trench, and, springing into it from the rear, cleared it single-handed, bayoneting the first two Turks he met (one an officer) and shooting five more. A number of other Turks[5] in the trench bolted, startled by the whirlwind attack, and Jacka shot two (in addition to the seven officially credited to him) as they were disappearing over the parapet. Jacka's many exploits with the 14th made him the hero of his native State, and on his return to Melbourne, at the end of the war, he received a public welcome that a prince might have envied. But, as was the case with other V.C. winners, his reputation aroused the spirit of jealousy in a number of petty minds, both inside and outside the A.I.F.

The morning of May 20 disclosed a revolting scene. The bodies of Turks were lying in heaps, and the sufferings of the wounded must have been appalling. Doubtless, in the main, our opponents were rough and illiterate men, but they had fought like heroes, and given their lives freely in the defence of their country. Their courage in this engagement won them the lasting respect of the Anzacs, and henceforward, though our own men and the enemy recognised each other as political opponents, the fighting was purely impersonal. The Turkish losses were computed at seven thousand, and the Australian casualties at one hundred killed and five hundred wounded. The result was an eloquent tribute to the fact that unless the defenders can be taken by surprise, or their morale first shattered by high explosives, the attack has no chance against modern weapons in the hands of resolute men. There are few instances in the Peninsula campaign of a successful offensive on either side when the element of surprise was lacking.

<small>Respect of Anzacs for the Turks.</small>

During the night of May 18-19 the 14th men had fired twenty-three thousand round[6] of ammunition. The losses of the battalion, which had taken an active part in the battle, were:—One officer (Lieut. Hamilton) and ten other ranks

---

[4]Pte. James McNally, No. 1293, D Company, labourer, West Leederville, Western Australia.

[5]Twenty-six Turkish rifles were afterwards picked up in the trench.

[6]The normal daily expenditure was from 300 to 600 rounds.

killed, and Lieut. Boyle and 69 other ranks wounded. Lieut. Hamilton was one of the most promising of the battalion's young officers, and his death was a great loss to the unit. He was a cadet from Duntroon College, and before going on duty had remarked that it would soon be his 21st birthday, and he hoped to live long enough to enjoy it. The other ranks killed included L.-Cpl. R. Sayers,[7] and Ptes A. Walker, W. A. Day, H. D. Cole, R. F. Osborne, D. Clement, R. Angus, J. Tyler, W. V. Mow, and F. S. Binns, of the machine gun detachment.

---

[7] L.-Cpl. Ralph Sayers, No. 1108, B Company, labourer, Wonthaggi, Victoria.

# CHAPTER VIII.

## LAST DAYS ON COURTNEY'S POST.

### 1915—May 20 to May 31.

After the great attack of May 19 a period of comparative calm set in, varied by the usual routine of regimental life. A divisional order appeared on the 21st containing the promotion of R.S.M. Blainey and C.S.M. Booth to be second lieutenants.[1] These were the first promotions from the ranks in the battalion. On this evening two Japanese trench mortars were fixed, one on either side of our firing line, and during the night covering fire was given to Quinn's Post. The weapons were a great improvement on the trench mortars previously used; their bombs rose to a great height, and burst with a deafening explosion, causing great consternation to the Turks among whom they fell. Unfortunately, they were accompanied by an insufficient supply of bombs, so that the effect they produced was far less potent than it should have been. The enemy had a "broomstick" bomb, also devastating in its effects, which was by no means popular with our men.

*Japanese Trench Mortars Utilised.*

On May 24 an armistice for nine hours was arranged to allow the Turks to bury the dead who had fallen in the great assault, and collect any wounded men that might still be alive. Burial parties went out from both sides, and buried, as far as possible, all the dead lying in No Man's Land. Some bodies had been lying for weeks, and could not be handled, so holes were dug beside them and the remains interred. The identification discs of Australians previously posted as missing—men whose mouldering remains had been lying in No Man's Land—were collected. Strange faces appeared this day at the front line, visitors from the navy and some of the headquarters staffs. Friends and foes exchanged cigarettes and greetings. Parties of stretcher-bearers, under the Red Cross and the Red Crescent, scoured the country in search of wounded men.

*Armistice.*

Some of the 14th men, enjoying a spell out of the trenches

---

[1]Vide Chapter II.- "Promotions."

in the rear on May 25, were horrified to find some of their
mates beside them, dead or wounded. During
the night a sniper, or snipers, had worked
round, and got these dugouts into a line of
fire. All the men in the exposed position had
to clear out, and make fresh dugouts behind a knoll. Amidst
the horrors of war, it is not everyone who can retain his sense
of proportion. A striking instance of the ability to do so is
furnished by the diary of a 14th Battalion officer, describing
the above incident. After recording casually that the snipers
"caused several casualties in our bivouac area," he adds,
gravely, coming to the climax, "and smashed a jar of rum in
the quartermaster's store!"

**Enemy Snipers. Active.**

On May 25 the fine warship Triumph was torpedoed and
sunk, within sight of Anzac. Her spectacular loss in full view
of thousands who lined the hills caused no
little excitement; but it is alleged that some
excellent wine, from bottles salved on the
beach, found its way down the throats of
certain 14th boys, thus verifying the old Shakespearian adage
that "there is some soul of goodness in things evil."

**H.M.S. Triumph Torpedoed.**

The battalion casualties already incurred had left room
for promotion, and on May 27 the following promotions
appeared in divisional orders:—Capt. Dare to
be major; Lieuts. Clark, Combes, Boyle, and
Groom to be captains; and Sgts. Dadson,
Hansen, Laloe, Sanders, Matthews, Macdermid, and Couttie
to be second lieutenants.[2] Some of the newly appointed
subalterns took an active part in the subsequent operations of
the battalion, whilst Capt. Boyle[3] is believed to have been the
youngest captain who ever held rank in the A.I.F.

**Promotions.**

Before daylight on May 29 all on Courtney's heard a
terrific explosion; the earth shook, and sand bags and debris
were flung into the air. Word was received
that the Turks had blown up a portion of
Quinn's Post on the left, and instantly charged
into it. Our machine guns gave covering fire,
and some of our men reinforced the garrison. The Turks were
finally driven back, after a brief but energetic struggle. The
attack, unfortunately, resulted in the death of a hero of the

**Struggle at Quinn's.**

---

[2]Vide Chapter II.—"Promotions."
[3]Captain H. N. Boyle, of Brunswick (Vic.). Born December 28, 1895.
Captain when 19 years and five months old. Educated at St. Patrick's
College, East Melbourne, and Royal Military College, Duntroon.

4th Brigade—Major Quinn, of the 15th, after whom the post was named, and one of the finest soldiers on the Peninsula. The 14th R.M.O., accompanied by Pte. Agar, was on Quinn's shortly after the explosion, assisting the wounded, one of whom, with both thighs broken, became delirious after morphia had been administered; he hopped about on the stumps of his legs, feeling no pain until he was secured to improvised splints. Shortly afterwards he died.

Our men had now become accustomed to their surroundings at Courtney's. The trenches were only a few yards from the summit. Communication trenches ran back from the firing line, and on the slopes at the back of the hill lived the supports, like rabbits, in the dugouts which honeycombed the ground. There was no room for physical exercise. Sports (which to the Australian are almost as necessary as food) in any form were impossible. Water at all times was as scarce as vermin was plentiful. Overhead, day and night, whined the winged messengers of death. Snipers were ever ready to take toll of those who ventured out of cover for any purpose. Sanitation was attended to under most difficult conditions. Food, though good, was monotonous, and the lack of variety made it nauseous.

<small>Conditions at Courtney's.</small>

As the heat increased various articles of clothing were discarded, and Anzac became peopled with bronzed, semi-nude athletes. Some wrote the names of their home towns with indelible pencil on the front of their hats; this enabled them to recognise and fraternise with fellow townsmen on the beach and elsewhere. Men came to know each other's worth under these primeval conditions, for all veneer was stripped off, and everyone was valued exactly for what he was. The men of action displaced the talkers, who are so prominent in civil and political life, and the joint facing of danger fostered friendships such as ordinary life rarely knows. All, too, had acquired a strong feelong of esprit de corps in their battalion. Every shade of political, religious, and social thought was represented in the ranks, and probably the one subject on which there was a consensus of opinion was the superiority of the 14th to all other battalions in the A.I.F. And the members of all the other A.I.F. battalions held the same opinion about their respective units.

On May 30 Lieut.-Col. Courtney[4] was evacuated sick,

---

[4]Lieut.-Col. R. E. Courtney, C.B., V.D., solicitor, of Melbourne. Born Castlemaine (Vic.) September 8, 1870. Died of illness at Melbourne, October 21, 1919.

and never rejoined the battalion.  He was its first commanding officer, and saw it develop from an
inexperienced body of untrained men into the
splendid battalion he commanded on Courtney's Post.  He was an excellent organiser, and
his work in that direction was valuable, but delicate health
made him incapable of standing the strain of the Peninsula
campaign.  His optimistic temperament, too, sometimes misled
him in the choice of subordinates.  He died at Melbourne
shortly after the conclusion of the war, and his death was
doubtless accelerated by the worries and strain he experienced
on Gallipoli.

*Colonel Courtney Evacuated.*

On May 31 the battalion was relieved by the New
Zealanders, and left Courtney's (with which its name will
ever be associated) never to return.  During
its five weeks' occupancy it had suffered
severely, and the men looked a motley crew
as they moved off, carrying all their belongings on their back.  Some had not changed
their clothes for weeks, and most were vermin-covered.  All
were worn out and anxious for a spell.  The romance of war
had passed.  It was found to consist of continual labour, an
ever ceaseless vigil, an absence of every civilising influence
that makes life pleasant, and the ever-present prospect of
sudden death or mutilation.  The golden thread that ran
through so much misery, discomfort, danger, and filth, was
the strong spirit of comradeship and self-sacrifice existing
among so many gallant men.  That spirit, probably, was
stronger among the Australians than among any other troops
that served in the war.

*14th Relieved by the New Zealanders.*

The Machine Gun Section, under Lieut. Blainey, remained
behind to assist the New Zealanders.  By this time a sap had
been dug down Shrapnel Gully to the beach, so the retirement was made, free from the attentions of snipers, and the
battalion marched to its new headquarters at Reserve (sometimes humorously called Rest) Gully.

## CHAPTER IX.

### RESERVE GULLY.

#### 1915—June 1 to August 6.

**Reserve Gully.** Reserve Gully, which was to be the home of the 14th for eight weeks, was a fissure between two ridges leading down to the beach from Russell's Top. The gully ran almost due east and west, the sea being at its western end. Looking seaward, there was a good view of Imbros, with its mountain range, and the sunsets in that direction were often superb. The view inland from the gully was blocked by Russell's Top, whilst Plugg's Plateau shut off the view towards Helles. The whole of the 4th Infantry Brigade was now congregated in the gully as divisional reserve. At this time it was a pleasant, shady spot, the steep banks being covered with green bushes; when the brigade left, in August, it was dusty and smelly, and all the bushes had been destroyed.

**Strenuous Work There.** The time spent at the gully was not by any means in the nature of a picnic. Work of a strenuous character was imposed. Three days out of every four the battalion supplied working parties, consisting of from ten to fourteen officers, and four to five hundred men, clad usually in fatigue dress (i.e., a hat, sleeveless shirt, a pair of pants like bathing drawers, boots, socks, and rifle), with picks and shovels, who dug communication trenches to No. 1 Outpost, and dumps for stores in Mule, Reserve, and Supply Gullies. This heavy manual labour proved a severe test to men unaccustomed to such work. **Beach Parties.** Beach parties were also detailed to unload barges, and work the water pumps, dangrous duty, often performed under shell fire. In one of these beach parties Pte. H. Havis,[1] author of "An Anzac's Diary," was wounded on the 4th August, whilst at another Pte. N. T. Wynne[2] received the M.M. for rescu-

---

[1] Sgt. Herbert Havis (A Company, No. 66), farm labourer, from London (Eng.).

[2] Pte. Nathaniel Thompson Wynne (B Company, No. 1307), carpenter, of Carlton (Vic.).

ing a sergeant-major of an Indian unit, on the beach on July 7, from beneath a stack of live shells, which had been set on fire by the enemy's artillery—a gallant act.

The battalion turned out each morning at 3.30, and every fourth day acted as brigade reserve, turning in again at dawn if everything was quiet. Sea bathing was enjoyed in spare time, often under fire. Some men, who objected to be Turkish targets, did their bathing at night. Though thousands bathed off the beach for months, and many were killed and wounded in the water by shell fire, there is no record of any man being attacked by sharks.

The casualties in the security of the gully were, fortunately, very few, but the weather had now become extremely hot, and the dust and flies were almost unbearable. The flies were innumerable, and swarmed into and poisoned the food. Water, too, was very scarce; most of it came from Alexandria in barges, and had to be treated with chloride of lime, which, though a good disinfectant, did not make it more palatable. The food was meagre and monotonous, consisting largely of bully beef, biscuits and jam, occasionally some cheese, bacon and potatoes. The lack of bread was felt severely. Large numbers of men, about this time, fell victims to dysentery and para-typhoid, and became covered with septic sores; but losses were made good by the arrival of reinforcements, and the return of slightly wounded men. Amongst others who now returned to the battalion were Capts. Boyle, Groom, Hutton and Henry, and Lieuts. Warren, Couttie and Sanders. Lieut Laloe arrived from Imbros, where he had been temporarily in charge of General Sir Ian Hamilton's bodyguard. Lieuts. Luscombe and Morehouse joined as reinforcements.

*Plague of Flies.*

*Dysentery and Typhoid Prevalent.*

The stay at Reserve Gully was broken pleasantly by a brief trip (July 11 to 14) to Imbros, which heartened all ranks. But even on the peaceful isle platoon and company attack movements were undertaken, verifying the old adage that there is "no rest for the wicked." The return of the battalion to the gully on July 14 resulted in a resumption of the old duties. Anzac Beach about this time presented daily an animated appearance. Enormous quantities of stores and ammunition had been landed, and neatly packed in recesses, specially dug for the purpose, in the steep face of the cliff. Water was being continually pumped by hand from barges near the shore, and

*Trip to Imbros.*

carts at the margin of the sea. Various headquarters had also been established, and a few Red Cross flags were evidence of the activity of the Army Medical Corps. Beach parties were there in abundance, and the shore often swarmed with bathers, anxious for a plunge.

Towards the end of July there were many indications of a big movement in active preparation. Vast quantities of ammunition were landed daily; staff officers were frequently seen going to the outposts on the left, and senior officers were taken out in destroyers to reconnoitre the country on the left flank. Our equipment was overhauled, and bombers were trained in each company, under the supervision of Lieut. Crabbe. A sinister portent was the arrival of several hospital ships, which lay off the coast for some days immediately prior to the great advance. The one topic of conversation was the big job ahead, and rumours of all kinds were rife as to the shape it would take. The men (with the exception of a few "cold-footers") were keen and eager for the fray, and (being Australians) were full of optimism as to the result.

*Preparations for Great Advance.*

The security of the gully from shell fire made it an ideal mustering place for reinforcements. At the beginning of August large numbers of troops were landed at Anzac every night; among the newcomers were the Indian Gurkhas—small, stumpy men, but very companionable and excellent fighters. They wore hats of the Australian pattern. Terraces were dug along the side of every hill to accommodate the British and Indian troops that were to co-operate in the forthcoming attack. On August 2 the 6th Reinforcements joined the battalion; many of these men had had very little training.

*Sixth Reinforcements.*

On August 5 the Brigadier (Col. Monash) assembled all the officers and N.C.O.'s of the Fourth Brigade, and, in his clear and lucid style, explained the proposed attack, its objects and effects. According to the plan, the First Brigade of the A.I.F. was to capture Lone Pine; the Light Horse and other units were to attack on their front, and there was to be an offensive from Helles, in the south. It was hoped by these attacks to engage the enemy's attention, and compel him to bring his reserves to those spots, leaving open the position at Sari Bair, on our left, where the New Zealand and Australian Division, under Major-General Godley, was to attack, assisted on the north by a British Expeditionary Force, to be

*Plan of Great Advance.*

thrown ashore at Suvla Bay. The attack of General Godley's column was to be the main one, and the intention was to capture the dominating height of Koja Chemen Tepe, advance on Maidos, and open up the Narrows, permitting the British fleet to get through the straights and dominate Constantinople. The other attacks, above referred to, were feints. The troops destined for this main attack were to be divided into four columns, including a right and left assaulting column, separated from one another, and advancing up different gullies. The assaulting columns were to be assisted by two covering columns, whose duties were to clear the ravines and foothills, and keep the flanks of the assaulting columns clear. The left assaulting column, to which the 4th Brigade was attached, was commanded by Brigadier-General H. V. Cox, a British officer and a very capable soldier, who was afterwards the first commanding officer of the 4th Australian Division.

<small>Fourth Brigade Attached to Left Assaulting Column.</small>

The operations against Sari Bair were of an exceedingly complicated character, and necessitated an exhausting night march through an unknown, intricate, and bewildering "jungle" of cliffs, hollows and ravines, manned by an enemy of unknown strength and undoubted bravery, and fighting fanatically for the defence of his capital. The attacking forces consisted of converging columns, separated from one another by ranges of hills, so that the delay of any one column might ruin the whole plain. Some of the guides were Levantines of doubtful character, whilst the terrain was so intricate that whole columns lost their way, and our men sometimes came under a murderous fire from their own artillery. Our troops, as was usual during the Peninsula operations, owing perhaps, in part, to the optimism of Sir Ian Hamilton, were set enormous objectives, and nothing could ensure success but the hardest of fighting, the closest and most active of co-operation, the ablest of leadership, and a considerable element of luck. In any case, whether the movement proved successful or otherwise, the casualties were certain to be very severe. On August 6 the battalion strength was 24 officers and 858 other ranks. Major Rankine was in command, and Major Dare second in command.

<small>Enormous Objectives Set.</small>

## CHAPTER X.

### THE BATTLE OF ABD-EL-RAHMAN BAIR.

#### 1915—August 7 and 8.

**Cosmopolitan Forces Utilised.**
The force destined for the Sari Bair operations was a cosmopolitan one—Australians, New Zealanders, "Tommies,"[1] Gurkhas, and Sikhs, but it was composed of excellent fighting material. It numbered, however, in all only about 12,000 men, whilst it required probably twice or thrice that number to give any reasonable prospect of success. White patches of calico were sewn on the back of all tunics, and also on each arm, to ensure recognition in the dark, and everyone was warned that the first, and possibly the second, night would be sleepless. The operation looked as if it was going to be an arduous one. A plentiful supply of iron rations[2] had been issued, and for the first time since the landing plenty of drinking water was available at the outset of the operation.

**Great Offensive Starts.**
The great offensive started on the afternoon of August 6. The 4th Brigade in Reserve Gully could hear the opening of the struggle down south at Lone Pine. The distant artillery fire sounded like continual peals of thunder, whilst close at hand cruisers were firing over Reserve Gully at the Turkish positions, and some British howitzers near the foot of the gully, also firing at the Turks, added to the din.

**4th Brigade Advances.**
At dusk all was ready in our lines for the advance. Blankets, great coats, and packs had all been stored so that the march might be hampered with as little equipment as possible. At about 9 p.m. the battalion fell in at the foot of the gully; the order to advance was given, and the brigade marched towards the sea in the following order:—13th, 14th, 15th, and 16th Battalions. Brigade headquarters followed the

---

[1]"Tommies."—The generic name by which the British Imperial troops are known.

[2]Iron rations are the emergency rations; only to be used if other rations are not available.

## The History of the 14th Battalion. 55

13th Battalion, and behind the 14th Infantry came the Battalion Machine Gun Section, and behind that again Capt. Loughran (the regimental medical officer), the stretcher-bearers, and Chaplain Gillison. Every precaution had been taken that the march through the enemy's country should be as silent as possible, and special instructions had been issued that the bayonet alone on this night march was to be the weapon for attack. Lights were not permitted, and both talking and smoking were prohibited.

It was a beautiful, though moonless, night, and the stars twinkled overhead. All marched with bayonets fixed, and rifles slung over their shoulders. Heavy salvoes of Turkish shrapnel were bursting round the British howitzers at the foot of the gully as the troops marched by, causing two or three casualties. The column turned to the right on reaching the beach, and marched north parallel to the coast. Some Light Horse scouts (who had recently been doing some scouting in the locality at night) were stationed at various points to assist in keeping direction. The cruisers out at sea were directing their searchlights over Turkish positions further inland, and Turkish shells aimed at the cruisers were passing high over head; the atmosphere soon became thick with smoke. The column was long, the night dark, and the pace in consequence slow.

**Marches North.**

Upon reaching No. 2 outpost[3] all lay down in the open and awaited further orders. Meanwhile, the right covering force of New Zealanders was forcing its way inland, and as a result the 4th Brigade could hear cheers and yells, the bursting of bombs, and machine gun and rifle fire as the New Zealanders closed with the enemy. After some delay the march of the left assaulting column was resumed, and proceeding further north it turned inland into the Chailak Dere, and following it up crossed the Aghyl Dere, and moving up it finally occupied a position near the Kaiajik Dere. Meanwhile the left covering force, acting in co-operation, seized some heights on the left. After leaving No. 2 outpost, all knew that they were in enemy's territory marching into the unknown, and had to be prepared for any contingency. The Indian Brigade, which was to co-operate with the 4th Brigade, and

**No. 2 Outpost Reached.**

**Brigade Turns Inland.**

---

[3]Lieut.-General Godley, who was in charge of the Sari Bair operations, subsequently fixed his headquarters here, and supplies of ammunition and water for the use of the fighting troops were organised on this spot.

56         *The Battle of Abd-el-Rahman Bair.*

ABDEL RAHMAN BAIR

to attack between it and the New Zealanders, had followed up behind.

The Fourth Brigade, about 11.30 p.m., was formed into two columns, the 13th and 14th comprising the left or outer column, and the 15th and 16th the right or inner column, the intention being to spread out the forces so as to clean up the whole valley in the advance. The 13th pushed ahead, and formed the screen of the outer column. The advance consisted of a series of marches, halts, and skirmishes, combined with a certain amount of running and ducking. The advance was up a wide valley in which, like islands, were some rugged, bushy hills. The valley flat was covered with soft grass; olive and other large trees were growing here and there, and the air was full of the scent of wild thyme. The fragrant surroundings and balmy air seemed like paradise after the dusty, treeless gully which the brigade had only just vacated. There was little organised opposition at first, as the Turks were obviously taken by surprise by this night march through their territory, but there were a few casualties from stray bullets. The 15th and 16th, however, had encountered some determined opposition in their advance on the right. Towards dawn the opposition in front of the 13th and 14th stiffened, and for a time the advance guard was held up, and two platoons of A company 14th (under Lieuts. Macdermid and Crabbe) were sent forward to assist the 13th. Meanwhile, the rest of the 14th moved to the left, filed past the 13th, and took up the advance just as dawn was breaking. The march had been delayed through the left covering column having been some hours behind schedule time. A party of about 50 Turks pushed towards our lines by the advance of the 15th and 16th Battalions were killed or dispersed by B Company men, some of them quite close to our position. Their water bottles were eagerly seized by our men. A few, however, escaped and commenced sniping our lines later on. About dawn some of our scouts reported troops digging in on our left. These were passed, and proved to be a regiment of "Tommies."

*Formed Into Two Columns.*

*Completion of Night March.*

The first part of the hazardous operation—the night march—planned for the Fourth Brigade, had been successfully and triumphantly achieved, and we were now in the heart of the enemy's country. This night march proved one of the most memorable exploits of the Fourth Brigade and a

*Fine Display of Discipline.*

proof of the high standard of its discipline, and of the nerve
and coolness of its personnel. There were some reinforcements in its ranks which had only joined a few days prior to
the march, and had never been under fire, yet all had marched
in a dark night, through enemy's territory, in the midst of a
raging artillery fire, with some wounded by bullets from an
unseen enemy, and even under these trying conditions orders
had been strictly carried out, not a shot had been fired, strict
silence had been maintained, and the prisoners taken were
captured unaware of our presence until they were taken sleeping in their bivouacs.

It was now broad daylight. The battalion had reached
a spot (known afterwards as Australia Valley) where there
was a deep gully in front, and across it a low
**Australia Valley.** hill. All ranks were exhausted by the night
march, and the consequent want of sleep, but
the panorama that lay spread before them was a recompense
for all their toil, and an augury for the success of the operation
which was intended to terminate the Peninsula campaign, and
capture Constantinople. Suvla Bay lay to the left rear, full
of cruisers and transports, with smaller vessels passing
between them and the shore. Battleships were pouring forth
broadsides, and the Suvla Bay area was full of smoke from
the bursting shells. A co-operating army was being thrown
ashore on the left flank. The tactical scheme was apparently
working out exactly as scheduled. The Turks had been
obviously surprised, and there did not seem to have been
anything to have prevented the Suvla Bay force from immediately seizing the commanding heights overlooking Suvla.
About a mile to the left rear were two red-roofed buildings
(Kabak Kuyu). Some of the Battalion signallers (always of
a roving disposition) walked over there, and returned with
fresh water and honeycomb.

There was some argument among the officers of the four
battalions as to where the brigade should entrench. The
maps of this part of the country were not very accurate, and
there seemed some uncertainty as to whether the brigade had
reached the scheduled spot for the day, for the men were too
exhausted by the night march to attack forthwith. It was,
however, finally decided to entrench on the
**Battalion** spot then reached, viz., a ridge fronting the
**Entrenches.** Kaiajik Dere—a big, dry watercourse with
precipitous banks. For some reason, the men
were instructed to dig in on the enemy's side of the ridge,
instead of the side facing the sea. The drive down the Dere

by the 4th Brigade had forced the Turks inland, and advantage was taken of their absence to construct trenches, and consolidate the position. There was not any interference with our men for nearly a couple of hours, but then the Turks, relieved of pressure by the halt of the brigade, returned and commenced firing from the next ridge. The sniping from inland grew hotter and hotter, with resultant casualties, and many of our men stopped digging, and hastily changed their position to the other side of the ridge, where they were under better cover. They dug little holes, without communication with one another, but sufficient to give protection to the occupants from fire, when lying flat. Here all passed a most trying day, waiting for night to release them from their cramped positions. Among the killed was Capt. Groom, O.C. of C Company (sniped when observing). Lieut. Warren then took over command of the company.

*Hot Enemy Sniping.*

*Capt. Groom Killed.*

During the day, Capt. Loughran (the R.M.O.) and the stretcher-bearers worked unceasingly for the wounded, often under fire,[4] and went out again at night and searched the ridges for any of the wounded that might have been overlooked.[5] It was after midnight before their labor ceased. Night also brought its duties, as fatigue parties had to make their way to a gully (about a mile in the rear) to help carry tins of water to the front. Exhaustion was now beginning to make itself felt. It was Saturday, and, since the previous Thursday night, sleep had been unobtainable. The interval had been varied by a surfeit of marching, fighting, and heavy digging with picks and shovels, whilst the meagre supply of water now available scarcely alleviated thirst. Advantage was taken of the darkness to deepen the holes and connect them by trenches. All were now able to move about without the danger of being sniped at.

*Battalion Exhausted.*

A hot day was followed by a cold night, and weary, hungry, dirty and cold (blankets and overcoats having been left behind), the men shivered through the dark hours. The conditions were such that, for the second successive night, sleep was almost unobtainable. Unfit as all were from physical

---

[4]The casualties for the day (August 7) consisted of one officer (Capt. Groom) and nine other ranks killed, and one officer (2nd Lieut. Neale) and 23 other ranks wounded.

[5]Pte. Raymond Phillips, one of the stretcher-bearers, lost a leg whilst carrying out his duties.

exhaustion for further effort, the battalion was to be called upon next day to attempt one of the hardest propositions ever given to Australian troops during the war. At 7.45 p.m. on August 7, C.O.'s and adjutants of the four battalions had attended at brigade headquarters and received orders to advance and attack next morning Koja Chemen Tepe, via the Abd-el Rahman Bair. The position, which was to be captured at all costs, was the highest and most dominating height on the Peninsula.

The line now ran as follows:—A Battalion of the British Division (5th Wiltshires) on the left, then the 13th, 14th, 15th and 16th Battalions in that order, with the 29th Indian Brigade on the right. The 13th Battalion was to be in reserve, and not to take part in the proposed attack, which was to be conducted (as far as the 4th Brigade was concerned) by the 14th, 15th, and 16th. The Gurkhas were to attack on the Brigade's right, and, further south, the New Zealanders of the right assaulting column were to continue their attack of the previous day. The newly arrived Suvla Bay force was to co-operate on the left of the 4th Brigade, and protect that flank.

**Orders for the Battle.**

August 8.

At 2.30 a.m. the exhausted men rose and fell in by companies and marched out in the dark on the new adventure. The 15th Battalion led the column, followed by the 14th, which was in its turn followed by the 16th. The troops slid down into the gully below and advanced in the direction of Hill 60. The approach of daylight disclosed the objective (Koja Chemen Tepe), and all recognised its capture entailed a formidable task on the brigade. Some of the more reflective thought that it might be possible for a handful to reach the summit, but the chance of any getting back seemed problematical. During the advance, General Godley's headquarters was at No. 2 Outpost. Brigade signallers during the action got through a telephone wire from brigade headquarters to Colonel Pope (16th Battalion), who was the senior 4th Brigade officer in the forward area. After an advance of some distance across hills and valleys, a turn was made to the right through a stubble patch known as the "cornfield," without any cover whatever. Here the Turks made their presence felt, and the brigade crossed this at the double under a terrific fire. Men were dropping everywhere, and the air was alive

**Advance of Brigade.**

**Terrific Enemy Fire.**

with missiles. After the dash across the "cornfield," the 14th deployed into four lines of companies. Major Rankine (who had been unwell) here fainted, and Major Dare took command of the 14th. A further advance brought the brigade on to ground commanded by enemy trenches on higher ground, and by machine guns admirably placed to bring enfilade fire on every movement. The 15th Battalion, in front, withered away under this concentrated fire, and the 14th, suffering heavy casualties, found itself confronting the enemy, whom it gradually pushed back. C and D Companies, which were in the lead, had got into position before A and B arrived. On arrival, they came in on the right of C and D, with the Indian Brigade on their own right.

*Major Dare Takes Command.*

The attack as planned provided for the co-operation of the Suvla Bay force on the left flank. This co-operation, however, failed to materialise, with the result that the left flank of the 4th Brigade was "in the air," and the Turks were thus able to concentrate their energies on the destruction of it. Great numbers of Turks, deploying behind a hill, came out and enfiladed our left flank, which was bent back to meet the attack. An attempt was made by our men to dig in, but that was not any protection against the enemy's shrapnel, which took a heavy toll. Fire was now coming, not only from the high slopes in front, but also from the left and right fronts, and the high slopes to the south. In the confused and chaotic fighting that ensued, units got intermingled, men separated from their officers, and there was a lack of co-ordination and control perhaps inevitable under the circumstances. It was manifestly impossible to push on with an unprotected flank, which was crumbling to pieces under the pressure of incessant counter-attacks, whilst adequate artillery support (which was essential for a successful advance) was not forthcoming.

*Failure of Suvla Bay Force.*

*Brigade Advance Checked.*

As the battalion was rapidly melting away without the possibility of advance, Capt. George Cooper, adjutant of the 14th, went back and acquainted the Brigadier with the serious position at the front.[7] General Monash, realising that the

---

[6] Exactly three years later (August 8, 1918) the 4th Brigade (whose present brigadier was then corps commander) participated in, on French soil, the famous battle which practically decided the war.

[7] Col. Cannan (C.O., 15th Battalion) and Lieut. Locke, of 4th Brigade Staff, made a verbal report to the Brigadier of an exactly similar character.

brigade, if left, was doomed to destruction, got into communication with General Cox, with the result that instructions were issued for the 4th Brigade to withdraw from its perilous position. About 7.30 a.m. instructions reached the firing line to retire. Major Dare was loath to do so, and sent back to say that, if support could be given to our left flank, we could hold the position captured, but a further message was received from Colonel Pope, stating that the whole brigade was retiring, and that the 14th must retire. The order was obeyed and the troops withdrew by platoons in a straggling formation, but without undue haste, some helping the wounded and others carrying back equipment. Unfortunately, some of the very severely wounded and all of the dead had to be left to fall into Turkish hands. Capts. Giles and Henry were in command of the 14th's rearguard. Very efficient covering fire was now given by the 4th Brigade Machine Gun Section, under Captain Rose; with him was Lieut. Blainey with his guns and men. There was an escort of about 50 men of various battalions with the machine gun section in the retreat, including Lieut Macdermid and Sgts. Norman Harris and Duffield, of the 14th. The presence and efficient handling of the machine gun section inflicted heavy casualties on the Turks, and probably saved the rearguard from destruction.

**Brigade Retires.**

Prior to the retirement, a small handful of C Company had forced its way into the Turkish position, and, after a vigorous struggle, been cut off and destroyed. Opposite our left flank were three small outlying ridges held by the Turks in front of their main position on the Abdel Rahman Bair. Lieut. Warren, O.C. of C Company—a man of keen and resolute character—promptly determined to attack them, but, falling mortally wounded, ordered Lieut. Luscombe (No. 9 Platoon) to push on. The Turks retreated behind the second ridge as Luscombe advanced with about a dozen men, reinforced a few minutes later by Lieut. Curlewis (No. 11 Platoon) with several more men. Curlewis was soon mortally wounded by machine gun fire. Reinforcements were badly wanted, and a 15th Battalion man[8] (one of the party) volunteered to carry back a message requesting them, but was killed by shrapnel while crossing the

**Death of Lieut. Warren.**

**Death of Lieut. Curlewis.**

---

[8]The name of this gallant man has unfortunately been lost.

**Lieut. Luscombe Wounded and Captured.**

ridge en route. The Turks now counter-attacked. The handful of Australians built a barricade of ammunition boxes which they had captured, and fought desperately until several had been killed, when the thirteen survivors (only two of whom were unwounded) surrendered. Sgt. Neyland, Cpl. Kerr, and Pte. Masterton did excellent work under very trying conditions. This little body of brave men[9] is believed to have made the furthest advance in the ranks of the 4th Brigade that day.

Meanwhile, the shattered relics of the 14th had returned to the camping ground of the morning, and moved up in rear of the 13th, which had not taken part in the action. Every one was in the last stage of exhaustion. Some had not had any sleep since they left Reserve Gully two days previously. Half of the personnel of the battalion was killed, wounded or missing. C and D Companies, acting on the

**Appalling Losses.** exposed left flank, and bearing the full weight of the Turkish counter-attacks, had been decimated. Every officer in C Company had been killed or wounded. A and B Companies, fighting more to the right, had far less casualties. The killed alone in the 14th, on August 8, was upwards of 100. With one exception,[10] it was the bloodiest day the battalion ever had. The 4th Brigade had fought in a manner worthy of its old renown, but the heroism of its personnel was hopeless against the difficulty of the terrain, the enormous objectives set, and the failure of co-operation by the Suvla Bay force.

Six officers had been killed, viz., Capt. Groom,[11] Lieuts. Warren,[12] Curlewis,[13] Harris,[14] Hill,[15] and Matthews.[16] Capt.

---

[9]The names of the gallant handful captured deserve to be remembered, and are :—Lieut. Leslie Luscombe, O.C., No. 9 Platoon, clerk, Kew, Victoria (wounded). No. 2192, Sgt. Niver Neyland, farmer, Ouyen, Victoria (wounded). No. 888, Cpl. G. E. Kerr, labourer, East Melbourne (wounded). No. 896, Pte. James Masterton, cook, Surrey Hills, Victoria (wounded). Also Ptes. H. N. Brown, W. Williams, W. H. Stringer, J. Passmore, H. Foxcroft, T. H. Dowell, W. E. Warnes, Henessy, P. O'Connor, all of the 14th Battalion; and Pte. J. Mathers of the 15th Battalion. To these must be added Pte. B. Calcutt, 14th Battalion, Williamstown, Victoria, also wounded, who died in the hands of the Turks.

[10]April 11, 1917.

[11]Capt. W. E. Groom, clerk, Brighton, Victoria. Killed in action August 7, 1915.

[12]Lieut. R. Warren, clerk, North Brunswick, Victoria. Killed in action August 8, 1915.

[13]Lieut. K. Curlewis, electrical engineer, Malvern, Victoria. Killed in action August 8, 1915. Three other members of the Curlewis family

**Details of Casualties.**

Groom and Lieut. Warren—both of C Company—were gallant men and capable officers, both of whom had already been wounded in prior engagements. The wounded officers included Capt. Boyle,[17] Lieuts. Morehouse, Luscombe, and 2nd Lieut. Neale. Capt. Boyle was a very intelligent young officer who had seen much fighting with the battalion. Capt. Hutton was also incapacitated by the re-opening of an old wound, and had to be evacuated. The battle had also fatal results for a large number of N.C.O.'s, including Sgts. Chippendale (E. Brunswick), Stokan (Malvern), Twose (Burnley), Quirke (Coburg), and McAllister (Scotland), also Cpls. Wells (St. Kilda), Whitteron (Kew), Hope (Queenscliff), Greengrass (Yarraville), Smith (Yarrawonga), White (Armadale), and Hewitt (Wedderburn); and L.-Cpls. Brewer (no details), Murphy (Bendigo), Allan (Williamstown), Goble (Scotland), Kneale (Armadale), Laker (England), Taylor (Corowa, N.S.W.), Negro (Richmond), and Cubitt (Abbotsford). Capable N.C.O.'s are the backbone of a battalion, and the loss of so many fine men was irreparable. Among the severely wounded were Sgts. R. H. Berry and H. Vernall, and Cpl. E. R. Davison—the two latter each losing an arm. Among the privates must be mentioned Pte. F. A. Boden, of the 3rd Reinforcements, who lost his life on an errand of mercy, when carrying a wounded Turkish officer to the beach on August 7.

---

(brothers or cousins of Lieut. K. Curlewis) lost their lives in the ranks of the A.I.F. at Gallipoli.

[14] Lieut. H. R. Harris, salesman, Maryborough, Victoria. Killed in action August 8, 1915.

[15] Lieut. T. N. Hill, Sandringham, Victoria. Killed in action August 8, 1915.

[16] Lieut. J. H. Matthews, postal official, Ararat, Victoria. Born Amherst, Victoria, December, 1894. Killed in action August 8, 1915.

[17] Capt. H. N. Boyle, Duntroon graduate. Vide footnote No. 9, Chapter VIII.

## CHAPTER XI.

### MISCELLANEOUS DUTIES.

#### 1915—August 9 to August 13.

During the battle of August 8 the dressing stations of the 14th and 15th Battalions were situated in a small "dere" running toward the Kaiajik Dere, and close to the "cornfield." The wounded soon kept pouring in, and the stretcher-bearers were very busy; few stretchers were available, and improvised ones of all kinds were called into use. Shortly before the retirement, a body of Turks appeared on the other side of the stubble field, and for a time things looked serious, for the fighting troops were not in the vicinity, and there was danger of the medical personnel being captured. Sgt.-Major Warburton, however, who was there, showed presence of mind, rallying some signallers who were at hand and distributing ammunition. The awkward position was relieved by the timely arrival of the Fourth Brigade Machine Gun Company, which opened fire and dispersed the Turks. The stretcher-bearers, signallers and other details then retired. The machine-gunners who covered the retreat assisted in getting back some of the wounded.

After the retirement on August 8, the survivors of the Battalion rested in Australia Gully for the remainder of the day, but next day were ordered to take over the trenches of a British unit—the 6th King's Own, a Lancashire regiment. This unit had suffered severe enfilade fire, through neglect to deepen the trenches, which were strewn with their dead bodies. The parapets, likewise, were covered with dead, and our men had to remove the corpses prior to deepening the trenches, which they worked at hard all night. The water question was always acute, but an unofficial issue was here appropriated, consisting of a small quantity left by the unfortunate dead "Tommies."

*Battalion Relieves 6th King's Own Regiment.*

On August 10, three officers and 100 other ranks, under Capt. A. R. Cox, were sent to support the Gurkhas on the right. They were absent three or four days, during which time Capt. Cox was wounded. Some days of comparative quiet then ensued, and was utilised in ordinary trench routine: the men were occupied in improving our trenches and communication trenches, in sapping toward the 13th Battalion on the left across the plateau, and in carrying food and ammunition to the trenches, from where the mule trains which carried these necessaries up from Anzac used to stop, about half-a-mile away. Parties were also despatched to Reserve Gully to bring the packs which had been left there on August 6, prior to the march north.

*Miscellaneous Duties.*

During this spell, Corporal Reg. Jones (whose aggressive spirit was always active) formed a sniping position known as the "shooting gallery," capable of holding four men, from which a great deal of very effective shooting was done, and much damage inflicted on the enemy. The Turks across the Dere were carrying bushes to erect a screen behind which to dig, and provided many good targets. Corporal Lewis and others were specially active here. The Turks, however, located the post on August 12 (through the presence of some staff officers who had made use of it temporarily as an observation post), and Jones was wounded that same afternoon in such a way as to prevent him from effectively sniping again. His intelligence and courage already stamped him as one of the very finest soldiers the A.I.F. ever possessed. He had done yeoman sniping work for the Battalion, and personally accounted for upwards of fifty Turks since his arrival on the Peninsula.

*The "Shooting Gallery."*

One of the most important days in the history of the battalion on the Peninsula was that on which the water trouble ceased. It is impossible to realise the sufferings that had been endured during the torrid summer months through the insufficiency of water, and the battalion owed a debt of gratitude to Sergeant Crapper,[1] an old miner, who at this time untiringly sunk wells for water. His successful efforts rejoiced hundreds, and assured a plentiful supply of splendid fresh water for the first time since the landing. The sergeant, who was 46 years of age, unfortunately died at Malta of illness brought on by his exertions.

*Sgt. Crapper's Successful Search for Fresh Water.*

*His Death.*

---

[1]Sgt. Charles Crapper (No. 969), miner, of Tandara (V.), Born at Raywood (Vic.) on May 8, 1869. A veteran of the South African War. Died of illness at Malta, September 27, 1915.

A phenomenon that occurred about this time was dropping bullets, which used to fall frequently in Australia Gully—probably Australian, fired too high at the Turks on Baby 700, and coming across the plateau and falling on our men. Sometimes at night they would come down like raindrops. Rapid musketry could be heard in the distance when this occurred, and several slight casualties resulted from them, but not anything serious.

**Dropping Bullets.**

A reaction after the excitement of the late engagement now set in, and the complaints which had been rampant when the battalion was in Reserve Gully—dysentery and septic sores, i.e., "Barcoo rot"[2]—again asserted themselves. The men were worn out. They began to be very weary of trenching, sapping, and carrying stores and ammunition. Excessive labour and lack of variety in their diet had brought them to the limit of their strength, and their best efforts had failed to attain success. Only their native courage and unquenchable optimism kept them from collapsing. Large numbers were so weak that they could hardly handle a rifle. But they were to be called upon for further effort and more severe fighting before the campaign ended.

**Battalion Worn Out.**

---

[2] Many men marched out to battle on August 6, suffering from "barcoo rot," and with bandages on. The worst cases were left with Major Young (quartermaster) as baggage guard over packs, greatcoats, etc.

# CHAPTER XII.

## ATTACKS ON HILL 60.

### 1915.—August 20 to September 2.

**Failure of Great Offensive.** The great offensive of the British Expeditionary Force of August 6 to 12, though illuminated by countless acts of heroism, and favoured with some local tactical successes, had failed. The attempt to get astride the Peninsula, open up the Narrows, and enable the British fleet to reach Constantinople, had not materialised. The Turks still held the key to the Peninsula. They were ably commanded, and fighting heroically, and the attempts to storm their strongly fortified positions had proved extremely costly. Optimism at Army Headquarters, however, was still pronounced, and the failure of the Suvla Bay contingent to make good on its front determined Sir Ian Hamilton to bring up from Helles the famous 29th British Division to attack Scimitar Hill, overlooking Suvla Bay. The attack was to be an extended one, reaching from Scimitar Hill to Hill 60, opposite the 4th Brigade positions. Portion of General Godley's force was ordered to co-operate in the proposed attack, and 500 men of the 4th Brigade, with other details, were temporarily **Operation against Hill 60.** detached from their immediate commands and placed under General Russell, of New Zealand, who was in charge of the local operation against Hill 60. The 4th Brigade detachment was chosen from the 13th and 14th Battalions in equal proportions. New Zealand troops were to attack further to the left. Hill 60 was unoccupied by the Turks during the 8th August battle, but had since been seized by them, strongly fortified and garrisoned.

The 14th quota, viz., 250 men (the fittest in the Battalion) was picked on August 20 for the attack, which was to take

## The History of the 14th Battalion. 69

**14th to Participate in Attack.** place the following day. On the 21st, the officers who were to take part reconnoitred the ground, and water, ammunition, tools, and sandbags were issued to the personnel. The 4th Brigade assaulting party had to advance from the 13th Battalion trenches (on the 14th's left) under cover of a little hill in the middle of the Kaiajik Dere (held by a few Turkish snipers), cross to and clean out this hill, and then charge across the Dere, climbing the opposite bank, and then advance and take a Turkish trench situated a little distance above the bank on the Turkish side of the Dere. As our men emerged from the shelter of the little hill in the Dere, they would come into full view of the Turks.

At 2 p.m. the bombardment opened. Naval and field guns shelled the Turkish trenches for upwards of an hour. A body of 14th Pioneers, light duty men,[1] cooks and batmen, under Lieut. McQueen, were left in our trenches to open a covering fire on the enemy's trenches and prevent movement behind his lines.

At 3.30 p.m. the bombardment ceased and the first wave, consisting of 150 men of the 13th under Lieut. Ford, charged.

**Charge by 14th Battalion.** Suffering heavy casualties crossing the Dere, they drew up at the foot of the hill just at the top of the other side of the Dere. A few minutes later came the turn of the 14th—the second wave of 150 men under Major Dare. A whistle blew, and down the hill they raced like madmen. The Turks were by this time thoroughly aroused and alert, and the moment the crest was passed by our men, artillery, machine-guns and rifles vomited death in their faces. Forty per cent. became casualties in that short, wild, frenzied charge.

**Lieuts. Crabbe and Duffield Killed.** Lieuts. Crabbe and Duffield were killed. Major Dare, Lieut. D. R. Macdermid, and Sgt. Ernie Hill got through unwounded. A timely and courageous display of leadership in this charge on the part of Sgt. Ernie Hill won the M.M. for that popular N.C.O. The survivors joined up with the 13th Battalion men who had stopped at the foot of the hill. It was impossible to complete the attack on the trench without artillery support, so Major Dare (who assumed command of the survivors of both waves) ordered the position to be con-

---

[1] The light-duty men, under normal conditions, should have been in hospital. Some were so ill that they could hardly hold a rifle. The regimental medical officers had been instructed not to evacuate anybody able to stand in a trench, and capable of holding a rifle.

solidated. Fortunately, though it was impossible either to advance or retreat, the position was immune from the Turkish frontal fire, being tucked away in the front of the hill. It now became the duty of the third wave of 200 men (consisting of 100 men each from the 13th and 14th Battalions) to repeat the attack made by the first two waves. It, however, proved impracticable. The Turkish machine-gun fire had now become so hot as to block all advance, and when the third wave attempted to charge it was brought to a standstill, with the exception of Sgt. Bertram Edmonstone and a handful of men, who charged through and survived the deadly fusilade. Many were hit immediately they appeared on the crest, and fell straight back into the gully. Some got a few yards and were wounded, or had to lie down in the scrub, the machine-gun bullets just grazing them. The fourth wave—consisting of a Hampshire battalion—had a similar experience. Scores were shot down, and it, too, failed to support the two leading waves, now isolated, and with no means of communication with their own lines, except over the fearful bullet-swept slope behind.

Major Dare was anxious to communicate with General Russell, to inform him where our lines had reached, and ask for artillery support. There were not any signallers available, and but one means of communication remained, viz., by runner. It looked like certain death to get a message through that bullet-swept valley, but there were not any dangers that Anzacs would not face. Young Geoffrey Veel,[2] of Bendigo (A Company), volunteered to take the message back to our lines. Every Turkish gun available opened on him as he rushed across the valley, but he dashed unharmed through a shower of bullets, only to fall dead when he reached our trench among his comrades, for whom the young hero had risked and given his life.

*Pte. Geoffrey Veel's Sacrifice.*

To add to the horrors of the day, an enemy shell set fire to the scrub on the hill just crossed by the attacking waves. As the fire spread it ignited the bombs carried by some of the dead lying scattered in the scrub, which, exploding, increased the area of fire. The plight of the hapless wounded was appalling. Some who tried to escape from the flames were shot down by the enemy's snipers. Little assistance could be rendered in daylight on the bullet-swept hill, though under cover of the smoke several wounded men were dragged away by the stretcher-bearers from near the fire. It was a night

---

[2] Pte. Geoffrey C. Veel (No. 668. A Coy.), grocer, of Bendigo (V.), Killed in action, August 21, 1915.

of horror; the cries of the wounded could be heard calling to their comrades. Captain Loughran and the stretcher-bearers scoured the hill at night, bringing in all the wounded they could find There were, however, some still among the bushes next morning. Sgt. Alick Swift[3] (Moonee Ponds, Vic.), of A Company, badly wounded, was seen working his way up a depression on his back, when a Turkish machine-gun was turned on him with fatal results. Other wounded, too, who sought safety were killed. On this day (August 22) the 14th suffered the greatest loss it had yet incurred in the death of any one man. Its popular and heroic Chaplain Andrew Gillison was mortally wounded when endeavouring to bring in a wounded man from the slopes of that horrible and bullet-swept hill.

**Death of Chaplain Gillison.**

Under cover of darkness (August 21), Major Herring, (13th Battalion) brought over to the captured position the remainder of the third wave, with picks and shovels, and the fire pits already dug by the first two waves were soon converted into a trench. During the night, the 14th and 15th Battalions dug a communication trench connecting our lines with the newly-captured position, with the result that food, ammunition, and water were brought across. On August 23 the 16th Battalion took over the trenches, and the worn out garrison retired.

**Relieves 14th. 16th Battalion**

The strength of the battalion had now shrunk from 24 officers and 838 other ranks (who had marched out from Reserve Gully on August 6) to 12 officers and 304 other ranks. The fighting strength of the battalion had been shattered. The last abortive attack had taken another heavy toll of its surviving manhood. The losses during the month had already been so heavy, and the survivors were so worn out with disease and suffering, that only the strongest and fittest men had been sent into the last engagement. The killed included Capt. (Chaplain) Gillison,[4] Lieuts. Crabbe[5] and Duffield,[6] Sgt. Swift, Cpls. Skilton (Williamstown), Johnston

---

[3] Phillip Schuler, in "Australia in Arms," page 274, describes Geoffrey Veel's sacrifice and Alick Swift's death. The incidents are described, but names are not mentioned.

[4] Captain Andrew Gillison, of East St. Kilda (V.), Presbyterian clergyman. Died of wounds, August 22, 1915.

[5] Lieut. Keith G. W. Crabbe, of St. Kilda (V.), clerk. Killed in action, August 21, 1915.

[6] 2nd-Lieut. Frank Duffield, of Oldham (Eng.), iron machinist. Killed in action, August 21, 1915.

(Balwyn, Vic.), O'Bryan (Mumbannar, Vic.), and some of the finest of the rank and file.

Captain Gillison was the first chaplain in the A.I.F. to be killed during the war. He had a most engaging personality, and was the most popular man in the 4th Brigade. A man of exceptional courage, his kindness had endeared him to all ranks, and his death on an errand of mercy sent a cold chill through the hearts of the whole battalion. There was not any personal incident in the whole campaign which caused a greater sensation or gave rise to more sincere regret in the battalion. Lieut. Crabbe was one of the most energetic of the battalion's young officers, who had distinguished himself in the defence of Quinn's, and was in charge of operations when L.-Cpl. Jacka won his V.C: Second-Lieut. Duffield had received his commission just prior to his death, but died unaware of his promotion. Sgt. Swift was one of the best of the N.C.O.'s. Among those who fell was Pte. Verswyvelt[7] ("Belgian Joe"), a man well over 40, who had taken an active part in co-operation with Cpl. Reg. Jones on Quinn's in dealing with enemy snipers. Pte. W. Hartigan (No. 1688) had reported to the R.M.O. as sick on the forenoon of the 21st, and had been marked "light duty," i.e., which meant that he was not to take part in the assault. His keeness, however, took him into the fight, and after its close the R.M.O. found him severely wounded in the abdomen. On being queried why he had gone into the attack when marked "light duty," his reply was: "If I hadn't stopped this (i.e., bullet) some other poor b—— would." The wounded included Lieuts. Couttie and Dadson (the latter severely).

Army Headquarters was apparently not even yet convinced of the inutility of a further offensive against Hill 60,

**Another Attack on Hill 60 Ordered.** and decided that, on August 27, another attempt should be made to take it. Major Adams was chosen to command the 4th Brigade section of the attack, which was to comprise representatives of the recently arrived 5th A.I.F. Brigade, New Zealand Mounted Rifles, Australian Light Horsemen, and Connaught Rangers—about 1000 men in all.

The 14th Battalion detachment consisted of four officers and 100 O.R.'s, and the 13th furnished a contingent of the

---

[7] Pte. Joseph William Verswyvelt (No. 141, A Co.), of Chelsea (V.), cook. Killed in action August 21, 1915. He refused to act as cook, though upwards of 40 years of age, and insisted on being an active combatant.

## The History of the 14th Battalion. 73

**14th Participates.** same size. A heavy artillery bombardment commenced at 4 p.m. to clear the way for the infantry assault, and our brigade machine guns opened to prevent movement in the enemy's trenches. Unfortunately, the artillery bombardment was just a "stand to arms" signal for the Turks; no shells[8] fell in the sector of trench to be attacked by the 13th and 14th. Our men had to climb out of the Dere with the object of advancing 100 yards across a stubble paddock (which had been crossed in the attack of August 8) to capture a Turkish trench almost parallel to the Dere, but converging a little towards it on the right. The bombardment ceased; it was now the infantry's turn, but the moment our men showed their heads above the skyline they were faced by a terrific rifle and machine-gun fire, and the parapet was sprinkled by bullets as from a **Terrible Carnage.** hose. Very few succeeded in getting out of the trenches; some fell back wounded at once; others were hit on the fingers trying to drag themselves over the parapet. With the exception of a handful on the extreme left, who got some concealment in a shallow ditch running along a hedge, no one got forward any distance. The attack was stillborn; it was blotted out before it materialised. Major Adams promptly stopped the carnage, and **Capt. Connelly** called off the attack. Capt. Connelly[9] was **Killed.** killed, and Capt. Graham[10] severely wounded.

Two 13th Battalion officers were also killed. Capt. Cooper[11] was wounded next day. Three-fourths of the attacking force had been blotted out in a few minutes.[12] Sgts. Jack (North Melbourne), Grant (Scotland), Stokan (South Yarra, Vic.), and Williams (Barrakee, Vic.); Cpls. Fegan (Bendigo, Vic.), Hart (Mildura, Vic.), and L.-Cpl. N. Baker (England), were killed or died of wounds. Among those killed this day was Pte. P. D. Annear,[13] of Elsternwick, a graduate of Melbourne University.

---

[8] Evidence of Capt. Loughran, who was a close witness of the bombardment.

[9] Capt. Clive E. Connelly, of Hampton (V.), solicitor. Killed in action, August 7, 1915.

[10] Capt. Reginald W. Graham, of Brighton (V.), clerk.

[11] Capt. George Cooper, M.C., of Forest (Tas.), member of Australian Permanent Forces.

[12] Three officers and 72 other ranks were casualties out of four officers and 100 other ranks.

[13] The registrar of the Melbourne University writes that 1850 graduates and undergraduates of that university enlisted for active service, of whom 218 lost their lives.

## Attacks on Hill 60.

This was the last serious fighting that the 14th had on the Peninsula. The three August attacks—8th, 21st and 27th—had been sheer massacres. The 4th Brigade was matched in each case against impossible odds, and its personnel never had a chance of success, though matchless heroism had been shown by all ranks. Some important changes were now made at battalion headquarters. On August 28 Major Adams was evacuated to hospital, and Major Dare was appointed C.O. of the battalion—a position he held for fifteen months. Capt. Stewart Hansen was appointed acting adjutant vice Capt. George Cooper (wounded).

*Major Dare Appointed C.O.*

Now that the excitement of action was over, sickness again asserted itself, and took a terrible toll of the survivors. The battalion was melting away. It was a positive relief when it handed over its sector on August 31 to the 6th Essex Battalion, and bivouacked for the night in the Aghyl Dere in the scrub. Next day the march was resumed, and a position (between the Aghyl and the Chailak Deres) taken over from a Staffordshire Regiment. The new trenches were in a bad state of repair, and work was immediately commenced by sapping forward, and then tunnelling to connect the saps. During the relief Capt. G. H. Clark (signalling officer) was wounded. This new camp—known as Durrant's Post[14]—became the home of the battalion during the remainder of its career on the Peninsula. It was the safest spot it had yet been in. The Turks were about half a mile distant, and both their position and Durrant's Post were practically impregnable. The 13th Battalion was on the same ridge, but more to the right. In front of the 13th was the cleared patch and small tiled house known as the "farm," and numbers of dead Turks—victims of the heavy fighting in the previous month—were lying there in plain view. Things became very quiet, and casualties practically unknown.

*Durrant's Post.*

---

[14] Named after the then adjutant and future C.O. of the 13th Battalion.

## CHAPTER XIII.

### DURRANT'S POST AND THE EVACUATION.

1915.—September 3 to December 31.

On September 3 the personnel of the battalion had shrunk to nine officers and 149 other ranks, which was the numerical low water mark in its history. Six drafts of reinforcements had already been absorbed into the battalion, and altogether upwards of 2000 men had up to that date passed through its ranks. Now after four months fighting less than eight per cent. of that number were fit to carry a rifle. Nearly 400 (including 16 officers) had paid the supreme penalty of war, whilst dysentery and typhoid had prostrated those whom the bullet had spared. The majority of the survivors still on the Peninsula were worn and haggard, with long hair and hollow cheeks, covered with dirt, vermin and sores, wearing brimless hats. with uniforms torn and stained. They had lived in daily commune with death for months, and even then their relief was only made possible by the arrival of the 2nd Australian Division, whose personnel presented a pleasing contrast to that of the ragged veterans whom they relieved. No one would recognise in the jaded handful of worn and weary men the remnants of that magnificent battalion—bronzed and bursting with vitality—which took part in the famous brigade route march through the streets of Melbourne on December 17, 1914. The old spirit still existed in the survivors, but the flesh was very, very weak. Only five officers of the thirty-two who had landed on the Peninsula were still with the battalion, viz., Major Dare, Capts. Loughran, Richardson, and Giles. and the veteran Quartermaster-Major Young. Among the officers promoted from the ranks there were still available Lieuts. Blainey, Macdermid, Hansen, and Hastain.

*Battalion's Personnel Reduced to 9 Officers and 149 Other Ranks.*

*Personnel Emaciated and Worn.*

During the next few days a track to the Chailak Dere was completed, trenches improved, and a well sunk for water.

## Durrant's Post and the Evacuation.

**Battalion Relieved.**
On September 13 came the well-earned rest. The trenches were handed over to the 25th Battalion (of the newly arrived 2nd A.I.F. Division), and this was immediately followed by a battalion march to Anzac Beach, and embarkation on lighters, which were towed out to the H.M.T. "Abassia," on which all got on board. Lemnos was headed

**Reaches Lemnos.**
for and reached on the 14th, and the battalion disembarked, and marched four miles to Sarpi rest camp. Heavy rain flooded the camp during the night. A week's spell (without parades) was spent exploring the island. At last the men were looked after and properly fed, and free for a time from the strain of waiting for death or wounds. The rations improved, and fresh bread, meat, and eggs were available.

Almost all now set to work to investigate the surroundings of their new home. Railways were found to be non-existent and roads few; vineyards, however, were

**Pleasant Surroundings.**
plentiful, and the landscape was dotted by quaint windmills propelled by sails. Much money was spent by the Anzacs, to the evident satisfaction of the islanders, the majority of whom were a simple people, living secluded from the world in their island home. Sometimes an impromptu battalion concert would be held in the evening round a blazing camp fire. Many Australian nurses were on duty in the neighbouring hospitals, and the sight of their brave countrywomen struck a home chord in the hearts of these veterans that had not been touched since they left Australia.

The spell lasted less than a week. Training recommenced on September 20, and on the following day the brigade was inspected and addressed by General Godley, who said that he relied on it, after its strength had been built up, to go back and fight its way to Constantinople!

On the 16th Captain Loughran and Lieut. Blainey were evacuated sick, and the valuable services of the former were permanently lost to the battalion. A few days subsequently the quartermaster, Major Young had to return to Australia through illness. Q.M.S. W. G. Laver was appointed quartermaster in his place. Later, Capts. Richardson and Giles, and Lieuts. Macdermid and Hansen were also evacuated sick. Major Dare was now the only officer who had been continuously with the battalion from the date of the landing.

On October 23 Lieuts. Davidson and Orr arrived with the 7th Reinforcements, bringing up the battalion strength to seven

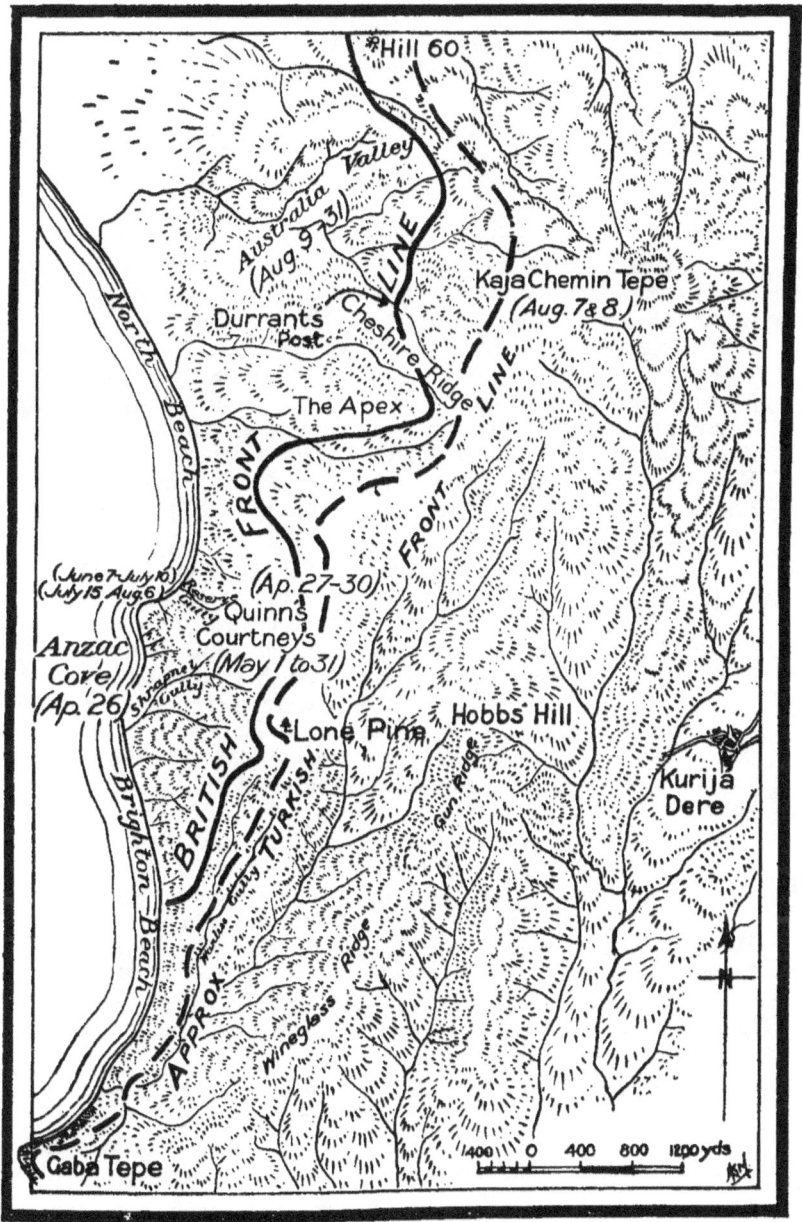

LOCALITY MAP OF THE PENINSULA

officers and 384 other ranks, and Captain R. C. Winn was appointed regimental medical officer in lieu of Captain Gerald Loughran.

Meanwhile, political events were taking place which were to have an important bearing on the Peninsula campaign. Bulgaria, encouraged by the failure of Ian Hamilton's August offensive, had formed an alliance with the Central Powers. The British War Cabinet, which had entered into the Peninsula campaign drifting on a sea of optimism, and had never taken the possibility of failure into consideration, was greatly perturbed by the want of success of the expedition, and determined to recall Sir Ian Hamilton. General Sir Charles Munro was sent out to report on the situation. The new general, after a careful survey of the whole position, unequivocally advocated a military withdrawal from the Peninsula, stating that the lines held possessed every possible military defect. Later Earl Kitchener visited the Peninsula, and confirmed that decision. On October 28 General Munro inspected the 4th Brigade camp at Lemnos.

The long and much appreciated spell at Lemnos terminated on October 31, when the battalion, greatly refreshed, embarked on the "Osmanieh" and left for the Peninsula. **Battalion Returns to Peninsula.** The sea was very choppy, and arriving off Anzac anchor was cast, but all hopes of disembarking that day were dispelled owing to heavy seas. Whilst at anchor here a stray Turkish bullet struck Pte. C. H. Coleman,[1] killing him instantly. **Pte. C. H. Coleman Killed.** The victim of this purely fortuitous accident had had a marvellous escape from death on Quinn's Post on April 27, receiving no less than six superficial machine gun wounds. After this untoward incident anchor was weighed, and the "Osmanieh" proceeded to Imbros, where it remained in the security **March to Durrant's Post.** of the harbour till next day, when it returned to the Peninsula. The battalion then disembarked at North Beach, and next day marched to Durrant's Post, and took over again the old trenches from the 28th Battalion.

It is unnecessary to linger on the remaining days on the Peninsula. Evacuation had been decided upon, though this was as yet unknown to the combatants. The weather was getting colder, and much tunnelling was undertaken to provide

---

[1] Pte. Claude Hamilton Coleman (No. 1343, 1st Reinforcements), labourer, of Newport (Vic.). Killed in action, November 1, 1915. Vide Chapter IV.

for shelter and winter quarters. On November 12 the 8th Reinforcements arrived, bringing the strength of the battalion up to nine officers and 535 other ranks. Chaplain Cope took the place of the late Chaplain Gillison, and Captain Fuhrmann arrived from Egypt, where he had been in charge of the transport since the date of the landing. Sgt. F. C. W. Symonds was appointed transport officer in his place. Trenches were now relieved every 24 instead of every 48 hours, and all available clothing was used to combat the increasing cold; there was a shortage of blankets and overcoats, however, which gave rise to much discomfort and caused many evacuations to the hospitals. Storms at Anzac about this time sometimes seriously interfered with the unloading of stores.

At the end of November snow fell freely, and many in the battalion saw it for the first time. A new scale of rations was adopted on December 4, the extras being much appreciated. A few days later it was noticed that troops were beginning to leave the Peninsula; the gullies were slowly emptying, and many sick men were sent away. Evacuation now began to be hinted at, but to the majority such a course seemed impossible after all the sacrifices made to attain and enlarge our hold on the Peninsula. Rumours, however, of all sorts were rife. Finally, on December 17, General Birdwood inspected the trenches, and stated that the evacuation rumours were correct, and that the battalion would leave the next day.

Rumours of Evacuation.

At dusk on the 18th the trenches were handed over to the 13th Battalion, and the 14th (the stretcher-bearers and machine gunners in the rear) marched down the Chailak Dere to No. 2 outpost, where all formed up on the beach and subsequently marched along the big sap parallel with the beach to Anzac after a final roll call. The Australian is deficient in imagination, but on this night the most thoughtless were full of reflections. It was a strangely silent march; each man was thinking deeply, and oblivious to all about him. They were giving up all that they had for months fought so hard and suffered so much for, and they were leaving the graves of their dead comrades[2] behind—that was the bitterest pill of all. In April everyone thought that Constantinople would be in their grasp in a few days, and now they were leaving the Peninsula surreptitiously like thieves in

Battalion Evacuates the Peninsula.

---

[2] This was brought home to all when passing the cemetery near No. 2 outpost.

the night. At the beach were smashed mule carts, burnt stores, and wrecked dugouts. The pier was covered with empty sandbags to deaden the noise of tramping feet. The battalion was taken off in motor barges, and subsequently transferred to the steamer "Hazel," which arrived at Lemnos about 6 a.m. on December 19. The retirement had been made without casualties. From the "Hazel" a transfer was effected to the battleship "Zealandia," where all were entertained by the crew. The jolly tars gave them a splendid reception, and treated them right royally. After leaving their new found hosts, a short march took the battalion to the new camp near Mudros. The next morning the "die-hards" (i.e., the last Anzacs to leave the Peninsula) arrived, and were given an enthusiastic and tumultuous reception. All were relieved to hear that the evacution had been bloodless, and that the humiliation of retirement had not been accentuated by a bloody massacre. The retirement had been most ably conducted, and will always stand as a brilliant piece of staff work. Christmas was spent at Lemnos, and was brightened by the receipt of presents from Australia, including billycans full of gifts. The cans, however, were encased in labels, on which were pictures of a kangaroo with a bayonet chasing a Turk off the Peninsula. This unintentional sarcasm coming within a week of the evacuation proved rather much for the feelings of some of the old hands.

*Reaches Mudros.*

*Christmas Spirit at Lemnos.*

Embarkation orders for Egypt were carried into effect on December 28, and Lemnos was left by the battalion for the last time. Alexandria was reached on the last day of 1915—a year ever memorable in the history of the Australian Commonwealth.

*Alexandria Reached.*

So ended the ill-starred Gallipoli Peninsula Expedition— the scene of so much futile heroism, the object of so much strenuous and unfruitful exertion. It is estimated to have cost the British Empire in cash about £300,000,000, whilst the British Expeditionary casualties[3] alone were about equal to those suffered by Germany in the war with France in 1870-71. The loss in prestige, especially in the East, cannot be over-estimated, whilst the war would have been abbreviated if the expedition had not been undertaken. Its failure had much to do with bringing Bulgaria into the war on the Germanic side. It was essentially a political expedition.

*The Gallipoli Campaign a Failure.*

---

[3] This does not include the French Peninsula casualties.

not justified by tactical reasons, and a "Strategical plan which ignores the tactical factor is foredoomed to failure."[4] The shortsightedness and false optimism of those responsible for the expedition were more than redeemed by the valour of the combatants—both Imperial troops and Anzacs. The shearers, miners, farmers, and artisans of Australia (transformed within a few months into soldiers) had given the world a marvellous exhibition of courage and fortitude under most adverse conditions, which was not surpassed by any troops in any campaign in the World War.

With the evacuation of the Peninsula the initial story of the 14th comes to a close. In future chapters will be told the birth of the 4th Division of the A.I.F. in Egypt, with which the 4th Brigade was afterwards incorporated, of its transfer to France, and of its vicissitudes there for nearly two and a half years until the termination of the war. It now only remains to epitomise very briefly the battalion's doings to date.

**Epitome of Battalion's Doings in 1914 and 1915.** The 14th became a live unit on October 1, 1914, when camp lines were laid for the new battalion at Broadmeadows, and until December 22 it put in a strenuous time there, making excellent progress under Col. Courtney's training. On December 17 the battalion participated in the famous route march of the 4th Brigade through the streets of Melbourne. Few who saw that march will ever forget it—thousands of picked Australians of magnificent physique and highly trained, marching with the confidence and bearing of veterans. From December 23, 1914, to the end of January, 1915, was occupied by the voyage to Egypt on the Ulysses, and on arrival there the battalion made its first acquaintance with the East. The home of the battalion in Egypt was the camp outside Heliopolis, near Cairo. An important change in its internal organisation here took place in the adoption of the double company system, E, F, G and H Companies being absorbed into A, B, C, and D respectively. The 4th Brigade became portion of the newly formed New Zealand and Australian Division. Much strenuous training was undertaken, and many trying marches made through the desert sand during the sojourn in Egypt.

On April 13 the battalion left Egypt on the "Seang Choon" for Lemnos, which was reached two days later. A few days at Mudros Harbour preceded the voyage to the Peninsula, which was reached on the afternoon of April 25. Next day the whole

---

[4] General Ludendorf.

of the battalion landed, and on the 27th detachments of it fought at Quinn's Post, Steele's Post, and Pope's Hill. On Quinn's, A and B Companies had a terrible experience from machine guns and snipers, resulting in the death of Capt. Hoggart and a number of non-commissioned officers and men. Then followed five strenuous weeks on Courtney's Post, repelling countless Turkish attacks, and losing many men from snipers' bullets, for many of the Turkish snipers showed considerable enterprise and unbounded pluck. A terrible Turkish attack on May 19 was successfully repulsed, but a brilliant young officer, Lieut. Hamilton, lost his life in the engagement. The battalion on that day gained great renown through the initiative and daring of L.-Cpl. Albert Jacka, who won the first V.C. awarded to any member of the A.I.F. during the war.

On May 31 the battalion left Courtney's, with which its name will ever be associated, and with its sister battalions made a home in Reserve Gully for a couple of months. Very strenuous work was put in digging and sapping, and many beach parties were supplied by the battalion. Disease here got a grip of the personnel, and hundreds of men were evacuated sick, the continuous labour, monotonous fare, and shortage of water, with a complete lack of recreation or rest, completing the work commenced by myriads of flies, which poisoned and contaminated the food.

The stay in the Gully was varied by a short spell at Imbros. In August a tremendous but unsuccessful effort was made by the Expeditionary Force to get astride the Peninsula and open up the Narrows. The 4th Brigade was set the task of making a night march into the heart of the enemy's territory, and then in co-operation with a new expeditionary force at Suvla Bay to attack and capture Koja Chemen Tepe, the key to the Turkish position. The expected support of the Suvla Bay force failed to materialise, and the 4th Brigade found the task without co-operation beyond its powers. On August 8 the 14th was cut to pieces, losing on that day alone upwards of one hundred killed, including a large number of officers and non-commissioned officers. Two subsequent abortive attacks were made on Hill 60, on August 21 and 27, by detachments of the 14th in conjunction with other units. Little resulted from these attacks but aggravated losses. On August 22 the battalion's heroic Chaplain Gillison—the most popular man in the 4th Brigade—lost his life in an endeavour to rescue a wounded man from a very exposed and dangerous position.

The battalion left Australia Gully on August 31, and made its way to Durrant's Post, which was the last home on the

Peninsula. On September 9 the battalion had been reduced by disease and the bullet to 9 officers and 149 other ranks. On the 13th of the same month the decimated remnants left for Lemnos, where they remained till October 31, enjoying a well-earned rest, though training was resumed after the first week. A return was then made to the Peninsula for the last time, when possession was taken of the old trenches at Durrant's Post. Here the battalion remained until the evacuation, doing much tunnelling and other heavy work. Then followed the evacuation of the Peninsula. Durrant's Post was vacated on the night of December 18, and Lemnos reached on the following day.

The following is a list of the "homes" occupied by the battalion up to the date of the evacuation of the Peninsula. It is needless to say that for comfort Broadmeadows stood in a class by itself:—

"Homes" of the Battalion in 1914 and 1915.
Broadmeadows Camp (near Melbourne), October 1 to December 21, 1914; H.M.A.S. "Ulysses" (voyage from Australia to Egypt), December 22 to January 31, 1915; Heliopolis (Egypt), February 1 to April 11; H.M.S. "Seang Choon" (transport), April 12 to April 25; Anzac Beach, April 26; Quinn's and adjacent posts, April 27 to April 30; Courtney's Post, May 1 to May 31; Reserve Gully, June 1 to July 10; Imbros (island), July 11 to July 14; Reserve Gully, July 15 to August 6; March north and attack on Koja Chemen Tepe, August 7-8; Australia Gully, August 9 to August 31; Durrant's Post, September 1 to September 13; Lemnos Island (Mudros), September 14 to October 31; Durrant's Post, November 1 to December 18.

## WITHDRAWN.

Landing in face of a terrible fire,
Storming the cliffs that rose higher and higher,
Determined to push on and never retire—
   Withdrawn!

Stubbornly facing the bullets that rained,
Paying in blood for each yard that was gained,
A ghastly picture of shattered and maimed—
   Withdrawn!

## Durrant's Post and the Evacuation.

Toiling and fighting for months in vain,
In scorching summer, snow, and rain,
Trials endured, yet little gain—
    Withdrawn!

Making a page in the history of fame,
Upholding Australia's glorious name;
Of one accord, one heart, one aim—
    Withdrawn!

'Twas hard to leave ground so possessed,
More so the graves where comrades rest,
But after all, 'twas for the best—
    Withdrawn!

—No. 1679, CPL. CHARLES SMITH,
3rd Reinforcements, No. 5 Platoon,
B Company, 14th Battalion.

## CHAPTER XIV.

#### SIDELIGHTS ON THE PENINSULA.

Perhaps the two most dominant passions on the Peninsula among the Anzacs were the physical craving for water and the mental craving for news from home. The sufferings endured for months by the 14th men through the inadequate water supply (meagre in quantity and wretched in quality) were almost intolerable, and Sgt. Crapper's successful efforts in August in finding copious quantities of the precious fluid of excellent quality earned the gratitude of hundreds, and rendered life once more worth living.

The craving for home news was the natural result arising out of a large body of men (the human cream of a continent) being temporarily detached from all home ties. During that long Peninsula campaign, so crowded with vicissitudes, and so full of interest, it is not any exaggeration to say that whilst the bodies of the 5,000,000 stay-at-home Australians were on their island continent, their hearts were on the Peninsula with their chosen representatives. Conversely, the Anzacs, though physically on the Peninsula, were mentally in Australia—their thoughts being largely concentrated on their homeland and loved ones far away. The arrival of the Australian mail on the Peninsula always created the greatest excitement, and the most commonplace news from home gave unlimited pleasure to the recipients. The unfortunates who did not receive correspondence felt at such times depressed and miserable. After home correspondence had been read everyone turned to the Australian papers. The accounts of engagements in which the readers had participated were read with particular interest.

One result of the Peninsula campaign was the mutual knowledge that the Australians and New Zealanders acquired for one another. The 4th Brigade was attached on the Peninsula to the same division as the New Zealanders, and stauncher comrades no men could wish to have.

Before ringing down the curtain on the Peninsula drama it will be advisable to devote some space to the consideration of the medical personnel, band, machine gunners, signallers, and other details of the battalion's work there.

"The morale of troops often depends on many extraneous conditions unconnected with discipline, such as an effective medical service, the quality and variety of food and its preparation, the quantity of water available, the presence or otherwise of tobacco, and various other incidental matters affecting health or comfort.

"One of the most remarkable features of war is the good effect on the morale of troops of an efficient medical service.

**Medical Personnel.** The knowledge that he has good doctors behind him cheers a man almost as much as the knowledge that his guns are efficient, or that there are plenty of men in reserve behind him."[1] The appalling sufferings undergone by the Australian wounded in the early stages on the Peninsula, largely owing to a grotesque under-estimate by the higher command of the number of casualties, is fully described in Captain Bean's admirable Australian Official History of the War, and will not be referred to here.

It is worthy of note, however, that whilst the fierce courage of the Anzacs in battle became world famous long before the end of the war, the fortitude, heroism, and unselfishness of the Australian wounded were less known, though even more commendable. The wounded indeed frequently displayed a contempt of death, a disregard of pain, and a chivalry and consideration for others which eclipsed even their valour and virility as combatants.

The 14th was fortunate throughout the war in the efficiency of its medical personnel and the personality of its regimental medical officers. Its first medical

**Medical Personnel.** officer was Captain Gerald Loughran, who acted during almost the whole of the Peninsula campaign. He was indefatigable and ubiquitous, and at all times displayed a disregard of danger and a remarkable coolness that had a steadying effect upon all those with whom he came in contact. He rendered invaluable services to the battalion, and set a high standard to his successors. He was supported by the following assistants:—

(1) One corporal and four orderlies (attached to and belonging to the Army Medical Corps).

(2) An orderly L/cpl. and sixteen stretcher-bearers (drawn from the battalion).

---

[1] "Times" History of the War. Vol. 7, p. 342.

# The History of the 14th Battalion.

It will be noted that the medical personnel was partly drawn from the Army Medical Corps, and partly from the infantry. The stretcher-bearers enjoyed immunity from certain fatigues, which was a stimulus and temptation to the infantry man to join their ranks. Some elaboration of the personnel is necessary.[2]

Sgt. Harris,[3] who did splendid work, was subsequently mentioned in despatches in France, attended an officers' training camp in England, received a commission, and fighting with the battalion died on April 12, 1917, of wounds received at the Battle of Bullecourt on the previous day.

Pte. Fraser, whose work also was of a high order, was prominent in France as well as on the Peninsula, whilst George Huse was mentioned in despatches, and received a commission in France. Williams died of wounds, whilst Phillips, Binger, Henshall, Manders, Noble and Ruschin were wounded, but the casualties among the stretcher-bearers were not heavy considering the risks they often incurred.

It may be stated briefly that the fine work done by the stretcher-bearers on the Peninsula, though highly appreciated

---

[2] The first A.M.C. L/Cpl. was E. A. Beardsley, who, however, transferred to the 4th Field Ambulance before the battalion reached the Peninsula, and his place was taken by Corporal Hudson, a medical student. The four orderlies were William Agar (Footscray), R. Tillson (England), Cecil Denholm (Bendigo), and J. H. Tierney (Watchem). Both Hudson and Agar were wounded and evacuated, whilst Denholm and Tierney got ill and had to leave the Peninsula.

[3] The first orderly L/Cpl. was No. 621 George Michie (Kyneton). He became Capt. Loughran's right-hand man, and though twice wounded refused to leave the Peninsula until stricken down with rheumatic fever on the 15th September, 1915. After the first day or two on the Peninsula, there never were the full stretcher-bearers available. The following acted during different times in 1915 as such, the first sixteen being the original stretcher-bearers:—

No. 1202, Sgt. A. J. Harris (Echuca)
No. 1203, Pte. D. H. Fraser (Benalla)
No. 1132, Pte. L. Ruschin (Carlton)
No. 1251, Pte. P. Williams (Flemington)
No. 1257, Pte. B. J. Binger (Nathalia)
No. 1218, Pte. H. S. Fredman (Williamstown)
No. 1198, Pte. A. M. Code (South Yarra)
No. 96, Pte. P. V. Manders (Leongatha)
No. 878, Pte. S. Henshall (Beulah)
No. 689, Pte. L. W. Bain (Seymour)
No. 111, Pte. R. Phillips (Mooroopna)
No. 680, Pte. C. T. Bell (Benalla)
No. 697, Pte. S. Colcott (Terang)
No. 1118, Pte. E. G. Noble (Mildura)
No. 1139, Pte. E. E. Marsh (Bacchus Marsh)
No. 60, Pte. W. Guy (Ringwood)
No. 613, Pte. W. H. Maskell (Terang)
No. 1138, Pte. R. Garford (E. Camberwell)
No. 1304, Pte. G. J. Huse (Stawell)
No. 617, Pte. G. S. Moore (Broadford)
No. 168, Pte. R. Bell (Windsor)
No. 145, Pte. E. S. Wearne (Middle Brighton)
No. 1143, Pte. H. E. Krutli (Numurkah)
No. 739, Pte. H. Lee (England).

Stretcher-bearing on the Peninsula was rendered exceptionally arduous owing to the rugged and precipitous character of the country over which the stretcher-bearers often had to carry their mutilated burdens, and dangerous on account of the frequent attentions of snipers.

by the combatants, was not, except in some very isolated cases,[4] recognised officially, and it was not really till the A.I.F. reached France that the gallant work of the stretcher-bearers received adequate official notice.

At Broadmeadows a 14th Battalion band was formed, from which the stretcher-bearers were selected. The bandsmen were trained there originally by the bandmaster of the 51st Infantry (an old militia unit). whose duties were subsequently taken over by Sgt. A. J. Harris. The Melbourne Grammar School, which always took an interest in the 14th, provided funds, and there were in addition private subscriptions towards the purchase of instruments. The regimental march was the famous folk song, "The Suwanne River"[5] (arranged as a march), and the strains of that inspiring air often stimulated the weary to the required exertion during the arduous route marches on the sands of the Egyptian desert. When the battalion embarked for the Peninsula the instruments were stored at Cairo, where many of them were stolen prior to the return of the unit to Egypt.

The Band.

The machine gun was a deadly weapon, which played an important part in the world war, and inflicted innumerable casualties on the combatants. Its practical value was first realised by the Germans. The 14th Machine Gunners were a body of experts who received special training prior to landing on the Peninsula. The 14th arrived on the Peninsula with two machine guns and the necessary personnel; they were used as an auxiliary to the front line rifle fire, and proved very efficient on May 19, tearing the Turkish assaulting column to pieces, and also on August 8, when the brigade rearguard was probably saved from destruction by the efficient handling of the machine gun sections. 2nd-Lieut. Rutland, the first O.C. of the section, was killed on May 1, and was succeeded by 2nd-Lieut. Arthur

Machine Gunners.

---

[3] 2nd-Lieut. Augustus J. Harris, born at Echuca (V.), on July 22, 1892. Educated at St. Mary's Primary School, Echuca. M.I.D., October 13, 1916. Died of wounds in France, April 12, 1917.

[4] Even Kirkpatrick (Simpson), the famous Peninsula stretcher-bearer with the donkeys, whose exploits and heroism were the talk of Anzac, was only mentioned in despatches. Similar work in France would have been rewarded with a decoration.

[5] The late Judge George L. Christian, of Richmond, Virginia, U.S.A., a Confederate veteran, wrote to the author that the "Suwanne River" was one of the favorite songs of the Confederate veterans of Lee and Stonewall Jackson, and was sung by them on the Rapidan, the Rappahannock, and elsewhere during the American Civil War of 1861-1865.

Blainey. The original N.C.O.'s were Sgt. A. Sutcliffe, Cpl. D. J. Hamilton, and L.-Cpls. E. W. Ballingall and Clarence Dight. The first member of the battalion to lose his life in the war was Pte. J. C. Hooke, a machine gunner.

An important branch of battalion organisation was signalling, which required more education than most army occupations. Efficient signalling is absolutely essential, as modern warfare is highly organised, and cannot be carried on without accurate information, which it is the duty of the signallers to maintain. The battalion signallers were originally trained at Broadmeadows under Sgt. Richmond, whilst Lieut. G. H. Clarke, of South Australia, was the commissioned officer. Further training was undergone on the "Ulysses" and in Egypt. At the outset of the Peninsula campaign visual signalling was employed, but had to be abandoned as unsuitable, owing to the hilly and wooded country there. Telephones were soon obtained and wires laid from 4th Brigade headquarters to the headquarters of the four battalions. Owing to casualties and sickness there were only four battalion signallers available at the date of the evacuation, viz., N. J. Bear, G. W. Orpwood, — Nowotna, and W. A. Gill. In addition to the battalion signallers, there were company signallers, whose duties were limited to the companies to which they were attached.

*Signallers.*

The cooking on the Peninsula was elementary, and not so well organised as in France. At Courtney's and Reserve Gully men cooked for themselves. Dixies were not available, and the men were accustomed to break up their biscuits on stones, and mixed them with bully beef and make rissoles. Later, at Durrant's Post, when dixies were available, and supplies of bread and Canadian frozen meat could be had, cooking was done by companies. Reliable men used to be provided with money, and sent by the various companies to Imbros to purchase stores. Sgt. M. O'Brien was the sergeant cook. He was put in charge of a tunnelling party at Durrant's Post, and the work was so excellently done that he was awarded the D.C.M. Among the cooks must be mentioned Pte. "Baldy" Pitts, who was very obliging, and an indefatigable worker.

*Cooks.*

During operations at Suvla Bay small numbers of Australians were sent, and temporarily attached to some of the Territorial British units in that locality, as scouts, bombers, or snipers. These specialists, on returning to their own Australian units, were almost invariably accompanied by orders

*Details on Special Service.*

of appreciation for valuable services rendered. Two very capable 14th men, Les. Guppy (No. 201) and Jack Garcia (No. 197), both of B Company, were detailed from the 14th to the Suvla Bay area, and did valuable work there. Garcia specialised in bombing, and was the inventor of a bomb carrier. He became a well-known personality in the 14th.

**Decorations.** Remarkably few decorations were awarded to the personnel of the 14th for the great amount of meritorious work performed on the Peninsula. Many decorations were earned there, but few granted. It seemed to be the rule throughout the war, in regard to the A.I.F., to bestow decorations freely as the result of successful operations. If troops were asked to do the impossible, and consequently failed, decorations were withheld. They were penalised for the shortcomings of those in higher command. Sometimes C.O.'s were to blame in not recommending deserving men. The decorations awarded to the battalion on the Peninsula were as follow:—

Victoria Cross.—L.-Cpl. Albert Jacka (Wedderburn, Vic.).

Companion of the Order of the Bath (C.B.).—Lieut.-Col. R. E. Courtney (Melbourne).

Distinguished Service Order (D.S.O.).—Major R. Rankine (St. Kilda, Vic.).

Military Cross (M.C.).—Captain George Cooper (Tasmania).

Distinguished Conduct Medal (D.C.M.).—Sgt. M. O'Brien (Bacchus Marsh).

Military Medal (M.M.] —80, Cpl. Reginald W. Jones (Essendon, Vic.); 1307, Pte. N. T. Wynne (Carlton, Vic.); 717, Sgt. E. P. Hill (Ballarat, Vic.).

Mentioned in Despatches.—Lieut.-Col. R. E. Courtney, C.B.; Major R. Rankine, D.S.O.; Capt. G. Cooper, Capt. (Chaplain) Gillison, Lieut.-Col. C. M. M. Dare, Sgt. M. O'Brien.

**Casualties.** The casualties in the 14th in Gallipoli and Egypt were the heaviest it suffered during any one of its four years' service abroad, and consisted of 16 officers and 387 other ranks killed or died of wounds. The casualties in the field were mostly suffered in the abortive but bloody fighting in August, while sickness got a terrible hold on the battalion in the summer. Comparatively few battalions in the Great War underwent a worse experience

## The History of the 14th Battalion. 91

in a limited time. The following is a list of officers and men in the 14th who were wounded more than once during the Peninsula campaign. The rank set out is that of the combatant when wounded on the last occasion:—

### OFFICERS.

Capt. H. N. Boyle, East Brunswick, V.
Lt. A. R. Cox, Box Hill, V.
Capt. Geo. Cooper, Tasmania.

### OTHER RANKS.

521 Pte. J. W. Field, Kent. Eng.
621 L/Cpl. G. Michie, Kyneton, V.
495 C.S.M. C. Scott,, Fitzroy, V.
595 S.M. G. A. Hare, Malvern, V.
1350 Pte. A. Cameron, St. Arnaud, V.
61 Pte. F. J. W. Harding, Footscray, V.
646 Pte. N. W. Raynor, Colac, V.
66 Pte. H. Havis, London, Eng.
1144 Pte. C. E. Dannock, Leongatha, V.
1910 Pte. E. Basterfield, Prahran, V.
329 Sgt. D. J. Hamilton, Hawthorn, V.
1422 Pte. F. E. Spencer, Carlton, V.
1406 Pte. K. Saber, Toorak, V.
810 A/Sgt. J. R. Bryan, Swan Hill, V.
1388 Pte. G. McKenzie, Scotland.
80 Sgt. R. W. Jones, Essendon, V.
1477 Pte. W. M. O'Connor, Auckland, N.Z.
1355 Pte. R. F. Edmonds, Preston, V.
619 Pte. J. J. Myers, Daylesford, V.
1403 Pte. L. H. Pascoe, S. Australia.
724 Pte. J. G. Hartley, London, Eng.
1058 Pte. J. McG. Stuart, Mirboo Nth., V.
726 Pte. W. Isbel, Ararat, V.
470 Cpl. J. Lewis, Launceston, Tas.
866 Pte. J. Gooder, England.
877 Pte. R. Hare, Gunbower, V.
1284 Pte. W. E. W. Porter, Tylden, V.
949 Cpl. W. Beach, England.
1750 Pte. E. W. Gilchrist, Moonee Ponds, V.
260 Pte. W. H. Saunders, Mickleham, V.
320 Cpl. H. Fegan, Bendigo, V.
718 Pte. H. R. Herrod, Yarra Junction, V.

953 Cpl. R. G. Bonwick, Auburn. V.
1184 L/Cpl. A. C. Hutton, South Melbourne.
45 Cpl. L. W. Cozens, Wellington, N.Z.
1353 Dvr. F. Dolan, Ireland.
2052 Pte. W. Bolton, N. Fitzroy, V.
90 L/Cpl. McLellan, Outtrim, V.
668 Pte. G. C. Veel, Bendigo, V.
129 Cpl. A. Stuckey, Yarraville, V.
708 Cpl. T. French, Geelong E.
753 Cpl. J. Menzies, Pt. Melbourne.
231 Pte. R. G. A. Lawson, Mildura. V.
852 Pte. P. A. Eville, South Yarra, V.
25 Pte. T. Auhl, South Morang, V.
826 L/Cpl. H. Bowen, Colac, V.
1377 Pte. D. Lareedo, Launceston. Tas.
1813 Pte. H. Ryan, Melbourne, V.
419 Pte. F. H. Boyes, Lardner, V.
674 Pte. E. A. Younger, Geelong, V.
1386 Pte. G. E. Murphy, Williamstown, V.
1578 Pte. L. Lee, Richmond, V.
1325 Pte. D. J. Cameron, Scotland.
1318 Pte. F. Brennan, N.S.W.
634 Pte. C. E. Pellitt, Glenferrie, V.
2173 Pte. C. G. Lander, Geelong, V.
72 Pte. W. Hood, Deniliquin, N.S.W.
1865 Pte. W. C. Moore, Balaclava, V.
2158 Pte. H. Heins, Port Melbourne.
1985 Pte. A. McArady, Clifton Hill, V.
1941 Pte. T. Garrity, England.
1346 Pte. V. Callanan, Albert Park, V.

## CHAPTER XV.

### EGYPT.
### THE BIRTH OF THE FOURTH DIVISION.

1916.—January 1 to May 31.

The battalion's second sojourn in Egypt lasted five months. The original Anzac brigades had been all decimated on the Peninsula, and the interlude in Egypt was a time of recuperation, organisation, absorption of reinforcements, and training.

The first camping ground of the 14th was near the Ismailia railway station (close to the Suez Canal)—a very picturesque spot. Shortly after reaching the new quarters all were delighted to see Sgt. Symonds (transport sergeant) appear with the regimental transport, which had not been seen since the departure of the battalion for the Peninsula on the previous April. Tents were not at first available, so waterproof sheets were requisitioned to provide cover at night. The opportunity now presented to everyone of purchasing and consuming rich food, after the monotonous Peninsula fare, was too great a temptation to be resisted, with the result that many suffered in consequence. After a few days without parades training commenced in earnest, including at first company and platoon field training, and later battalion exercises and route marches, which latter were often undertaken at night.

Ismailia.

On January 21 tents were struck, and the camp moved to Moascar. Here brigade training and divisional exercises also became part of the routine. Arduous training, however, was varied by most enjoyable bathes in Lake Timsah. On January 26 Capt. N. D. Fethers transferred to the 14th from the 12th Battalion. This was the first (but by no means the last) occasion on which senior officers from outside units were drafted into the 14th.

Moascar.

A further change of camp took place on February 27, when the battalion left Moascar for Tel-el-kebir. The brigade

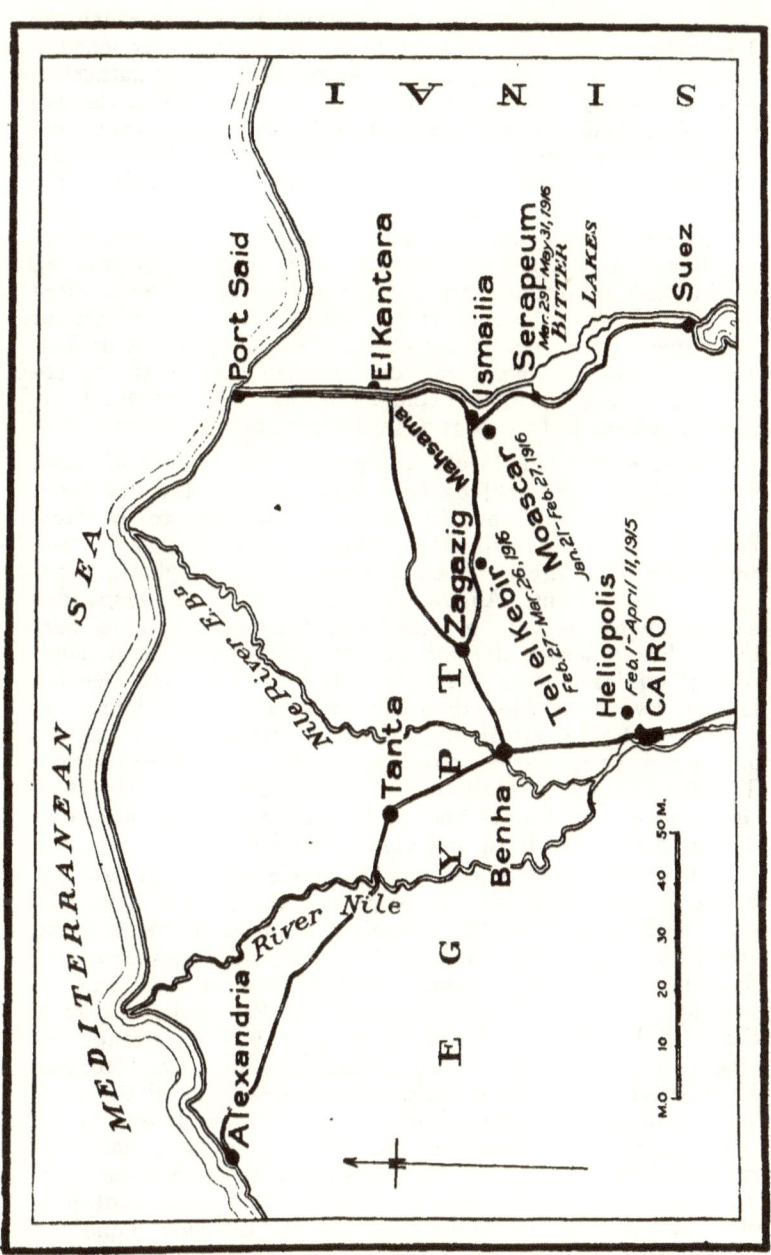

LOCALITY MAP OF EGYPT

here finally parted with their old comrades, the New Zealanders, and the parting was consummated by a much enjoyed convivial gathering. The new camp was in the middle of the desert, and the site of a battle fought in 1882. Various other Australian units were camped in the vicinity, and the neighbourhood took on quite an Australian character—one, too, which was free from the temptations of Cairo. Large numbers of Australian reinforcements were weekly pouring into the camp, among whom the old hands had numerous friends. After the day's training was completed accordingly many old friendships were often renewed, or new ones formed, whilst numerous places of amusement were nightly crowded. The month spent at Tel-el-kebir was an important one in the history of the 4th Brigade on account of it being incorporated in the 4th Division, to whose birth a passing reference must be made.

*Tel-el-kebir.*

During the Peninsula campaign, Australia had been represented in the field by two divisions (the 1st and 2nd), and the 4th Brigade (attached to the New Zealanders). Many reinforcements had already been absorbed by the fighting units, but Australia's manhood had responded splendidly to the call to arms, with the result that, in spite of the heavy losses already incurred, there were large numbers of reinforcements available in Egypt, and it was decided to form two more Australian divisions (afterwards known as the 4th and 5th) out of the reinforcements already in Egypt, and a fifth (afterwards known as the 3rd) in Australia itself. The 4th Brigade was allotted to the newly formed 4th Division, which earned, even among Australian divisions, a reputation in France for hard and continuous fighting.

*Birth of 4th Division.*

Its commanding officer was Major-General Sir H. V. Cox, of the Indian Army, a very competent officer. The new division, in addition to the 4th, comprised the recently formed 12th and 13th Infantry Brigades, and it was considered necessary that the new brigades should contain a strong nucleus of veterans who had already fought on the Peninsula. To form the 12th Brigade the 4th Brigade gave half its strength of officers and men, with the result that the 13th, 14th, 15th, and 16th Battalions provided the nucleus respectively of the 45th, 46th, 47th, and 48th Battalions. Three officers (Capt. G. H. Clarke and Lieuts. Simonsen and Morehouse) and 400 other ranks left the 14th to join the 46th Battalion, and large numbers also left it to join the newly formed 4th Pioneer Battalion, 4th Machine Gun Company, and the 4th Division Signalling Company.

The permanent loss of so many veterans was a great blow to the battalion, but the 9th, 10th, 11th, 12th, and 13th reinforcements joined with many new officers, including Lieuts. W. R. Wadsworth and B. T Smith, and 2nd-Lieuts. J. Mackay, M. R. Walker, A. T. Harvey, H. B. Wanliss, C. R. T. Cole, and H. S. Dobbie. Some well-deserved promotions to commissioned rank took place, including C.S.M.'s J. B. Roderick and Albert Jacka, V.C., and Sgts. A. Williamson, R. W. Jones, M.M.; N. Wilson, R. D. Julian, A. R. Dean, and J. S. Rogers.

**Reinforcements and Promotions.**

On March 22 the battalion was inspected by the Prince of Wales, and on the following day the battalion took part in brigade sports. The brigadier presented a cup for the best platoon in the brigade, and Lieut. "Lofty" Williamson's platoon (No. 13 of C Company) was only beaten by four points.

Towards the end of March the newly formed 4th Division was allotted a portion of the Suez Canal defences, and the 4th Brigade was instructed to move to the canal zone on the 26th of that month. This entailed a three days' march through the desert from Tel-el-kebir to Serapeum, via Mashama and Moascar, a distance of 43 miles. Few who participated in that march will ever forget it—especially the third day. It was carried out in full "marching order," i.e., each man had to carry his pack (containing change of clothing, extra boots, souvenirs, etc.), also food, water bottle, field dressing, rifle, bayonet, trenching tool, and ammunition. The heat was intense. There was not any shelter, and every footstep was through heavy sand. Many were tortured by new and badly fitting boots, or chafed by ill-fitting recently issued khaki trousers. The stifling desert wind drove the sand in their sweat-covered faces. Some, nearly crazy with thirst, lurched along with their tongues out like dogs. Intense irritation was caused by the sight of empty trains running past in the same direction as the march. Some few, absolutely prostrated, fell out, but nearly all joined up the battalion after dark. This march was one of the most trying experiences that the newly formed division ever had.

**Desert March to Serapeum.**

The new camp was on the Sinai Peninsula, about a couple of miles east of the Canal, and training was occasionally varied by bathing in its waters. Anzac Day— the first anniversary of the landing on the Peninsula—was fittingly observed. A brigade

**Anzac Day.**

church parade was held in the forenoon, and swimming sports in the Canal in the afternoon. There were several decorated boats, and when steamers passed through the Canal many plunged in and swam out near them.

**Training.** Meanwhile, training was going on apace. Every man was put through a course of musketry, and schools for junior N.C.O.'s formed. A bombing platoon was started, and the adoption of the light Lewis machine gun marked an improvement much appreciated by the machine gun section. Stokes guns and Mills bombs were novelties, which excited a considerable amount of interest.

It was now an open secret that the battalion's destination was France, and that rumour gave great satisfaction. All were tired of Egypt, and anxious to meet the Germans, whose Government was credited with having originated the war. Preparations were now actively made for leaving Egypt. Sun helmets were set aside for the Australian felt hats so well known afterwards in France. On May 17 Col. Dare obtained leave to get married, but resumed duty prior to leaving Egypt. Major N. D. Fethers took over temporary command in his absence.

On May 29 a grand review of the 4th Division was held by the commander-in-chief, in which the 4th and 12th Brigades took part. Capt. Wadsworth and some other ranks about this time left for Marseilles to make arrangements for the disembarkation of the battalion on arrival there. The last few days of May were taken up with the packing of kit bags and stores. Everything was now ready for departure, and the 14th was once again a battalion complete in every detail. On May 31 at dusk all marched to Serapeum, crossed the pontoon bridge, and travelling all night in railway trucks, arrived at Alexandria next morning, and embarked on board the s.s. "Transylvania" for Marseilles. The regimental transport was carried on the s.s. "Hereford." The Peninsula campaign was thus but a prelude to the greater drama in France, where the battalion was to have a chequered career for upwards of two and a half years. It had entered the Peninsula as an untried unit; it was to enter France as a veteran battalion having traditions and achievements behind it. The following is a list of the commissioned officers on May 11, 1916, immediately prior to leaving Egypt:—

**Train to Alexandria and Embarkation for France.**

Headquarters.—Lieut.-Col. C. M. M. Dare, Moreland, Vic., Commanding Officer; Major N. D. Fethers, 2nd in com-

Capt. Harold B. Wanliss, D.S.O.

Capt. Albert Jacka, V.C., M.C. and Bar.

Capt. Reginald W. Jones, M.C., M.M.

**Commissioned Officers.**
mand; Capt. A. R. Blainey, England, Adjutant; Capt. R. C. Winn, Sydney, N.S.W., Medical Officer; Capt. J. L. Cope, Carlton, Vic., Chaplain; Lieut. W. G. Laver, Kew, Vic., Quartermaster; Lieut. C. R. T. Cole, Malvern, Vic., Machine Gun Officer.

A Company.—Capt. A. R. Cox, Boxhill, Vic., Officer Commanding; Capt. R. W. Orr, Footscray, Vic.; Lieut. H. B. Wanliss, Ballarat, Vic.; 2nd-Lieut. J. B. Roderick, Glenferrie, Vic.; 2nd-Lieut. R. D. Julian, Geelong, Vic.

B Company.—Major O. C. W. Fuhrmann, South Melbourne, Officer Commanding; Capt. W. R. Wadsworth, Castlemaine, Vic.; Lieut. A. T. Harvey, Bundaberg, Qld.; 2nd-Lieut. F. C. W. Symonds, South Camberwell, Vic., transport officer (attached to B Company); 2nd-Lieut. A. Jacka, V.C., Wedderburn, Vic.

C Company.—Capt. S. M. Hansen, Williamstown, Vic., Officer Commanding; Capt. B. T. Smith, Auburn, Vic.; Lieut. M. R. Walker, South Yarra, Vic.; Lieut. P. J. Hayes, Marrickville, N.S.W.; 2nd-Lieut. N. Wilson, Auburn, Vic.; 2nd-Lieut. A. R. Dean, Sydney, N.S.W.

D Company.—Capt. C. R. M. Cox, Box Hill, Vic., Officer Commanding; Capt. F. B. Stanton, Stawell, Vic.; Lieut. S. H. Dobbie, Footscray, Vic.; Lieut. A. Williamson, Tongabbie, Vic.; Lieut. J. Mackay, South Melbourne, Vic.; 2nd-Lieut. R. W. Jones, M.M. Essendon, Vic.

Only four of the above 29 officers had held commissioned rank in the battalion at the commencement of the Peninsula campaign, viz., Lieut.-Col. Dare, Major Fuhrmann, and the Cox brothers, whilst, excluding the chaplain, only four (viz., Capt. Blainey and Lieuts. Symonds, Hayes and Dean) were over thirty years of age. It was a young man's war. If a comparison is justifiable between the merits of the 14th Battalion commissioned officers of April, 1915, and those of May, 1916, most of the battalions' old hands would probably vote for the latter as having a higher average standard of excellence. Jones and Jacka were two jewels of the first water, and some of the reinforcement officers were men of great promise.

The following is a list of the non-commissioned officers[1] on the battalion strength on April 20, 1916, and it would be

---

[1] The author is indebted for the list to a record among Col. Dare's papers. The initials, regimental numbers, and addresses were furnished by the author.

**Non-commissioned Officers.** difficult to find a finer body of N.C.O.'s in any battalion in the A.I.F. Some were men of exceptional personality, whilst most were keen and resolute soldiers who had been often tested, and not found wanting. It was a peculiarity, however, noticeable among all ranks that a few who had shown energy and enterprise on the Peninsula, seemed to lose some of their initiative in France; their fund of vitality appeared exhausted.

### N.C.O.'s ON BATTALION STRENGTH ON APRIL 20, 1916.

A Company.—Company Sgt.-Major (No. 551) W. R. Beamond (Geelong, V.), Company Q.M.S. (No. 1747) L. H. Gill (Melbourne), Sgt. (No. 611) J. Millis (Middle Brighton, V.), Sgt. (No. 63) N. C. Harris (Canada), Sgt. (No. 1810) A. Rich (Ballarat, V.), Sgt. (No. 49) S. D'Arango (Bendigo, V.), Sgt. (No. 2553) S. J. J. Garton (Brunswick, V.), Sgt. (No. 545) F. Anderson (Buangor, V.), Sgt. (No. 46) H. Croft (Elmhurst, V.), Sgt. (No. 2551) A. J. K. Ayre (Essex, Eng.), L.-Sgt. (No. 2554) M. Kohlmann (Canterbury, V.), Cpl. (No. 559) J. A. Brotchie (Fitzroy, V.), Cpl. (No. 1405) J. Pearce (Trawalla, V.), Cpl. (No. 2926) G. F. Wilson (Auburn, V.), Cpl. (No. 2416) A. J. Naylor (Camberwell, V.), Cpl. (No. 2778) W. C. Fulton (Footscray, V.), Cpl. (No. 3543) C. F. Ross (Bendigo, V.), Cpl. (No. 952) C. A. Bruckner (Bairnsdale, V.), Cpl. (No. 103) S. Nicholls (Balaclava, V.).

B Company.—Company Sgt.-Major (No. 795) G. T. Trewheela (Geelong, V.); Company Q.M.S. (No. 717) E. P. Hill, M.M. (Ballarat, V.); Sgt. (No. 201) A. L. Guppy (Benalla, V.), Sgt. (No. 736) H. Lewis (Port Melbourne, V.), Sgt. (No. 178) E. R. Chubb (Chiltern, V.), Sgt. (No. 2043) W. V. Field (England), Sgt. (No. 2144) B. I. Griffiths (Frankston, V.), Sgt. (No. 2344) L. C. Barnes (Nhill), Sgt. (No. 1779) S. B. Thompson (St. Kilda, V.), Sgt. (No. 1780) L. B. Thompson (St. Kilda), L.-Sgt. (No. 797) J. Turner (Melbourne, V.), L.-Sgt. (No. 2446) H. D. Mortimer (Teneva, V.), Cpl. (No. 162) R. S. Blamey (Albert Park, V.), Cpl. (No. 79) R. L. Jones (Essendon, V.), Cpl. (No. 4197) W. C. Groves (Sebastopol, V.), Cpl. (No. 1330) F. J. Banyard (England), Cpl. (No. 3496) F. Smith (England); Cpl. (No. 2450) A. D. J. Waddell (Beechworth, V.), Cpl. (No. 914) C. L. Russell (Geelong, V.), A.-Cpl. R. E. Sanders.

C Company.—Company Sgt.-Major (No. 465) A. Jacka, V.C. (Wedderburn, V.); Company Q.M.S. (No. 1090) F. Larter (West Melbourne, V.), Sgt. (No. 391) H. W. Thompson (N. Melbourne, V.), Sgt. (No. 316) B. Edmondstone (Ararat, V.), Sgt. (No. 323) L. Garcia (Fitzroy. V.), Sgt. (No. 817) R. H. Berry (Elsternwick, V.), Sgt. (No. 3007) F. W. Appleton (Balaclava, V.). Sgt. (No. 374) G. A. Ross (Fitzroy, V.). Sgt. (No. ) Davies. Sgt. (No. 1093) T. H. Loughead (Port Melbourne, V.). L.-Sgt. (No. 922) R. Stanley (Mornington, V.), L.-Sgt. (No. 1777) W. E. Manie (Windsor, V.). Cpl. (No. 2636) E. J. Rule (Cobar. N.S.W.), Cpl. (No. 823) S. Booley (Nyang V.). Cpl. (No. 269) J. S. Stewart (Hamilton, V.), Cpl. (No. 2777) G. Bailey (Northcote. V.). Cpl. (No. 2362) E. A. Cleary (Hawthorn. V.), Cpl. (No. 1691) J. Horricks (England), Cpl. (No. 3359) P. T. Harris (England), Cpl. (No. 2598) G. A. Hilford (Surrey Hills, V.).

D Company.—Company Sgt.-Major (No. 1532) D. E. Docwra (England). Company Q.M.S. (No. 1009) N. A. Kent (Narre Warren, V.), Sgt. (No. 526) W. Oram (Foster, V.). Sgt. (No. 419) F. H. Boyes (Lardner, V.), Sgt. (No. 2925) J. S. Rogers (Wonthaggi, V.),, Sgt. (No. 1184) A. C. Hutton (S. Melbourne, V.), Sgt. (No. 1043) T. A. Rose (Rochester, V.), Sgt. (No. 2561) W. Pearce (Piercedale, V.), Sgt. (No. 2560) N. McKenzie (Armadale. V.), Sgt. (No. 1990) T. T. O'Brien (South Melbourne, V.), L.-Sgt. (No. 2579) F. W. Dalitz (Dimboola, V.), L.-Sgt. (No. 2782) R. R. Neale (Castlemaine, V.), Cpl. (No. 454) W. J. Horne (Collingwood. V.), Cpl. (No. 2028) A. Urie (Scotland), Cpl. (No. 4172) D. Drummond (Sebastopol, V.), Cpl. (No. 2578) A. Dalitz (Dimboola, V.), Cpl. (No. 3484) M. N. Robertson (Coburg, V.), Cpl. (No. 1230a) W. Jacka (Wedderburn, V.), Cpl. (No. 2365) W. J. Douglas (Williamstown, V.), Cpl. (No. 1063) G. D. Thompson (England).

**HEADQUARTERS.**

Rgt.-Sgt.-Major (No. 1807) A. Pringle (Glenferrie. V.); Rgt. Q.M.S. (No. 872) D. H. L. Hawkins (Caulfield, V.); Sgt. (No. 1022) O. G. McAllan (Albert Park, V.), Pioneer; Sgt. (No. 1100) H. G. Raper (Windsor, V.), Armourer; Sgt. (No. 1354) J. O. Elliott (Warracknabeal. V.), Shoemaker; Sgt. (No. 1202) A. J. Harris (Echuca. V.), Band; Sgt. (No. 778) H. J. Schultz (Albert Park. V.), Transport; Sgt. (No. 336) A. King (Albert Park. V.), Machine Gun; Sgt. (No. 416) D. Blackburn (Camperdown V.). Machine Gun; Sgt. (No. ) M. O'Brien, D.C.M. (Bacchus Marsh. V.), Cook; L.-Sgt. (No. 14) N. J. Bear (Spotswood, V.). Signalling; Cpl. (No. 1376) J. H. Laidlaw (Portland, V.).

Machine Gun; Cpl. (No. 8) W. W. Goodwin (Melbourne, V.), Signalling; Cpl. (No. 952) C. A. Bruckner (Bairnsdale, V.), attached to A Company; Cpl. (No. 914) C. L. Russell (Geelong, V.), attached to B Company; A.-Cpl. (No. 943) Andrews (Suffolk, Eng.).

## CHAPTER XVI.

### ARRIVAL IN FRANCE.

#### 1916.—June 1 to June 10.

From March to June, 1916, scores of thousands of bronzed Australians (many of them veterans) poured across
**Mediterranean.** the Mediterranean from Egypt to the battle zone of Northern France. This entailed a sea journey to Marseilles of about 1700 miles, followed by a land trip through France of upwards of 600 miles. This journey now faced the troops of the 4th Division of the A.I.F., in common with their comrades of the 1st and 2nd Divisions who had preceded them. The voyage through the Mediterranean was through the most interesting sea in the world, bordered by lands which were the cradle of Western civilisation, and studded with historic isles of great scenic beauty. At this time, too, there was an added
**Submarines.** tonic of excitement (for excitement is as essential to the Australian as the air he breathes), since the Mediterranean during the war swarmed with submarines, and many a good ship[1] was sent to the bottom through their agency.

The "Transylvania" carried not only the 14th,[2] but the 13th and 15th Battalions, together with Brigade Headquarters —a grand total of about 3000 men. Embarkation was completed about mid-day on June 1, but the transport lay at the wharf all day with sentries posted on the gangways. At
**Route.** 10 a.m. next day she moved out from the wharf and started for Marseilles. The route lay north of Crete, south of Malta, and along the coast of Sardinia, and the journey lasted almost exactly five days. It was made under ideal conditions, and resembled

---

[1] Among them was the "Transylvania," which was torpedoed on a subsequent trip in the Mediterranean on May 4, 1917, and sunk with a loss of 413 lives.

[2] Strength of 14th Battalion at this time, 27 officers and 958 other ranks.

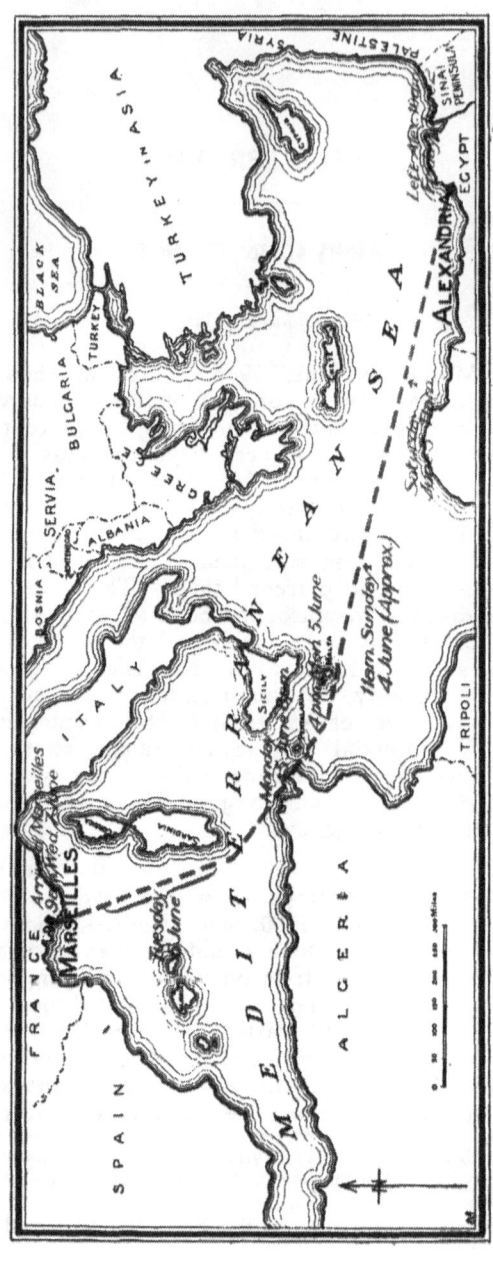

ROUTE THROUGH THE MEDITERRANEAN

*The History of the 14th Battalion.*

**Ideal Conditions.** a trip through an island-studded lake; the sea was calm, the weather delightful, and it was rendered more comfortable because it was not necessary to sleep haphazard on deck; each man had a bunk to himself. Three sittings were required at each meal to enable all troops on board to dine. At the sergeant's mess the voice of the popular "Curly" Croft[3] could be heard above all others laughing and joking. A good deal
**Voyage.** of leisure was accorded, and everyone had the opportunity of enjoying the surroundings. An exceptionally sharp look-out was kept for submarines during daylight, and, as an additional precaution, a zig-zag course was steered. No lights were visible on deck at night. Practice submarine alarms were held to accustom all ranks to their boat stations, and there were the usual ship inspections. A church parade was held on Sunday, June 4. A huge letter-box was opened for the reception of letters, and full advantage was taken of the opportunity for correspondence. All were keen to get a first glimpse of the French coast, for the thoughts of the whole world had been focussed on that country during the preceding two years. At length, on the morning of the 7th, land was sighted, and the
**Marseilles.** picturesque harbour of Marseilles entered, with its abrupt cliffs, verdant hills, and red-tiled houses. Trains and trams were visible from on board, and as the troopship (about 10 a.m.) steamed slowly alongside the wharf a tumultuous welcome was
**French Welcome.** accorded by the French people ashore. The tangible proofs of war (afterwards so much in evidence) were not here visible, but the toll it had taken of the French population was at once evident in the almost complete absence of able-bodied men, and the vast number of women in mourning.[4]

During those five days at sea two startling items of news had been received by wireless. The first was the account of the naval battle of Jutland, and the other the
**Death of** death, under dramatic circumstances, of Lord
**Lord Kitchener.** Kitchener. His sudden demise came as a shock to all Australians, for he was the most prominent personality in the British Empire at that time. The Empire was indebted to him for many important and varied

---

[3] A platoon sergeant in A Company, 14th Battalion. Vide Chap. 18.

[4] In Britain, on the contrary, mourning was not worn to any extent for battle-slain relatives; there was not anything in the dress of the people there to call attention to the existence of war.

public services, and he was a man of majestic appearance and great driving power. It must be admitted, however, that he was responsible in a large degree for the tragic Gallipoli campaign, and that his abilities were over-rated. He camouflaged his lack of knowledge by silence.

The voyage just terminated remained ever a bright spot in the memory of those who participated in it, but it was only a prelude to a railway journey through France which for charm, novelty, and enjoyment eclipsed any other experience that the battalion ever underwent abroad. On arrival at Marseilles Capt. W. R. Wadsworth, the embarkation officer, met the troopship with orders to disembark right away, and A and D Companies left by train for the north at 3.30 p.m. (June 7), whilst Headquarters with B and C Companies followed at 10 o'clock next morning. Lieut. J. Mackay and 2nd-Lieut. A. R. Dean, with 35 other ranks, remained behind at Marseilles as corps rearguard. The march of the battalion through the narrow streets to the railway station attracted much attention from the local populace.

**Journey Through France.**
The journey north lasted upwards of 60 hours, and as equipment and rifles were taken into the carriages there was not much spare room, and sleeping accommodation was decidely cramped. The troop trains moved slowly north, making frequent halts at railway sidings to enable express trains to fly past south. French sentries were posted at about quarter mile intervals, and all bridges, viaducts, and tunnels were closely guarded.

It would be difficult to apportion the sensations enjoyed by our men on this journey, and state definitely whether the charm of the scenery (doubly enchanting after the sand and heat of the Egyptian desert), or the enthusiasm and hospitality of the French people most appealed to them.

The initial journey lay through the valley of the rapid and turbid Rhone, and it was like a succession of cinematographic views of Paradise. Round hills or through tunnels swept the train, affording fleeting glimpses of the noble river, parallel to which ran a magnificent road as white and (apparently) as smooth as marble flanked by avenues of trees clad in gorgeous foliage. Rows of hills covered with crops, and dotted here and there with sheep and cattle, filled in the picture. Everywhere was verdure. Occasional glimpses could be caught of far away mountain spurs to the east, of chateaux

**The Rhone Valley.**

**Its Charm.**

perched on crags, of grape vines, orange groves and creepers, of towns and villages. It was June. The air was sweet and balmy, and the sky seemed to vie with the landscape in adding to the beauty of the scene. Few had ever seen, or will ever see, a fairer picture. The enthusiasm of the inhabitants rivalled the charm of the landscape. Peasants left their work and waved salutations. The towns were crowded with onlookers, who cheered and waved handkerchiefs and flags as the troop trains swept past. The fair daughters of France flashed glances of admiration, whilst ragged urchins ran along the track shouting for bully beef and souvenirs, both of which were thrown to them in generous profusion. At the stopping places the residents crowded to the railway stations to supply refreshments, and exchange compliments with the Anzacs.

*Enthusiasm of the French.*

The heart of France was stirred by the sight of those bronzed, hatchet-faced men who had come so far to fight for its freedom, and its inhabitants took every opportunity of expressing their admiration and gratitude. The entente cordiale with the French here commenced, was never broken, and of all foreign troops who fought on French soil probably the Australians were the most popular.[5]

The Australian is not emotional; at all events, his emotions are not on the surface, but our men would not have been human had they remained unmoved by the scenes of beauty and enthusiasm through which they were passing. Nor were they; indeed, they were intoxicated by it, and gave vent to their feelings in boisterous Australian fashion. They crowded to the carriage windows; they sang "The Marseillaise" and "Australia Will Be There;" they cheered, laughed, yelled, and roared greetings and salutations to the French, and at all stopping places animated and spirited attempts at conversation with the inhabitants took place. It was the trip of a life-time, and sent a glow of enthusiasm through the ranks of the 4th Brigade. Never will it be forgotten by those who took part in it.

*Enthusiasm of the Australians.*

The route lay through Arles, Tarascon, Avignon, Orange, Macon, Les Laumes, Lyons, Dijon, Montereau, and the environs of Paris, Creil, Clermont, Amiens (afterwards so well known), Abbeville, Etaples, Boulogne, near Calais, St. Omer, Hazebrouck,

*The Route.*

---

[5] Nevertheless our men all through their French campaigns had frequently to put up with extortionate demands and overcharges from the local population.

and Baillieul. There was great excitement as Paris was approached, but to the disappointment of all little was seen beyond a glimpse of the Eiffel Tower. The temperature got decidedly lower on the approach north, and the landscape lacked the luxuriant charm of the Rhone valley. Baillieul was reached on June 10, and after a drink of hot tea the battalion was met by guides, who led the way through narrow lanes to the billets which were to be the home of the battalion for a week. Lieut. P. J. Hayes and 35 other ranks had been left with the transport vehicles at Abbeville.

So ended the long journey by land and sea of about 2300 miles, crowded with novelty, incident, and excitement—the most delightful and enjoyable week ever experienced by the battalion abroad, and the record of which appears like a gleam of sunshine amidst stories of hardships endured, casualties suffered, and records of death, mutilation, and disease.

BATTALION'S ROUTE THROUGH FRANCE

## CHAPTER XVII.

### INITIAL DAYS IN FRANCE.

**Battalion in Battle Zone.**
The 4th Brigade was at last in the French battle zone, the object of its ambition, and where it might have been upwards of a year earlier but for having been side-tracked to the Peninsula. Conditions in rrance, both in and out of the line, were different from previous experience. The Peninsula—climatically, geologically, and in the sparseness of its population—was more akin to Australia than perhaps any other portion of Europe; in France, on the contrary, the battalion found itself in a densely populated country, and when out of the line the men were billeted among the local population. The district where it was now located was an agricultural one, and the men were assigned billets in the barns and out-houses of the French farms, which were sometimes draughty, and often vermin-infested and uncomfortable. The farms in this part of France bore a certain family resemblance; the fowl-houses, barns, and pigstys were usually in close propinquity to the living quarters (often built in quadrangular form), with the inevitable manure heap and stagnant pool in the centre. The 14th men, with Australian adaptability, settled down to the novel conditions, and were soon on terms of intimacy with their French hosts, who were remunerated for the lodgings provided. The first week in France was principally devoted to arranging billets and cook-houses, and constructing latrines, together with the inevitable training and route marching.

**Personnel Billeted in French Farms.**

**German Army Highly Trained.**
The fighting conditions in France, too, were different to those of the Peninsula. Our opponents here were a highly educated people whose rulers had made war their particular hobby for generations. The whole German population was permanently trained to arms, and the best brains of the country were devoted to the study and practice of the art of

war. This army, against which the Australians were now pitted, was the most highly trained in the world; it had great achievements behind it, and fondly looked on itself as invincible. Before the war ended it tacitly acknowledged the A.I.F. as about the most formidable of all the opponents it had ever had to face.

On the Western front the contending armies in 1916 faced each other on a line of enormous length (upwards of 400 miles), extending like a long winding river from the borders of Switzerland to the sea, and it was on the northern sector of this line that our men now found themselves. The war had developed into what was known as trench warfare. Both opponents dug themselves in, and strengthened their positions by every device known to military science.

*Trench Warfare.*

It was considered advisable by General Headquarters to allow the Australians a little experience in the new warfare before employing them in major operations. Poisoned gas (unknown on the Peninsula) was a common object of offence in France, and accordingly gas respirators with steel shrapnel helmets were issued by the quartermaster on June 15, and next day, clad in helmets and respirators, the 14th men made a march through a cloud of gas to give confidence in the efficiency of their new anti-gas equipment.

*Gas Respirators.*

After a week spent in the vicinity of Bailleul, the battalion marched on the 17th about eight miles to Fort Rompu, near Armentieres, the cooking utensils and stores being conveyed by motor lorry. Here the battalion was rejoined by Capt. Wadsworth, and also by Lieut. Symonds with the transport vehicles.

*March to Fort Rompu.*

The 4th Brigade was at length, after months of training, about to come to grips with the enemy. The men were tired of continual preparation, and anxious to measure themselves against their redoubtable opponents. The move to the front line, so long anticipated, was about to become a reality, and the 14th, highly trained, full of fight, and strongly seasoned with veteran troops, was now a formidable fighting machine. It was now in what was known as the Bois Grenier[1] sector, the 4th Brigade being the reserve brigade, and on June 19 and 20 the 14th supplied working parties of four

*Battalion in Bois Grenier Sector.*

---

[1] Bois Grenier, a little village about four miles south of Armentieres.

officers and 400 other ranks for work behind the lines, and here it suffered its first casualty in France, one man being wounded. The 19th Battalion of the 2nd Division was holding the line, and on the 21st several officers and three platoons of the 14th moved into the front line trenches for a few days to gain experience alongside the 19th Battalion men. A spectacular sight was witnessed one afternoon, when a British plane, under intense shell fire, brought down over the enemy's lines five of his observation ("sausage") balloons, and returned back in safety. On the 27th three more platoons of the 14th moved into the line, relieving three platoons of the 19th, and on the 28th the remainder of the 14th marched out about 7 p.m. and took over, about 10 p.m., the whole of the front line trenches, hitherto held by the 19th Battalion, B, C, and D Companies being in the front and support lines, and A Company in reserve. The relief was completed by midnight (the Lewis gun section of the 19th Battalion remaining in the line), and the 14th was holding for the first time a section of front line trenches in France, extending from "Burnt" Farm to "Inflamingerie" Farm.

The relief, however, was barely completed before a small party of C Company men ran into a patrol fight. C.S.M. Harold Thompson, Sgt. E. J. Rule, Pte. Bert Showers, and three or four others (accompanied by Capt. McGill, of the 19th Battalion, as a guide), went out to establish a listening post in front of our wire. A body of Germans, aware of the locality of the post, had laid a trap, and were awaiting them, and our party had barely left our wire when a volley, fired at point blank range, mortally wounded McGill and severely wounded Thompson. The unwounded members of the party, though startled by the unexpected attack, brought bombs and rifles into play, with the result that three Germans were severely wounded. Lieut. Jacka, V.C. (B Company) went out subsequently with a party, and brought back the three wounded Germans as prisoners; they proved to be members of the 231st Prussian Reserve. That was the first brush with the enemy in France. The same night Pte. Bertie Pring[2] was mortally wounded by a sniper, and died next day. He was the first member of the 14th to be killed in France.

Patrol Fight.

The right flank of the 14th sector was held by the 13th Battalion, whilst battalions of the 6th A.I.F. Brigade were

---

[2] Pte. Bertie Pring (No. 3455), of Ballarat (V.), labourer. Died of wounds, June 29, 1916.

**Description of Sector.**

posted on the left. The country here was low lying and blessed (or rather cursed) with such a superabundant rainfall that the whole neighbourhood was permanently saturated with moisture. It was useless to dig trenches—they immediately filled with water. Consequently, it became necessary to build earthworks, and thousands of bags full of earth were employed for that purpose, and piled up six or seven feet high in front of our lines. This entailed enormous labour, and as they were constantly being destroyed by the enemy's artillery they had to be continually renewed. There was one sally port in front of each company in the front line used by patrols entering and returning from No Man's Land.

The Germans had a very powerful searchlight somewhere close to la Houssoie, which they used to flash on No Man's Land at night, and which made the work of patrolling dangerous. Access to the battalion's front line from the rear was mostly by Tramline Avenue, a means of communication which traversed the battalion sector, and was both commodious and safe, besides being well duck-boarded. Rations were brought up at night by our transport to a dump about a mile from our trenches, and from there were taken by detailed parties of our men on trollies to the front line trenches and distributed.

On June 29 the rearguard which had been left at Marseilles rejoined the battalion.[3] On the same date Lieut. Reg. Jones (who with two other ranks had just returned from a sniping school) was appointed battalion sniping and scout officer, and immediately commenced the organisation of the sniping section. Unfortunately it was short lived, for that same evening Jones was detailed to take out a party to protect the right flank of a 6th Brigade raiding party, operating on the left of the battalion sector. Jones was severely wounded during the raid, but characteristically refused to have his wounds attended to until he had written out his report. One member of his party was overlooked, and lay for two days in No Man's Land.

**Lieut. Jones Wounded.**

---

[3] The Marseilles divisional rearguard was composed of D Company men, and included the following well-known personalities:—Sgts. John O'Brien and W. H. Pearce, Cpl. A. Urie, and Ptes. Eric Fulton, W. H. Boyes, R. Scanlan, and F. Wright. (Vide Chap. 16.)

## CHAPTER XVIII.

### THE FIRST TRENCH RAID OF THE FOURTH DIVISION.[1]

1916.—July 2 and 3.

Among other means of offence on the Western front were infantry raids on the enemy's trenches, which were much in vogue in the A.I.F., and whose records teem with descriptions of them. These "minor enterprises" were usually carried out between major operations, and all bore a strong family resemblance. They were almost invariably conducted under cover of darkness, and usually opened with an artillery barrage of more or less intensity, followed by a rush of the raiding party on the enemy's trenches, where the raiders dealt out death and destruction, and then returned—those who were left of them—with what prisoners or loot they had captured. Their ostensible objects were to inflict casualties on the enemy, "keep up the morale of our troops," and obtain identification and information of the enemy's units opposite, and they were much favoured by some of the leading generals on the Western front. They undoubtedly inflicted considerable loss, and a certain amount of demoralisation among the Germans, but many of them were costly adventures, for any accident might lead to a tragedy,[2] and it is a moot point if the necessary information could not have been obtained practically without loss by enterprising scouts, and whether it was advisable to fritter away the lives of priceless men on minor operations which could have no decisive influence on the war as a whole. They were also not required to keep up the morale of Australian troops.

In all units there were a handful of exceptionally brave men (born leaders) whose personality and courage inspired the others. Australian raids were almost always conducted by volunteers, and the raiders were recruited almost wholly from this handful (for only the bravest were chosen for

*Object of Raids.*

*Raiders the Cream of the A.I.F.*

---

[1] The first raid of the 5th Division took place on August 19, 1916.
[2] This was strikingly exemplified in the present raid.

this dangerous work), so that the losses among raiders cannot be calculated solely on a numerical basis. They were the flower of the A.I.F., and their losses were very difficult to replace, so that raids could only be considered successful when the losses inflicted on the enemy were out of all proportion to those suffered by the raiders.

Shortly after the arrival of the 4th Division in France it was decided by General Godley, commanding the 2nd Anzac Corps (to which the 4th Division was attached) that a trench raid by that division should be carried out, and the brigadier of the 4th Brigade (General Monash) was instructed to do so. General Monash decided that it should be conducted by the 14th Battalion, and that it should be a company raid, as it was considered that if the raiders were chosen from one company they would be more homogeneous and better acquainted with one another. Colonel Dare was consulted as to the choice of a company, and he selected A Company, and Capt. A. R. Cox (O.C. of A Company) was put in charge of the operation.[3]

"A" Company Selected.

In pursuance of this arrangement A Company paraded on June 19 at Fort Rompu, and volunteers for a raiding party called for.[4] There was not any lack of volunteers, almost the whole company stepping forward as one man, one of the very oldest men in the company jumping forward in his eagerness, but he was not selected, as it was a young man's job. The pick of the volunteers were subsequently chosen by Capt. Cox and his platoon commanders. After the raiders had been selected they marched next day to the front line at Bois Grenier, where the raid was to take place, and were left there for four or five days to get used to the shelling, and to familiarise themselves with No Man's Land both by day and night. They then left the front line and went into wooden huts about three miles behind the line, and started preparing for the raid. The preparation and organisation was directed by Capt. Cox.

Volunteers Called For.

Raiders Chosen.

Training.

---

[3] Communicated to the author by Lieut.-Col. J. M. A. Durrant, C.M.G., D.S.O., then brigade major of the 4th Brigade.

[4] A spirited account of this raid was written by Scout Alan Davies to his father. It was printed in the Melbourne "Argus" of August 26, 1916, and entitled "Raid on a Trench." No. 5362, Alan Davies, born at Heidelberg (Vic.) on March 6, 1893. Wounded in the raid, and subsequently joined the 25th Battalion, and killed in action July 18, 1918.

assisted by the platoon officers. It consisted of physical training, bayonet fighting, revolver practice, with football, hot and cold baths, and three good meals a day. At the end of a few days all had attained a high standard of technical efficiency, and were physically as fit as picked athletes. There was much enthusiasm that A Company had been chosen for the raid out of the forty-eight companies in the 4th Division. The success of the raid depended on each man knowing exactly what he had to do when he reached the German lines, and sham attacks were made on trenches as nearly like the one to be raided as possible, and laid out by the engineers. Lectures were also given on the raid and plans of the trenches to be attacked shown. The raiders were allotted to their various sections, and told exactly what to do, just as in a football team. Each man was also given a number by which he was to be known.

The raiders may be divided roughly into two sections: (a) The assault party proper, consisting of four officers and 56 men, subdivided into right and left parties, who were to turn in those respective directions on reaching the German trenches. Each of these parties contained a bombing, parapet, and blocking party, stretcher-bearers, prisoners' escort, an intelligence N.C.O., an engineer, and machine gunner. There were also the scouts, who had done important work patrolling No Man's Land. (b) The covering party, position party, and reserves, whose duties were incidental and accessory to the raid, but who did not take an actual part in the assault on the trenches.

Assault Party.

Capt. A. R. Cox was officer commanding attack, and with Capt. Stanton as understudy directed operations from company headquarters in our lines. The officer commanding assault, who was in charge of, and responsible for the actual fighting operations, was Lieut. Harold B. Wanliss, of Ballarat, who was O.C. of No. 3 Platoon. The important position of scouts' officer was allotted to Lieut. A. T. Harvey,[5] of Bundaberg (Q.), whilst 2nd-Lieuts. R. D. Julian (Geelong) and J. B. Roderick (Glenferrie) were in charge of the right and left parties respectively. Lieut. Roderick was an "original," and the only one of the four officers who had been in action before.

O.C. Attack.

O.C. Assault.

---

[5] Lieut. A. T. Harvey and Sgt. R. J. Garcia (N.C.O. in charge of right bombing party) were the only raiders who did not belong to A Company. They were both B Company men.

## First Trench Raid of 4th Division.

**Peninsula Veterans.**
Most of the raiders consisted of recent reinforcements who had joined up in Egypt, and had no war experience, but the quota also contained a handful of Peninsula veterans, including Sgts. Norman Harris, Jack Garcia, "Curly" Croft, John Pearce, Arnold Rich, Fred Anderson, and Steve de'Arango, Cpls. J. J. Myers, F. P. Ryan, and C. Farnbach, L/Cpls. T. E. Ross, George Bullen, and B. Brodal, and Ptes. G. Huse, P. Manders, W. H. Pike, H. J. Wright, J. Boulton, W. A. Smith, and L. Davis.

**Weapons.**
The weapons consisted of rifles, revolvers, bayonets, bombs, and knob-kerries.[6] Wire cutters were carried by the scouts and officers. Some had electric torches. All bayonets were painted black to prevent them shining in the dark.

On July 2 the raiders were informed that the raid would be that evening, and that everything must be ready! This consisted in destroying all old letters and writing farewell ones home, and packing valuables in small parcels in case the owners were posted missing next morning. Identification discs, paybooks and badges were left behind, and all the raiders put on British uniforms and dark woollen caps in place of helmets, so that if their bodies were left in the German trenches they would be unidentifiable.

**Description of No Man's Land.**
The place of the raid had been chosen by General Monash, who himself worked out the details.[7] His work was, as ever, efficient. The raid took place a little to the left of the 14th Battalion's sector, and close to where the 23rd Battalion was then in the line. No Man's Land[8] was here about 300 yards wide, and was bisected by the Coureau River from 3 to 10 yards wide and from 3 to 10 feet deep. This had to be crossed by the raiders both in the advance and retirement, and was a formidable obstacle to get wounded across. The scouts who had patrolled No Man's Land had chosen a crossing place where the water was about 4 feet deep. In front of our parapet was our own wire about 20 to 30 yards wide; a shallow ditch (or irrigation channel), partly filled with water, about 18 inches deep and about 2 feet

---

[6] "Knob-kerries" consisted of entrenching tool handles with iron cogwheels on the end; they were ugly weapons in trench fighting.

[7] Sometimes the details of raids were worked out at battalion headquarters. In this case the brigadier undertook the work in person.

[8] No Man's Land, i.e., the land between the German trenches and our own.

wide, ran at a slight angle from near our wire to the River Coureau. The raiders (including several wounded) found a refuge in this ditch on their return to our lines. No Man's Land was covered with shell holes and grass two feet high (which offered concealment if not protection) on our side of the river. Along the banks were a number of willow trees torn by shells. On the far bank and on slightly rising ground almost bare of trees was the German barbed wire, consisting of three belts, each several yards wide; first a trip wire close to the ground, then a space of a few yards and a belt of high loose wire; then a further space and another belt of loose wire. In addition to these formidable defences the Germans had their very efficient and powerful artillery, and two machine guns, one on each flank, in a position to enfilade their own wire and parapet; these machine guns took a heavy toll of the raiders during the engagement. There had been a big trench raid on the sector by the Sixth Brigade A.I.F. on June 29,[9] which doubtless put the Germans on their guard, and caused them to strengthen their wire. It also tended to make them alert and suspicious.

*German Defences.*

The artillery[10] support of the raid consisted of a "box" barrage so arranged that the shells should explode for three minutes on the German parapet, and then move back to their support and communication trenches, forming an iron ring round the point raided, so as to keep enemy supports from coming up. There were also to be artillery diversions on both flanks to divert attention from the main attack, whilst the 4th Machine Gun Co. was to attempt to enfilade the enemy's communication trenches, and engage any hostile machine guns that should open fire on our men. The destruction of the enemy's wire, which it was essential for the raiders to pass through to reach the enemy's parapet, was entrusted to the 6th Brigade Trench Mortar Battery. Theoretically everything was arranged to perfection; the result depended on the practical and successful working out of the scheme, and the action of the enemy. Emphasis must be laid on the fact that everything had to be worked out to an unalterable time-table. Ten minutes after the assault opened was the maximum time allowed for our men to be in the enemy's trenches; our artillery barrage then turned again on the enemy's parapet, so that if the raiders

*Artillery Support.*

*An Unalterable Time-table.*

---

[9] Alluded to at the end of Chap. xvii.
[10] The artillery of the 2nd Division co-operated in the barrage.

were not then all out by that time they would come under the fire of their own barrage as well as that of their opponents. All the officers carried luminous watches, which were synchronised with 4th Brigade Headquarters shortly before zero time.

Towards evening, after receiving final instructions, all formed up into raiding formation, and about 8 p.m. marched off towards the front line trenches. They were full of enthusiasm, as if going off to a picnic. Jokes, chaff, and witticisms were bandied about freely. The result of nearly a fortnight's training was to be crammed into ten minutes work.

**Enthusiasm of Raiders.**

On the way to the front all stopped at an old cottage and blackened each other's faces with burnt corks, so that they would be more difficult to see in the dark. On reaching the front line all moved along to the place where they had to crawl out over our parapet, passing en route the trench mortars with their piles of bombs (known as "plum puddings"), which were to be utilised to bombard the German wire.

**All Faces Blackened.**

The reserve party was here left in our trenches, and the residue of the raiders, in their formation number, and one behind another in single file, like a huge human serpent, headed by the O.C. Assault, crept one by one over our parapet, and through our wire by a path which had been cut in it to let them out, then literally ventre a terre crawled across the shallow ditch, and bearing away to the right until they came directly in front of the position to be attacked, where they laid down and waited in the long grass for our barrage to open, the scouts who had been investigating having reported that all was clear. The German machine gun on the left flank was firing just over them, sweeping the parapet behind, and every now and then putting a burst into No Man's Land, some of the bullets passing very close over the raiders. At short intervals a flare would be sent up from the German lines, and would light up No Man's Land, some of them falling within a few yards of the expectant party. A German wiring party could be distinctly heard strengthening the wire in front, but these men were all killed, and their bodies seen along their wire when our men attacked. Meanwhile the linesman had taken out a telephone wire to the raiders' jumping-off

**Wait in No Man's Land.**

**German Wiring Party.**

place, and one message was got through to Capt. Cox before it was destroyed by shell fire.

The long wait of about half an hour was very trying to men keyed up to a high pitch of enthusiasm, and whose nerves were strung up awaiting action, though even here some of these irrepressible Australians could not forbear indulging in jokes. They laid with their eyes glued in the direction of the German parapet veiled in darkness in front of them. Suddenly at 11.35 p.m. our barrage opened with a crash just over their heads, and the hitherto sombre parapet became a mass of living flame from the bursting shells.

Simultaneously the trench mortars also opened, and their concussion nearly lifted the raiders off the ground, the mortars bursting with a roar, whilst the handles (about 2 ft. 6 in.) came flying back over them. Three minutes of this tornado and the parapet suddenly grew dark again—the barrage had moved back to the communication trenches. Up then they rose like one man, the signal was given, and **Rush of** rapidly but in good order, yelling like mad- **Attacking Party.** men they rushed for the river—here up to their armpits—and plunging into the icy cold water like a lot of frogs, scrambled up the other bank and made for the openings in the wire, for the time allotted was short, and "time was the essence of the contract." Thirty seconds had been allowed for getting through the gaps in the enemy's wire, but on reaching it the raiders found there were not any gaps. The wire was practically **Failure of** uncut. The trench mortars had failed to do **Trench Mortars.** what was allotted to them. Their bombs. instead of bursting in the wire, had landed on and beyond the enemy's parapet, or between, instead of in, the belts of wire. The whole raid was now out of gear, and the result of this error, as ever throughout the war, fell, not on the unintentional authors of it, but on the unfortunate infantry, who always paid the price with their blood for the mistakes or failures of others.

It now became a perfect inferno. The German artillery, with extraordinary promptitude and accuracy, opened a tremendous fusilade on their own wire, whilst **German Artillery** their machine guns were also putting in bursts **Opens on Own** of fire and spraying the wire with bullets. **Wire.** Searchlights and Verey lights went up from the German lines in all directions, with the result that it became as bright as day, whilst the din was so deafening that one could shout in his neighbour's ear and not be heard. There was not any intention of relinquishing the enterprise in spite of the now desperate condition of affairs; the blood of the Australians was up, and nothing could stop them. Led by their young chief and Lieut. Harvey, they hurled themselves on the barbed wire, the scouts and officers using their wire cutters with the greatest energy. Men were thrown down by the trip wire, sprang to their feet, and were thrown down again, whilst others from behind crawled over the top of them, and were then themselves thrown down and used in turn as human bridges by others. Meanwhile many were wounded, and all had their clothes torn to tatters, and their arms, faces and legs ripped and gashed by the barbed wire. How they got through no one could say, but they did get through, cursing, tripping, yelling, falling and battling like a set of furies, whilst all experienced to the full in this desperate struggle the noise and blinding effect of the bursting shells which were exploding on all sides of them. "They went through that wire," said Sgt. de'Arango,[11] "as through a field of wheat." Lieut. Harvey,[12] who had shown great gallantry, was desperately wounded close to the German parapet. A German sallyport was now fortunately discovered a little to the left of the point of entry to the last belt of wire, and through it the survivors of the raiders rushed for the German trenches. There was not the least confusion; as each man arrived he went methodically to the point previously allotted to him as if at drill; seldom has the advantage of training and organisation been more evidenced.

*Raiders Rush Through Uncut Barbed Wire.*

*Survivors Reach German Trenches.*

The time available was now very short, as our barrage was timed to re-open on the German parapet at 11.48 p.m., and the struggle through the wire had taken some minutes. The enemy's parapet was between 9 and 10 feet deep, and their dugouts were under the parapet, with openings which had covers which our bombers lifted and threw bombs in. The story of the few strenuous minutes in the German trenches is difficult to disentangle, for men had different impressions and varied experiences. Some did not see a live German, but both right

*Dugouts Bombed.*

---

[11] Sgt. Steve de Arango (vide Chap. vii., note 4) was in charge of the covering party in No Man's Land, and from his propinquity the spectator best fitted of all to see the rush of the attacking party.

[12] Lieut. A. T. Harvey, of Bundaberg (Q.), clerk. Born Maryborough (Q.) on March 20, 1888. Educated at Central Boys' School, Bundaberg.

and left bombing parties claim to have bombed dugouts full of Germans, and to have heard screams and yells as the bombs exploded. It was affirmed that two Germans here killed were officers. One man blew up a German bomb store. Just prior to the retirement some bombs were thrown by Germans from behind their parados, but our men were not able to get to grips with these bombers, as the time limit had arrived, and the "out" signal was given. Meanwhile Sgt. Norman Harris, of the Scouts, had attached a luminous tape from the point of entry towards the German parapet, and ran it through the best passage in the barbed wire towards the river. This served as a beacon to the returning raiders, and doubtless' saved many lives.

**Luminous Tape Through Wire.**

When the assault party advanced to the attack, the covering party, under Sgt. de'Arango, and Cpls. C. F. Ross and J. C. Blair, having crossed the river, spread out fan-like in No Man's Land, to protect its flank and rear, and during the retirement was able to render valuable aid to the wounded.

**Covering Party.**

The raiders had been instructed when their work was completed to get back as best they could, and they now came rushing back through the wire in twos and threes just in front of our barrage, which had re-opened on the parapet just vacated. Lieut. Wanliss, who had been severaly wounded in the advance, but had nevertheless remained on the German parapet in full control of operations, and had given the "out" signal, was again severely wounded, and was the last man to retire, and then only after he had seen every one of his surviving men go back. He was wounded a third time during the withdrawal, and finally collapsed, being brought back to our lines more dead than alive. He had been the first man to reach the German parapet in the advance.

**Retirement.**

**O.C. Assault Wounded.**

The retirement was even more difficult than the advance, on account of the numerous wounded (continually being increased by the enemy's fire) who had to be got in. Many who had been previously wounded were wounded now a second or third time. There was the same hard struggle to get back through the wire, and it was during the early retirement that young Julian was killed, and Sgt. Croft mortally wounded. After negotiating the wire, and leaving the luminous tape, all who could struggled towards the river (the unwounded and less severely wounded helping

**Death of 2nd-Lieut. Julian and Sgt. Croft.**

the more severely wounded), where all jumped in and most took refuge in the shallow drain which ran towards our lines.

After all the raiders had suffered they had to undergo another terrible experience before they got back to safety.

**Terrible Experience in No Man's Land.** The Germans, realising that the retirement was taking place, opened up an intense barrage on No Man's Land and our front line trench, cutting off the retreat of the raiders.

Flares were going up every minute, rendering everything visible, while the air was alive with missiles; the slightest movement by our men would have attracted attention, and resulted in their consequent annihilation, and for about an hour all had to lie concealed full length in a shallow ditch, half-full of icy water, with only their faces out; the tortures of the wounded (and the majority were wounded) under these conditions can be better imagined than described. Machine gun bullets kept sweeping a few inches over their heads, and occasionally a shell would land right in the ditch; but owing to the mud and water, its effect was fortunately purely local. At length the barrage ceased, though shells still kept coming over, and machine gun bullets still swept No Man's Land. So cramped were all with the cold that it was some time before even the strongest could crawl.

The greatest difficulty was now experienced in getting back the wounded, and many splendid acts of heroism[13] were performed by men who, after participating in all the strain and struggle of the engagement, risked their lives again and again, amidst the flying bullets, to rescue wounded comrades.

**Acts of Heroism.**

The wounded could not, under these circumstances, be handled carefully, and sometimes rescuers and wounded fell headlong into shell holes together. Nor must the fortitude of the wounded be forgotten. Some, shot to pieces, and suffering untold tortures, did not utter a complaint. Special reference must be made to the work here done by Sgts. Fred Anderson[14] (who rescued and carried back fourteen men), Norman Harris,[15] Steve d'Arango, Cpls. Charlie Ross[16] and

---

[13] "Australians will do for me," wrote Scout Alan Davies, "after what I saw them do that night."

[14] Capt. Fred. Anderson (A Company, No. 545), forest foreman, of Buangor (V.). Born July 15, 1893, at Buangor (V.).

[15] Lieut. Norman C. Harris (A Company, No. 63), farmer, of British Columbia (Canada).

[16] Sgt. Chas. Ross (A Company, No. 3543), stationmaster, of Bendigo (V.). Born May 5, 1890, at Bendigo (V.). Killed in action at Bullecourt on April 11, 1917.

F. P. Ryan,[17] Pte. Geo. Huse,[18] and others, in assisting their stricken comrades. It can be recorded with just pride, that, in spite of the appalling difficulties of the retirement, only one wounded man (Sgt. Croft) was left in the enemy's hands, and that only because he (tangled up in the enemy's wire with broken legs) was again struck by a shell when being dragged back by some of our men, who only then left him because they thought he had been killed outright. Several, some of them severely wounded, had tried to save him.

The Germans, as often throughout the war, made no attempt to come to personal grips with our men, whom they should have annihilated, but their artillery and machine gun fire was prompt, accurate, and effective. Our casualties were very heavy.[19] All the officers[20] and three-fourths of the other ranks of the assault party were casualties,[21] including four out of five scouts, the two runners (both killed), the two engineers (both severely wounded), fourteen out of sixteen bombers, and seven out of nine of the blocking parties. The German casualties were officially estimated at a minimum of fifty-one men, but that is probably an over-estimate; at all events the conditions were such that an accurate estimate was impossible. Their casualties probably contained many killed, for little quarter was given, and it was impossible under the circumstances to bring back prisoners. Lieuts. Harvey and Julian[22] were two most promising officers, and were a great loss to the battalion. The death of the veteran Sgt. "Curly" Croft,[23] too, was severely felt. He was a great N.C.O.—one of the finest, indeed, in the A.I.F. A man of exceptional personality, with great initiative and driving power, he enforced

*Heavy Casualties.*

---

[17] Cpl. F. P. Ryan (A Company, No. 643), labourer, of Werribee (V.).

[18] Lieut. Geo. Huse. Vide Chap. xiv. (list of stretcher-bearers).

[19] All the casualties were confined to the assault party; there were not any casualties among the covering party, position party, or reserves.

[20] The officer commanding assault was the only one of the four officers who was able to go into action again.

[21] Among our killed was Pte. James Pender (A Company, No. 3458), of Geelong. He was batman to Lieut. Julian, and it was universally stated and believed at the time that he had returned to our lines after the assault when he heard that Lieut. Julian was missing, and then went back to recover his body, losing his life in the attempt. The author cannot find any confirmation of this story.

[22] 2nd-Lieut. R. D. Julian (A Company, No. 3571), ironmonger, of Geelong (V.). Killed in action, July 2, 1916.

[23] Sgt. Harold Croft (A Company, No. 46), of Elmhurst (V.), shearer. Born Elmhurst, April 14, 1890. Died of wounds at Lille on July 8, 1916. Known as "Curly," from his close-cropped curly hair. (Vide Chap. xvi.)

discipline by sheer force of character. He was always cheerful, even under depressing conditions, and was one of the most popular N.C.O.'s in the whole 4th Brigade. The wounded, after receiving local attention from the R.M.O. were sent to hospital at Bailleul, and subsequently many of them were sent on to England for treatment and recuperation. The unwounded reported at Headquarters dugout, had a tot of rum, went back to billets, got out of their wet clothes, had a sleep, and that same evening went back to the trenches with no other reward for their splendid achievement than the consciousness of duty done.[24]

**Decorations.** Three decorations were awarded—the D.S.O. to Lieut. H. B. Wanliss, the O.C. Assault, being the first occasion during the war that that decoration was awarded to a subaltern in the A.I.F.; the hardbitten Jack Garcia[25] secured the D.C.M.,

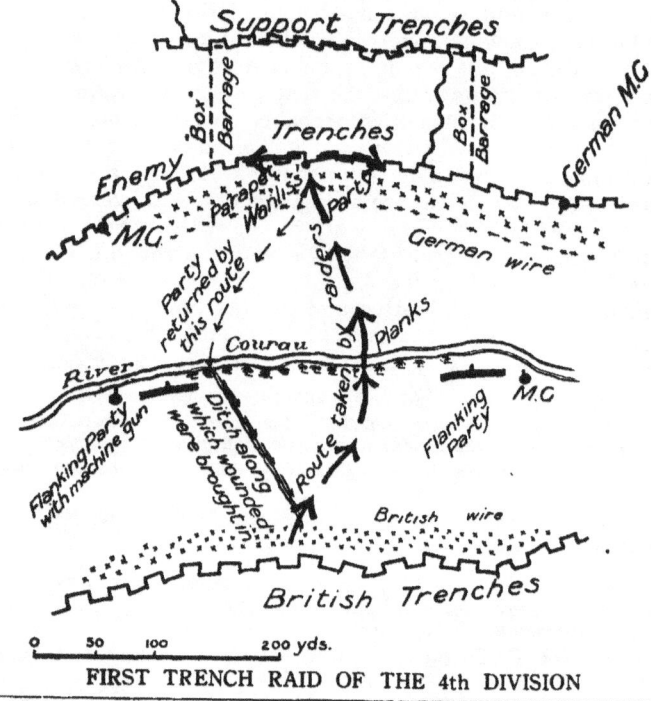

FIRST TRENCH RAID OF THE 4th DIVISION

[24] It seems curious throughout the war that special work was not recognised by special leave.
[25] Vide Chap. 14.

whilst Sgt. Fred Anderson by his exceptional work richly earned the M.M. Owing to all the officers in the assault becoming serious casualties, some men who should have received decorations failed to be recommended.

**Battalion's First Engagement in France.**
So ended the first engagement of the 14th in France—an operation that greatly enhanced the reputation of the battalion, and caused it to be held up as an example to the whole 4th Division. It was an exceptional piece of work, rarely equalled even in the annals of the A.I.F., and memorable on account of the apparently insurmountable difficulties successfully overcome, and the extraordinary coolness and nerve of the personnel.

**Its Exceptional Character.**
It was more remarkable owing to the fact that three-fourths of the officers and men engaged in the actual assault had never been in action before. It was their baptism of fire—and of blood.

**Encomiums of Generals Monash and Birdwood.**
The operation received high encomiums from leading generals. The Brigadier wrote:—"I consider the resolution and determination of the party in persevering to force their way into enemy trenches, through uncut wire, under heavy fire, worthy of the highest praise, and reflecting the greatest credit upon their offensive spirit"; and on July 5 the Corps Commander, General Birdwood, made the raid a subject of routine orders.[26]

**APPENDIX A.**

As the above was the 4th Division's first trench raid in France, a list of the personnel of the assault party, with attendant casualties, is set out hereunder. The author is indebted for the raiders' names to a list among General Monash's papers. The following abbreviations are used:—K.I.A. (killed in action), D.W. (died of wounds), W. (wounded).
Scouting Party.—Lieut. A. T. Harvey, W; Sgt. N. C. Harris; Pte. H. Hibbert, W.; Pte. L. Davis, K.I.A.; L/Cpl. T. E. Ross, W.; Pte. A. Davies, W. Stretcher Bearers.—Left Party—Pte. G. Huse; Pte. C. Ward; Right Party—Pte. P. Manders, W.; Pte. J. A. C. Snow, D.W. Assault Party.—Officer commanding, Lieut. H. B. Wanliss, W. Runners to Assault Party—Pte. R. Easton, D.W.; Pte. T. Brocklebank, K.I.A.; Sgt. G. Wilson, W. Telephonists to O.C. Assault—L/Cpl. B. Brodal, W.; Pte. R. P. Hallett. Linesman to O.C. Assault—Pte. M. H. Griffiths, W. Positions and details of the remainder of the party:—Left Parties—Officer commanding, Lieut. J. B. Roderick, W. Bombing Party—Sgt. J. Pearce, Pte. T. Trevilian, W; Pte. R. Sparks, W.; Pte. J. C. Donnelly, W.; Pte. T. H. Gray, W.; Pte. L. Cronin, W.; Pte. J. Beggs, K.I.A.; Pte. M. Bourke, W.

---

[26] A list of the members of the assault party appears in Appendix A to this chapter.

124        *First Trench Raid of 4th Division.*

Parapet Party.—Left Parties—Sgt. A. Rich, W.; Pte. A. H. Bruce, W.; Pte. R. J. H. Hyatt, W. Blocking Party—Cpl. J. Myers, W.; Pte. O. Anderson; Pte. J. Gray, W.; Pte. J. Keane, W. Intelligence N.C.O.—Cpl. F. J. Weston, W. Machine Gunner—Pte. W. A. Smith, W. Engineer—Sapper J. Dadsey, W. Prisoners' Escort—Pte. R. J. Ramsay, W.; Pte. G. H. Dietrich. Right Parties—Officer commanding, Lieut. R. D. Julian, K.I.A. Bombing Party.—Sgt. R. J. Garcia, W.; Pte. G. M. Quigley, W.; Pte. H. White, W.; Pte. H. J. Wright, W.; Pte. H. J. Armstrong; Pte. R. Boyle, W.; Pte. W. Pike, W.; Pte. J. Boulton, W. Parapet Party—Sgt. H. Croft, D.W.; Pte. W. H. Watts; Pte. V. Lacon. Blocking Party—Cpl. F. P. Ryan, W.; Pte. W. J. Earll, W.; L/Cpl. G. Bullen; Pte. L. Best, W.; Pte. F. Blight, W. Intelligence N.C.O.—Sgt. F. Anderson. Machine Gunner—Cpl. C. Farnbach. Engineer 4th Field Company—Sapper F. Paton, W. Prisoners' Escort—Pte. J. Pender, K.I.A.; Pte. Bert Mason.

## APPENDIX B.

Since the above chapter has been written, through the courtesy of Mr. C. E. W. Bean, the Australian official historian of the war, the author has been furnished with the German official account of the above raid, which is hereunder set out. It must be noted that the apparent discrepancy in the time is accounted for by the fact that German time is one hour ahead of the British. It was the 50th (Prussian) Reserve Division which faced the raid. Its account is as follows:—

"During the night (of July 2, 3) enemy infantry and machine gun fire was lively. At 12.30 a.m. heavy hostile artillery and trench mortar fire was put down in vii B, viii, and ix a.b. The fire was heaviest in viii A. Our batteries opened out immediately in reply to the enemy fire. An enemy patrol, 50 or 60 strong, which advanced in viii A c against our trenches, was caught in a searchlight, and as it reached our wire was shot up with infantry and machine gun fire. The enemy fled, leaving about 15 dead in our wire. Towards 1.30 a.m. all was quiet on the Divisional front. Our losses in this engagement were: 6 dead, 47 wounded."

## CHAPTER XIX.

### THE GERMAN COUNTER RAID.

#### 1916.—July 3.

Our raid described in the last chapter was a direct challenge to the Germans, and could not be passed over by their leaders. Consequently next day they retaliated by a raid on our trenches. B Company held the right, C Company the centre, and D Company the left of the line; the blow fell on the latter. D Company platoons were arranged that day as follows:—

14th Platoon, on the left: Officer commanding, Lieut. J. Mackay; platoon Sgt. T. A. Rose.

16th Platoon, in the centre, under Sgt. A. C. Hutton.

13th Platoon, on the right : Officer commanding, Lieut. Stanley Rogers; platoon Sgt. W. Oram.

15th Platoon, in reserve, under Sgt. N. McKenzie, about a quarter of a mile in rear of No. 13 Platoon.

During the afternoon the enemy fired over a certain number of range finders, and also an aerial torpedo to find the range of our wire. The Peninsula veterans anticipated trouble, but the reinforcements, new to battle, did not realise the serious results that these range finders portended.[1]

*Enemy Fires Range Finders.*

Lieut. Williamson (2nd in command of D Company) detailed Sgt. T. A. Rose and Sgt.-Major F. H. Boyes to make a thorough inspection of the wire entanglements along the battalion's lines that night, with the result that preparations for an attack were made, and all advised to keep a close watch.

After dark everything was quiet, and there was not a breath of wind. Suddenly, at 10.23 p.m., the German bombardment opened with a terrific roar, and for about an hour a torrent of missiles of every description—high explosive 5.9 and 4.2 shells, minenwerfers, shrapnel and machine gun fire—

*German Bombardment Opens.*

---

[1] In view of these unmistakable portents, whether it would not have been advisable to have withdrawn the bulk of the garrison from the threatened sector, and allow the Germans to expend their fury and ammunition on empty trenches, need not be discussed.

was concentrated on the 150 yards of trench held by the 14th Platoon of D Company. It was here that the 14th men made their first acquaintance with the minenwerfers **The Minenwerfers.** (or "aerial torpedoes," as they called them), a missile of the same description as our mortars, which combined deadly accuracy with enormous explosive power. Their accuracy on this date indeed was a painful contrast to the complete failure of our own trench mortars the night before; their course through the air could be traced like comets, but their explosion on landing was most demoralising. Our line was illuminated with the bursting shells, whilst the noise of their rush through the air, the concussion, and the fumes of the high explosives made an **Violent and** inferno that it is difficult to imagine. It mostly **Destructive** fell on the 14th Platoon, which held that part **Effects of** of the line, and few experiencing it expected **Bombardment.** to get out alive. Many were buried and dug out; others were buried and could not be dug out. Everything was reduced to chaos, and the trenches flattened out. The behaviour of the D Company men, under these trying conditions, could not have been **Gallantry of** surpassed; they behaved with the greatest **D Company.** gallantry, and did not retire to their dugouts, but clustering in the "bays" took it in turn to observe. One would hop on to the fire step, observe for a few seconds or minutes, according to his courage or temperament, then down and under the step, and his place would be taken by another.

Shortly after the barrage opened Capt. C. R. M. Cox (O.C. of D Company) tried to raise headquarters on the phone, but found all wires had been cut; **Germans Attack.** he then sent up the S.O.S. signal, but it was some considerable time before our artillery retaliated. Suddenly, after an hour's duration,[2] the barrage lifted on to our support lines, and the enemy were seen advancing on our position. The 19th Battalion Lewis gun team, which had been left in our line, did excellent work, firing about 700 rounds on the advancing enemy, causing heavy casualties, and our boys sprang to the fire pits, and using their rifles effectively, with the result that the enemy was badly cut up, and only a handful reached our lines: They

---

[2] Our barrage during the raid of the previous night had lasted only three minutes, in contradistinction to the present one, which lasted an hour. The success of our raid depended on surprise, theirs on the demoralisation caused to our personnel by an excessive and overwhelming bombardment.

scored one success. One of our "bays," tenanted by Lieut. J. Mackay, Cpl. Urie, and Ptes. Duffy, Robinson and Stephens, had been hit by a shell during the bombardment, burying Mackay and Urie up to their shoulders in the debris. The three privates, when endeavouring to release their comrades, were surprised by the sudden appearance of the Germans, who bombed the pit, killing Duffy, mortally wounding Robinson, and severely wounding Stephens, who lost an eye, and was dragged away half dazed as a prisoner. They also endeavoured to drag out Mackay and Urie, but failing, threw five bombs at the helpless and imprisoned men, which fortunately failed to explode. Both were subsequently released by their comrades. Meanwhile, in an adjacent "bay," Pte. W. H. Boyes,[4] who had sprung over the top when the barrage ceased, met several of the Germans face to face, and shot two at very close range, one of whom appeared to be the leader of the party.

The flares had now ceased, and a few German survivors retreated in the darkness, taking Stephens with them. Sgt. Rose, who was on the right, collected a few men, and going over the parapet, made an attempt to cut off the retreat of the raiders, but was too late, though some of their equipment was brought back. The wounded and buried men next claimed attention. The bombarded trenches were level with the ground, and practically every man had been buried. The trench was opened up, the dead removed, and the others released. One element of humour lightened the tragedy; it arose from the last man released. One of the rescuers, putting his head under the timber to see if there were any more men alive, called out, "Are there any more men under here?" A sepulchral voice from the other end (recognised as that of Pte. W. Devereau, of Warragul) replied, "My oath, there is!" The man who can joke under these conditions is an asset to the battalion.

**Buried Men Released.**

The wounded and buried having been removed, and a roll called, an effort was made to repair the trenches before daybreak. "A" Company was brought up from reserve to assist, and all available men were organised into fatigue parties to repair the shattered trenches; a wiring party was also

**Trenches Repaired.**

---

[3] No. 4314, Pte. Arthur A. Stephens, of Lorquon (V.), labourer. Born Lorquon December 6, 1896.

[4] Pte. William Harold Boyes, of Lardner (V.), farmer. (Vide also Chap. 40.)

detailed by Lieut. Williamson to fix up the wire in front. Lieut. Williamson was indefatigable, and took a very active part both in the relief of the wounded and reorganising the defences. Lieut. Stanley Rogers also co-operated.

The stretcher-bearers, under Capt. Winn (R.M.O.) and Sgt. A. J. ("Gus") Harris, worked till daylight attending to the wounded. Valuable aid was also rendered at the regimental aid post by Major Welch, of the Fourth Field Ambulance. Daylight presented a gruesome spectacle. Section 57 of our defences (held by D Company) was a wreck, and the area was covered with debris, shell holes, and human remains.

<small>Attention to Wounded.</small>

A fatigue party of A Company, sent up to the front line during the night with picks and shovels, but unarmed, was caught in the barrage, and severely mauled, suffering several casualties, including the two Moores[5] (twins), of Ballarat, killed. A patrol sent out from C Company lines under Sgt. Bertram Edmonstone[6] about 10 p.m. was cut off by the barrage from our lines, and was unable to return. The sergeant, a very fine soldier, was mortally wounded, but was carried back through the barrage by Pte. F. Calway,[7] and placed in our trenches. Calway then returned through the barrage to look for the patrol.

Our casualties were upwards of forty, and included Capt. C. R. M. Cox and Lieut. J. Mackay wounded, Sgts. Edmonstone and W. H. Pearce[8] (the bombing sergeant of D Company, and an excellent soldier) mortally wounded, Cpl. W. J. Horne[9] (severely wounded and evacuated to Australia), besides several killed and many more wounded. Among the killed was an old man known as "Dad"

<small>Our Casualties. Capt. C. R. M. Cox Wounded.</small>

---

[5] No. 4256, Ina Moore, of Ballarat (V.), engine driver, and No. 4257, Clement Moore, of Ballarat, carpenter. They entered and left the world together. The author is not aware of any similar incident occurring in the annals of the A.I.F., of twins being killed on the same day. (Vide Chap. 42.)

[6] No. 316, Sgt. Bertram Edmonstone, of Ararat (V.), grocer. Died of wounds, July 5, 1916. Known as "darkey," a brave and popular soldier, who distinguished himself in the attack on Hill 60 (vide Chap. 12). Before the war he was a prominent member of the Ballarat Imperial football team. He had a brother who was a sergeant in the 14th Battalion.

[7] No. 3295, Pte. Francis G. Calway, fireman, of Leigh Creek (V.).

[8] No. 2561, Sgt. W. Pearce, labourer, of Piercedale (V.).

[9] No. 454, Cpl. William J. Horne, driver, of Collingwood (V.), an original," and always known as "Collie." He proved an excellent forager on the Peninsula, and was always a great optimist.

O'Shea.[10] Old men whose keenness led them into the ranks of the A.I.F., if genial in their temperament, were always regarded in a kindly and almost affectionate spirit by their younger comrades. The number of the German casualties was unknown, but must have been heavy.

There were numerous instances of devotion to duty, but the following were specially mentioned for their fine work by the battalion commanding officer:—Pte. R. W. Scanlan,[11] L.-Cpl. A. L. Francis,[12] Pte. F. L. Wright,[13] and Pte. W. H. Boyes. L.-Cpl. J. H. Mitchell and Pte. E. L. Luke, of the 19th Battalion Lewis gun crew, also did excellent work, whilst Signaller R. M. Downes showed fine devotion to duty.

**Men Specially Commended.**

The 14th had held the front line trenches for less than a week, and the casualties had already passed the century, and many valuable officers and N.C.O.'s been put out of action, including Capt. C. R. M. Cox, Lieuts. J. Mackay, H. B. Wanliss, R. W. Jones, J. B. Roderick, A. H. Harvey, and R. D. Julian, the three latter being permanent losses to the battalion. A number of excellent N.C.O.'s had also become casualties, including C.Q.M.S. Ernie Hill, M.M., C.S.M. Harold Thompson, Sgts. R. J. Garcia, "Curly" Croft, A. Rich, G. F. Wilson, B. Edmonstone, W. H. Pearce, Cpls. W. J. Horne, F. P. Ryan, F. H. Weston, J. J. Myers, and L.-Cpls. B. Brodal, H. Carrick, T. E. Ross, and G. W. Eddy.

The 14th Battalion men, in incurring casualties, however, had also gained experience, for experience in war has always to be purchased by blood. They recognised the excellence of the German artillery, the exactitude and devastating power of his minenwerfers, and the deadliness of his machine gun fire—the high standard, in short, of our opponents on the mechanical side of war, but already there was the feeling—so marked throughout the war—that the Australian was his master in man to man fighting, and that his troops in the main, though highly trained, were less aggressive and self-reliant than our own.

**Excellence of German War Mechanism.**

---

[10] No. 3122, Pte. William O'Shea, iron fitter, of Clifton Hill (V.), known as "Dad," aged 44. Died of wounds, July 4, 1916.

[11] 2nd-Lieut. Roger Scanlan, labourer, of Sebastopol (V.). He was a prominent and capable N.C.O. of D Company throughout the war.

[12] No. 1739, L.-Cpl. A. L. Francis, farmer, of Sussex (England).

[13] No. 512, Pte. F. L. Wright, labourer, of Moonee Ponds (V.).

## CHAPTER XX.

### AN INTERLUDE.

#### 1916.—July 4 to August 5.

After the German raid of July 3 little of moment occurred till the 14th was relieved. The casualties among officers having created vacancies, C.S.M. W. R. Beamond, C.S.M. J. Millis, and Sgt. F. W. Appleton were appointed 2nd.-Lieuts. On the 5th, Generals Godley, Cox, and Monash paid a visit to the battalion's trenches. There was some mutual shelling during the next few days, with little material loss, the battalion's last fatal casualty for the month being No. 3516, Pte. A. Vincent, of A Company, who was shot on the 9th, through a loopholed position by a German sniper.

*Promotion of N.C.O.'s.*

Finally, on the 10th, eight platoons of the 30th Battalion (5th Division) relieved the same number of platoons of the 14th, and on midnight of the 11th the other eight platoons of the 30th marched in and took over the line. The recently formed 5th Division, A.I.F., which now took over the sector, had a fearful blooding a week later at Fleurbaix, which cost it over 5000 casualties.

*Relief by 5th Division.*

On the 12th the battalion marched to its former billets at Bailleul, and on the following day entrained at 9 a.m. for Candas (a village adjacent to and south-west of Doullens), which was reached after a long journey at 3 p.m. This journey was necessitated owing to the 4th Division being under orders to proceed to the Somme, where a tremendous battle had been proceeding since the first of the month, and in which the Australians ultimately took a prominent part. The battalion detrained at Candas, and marched to Domart, arriving there at 7 p.m., after one of the most exhausting marches the battalion ever had, and going into billets in the town. The 4th Division was now in what is known as the department of the Somme,

*Departure for the Somme.*

*Domart.*

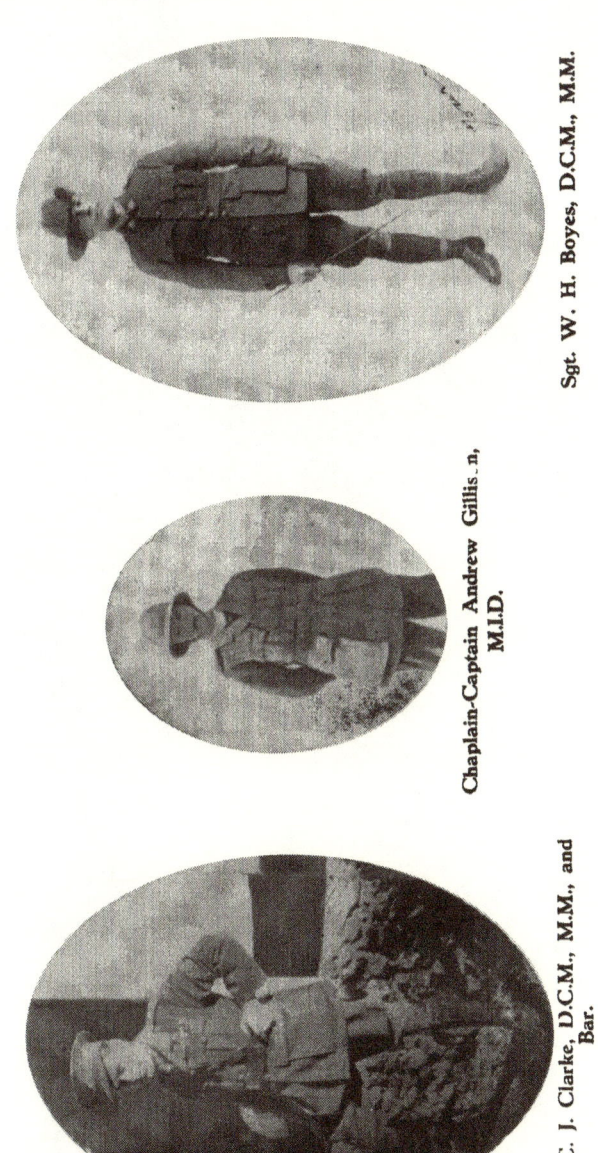

Sgt. W. H. Boyes, D.C.M., M.M.

Chaplain-Captain Andrew Gillis_n, M.I.D.

Sgt. C. J. Clarke, D.C.M., M.M., and Bar.

which was henceforth to be the scene of much of its activities, and which contains numerous battlefields famous in the history of the A.I.F.

On the following day (the 14th), the 4th Brigade lost its able and brilliant chief (Brigadier-General Monash), who relinquished the command of the brigade to take over command of the newly formed Third Australian Division. A brigade will always respond to a strong personality, and the capable and vigorous leadership of its great chief gave the brigade a reputation second to none even among the virile brigades of the A.I.F. General Monash had been working in France in conjunction with Major-General Sir H. V. Cox (G.O.C. of the 4th Division), and the two made a very powerful combination—a combination of excellence that was perhaps unequalled in the A.I.F. during the war. His successor, Colonel Brand, was an energetic officer who had shown initiative on the Peninsula, but he lacked the wide range of mind of his famous predecessor.

*Brig.-General Monash Relinquishes Command of 4th Brigade.*

*His Personality.*

On the 16th the battalion marched to Naours, where the men were allocated billets. Here the battalion remained for nine days indulging in route marching, and company and field training. There was an old subterranean city in the neighbourhood which was an object of interest to some of the troops. On the 20th a party of 150 men—17th Reinforcements and details—joined up.

*Naours.*

. It was during the stay here that the bombers were put on a different footing. Each battalion in the brigade was ordered to form a platoon of 40 picked men to be trained as bomb fighters pure and simple. The platoon was divided into four sections of ten each, each section representing a company. 2nd-Lieut. A. R. Dean was made O.C. of the platoon, with Sgt. E. J. Rule second in command, whilst Sgt. John Pearce was put in charge of A and B sections. After some strenuous training the platoon proved a very efficient body of men.

*Battalion Bombing Platoon.*

On the 25th the 4th Brigade marched out complete with all transport for Herissart, and billets were allotted on arrival there. The battalion marched for Warloy on the 27th, reaching it about 3 p.m. It was now approaching the battle zone, and the specialists —bombers, Lewis gunners, wiring parties, signallers, and runners—were being energetically trained for the warm work ahead. The distance from the firing line was now only about 12 miles; the roar of the guns at the front could be plainly and incessantly heard, some of the explosions shaking the village buildings. Rumours of the great battle, and the part played in it by the 1st and 2nd Divisions of the A.I.F., came dribbling through, but in spite of the rumours of appalling losses, the vast majority of the 14th men were eager and keen to get in, and have their turn in the struggle. Australian optimism and Australian lack of imagination stood them in good stead in this crisis. The Peninsula veterans had little to say; they had become hardened to war, and took all things as a matter of course. The recent reinforcements vainly endeavoured to imagine what war would be like, and how they would feel and act in their baptism of fire. All knew by this time that their turn would soon come. A foretaste of what they might expect was revealed to them one morning, when some of the 1st Division men, hot from the fighting at Pozieres, marched by. Their experiences at the front could be judged by their appearance and demeanour. All looked drawn and haggard, whilst some were so dazed that they appeared to be walking as if in a dream, with glassy, staring eyes. A few seemed even affected mentally. Some companies appeared to have been almost obliterated.

<small>Herissart. Warloy.</small>

<small>Battle Psychology.</small>

On the 30th 2nd-Lieut. Craven joined the battalion as signalling officer. He was originally a 15th Battalion man, and had won the D.C.M. for gallantry on the Peninsula. On the following day Lieut D. R. Macdermid rejoined the battalion after having been evacuated from the Peninsula. Meanwhile, training was going on apace. Packs, spare gear, and overcoats were dumped; nothing was retained by each man but a blanket and a waterproof sheet. The company commanders were:—A Company, Capt. A. R. Cox; B Company, Major O. C. W. Fuhrmann; C Company, Capt. Stewart Hansen; and D Company, Capt. R. W. Orr.

<small>Signalling Officer Appointed.</small>

<small>Company Commanders.</small>

August 4 was the second anniversary of the entry of Great Britain into the war, and that date raised reflections

**March to Albert.** among many. The Peninsula veterans, too, remembered that the first week of August, 1915, had also been a week of preparation for a big enterprise, that was then fondly supposed would result in the capture of Constantinople. On the same evening, at 9 p.m., the 4th Brigade left Warloy, and, fully equipped, marched through Senlis to Albert, reaching it about midnight, and bivouacked on an open piece of ground known as the brickfields, an elevation overlooking the ruins of Albert. The march was spectacular, for though the night was pitch dark, the sky was lit up with the countless flashes of the artillery, and the continual explosion of shells, whilst the thousands of flares, and many coloured rockets flashing through the heavens, gave the impression of a display of fireworks on a gigantic scale, whilst the eternal roar of the artillery sounded like a tropical thunderstorm. Both eyes and ears were satiated with sensations.

**Its Spectacular Character.**

Daylight disclosed Albert, and also no less than fourteen of our observation balloons floating in the sky, a sure sign of the activity of the sector. The battalion remained here all day, and an additional hundred rounds of ammunition was issued to each man, who now carried 220 rounds of S.A.A., two Mills bombs, and two days' iron rations, in addition to the 24 hours' ordinary rations. Everything was now ready. The battalion was about to take part in its first great battle in France.

**Battalion Ready for Action.**

## CHAPTER XXI.

### POZIERES RIDGE.

#### 1916.—August 6 to August 16.

**British Attack Launched.** The great British attack had been launched on July 1, 1916, on a wide front facing Bapaume, whilst the French fought at the same time on the immediate right flank. The position attacked was one of extraordinary strength—the best engineering talent in the German army having been engaged for nearly two years in strengthening it—and the British losses were appalling,[1] the enemy holding his ground with the greatest tenacity. The tactics adopted by the British High Command had been primitive. Brigade after brigade, like enormous human waves, were hurled against almost impregnable positions, were torn to pieces by artillery and machine gun fire, and the survivors were then drawn out, to be replaced by other units, which underwent similar experiences. Every yard gained was purchased by a profuse expenditure of human blood.

It took upwards of three weeks to capture Pozieres, a small town situated on elevated ground on the Albert-Bapaume road, and the higher ground behind the ridge was still in the enemy's possession when the 14th reached Albert. Many Australian units of the 1st and 2nd Divisions had been engaged in the struggle prior to the arrival of the 4th Division on the scene, and had been cut to ribbons by the awful artillery fire, which levelled trenches, buried men, and turned the battle area into a heaving volcano. What Australians endured in this Hell will probably never be thoroughly understood or appreciated by their countrymen.

At 1.40 p.m. on August 6 orders were received at battalion headquarters for the 14th to march out at once and

---

[1] The British (which, of course, includes Dominion) casualties for July, 1916, was 8,709 officers and 187,373 other ranks, being at the average rate of upwards of 6,000 casualties a day.

## The History of the 14th Battalion. 135

**14th Ordered to the Front.** relieve the 26th and 28th Battalions, then in the front line on Pozieres Ridge. The 14th and 15th were to go into the front line, with the 13th and 16th in support. At 2.30 p.m. the battalion moved off by companies with ten minutes interval between. The route lay through Albert via Tara Hill, then through Sausage Valley, leaving the chalk pit on the right, then through saps and supports (near the ruins of Pozieres), then to the right along a communication trench, and finally across about 150 yards of open country to the firing line.

**Route Followed.**

The commanding officer (Lieut.-Colonel C. M. M. Dare, D.S.O.), had decided to hold the firing line with one company only, having another in support, and two in reserve. B Company took over the line, with C in support, whilst A and D were held in reserve in Gun Trench. Thus the majority of the men were behind the line, and each company had one day in the firing line, one day in support, and two in reserve. This was eminently sound tactics, though contrary to the practice then in vogue.* It was impossible to avoid very heavy casualties if men were crowded into imperfect front line trenches, for they simply became targets for the enemy's artillery, since trenches were blown in as fast as they were dug. It was far better to risk a temporary penetration of the line, than to suffer heavy casualties from the enemy's shell fire on a congested front.

**The Front Line Thinly Held.**

The march to the front line gave a foretaste of future events. Sausage Valley, the long depression running towards Contalmaison, was the main entry to the forward positions. It was full of life, but it also had its daily quota of death. To many Australians it was their first and last glimpse of battle. Artillery, transport lines, cook houses, ammunition dumps, columns of moving troops were all represented, and the terrific German bombardments took their daily toll even here, far back from the front line. B Company in advance marched through the valley, and at length reached Pioneer trench, and passed along it in single file; it was particularly long and uncomfortably narrow. Ghastly sights were witnessed on the journey. Scores of bodies had been partially buried in the soft earth, and bloody hands and feet protruded at frequent intervals. Boxes of ammunition and rations lay scattered about where fatigue parties had been annihilated by artillery fire. It was dusk

**Sausage Valley.**

**Sights en Route to Front Line.**

---
* Vide Appendix at end of this chapter.

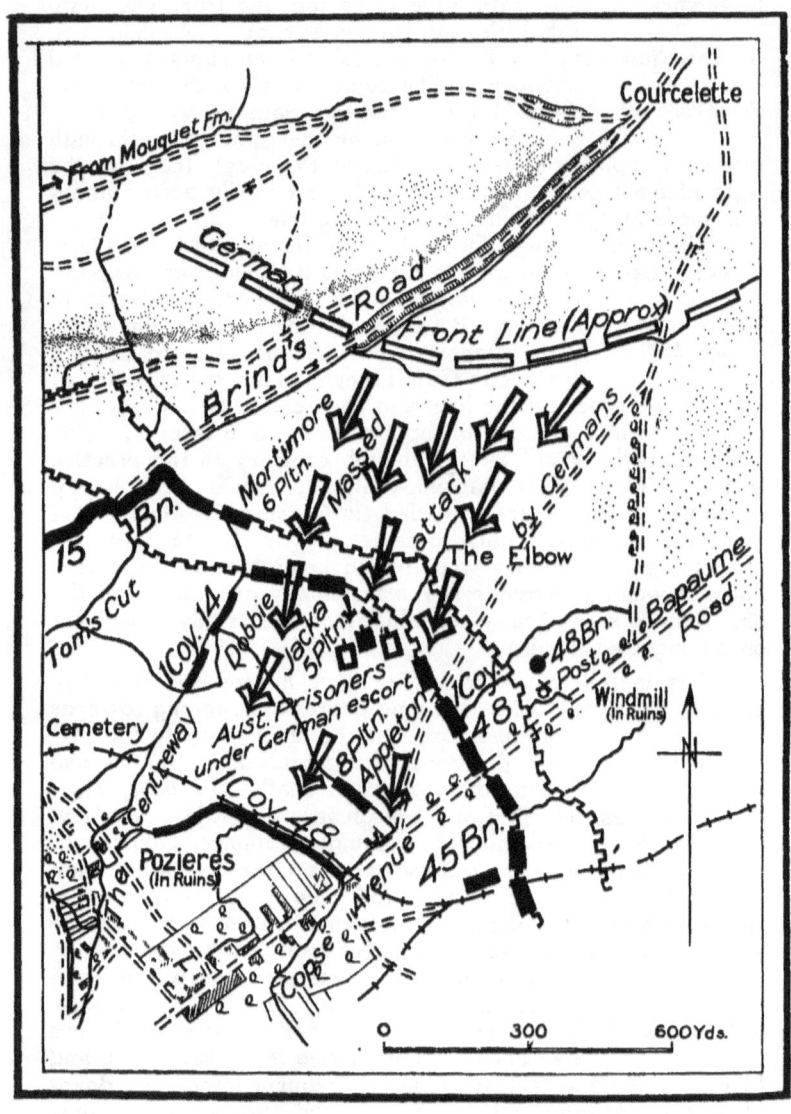

BATTLE OF POZIERES RIDGE

when B Company reached the end of the sap—a dead end—but the firing line was not far distant, though access to it was across the open. Here, again, the sights visible were mute evidence of what the 2nd A.I.F. Division (now about to be relieved) had just gone through, and included broken trenches, twisted barbed wire, stretchers containing dead bodies, and in many cases surrounded by dead stretcher-bearers. Many of the men relieved seemed dazed by their awful experiences.

**B Company Takes Over Front Line** — B Company men doubled across the open in twos and threes, and took over the so-called trenches allotted to them, which were simply shell holes connected together by shallow trenches, in places only a foot or two deep. The original trenches had been blown out of existence by the artillery of both armies. Dead bodies were everywhere, and large numbers had evidently been killed by concussion alone. Before the trenches could be deepened the numerous dead had to be ejected, and then a vigorous attempt was made to improve them.

The position along the front line was now as follows:—On the left flank was the 15th Battalion, then the 6th Platoon of the 14th, under 2nd-Lieut. H. S. Dobbie (a **Position at Front.** portion of the 6th Platoon under the platoon Sgt. Douglas Mortimer, holding an advanced position about 100 yards in front of the rest of the platoon), then a considerable gap on the right, then the 5th Platoon under 2nd-Lieut. Albert Jackt, V.C., with its right near the remains of an old windmill; then a further gap, and then the 48th Battalion of the 12th Brigade. Appleton's Platoon (No. 8) was in support. The officer commanding B Company (Major O. C. W. Fuhrmann) had his headquarters in a capacious dugout about 300 yards behind the front line, whilst battalion headquarters was on the forward side of the ruins of Pozieres. There were a few Lewis guns in the front line, one of which was placed in the space between the 5th Platoon and the 48th Battalion. The gaps in the line were tenanted by a few posts under N.C.O.'s.

It will be noted that the front was very thinly held, one company really being responsible for a battalion frontage. The **Front Line to be Held "At All Costs."** stereotyped instructions were that the front line was to be held, and to be held "at all costs." These instructions meant much on Pozieres Ridge. B Company men fortunately reached the front line with very few casualties.

About 9 p.m. the German artillery opened up a fearful bombardment. Their guns were innumerable, and were exactly ranged. The drum fire was incessant, and continued all night with unabated fury. 14th men had afterwards many experiences of enemy bombardments, but those who experienced this one always recalled it as surpassing anything that they ever faced, both in its fury and continuity. There were shells from the big 12-inch howitzers down to the little nerve-racking "whizbangs"; there were high explosive shells with sulphur fumes, which burnt immediately overhead, and there were other shells with neither fumes nor smoke. There was not only a frontal fire. but an enfilade fire from the direction of Thiepval. The very earth, lacerated and torn, rocked and dissolved under the weight and force of the metal blown into it. Both the earth and the heavens seemed rent by this concentrated effort of man's fury. Some men were blown to fragments; others were stunned by concussion alone. The appalling uproar rendered speech useless, whilst trenches were blown in, and communications severed. Most of the men fortunately found cover in some untenanted and commodious German dugouts which had survived previous bombardments. The 14th men, though severely shaken; faced this storm with that fortitude which Australians almost invariably display in battle.

*Terrific German Bombardment.*

*Its Character.*

This intense bombardment lasted nearly eight hours. About 4.45 a.m. it gradually lifted off our front lines, its cessatic being a prelude to a grand German counter-attack, delivered in the semi-dusk of the summer morning. This attack came on wave after wave, on a narrow frontage, in great depth, and the full force of it fell on the survivors of the 5th Platoon. and the left flank of the 48th Battalion. The first German wave of the attack, advancing in semi-darkness. was up to and into our line before our troops had grasped the significance of what had occurred, but the succeeding waves were badly cut up by flank enfilade fire from a platoon of C Company of the 15th Battalion, under Lieut. D. Dunworth,[2] and Douglas Mortimer's[3] men of the 6th Platoon of the 14th. These flanking bodies were outside the

*Lasts All Night.*

*Great German Counter-attack.*

---

[2] Capt. David Dunworth, M.C., afterwards wounded and captured at the Battle of Bullecourt on April 11, 1917.

[3] No. 2446, Sgt. H. D. Mortimer, grazier, of Laneva West (V.), Wounded and evacuated to Australia.

line of the German attack, and the men stationed there took full advantage of the magnificent target presented to them, and cut up the right flank of the attacking force severely.

Meanwhile, the 5th Platoon men, emerging in the twilight from the dugouts in which they had taken shelter from the bombardment, found Germans among them. Daybreak disclosed a condition of things rarely seen in this war, and an unknown experience in the ranks of the 14th. Germans were everywhere, and were mixed up with our men like players in rival football teams during a match.

*Penetrates Our Front Line.*

The 5th Platoon held firm, but a number of the Germans, pressing on, and passing round the line held by the 14th, turned half left, and attacking the left flank of the 48th Battalion, captured two officers and a considerable body of men of that unit. A German column, guarding and escorting these prisoners, was returning towards its own lines, when it was suddenly attacked by Lieut. Jacka with seven[4] men. Lying concealed, he allowed the Germans to approach within about thirty yards, when he sprang over the parados with his handful. A sensational and desperate fight occurred, the odds against the Australians being at least twenty to one. Every one of the eight as he sprang up was hit by rifle bullets, for they were surrounded by a circle of fire, but it was fought out to a finish. Some 48th Battalion men under Sgt. Beck (killed) came up and co-operated in the attack. Jacka,[5] hurled off his feet on different occasions by the terrific impact of rifle bullets fired at close range, was seven times wounded, once being knocked down by a bullet that passed through his body under the right shoulder, and twice partially stunned by head wounds. He fairly surpassed him-

*Captures Australian Prisoners.*

*Lieut. Jacka's Furious Counter-attack.*

*Jacka Seven Times Wounded.*

---

[4] 5th Platoon men who co-operated with Lieut. Jacka in this counter-attack comprised the following:—No. 2025, Pte. C. C. J. Taylor, hairdresser, Oakleigh (V.); No. 1327, Pte. H. L. Carroll, bricklayer, Pleasant Street, Ballarat (V.); No. 1380, Pte. F. G. Miller, biograph operator, Bendigo (V.); No. 1675, Pte. W. J. C. Williams, Rochester (V.); No. 3758, Pte. H. Fitzpatrick, South Melbourne (V.); and No. 3751, Pte. J. A. Finlay, East Malvern (V.). The name of the seventh man in the party is unknown. Williams and Miller are still alive.

[5] Capt. Albert Jacka, V.C., M.C., and bar. He won the first V.C. won by an Australian during the war (vide Chapter 7). He was awarded the M.C. for his conduct in this operation. The feeling in the battalion was that he had earned a bar to his V.C.

self this day, and killed upwards of a score of Germans with his own hand, including some with the bayonet. The bayonet was freely used in this encounter, being one of the very few occasions during the war that it came into operation. The superiority of our men, active as cats, over their opponents (who were picked troops) in this hand-to-hand fighting was most marked. This brilliant counter-attack against an overwhelming and triumphant enemy was completely successful—all the Australian prisoners were released, the whole of the German escort guarding them was killed or dispersed, and in addition 42 unwounded Germans (including two officers), the survivors of the German escort, were captured. It was a marvellous piece of work, bold in conception, brilliant and heroic in execution, smashing and demoralising to the enemy, and fruitful in its results—a splendid piece of bluff carried to a successful and glorious conclusion by a handful of men who had already endured a nerve-racking bombardment of several hours. The records of the A.I.F. teem with successful exploits in the face of great odds, but they do not contain anything which surpasses (if anything quite equals) the work of Jacka and his seven on Pozieres' Ridge.

*Its Success.*

*Its Marvellous Character.*

When these stirring events were taking place, our artillery barrage came down and destroyed large numbers of the enemy waiting behind the ridge to follow up and exploit the successes of the first wave.

*Our Artillery Barrage.*

The position was now as follows:—The first German waves, arriving under cover of darkness, had entered the Australian lines, and though portion of it had been smashed by Jacka's violent attack, other portions were still scattered about our front. The succeeding waves, received by a hot fire, had been mostly destroyed or driven back, whilst their reserves, cut up by our artillery barrage, was unable to follow up the success of the first waves.

Major Fuhrmann, realising the serious condition of affairs, ordered up Appleton's support platoon (No. 8), and its advent made the position secure. The Germans who had reached our lines, finding themselves attacked on all sides, mostly took cover in shell holes, and finally, after some fighting, surrendered, though a few, including some of the machine-gunners, fought to the death. Sgt. Douglas Mortimer, at considerable personal risk (being shot

*Advance of Appleton's Platoon.*

at at close range), induced about a dozen, including two officers, to surrender. Some of Appleton's men attacked and bayoneted a German machine-gunner who was quite 200 yards in rear of our front line, and causing casualties. Finally all the Germans who had reached our lines were killed or captured by Appleton's and Dobbie's men, and the survivors of the 5th Platoon. The position of the Germans thus thrust into our lines was obviously hopeless when their supports failed them, and it is doubtful if any who penetrated our lines got back to their own that day. The German counter-attack had failed, and their losses were tremendous, the ground being everywhere strewn with their bodies. Both sides were too exhausted fo: further effort, and beyond some shelling t rest of the day passed quietly, the stretcher-bearers being very busy getting our wounded to the dressi station. B Company was relieved by D Company on the evening of the 7th, and the shattered remnants of that company made their way back towards Sausage Valley and occupied some big German dugouts for the night. No. 5 Platoon, after taking a fearful toll of its enemies, had simply disappeared. It marched in 52 strong on the 6th, and came with four unwounded men on the 7th. Lieut. Jacka, its O.C., severely wounded; its platoon sergeant, H. Lewis,[6] killed; Sgt. J. Turner[7] severely wounded and evacuated to Australia, L.-Sgt. Ryan[8] wounded, Cpl. F. Smith[9] killed, L.-Cpl. R. H. S. Dean killed, and L.-Cpl. W. M. McKissack killed.

**German Counter-attack Annihilated.**

**B Company Relieved.**

**Appalling Losses of No. 5 Platoon.**

The engagement of August 7 was the third operation in which the 14th had participated on French soil, and every

---

[6] No. 736, Sgt. Hugh Lewis, packer, of Port Melbourne (V.). Killed in action, August 7, 1916. A brother, Pte. P. W. Lewis, was killed in action fighting with the battalion at the Battle of Bullecourt, April 11, 1917.

[7] No. 797, Sgt. James Turner, labourer, of Melbourne. Born May 25, 1883, at Mt. Macedon (V.).

[8] No. 769, L.-Sgt. Gerald Ryan, salesmen, of Horsham (V.). Afterwards accidentally killed skating in England, on February 6, 1917.

[9] No. 3496, Cpl. Frank Smith, driver, of Birmingham (Eng.) Killed in action, August 7, 1916.

[10] L.-Cpl. R. H. S. Dean, moulder, of Ballarat (V.). Killed in action, August 7, 1916.

[11] No. 761, L.-Cpl. W. M. McKissack, labourer, of Metcalfe (V.). Killed in action, August 7, 1916.

## Pozieres Ridge.

**The Battalion's Third Engagement in France.**
one of them had been star performances of the very first rank. The intrepidity and élan of the A Company men on July 2, the fortitude and grim resolution of the 14th Platoon on July 3, and the reckless, death-defying valour of the 5th Platoon on August 7, were worthy of the highest traditions of the finest troops in the war. Few units can have started any campaign in the great war with three finer initial records to their credit.

**Three Meritorious Operations.**

D Company reached the front line fortunately without casualties. On the way to the front a stretcher party was met carrying back Lieut. Jacka, desperately wounded, and his old comrades of D Company, who knew him so well, wondered what hot work he had been in. Unburied corpses lay everywhere; there had not been time to bury the dead. The relief was completed by about 7.30 p.m. The 47th Battalion relieved the 48th Battalion on the right flank. The Germans, irritated by the repulse of their counter-attack, wreaked their fury on our trenches by a concentrated bombardment, but as the trenches had been improved, the casualties were less heavy than might have been expected.

**D Company Takes Over Line.**

**Heavy German Bombardment.**

During the next day (August 8) the O.C. of D Company (Capt. R. W. Orr) sent a runner, Pte. G. A. Willison[12] with a message to Battalion Headquarters. He returned almost immediately without a thumb, which had been blown off by a piece of shell. Although suffering intensely, he refused to allow the O.C. and the C.S.M. to bind up his lacerated hand until he had turned over the message to another runner, and given him explicit instructions as to the route to Battalion Headquarters. He was afterwards awarded the M.M. for his soldierly conduct.

**Pte. Willison's Soldierly Conduct.**

The 14th Platoon held the extreme right of the position, and some of our men brought in a number of wounded Germans—victims of the fighting of the previous day. L/Cpl. F. Wright[13] was prominent in this humane work, making several trips far out into No Man's Land to bring in wounded enemies. Sgt. T. A. Rose[14] was wounded during the day. In the afternoon A Company

**14th Platoon Rescues Wounded Germans.**

---

[12] No. 4331, Pte. George Arthur Willison, labourer, of Manchester
[13] L.-Cpl. F. L. Wright (vide Chap. XIX., note 13).    (Eng.).
[14] No. 1043, Sgt. T. A. Rose (vide Chap. XIX.).

relieved D Company in the firing line, and D Company relieved C Company in support. D Company, however, was subjected to intense shelling during the night, and suffered heavy casualties. No. 16 Platoon suffered particularly, many men being buried alive. Its Platoon Sgt., A. C. Hutton,[15] rendered great service that night in digging out wounded and buried comrades under the torrential shelling. There was little or no rest at Pozieres. Even the reserve company, temporarily out of the line, had to furnish fatigue parties to convey rations and ammunition to the other companies. The ceaseless bombardments had destroyed all roads in the forward areas, consequently all stores and casualties had to be man-handled, so that even the infantry which was not actually for the moment in the line was worn out by excessive and continuous manual labour.

16th Platoon Severely Handled. Sgt. A. C. Hutton's Services.

A Company (O.C. Capt. Roy Cox) took possession of the front line trenches on the evening of the 8th. A heavy bombardment by our artillery preceded a night attack by the 15th Battalion on our left flank. This attack necessitated the left flank of A Company (comprising Platoons 3 and 4, under 2nd Lieut. W. R. Beamond, with Sgt. F. Anderson, M.M., and Cpl. Fisher as senior N.C.O.'s), connecting up with the right of the 15th. The objective of this party was to establish a strong point on the right of the 15th's captured position, and to dig a sap back to the 14th's left flank, thus linking up the line. The digging continued all night, during which time Lieut. Beamond was severely wounded. The Germans made some show of counter-attacking next morning, but it was not pushed home. Owing to the failure of a British unit, attacking on the left of the 15th, to reach its objective, the left flank of the 15th was exposed,[16] so that it had to fall back, bringing the left of A Company back with it.

A Company Takes Over Line.

2nd-Lieut. Beamond Wounded.

Meanwhile the other two platoons (1 and 2), under 2nd Lieut. L. Ebbott, linked up the shell holes as best they

---

[15] No. 1184, Sgt. A. C. Hutton. Killed in action September 26, 1917. (Vide Chap. 32.)

[16] It was alleged that heavy shelling of the 15th Battalion's new position by our own guns helped to compel the withdrawal of that battalion.—(4th Brigade War Diary: Narrative of operations, 5/8/16 to 15/8/16.)

## Pozieres Ridge.

could, the enemy keeping up a heavy artillery fire all night. Lieut. Ebbott was wounded. At dawn all set to work to repair the damage done by the enemy retaliation artillery fire.

*Lieut. Ebbott Wounded.*

On the 9th C Company (O.C. Capt. Stewart Hansen) relieved A Company in the firing line, and A Company relieved D Company in support. The relief was completed by 6 p.m. C Company experienced a night of tremendous shelling. About midnight, after a bombardment from our artillery, the 15th again advanced, and took their objective, one platoon of C Company being placed at the disposal of the C.O. of the 15th, and our left was again swung forward and touch obtained with the 15th's right flank. The position was consolidated, and strong points created, manned by Lewis gunners and bombers. Our trenches were badly damaged by shell fire during the night, and an attempt was made to repair them during daylight.

*C Company in Front Line.*

All companies had now been through the inferno, and the men were showing signs of exhaustion, for the incessant drum fire rendered it very difficult to obtain sleep, and several had been evacuated for nervous breakdowns. The continual strain was telling on all ranks, but the 14th was not yet done with Pozieres ridge.

On the 10th 2nd Lieut. H. R. McKinley and 83 other ranks joined up as reinforcements, most of them being absorbed by B Company, whose ranks had been greatly depleted during the recent fighting. The same afternoon B Company again took over the firing line (S.M. H. Thompson and Sgt. T. H. Loughead having received commissions, and been posted to the Company). C Company moved back into support. The 13th Battalion relieved the 15th on our left. Our trenches were again heavily shelled, and among the casualties was Sgt. W. V. Field, of B Company, a very sound N.C.O., who lost a leg. He was a man upwards of 40 years of age. One enormous shell[17] smashed in the roof of an old German dugout tenanted by 2nd Lieut. A. R. Dean and about twenty of his bombers. It smashed through five feet of earth sup-

*Reinforcements Join Up.*

*B Company Again in Front Line.*

*Sgt. Field Wounded.*

---

[17] Extract from letter from the late 2nd-Lieut. A. R. Dean to Capt. McWilliam, father of one of the bombers who was killed here.

*The History of the 14th Battalion.* 145

Bombers Buried.
Sgt. Pearce Killed.
Cooks Killed.

ported by huge beams and tree trunks, and buried the whole party, killing three, and wounding six of the bombers. Sgt. John Pearce[18] was killed here. On the 11th the enemy kept up a heavy barrage on all our communication trenches. One shell, landing in Sausage Valley, among the cookers, killed Ptes. W. F. Malcolmson and H. Campbell, two of B Company cooks.

D Company Again in Front Line.

During the afternoon of the 11th, D Company took over the front line again, the men working their way forward through some old saps. The pounding of the shells never ceased. Little improvement could be made to the trenches during the night, owing to the heavy bombardment, but small patrols sent out into No Man's Land found everything quiet within 400 yards of our trenches. At daylight on the 12th a fairly thick fog settled over our front, and through it (about 5 a.m.) an enemy patrol of four men wandered into our lines. They were encountered singlehanded by Pte. Alfred Gray,[19] a Korumburra miner, of No. 15 Platoon, who was at the time unarmed, but seizing a shovel he made a bulldog rush at the party, hitting one of them over the head. All the members of the patrol dropped their rifles, and surrendered to him, one of them being a corporal decorated with the Iron Cross. Pte. Gray was an immensely proud man when he marched his prisoners down to Headquarters. He was awarded the M.M. for his spirited action. All day much work was done improving the trenches. Another night of heavy bombardment again badly damaged them, and again on the 13th the eternal work of repairing them recommenced.

Nerve of Pte. Gray Captures Four Prisoners.

Relief for the 14th was at last due, and guides from our four companies reported at Tara Hill on the 13th, and guided up to our trenches the 49th Battalion, which relieved our men on that date. the relief being completed by 11.15 a.m. The companies as

14th Relieved.

---

[18] No. 1405, Sgt. John Pearce, labourer, of Trawalla (V.). He had been in charge of the left section of the bombers in the raid of July 2, 1916. Only two out of 16 bombers on that occasion escaped becoming casualties, and both of them (Sgt. Pearce and L.-Cpl. H. J. Armstrong) were killed in this engagement. Sgt. W. H. Pearce (bombing Sgt. of D Company) died of wounds, July 4. 1916.

[19] No. 4203, Pte. Alfred ("Dolly") Gray, miner, of Korumburra (V.).

relieved marched back from the filth, stench, and blood of the trenches to the Brickfields (Albert). A few shells landed round the camping ground at night, but fortunately no casualties resulted. The week of stress was over. Haggard, worn, and exhausted, with faces bearing signs of the storm and stress of the nerve-racking days and nights they had endured, the remnants of the decimated companies had indeed earned a spell. The battalion had gone through the most severe test on the morale of the men that could be experienced, yet no task had been too severe for the majority[20] of them to face, no danger too great to be endured. Now that the reaction had come, all craved for rest and sleep. Pozieres Ridge, except in some rare instances, did not lend itself to spectacular heroism. It was rather a grim holding on to ground that was particularly accessible to the missiles from the enemy's heavy guns, our infantry simply providing targets for their artillery. All the sacrifices made by the battalion there did not appear to have done much towards carrying on the war, but the programme allotted had been faithfully carried out, the line had been held, and held "at all costs." It was the battalion's baptism of fire in France, and the new recruits had worthily upheld the reputation of the battalion won by the fighting of the veterans on the Peninsula. The dangers endured in common had welded all ranks together in a way that only war can. The battalion had gone through the worst trials that war could mete out to it, and had emerged triumphant, if bruised and battered. Some of the flower of the peninsula man had been killed or permanently incapacitated, and their loss was, of course, irreparable. The strength of the strong had been proved, and the weakness of the weak exposed. The men had now found their true leaders, for war always brings out surprises in its exposure of the strength and weakness of character. The battalion emerged lacerated, chastened, experienced, and thoughtful from Pozieres Ridge.

**Trials Endured.**

General Birdwood addressed the battalion on the 14th in one of his usual congratulatory speeches. That same afternoon the march was continued to Warloy. All now found time to recount incidents of the recent fighting, and many wrote letters to relatives of deceased comrades relating how they had been killed. Four N.C.O.'s were promoted to commissioned rank about this time, viz.:—Sgts. F. Anderson, M.M. (A

**Promotions.**

---

[20] As in all units, there were some 14th men who broke up under the strain.

Company), L. B. Thompson and S. B. Thompson (twins, of B Company), and W. Jacka (brother of Albert Jacka, V.C.), of D Company.

Some reference must be made to necessary though incidental work during the battle, without which the fighting men in the front line would have been unable to carry on.

Great and strenuous work, under most trying conditions, was rendered by the stretcher-bearers during the week of battle. The battalion R.M.O. (Capt. R. Winn) worked in a sap at the entrance to the dugout occupied by Battalion Headquarters.

**Work of the Stretcher-Bearers.**

On the Peninsula only four stretcher-bearers had been allotted to each company, but at Pozieres Ridge this number was largely increased, and amounted to no less than forty-five stretcher-bearers (including the band and five medical orderlies), in addition to sixteen partly trained men whose services were utilised when occasion required. Sgt. Gus Harris,[21] the N.C.O. in charge, was, as ever, bravery and efficiency personified, whilst the following were specially mentioned for their work:—Ptes. D. H. Fraser,[22] R. Garford,[23] S. Henshall,[23] S. A. Markham, A. R. Dodemaide, and T. V. Hughes. Young Hughes, though a mere lad, took charge of the stretcher squad of his company after all the senior members had been wounded. The following stretcher-bearers were wounded during the battle, viz.:—Ptes. J. C. Meredith, T. O'Keefe, H. W. Hodges, C. Ward, L. W. Bain, H. Lee, A. McKissock, and J. L. Pulbrook.

Both the signallers and the runners were kept very busy, for the continual bombardments frequently destroyed the telephone wires, which had to be repaired, often under heavy fire, and the runners were sometimes the only means of communication between the firing line and Battalion Headquarters.

**Signallers and Runners.**

The bombing platoon, though not utilised to any extent, was sent up to the line on August 7, during the German counter attack, but on arrival at B Company Headquarters it was ascertained that the infantry had the situation in hand, so the services of the bombers were not required. C and D sections, however, acted as reserves to the 15th

**The Bombing Platoon.**

---

[21] Sgt. Gus. Harris (vide Chap. XIV.).
[22] Pte. D. H. Fraser (vide Chap. XIV.).
[23] Vide Chap. XIV. (medical personnel).

Battalion bombers in the attack made by that battalion, and which has already been referred to.

**4th Brigade Canteen.** A 4th Brigade canteen was formed at Bois Grenier by a joint money contribution from each of the battalions. It was a kind of co-operative tuckshop, run by and on behalf of the personnel of the brigade. All profits were returned to the battalions, enabling them to provide prizes for sports, and obtain other benefits. It had the double advantage of providing the men with delicacies, which helped to make their lot more tolerable, and also prevented them being robbed by that class of shopkeeper which takes advantage of war conditions to plunder soldiers. The canteen, which was in charge of "Dad" Brotchie,[24] a 14th Battalion original, was placed in Sausage Gully during the battle amidst British guns, and its presence did at least something to alleviate the misery and strain endured by all during that trying week.

**Casualties.** The total number of casualties of the 4th Brigade during the operations on Pozieres Ridge (as set out in the 4th Brigade war diary) reached the enormous total of 49 officers and 1614 other ranks, made up as follows:—

|  | Officers. | Other Ranks. |
|---|---|---|
| Killed | 5 | 188 |
| Wounded | 39 | 1294 |
| Missing | 4 | 111 |
| Prisoner of war | 1 | 1 |
| Shell shock | — | 20 |
|  | 49 | 1614 |

The casualties of the 14th during the same period were set out as 6 officers and 399 other ranks, made up as follows:—

|  | Officers. | Other Ranks. |
|---|---|---|
| Killed | 1 | 49 |
| Wounded | 5 | 320 |
| Missing | — | 30 |
|  | 6 | 399 |

The "missing" in the battalion were practically all killed, and several wounded subsequently dying of wounds raised

---

[24] L.-Sgt. Brotchie (No. 559), of Fitzroy, agent. Born Fitzroy (V.), October 22, 1870. (See also Chap. 42).

the fatal casualties of the battalion during the week of battle to 87.[25]

One officer, 2nd-Lieut. H. S. Dobbie,[26] died of wounds, whilst five (2nd-Lieuts. A. Jacka, V.C., W. A. Appleton, J. Millis, W. R. M. Beamond, and L. H. Ebbott) were wounded. Twelve N.C.O.s (including Sgts. Hugh Lewis and John Pearce) were killed or died or wounds, and 44 were wounded. Amongst the wounded N.C.O.'s, in addition to those already mentioned, were Sgts.: 2446, D. H. Mortimer; 1779, S. B. Thompson; 922, R. Stanley; 2777, G. Bailey; 310, F. A. Dawes; 416, D. Blackburn (Lewis gunner); 213, A. McK. Hepburn; 1345, J. B. Cheyne; and L.-Sgt. (2782) R. R. Neal. Almost all the N.C.O.'s in B Company were casualties. The following were also included among the wounded, viz.:—Cpls.: 1330, F. J. Banyard; 4172, D. Drummond; and 943, R. Andrews; and L.-Cpls.: 1307, N. Wynne, M.M.;[27] 989, E. E. Frost; 512, F. L. Wright; 3388, J. McRae; and 533, Pte. J. Bickley,[28] who had been one of the four volunteers for the bayonet charge on May 19, 1915, when Capt. (then L.-Cpl.) A. Jacka won the V.C.

**Decorations Awarded.** The following decorations were awarded for the Pozieres Ridge operations:—

### M.C.
2nd-Lieut. A. Jacka, V.C. (Wedderburn, V.).
2nd-Lieut. H. S. Dobbie (Brunswick, V.).

### D.C.M.
2553, Sgt. S. J. J. Garton (Brunswick, V.).
3388, Pte. J. McRae (Bairnsdale, V.).

### M.M.
994, Pte. W. Gill (Canada), signaller.
1513, L.-Cpl. C. J. Clarke (Tasmania), signaller.
2607, Pte. T. V. Hughes (Ararat, V.), stretcher-bearer.
3312, Pte. A. R. Dodemaide (Mildura, V.), stretcher-bearer.

---

[25] There were 1049 fatal casualties in the battalion during the war up to the end of February, 1919, according to official figures. Some have also died as the result of injuries since that date.

[26] 2nd-Lieut. H. S. Dobbie, of Brunswick (V.), clerk. Born July 7.

[27] L./Cpl. N. Wynne (vide Chap. IX.).

[28] Pte. J. Bickley (No. 533). (Vide Chap. VII., footnote 4.)

1598, Pte. S. A. Markham (Flemington, V.), stretcher-
bearer.
4552, Pte. G. A. Willison (Manchaster, Eng.), runner.
4203, Pte. A. Gray (Korumburra, V.).

## APPENDIX.

Though the thinning of the front line garrison by Colonel Dare was contrary to the practice in vogue, it was in accordance with the orders constantly sent from the higher staffs. The majority or the commanders at the front, however, either found it necessary to retain the men in order to dig the trenches, or were nervous about carrying out the instructions. —(Communicated to the author by Mr. C. E. W. Bean, the Australian historian of the war.)

# CHAPTER XXII.

## MOUQUET FARM.

### 1916.—August 17 to August 31.

The Australian brigades, during the operations on the Somme, were utilised like cabs in a cab rank. They were sent into the line methodically, one after another, **A.I.F. Procedure on the Somme.** and after desperate and strenuous fighting the survivors were taken out, given a few days for recuperation and organisation, and then (with reinforcements that could be scraped together in the meantime) were again sent into the line. This procedure was now adopted with the 4th Brigade. It was taken out of the line for a few days, and sent on a short circular tour to enable it, metaphorically, to recover its breath and reorganise, before being again thrown into the struggle.

The brigade left Warloy on August 17, and marched to La Vicogne, and on the following day continued the march to Pernois. Capt. C. R. M. Cox rejoined on the **A Few Days' Breathing Time.** 19th, and on the following day Lieut.-General Sir H. V. Cox (G.O.C. of the 4th Division) presented cards to all officers and others who had been recommended during the recent fighting at Pozieres Ridge. The next move was to Talmas, and then to Vadencourt, and from there to Albert, where the battalion arrived about mid-day on August 26, and was again within hearing of the guns. During this time the reorganisation of the battalion, and the training of specialists, had been attempted, but the weather had been unpropitious, and rain had considerably interfered with training. The strength of the battalion at this time was 34 officers and 751 other ranks.

The task now allotted to the battalion was to relieve the 21st and 22nd Battalions, A.I.F., and take over the trenches held by them. These units had been engaged **Battalion Again in the Line.** in operations against a German strong point known as Mouquet Farm, which was very strongly held, and surrounded by a system of cleverly constructed secret tunnels, the existence of which was then unknown to the assailants. The battalion left Albert at 8 p.m. (26th), and at La Boiselle was meet by guides, who took C and D Companies to the trenches, the relief being completed by 3 a.m. The night was pitch dark, and it was pouring with rain. The position was now as follows:—

C and D Companies (O.C.'s, Capts. Stewart Hansen and C. R. M. Cox respectively), in the front line.

B Company (O.C., Major O. C. W. Fuhrmann), in support.

A Company (O.C., Capt. A. R. Cox), in reserve (the reserve company supplied carrying and fatigue parties, its duties being of an incidental character).

Two sections of bombers were attached to C and D Companies, and two sections to A and B. Efforts were at once made by C and D Companies to deepen and improve the trenches taken over, which were not in a good condition. The 21st Battalion had had a strong point about 200 yards in front of their line, but all touch with its garrison had been lost, and they were thought to have been all killed or wounded. An advance in extended order by the 14th men, however, discovered the survivors of the 21st Battalion party in some shell holes, and they were immediately released and sent back. Work was immediately commenced to consolidate this strong point (known as 77), and two N.C.O.'s with a Lewis gun, and a proportion of bombers under Sgt. Selwyn Stewart (of Hamilton) were detailed to dig themselves in. An officer and 28 other ranks were put on to dig a communication trench from this strong point to our lines, and as the soil was calcarious the job was arduous. Work was also commenced to sap towards the 15th Battalion on our right.

Battalion headquarters was in the cemetery at Pozieres. whilst C Company headquarters was in a quarry, and the front line ran along its northern edge. The tactical situation was a curious one. There was a gap without trenches between our right flank and the left flank of the 15th Battalion, which was stationed on our right. There was also a large gap in the line between our left and British troops on our left rear. In addition, there was a strong point (77) held by our men, well forward from the centre of our line, whilst the enemy held Mouquet Farm, itself an immensely strong point, and the strong points 54 and 27 on either side of 77.

*Curious Tactical Situation.*

## The History of the 14th Battalion. 153

On the 27th a brigade operation order was received directing the 14th to capture the enemy's strong points at 54 and 27, and to dig a trench connecting them with 77, and also with the 15th Battalion on the right. This had to be carried out the same night, August 27-28. C Company, under Capt. Hansen (a very intelligent officer, who had done much useful work on the Peninsula), was chosen for the task, and two platoons of D Company were detailed to assist. The remaining two platoons of D Company (Nos. 13 and 14), together with B Company, were to man the front line trenches, and give whatever assistance was possible. Very little information, in the short time available, could be obtained of the exact strength of the enemy in the various positions to be attacked, and Capt. Hansen, with inadequate information, made the most careful and elaborate arrangements possible under the circumstances, which, however, owing to the scanty number of the attackers, were doomed to failure. The attack was divided into three parts (left, centre, and right).

*C Company's Task.*

(1) The left, to attack strong point 54, comprised two sections of headquarters bombers under Sgt. E. J. Rule, supported by two platoons (C Company), under Lieut. P. J. Hayes.

(2) The centre, to attack from strong points 77 to 27, comprised two platoons (C Company) under 2nd-Lieut. F. Anderson.

*Details of Attack.*

(3) The right, to attack 27, comprised two sections of headquarters bombers under 2nd-Lieut. A. R. Dean, supported by two platoons (D Company) under 2nd-Lieut. Quinn.

Stretcher-bearers and a Lewis gun were sent with each party. It will be noted that Lieut. Deans's bombers were now getting their opportunity, the main portion of the work being assigned to them, whilst the infantry was to take over and consolidate the positions.

The German artillery shelled the quarry containing C Company headquarters for about two hours in the afternoon, and opened fire again at dusk. Considerable damage was done to our saps and trenches by the enemy's bombardment.

The battalion's attack was timed for midnight, and was to be preceded by a five minutes' barrage of the objective. There was also to be co-operation by the 4th Trench Light Mortar Battery. Our bombardment opened at 11.55 p.m., and during it the bombers crept up as close as possible to the barrage,

*Attack by Bombing Platoon.*

and the moment it lifted rushed their objectives with true Australian impetuosity, and bombed the strong points and communication trenches. Three large enemy dugouts were successfully bombed, and heavy casualties inflicted. The attackers, however, were but a handful, and their opponents innumerable. The latter were at first demoralised by the impetuosity of the Australian attack, but, supported by their artillery in response to their distress signals, they emerged in great strength from numerous dugouts like a swarm of bees, and bombarded and swamped the few Australians by sheer force of numbers. Both right and left columns had the same experience, and had to withdraw before a greatly superior force, for the captured trenches wrecked by our artillery fire did not give any cover to our men. The centre column, with admirable tenacity, though nearly surrounded, clung to and held strong point 77. It was discovered that strong point 27 was connected with the main trench leading into Mouquet Farm. Both strong points 54 and 27 were found to be well entrenched and strongly held, the garrisons being accommodated in spacious dugouts. Meanwhile, strong point 77 successfully repelled two enemy counter-attacks on the night of the 27th-28th, and another on the night of the 28th-29th, the tenacity of the little garrison being highly commendable. Just prior to its relief, Sgt. S. Stewart, the N.C.O. in charge, was severely wounded, losing a leg.

*Attack Unsuccessful.*

Cpl. J. J. Myers (Daylesford, V.), Ptes. J. Roberts (Collingwood, V.), W. Mayne (South Yarra, V.), and E. L. Kohls (Richmond, V.), all of whom were wounded, were prominent in this bomb fighting. Lieut. P. J. Hayes was severely, and 2nd-Lieut. A. R. Dean[1] mortally, wounded. Lieut. Dean was a gallant officer, and very popular with his men; he refused medical attention until other wounded had been dressed.

*Lieut. Dean Mortally Wounded.*

Whilst the attack, as projected, had failed, information was gained which would have been invaluable had it been appreciated and utilised by the High Command. There was not any doubt to anyone who had participated in the attack that the capture of Mouquet Farm and the adjacent strong points required an immensely strong force, backed up

*Information Gained.*

---

[1] 2nd-Lieut. A. R. Dean, of Sydney (N.S.W.). Born November 10, 1883. Died of wounds, December 2, 1916.

by adequate artillery preparation, and general surprise was excited in view of these facts by the information that the 14th was expected, in its present depleted state, to attack and capture the next evening the strong points that it had failed to capture on the previous night. Colonel Dare was convinced by the representations of Capt. Hansen, who had been in charge of the operations, that a renewed attempt by the battalion under these conditions would only result in a useless squandering of valuable lives, and protested strongly against a renewed attack. Optimism, as usual, however, in the High Command was rampant, but Colonel Dare, who had the support of his officers, was firm and insistent, with the result that the proposed attack was undertaken by the 16th and 13th Battalions. In response to a request for assistance by the 16th, A Company of the 14th was detailed to assist the operations of that battalion.

On the night of 28th-29th, the line was taken over by the 16th Battalion (the 13th relieving the 15th Battalion on the right). Heavy rain set in on the 29th, reducing the trenches to little better than quagmires, and on the night of the 30th-31st the 16th and 13th, under cover of an intense artillery barrage, attacked Mouquet Farm and the adjacent trenches. The attack was an exact repetition of the attack by the 14th on the 27th. The positions were captured, but could not be held, and both units had to return to the jumping off trenches after suffering heavy losses. Meantime, A Company, 14th Battalion, in reserve, the men up to their knees in water, remained in the trench under shell fire awaiting the next move. After the failure of the 16th Battalion, there was some intention of sending in A Company to attempt to take the objective that had proved too strong for a whole battalion. Fortunately, better counsels prevailed, and the proposed attack was countermanded. A and B Companies subsequently rejoined the rest of the battalion at La Boiselle.

**Attack by 13th and 16th Battalions.**

Mouquet Farm was attacked again by the 13th Brigade. A.I.F., on September 3, and captured, but again the assailants were forced to retire through intense artillery fire. It was again attacked by the 13th Brigade, in conjunction with the Canadians, on September 5, and was only finally occupied on September 25, after most desperate fighting, and after thousands of men had been thrown against it. The expectation of capturing such a position by means of three or four dozen bombers, supported by half a dozen

**Further Attacks on Mouquet Farm.**

156        *Mouquet Farm.*

infantry platoons, conclusively proves the grotesque optimism then prevalent, and how little had been learnt of German methods and German strength after two years of continual warfare by those responsible for such tactics.

Thus ended the battalion's second enterprise on the Somme. The losses of the 14th for that period (as set out in the 4th Brigade war diary), were fortunately less than on the previous occasion, and consisted of 4 officers wounded, and 15 other ranks killed, 99 wounded,[2] and 1 missing. Among the killed or mortally wounded, in addition to those already mentioned, were:—Ptes. D. E. Docwra, an excellent soldier in the line (who had formally held non-commissioned rank), J. C. Ronald (son of an ex-member of the Australian Federal House of Representatives), and C. S. Holland,[3] the second of two brothers who had lost their lives within two months' fighting in the ranks of the battalion.

**Battalion Casualties.**

The dressing station was in a dug-out near the cemetery, and two stretcher-bearers lost their lives in this operation, viz., Ptes. A. R. Dodemaide (who had won the M.M.[4] earlier in the month) and G. Osborne. Among the wounded were:— Sgts. E. J. Rule, S. Booley, J. S. Stewart, W. Oram, A. C. Dalitz, J. T. O'Brien, and A. Urie; Cpls. A. G. Ansett, W. J. Orr, A. J. Slade, J. J. Myers, J. C. Blair, F. J. Brasch (machine gun section), W. J. Jackson, F. A. Goode, G. F. Harrison, W. A. Smith (machine gun section), and J. S. Wheeler; and L.-Cpls. C. Smith, R. L. Trickey, J. F. McPherson, G. Mills, G. Brown, V. A. Crougey, G. D. Radnell, and L. J. Fisher; also Pte. E. J. Graham,[5] of A Company, who is said to have been the youngest "original" in the battalion, having joined up at 16 years of age.

The non-commissioned officers of the battalion had shown the greatest initiative and daring in the two Somme opera-

---

[2] Some of the wounded subsequently died. The casualty list for this period discloses one officer and 23 other ranks killed or died of wounds. The total deaths in the two Somme enterprises (chapters 21 and 22) were 111 out of 1049 deaths suffered by the battalion during the war.

[3] Vide Appendix G.

[4] Pte. A. R. Dodemaide. (Vide Chap. 21, "Decorations.")

[5] Pte. E. J. Graham (No. 1252, A Company), printer, of Elsternwick (V.).

# The History of the 14th Battalion. 157

**Reputation of Australian N.C.O.'s.** — tions, and had suffered accordingly. The reputation of the Australian officers is world-wide, but Australia has not yet learnt to appreciate the tribute it owes to its non-commissioned officers, who were among the finest in the Great War.

**Decorations.** — The following decorations were awarded in respect of the above operations:—

### M.C.

Captain and Adjutant A. R. Blainey (England).
Captain Stewart M. Hansen (Williamstown, V.).
2nd-Lieut. Archibald Robert Dean (Sydney, N.S.W.).

### D.C.M.

374, Sgt. G. A. Ross (Fitzroy, V.).
269, Sgt. J. Selwyn Stewart (Hamilton, V.).

### M.M.

2636, Sgt. E. J. Rule (Cobar, N.S.W.), bomber.
619, Cpl. J. J. Myers (Daylesford, V.). bomber.
840, Pte. W. A. Cox (Carlton, V.).
5129, Pte. W. J. Jackson (Numurkah, V.), observer and scout.
3377, Pte. E. L. Kohls[6] (Richmond, V.), bomber.
528, L/Cpl. Roger Scanlon (Sebastopol, V.).
8, Cpl. W. W. Goodwin (Melbourne, V.), signaller.
4238, Pte. K. N. McNamee (Ballarat, V.), company runner.

### MENTIONED IN DESPATCHES.

1202, Sgt. A. J. Harris (Echuca, V.), stretcher-bearer.
49, C.S.M. Stephen de Arango (Bendigo, V.).
526, Sgt. William Oram (Foster, V.).
419, C.S.M. F. H. Boyes (Lardner, V.).

---

[6] Pte. E. L. Kohls, born Antwerp, Belgium, December 26, 1878. It was almost wholly through his initiative and courage that several of the bombing platoon who had been buried were rescued (vide. Chap. 21). He was the first man to enter Strong Point 27 on the night of August 27-28, and subsequently dressed the wounds of Lieut. Dean under a heavy shell fire and carried him to a place of safety.

## CHAPTER XXIII.

### CARE AND DISTRIBUTION OF THE WOUNDED.

**Battalion's Numerous Wounded.**
There were few of the front line A.I.F. infantry who escaped being wounded during the war; some, indeed, two, three, and four times. The wounded and injured of the 14th Battalion during the continuance of hostilities amounted to no fewer than 2323.[1] Some details have been given in a previous chapter[2] of the work of the 14th's medical personnel on the Peninsula, but local conditions in France being more favourable enabled the medical side of the battalion to be more thoroughly and completely organised, and the treatment of the wounded to be placed on a more elaborate and scientific basis. This important side of battalion organisation in France must be briefly but specifically alluded to.

**First Field Dressing.**
Every Australian soldier, on going into action, carried with him a first field dressing, which he was taught how to use, and which was adequate for first dressing. When a combatant was wounded during an engagement, if his advance had carried him beyond the reach of the stretcher-bearers, he applied his field dressing, or, if unable to do so, got a (wounded) comrade (if available) to do it for him. He then made his way, or was assisted, to the regimental aid post. This comprised the battalion medical officer and the battalion A.M.C. men, and was established close behind the lines. There the wounded received as much attention as could be given under the stress of circumstances, for the locality was often under shell fire, and the accommodation congested. The

**Regimental Aid Post.**

---

[1] This does not include 357 who were gassed. 786 were wounded on the Peninsula and the remainder in France.
[2] Vide Chapter 14.

## The History of the 14th Battalion. 159

aid post might be described as the battalion medical unit. From there the wounded were either assisted by stretcher-bearers, or (if capable) walked to the advanced dressing station, which was situated a little further back. Wounds were here diagnosed and more complete attention given. The wounded were then sent back from the advanced to the main dressing station (situated usually two or three miles from the front line), where they received still further attention. The stress on the staff was here less severe, and the locality less disturbed by shell fire. Every wounded man who reached the main dressing station was injected with anti-tetanus serum, for the French soil is full of germs, which tend to produce tetanus, or lock-jaw. The two dressing stations (the advanced and the main) were known as the Field Ambulance, which might be described as the brigade medical unit.

*Advanced Dressing Station.*

*Main Dressing Station.*

The wounded were next moved (usually by motor ambulance) to the casualty clearing station (situated, perhaps, seven or eight miles in the rear). Previous attention had been temporary; here it was complete. The staff was thoroughly organised and qualified. Nurses were now seen for the first time, and urgent operations were performed. Organisation of the wounded was also attempted, and they were sorted out for distribution to the various French bases. They journeyed by hospital trains to those base hospitals which were scattered all over the north of France; en route they were attended by nurses, who looked after the comfort of their charges. Sometimes, if canals were available, the wounded were taken on barges. At each of the above separate stations cigarettes were distributed, and hot cocoa given to the wounded to drink. They were now finally removed from the atmosphere of the battlefield, with its unmentionable horrors and ghastly sourroundings. When the train or barge arrived at its destination (the base), the wounded were put in hospitals, and the less urgent operations (such as the extraction of bullets) were frequently carried out. Two classes of the wounded were retained temporarily at the French bases—(1) the very slightly wounded, who remained for a short time till they could return to their battalions; (2) the very severely wounded, who remained till they were fit to be moved. Sometimes, however, if a big battle was expected, the very slightly

*Casualty Clearing Station.*

*French Base Hospitals.*

160    *Care and Distribution of the Wounded.*

**Voyage Across the Channel.**

**English General Hospitals.**

wounded were cleared out of the hospitals to make room, and were sent to England. The remainder of the wounded (outside these two classes) were sent across the Channel to England on hospital ships (convoyed by destroyers), and on arrival on British soil were distributed among the different general hospitals, scattered all over England. as vacancies occurred.

**Auxiliary Hospitals.**

**Convalescent Camps.**

**Fourteen Days' Furlough.**

**Command Depot.**

**French Base.**

**Return to Unit.**

After a period in a general hospital the wounded were transferred to an auxiliary hospital (of which there were scores), and after a spell there were forwarded to a convalescent camp, such as Harefield or Dartford. The great majority of the convalescents. after a sojourn at these camps, got fourteen days' furlough, to enable them to recoup. On the completion of the furlough, if then cured, the convalescents were forwarded to a command depot (such as Perham Downs), where. after a period of training, they were transferred to France, and went to one of the French bases, wnere, after a further short period of training, they returned to their old battalions, or to any other units to which they had been assigned. A brief summary of the stages through which the wounded passed is as follows:—

**Recapitulation.**

1. First field dressing  
2. Regimental aid post  } Vicinity
3. Advanced dressing station } of
4. Main dressing station  } Battlefield.
5. Casualty clearing station

6. Hospital train or barge } North of France
7. Base Hospital

8. General Hospita.
9. Auxiliary Hospital  }
10. Convalescent camp  } England
11. Fourteen days' furlough
12. Command depot (England)

13. French base (training), France
14. Return to unit.

There was, however, a class of more severely wounded, who were unfit for service permanently, or for a long period.

**Wounded Permanently Unfit for Service.**
This class was almost invariably sent to Weymouth, on the Dorsetshire coast, in the south of England, where the members were sifted out. The less dangerously wounded were (after a long spell) returned to France, and again entered the fighting line. The remainder (who were permanently unfit for service) were either given base jobs in England or were returned to Australia.

The awful scenes visible at the clearing stations and hospitals can only be referred to here, but it may be added,

**Reflections.**
in conclusion, that the Army Medical personnel and the brave nurses learnt the inner meaning and utter abomination of war in a way that politicians, newspaper editors, captains of industry, munition workers, and others who make and prolong wars, and those vultures of commerce and industry who fatten and get rich on war, never do, because the former saw its results at first hand, and its horrors were brought home to them in a way that the latter never realised.

## CHAPTER XXIV.

### FLANDERS AND RETURN TO THE SOMME.

#### 1916.—September 1 to December 14.

Flanders was an area where the flames of war at times burst out with furious and volcanic intensity, varied by long intervals when little eventuated. The autumn of 1916 was one of its calm periods, and the shattered Australian divisions were withdrawn from the shambles of the Somme, and sent there to recruit. The 1st Australian Division went north on August 23, and the 2nd and 4th Divisions followed shortly after.

The 14th marched to Warloy on September 1, all showing signs of what they had passed through, the majority covered with mud from head to foot, and many without puttees, and with clothes ragged and torn. A division of Canadians marching for the Somme area was passed en route. A week was subsequently spent in various villages north of Amiens, and during that time General Birdwood presented medals to those who had won them at Pozieres Ridge. Doullens was reached on the 8th, and here the battalion entrained for the north, and on arrival there marched to Zevecoten, near Poperinghe, and billeted in wooden huts. There were many hop plantations in the neighbourhood, and the inhabitants were busy picking the plants. The battalion was now for the first time in Belgium. A pleasant innovation was introduced in the middle of the month (September), when leave to Great Britain was inaugurated. It was only ten days' leave, but the system remained in force till the end of the war, and was much appreciated, as the prospect of it helped to make life at the front more tolerable. Some visited the homes of their ancestors, whilst many friendships were formed with residents in the Motherland, some of which ultimately resulted in matrimonial alliances. General Sir H. V. Cox (G.O.C., 4th Division) distributed

*Battalion Leaves for Flanders.*

*Blighty Leave Inaugurated.*

cards on the 13th to officers and men who had been recommended for conspicuous work while in the trenches near Mouquet Farm. The battalion marched on the 15th to Dickebusch as reserve battalion, A and one half of B Company being detailed to Vermezele. It was during the stay at Dickebusch that the new chaplain, Captain F. W. Rolland, joined the battalion, taking the place of Chaplain-Captain Cope, and before long became a well-known and popular figure in the unit.

**Chaplain Rolland Joins.**

During the next few weeks the whole battalion was utilised largely as a labour battalion, both by day and by night, being organised into working parties, and engaged mending roads, improving trenches, constructing defences, erecting firesteps and duckboarding floors. This work was not popular; the men knew they were looked to and called upon as storm troops when desperate fighting was wanted, and they resented being utilised in addition to work as navvies when in quiet sectors, especially when they noticed that some storm troops, such as the Guards, received differential treatment.

Some of the officers and men wounded in the summer fighting now began to return from hospital. On the 27th Lieuts. J. Mackay, H. B. Wanliss, D.S.O., and 2nd-Lieut. R. E. Sanders, and on the following day the veteran 2nd-Lieut. Reg. Jones, M.M., returned to the battalion. On October 1 a stray bullet killed Pte. Percy Pigot,[1] who had been batman on the Peninsula to Chaplain-Captain Gillison, and subsequently to Lieut.-Colonel Dare; and on the 5th Sgt. Jack Garcia, D.C.M., was wounded. On the 6th Lieut. H. B. Wanliss and 2nd-Lieut. S. B. Thompson, with 100 other ranks, were detailed to assist the 1st Canadian Tunnelling Company at La Clytte. They remained with the Canadians for about a fortnight, and their co-operation was much appreciated. The 50th Battalion relieved the 14th on the 8th, and our men moved to Zevecoten, where they again occupied Alberta camp. There was a brigade inspection here by General Plumer (G.O.C. of the 2nd Army) on the 11th, followed by a march past in column of route.

**Return of Wounded to Battalion.**

The battalion moved into trenches in the Ypres salient on the 13th (with the 15th Battalion on the left flank), and

---

[1] Percy Pigot, labourer, of Mount Gambier (S.A.). Killed in action, October 1, 1916.

164   *Flanders and Return to the Somme.*

**Ypres Salient.** remained there for six days. There was some desultory shelling on both sides, with few casualties, though Capt. A. R. Cox (O.C. of A Company) was wounded (Capt. D. R. Macdermid taking over command of the company), and Sgt. G. A. Ross,[2] of C Company (who had won the D.C.M. at Mouquet **Sgt. G. A. Ross** 1 arm) was killed. When relieved, the bat- **Killed.** talion returned to Alberta camp. Capts. Henry and Richardson (ex-14th Peninsula officers) here rejoined the battalion with 69 reinforcements, and the ranks, depleted at Pozieres, were gradually filling up again.

It was about this time that the "conscription vote" was taken in the A.I.F., and its result was one of the enigmas of the war, and impossible to understand unless **Conscription** one realises the complexities of the Australian **Vote.** character. War had decimated the ranks of the Australian infantry, and a referendum was taken by the Australian people to decide whether conscription was to be enforced on the crowds of shirkers in Australia who had refused to enlist, and had not any intention of doing so. The subject is too wide to be dealt with here, but it can be said briefly that the fighting members of the **Rejected by** A.I.F. (except the officers) voted overwhelm- **Fighting Men.** ingly "No." Various alleged reasons[3] were given for this vote, but the following explanation perhaps gets at the root of the matter. The average Australian views national questions largely from a personal standpoint. The Australian troops (like all troops in war time) had many grievances, some certainly imaginary, but others very genuine. The origin of these grievances were somewhat vaguely attributed by them to the "Heads," i.e., their military and political chiefs, and as they knew the "Heads" wanted an affirmative vote they voted in the negative. There was a large "Yes" vote in the A.I.F., but it came from the non-fighting sections of that organisation **Non-fighting Men** —the men in the base camps, the Horseferry[4] **Vote "Yes."** Road clerks, the pay corps, the bakery corps, the Army Service Corps, and other non-

---

[2] Sgt. G. A. Ross. (Vide Chap. 22, "Decorations.")

[3] One potent reason undoubtedly was the fear among many that conscripts were not to be relied on, and would "let down" their comrades in the fighting line.

[4] The Australian Headquarters in London was situated in Horseferry Road. There were a very large number of clerks (members of the A.I.F.) employed there.

fighting elements. These men, in the great majority of cases, had safe, remunerative, and comfortable billets, and participated in the glories of the A.I.F. without sharing in its dangers and hardships. They feared that the dwindling of reinforcements would result in them being sent to the front, and voted "Yes" accordingly to obviate the danger of such an unpleasant contingency.

The battalion, on October 21, crossed the Belgian frontier, and entered France, billets being found in farms near Steenvorde. The first draft of N.C.O.'s left the battalion on the 26th to proceed to the 4th Training Battalion as a training cadre. (Hitherto the 14th's reinforcements had been trained by N.C.O.'s who had not seen service.) Some specialist and company training preceded the return of the battalion to the old Somme battle-ground. The great offensive which had commenced there on July 1 still continued—one long battle, lasting nearly five months, and which during that time cost the A.I.F. upwards of 30,000 casualties. The 14th was destined to take part in the last phase of the 1916 offensive. The return south took place on the 26th, when the 14th marched to Caestre, and entrained for Port Remy, in the lower Somme area, and on arrival marched to billets at Bellancourt. It was a night journey by train, and the destination was reached (after a march) in the early hours of a bleak morning. The scenery in this district was of a more picturesque character than that of the monotonous, damp, and dreary northern country which had just been vacated. Company and specialist training were carried on for a few days, and here the battalion was joined by 2nd-Lieuts. Edmonds, Mitchell (afterwards adjutant), and Aldridge, and 26 other ranks.

*Return to the Somme.*

*Officers Join Battalion.*

After a few days in neighbouring villages, the battalion, on November 8, marched to Picqueny, where it was allotted motor 'buses supplied by the French Army, and driven by French colonial natives. This was a novelty for the 4th Brigade, for hitherto its means of locomotion to and from the line had been on foot. The 'buses, loaded with their human cargoes, swept through villages along the Somme valley, and passing through the outskirts of Amiens, where some of the 'buses broke down, arrived at their destination, Ribemont, a village where the battalion was to spend a good deal of its time before the war ended. The surroundings were cheerless; everything was in deep mud, and the billets were poor and dirty. Squads of German prisoners were employed in the locality cleaning up the roads and keeping them in repair. They saluted our officers punctiliously.

Packs were stored on the 13th, and the 4th Brigade marched to Dernancourt.[5] On the road the 5th Battalion, A.I.F,. was met returning from the trenches, and many greetings took place between the two Victorian units, for many members of each unit had friends in the other. The battalion was now approaching the old battle-ground of the Somme offensive. The Germans had been pushed back somewhat during the absence of the 4th Brigade in Flanders, and the battalion's route was different from its previous advance in August. The 4th Brigade marched on the 14th through Meaulte, and the ruins of Fricourt on to Montauban, and finally reached its destination at Bernafray Wood, about five miles from the ruins of Pozieres. The roads and railways had been torn to pieces by artillery fire, and the improvised means of communication were totally inadequate and fearfully congested. Locomotion was consequently slow. The so-called wood had been blow to pieces, and consisted of torn tree stumps and a mass of shell holes. The battalion bivouacked and remained here for a week, during which time from six to seven hundred men were engaged daily in working and fatigue parties. There were heavy frosts at night, and many of the reinforcements saw snow for the first time. Men went about clad in sheepskin waistcoats. Captain Hansen, M.C.,. left for a Divisional school on the 22nd, and Captain "Lofty" Williamson assumed temporary command of C Company. The battalion had now been built up by reinforcements to its full strength. Another move took place on the 23rd, when the battalion marched to Carlton camp, near Bazentin. The accommodation here was wretched, but dugouts were made of what material was available. Working parties to the number of 700 were supplied by the battalion on the following day. Rain fell in torrents.

A and C Companies marched out on the 26th, and relieved two companies of the 48th Battalion in support at Bull Road, near Flers, and next day took over the front from that battalion, B and D Companies taking over the support lines. The relief of the front line took eight hours to complete, owing to the awful state of the saps and trenches, the mud and slush being up to the men's waists. Many lost their gum boots in the mud, and arrived at the front barefooted. Some fell into the mud and had to be dug out en

---

[5] Dernancourt, the scene of a great 4th Division victory on April 5, 1918.

route. Nine men were stuck in the mud all night, and were found nearly frozen to death.

The disposition on the front was now as follows:—Front line, five platoons and eight Lewis guns, with two platoons in support in Cheese road. The Germans, however, were no longer the chief enemy; it was the weather. Words fail to describe the conditions during the Somme winter of 1916-17. It was considered by many the most trying experience of our men during the whole war. The winter was one of unparalleled severity, and the continuous rain had turned the whole country into an ocean of oozing mud. Laden with equipment, all had to struggle through this, going to and returning from the trenches. Some men fainted from exhaustion. The roads were littered with dead animals and vehicles which could not be extracted from the mire. The trenches themselves were merely shell holes half full of freezing water, where the long-suffering infantry, who could get no exercise, lay crouching, exposed to the weather and the enemy's artillery fire. "Trench feet" made its appearance, and threatened to decimate the A.I.F. It was only by the greatest exertions that the men could be fed and kept alive. "Tommy Cookers" now made their first appearance, and the rum issue was much appreciated. The battalion cooks did their best, under adverse conditions, to alleviate the men's sufferings. The Australian character, full of innate grit, was seen at its best under conditions such as these, and the 14th men faced the appalling misery of that winter as they had faced the German artillery fire at Pozieres Ridge. Decimated as they had been on the Peninsula by enteric, dysentery, and scurvy, they now had to face conditions as trying, but of an absolutely diverse character. Those 14th men who had come through the Peninsula and the Somme winter had little to learn of the depths of human wretchedness and misery.

*Appalling Conditions During 1916-17 Winter.*

*Faced with Fortitude.*

An unfortunate incident occurerd on December 1, when a brigade operation order, with accompanying plans, which had been received at battalion headquarters, was forwarded to the O.C. of B Company for his perusal. That officer then took the responsibility of giving them to one of his platoon commanders to peruse. The latter took them to his dugout near Goodwin's Post, and after perusal sent them back by a runner to the O.C. of B Company. The runner, new to the trenches, attempted to take a short cut, and missing

*An Unfortunate Incident.*

his way in a mist, walked into the German lines with these important papers on his person, and was captured. Consequentially the proposed operation—an attack by the 16th Battalion supported by the 14th—had to be abandoned. This incident led to an inquiry, with consequential remedial measures.

A break with the early history of the battalion occurred on December 2, when Lieut.-Colonel Dare[5] relinquished the command of the 14th, with which he had been connected since its inception, first as adjutant and subsequently as C.O. On his appointment as C.O. he had been the youngest colonel in the A.I.F. Major N. D. Fethers took temporary command, and on the 3rd the 14th was relieved by the 16th and moved back to the reserve line. The 4th Brigade was relieved on the 6th, and moved back to Ribemont, where the packs had been stored, and all were able to indulge in the luxury of a change of clothing. Lieut. A. Jacka, V.C., M.C., who had returned to the unit, was appointed assistant adjutant to Capt. Blainey.

*Lieut.-Col. Dare Relinquishes Command.*

A large number of sick were evacuated about this time, but there were, fortunately, few casualties in the line, though among the wounded, on December 1, was L.-Sgt. M. Bronson, of A Company, who had been in charge of the burial party at Quinn's Post on April 30, 1915.[*]

*Many Sick Evacuated.*

The first few days at Ribemont were spent in overhauling equipment, varied by company training and inspections. Capt. Winn,[7] who had been attached to the battalion for upwards of thirteen months, and actively engaged in all its battles in France, left to join the 4th Field Ambulance, and his place was taken by Major Fletcher, who remained with the battalion till September, 1917. Speculation was now rife in the 14th as to who was to be Colonel Dare's successor, and on the 14th rumour was translated into fact when Major J. H. Peck took charge as C.O. of the battalion. A better

*Capt. Winn, R.M.O., Leaves.*

*Major Fletcher Takes His Place.*

---

[6] Lieut.-Colonel C. M. M. Dare, D.S.O., architect. Born at Moreland (V.), May 27, 1888.

[7] L.-Sgt. M. Bronson (vide Chap. IV.).

[8] Captain R. C. Winn. Subsequently leaving the battalion, he was severely wounded and evacuated.

*Major Peck Becomes C.O. of the 14th.*

*His Outstanding Ability.*

choice could not have been made. The new C.O. had fought at the landing on the Peninsula in the 11th Battalion, and later as brigade major of the 4th Brigade. He was, perhaps, the ablest man who commanded a battalion of the A.I.F. in France. Under the virile leadership of its new and capable chief the 14th attained the high-water mark of discipline, efficiency, reputation, and contentment.

# CHAPTER XXV.

## A NEW REGIME.

### 1916.—December 15 to December 31.

After nine days spent at Ribemont a long march of about fourteen miles was made on December 16 to Rainneville (the blankets being carried by transport). The usual training and route marching during the next few days was varied by a battalion sports, held on Christmas Day, followed by a Christmas dinner of excellent quality. A letter and parcel mail from Australia added to the enjoyment.

**Christmas Day.**

The transformation in the morale of the battalion effected by Major J. H. Peck was so pronounced that some reference in detail must be made to it. The prolonged indecisive fighting and heavy losses of the summer, followed by the appalling conditions and cold of an exceptionally severe winter, had resulted in a certain amount of mental dry rot, which had more or less affected all ranks. Enthusiasm had vanished, and ideals required reviving. The new C.O. was a permanent soldier, who had mastered his profession in every detail, whilst his dominant personality appealed to everyone with whom he came in contact. He made it his first business to get to know all the officers and N.C.O.'s, and then set out at once to reorganise the battalion. Work at headquarters was systematised, and Captain A. R. Blainey, who had been adjutant for a long time, leaving for a training battalion in England, his place was taken by Lieut. H. B. Wanliss. The front lines were henceforth regularly visited by the C.O. or adjutant, and many matters of internal organisation, formerly left to junior officers, were dealt with by the C.O. in person.

**Improvement of Morale.**

**Reorganisation of Battalion.**

A vigorous programme of training was introduced. Battalion drill and brigade manœuvres were made interesting and informative. Officers were encouraged to come to battalion

**Vigorous Training Introduced.**

**Sports Encouraged.**

headquarters, and advice on any subject, when asked, was freely given. Sports were encouraged, and a lot of the useless barrack yard drill cut out. The welfare and comfort of the men were studied, and care taken that they were well fed and clothed. When out of the line, classes were held for the officers, with resulting examinations, whilst company and platoon commanders had to lecture to their companies and platoons. The intellectual side of the men was not neglected, and debates were organised and held in the evenings, in which much good oratory was displayed. The excellent N.C.O.'s of the battalion received more consideration and encouragement than had ever been extended to them. Whilst everything was done to raise the battalion to a high state of discipline and organisation the new C.O. was too strong a man to brook any unauthorised interference. The result was that the battalion was worked up to concert pitch, every one was interested in his work, all were happy and contented, and when the Battle of Bullecourt took place four months later there was not any infantry unit in the A.I.F. which surpassed, if any quite equalled, the 14th Battalion.

**Examinations and Lectures.**

**Debates Organised.**

**N.C.O.'s Encouraged.**

**Results of Training.**

The 2nd and 5th Divisions of the A.I.F. changed their G.O.C.'s during December, and on the last day of the year Brigadier-General Holmes became G.O.C. of the 4th Division, vice Major-General Sir H. V. Cox. The retiring general (formerly a British officer in the Indian army) was an excellent soldier, as well as a strict disciplinarian, and was continually in the front line seeing things for himself. The division owed much to him for able and capable leadership.

**Brig.-Gen. Holmes Becomes G.O.C. of the 4th Division.**

The conclusion of the year 1916 renders it advisable to give a brief epitome of the battalion's doings during the preceding twelve months.

January 1, 1916, found the battalion just arrived in Egypt after the evacuation of the Peninsula. Its first camping ground was Ismailia, near the Suez Canal, where all recruited after the hardships of the Peninsula campaign. On January 21 a movement was made to Moascar, and on February

**Epitome of Year 1916.**

**Egypt.** 27 a further move to Tel-el-Kebir, where the 4th Australian Division was formed, and the 4th Brigade allotted to it. Several promotions from the ranks took place about this time, and many reinforcements were received. The newly-formed division made a three days' march through the desert to Serapeum, which proved one of the most trying experiences in its existence. A grand review of the 4th Division was held on May 29, and on June 1 the battalion embarked on the S.S. "Trannsylvania" for Marseilles. The voyage through the Mediter-
**Voyage to** ranean and the trip through France—from
**France.** Marseilles to Baillieul—was the most delightful experience that the battalion had during its four years abroad. On its arrival north the battalion was located in the Bois Grenier sector of the line, near Armentieres, and here it suffered its first casualties. On July 2 "A" Company carried out the first trench raid
**First Raid of** made by the 4th Division in France. The
**4th Division.** German wire was uncut by our trench mortars, but the assaulting party, splendidly led by its young officers, forced its way through the uncut wire and carried out the operation at the cost of almost eighty per cent. of its numbers. Among the fatal casualties were 2nd-Lieut. Robert Julian and Sgt. "Curly" Croft. Next day the Germans responded with a counter-raid after a terrific
**German** and prolonged bombardment, in which the
**Counter Raid.** 14th Platoon suffered severely. The German attack was repulsed, and again great courage and fortitude were shown by our men. Sgts. W. H. Pearce and "Darky" Edmonstone were killed. On July 10 and 11 the 14th was relieved by the 30th Battalion, and on the 13th it entrained for the Somme area. After some arduous training the 14th relieved the 26th and 28th Battalions on August 6 on Pozieres Ridge, and at dawn on the
**Pozieres Ridge.** following morning, after suffering a terrific all night bombardment, B Company, with some assistance from adjoining units, broke up a great German counter-attack, 2nd-Lieut. Albert Jacka capping his V.C. performance by a feat of arms which was not surpassed in the war. The battalion held the trenches on Pozieres Ridge for a week under adverse conditions that have been rarely equalled even on the western front. 2nd Lieut. H. S. Dobbie was killed, and the majority of the N.C.O.'s of the battalion were killed or wounded. After a few days out of the line the battalion returned to the battlefield, and on August 28 the

**Mouquet Farm.** bombing section, supported by C Company, attacked the enemy's strong points near Mouquet Farm. The attacking force was numerically grossly inadequate, and after some preliminary success had to retire, though Sgt. J. S. Stewart, with a few men, successfully held strong point 77. 2nd-Lieut. A. R. Dean was mortally wounded during this operation. The battalion was relieved on August 29, and on September 8 entrained for the north, where a comparatively uneventful time was spent, varied by much hard manual labour, including road mending and trench improvement. The conscription vote was taken during the stay here. On October 26 the 14th returned south and took part in the last phase of the Somme offensive. The winter of 1916-17 was one of extraordinary severity, and the hardships undergone remained almost a nightmare to those enduring them. Major J. H. Peck took over command of the battalion on December 14, and under his handling it rapidly attained a high standard of discipline and efficiency.

## CHAPTER XXVI.

### STORMY TRENCH.

#### 1917—January 1 to February 7.

The year 1917 opened with a very successful brigade sports meeting held at Rainneville, on the first day of the year, the 16th Battalion beating the 14th by five
**Brigade Sports.** points in the aggregate for places won. During these athletic contests all temporarily forgot the war, and felt as if they were back in Australia again. Next morning the battalion left for Rainneville in full marching order, and arrived at Ribemont, where a few days were spent, and then followed a further move to Mametz and Bazentin. The war traffic in this part of France was so tremendous that the roads required continual repair, and as the severity of the weather imposed a restriction on combative operations, the month of January was largely devoted by the 14th to supplying working parties, consisting of several officers and many hundred men, who were
**Battalion Supplies** daily employed mending and widening roads,
**Working Parties.** spreading metal, and clearing embankments. Meanwhile, reinforcements continued to be absorbed until the battalion was over strength; some of the details were old battalion men who had been away from the unit for over twelve months. On January 23 A and B Companies, with a proportion of specialists, took over the reserve line from the 47th Battalion near Flers. The ground was now frozen to a depth of several feet, but though the cold was intense the men could keep their feet dry, as mud and water were solid, and not liquid. Few fatal casualties were suffered during this term in the trenches, but on the 28th, as the result of a reconnaisance the enemy's retaliatory fire was unwisely drawn, with the result that Captain D. L. K. Richardson[1] (O.C. of A Company) was slightly, and No. 5129, Cpl. W. J. Jackson,[2] (intelligence corporal of A Com-
**Cpl. Jackson** pany, and a gallant and popular N.C.O.)
**Killed.** mortally, wounded. Sgt. A. J. K. Ayre was wounded on January 31. The temporary cut-

---

[1] Captain D. L. K. Richardson, accountant, of Footscray (Vic.). (Vide Chapter 2, original officers of D Company, 14th Battalion.)
[2] No. 5129, Cpl. W. J. Jackson, of Numurkah (Vic.), labourer. Killed in action, January 28, 1917.

## The History of the 14th Battalion.    175

ting out of the battalion rum issue about this time caused much comment and considerable profanity. It was, however, renewed towards the end of January, for its absence under the climatic conditions then prevailing caused much hardship.

On February 1 two companies of the 15th Battalion, stationed on our right flank, raided the German position at
<br>Stormy Trench. The attacking party (as
**15th Battalion** was so frequent in our offensives throughout
**Assaults Stormy** the war), was numerically too weak for the
**Trench.** job, and though the trenches were captured
they could not be held against powerful counter-attacks launched by the enemy, especially as the 15th's supply of bombs ran out. Next day the 14th was relieved by the 16th Battalion, the relief being completed by 9.45 p.m. The term in the trenches just vacated had been uneventful, but uncomfortable; the trenches were icebound, with unthawed
<br>snow lying everywhere; the cold had been
**Severe Cold.** such as the great mass of the 14th men had
never before experienced. On relief the battalion marched to support lines about one and a half miles further back; here all expected to enjoy a little rest, and started making dugouts and shelters to protect them from the biting winds. As far as C Company was concerned these expectations of rest were not realised. On February 3 Major Peck left for ten days' leave to the United Kingdom.

Meanwhile the High Command had resolved on another attack by the 4th Brigade on Stormy Trench, and on February
<br>3 Colonel Durrant (C.O. of the 13th Battalion)
**13th Battalion** received orders for his unit to attack that
**Detailed** position on the night of February 4-5. He
**to Attack** was offered the choice of any company in the
**Stormy Trench.** 4th Brigade to co-operate in the attack, and
he selected C Company, of the 14th. The
**C Company 14th** time for preparation was very short, but
**to Co-operate.** Colonel Durrant acted with great energy. His
company commanders were called together, and the details of the proposed attack outlined and explained; the terrain to be attacked was reconnoitred by the officers;
<br>strong artillery support was arranged for;
**Preparations.** enormous quantities of bombs and grenades
were carried into the forward trenches, and each company provided twenty carriers to carry the bombs to the captured position. The German egg-bombs, being much lighter than our Mills bombs, could consequently be thrown much further; this disadvantage was obviated by screwing

small rods into the bases of the Mills, and firing them out of rifles with blank cartridges. This procedure proved very effective in action. Our barrage was to open at 10 p.m. 13th Battalion headquarters was in a chalk quarry.

It came somewhat as a shock to the C Company personnel when it was learnt that the company was to be sent back immediately to the line, but the confidence and compliment implied in the choice of the company was recognised, and all determined to uphold the reputation that its record had inspired. February 4 was spent in issuing ammunition and bombs, cleaning and oiling rifles, and making all preparations for the work ahead.

The role of C Company in the proposed operation was to be a subsidiary one; it was to be in support, and its duty was to file into the front line trenches vacated by the 13th on the opening of the attack, and be prepared to assist that unit in any direction in which its services might be required. Captain Stewart Hansen was O.C., and Captain "Lofty" Williamson second in command of the company. The former took charge of Platoons 11 and 12, and the latter of Platoons 9 and 10. Four Lewis gun sections—Smith's, Finger's, Perry's, and Muir's—took part in the operation. The night of the attack was bitterly cold—the kind of night a wounded man dreads, for it adds to his tortures.

*C Company Moves Off.*

About 7.30 p.m. the four platoons of C Company moved off along the duckboard track at intervals of about one hundred yards, a box of bombs being carried between every two or three men. Captain Hansen moved up with the rear platoon. On C Company's arrival at the 13th Battalion's support company's position in a sunken road near the chalk quarry (where its battalion headquarters was situated), the support company was just leaving the position to join the other companies for the attack, so that some delay arose before it was clear. When it was clear C Company moved into the communication trench, which led from near the quarry to the front line. There were long and frequent delays in the communication trench, but finally, as the 13th Battalion vacated the front line to creep into No Man's Land, C Company filed into Shrine Trench. Captain "Lofty" Williamson and Lieut. Peter McCallum, with platoons 9 and 10, then moved to the left to Grease Trench, while Captain Hansen and Lieut. Norman ("Pongo") Wilson remained with

*Enters Communication Trench.*

*Enters Shrine and Grease Trenches.*

platoons 11 and 12 in Shrine Trench. In order that the front line might not be too congested, some of the men (including most of the 12th Platoon and Perry's Lewis Gun Section) remained in the communication trench near its junction with Shrine Trench. Meanwhile, A, B, and D Companies, 14th Battalion, had moved to Possum Trench as a reserve.

At 10 p.m. our barrage, projected from many hundreds of guns, opened with a terrific crash and moved across No Man's Land at the rate of fifty yards a minute. Just behind the fringe of the innumerable hissing balls of fire which marked its progress advanced the long serried line of the 13th Battalion, and the moment the barrage lifted the 13th men were over and into the German trenches the dazed occupants of which mostly surrendered promptly, but some on the right showed fight, and had to be killed. The initial success had been cheaply gained, but the struggle was only commencing, for the Germans had expected an attack, and were prepared. Their barrage fell promptly, and with terrific violence. Shrine Trench was well known to the enemy, and it received the full blast of the storm. Missiles of every description rained upon it. Many of the survivors of the two platoons stationed there considered it their worst experience in the war. They were trapped in a wall of fire and steel.

*Our Barrage Opens.*

*German Barrage Opens.*

*Its Intensity.*

There was little shelter; men hugged the bottom of the trench for some protection. The ground was frozen hard, and huge blocks of ice, loosened and lifted by the explosions, were hurled into the air. Several boxes of bombs in the trench were exploded by the bombardment. The unearthly din arising from the two concentrated barrages was awe-inspiring. The trench soon became a shambles, from which few expected to escape alive. There was no excitement of action; it was a continual passive expectation of death or mutilation. About seventy per cent. in Shrine and the communication trench became casualties. No. 12 Platoon was almost blotted out. Capt. Hansen was mortally wounded, whilst Cpl. H. Perry and the whole of his Lewis gun section were killed and buried by one trench mortar shell. Wounded men were struggling over the dead in their efforts to crawl out of this inferno, whilst some 13th Battalion men, wounded during the assault, crawled back to the trench, and added to the misery and congestion there. For seven long hours this pitiless

*Heavy Casualties.*

*Captain Hansen Mortally Wounded.*

storm continued, but towards daylight it slackened and died down. Fortunately Platoons 9 and 10 in Grease Trench on the left were out of the direct range of the barrage, and escaped with comparatively few casualties.

Meanwhile during the whole night the 13th Battalion men were fighting for their lives to retain the trenches they had seized, the enemy, assisted by their heavy barrage, delivering counter-attack after counter-attack with the greatest determination.

*Severe Fighting by 13th Battalion.*

The heaviest pressure was on the right flank, where A Company was stationed, and here the struggle was tremendous, and almost hand to hand, but the 13th men fought in a manner that was beyond all praise, led by their O.C. (Capt. Harry Murray), who was one of the grandest heroes in the A.I.F. The Germans were fought to a standstill, though A Company lost two-thirds of its members.

The 13th Battalion carrying parties were meantime working feverishly, and losing heavily, getting bombs across No Man's Land to the new position. Captain Williamson, noting this, detailed a number of C Company men to supplement the work of the 13th carriers, and all night long the C Company men worked backward and forwards through the barrage, suffering many casualties, but carrying several thousands of bombs to the hard-pressed front line; their work was of the greatest value, and was possibly the means of rendering the position secure.

*C Company Supplies Carrying Parties.*

Shortly after the attack commenced a message came through to Captain Hansen from the front line for a Lewis gun section to be forwarded to Capt. Murray's company, and L.-Cpl. Percy Muir[3] led his section through the raging barrage and was posted on the extreme right of A Company, 13th. Here it took a very prominent part in the very hottest of the fighting, Muir firing his gun into the enemy until his hands were burnt with the heat from the casing. Later in the night Smith's and Finger's Lewis gun sections were detailed by Capt. Williamson to join the 13th on the left of their line. They, too, did useful work, but had a comparatively quiet time, the right flank of the 13th being the storm centre.

*Company Lewis Gun Sections Co-operate in Front Line.*

After dawn the stretcher-bearers were able to move more

---

[3] No. 3424, L.-Cpl. Percy Frederick Muir, orchardist, of Mt. Waverley (Vic.).

freely and were enabled to carry the wounded away. About 8 a.m. (February 5) word was received from the 13th Battalion that all was quiet, and that there was no longer any need for C Company to remain in close support, and the shattered remnants of the company then left the trench and joined up with the remainder of the battalion.

Later in the day C Company Sgt.-Mjr., Les Bain, was detailed to take the Battalion Pioneers and bury our dead, which was not an easy task as the ground was frozen hard and impervious even to picks. The bodies had consequently to be buried in shell holes, and covered with loose earth broken up by the bombardment. Capt. Hansen, though he never regained consciousness, did not die till February 7 (his birthday). His remains were buried at Warloy, alongside Lieut. Dobbie. Volunteers were called for to assist in digging a communication trench (afterwards known as Fourteenth Alley), to the newly-captured position, and one hundred men, under Lieuts. Aldridge and Edmonds, volunteered, and the risky work was completed after ten hours labour, on the night of February 6-7, with only one casualty.

Our Dead Buried.

Communication Trench Dug.

The capture of Stormy Trench was one of the finest bits of work—both in conception and execution—ever carried out by the 4th Brigade. Its success was due to four main causes: the excellent arrangements and forethought of Col. Durrant, the splendid fighting qualities of the 13th Battalion personnel (especially A Company), the prompt and excellent co-operation of our artillery, and the initiative and intrepidity of C Company, 14th Battalion, whose services were handsomely acknowledged by Col. Durrant[4] in his lucid report on the operation. General satisfaction was caused throughout the brigade by the award of the V.C. to Capt. Murray for his conduct in the struggle.

Captain Murray, 13th Battalion, Wins V.C.

The total casualties of the battalion in connection with the operation were seventy-two,[5] of whom twenty-seven were killed or died of wounds, many of them being 18th and 19th

---

[4] He stated: "The bravery and devotion to duty of C Company, 14th Battalion, in support, was most commendable, and their carrying of bombs over to the front line largely contributed to success." Also, in a recommendation of Captain "Lofty" Williamson for a decoration, he added: "I cannot speak too highly of him and the work of his men."

[5] The 13th Battalion casualties during the engagement were 233.

180                    *Stormy Trench.*

reinforcement men who had recently joined up. The fatal casualties included Captain Hansen,[6] Cpl. Harold Perry (109),[7] and L.-Cpls. J. Mattinson (5415),[8] G. Ritchie (1414),[9] and H. J. Hassett (876).[10] Stewart Hansen was one of the outstanding personalities of the 14th Bat-
Captain Hansen's talion. An "original," he was prominent for
Record. his work on the Peninsula, and for some time acted as adjutant. He landed in France as the O.C. of C Company, and was in charge of the operations against Mouquet Farm, which he conducted with marked ability, and for which he was decorated. Clean living, capable, courageous, and cheerful, he set a high standard of life and conduct, and was one of the battalion's finest and post popular officers. His loss was deeply felt by all ranks.

The wounded included Sgts. J. Bailey (2777) and P. Harris (3359); L.-Cpl. A. S. Smith (293); and Ptes. T. V. Hughes, M.M. (2607), and E. L. Kohls, M.M.

Decorations. The following decorations were awarded in respect of the Stormy Trench operations:—

MILITARY MEDAL.

3424, L.-Cpl. Percy F. Muir, Mount Waverley (Vic.), Lewis gunner.

1692, Cpl. Percy G. Hume, Liverpool (Eng.), stretcher-bearer.

---

[6] Captain Stewart Murray Hansen, M.C., architect, of Williamstown (Vic.). Born February 7, 1892. Died of wounds, February 7, 1917.

[7] No. 109, Cpl. Harold Perry, railway employee, of Deer Park (Vic.). Killed in action, February 5, 1917.

[8] No. 5415, L.-Cpl. James Mattinson, farmer (Scotland). Killed in action, February 5, 1917.

[9] L.-Cpl. G. Ritchie, carpenter, of Hamilton (Vic.). Killed in action, February 5, 1917.

[10] No. 876, L.-Cpl. H. J. Hassett, bootmaker, of Hobart (Tas.). Died of wounds, February 17, 1917.

## CHAPTER XXVII.

### PREPARATION AND TRAINING.

#### 1917.—February 8 to April 8.

The 12th A.I.F. Brigade relieved the 4th on February 8, and on that date the battalion moved back to Mametz. 2nd-Lieuts. L. H. Mullett and R. E. Hayes, reinforcement officers, marched in next morning, and were allotted to B Company, of which about this time Captain Stanton became O.C. Lieut. Reg. Jones, M.M., left for a training camp in England on the 15th, and on the following day one of the enemy's planes dropped a bomb on an ammunition dump at Montauban, in the vicinity of the battalion, and all day the air was rent by the explosion of thousands of shells and bombs. On the 17th Colonel Peck returned from leave, and Major Fuhrmann became temporarily brigade major of the 4th Brigade.

The battalion marched to Ribemont on February 22, where it remained about a month. There were few (if any) villages in France where the battalion passed more time than in Ribemont, or where there were more cordial relations between the battalion representatives and the inhabitants. Like all French villages, it contained numerous estaminets, where the men put in much of their spare time when off duty. The billets which were allotted to them for lodging during their peregrinations through France, and where their belongings were stored (often mere huts and farm sheds), were usually cheerless, draughty, and congested, and frequently vermin-infested and uncomfortable. The estaminets, on the contrary, were more like their own Australian homes—warm, well lit, and clean, and were filled with little tables, where all were free to remain throughout the evening, smoking, absorbing refreshments, and discussing their many adventures. The usual staple subjects of conversation were Australia, and life and sport there, but there was much argument about places of interest in Europe, whilst the characteristics and peculiarities of their

*Ribemont.*

*The French Estaminets.*

officers were analysed with true Australian freedom. Their discussions were interspersed with the consumption of chips, and fried eggs, and innumerable cups of coffee, sometimes flavoured with rum. French women are, perhaps, the world's best cooks, and it was generally a woman who presided at the estaminet, which became in reality a soldiers' club. Among the local celebrities at Ribemont was the village idiot, known as "Incinerator Kate" (usually seen trundling a huge barrow), whose eccentricities were a perennial source of amusement to all.

It was universally recognised that in the spring, when milder weather would render active operations on a large scale possible, a desperate effort would be made on the British front to break through the German line of defence. The recent Somme summer offensive, though a few tactical successes had been gained at enormous cost, had been a strategic failure in the sense that there had not been a break through, and all realised that the fighting in the spring would be desperate. Accordingly a strenuous course of training, both practical and theoretical, was now adopted to prepare the battalion for open warfare offensive action; it proceeded on progressive lines, and was divided into four periods:

*Open Warfare Training.*

1. Platoon, section and specialist.
2. Company.
3. Battalion.
4. Brigade.

The results of the above training, alternated with sport, and also with leave, which was freely given, enabled all to rapidly recover from the almost intolerable sufferings which had been endured during the terrible preceding winter. When the day's work was done a series of entertainments and debates were provided each night at the school house by Chaplain-Captain F. W. Rolland, who was indefatigable in his efforts to stimulate the intellectual side of the combatants. Hundreds (including men from other units in the brigade) attended these gatherings, which were thoroughly organised, refreshments being distributed towards the close of the evening. The debates were full of life, humour, and light. The two battalion star speakers were Cpl. Allan McDonald[1] and Pte.

*Battalion Intellectual Entertainments and Debates.*

---

[1] Sgt. Allan M. McDonald (No. 6401), farmer, of Winchelsea (V.). Wounded at the Battle of Bullecourt. Subsequent to the war he twice unsuccessfully contested the Corangamite electorate for the Federal House of Representatives.

Bert Bott.[2] These evenings were highly appreciated and most enjoyable, and as officers and other ranks here met on common grounds, they had a marked effect in stimulating that strong feeling of comradeship among all ranks which was so pronounced a feature at this time in the 14th Battalion. They were also somewhat of a novelty during this period in the A.I.F., for hitherto the intellectual side of the combatants had not received that attention from the authorities that it should have done. The 14th was probably the first unit in the A.I.F. which looked forward to the days of peace, and sought to train men for the realities of life after the war. An army educational scheme was adopted and put in force in the battalion, classes being formed in which many subjects were dealt with. This scheme in a somewhat altered form was subsequently adopted by the higher authorities, and applied at the termination of the war to the whole A.I.F.

*Their Effect on Battalion's Morale.*

*Battalion Educational Scheme.*

Before dealing with the heavy fighting in the ensuing spring, it will be advisable to set out a list of the officers with the battalion on February 28, 1917. Their domicile and decorations are appended, and if at an officers' school on this date the fact is referred to. It will be noted that they were almost all Victorians:—

*List of Battalion Officers.*

Lieut.-Colonel J. H. Peck (Grenfell, N.S.W.), C.O.
Major N. D. Fethers (Victoria).
   ,,    O. C. W. Fuhrmann (South Melbourne, V.)., assistant brigade major.
Capt. W. R. Wadsworth (Castlemaine, V.). (School.)
   ,,   R. W. Orr (Footscray, V.).
   ,,   F. B. Stanton (Stawell, V.).
   ,,   A. Williamson (Toongabbie, V.).
Hon. Capt. W. G. Laver (Kew, V.).
Capt. D. R. Macdermid (Newstead, V.).
Lieut. W. G. McQueen (Hamilton, V.).
   ,,   H. B. Wanliss, D.S.O. (Ballarat, V.).
   ,,   C. R. T. Cole (Malvern, V.).
   ,,   F. W. Symonds (South Camberwell, V.).
   ,,   R. W. Jones, M.M. (Essendon, V.), 4th T.B.
   ,,   N. Wilson (Auburn, V.).

---

[2] Pte. A. B. Bott (No. 6225), salesman, of Brunswick (V.). Killed in action at the Battle of Bullecourt, April 11, 1917.

",, A. Jacka, V.C., M.C. (Wedderburn, V.).
,, P. McCallum (Birregurra, V.).
,, R. E. Sanders (London, England), 4th A.L.T.M.
,, H. R. McKinley (Hawthorn, V.). (School.)
,, O. C. D. Gower (Sandringham, V.).
2nd-Lieut. F. H. Dadson (England).
,, A. L. Hudson (Glenroy, V.).
,, W. J. G. Lyon (Surrey Hills, V.).
,, J. A. Mitchell (Royal Park, V.).
,, N. C. Aldridge (Hawthorn, V.).
,, E. J. L. Edmonds (St. Kilda, V.).
,, L. H. Mullett (East Malvern, V.).
,, R. E. Hayes (Ballarat, V.).
,, M. O'Donnell (Gisborne, V.)
,, W. R. M. Beamond (Geelong, V.).
,, F. W. Appleton (Balaclava, V.).
,, J. Craven (Yorkshire, England). (School.)
,, H. W. Thompson (North Melbourne, V.), 4 T.B.
,, S. B. Thompson (St. Kilda, V.).
,, F. Anderson (Buangor, V.). (School.)
,, W. Jacka (Wedderburn, V.).

The first three weeks of March were spent at Ribemont, the battalion being actively engaged in training and battle tactics. The weather was still cold and bitter.

**Advent of Hindenberg in the West.** Meanwhile, important events were happening on the Western front. Hindenberg, the idol of Germany, and the hero of the Battle of the Tannenberg, had been appointed its chief of staff. He had won brilliant successes against the Russians in the East, and there is no doubt that his advent to the Western theatre of war had a stiffening and vivifying effect on the German personnel there. Their troops seldom fought as well as they did in the spring of 1917. The new chief decided on a withdrawal of the German line to more favourable country in the rear along the position Arras-St. Quentin-Soissons. The enemy retirement

**German Retirement.** on a grand scale began on March 16, and was admirably carried out. Bapaume was captured on March 17 by the 6th A.I.F.

**Capture of Bapaume.** Brigade, and the news acted like a tonic on our men. Some of the optimists foresaw a speedy end of the war.

A very successful and well-arranged battalion sports was held on March 15, the affair going off with great swing.

**Battalion Sports.** Pte. "Tug" Paterson, a Western District athlete, won the 100, 220, and 440 yards; C.S.M. N. McKenzie the half mile; Pte. H. Burns the 120 yards hurdles, and Pte. P. Manders the bandsmen's race.

**Departure from Ribemont.** The battalion left Ribemont on March 22 for the forward area. It was now a thoroughly rejuvenated battalion, and all were full of confidence. The first resting place was Mametz camp, where a stay was made for a few days, and on the 26th Bazentin-le-petit was reached, where the heavy surplus stores were dumped, and left under guard in charge of Sgt. Dobbie.[3] The battalion left Bazentin on the following day, and reached the Bapaume road, and passing the remains of Sars and the Butte de Warlencourt, arrived at Bapaume, then in ruins. The scenes in the advance were inspiring. All the equipment of war was in motion—motor waggons carrying material and ammunition, limbers with rations, and tractors hauling howitzers were all on the forward move, whilst batches of enemy prisoners were being escorted to the rear. The desolation of the Somme was being left behind; all was excitement, and victory seemed in the air. After nine months of the misery and monotony of trench warfare the battalion seemed coming into its own again. The Germans, however, had left the villages in ruins; the wells were filled with filth, and even the fruit trees were destroyed. Many traps were left for our men, and souvenirs were left lying about attached by cords to hidden explosives. The 14th was soon to have a dramatic illustration of German traps.

**Entry to Bapaume.**

**Inspiring Scenes in Advance.**

**Beugnatre.** Bapaume was still in flames when the battalion marched through the ruins to the stirring strains of the regimental march "The Suwanne River." Leaving Bapaume behind, the battalion reached Beugnatre at 1 p.m. on March 27, and bivouacked among the ruins of that village. Battalion headquarters was located in a roofed stable, a substantial building, and about the only one left standing in the locality. Adjoining the stable was a cellar, tenanted on the evening of the

---

[3] Brother of 2nd-Lieut. H. S. Dobbie, of B Company, who died of wounds received on Pozieres Ridge. (Vide Chapter 21.)

28th-29th by Lieut. McQueen, his batman, Tom Young, and two signallers. About 6.30 a.m. on the 29th a terrific explosion rent the air. It was caused by a delayed mine left by the Germans in the cellar. McQueen and Young were blow to fragments, whilst Cpl. W. W. Goodwin, M.M., and Pte. F. A. Thorn (signallers) were also killed, and Lieut. Craven (signalling officer at adjoining battalion headquarters) and three other ranks were severely shocked and buried. Had the mine exploded a day earlier all of A company officers would have been victims, as they had inhabited the cellar the previous night. McQueen had just received instructions to report for six months' duty at the base at Etaples. Lieut. Norman ("Pongo") Wilson proceeded to the Bull Ring (Etaples) in McQueen's stead. One of the signallers killed was Cpl. W. W. Goodwin,[4] M.M., an original (No. 8), a brave man who had been decorated for his fine work at Pozieres. After this dramatic exhibition of German ingenuity a fatigue party was detailed to dig out a site for headquarters in the open fields near by.

*Cellar Adjoining Battalion Headquarters Blown Up.*

*Lieut. McQueen and Cpl. W. W. Goodwin Killed.*

Some well-deserved promotions among commissioned ranks took place during March, probably the three finest subalterns the battalion ever had being appointed captains, viz., the adjutant, Lieut. Harold Wanliss, D.S.O. (on the 6th), and Lieuts. Reg. Jones, M.M., and Albert Jacka, V.C., M.C. (on the 13th).

*Lieuts. Wanliss, Jones, and Jacka Appointed Captains.*

The first week in April was spent near Beugnatre, the battalion being kept busy in filling up mine craters (legacies of the German withdrawal), constructing strong points, burying cable, and preparing for a forward move. It was fairly quiet, but one dramatic incident caused universal excitement. Baron von Richthofen's[5] "circus" was much in evidence about this time, and on April 3 one of their machines, said by some to have been manned by Richthofen himself, flew over our lines and downed two of our observation balloons in quick succession. The little red-bellied machine flew very low in the performance of its work, and hundreds of our rifles and machine guns were turned on it. Though the focus of a tremendous fusilade, it escaped to the accompaniment of

*Feat of German Flying Men.*

---

[4] Cpl. W. W. Goodwin, M.M. (No. 8), steward, of Melbourne.

[5] Baron von Richthofen, the famous German "ace," the machines of whose "circus" were painted red. He was killed in action on April 21, 1918. He is credited with 80 victims in his aerial fights.

loud Australian cheers, the admiration and sporting instincts of our men overcoming all political animosity.

On April 7 the battalion moved forward to Noreuil, relieving the 51st Battalion. The relief was not effected without casualties. As the 15th Platoon was making its way through a cutting it came under shell fire, losing three killed and 13 wounded, in addition to Sgt. A. G. Ansett[6] (orderly sergeant) killed. He was a good soldier, and had been wounded in the operations at Mouquet Farm in 1916. Sgt. Hugo F. S. Stach (No. 2650) was appointed orderly sergeant in his stead.

*Battalion Moves to Forward Area.*

*Sgt. Ansett Killed.*

The 14th was now facing the famous Hindenberg line, where the enemy had come to a standstill behind a position of enormous strength, designed by the best engineering talent in his army, and carried out largely by forced labour. The 16th Battalion was on our right, and the 46th on the left. Lieut.-Colonel Peck attended on the 7th a conference at brigade headquarters in reference to a proposed attack on the Hindenberg line.

The 14th Battalion at this period of its history was absolutely at its zenith, both in discipline and efficiency. It had then in its ranks the finest officers it ever had. It was ably commanded, strong numerically, highly trained, and almost bursting with vitality and confidence. What applied to the 14th Battalion also applied at that time to the whole 4th Brigade.[7] In Durrant, Peck, McSharry, and Brockman (C.O.'s respectively of the 13th, 14th, 15th, and 16th), the brigade had a quartette of C.O.'s that would be hard to beat in the A.I.F. The foundations and traditions of the brigade, in the first instance, too, had been well and truly laid by John Monash, who was to become world famous ere the war ended. It was now a magnificent fighting machine (probably unsurpassed on the Western front), with a long line of splendid achievements behind it, and required but one thing to utilise to the best advantage its magnificent vitality and confidence, viz., army leadership of a high order. That very necessary essential to success, however, was unfortunately denied to it, in this the climax of its fortunes, as the next chapter will show.

*Battalion at Zenith of Strength and Efficiency.*

*Splendid Efficiency of 4th Brigade.*

---

[6] Sgt. A. G. Ansett (No. 3229), of Clifton Hill (V.).

[7] Capt. T. A. White, in "The Fighting Thirteenth," emphasises the fact that, at that time, the 13th Battalion was never in its history in a higher state of efficiency.

## CHAPTER XXVIII.

### BATTLE OF BULLECOURT.

#### 1917—April 11.

The three days prior to the Battle of Bullecourt were spent in preparations and reconnaissances. The officers, knowing an engagement was to come off shortly, spent a lot of time viewing the country ahead. The continuous snowing (for the winter seemed as if it would never cease) made the half-completed trenches abodes of misery.

**Captain Jacka, Intelligence Officer.** Captain Jacka had been appointed Intelligence Officer, and his work was particularly good. Immediately on the 4th Brigade taking over the line, he discovered, by means of a night reconnaissance, that the sunken road situated about 300 yards north of the railway line was not held by the enemy, with the result that the 46th, 14th and 16th Battalions at 9 p.m. on April 8 occupied it. Patrols were sent out at night, and snipers during the day. Meanwhile the enemy kept very quiet, and was apparently not desirous of disclosing the strength of his position until it was attacked in force. The Battalion Staff was working at high pressure over the final preparations, and everything was completed to the smallest detail with a thoroughness that could not be surpassed. A general spirit of optimism prevailed—perfectly natural when the high state of efficiency of the Brigade is considered—and pleasure was felt that for the first time in France the Brigade was to make the proposed attack as a Brigade, and not piecemeal, as hitherto.

**Excellent Battalion Staff Work.**

Meanwhile on April 9 the long-expected British attack opened on the Third Army front at Arras, a few miles north of the 4th Brigade's position. Aided by a tremendous artillery preparation it had some initial success, and the news of this success, possibly exaggerated, seems to have influenced with undue optimism the Fifth British Army staff, under whose

**British Attack at Arras.**

orders the 4th Australian Division then was. At all events, as if struck by some sudden inspiration, that staff suddenly issued orders on the afternoon of April 9, to the headquarters of the 4th Australian Division, to be prepared to attack the Hindenburg line on its immediate front at 4.30 a.m. on the following morning. Previous orders were countermanded, and this attack was to dispense with direct artillery support, and to rely on the co-operation of twelve tanks, which were to precede the infantry, break down the enormous strands of barbed wire fronting the German defences, and generally to do the work usually assigned to the artillery. The extreme shortness of notice did not give the Australians time either to issue the necessary orders, or arrange for reconnaissances, or make the necessary administrative arrangements. It was only the excellent discipline and training of the Australian units that enabled the orders to be carried out in such a short time. The position to be attacked was one of enormous strength, whilst the few tanks, on which so much reliance was placed, were mechanically deficient, the crews were half trained and new to battle, had never co-operated with infantry, and there were far too few of them.[1] In addition, in order to reach the rendezvous in time to take part in the engagement, the tanks and their crews had to travel all night in a violent snow storm. The crews naturally arrived worn, tired out and dispirited. Clogged with all these disadvantages, the tanks were expected to work miracles. Briefly, "the tanks were employed in a manner continually condemned by every officer in the Tank Corps itself."[2]

*Order for Immediate Attack.*

*Artillery Support Dispensed With.*

*Tanks to be Utilised.*

*No Time to Make Proper Arrangements.*

*Deficiencies of Tanks and Crews.*

This company of tanks, too, had not only never co-operated with infantry in battle, but the infantry of the 4th and 12th Australian Brigades, earmarked for the engagement, had never co-operated with tanks, or even seen one in action. The 4th Brigade had every confidence in its ability to follow the orthodox mode of attack, i.e., a

*Infantry Never Co-operated with Tanks.*

---

[1] At Cambrai, in November, 1917, about 400 were employed. On this occasion there were only twelve.

[2] A quotation from one of the Tank historians in reference to the employment of the tanks in this battle, vide "The Tank in Action," by Capt. D. G. Brown, M.C., page 63.

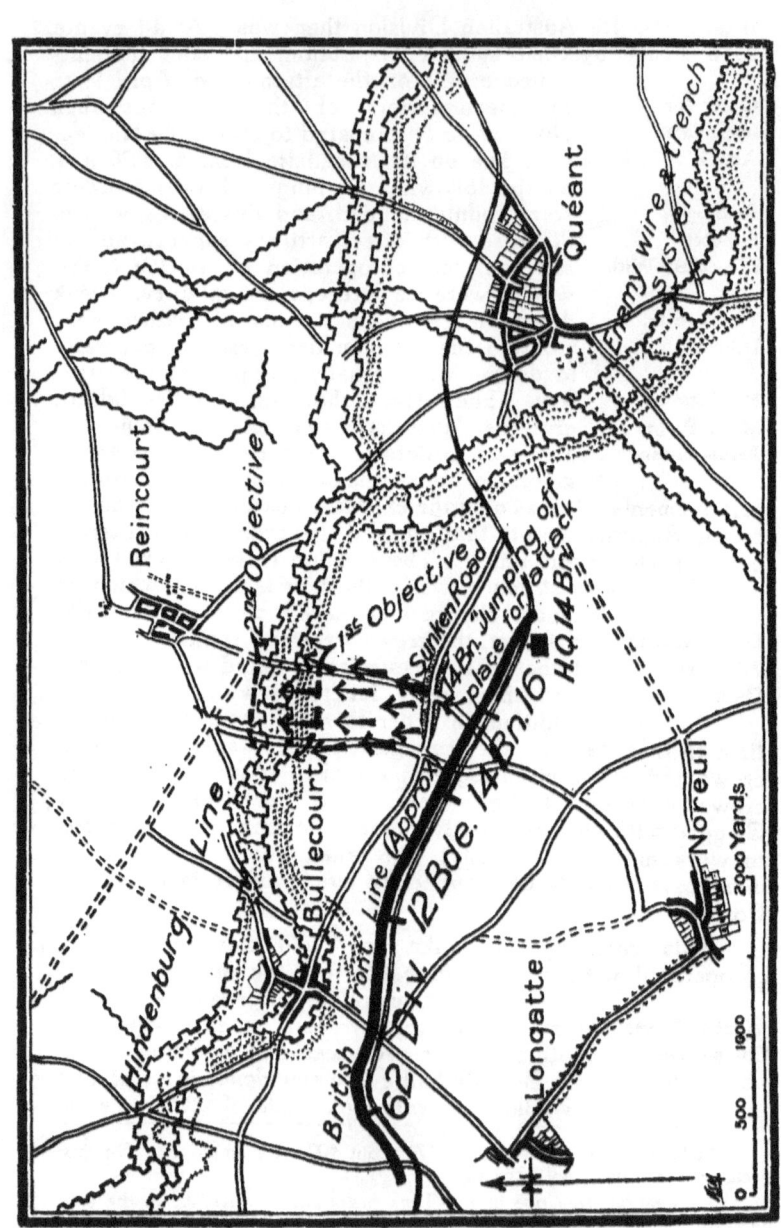

BATTLE OF BULLECOURT

barrage. "The 4th Brigade," it was said, "leans up against the barrage, and when it lifts, falls on the top of the enemy."

**Sudden Change of Plans Cause Irritation.**
The sudden alteration of all plans at the very last moment caused intense irritation. No one in authority among the Australians appears to have believed in the feasibility of the scheme, and protests are understood to have been lodged against it, but, if so, all to no purpose.

In co-operation with, and on the left of, the Australians was stationed an English Division (the 62nd). The part assigned to it in the battle was a comparatively subordinate one. It was not to attack until the Australians had cleared out the German front trenches, and some of the tanks, followed by an Australian Battalion, had reached Bullecourt and mopped it up. It was then to advance and assist the Australians to exploit their success. The tanks did not reach Bullecourt, so it necessarily remained quiescent. Its participation in the battle was therefore purely negligible. The Australians single-handed had "to do the trick."

**Subordinate Position Assigned to 62nd Division.**

**Attack Exposed on Both Flanks.**
The attack, contrary to military precedent, was to be pushed through on a narrow front, without support on either flank, except some desultory shelling, so that in addition to a tremendous frontal fire, the Australians in their advance were exposed to a terrific enfilade fire from Queant and Bullecourt which tore them to ribbons. Even if successful the result would have been merely a salient pushed into the enemy's line and liable to attack from three sides; it could have little hope of permanence. The strategical intention of General Gough and his advisers was doubtless to co-operate with the Third Army attack up at Arras, and by breaking through the Hindenburg line near Bullecourt capture thousands of prisoners between the two points. This was strategically sound—if the facts on which it was based had been correct—but even sound strategy is foredoomed to failure if the tactical factor be ignored, as it was in the present instance.

**Sound Strategy but Faulty Tactics.**

**Officers' Patrol**
An officers' patrol, consisting of Jacka (14th) and Bradley and Wadge (16th), set out on the night of the 9th to examine and report on the German wire opposite the 4th Brigade. A daring reconnaissance right inside the German wire led them to report that it was useless to attack the Hindenburg line without

artillery support, and until the wire was thoroughly cut; they also reported that the garrison of the Hindenburg line was very strong. What use was made of the report of those highly competent officers, is not known, but evidently little or no notice was taken of it. Jacka and Bradley on their return to our lines cleverly captured a Wurtemburg officer and his orderly patrolling No Man's Land quite close to the German wire. The officer proved recalcitrant, and Jacka had to adopt vigorous measures to induce him to accompany his captors.[3] When brought before Colonel Peck for examination the officer complained of the rough treatment he had received. The C.O. told him dryly that if he had been through Jacka's hands he could thank God he was still alive. Jacka received a bar to his M.C. (his third decoration) for his work at Bullecourt.

*German Officer Captured.*

Time was now getting on, and at midnight the companies converged on the hopping-off place, and got into their positions in four waves. Everybody was now calmly and confidently awaiting zero hour (4.45 a.m.). Conversation was carried on in hushed whispers, and many jokes were passed, for no conditions damp the Australian sense of humour. Patrols were meanwhile covering the 1000 yards between our men and their objective. The adjutant, an active and popular figure, passed up and down the line seeing that everything was right. The weather was bitterly cold, and as the night wore on everybody became somewhat quieter; the strain of waiting was beginning to tell. One unfortunate incident marred this long vigil. 2nd Lieut. N. McKenzie, returning from No Man's Land to our lines with his patrol, was mistakenly fired on by some of our Lewis gunners, and the Lieutenant and two of his men were severely wounded.

*14th on J.O.T.*

*2nd Lieut. McKenzie Wounded.*

The tanks were to lead the attack, and as zero hour approached, and there was not any sign of their appearance, all ears were strained listening for their advent. They had had a night journey to perform, and the time allotted to them by the Fifth Army Staff for its accomplishment having been too short, the shivering infantry listened in vain. The approaching daylight, however, did not wait, and as the first

*Non-arrival of Tanks.*

---

[3]The automatic pistol taken from this officer by Captain Jacka is now an exhibit at the Australian War Museum.

faint streaks of dawn raced across the leaden clouds, the adjutant arrived post haste from Battalion Headquarters with the order that, as the tanks could not get up in time, the proposed attack was cancelled, and for all to get back as best and as fast as they could to Noreuil. Cold, cramped, and stiff, feeling the reaction after being keyed up for hours to a concert pitch of expectation, all (except D Company, which remained all day at the sunken road) started back to the Noreuil Valley, just like a football crowd after a big match, cursing the tanks and everybody connected with them. All were intensely soured and disgusted. The bungling that had resulted in this grotesque fiasco was evident to everyone, and confidence in the higher leadership was badly shaken. It was due more to good luck than to good management that the retirement had not ended in an Australian shambles. Upwards of 4000 Australians (including the two battalions of the 12th Brigade on the left) were within easy artillery range of the Germans, in rapidly increasing daylight, when fortunately a heavy fall of snow occurred, rendering all objects indistinct, and enabling our men to get back with remarkably few casualties.

*Attack Cancelled.*

*Withdrawal of Battalion from J.O.T.*

*Confidence in Higher Leadership Lost.*

The enemy apparently saw the withdrawal,[4] and became aware that a formidable attack on his trenches had been intended, and for some purpose abandoned. As ever throughout the war, he profited by his experience, and, during the day, his immensely strong position was further strengthened by rushing up large numbers of storm troops, and increasing the number of his machine guns.

*Enemy. Warned and Strengthens His Position.*

The whole theory of the proposed assault had been that of a surprise attack, and now that the plan had been disclosed to the enemy, who was very much on the alert, it is difficult to understand why the Fifth Army Staff still persisted in ordering the attack to be carried out on the following morn-

*Renewal of Attack Ordered.*

---

[4]Some doubt has been expressed as to whether the Germans saw the withdrawal. They could hardly fail to do so, but Captain Dunworth (15th Battalion), Sgt. Dalitz (14th Battalion) and others taken prisoners in the battle were specifically informed by their captors that our withdrawal was seen, and the presence of the cavalry noted, and in consequence that their position was immensely strengthened both by storm troops and machine guns during the day. Vide also the evidence of Captain D. P. Wells, of the 13th Battalion (Captain T. A. White's "The Fighting Thirteenth," p. 100).

ing, under practically the same conditions, not even allowing the attacking infantry the protection of a barrage. During the day, the troops, who had all passed a sleepless and exhausting night in the snow, endeavoured to snatch a little rest. There were rumours (correct in this instance) that Colonel Peck was strongly against the attack. Some desultory shelling by the enemy occurred before the attack of next day, causing a few casualties, among them Sgt. A. C. Francis, the platoon sergeant of No. 14 Platoon, but in the main he laid low, not wishing to do anything to discourage the attack he saw imminent, and wished for, on his immensely strong position.

<small>Sgt. A. C. Francis Wounded.</small>

Towards evening, it became known to all that the attack was to be made the following morning. This meant that, for the second night in succession, and immediately before the bloodiest battle the Brigade was ever called upon to face, and when all required every ounce of strength and vigour, the troops were compelled to pass another night without sleep amidst their snow-clad surroundings. The 13th and 15th Battalions, in addition to two sleepless nights, had also to march, on April 10, to Favreuil and back, a distance of 16 miles over the snow, and only got back to the jumping-off tape just in time to begin the battle.

<small>Exhaustion of Personnel.</small>

At 3.30 a.m. the Battalion was again in position on the jumping-off tape, awaiting zero hour in the sunken road. The attack by the 4th Brigade was made on a frontage of about half a mile. As usual, enormous objectives were set. The first and second objectives (being respectively the first and second line of German trenches) were to be taken by the 14th and 16th Battalions, advancing side by side—the former on the left, the latter on the right. The 15th and 13th Battalions were to go through the 14th and 16th respectively, capture Riencourt, and finally take up a position in front of it, about 1500 yards distant from the first objective. A, B, C, and D Companies of the 14th advanced in that order from right to left. The advance was made in four "waves," each "wave" being represented by a platoon. The capture of the first objective was allotted to the first two waves, whilst the third and fourth waves had to take the second objective. There was from about two to three yards between each individual man, and

<small>Battalion on J.O.T.

Enormous Objectives Set.

Advance in Four Waves.</small>

Ribemont-sur Ancre

Deconinck Farm (Messines)
(Australian War Museum Official Photo.)

## The History of the 14th Battalion.

about twenty yards between each separate wave. Sgt. D. W. Blackburn's Lewis gunners went over with the second wave, whilst four trench-mortars were detailed to support the Brigade attack. The 4th Machine Gun Company, too, took a very active and honorable part in the battle. Some British cavalry was also at hand to ride down the fleeing Germans and exploit the Australians' success. On the left of the 4th Brigade two battalions of the 12th A.I.F. Brigade (the 46th and 48th) attacked, but their attack was not made contiguous to the 4th Brigade, a gap of 400 yards being left between the two brigades, which the Germans held during the whole battle, and from where they were enabled to enfilade both brigades.

*Gap Left in Advance.*

The 14th Battalion Headquarters was situated in the railway cutting alongside that of the 16th, with the 13th a little further away. The 14th Regimental Aid Post was also in the railway cutting. The following is the list of 14th Battalion officers who took part in the attack. It will be noted that only three officers taking part in the assault got back to the Battalion unwounded, and that ten officers (including three captains) were killed in action or died of wounds.

*Battalion Headquarters and Aid Post.*

*Battalion Officers in the Attack.*

A Company—O.C., Capt. W. R. Wadsworth; Lieut. F. H. Dadson, K.I.A.; 2nd-Lieut. E. J. L. Edmonds, P.W.; 2nd-Lieut. A. J. Harris, D.W. B Company—O.C., Capt. F. B. Stanton, K.I.A.; 2nd-Lieut. G. H. Clarendon-Hyde, 2nd-Lieut. M. O'Donnell, K.I.A.; 2nd-Lieut. R. E. Hayes, 2nd-Lieut. L. H. Mullett, K.I.A. C Company—O.C., Capt. A. Williamson, K.I.A.; Lieut. F. W. Appleton, W.; Lieut. Peter McCallum, W. and P.W.; 2nd-Lieut. W. J. G. Lyon, P.W.; Lieut. O. C. D. Gower, W. and P.W. D Company—O.C., Capt. R. W. Orr, K.I.A.; 2nd-Lieut. S. B. Thompson, K.I.A.; 2nd-Lieut. N. McKenzie, W.; Lieut. J. A. Mitchell, W.; Lieut. N. Kent, D.W.; Lieut. A. J. McQuiggan, W. and P.W. Headquarters—Lieut.-Col. J. H. Peck, C.O.; Capt. H. B. Wanliss, D.S.O., Adjutant; Capt. A. Jacka, V.C., M.C., Intelligence Officer; Lieut. H. R. McKinley, Assistant I.O., D.W.; Lieut. J. Craven, D.C.M., Signalling Officer, W.; Capt. D. R. Macdermid, O.C. Carrying Party; 2nd-Lieut. F. Anderson, M.M., Transport Officer; Major W. M. A. Fletcher, Medical Officer; Capt. F. W. Rolland, Chaplain.

Zero hour (4.45 a.m.) was now rapidly approaching. The tanks finally advanced emitting showers of sparks, and making so much noise that their advent must have become known to the enemy. Artillery fire sufficient to deaden their noise had been asked for by the Brigadier, and promised, but was not forthcoming. It may be said, briefly, that the optimism of General Gough and his staff in reference to the tanks was not shared by the majority of the tank officers themselves. Six tanks[5] were allotted to the 4th Brigade, but three of them were out of action before the battle opened—accidents, engine trouble, and other reasons being assigned. One tank only reached the first objective (and that after the infantry had been some time engaged), and did good work, but was almost immediately put out of action by direct hits from a gun at Riencourt. Though the tanks were, consequently, not of any direct assistance to the 4th Brigade, in breaking down the wire, they were tempting targets, and certainly attracted a great deal of enemy machine-gun fire, which would otherwise have been concentrated on the infantry. To that extent, they doubtless assisted the passage of the infantry through the wire. The latter, confronted with a practically impossible task, now knew that, without direct assistance of any kind whatever, it had to face the problem alone.

*Failure of Tanks.*

While the Brigade was waiting for zero hour in the sunken road, the Germans scored one distinct success. Sandwiched between the 14th and 16th Battalions were two of the four trench-mortars and their crews, allotted to the Brigade for the battle. About ten minutes before zero, a 9.2 German shell, from the direction of Queant, landed right in their midst, blotting out almost the whole personnel of the battery, and killing and wounding several of the 14th and 16th men adjacent. This shell caused between thirty and forty casualties, and put the two trench-mortars completely out of action.[6] Shortly prior to this, the assistant Intelligence Officer (Lieut. H. R. McKinley) had been mortally wounded by the explosion of a shell, the concussion of which hurled the I.O. (Capt. Jacka) off his feet.

*Trench-mortar Crew Blotted Out.*

It was a bitterly cold morning, and snow had just commenced to fall, when "one minute to go" was passed along the line. Mates gripped hands, a murmured "Good luck, old man!" and then the order to advance.[7] There were about

---

[5]Captain Jacka had been detailed to advise and assist the tank officers with his expert knowledge gained by intelligence work. He was assiduous in his efforts to help them, but his advice was disregarded by some of the tank officers, with disastrous results.

[6]Communicated by Captain Jacka, who was a spectator of the incident.

[7]Friendships formed under those conditions are perhaps the strongest human tie that binds men together.

1000 yards to reach the first objective; there was not any cover —the ground was as flat as a billiard table. Unprotected by a barrage, the attacking force was absolutely at the enemy's mercy until it reached his wire; there could not be any retaliation until it got to grips with its opponent; the first problem was how many would survive to do so.

It was a magnificent sight—those four long perfect lines of matchless Australian infantry, advancing in the semi-twilight over the snow-covered ground, in perfect order, and as steadily as if on parade, but with a certain deliberate grimness that boded ill for their opponents. The 4th was a national and not a State Brigade; every State in the Commonwealth was represented in those long lines of brave men. They were the choicest flower of Australian manhood. All went well for the first 300 yards; then the sky was lit up by a marvellous display of fireworks—thousands of rockets of every description and colour flashed through the heavens. Our advance had been discovered; it was Fritz's S.O.S. call to his artillery. It was now 4.50 a.m. The first Battle of Bullecourt had opened.

*Splendid Spirit of the Personnel.*

*Fritz's S.O.S. Signal.*

The Germans got to work with a promptitude that showed that the attack was expected, and opened out with every shot in their armoury. Their artillery got busy, the boom of guns and the shriek of shells growing ever louder and more incessant. It was both frontal and enfilade. Men were hurled in all directions as shells burst in their midst. An immense number of machine guns, many of them admirably sited in dominant positions, vomited blizzards of lead into our ranks. This fire at first was rather high, but as the advance proceeded it grew hotter and more deadly, and men were falling in all directions; the snow was dotted with their bodies. Nearing the German lines, too, hordes of their infantry could be seen, confident in their security behind their wire, and undisturbed by our artillery, standing shoulder to shoulder and waist high over their parapet picking off our men like rabbits. Meanwhile two 14th officers never reached the first objective. Capt. R. W. Orr on the left was wounded when about 300 yards from our lines, and taking refuge in a shell hole was there subsequently killed by an enemy's

*German Artillery Opens.*

*Advance Through a Hail of Lead.*

*Captain Orr Killed.*

## Battle of Bullecourt.

**Lieut. Dadson Killed.**
whizbang. Lieut. F. H. Dadson on the right fell dead from a machine gun bullet just before reaching the German wire.

D Company on the extreme left of the Brigade, and on its exposed flank, perhaps had the hardest task of all. It encountered in the advance some opposition from a German "listening post," but that was soon disposed of, and several prisoners captured there were sent to the rear, but the majority were killed by their own machine-gun fire. As the advance proceeded, D Company came under a half flank, as well as a direct fire, and could not advance so quickly as the centre, which calmly paused amidst the hail of lead, on more than one occasion, to enable the alignment to be corrected, displaying under these nerve-racking conditions a steadiness and coolness that could not have been excelled on the parade ground. Nothing could have been finer than this advance—terrific punishment to which there was no means of responding—being taken without flinching. It reflected the highest traditions of our race. "It was magnificent—but it was not war."[8] With great gaps in their ranks, terribly bruised and mauled, the survivors were now rapidly approaching the tremendous belt of wire entanglements which protected the German front trenches. It was about 60 or 70 feet wide, breast high, with enormous protruding one-inch barbs, and so thick that anyone lying down could not see through it, and was also admirably sited so as to enable the German machine-gunners to fire along its fringe. The wire in places had been sufficiently destroyed by certain shell-bursts to enable the passage to be made. Otherwise, the gaps were few and far between, consisting of sally-ports of a corkscrew shape, through which one had to make his way in and out. Machine-guns concentrated their fire on these gaps, so that many lost their lives attempting to get through them.

**Nerve and Heroism Displayed in Advance.**

**Heavy Casualties Incurred.**

**Tremendous Strength of German Front Belt of Wire.**

When about 30 yards distant from the enemy's wire, a swing was made for the gaps, where numbers of our men fell under the deadly concentrated machine-gun fire. Those who got through were at last at grips with the enemy, and they rushed at and sprang into the trench facing them. Pockets

**German Wire Rushed.**

---

[8] A phrase used by a French officer in reference to the Balaclava Charge.

## The History of the 14th Battalion.

of Germans in places disputed possession, and a fierce hand-to-hand conflict took place which was speedily decided in our favour—as ever throughout the war when it came to close quarter fighting. Our Mills bombs did deadly work in those close contests. Several prisoners were sent to the rear but they were shot down, apparently intentionally, by their own machine guns. The surviving Germans scuttled like rabbits through their communication trenches to their second line. The first objective was ours. D Company, owing to its exposed left flank, had suffered probably most severely of all. Platoon Sgt. C. H. Mayer, on the extreme left of the Brigade, rushed through the wire, followed by about a dozen men—the sole survivors of his platoon, No. 16—and was soon severely wounded after killing a German at close quarters. Many more men were casualties before the first trench was cleared. Lieuts. J. A. Mitchell[9] and A. J. McQuiggan, together with the veteran Sgt. Urie (all of D Company) and Lieuts. Peter McCallum and O. C. D. Gower (of C Company) were here severely wounded and put out of action. Four trench-mortars had been allotted to the Fourth Brigade to co-operate, but only one reached the first objective. It accompanied D Company on the extreme left. It was now about 5.15 a.m. In that eventful first half-hour No Man's Land had been crossed, and the first objective taken; the work and conduct of all had been beyond praise, but the price paid had been heavy. A large proportion of the Battalion had been put out of action. The first phase of the battle was over.

*First Objective Captured.*

*First Phase of Battle Completed.*

As the above struggle in the first objective was nearing completion, the 15th Battalion in support came rapidly into the battle, and the survivors of the two units, now intermixed, rushed up the communication trenches, and attacked the second objective. Captain Stanton, leaving 2nd-Lieut. R. E. Hayes (2nd in command of B Company) with Company Headquarters at the first objective, gallantly called on his men to follow, and, whilst setting a splendid example, fell, shot dead shortly after. The second objective was also protected by heavy belts of intact barbed wire, unbroken except for certain passages left for patrols.

*Advent of 15th Battalion.*

*Attack on Second Objective.*

*Capt. Stanton Killed.*

---

[9]Lieuts. Mitchell and F. W. Appleton, though wounded, managed to crawl back about 1200 yards through the snow to our lines, and thus avoided capture.

## Battle of Bullecourt.

Some of our men sought desperately to clamber over the top, springing from strand to strand. Numbers were killed in this way, and lay hanging on the barbs. The fighting was very severe, and every available man was pushed up from the first objective to assist. Many futile acts of heroism were now performed by brave men who sought by the reckless sacrifice of their own lives to atone for the faults of the Higher Leadership. Capt. "Lofty" Williamson was mortally wounded in this struggle, and 2nd-Lieuts. Mullett, O'Donnell and Thompson killed, while some of the finest N.C.O.'s and men in the Battalion became casualties. Finally the second objective was captured, but at a heavy cost, the enemy's machine guns and snipers causing severe losses. All units, too, had become much mixed up in the confused and chaotic fighting that had taken place. It was now about 6.45 a.m., and the second phase of the battle was over.

*Heavy Fighting.*

*Capt. Williamson and 2nd Lieuts. Mullet, O'Donnell and Thompson Killed.*

*Second Objective Captured.*

Somewhat of a pause occurred after the taking of the second objective. Our men, exhausted by their stupendous efforts, and weakened by their heavy losses, set about consolidating their gains, whilst the Germans, startled by the impetuosity and fury of the assault, and the desperate character of their assailants were concentrating their reinforcements, and getting ready to organise counter-attacks. They had the inestimable advantage, too, of being undisturbed by artillery fire at this critical period of the battle. Though the first two objectives had been captured, much more remained to be done before the task set the 4th Brigade had been accomplished. The third objective was Riencourt, whose capture was destined for the 15th and 13th Battalions. These units, however, had been badly cut up assisting the 14th and 16th to capture the first two objectives, and the decimated Brigade now had that difficult problem to face. Riencourt was crammed with storm troops, backed up by numerous machine guns, and the few surviving Australian officers intuitively recognised that the task—in their present weakened condition—was far beyond their powers, and that the most they could hope for was the consolidation and retention of what had already been captured. Every effort was accordingly made for that purpose. The two objectives captured were like a rabbit warren, a bewildering combination of trenches, dugouts, communication trenches, and secret tunnels

*Third Objective Not Yet Taken.*

*Efforts at Consolidation.*

perfectly well known to their opponents, but a terra incognita to the captors. It could not be held strongly, for the attacking force was now too weak, but blocks were put in, fire steps cut, and machine guns hoisted into favourable positions. Some of these guns got an enfilade fire on enemy reinforcements streaming into Riencourt, and cut them up severely. Every effort, too, was made to get in our wounded, numbers of whom were lying out in the open, and place them in safety in the deep dugouts. Large numbers of the regimental stretcher-bearers had been shot down, and many men now acted as volunteer bearers; it was dangerous work, and many were killed attempting to succour wounded comrades. Captain H. Murray, V.C., of the 13th, became henceforth a kind of unofficial O.C. of the second objective, and was ubiquitous, visiting all parts of the Brigade front, giving advice and suggestions, besides posting men and guns.

*Efforts to Succour Wounded.*

*Capt. Murray, V.C., Organises Second Objective.*

He then sent back to Headquarters a message asking for artillery support. In spite of the appalling odds in front, there were small bodies of resolute men determined on pushing on. Capt. David Dunworth, of the 15th Battalion, after despatching a message to Headquarters by pigeon, advanced towards Riencourt, followed by a handful of 14th and 15th Battalion men.[10] He fell severely wounded close to that village, and the brave handful following him were all killed by machine gun fire—it being concentrated on them till they were all dead. That was probably the furthest organised advance made by the 4th Brigade that day.[11] All efforts to reach Riencourt, however, proved unavailing. It only ended in the destruction of all who made the attempt. The effort was beyond our strength.

*Capt. Dunworth's Effort to Reach Riencourt.*

When the above desperate struggle was taking place the Germans deluged No Man's Land for hours with missiles of every description right back to the cutting. One shell about 7 a.m. landed on the 13th Battalion Headquarters, causing numerous casualties, whilst another struck the 14th

*Germans Barrage No Man's Land.*

---

[10] It is regretted that the names of these brave men are not known.

[11] This recalls the advance of Lieut. Leslie Luscombe also with a handful of 14th and 15th Battalion men on August 8, 1915. Vide Chap. 10.

*14th Battalion Headquarters Hit.* Headquarters, putting out the lights, but fortunately without causing any casualties. The enfilade machine-gun fire, too, in this area was so severe that hardly anyone could pass through it. Two 15th Battalion carrying parties attempting to take ammunition and bombs to the front were absolutely blotted out, not one returning. Dumps had been formed in the forward area for transmission of ammunition to the fighting men, but Col. Peck, realising the futility of such attempts, refused to squander his men's lives in the effort.

The result of this barrage was that the hard pressed fighting men were cut off from any hope of reinforcements or ammunition. They had been heedlessly pushed into a trap—one of the most cleverly conceived and elaborately constructed traps on the whole western front—and had now been fought to a standstill, with the Germans on three sides of them in greatly superior numbers, their retreat cut off, and their supply of ammunition running dangerously low. The position could not have been more serious. The Germans had, in addition to all their other advantages, greatly superior numbers, an unlimited supply of munitions and material, intimate local knowledge, together with knowledge of the time and place of the attack—the assistance of heavy and continuous artillery support—a support which was completely lacking all day to our hard-pressed troops. Eighteen times had the S.O.S. signal for artillery assistance been sent up by our men. It was either not seen or disregarded—probably the former. Urgent messages for assistance, too, were got through by Murray (13th), Wadsworth (14th), and Dunworth (15th). Fourth Brigade Headquarters was thoroughly convinced of the critical position at the front, but the 4th Division Artillery group officers were misled by, and preferred to believe, the reports of the British Flying Corps to direct evidence from the front line, and refused to co-operate. The flying men reported that the "Australians had taken Riencourt," and that "two tanks, followed by cheering Australians, are going towards Hendicourt." No Australians got within 100 yards of Riencourt except as prisoners, and none of the tanks ever got within miles of Hendicourt. Rosenthal's

*Barrage Cuts Off Supplies of Ammunition from Front Line.*

*Serious Position.*

*Shortage of Ammunition.*

*Failure of Our Artillery to Co-operate.*

*Grotesque Reports of the R.F.C.*

forward observing officer, too, reported Australians in Riencourt. In short there was not that intimate collaboration between the infantry and artillery which had been so much in evidence at Stormy Trench on the previous February 5. There had not been time in this engagement to make proper administrative arrangements.

*Lack of Collaboration Between Infantry and Artillery.*

The third phase of the battle now commenced. The Germans, realising that the attack had come to a standstill, and recognising the numerical weakness of their opponents, set to work to organise counter-attacks, working down the communication trenches, and utilising the exposed left flank of the Brigade. The enemy bombing attacks were met with great spirit by our men, Cpl. Charles Thompson (Original), Ptes. H. J. Lamprell, F. Barker (Original), F. H. G. Bowell, J. J. Casson, and many others doing great work under severe retaliation. All their attacks were beaten off with heavy loss, but the Australians were melting away under the continuous showers of bombs, whilst the enemy had unlimited supplies of men and munitions at his disposal. Our bombs were running dangerously short, and though some were collected from the dead and wounded, the supply was painfully inadequate. Between 10 and 11 a.m. the German attacks became stronger, and Capt. Wadsworth, the senior battalion officer in the line, instructed C.S.M. W. Boland to send a messenger acquainting Battalion Headquarters with the serious position at the front. Three runners in succession made the attempt, but all were killed crossing No Man's Land.[12] Boland then courageously undertook the perilous job himself, and by a miracle got through. He was awarded the M.C. for his gallantry, being one of the first (if not the first) warrant-officer in the A.I.F. to receive that decoration.

*Third Phase of Battle Commences.*

*German Counter-attacks.*

*C.S.M. Boland Carries a Message Through No Man's Land.*

Meanwhile, the 46th Battalion (of the 12th Brigade on the left), about 11.30 a.m. could be seen retiring and being cut to pieces by machine-gun fire in the process. This enabled the enemy to bring extra pressure on the 4th Brigade. There is no need to dwell on the death agony of the battle. As long as our ammunition lasted the enemy was

*Retirement of 46th Battalion.*

---

[12] It is regretted that the names of these men are unknown. Compare Geoffrey Veal's sacrifice on August 22, 1915. Vide Chap. 12.

driven back. Even when almost defenceless, men—rallied by their officers and N.C.O.'s—fought on when all hope had fled. The Germans, after a terrific machine-gun barrage, which played up and down the trenches for several minutes, and tore inches off the parados, made an attempt to bomb up the first objective in the endeavour to cut off those in the second objective. That was frustrated with a final effort (many of our men coming back from the second objective to assist, though some were cut off in the attempt), but ammunition was now used up. There were only bayonets to rely on. Ardent Australians then attempted to go along the top and get at the enemy with the bayonet, but were immediately cut down by machine-gun fire. 16th Battalion men speak with admiration of a 14th Battalion corporal who acted like a superman this day.[13] No one knows his name, but a man of that character was not likely to have survived the fight. 2nd-Lieut. Norman Kent, one of the few surviving officers, was mortally wounded about this time. Many acts of heroism were now performed, of which no record remains. Enemy snipers lying in the open were picking off our defenceless men like pigeons, and man after man was shot without any chance of retaliation. The wires were covered with dead Australians hanging on them like clothes pegs, while the snow was stained with pools of blood. The Germans now swarmed in on all sides, and little pockets of unarmed Australians found themselves surrounded by armed enemies, leaving them no alternative but surrender. It was now about 11.45 a.m., and the order was given to retire. Those who could, discarded equipment, and, bolting back through the wire, made an effort to reach our lines, but large numbers were cut down in No Man's Land by the merciless machine-gun fire, and more casualties were added to the already appalling list.

*Australian Ammunition Exhausted.*

*Futile Attempts with the Bayonet.*

*An Unknown Hero.*

*2nd Lieut. Kent Mortally Wounded.*

*Awful Scenes.*

*Order to Retire.*

Mention must now be made of the work of the Battalion Lewis gunners, whose exploits on this day have seldom been surpassed on the battlefield. They were picked men, ably handled, and their work was superb. Fighting all day with reckless courage, they at times cut the enemy up

*Battalion Lewis Gunners.*

---

[13]Communicated by Lieut. E. J. Rule, of C Company. Some think this unknown hero was J. T. Jenkins, whose work throughout the whole day was superb.

severely, held him long at bay, frequently gave the co-operating infantry breathing space, and when the end came, in a magnificent spirit of self-sacrifice remained for

**Superb Work.** five minutes after their comrades had retreated and, with a small stock of ammunition which had been carefully reserved for this crisis, mowed down the enemy in his hour of triumph.   The locks were then taken out of most of the guns, and the few surviving gunners, almost encircled by enemies, rushed through a tornado of machine gun and rifle fire, following the infantry back to our lines.   Pte. Wm. Amor, endeavouring to carry back his gun, had the radiator pierced with a piece of shrapnel, and the butt knocked off.   About 80 per cent. of the Lewis gunners were casualties before the battle ended.   Sgt. A. A. Hore, L/Cpl. Joe Bamford (Camperdown, V.), and Ptes. Wm. Amor (Ballarat), Merl Cartledge (Ballarat), H. Finger (Wantirna, V.), J. T. Jenkins (Canterbury, V.), and several others fought heroically.   Very few got back.

As there was a danger of the Germans following up their success by a vigorous counter-attack which might have swept everything before it, Colonel Peck

**Adjutant Rallies** instructed the Adjutant to rally and organise
**Survivors.** the survivors in the cutting, which that energetic officer did forthwith, gathering together a few score of men prepared to fight to the last; the expected counter-attack, however, did not eventuate.

The work of the signallers during the engagement was naturally circumscribed, owing to its unfortunate termination. About five minutes before zero hour on April

**The Signallers.** 10, the Battalion signaller on duty received a message cancelling operations for the day. Prior to the advance on the 11th, telephone lines were laid from Battalion Headquarters to the jumping-off position, and signallers J. T. Gifford and R. V. Gubby were detailed as telephonist and linesman respectively, to follow the fourth wave and maintain communication during the advance. Touch was kept with Headquarters until the first belt of barbed wire was reached, but the outcome of the

**Lieut. Craven** battle was such that the efforts of the signallers
**and Sgt. Pellett** were rendered nugatory. Lieut. J. Craven and
**Wounded.** Sgt. "Curly" Pellett were wounded prior to the hop over.

The medical personnel of the Battalion had a tremendous strain thrown upon it during the battle. The regimental aid

**Location of the R.A.P.**

post was located on April 11 in the railway cutting, a rough shelter having been built from old railway sleepers by Cpl. T. Carberry and L/Cpl. A. J. A'Court, assisted by a regimental fatigue party. Here the R.M.O. (Major W. M. A. Fletcher) worked all day like a Trojan, under most dangerous and difficult conditions, assisted by Carberry and A'Court, and Ptes. Giroud and Patten. Chaplain Rolland, too, distributed cocoa alongside the R.A.P. to the wounded, either awaiting dressing or evacuation to the Field Ambulance. The 14th regimental stretcher-bearers were among the finest in the A.I.F., and on this occasion they more than upheld their high reputation. All day long (both during and after the battle) they worked indefatigably, and with an absolute disregard for their own safety, attending to and carrying the wounded. Many paid the penalty for their courage and devotion. Among some whose work was outstanding may be mentioned Ptes. Wm. Watson, Wm. Porter (an Original twice wounded on the Peninsula, and again in this battle), "Darkey" Rowse, "Tales" Alexander, S. A. Markham, Robert Seaborne, and L/Cpl. John Snuggs, in charge of C Company squad of bearers, and who, refusing to leave the wounded, was captured and taken prisoner. After the battle the Germans showed consideration to many of the wounded, and allowed some of the worst cases to be removed to our lines. Reference must be made to the work of Lieut. Julien, of the 52nd Battalion, who lent valuable aid organising stretcher parties, and seeing that none of the wounded were left out in the snow.

**The R.M.O. and His Assistants.**

**Superb Work of Regimental S.B.'s.**

About 12 noon our artillery (which had been silent almost all day), at length opened fire, though about half an hour too late to effectively cover the retreat. A heavy barrage was put down on the position our men had lately occupied. Its immediate result was to kill a large number of our severely wounded men who were lying out in the snow, and to render casualties many of our unwounded who had just been taken prisoners. It was the last ghastly tragedy suffered by our much-tried men that day. However, it kept the Germans down, and allowed some of our men who were late retiring to get back. It began snowing in the afternoon, causing untold tortures to the wounded who happened to be still in the open.

**Artillery at Last Opens Fire.**

**Its Immediate Result.**

During the afternoon some of the 13th Brigade took over

## The History of the 14th Battalion.

*Survivors March to Noreuil Valley.*

*Germans Shell Valley.*

*Headquarters Dugout Demolished.*

*March to Beaugnetre.*

the front line, and the survivors of the Battalion were sent on to Noreuil Valley. Even there their troubles were not over, as the valley was heavily shelled by the enemy, and most of the cooks and their assistants became casualties, whilst Sgt. A. McLellan (Original), one of the Battalion's best N.C.O.'s, was mortally wounded. Late in the afternoon Colonel Peck, with the staff and surviving officers, followed the rest back to Noreuil. The Headquarters dugout had been barely vacated when it was demolished by a direct hit from a German shell. After reaching Noreuil orders were issued for the survivors to march back to Beaugnetre. There has seldom been a more melancholy march. The distance was only four or five miles, but it was snowing all the time; officers and men had had two successive nights without sleep, and in addition had just survived a bloody and disastrous battle.

*Absolute Exhaustion of All.*

Everyone was absolutely exhausted, and it was only by the greatest effort of will that the destination was finally reached. Here the Battalion rested till next day, when it marched to Bapaume, and entrained for Albert, and thence to Mametz.

So ended the Battle of Bullecourt, the most disastrous, the most bloody, yet perhaps the most glorious day in the history of the 4th Brigade. Four Australian battalions,

*Battle Disastrous but Glorious.*

*Wonderful Effort of 4th Brigade.*

after two sleepless nights, with only rifles and bombs to rely on, advanced nearly three-quarters of a mile over absolutely open country, under hellish frontal and enfilade fire, forced their way through wire, seized the famous Hindenburg line, and, though cut off from reinforcements or assistance of any kind, held it without artillery support for seven hours, repelling innumerable counter-attacks from a far more numerous enemy, backed up by a powerful artillery. Even then it was only against unarmed men that the enemy gained any success, for it was the failure of our ammunition that finally led to the evacuation of the position. Never was the morale of the 4th Brigade so high, never did its personnel fight better. Bullecourt will ever remain an imperishable monument to the heroism, the fortitude, and the unflinching hardihood of the Australian race. As a mere feat of arms there was not anything

*Nothing Finer in the War.*

finer in the war. It bears in many of its aspects a strong resemblance to probably the finest infantry charge of last century, that of Pickett's magnificent Virginian Division at Gettysburg on July 3, 1863, with which, in its heroic features, it may be not unfairly bracketed. Australians will be content to leave it at that.

*Compared to Pickett's Charge at Gettysburg.*

The fighting effort of the troops, too, was backed up by Battalion staff work of the finest quality. Colonel Peck's grasp and thoroughness throughout were efficiency personified, whilst the gallantry, energy, and capacity of Capts. A. Jacka (I.O.), H. B. Wanliss (Adjt.), and D. R. Macdermid (O.C., Carrying Party) were of the highest order.

*Fine Battalion Staff Work.*

Officially, the loss of the battle was attributed principally to the failure of the tanks, but the real cause lay deeper than that. It was the extraordinary optimism of the Fifth Army Staff in depending solely on the success of the operation upon an experiment with them, and the entirely inadequate conception of that staff of the magnitude of the task in hand. The whole plan seems to have been based on numerous misconceptions, and was evidently the handiwork of someone dominated, not by reason, but by impulse. The decision to persist in the attack on April 11, under the same original conditions after the fiasco of the previous day, was a lamentable and unfortunate error of judgment, entailing most disastrous consequences. It seems inexplicable, and can only be explained as another example of that intense spirit of optimism which permeated British leadership throughout the whole war, and which seemed almost always immune to the many and bitter fruits of experience. Though the battle was splendidly fought, it was crudely planned.[14]

*Official Reasons for Failure.*

*The True Reason.*

The result of the battle was carefully camouflaged by the military authorities (the press being muzzled during the war by the censorship), and even to this day knowledge of its incidents may be said to be practically limited to those who participated in it. The British histories of the war pass

*Result of Battle Camouflaged.*

---

[14]The reader is referred to "A Company of Tanks," by Major Watson, for an inside picture of the battle.

**Reference in Field-Marshal's Despatch.**

it over with the barest references, and Field-Marshal Haig's despatch covering it, refers to "the Australian and West Riding Battalions[15] engaged showed great gallantry in executing a very difficult task across a wide extent of open country."

The Germans naturally did not conceal their exultation at the destruction of the Brigade which had dealt them so many staggering blows, and which they feared as they feared few brigades on the Western Front. Their morale was naturally greatly strengthened by such a victory. Bullecourt was but one of many battles in which the Australians participated during the war which never should have been fought, as the attacking forces were matched against odds which made success impossible.

**Battle Should Not Have Been Fought.**

The losses of the 4th Brigade in this battle were appalling, for its valour had been quenched in blood, and but few of the personnel remained. Its casualties for the battle were set out officially as:—

**Official Brigade Losses.**

| Unit. | Officers. | Other Ranks. |
| --- | --- | --- |
| 13th Battalion .. .. .. | 21 | 546 |
| 14th Battalion .. .. .. | 19 | 582 |
| 15th Battalion .. .. .. | 20 | 380 |
| 16th Battalion .. .. .. | 13 | 623 |
| 4th M.G. Company .. | 5 | 99 |
| 4th A.L.T.M. Bty. .. .. | 1 | 30 |
| Total | 79 | 2260 |

Only nine officers of the four battalions got back unwounded, or slightly wounded, viz.: Murray, Parsonage, and Rose, of the 13th; Wadsworth, Hayes and Clarendon-Hyde, of the 14th; and Kerr, Burrows, and Aarons, of the 16th. All officers in the 15th were casualties, and only 52 O.R.'s got back. The greatest individual loss in the Brigade that day was that of Major Percy Black, D.S.O., the outstanding hero of the 16th Battalion, who was killed near the second objective. "None fell that day with more glory, yet many fell and there was much glory." A Victorian

**Death of Major Percy Black.**

---

[15] It has already been pointed out that the participation of the West Riding Battalions (i.e., 62nd Division) in the battle was contemplative only.

by birth, he was a marvellous fighter, and must be bracketed with Jacka and Murray for daring and resource.[16]

This fatal battle was responsible for the deaths of almost twenty-five per cent. of the officers, and fifteen per cent. of the other ranks, who lost their lives in the 14th during the war. Among the fatal officer casualties were Capt. "Lofty" Williamson, a lion-hearted man of magnificent physique, and who though always prominent in action was one of the undecorated heroes of the Battalion; Lieut. F. H. Dadson (Original), an Englishman with a varied career, and South African War experience; 2nd-Lieut. Gus Harris (Original), was the original stretcher-bearer sergeant at Broadmeadows. Modest and unassuming in bearing, he was absolutely fearless, and remarkably efficient. The Battalion stretcher-bearers owed their exceptional efficiency largely to his training. 2nd-Lieut. Norman Kent (Original) combined high principles with fine soldierly instincts.

**Officers' Killed.**

Among the N.C.O.'s killed was Platoon-Sgt. Raymond Jones (Original of A Company), a brother of Capt. Reg. Jones, who had had a marvellous escape from death at Quinn's Post; the veteran Platoon-Sgt. "Jock" Urie, D.C.M., of D Company; L/Sgt. J. McRae, D.C.M., of C Company; Platoon-Sgt. C. F. Ross (A Company), one of the bravest and most capable N.C.O.'s that the Battalion ever had; Sgt. A. E. Schultz, killed attempting to rescue the wounded; Sgt. R. H. Berry (Original), of C Company; Sgt. R. S. Blamey (Original), of B Company, who was both popular and efficient; Platoon-Sgt. F. Collins (D Company); L/Sgt. A. S. Glen (Original), of A Company; Sgt. R. N. S. McDonald; Sgt. W. J. Orr; L/Sgt. R. H. Catterson (D Company), and Sgt. L. Ridge; Cpl. A. L. Whitfield (Original), L/Cpl. L. Coward (a fine athlete), L/Cpl. J. B. Le Brun, Cpl. J. H. Moir (B Company), Cpl. Storer (A Company), Cpl. C. B. Postlewaite, L/Cpl. P. E. Greene (a theological student), Cpl. R. Jones (A Company clerk), and L/Cpl. Bott (the Battalion's well-known debater). Among those who had not attained non-commissioned rank were Ptes. J. Stewart (Original), of D Company; P. W. Lewis (whose brother, Sgt. Lewis, had been killed at Pozieres), A. Markham, K. N. McNamee, M.M. (Company runner), and Wm. Isbel

**N.C.O.'s Killed.**

---

[16] If there was any other brigade in the A.I.F. (or out of it) which contained three greater fighting men than Harry Murray of the 13th, Albert Jacka of the 14th, and Percy Black of the 16th, it is unknown to the author.

(Original), whose athletic prowess secured the presentation cup for F Company at the Battalion sports held at Broadmeadows on October 21, 1914.[17] Many of these no less by their lives than by the manner of their deaths had formed those high traditions which are bound up in the history of the 14th. It is to be hoped that the memory of them and their exploits will never be forgotten by a grateful country.

Bullecourt was the only occasion in the whole war in which the Germans captured any considerable number of Australian prisoners. They claimed 1300, and considering the large number of wounded in the six battalions engaged who had to be abandoned the claim may not be exaggerated. Among those of the 14th captured by the enemy were Lieuts. McCallum, Gower, McQuiggan, Lyon and Edmonds (the three former severely wounded); C.Q.M.S. Leslie Guppy (Original), of B Company; L/Cpl. W. D. Howard[18] (Original), of A Company, who co-operated with Capt. (then L/Cpl.) A. Jacka when he won the V.C. on the Peninsula; Sgt. W. C. Groves, of B Company (alleged by some to have been the youngest sergeant in the A.I.F.); Platoon-Sgt. Stan Thomas (Original), of B Company; L/Cpl. R. A. Stephens, D Company runner; Sgt. A. C. Dalitz, of D Company; L/Cpl. F. L. Wright (Original), of D Company; and Pte. "Tug" Patterson, the well-known athlete.

*14th Battalion Prisoners.*

The following decorations were awarded in respect of the battle; the valiant dead, unfortunately, according to custom, were not awarded posthumous decorations: — Bar to Military Cross — Capt. A. Jacka V.C., M.C. (Wedderburn, V.). Military Cross—Capt. W. R. Wadsworth (Castlemaine, V.); Lieut. J. A. Mitchell (Royal Park, V.); No. 2336, C.S.M. W. Boland (Lancefield, V.). D.C.M.—3409, Sgt. C. H. Mayer (South Melbourne, V.). Bar to M.M.—1598, L/Cpl. S. A. Markham, M.M. (Flemington, V.), stretcher-bearer. M.M.— 392, Cpl. Chas. Thompson (Orbost, V.); 1363, L/Sgt. Thomas Carberry (afterwards R.Q.M.S., Perth, W.A.), A.M.C.; 1700, Pte. J. M. Deacon (Preston, V.); 6052, Pte. G. K. Lovekin (Warrnambool, V.); 487, L/Cpl. B. H. Perry (Worcestershire, Eng.); 2784, Pte. Wm. Amor (Ballarat, V.), Lewis gunner; 5398a, Pte. H. J. Lamprell (Wonthaggi, V.), bomber;

*Decorations.*

---

[17] Vide Chap. 1.
[18] Vide Chap. 7.

2734, Pte. J. G. Casson (North Melbourne, V.); 1284, L/Cpl.
W. Porter (Tylden, V.), stretcher-bearer; 6122, Pte. Wm.
Watson (Orford, V.), stretcher-bearer; 2005, Pte. W. Rowse
(Emmaville, N.S.W.), stretcher-bearer; 3226, L/Cpl. A. J.
a'Court (England), A.M.C.; 2579, Sgt. F. W. Dalitz (Dimboola, V.); 1339, Pte. E. J. Davis (Stewarton, V.), transport;
3811, Sgt. A. A. Hore (Albury, N.S.W.), Lewis gunner.

## CHAPTER XXIX.

### RECUPERATION.

#### 1917—April 12 to May 29.

After a stupendous disaster like Bullecourt, when the Battalion's casualties were numbered by hundreds, it was some days before life became normal again.

**Common Misfortune Renders Personal Differences Forgotten.** Incidents of the battle were recounted and recalled, threats of vengeance made against the enemy, inquiries instituted as to the fate of killed or missing comrades, and letters of sympathy sent to the friends and relatives of deceased soldiers, giving details of their deaths. The common misfortune made all personal differences forgotten for a short time, until once again battalion life settled down to the old routine.

Before the Battalion left Mametz it participated on April 14 in a ceremonial parade, followed by an address by General Birdwood, who conveyed a message of congratulation from the Commander-in-Chief on the Brigade's work in the recent engagement.

**Address by General Birdwood.**

General Birdwood may be frankly absolved from any responsibility for the tactics at Bullecourt, but his address to the Brigade on this occasion was utterly out of harmony with the feelings of those addressed, and, under any circumstances, peculiarly misappropriate.

On the 19th the Battalion marched from Mametz to Ribemont, where so much of its time in France was spent.

**Return to Ribemont.** The homecoming (for such it was), was a sad one. When the villagers realised that the small party returning, weary and war-battered, was all that remained of the proud and imposing unit which had marched away less than a month before, expressions of grief and sympathy were heard from them on all sides, mingled with inquiries as to the fate of their numerous friends.

**Anzac Day Celebrated.**

April 25 was the second anniversary of the historic landing on the Gallipoli Peninsula, and that event was celebrated by a church parade in the morning, and a brigade sports in the afternoon.

The paramount concern of the C.O. at this time was to restore the morale of the Battalion, and build it up again numerically. The number of officers killed at Bullecourt left many vacancies, with the result that several recommendations for commissions were sent in. On April 20 the following twelve appointments of 2nd-Lieuts. were made, viz.:—D. H. L. Hawkins, G. T. Trewheela, W. P. Boland, S. J. J. Garton, A. King, L. Garcia, L. H. Gill, H. J. A. Schutz, E. P. Hill, E. J. Rule, W. C. Fulton, and E. R. Chubb.

**Twelve Commissions Granted.**

On April 30 the veteran Capt. A. R. Cox, and two reinforcement officers, T. G. Griffith and J. H. Johnson, reported for duty. The last-named proved one of the finest officers the 14th ever had. The Battalion was strengthened about this time, too, by the arrival of the 22nd reinforcements, which was peculiar, in that it was a New South Wales detachment, and practically wholly recruited in that State. This was the only body of reinforcements which ever joined the Battalion which was not essentially Victorian in origin. The newcomers, however, proved a particularly fine body of men, who soon thoroughly identified themselves with the unit, and took an active and prominent part in its activities. The 23rd reinforcements joined shortly after, and the war gaps in the ranks began to fill up.

**Arrival of 22nd Reinforcements.**

**A New South Wales Detachment.**

The stay at Ribemont lasted about four weeks, and was filled in by the usual routine of training and lectures, which were always resumed when the Battalion was in a rest area. Any unit which expected to have a high standard of efficiency had to indulge in continual training. Colonel Peck, whilst always encouraging sports, was also a strong believer in appealing to the intellectual side of his men, since knowledge always made their work more interesting. The officers were accordingly instructed to lecture on subjects on which they were severally proficient. Among subjects upon which lectures were given about this time were:— "Methods of teaching Physical Training," "The Fighting Troops and Their Characteristics,"

**Ribemont.**

**List of Military Lectures.**

"Orders and Reports," "Methods of Teaching Drill," "Intercommunication," "Quarters," "Methods of Teaching Musketry," "The Lewis Gun," "Bayonet Fighting," and "Information." These lectures were sometimes delivered to all ranks, and sometimes merely to non-commissioned officers. In addition much time was spent in training or route marching, and recreation filled in what spare time there was. Even in the so-called rest areas the front line Australian soldiers had little time for ennui.

The long winter had at last disappeared, and some beautiful weather greeted the advent of May. Advantage was taken of this by the "heads" to arrange a series of athletic and military competitions. A transport competition (won by the 16th Battalion) was held on the 7th, a divisional boxing tournament on the 8th, and a divisional rifle competition on the 8th and 9th. L/Cpl. James Grieves, of Ballan (A Company, No. 3328), obtained second place in the open divisional rifle championship.

*Inter-Battalion Competitions.*

On the 12th, a divisional parade was held, at which General Birdwood (G.O.C. 1st Anzac Corps) said farewell to the Fourth Division and distributed medals. The Division, in spite of its recent rough handling at Bullecourt, presented a fine appearance at the parade. It was then announced that the Division was to leave the 1st Anzac Corps (comprising at that time the 1st, 2nd, 4th, and 5th A.I.F. Divisions), and be attached to the 2nd Anzac Corps, which was then operating in the extreme north of France. The reason for the transfer was that the Commander-in-Chief had decided to abandon all further fighting on the Bullecourt front, where so much Australian blood had been shed, and effort expended, and attempt a new offensive in the north. The 4th Division, after its recent holocaust, was being transferred there for the purpose of participating in the forthcoming battle.

*Transfer of 4th Division to 2nd Anzac Corps.*

Training continued for two or three more days at Ribemont, and on the evening of the 15th, the Battalion entrained north for Baillieul (passing circuitously through Amiens, Abbeville, St. Omer, and Hazebrouk), and reached its destination next morning about 10.30 a.m. Disentraining, a march of about eight miles brought the Battalion to Doulieu, near Estaires, and it was once more in the locality which marked its first permanent billets in France. The men settled down in the scattered farms of the neighbourhood. The

*Departure for the North.*

country in which they found themselves looked less war-ridden and more prosperous than localities on the Somme. Training was resumed in the new area, one section in each platoon specialising in grenade work.

The Fourth Division was now attached to the Second British Army, whose G.O.C. was General Plumer, whilst the Second Anzac Corps commander was Major-General Sir A. J. Godley, with whom the 4th Brigade had been associated on the Peninsula in 1915. The Second British Army was famed for the excellence of its staff work, so that under its guidance there was little chance of the Division's training and fighting qualities being dissipated through futile leadership. The accession of this fine Division to his forces was doubtless a source of satisfaction to General Plumer, who met the Battalion C.O.'s at 4th Brigade Headquarters on the 22nd, and subsequently inspected the 14th Battalion, which had been selected as the representative battalion of the 4th Brigade. The Corps Commander inspected the 4th Brigade on the 26th, and expressed his satisfaction at its appearance.

*4th Division Attached to 2nd British Army.*

*14th Selected as Representative Battalion of Brigade.*

On May 29 the Battalion received about the worst blow that could have befallen it in the relinquishment of its command by Colonel Peck, who was on that date transferred to the staff of the Third Australian Division. He had been five and a half months C.O. of the unit. There is not any profession where personality is more necessary than in the army, and the departing C.O.'s personality was outstanding. He combined a wide range of intellect with an extraordinary grasp of facts, whilst the lectures on military subjects which he delivered in the Battalion were an education in themselves. On all questions of military procedure he was a past master. He was, too, the soul of all the Battalion's activities, and his popularity with all ranks was unbounded. Everyone recognised the efficient leadership, the sound judgment, and the strength of will which had raised the Battalion to the zenith of its discipline and efficiency. Regret at his departure was universal, and whilst his association with the unit was perhaps the happiest period of his life, conversely there was not a happier unit in the A.I.F. than the 14th during his connection with it.[1]

*Transfer of Col. Peck to 3rd A.I.F. Division.*

---

[1] The late Lieut.-General Sir H. V. Cox (formerly G.O.C. of the 4th Australian Division) informed the author that he was responsible for the selection of Colonel Peck as C.O. of the 14th.

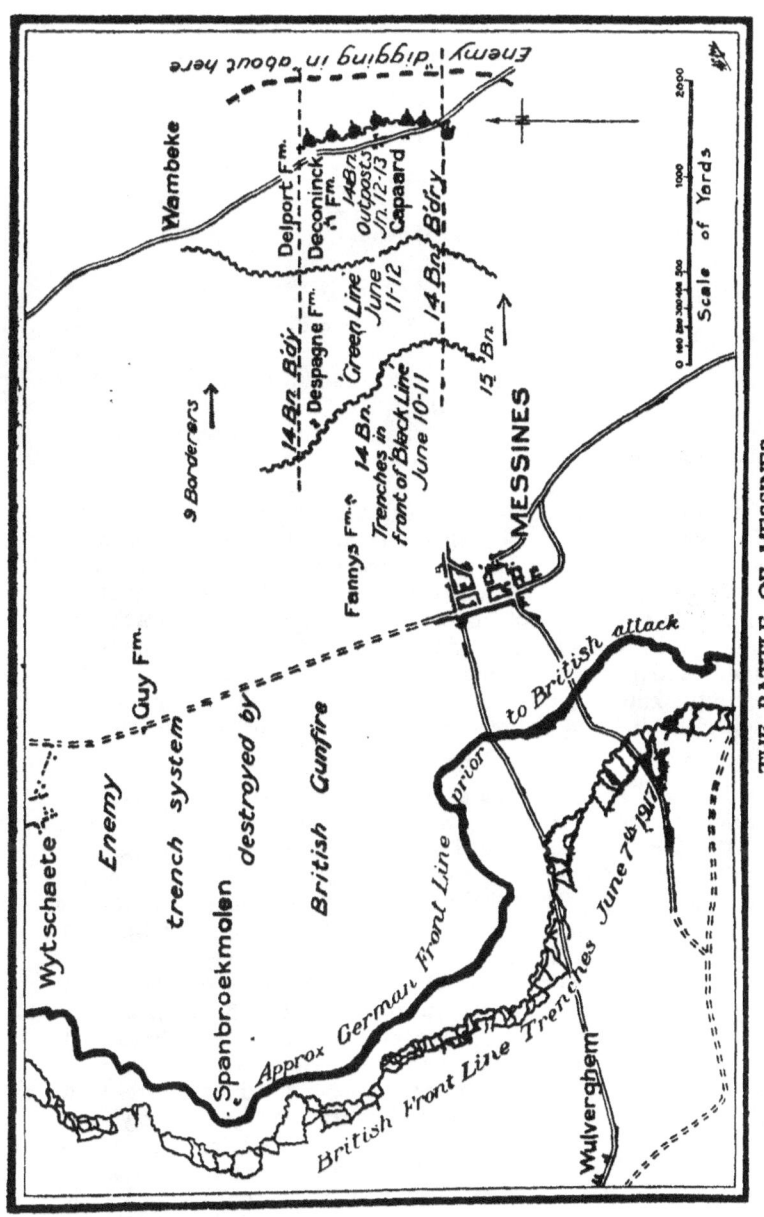

THE BATTLE OF MESSINES

# CHAPTER XXX.

## MESSINES.

### 1917—May 30 to June 26.

**Major Fuhrmann Takes Over Temporary Command of Battalion.**

The vacancy caused by the promotion of Colonel Peck was temporarily filled by Major O. C. W. Fuhrmann, who had been Battalion Transport Officer in Egypt in 1915. On May 31st the Battalion left Doulieu, and marched about eight miles to Dranoutre, across the Belgian frontier, camping on arrival in the adjoining fields at a place known as Crucifix Corner. A stay here of eight days was filled in by the usual training, varied by the sight of aeroplane fights and attacks on sausage balloons. One day a German airman dropped a bomb and exploded a big railway ammunition dump in the vicinity, killing a number of the attendant British guard and workmen, besides shattering many of the roofs and windows in the town, and causing general confusion.

It now became known that a major operation on a large scale was shortly intended, having for its objective the capture of the Messines ridge, and everyone had a pretty good idea that the 4th Brigade—in spite of its recent holocaust—would be again in it. This feeling received practical confirmation on the 6th, when each company of the Battalion in turn was detailed to inspect a contour map of the proposed Messines battlefield. It was fenced in and covered about an acre of ground. Everything—such as valleys, villages, hills and trees—was set out true to detail, whilst streams were represented by blue earth. In short, it was a very fine piece of work, and gave everyone a splendid idea of the terrain of the battlefield. It was a tactical novelty as far as the Australians were concerned, but nevertheless the foresight displayed in its conception by the

**Inspection of Contour Map of Messines Battlefield.**

---

* Vide photograph facing page 226

Second Army Staff excited confidence that the operation would be carried out by that staff to a successful issue.

**Attack on Messines Ridge.**

**Colossal Mine Explosions.**

The attack on the Messines ridge was carried out by the Second Anzac Army Corps, the first phase of the battle being an advance by the New Zealanders and Third Australian Division with British troops on the left. The battle opened at 3.10 a.m. on June 7 by the explosion of nineteen mines, containing upwards of 400 tons of explosives, immediately followed by a terrific barrage. The effect of the simultaneous discharge of these mines was indescribable, the German front lines and their personnel being simply obliterated. The result was that the casualties in the attacking infantry were trifling, the surviving Germans being too dazed to offer serious opposition. The explosion that initiated the battle seemed to cause the ground near the 14th to rise up and go down, whilst the tremendous barrage, though distant, could be distinctly heard, the roar of the great naval guns being prominent in the din. The role allotted to the 4th Brigade in the battle was that of a reserve brigade, but had the victory been less crushing it might have been engaged in the fighting.

**Battalion Marches to Reserve Line.**

**Major Margolin Takes Command of Battalion.**

The Battalion was standing by all day on the 7th, and was inspected in fighting order. The good news came to hand that the New Zealanders and 3rd ("Eggs-a-Cook") Division had taken their objectives, and several batches of German prisoners were seen going past to the rear. At midnight the 14th moved forward to the reserve line at Messines, arriving about 3 a.m. (8th) at a position known as the "subsidiary" line, not far from the village of Wulverghem. The day was spent improving trenches and awaiting orders. Major E. L. Margolin, D.S.O. (formerly of the 16th Battalion) here took over command of the 14th from Major Fuhrmann.

**Captain Macdermid Wounded.**

On the 9th, orders having been received to relieve the New Zealanders, then in the support lines, the position was reconnoitred during the day by company commanders and others. Whilst engaged in this duty, Capt. D. R. Macdermid, O.C. of C Company, was so severely wounded as to be put out of action during the remainder of the war. An Original, he had been prominent at Quinn's Post and Hill 60 on the Peninsula, and again at Bullecourt, in France.

Capable, courageous, and popular with all ranks, his loss was severely felt in the Battalion. At 9 p.m. the 14th moved up to the support trenches, the relief being completed at 4 a.m. next morning. There was some heavy enemy shelling on the 10th, and Pte. Martin Rollins[1] (No. 5441), one of the Headquarters runners, was blown to pieces. As a result of the appearance of enemy aeroplanes over our advanced posts about daybreak on the 11th, a hostile barrage was shortly after put over our lines. Orders were received early in the day that the 14th was to relieve the 50th Battalion in the front line (known officially as the "green line"), and being the extreme left sector of the 4th Division, B and D Companies were detailed for the advance, with A and C in support. The Germans, badly shattered, had retired somewhat, leaving behind snipers and machine-gun crews to cover their retreat.

*Battalion Moves into Support Trenches.*

*Orders for B and D Companies to Take Over Front Line.*

B and D Companies were commanded by those splendid soldiers, Capts. Reg. Jones and Albert Jacka respectively, and their work during the engagement was quite in accord with their great reputations. These two officers personally reconnoitred the "green line" in the afternoon, and towards night they detailed two patrols of a dozen men each (under 2nd-Lieuts. V. G. Garner, of B, and E. P. Hill, of D Company), to reconnoitre the Gapaard Road. The patrols advanced several hundred yards, being sniped at en route, and sighted several of the enemy, who retired; they then subsequently returned, and rejoined the remainder of the unit. About 11 p.m. B and D Companies moved forward to the front line, which was occupied at midnight. The ground was very sloppy, and the trenches required continual baling and deepening. The men were busy all night consolidating the position, whilst patrols were pushed forward, and numerous outposts established. Daylight next morning disclosed no signs of the enemy, though large numbers of his dead could be seen lying everywhere; his artillery fire, too, which had been severe during the two previous days, had now ceased. Our signallers,

*Two Patrols Sent Out.*

*B and D Companies Take Over Line.*

*Consolidation.*

*Outposts Established.*

*Germans Retire.*

---

[1] Private Martin Rollins, of Curlewis (near Geelong), labourer. He had been buried at Beaugnetre as the result of the explosion of the mine in the cellar (vide Chap. 27), and was evacuated for three days, returning in time, however, to do fine work in evacuating our wounded at Bullecourt. He was sitting outside Battalion Headquarters on June 10, when he was killed by a 5.9.

unhampered by the enemy's fire, were busy connecting the various scattered posts by telephone with Battalion Headquarters at Blauen Molen. All ranks were ordered not to show themselves unnecessarily. Australian troops temperamentally are essentially aggressive, and on this occasion there was a feeling among all ranks that a great opportunity—such as had never before presented itself to the A.I.F. in France—was being lost. A great victory had been gained: there was indisputable ocular evidence both of the enemy's heavy losses and demoralisation, and all were eager to push forward and exploit the victory. They were, much to their disappointment, held back, however, spending a precious day in inactivity, and the opportunity[2] was allowed to pass. The great tactical victory yielded only local results, and little strategical use was made of it by the General Headquarters Staff.

*Enemy's Demoralisation.*

*Opportunity Lost.*

In contradistinction to the general inactivity, however, Capts. Jones and Jacka spent a very active day. Leaving their commands in the line, they pushed forward alone in broad daylight, at great personal risk, reconnoitring the country ahead. Jacka, as a result of his reconnaissance, established posts in Deconinick and Delporto farms, seized a field and machine gun, established a strong line of outposts, and occupied several hundred yards of country in front of the "green line," arranging also for the co-operation of British troops on our left flank, and having them brought forward to correspond with our advance.

*Activities of Captains Jones and Jacka.*

Jones's work on the right was equally good. He crossed nearly 800 yards swept by machine-gun and snipers' fire, and examined the ruins of Gapaard farm, knowing that it meant almost certain death if the farm should happen to be tenanted by a hidden enemy. He then returned to his company, and led forward a small party which occupied the farm, shot down several snipers from the trees in front, and seized three enemy field guns and a large quantity of ammunition. Jones[3] also established a line of outposts and improved and reorganised his main line. Jones' and Jacka's activities resulted in an

---

[2] It has been aptly observed that the opportunity of a lifetime must be taken advantage of during the lifetime of the opportunity.

[3] Jones combined intellectuality with capacity and intrepidity. His able report on the above operations is a model of clarity and lucidity. Vide 14th Battalion Official Diary, June 12, 1917, in which his report is set out in full.

advance of the Battalion nearly half a mile into hostile territory, the work of these two intrepid and able officers being typical of Australian commissioned officers' work at its very best.

*High Standard of Their Work.*

Two other officers prominent in the engagement were the I.O. 2nd-Lieut. J. H. Johnson (who had just been appointed to that important position), and the Adjutant, both of whom did valuable reconnaissance work. The former received active co-operation from Cpl. "Sarto" Anderson (an Original), and his battalion scouts. Anderson's coolness and judgment in guiding relieving troops into their positions over the shell-swept roads during darkness was most marked. Other prominent N.C.O.'s were Sgts. Frederick Goode and D. Drummond (both of D Company), Sgt. J. C. Duxbury, of A Company, and Sgt. Signaller N. J. Bear, who was indefatigable in the discharge of his dangerous and arduous duties.

*Others Prominent.*

The R.A.P. during the first night in the line was in one of the old German front line trenches, with very little cover; on the following night it was moved forward over the ridge a little beyond and to the left of the Battalion Headquarters at Blauen Molen, where a small pillbox was occupied, with its opening facing the enemy, and at times a target for his salvoes of high explosives. Major Fletcher, the R.M.O., and his medical personnel worked throughout with their usual thoroughness.

*Location of R.A.P.*

On the 13th the Battalion moved back to the "subsidiary line" after a very satisfactory tour of duty. There had been only two days spent in the front line, but during that time a permanent advance into the enemy's territory of about half a mile had been made, and the unit's work had been not only clean, crisp and efficient, but of a distinctly high order, the Corps Commander (General Godley) sending a congratulatory message on the capture of Gapaard.

*Battalion Relieved.*

*Its Fine Work.*

Messines was the one battle in France prior to 1918 on which Australians can look back with unqualified satisfaction. The Staff work of the Second Army had been well-nigh perfect. The gains were substantial and cheaply purchased, the enemy's casualties being far in excess of our own. The Battalion's casualties during the engagement were only five killed and forty-five wounded, included in the latter being two

*Battalion Casualties.*

officers, viz., Capt. D. R. Macdermid and Lieut. N. C. Harris (D Company). L/Cpl. (No. 1598) S. A. Markham, M.M. and Bar,[4] a very fine stretcher-bearer, was among the killed. He was the only man in the Battalion at the time of his death (except Capt. Jacka) who had been awarded more than one decoration. The following decorations were awarded to the Battalion in connection with the above tour of duty.

**Death of L/Cpl. S. A. Markham.**

Military Cross—Capt. Reg. W. Jones, M.M. (Essendon, Vic.). Military Medals—No. 676, Cpl. H. A. Anderson (Collingwood, Vic.), Scout; No. 4172, Sgt. David Drummond (Ballarat, Vic.); No. 4200, Sgt. Fredk. A. Goode (Beaufort, Vic.); No. 14, Sgt. N. J. Bear (Spotswood, Vic.), Signaller.

**Decorations Allotted.**

The 14th remained at the "subsidiary line" from June 13 to 17, when a further move back was made to the green fields near Neuve Eglise. A stay here was made for about ten days. The locality was practically out of shell fire, and as the brigade canteen had been established nearby, there was every opportunity for varying the regulation diet. Specialist training and road-making on the ridge comprised the Battalion's activities here. The roadmaking consisted of laying wooden tracks for the transport to pass over, and many became quite expert at this work. Several British aeroplanes had been wrecked in this sector, and lay about just as they had crashed to earth.

**Neuve Eglise.**

The Duke of Connaught (an uncle of King George) was visiting the front about this time, and an inspection of representative members of the 4th Brigade was arranged in his honour, and held at Baillieul on June 26. The representatives (seven officers and seventeen other ranks), were the elite of the Brigade (all men specially chosen for their distinguished records), and comprised no less than three V.C. winners, viz., Murray (13th), Jacka (14th), and O'Meara (16th Battalions). A finer body of men has seldom

**Duke of Connaught's Inspection.**

---

[4] L/Cpl. Steven Arthur Markham. Labourer. Born Riddell's Creek (Vic.). K.I.A., June 11, 1917. Won M.M. at Pozieres and bar to M.M. at Bullecourt. A brother, No. 4247 Pte. Andrew Markham, was also K.I.A. in the ranks of the 14th Battalion at Bullecourt on April 11, 1917.

been gathered together. The 14th Battalion representatives in this unique little gathering were:—Capt. A. Jacka, V.C., M.C. and Bar (Wedderburn, V.); Capt. Reg. W. Jones, M.C., M.M. (Essendon, V.); A Company, No. 619, C.S.M. J. J. Myers, M.M. (Daylesford, V.); B Company, No. 197, Sgt. R. J. Garcia, D.C.M. (Yarraville, V.); C Company, No. 2005, Pte. W. ("Darkey") Rowse, M.M. (Glenlyon, V.); D Company, No. 5398, Pte. H. J. Lamprell, M.M. (Wonthaggi, V.). All had obtained decorations, and all were men of exceptional military merit. Myers, Rowse, and Lamprell were killed in action before the war terminated, on the following dates:—Myers, K.I.A. May 5, 1918; Rowse, K.I.A. Sept. 27, 1917; Lamprell, K.I.A. August 8, 1918.

<small>Battalion Representatives.</small>

<small>Their High Military Attainments.</small>

## CHAPTER XXXI.

### PLOEGSTEERT AND GAPAARD.

#### 1917—June 27 to August 31.

The 14th was destined to spend practically the whole summer of 1917 on the Messines front, consequently the short spell at Neuve Eglise was but a prelude to another tour of duty in the line. On June 28 the Battalion left reserves, and marched in the direction of the line, occupying billets that night near what was known as the "catacombs," i.e., huge dugouts on the reverse slope of a hill facing the German lines, and situated near Ploegsteert Wood. All who could get into the tunnels, whilst the others (mostly new recruits) found shelter in some half-ruined huts in the vicinity. There was hostile shelling on and off all night, and though several trees in close proximity were smashed up, fortunately no casualties resulted. The Battalion moved forward on the following morning to the reserve line, Battalion Headquarters being situated in an old cellar on the site of the former St. Ives post office. The New Zealanders whom the 4th Brigade here relieved were their old comrades of the Peninsula campaign.

*Battalion Returns to Messines Front.*

*Moves into Reserve Line.*

Ploegsteert Wood, near where the Battalion now found itself, was one of the best known spots on the British front. Prior to the war it had been a game reserve of the King of Belgium. The woods (smashed by gun fire) were intersected by avenues, at this time named after London streets, whilst the green sward under foot was carpeted at this season with wild flowers—poppies, cornflowers, daisies and buttercups. The weather, too, was mild and genial (when it was not raining), and the only fly in the ointment was that the German artillery had the locality under direct fire, and their bar-

*Ploegsteert Wood.*

*Pleasant Climatic Conditions.*

rages frequently made holes in the neighbourhood in which small cottages could be comfortably deposited.

The system of reserve trenches taken possession of by the Battalion here were fairly comfortable, though subject at times to artillery fire; they were constructed partly on the "breastwork" principle, i.e., built up from the ground. Most of the Battalion's personnel was detailed here for trenching fatigues in the forward support lines. These support line trenches, however, in addition to being knee-deep in mud, were in a frightful state of repair, largely owing to the previous attentions of our artillery. The ground had been recently fought over, and the smell was consequently vile, the earth being mixed with decaying bodies, rotting sandbags, stagnant green water, and other abominations, whilst it also abounded in rats and smaller vermin.

**Loathsome Condition of Support Trenches.**

The Germans, who had been allowed to recover from the staggering results of the Messines battle, were again displaying vitality, and deluging our area with artillery barrages and machine-gun fire. As many of the roads were under enemy observation, all work by our men had to be done at night, and sleep snatched during the day. During one of these hostile barrages Major-General Holmes (G.O.C. of the 4th A.I.F. Division), was killed on July 2, near Ploegsteert Wood, whilst taking the Premier of New South Wales on a visit to some of the 4th Brigade trenches. A curious incident occurred near Bonhill Row on July 5, when two of C Company cooks, Ptes. James Campbell (No. 2575) and Bob Jennings (No. 5399), after being slightly wounded early in the day, and had their wounds dressed, returned to duty only to be again both severely wounded a few hours later. Two Originals were killed about this time, viz., Cpl. R. E. Antill (No. 1228) on the 5th, and Pte. W. R. Colwyn-Stevens (No. 539) on the 6th.

**Death of G.O.C. of 4th Division A.I.F.**

The Battalion relieved the 15th in the front line on the night of the 7th, the Companies being allotted as follows: C on the right, B in the centre, and D on the left, with A in support. Rain fell for several days adding to the discomfort of everyone. There was not any actual front line in this sector—merely a system of out-posts, support lines, and reserves. The ground was intersected by hedges.

**Battalion Takes Over Front.**

The outpost system here, (a legacy from previous occupation), was insecure and tactically unsound, with the result

Men of the 14th Battalion (soft hats) studying a Raised Plan of Messines
(Australian War Museum Official Photo.)

*Standing Patrol Rushed by Enemy*

that almost immediately after taking over a standing patrol of the 6th platoon at post 4 was attacked at night by a large body of the enemy, and our handful of men driven out by sheer weight of numbers, after two had been killed and several wounded. The post was re-occupied by our men two days later, and in the meantime the problem had been taken in hand by the Adjutant with characteristic energy. He made a thorough personal reconnaisance of the front and, assisted by the Intelligence Officer and Captain Reg. Jones, thoroughly reorganised the whole of the outpost system.

*Outpost System Reorganised.*

No. 3 post which was in a tactically unsound position was removed to a better site. Strong fighting posts were established with good fields of fire, and mutual cross fire support with Lewis guns, whilst a series of listening posts were pushed forward in the form of a screen in front of the fighting posts with which they were connected by tug wires. These measures proved efficacious, and the enemy, who had been evidently meditating aggression, realised that quietude was the better policy.

On the 9th two veteran officers were wounded: Capt. Jacka (O.C. of D Coy.), who had been visiting an outpost in company with Sgt. R. Scanlon. was sniped in the leg; whilst Capt. A. R. Cox (O.C. of A Coy.), was slightly wounded in the neck.

*Capts. Cox and Jacka Wounded.*

The Battalion held the front line till the 13th. when it was relieved by the 51st Battalion. The men of that unit, instead of following the usual custom of waiting till it was dark, started from their camp in broad daylight. and were seen by the enemy, who in consequence subsequently opened a heavy barrage. hoping to catch our men on retirement. The latter fortunately got away without casualties, and marched to billets near Neuve Eglise. The personnel of the whole 4th Brigade was becoming worn out and required a spell. The casualties for the fortnight were set out officially as five killed, forty-six wounded and two missing (i.e., killed). There were also a good many evacuations for sickness about this time.

*4th Brigade Worn Out.*

After a few days at Neuve Eglise the Battalion on the 19th moved to the Vieu Berquin area. Its strength at this time was set out as 29 officers and 742 other ranks. The 4th Brigade was inspected by General Plumer on the 27th, and on the following day a very successful and enjoyable Battalion sports was held.

## Ploegsteert and Gapaard.

<small>List of Battalion Officers.</small>

The following is a list of officers with the Battalion on August 1, 1917:—Headquarters:—Major E. L. Margolin, D.S.O., (Russia), C.O.; Major O. C. W. Fuhrmann, (South Melbourne), Second in Command; Major W. M. A. Fletcher, (N.S.W.), Medical Officer; Capt. H. B. Wanliss, D.S.O., (Ballarat, V.), Adjutant; Capt. F. W. Rolland, (Noorat, V.), Chaplain; Lieut. C. R. T. Cole, (Malvern V.), L.G. Officer; Lieut. L. H. Ebbott, (Malvern, V.), Ass. Adjutant; Lieut. R. E. Hayes, (Ballarat, V.), Quartermaster; Lieut. F. C. W. Symonds, (S. Camberwell, V.), Transport Officer; 2nd-Lieut. J. H. Johnson, (Beeac, V.), Intelligence Officer; 2nd-Lieut. N. J. Bear (Spotswood, V.), Signalling Officer.

A Company—Capt. A. R. Cox (Box Hill, V.); Lieut. W. R. M. Beamond (Geelong, V.), Lieut. N. C. Aldridge (Hawthorn, V.), 2nd-Lieut. W. G. Fulton (Footscray, V.), 2nd-Lieut. L. H. Gill (Melbourne, V.), 2nd-Lieut. L. J. Le Fevre (Sydney, N.S.W.), 2nd-Lieut. L. G. Stevens (Warrnambool, V.), 2nd-Lieut. A. J. Naylor (Camberwell, V.).

B Company—Capt. J. Mackay (South Melbourne, V.), Lieut. W. Jacka (Wedderburn, V.), 2nd-Lieut. H. J. A. Schutz (Albert Park, V.), 2nd-Lieut. S. J. J. Garton (Brunswick, V.), 2nd-Lieut. W. P. Boland, M.C. (Seymour, V.), 2nd-Lieut. C. G. George (Clifton Hill, V.), 2nd-Lieut. G. Clarendon Hyde (London, Eng.), 2nd-Lieut. H. B. Jackson (Carlton, V.), 2nd-Lieut. G. Lansberg (Holland), Interpreter.

C Company—Capt. R. W. Jones, M.C., M.M. (Essendon, V.), Capt. A .R. Blainey, M.C. (Newcastle, Eng.), Capt. P. J. Hayes (Marrickville, N.S.W.), Lieut. T. N. Templeton (Yea, V.), Lieut. E. J. Rule (Cobar, N.S.W.), Lieut. D. H. L. Hawkins (Caulfield, V.), Lieut. V. G. Garner (Essendon, V.), Lieut. F. G. Hyett (Exeter, Eng.), Lieut. H. V. Walklate (Malvern, V.).

D Company—Lieut. G. Quinn (Camberwell, V.), Lieut. A. King (Albert Park, V.), Lieut. G. T. Trewheela (Geelong,

---

<small>[1] The officers of a battalion are continually in a state of flux. There are some always away sick, wounded, on detached duty, or at officers' schools. It is surprising how little front line service is actually performed by some, whilst others are continually in the line. In connection with the above list, it will be noted that Captain Jacka (O.C. of D Company) was away wounded. Captain Blainey returned to the Battalion on August 1, 1917, after six months' absence at a training battalion in England. Captain Wadsworth was also temporarily absent. Compare above with lists of battalion officers set out in Chapters 2, 15 and 27.</small>

V.), Lieut. E. P. Hill (Ballarat, V.), Lieut. R. O. Roxburgh (South Yarra, V.), Lieut. W. J. Hodges (Rosedale, V.), Lieut. R. Wood (Carlisle, Eng.).

Wet weather greeted the advent of August, and continued for some days. On the 3rd the Battalion marched to Neuve Eglise, billeting in some of the shell-torn houses of that village. The usual training followed for a few days. On the 4th a special order was received from the Commander-in-Chief referring to the beginning of the fourth year of the war.

**Battalion Takes Over Front Line at Gapaard.**

The 14th relieved the 16th Battalion on the 8th in the front line at Gapaard, near the scene of the Battalion's activities in the previous June. The relief took place during a tremendous thunderstorm. Lieut. Viv. Garner, of C Company (12th platoon) was killed (sniped) whilst reconnoitring an outpost during the relief. An Original, he was a brave, gallant and popular officer who had been wounded at Quinn's Post[2] immediately the Battalion went into action on the Peninsula, and only recently had returned to the unit after a long spell in England. Two days later A Company's personnel received special attention from the enemy's artillery at Warneton following a visit of inspection to our lines by one of his planes. A Company's Headquarters was demolished, and Lieut. Le Fevre wounded, whilst another shell, bursting in a bay tenanted by five A Company men, made them all casualties, killing Cpl. Arthur Oakley and Pte. E. Guest, mortally wounding Ptes. T. Hale and T. Y. E. Clifford, and wounding L/Cpl. F. S. Ross. Stretcher-bearer Thos. Connors and his assistants, disregarding the shelling, cleared the post of the wounded. One night a shell dropped in the centre of a ration-carrying party of C Company men taking rations to the front line; eight casualties was the result, including three N.C.O.'s. Sgt. Fred Goode carried several of the wounded back under shell fire.

**Death of Lieut. Viv. Garner.**

**Fatal Shell Burst.**

The Lewis gunners in one of our outposts on two occasions during this time inflicted severe casualties on the enemy's wiring parties working in the vicinity. Among the casualties

---

[2]Vide Chap. 4. A full and complete account of Garner's death appears in Lieut. E. J. Rule's diary. Rule at great personal risk, assisted by Sgts. F. A. Dawes (No. 310 of 11th Platoon) and G. F. Harrison (No. 2398 of 12th Platoon) recovered his body immediately after he was killed. Lieut. Vivian Gilbert Garner, of Essendon, Vict. railway clerk.

**Pioneer Sgt.
Wounded.**
during this tour of duty in the line was No. 2566, Sgt. P. C. Bland, of Carisbrook, V.), the Battalion's pioneer sergeant, who lost a leg through the explosion of a whizbang. He was succeeded by No. 1022, Sgt. O. McAllan, who died of wounds on February 1, 1918. The Battalion pioneers were
**Duties of Battalion Pioneers.**
a body of men who did much useful and arduous work for the unit. They were in reality its handy men, and consisted of a sergeant and about ten men, including three carpenters, one tinsmith, a signwriter, and some hefty pick and shovel men. In the line they built dugouts, buried the dead, and carried rations and ammunition. When out of the line they prepared billets for the Battalion, kept the place tidy, made targets for rifle practice, and also prepared crosses for the Battalion's dead.

During peace, day is the time for man's activities, and night for recreation and rest, but on the Western front in the vicinity of the front line, this was reversed.
**Night the Time for Battalion Activities in the Line.**
During the daytime there was not any movement, for movement meant detection by the enemy, and detection meant possibly death or mutilation. Men slept or rested then. Darkness brought life. Work was resumed, meals consumed, men moved about everywhere, engaged in their various duties, and No Man's Land, deserted in daylight, became alive with patrols and scouts, and those daring fighting officers and N.C.O.'s who sought information or adventure.

The first fortnight in August witnessed some changes among the Battalion officers. Capt. Reg. Jones ("Jones of the 14th") was promoted to be Assistant Brigade Major of the 12th Brigade. Jones takes a place in the very front of the 14th Battalion officers. An Original, he enlisted as a private, but his ability soon brought him to the front. A deadly rifle shot, he did much effective sniping on the Peninsula. He had been wounded several times, but it never altered his outlook on life. He was noted for his daring in a Brigade of brave men, but his daring was always controlled by intelligence. Much scouting[3] and reconnaissance work must be placed to his

**Capt. Reg. Jones Promoted.**

**His Character.**

---

[3]Scouting gets little limelight, though it is invaluable work, and military operations cannot be carried on without it. No work is more dangerous or less spectacular. It entails the greatest risks and earns very few decorations.

credit during his long and honourable career with the Battalion. He was succeeded as O.C. of C Company by Captain A. R. Blainey, also an Original, but whose military ideals were not identical with those of his predecessor.

**The Adjutant Takes Over a Company.** Capt. Harold Wanliss relinquished the Battalion adjutancy, which he had held for seven months, on August 13, to take command of a company. He had set a high standard both of efficiency and conduct, and his inspiring personality had permeated the whole Battalion. During the summer of 1917 he had been responsible for much of the Battalion's activities, and he was also continually among the outposts at night—dangerous work voluntarily undertaken in addition to and outside the scope of his actual duties.

The 14th was relieved by the 15th Battalion on the night of August 14-15, and moved back to reserve, where it remained for about a fortnight doing fatigue work on Messines Ridge—chiefly road making and sometimes salvaging. It was slogging work, but did not entail the same strain or risk as front line activities. On the 28th the 17th Manchesters, of the British Army — men of less stalwart physique than the Australians—relieved the 14th, and our men moved out of the mud and filth of the trenches for their well-earned rest.

**14th Relieved.**

**Casualties.** The casualties for the period August 8 to 20 were set out as one officer and seven other ranks killed, two officers and 44 other ranks wounded,[4] and one missing.

**Climatic Conditions in Flanders.** Flanders, that portion of France in which the Messines sector is situated, is one of the wettest portions of Europe, and operations had to be carried on in a flat country that was almost a semi-swamp, and under climatic conditions of a most unpleasant character—conditions that added greatly to the exhaustion and discomfort of the troops. The latter, however, were at this time buoyed up by the prospects of a three-months' spell, which had been continually promised to them by their responsible heads, and which all now eagerly looked for to enable them to recover from the appalling losses and hardships which they had endured during the fifteen months that they had been in France.

---

[4]Some set out as wounded subsequently died of wounds. The official casualty list for that period shows a total of one officer and eleven other ranks killed or died of wounds. There were other fatal casualties towards the end of August.

After relief the 14th marched to Neuve Eglise, where a stay was made for three days, and all enjoyed the unwonted luxury of hot baths, clean underclothing, and **Hot Baths and** resumed their Australian headgear (getting **General Clean Up.** temporarily rid of their steel helmets), and discussed the long-promised three months rest which all thought they were at last really going to get. On the last day of the month, a march of about eleven miles brought the Battalion to billets near La Motte.

## APPENDIX.

In "Diggers' Abroad," a book written by Captain T. A. White (the 13th Battalion historian), reference is made on p. 59 to two 14th Battalion men who were killed near Gapaard Farm by a machine gun and buried by the 13th men. These two casualties were evidently Privates C. W. Cook (South Melbourne) and C. Gaudin (Warragul).

## CHAPTER XXXII.

### BATTLE OF POLYGON WOOD.

#### 1917—September 1 to September 30.

On September 1 Lieut.-Col. W. J. Smith, formerly of the 37th Battalion, marched in and assumed command of the 14th, in lieu of Major Margolin, who had had charge of the Battalion during the preceding three months. About this time, too, Major O. C. W. Fuhrmann, the unit's second-in-command, parted company with it to go to the Fifth A.I.F. Division. He was succeeded by Major D. Thompson, an officer brought in from an outside unit, whose advent naturally blocked the promotion of 14th officers of long standing whose efforts had largely made the Battalion what it was. Fuhrmann was an excellent administrative officer, though he had seen little front line service during his long connection with the unit. His departure broke another link with the formation of the Battalion, for he was one of the 32 original officers[1] who left Australia in 1914. Only two (the Cox brothers) now remained. The experience of the 14th of the wastage of war was identical with that of every other Australian infantry unit. There was not any portion of the A.I.F. of which the war took a more terrible toll than the junior fighting commissioned officers of the infantry. The pick of them were the flower of the continent, always respected, and in some cases idolised by their men—heroes in the line and gentlemen out of it. Few of that type came back, and among the handful of survivors not many returned normal—the strain had been too great. Australia never has—perhaps never will—realise her losses in this war other than numerically.

*Lieut. Col. W. J. Smith Assumes Command of the Battalion.*

*Departure of Major O. C. W. Fuhrmann.*

*An Original Officer.*

*War Toll of A.I.F. Fighting Officers.*

*Non-realisation of Exceptional Quality of Many Australian Casualties.*

---

[1] See list of battalion officers in Chap. 2.

## Battle of Polygon Wood.

On September 2 the Battalion's personnel boarded motor lorries, and travelled about twenty miles in a south-westerly direction to Lisbourg, and alighting here marched a couple of miles to Fontaine-les-Boulans [2] a quaint little village well behind the battle area. Here all were billeted in huge barns—a company to a barn—and settled down for a spell from the trenches. The inhabitants had never seen Australians before, and being out of the battle area were on that account exceedingly hospitable and kindly. All looked forward to at length enjoying their long-promised three months rest in those congenial surroundings. These pleasant conditions and anticipations were, however, shortlived. On the afternoon of September 4, at a parade of officers and N.C.O.'s the Brigadier informed them that they were to get into harness again, and to prepare immediately to take part in the big offensive then going on near Ypres. The 4th Brigade had now spent fifteen months in France, and during that time few, if any, brigades on the British Western Front had had a more continuous front line service. It had been fought and worked to the limit of its endurance, and was "fed up" by continual but elusive promises of a spell. The scant consideration[3] now shown it after its splendid and continuous service evoked considerable resentment, and some strong oath-provoking expressions of opinion. However, after some very natural grumbling, all accepted the inevitable, and threw themselves with great energy into the training.

*Battalion Reaches Fontaine-les-Boulans.*

*Hope Entertained for Long Promised Three Months' Rest.*

*Disillusionised.*

*4th Brigade's Splendid Record.*

*Scant Consideration Shown It.*

An unfortunate incident occurred during the next few days to which a reference must be made. The Brigadier during a visit to the lines—evidently unaware of the fact that the company commanders at the time were carrying on their training in accordance with the schedule issued by the C.O.—made reflections, not only on the officers involved, who

*Difference with Brigadier.*

---

[2] Prior to this, orders had been received that the Battalion was to march to Staples, and before these orders were countermanded, the Battalion transport officer had forwarded a lot of gear, including all the Lewis guns, to that spot.

[3] It was rumoured that Major-Gen. MacLagan (G.O.C. of the 4th A I.F. Division) protested vainly against the 4th Division being again put into action. All other Australian Divisions (except the 4th) which had been engaged in the Bullecourt sector had been out of the line during the summer.

were extremely capable, but on the unit generally. The slur on the reputation of the Battalion was an attack on that unit's pride which was so pronounced throughout the whole of the A.I.F., so that the remarks—which were considered unwarranted — caused resentment throughout the whole Battalion. The officers of the unit, acting promptly and with practical unanimity, made a very determined protest, with the consequent result that a withdrawal was made of the remarks objected to.

*Determined Stand of 14th Officers.*

Battalion and company training took place for some days, followed on the 14th by a brigade sham attack scheme, carried out in the presence of the Army Commander (General Plumer) and the Divisional Commander (Major-General McLagan). After its termination General Plumer held a parade of officers, and expressed his appreciation of what he had seen, and his opinion that the Brigade would uphold its reputation, and accomplish its task in the coming battle.

*Training.*

*Army Commander's Expression of Opinion.*

Next day a battalion sports meeting was held in the afternoon in delightful weather. These festive gatherings caused everyone to forget the war, and made all feel as if they were back in Australia again. Much money changed hands, and in addition to the orthodox sporting events there were heterodox items provocative of much hilarity to the spectators. A Company's personnel was successful in scoring twice the aggregate points of any other company. It was the last day of unalloyed happiness in this life for some of the Battalion's finest soldiers.

*Battalion Sports Meeting.*

On the 18th the Battalion (much to the regret of the French villagers) left Fontaine-les-Boulans, the personnel travelling by motor lorries thirty miles to Staples. Next day Capt. A. R. Blainey, who had shortly before returned to the unit after six months in England, was appointed adjutant, a position which he had previously held for a long period. On the 20th a further forward move was made to Steenvorde, where the men were billeted in barns. Capt. Hugh Trumble (nephew and namesake of the famous international cricketer) marched in on the same day and took over the duties of R.M.O. The Battalion was indebted for much excellent

*Battalion Leaves Fontaine-les-Boulans.*

*Capt. Blainey Appointed Adjutant.*

*Capt. Trumble Becomes R.M.O.*

work to his predecessor, Major W. M. A. Fletcher, during his long connection with the unit. All surplus gear was dumped here, and the thirty-three per cent. details not going into action went to Caestre and remained there until the Battalion came out of the line.

A further move on Saturday, the 22nd, brought the Battalion to a place known as Belgian Chateau, on the outskirts of Ypres, and near where a violent battle (known as the 3rd Battle of Ypres) had been already intermittently waging for almost two months. It was in this neighbourhood that the "Old Contemptibles" had covered themselves with glory in 1914. The sector had been fought over for years, with the result that the whole countryside had been reduced to a desert. The traffic on the lines of communication was tremendous, the noise being deafening. The maintenance of the roads entailed enormous labour. The Germans had the ground accurately registered, and made certain danger zones, through which traffic had to pass, perfect hells of raging shells, where men and transport were continually blown to fragments. At night, too, the flashing and roaring of the guns combined with Fritz's innumerable star shells, made the whole surroundings weird and unearthly.

*Belgian Chateau.*

*3rd Battle of Ypres.*

The position about to be attacked by the Anzacs was immensely strong, and had already held up the attacks for several weeks. The Australians had now been brought into the fight, and a brilliant attack by the 1st and 2nd Divisions of the A.I.F. on September 20, acting in conjunction with British troops on both flanks, while suffering heavy casualties, had gained a brilliant victory. It was now the turn of the 4th and 5th Divisions to carry on the work so auspiciously begun. Our men had to advance across the open through swamps and mud where it was difficult to obtain a foothold. The Germans, on the other hand, operated from comparatively dry points on the hill tops, and their defences had been elaborately organised by the best engineering talent in their army, backed by the immense mechanical resources of their empire. Their troops, too, were the pick of their army, sturdy and well trained men. The German defence relied largely on a countless number of concrete blockhouses (known as "pill boxes"), manned by machine gunners,[4] and planted thickly over the forward

*Difficulties to be Faced.*

*Elaborate German Defences.*

*"Pill Boxes."*

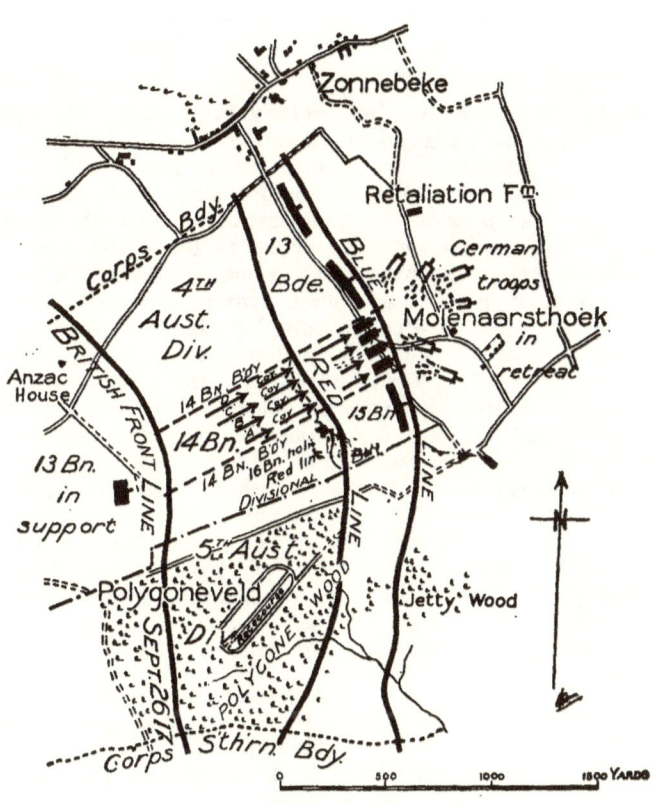

BATTLE OF POLYGON WOOD

area, and to a great depth behind. These pill boxes were immune from all save the very heaviest shells, and were so numerous and widely scattered as to be difficult for the artillery to deal with. It will be seen that the problem to be faced was one that called for all the nerve, initiative, and élan for which the A.I.F. was so well known. The pill boxes had not previously been faced by Australian troops. The staff work of the 2nd Army with which our men were now associated was always of the highest quality, and that knowledge created great confidence.

On the 23rd, shortly after midday, the Battalion left Belgian Chateau and arrived at China Wall via the well-known Menin road. It was here well under shell fire, and all had to settle down as well as possible near our artillery. On the 24th an official photographer, who happened to be in the sector, took a photograph of a number of our men (mostly B Company), having lunch.[5] Two officers and 100 men were engaged duckboarding during the forenoon. Lieut. T. H. Templeton (C Company) was killed in action during the day. He was the fourth C Company officer killed during 1917 up to that time.[6] There was some heavy enemy shelling during the day, and an ammunition dump was blown up, causing some casualties. On the 25th there was more heavy shelling in the vicinity of A Company. Meanwhile the Battalion officers about to take part in the engagement reconnoitred the route to be taken to the front line. When the A Company officers and some other ranks were making their reconnaissance a German shell landed in the midst of them, killing Cpl. D. Watson, and severely wounding Sgt. J. L. Blair.

*China Wall.*

*Lieut. Templeton Killed.*

The battle to which the 4th Brigade was now committed was fixed for the 26th. The following extracts from orders dated the 24th, and issued to the units engaged, give particulars of the operation as follows:—"The 4th Brigade, in conjunction with the 14th Brigade on the right, and 13th Brigade on the left, will assume offensive operations in two

*Orders for the Engagement.*

---

[4]The German machine gunners were picked men, the flower of their army, who frequently fought to the death.

[5]Vide photo facing page 290

[6]The others were Capt. Stewart Hansen mortally wounded at Stormy trench, Capt. "Lofty" Williamson killed at Bullecourt, and Lieut. Viv. Garner killed at Gapaard.

stages. 1st stage (red line), 2nd stage (blue line). 16th Battalion will secure the red line. 15th and 14th Battalions on a frontage of about 500 yards will secure the blue line. 13th Battalion will be in reserve in position now occupied. The barrage will be put down 150 yards in front of our forming up line at zero. It will begin to advance at zero plus three minutes, at the rate of 100 yards in four minutes for 200 yards; thereafter and up to the red line, the rate will be 100 yards in six minutes. Just prior to movement from red line it will increase in intensity, and troops will move up close under it."

*Company and Platoon Commanders.*

The following is a list of the company and platoon commanders who took part in the battle:—A Company—O.C., Capt. Harold B. Wanliss, D.S.O.; Platoons: (1) 2nd-Lieut. L. G. Stevens, (2) Lieut. N. C. Aldridge, (3) an N.C.O. (not known), (4) 2nd-Lieut. G. F. Wilson. B Company—O.C., Capt. P. J. Hayes; Platoons: (5) 2nd-Lieut. Lloyd Gill, (6) 2nd-Lieut. Cyril George, (7) Sgt. W. H. Fletcher, (8) 2nd-Lieut. H. J. Schutz. C Company—O.C., Captain J. A. Mitchell, M.C.; Platoons: (9) 2nd-Lieut. F. G. Hyett, (10) 2nd-Lieut. Leslie Bain, (11) Sgt. W. E. Manie, (12) 2nd-Lieut. W. C. Fulton. D Company—O.C., Capt. Albert Jacka, V.C., M.C. and Bar; Platoons: (13) 2nd-Lieut. Ramsay Wood, (14) 2nd-Lieut. W. J. Hodges, (15) Sgt. G. F. H. Grundy, (16) 2nd-Lieut. R. O. Roxburgh.

*March to the J.O.T.*

*Adverse Conditions en route.*

The preparations for the attack were now completed, and at 12.15 a.m. on September 26 A Company led the way to the jumping-off position, followed by B, C, and D Companies, in that order. The route for a long distance followed a corduroy track which was crammed with traffic, necessitating the advancing troops leaving it, and ploughing their way through the thick mud adjoining the roadside. Leaving the so-called road, the march continued along an ill-marked pathway. After sundry stoppages caused by the intense darkness, and the difficulty of marching over rough shell-torn ground, all companies finally reached the point of deployment (B Company arriving somewhat late). Companies then moved off to their positions, an irregular line of shell holes along which a white tape had been stretched by the battalion intelligence officer to mark the position, and just behind the line held by the 13th Battalion. Companies were then formed up in line of sections, and all preparations for the attack completed by 4.45 a.m.—one hour before zero. Fortunately the anxieties of the trying night march had not been accentuated by attentions from the enemy's artillery, though it shelled the positions behind the 4th Brigade. Men were ordered to take shelter in shell holes where possible until zero hour.

The first objective (red line), allotted to the 16th Battalion, was about 800 yards from the J.O.T., whilst the second objective, allotted to the 14th and 15th (the former on the left, and the latter on the right), was about 350 yards further on. The companies of the 14th Battalion advanced from right to left, as follows: A, B, C, D,[7] a frontage of 62 yards being allotted to each company. The first platoon of each company formed the first wave, the second the moppers up, the third the supporting wave, and the fourth the carrying party. Two trench mortars and two machine guns of the famous 4th Machine Gun Company had been allotted to the 14th for the battle. Among the combatants were many seasoned veterans, whilst some were now taking part in their first hop-over. Zero time (5.50 a.m.) was now rapidly approaching. Men talked in subdued whispers. Immediately before zero all conversation ceased, and then, just before daybreak, with a stupendous roar, our barrage fell upon No Man's Land just in front of the J.O.T. The 4th Brigade had had previous experience of barrages, but this transcended anything it had ever fought under. It was the acme of perfection—a gigantic thunderstorm of bursting steel hurled out of the lips of thousands of guns, and grinding No Man's Land to powder. So close overhead was it, that the warm air caused by the friction of the shells could be distinctly felt. In addition an excellent machine-gun barrage was maintained by the 4th Machine Gun Company on the back portion of the enemy's line.[8] The morning was misty, making visibility difficult. Skyward were aeroplanes on business bent, immediately overhead the hurricane of flying lead, and beneath and behind it the long serried lines of the 4th Brigade, the West Australians of the 16th Battalion in front, and close behind them, side by side, the Victorians and Queenslanders of the 14th and

*Battle Arrangements.*

*Our Barrage Opens.*

*Its Stupendous Character.*

*Advance of 4th Brigade.*

---

This mode of attack (i.e., A Company on the right and D Company on the extreme left) was frequently adhered to in battles in which the 14th participated—e.g., August 8, 1915; Bullecourt, August 8, 1918.

[8] L/Sgt. "Dad" Brotchie (A Company) was put in command of a party detailed to bring up ammunition for the 4th Machine gunners during the engagement.

15th respectively—hundreds of grim, tigerish figures advancing resolutely upon the foe, many of them with cigarettes in their lips. Seldom has an assault been delivered with grander enthusiasm. The excellence of our artillery barrage, and the absence of effective enemy artillery retaliation, had put all in great heart, and in addition the 14th was that day led by Company Commanders some of whom were unsurpassed in the A.I.F. All were full of confidence; nothing short of annihilation would have checked the onset of the 14th that morning. The ground over which the attack took place was in a frightful state, in places knee-deep in mud.

**Frightful Condition of Terrain.** There were shell holes every few yards, most of them filled with water. These conditions made the going very arduous, particularly as little sleep had been obtained by the combatants on the previous night. Excitement and the prospect of victory, however, supplied the necessary tonic to face the difficulties ahead. The first fatal casualty of the unit in the battle seems to have been No. 7035, Pte. Dan Kearney, of Geelong, who was killed by one of our own shells falling short about five minutes after the barrage opened. On rolled the advance towards the first objective. A spraying machine-gun fire from the enemy was causing casualties, but not more than were expected. The foe seemed dazed by the violence of the barrage, but strong opposition was experienced by the 16th Battalion from a series of concrete pill boxes on the extreme left flank which hung up the attack in that quarter. Captain Jacka immediately sized up the position, and acting with his usual promptitude, led a number of 14th men to the assistance of the 16th. The co-operative work of these two fine units proved entirely successful, the pill boxes were captured, and the occupants either killed or sent back as

**Capture of First Objective.** prisoners. After the capture of the first objective the barrage remained stationary for some considerable time, and here the West Australians remained, digging in and consolidating the position. They had reached their objective. The Victorians and Queenslanders were now responsible for the completion of the battle, and when the barrage moved on the 14th followed, the first wave getting as close under it as was safe. As the advance progressed the opposition stiffened, and the machine-gun fire of the enemy became greater, causing a fair number of casualties. Several enemy machine-guns and their crews were captured, one machine-gunner captured being chained to his gun. Few of the enemy outside the pill boxes waited for our barrage, though some did, and occasionally a German would fly up skyward as one of our shells lobbed in a shell hole beside him. The majority, however, either bolted through the barrage, or retired before its advent, forming excellent targets for our men, of which they took full advantage.

*Stirring Incidents in the Advance.* L/Cpl. R. Spearing (D Company) among others showed great initiative and daring, rushing out with his Lewis gun in front of his comrades under a heavy hostile fire and cutting up the retreating enemy. Cpl. Bill Fergus (D Company) and some of his moppers-up rushed a blockhouse under heavy fire, and captured twelve prisoners, whilst Cpl. T. H. French (B Company) and a handful of men captured a strong point that was holding up the attack. Cpl. "Sarto" Anderson, of the Scouts, rendered great assistance to the Intelligence Officer in the advance, and showed his usual courage and determination in leading an attack on a post, the inmates of which were all killed or captured. Pte. George Radnell (A Company) with seven men rushed an enemy's post, killing four of the occupants, and taking six prisoners. Many other acts of heroism were performed before the second objective was won.

The very keenness of the attack, however, might have led to disaster. The barrage paused for a short time to bombard some enemy strong points. The first wave, pressing on too impetuously, failed to observe that the barrage was stationary until almost under it. Orders were given to retire from the danger zone and take cover. Succeeding waves, seeing the leaders turn back, turned also. The position for a moment looked serious, but Capt. Jacka, with consummate courage, disregarding the barrage, rushed forward, rallying the men and signalling them to follow. The second *Capture of Second Objective.* objective, a small road running across our front, was reached about 8 a.m., but instead of digging in there, the Battalion moved forward some 40 or 50 yards, and the wisdom of the company commanders in carrying out this move was proved later. Just after the second objective was reached Capt. *Capt. Wanliss Killed.* Harold Wanliss was killed at the head of his men, falling in the moment of victory to which his inspiring leadership had so largely contributed. Lieut. N. C. Aldridge immediately took charge of A Company. Sgt.-Major Ayre (4th Platoon), and Sgts. Andrew Hutton and "Winch" Williams (both of D Company) had also been killed in the advance, whilst 2nd-Lieuts. G. F. Wilson, Cyril George, and W. C. Fulton had been wounded, the two former by missiles from our own artillery.

**Enemy Retire from Brodseinde Ridge.**
At this juncture the enemy were seen streaming back over Brodseinde Ridge, and there seems little doubt that that commanding position could have been captured and held that day by the 4th Brigade. Unfortunately, the system of limited objectives, invariably adopted by the higher command, prevented this favourable opportunity from being utilised, and as our men were consolidating, they were compelled to watch the enemy returning. Another costly attack had to be delivered on a subsequent occasion to oust our opponents from a position that had actually been vacated by them on the 26th.

**German Prisoners.**
Many scores of German prisoners were straggling back, some looking objects of abject misery as the result of their experience under our barrage, but others looking profoundly relieved at being captured. Many were killed by their own artillery fire before they reached safety. Some were rounded up into stretcher-parties, and cheerfully assisted in carrying back our wounded.

Our barrage remained stationary for some time at the second objective to give cover, whilst our men were digging in and consolidating the position, and though harassed by machine-gun fire, a respectable trench was dug by the time the covering barrage eased off. The enemy had meanwhile returned, and his machine-gun fire increased, while the missiles from one of his trench mortars of large calibre caused D Company some trouble.

About 3 p.m. the Germans formed up in front of D Company for a counter-attack, preceded as usual by a 5.9 bombardment, but the majority of the shells fell, fortunately, with great accuracy on the road just behind our line, and the foresight displayed in pushing forward for a few yards beyond it had saved the situation.

**A German Counter-attack Repulsed.**

Capt. Jacka, who had taken charge of the front line, allowed them to form up about 350 yards away, and then the S.O.S. signal went up. Our artillery put up a very solid barrage, which, combined with the machine-gun and rifle fire of our men, mowed them down in hundreds; only one man among them succeeded in getting as close as about 70 yards from our line. The German stretcher-bearers were busy the whole afternoon, and probably four or five hundred of the enemy were killed on the battalion front in that counter-attack alone. The attack appeared to have been made diagonally across our front, and the survivors bolted over the high ground on the right in front of the 15th Battalion. Again about 6 p.m.

another heavy enemy barrage opened on our front line, but the S.O.S. signal went up, and our barrage opened quickly. The hostile attack failed to develop, our Lewis guns and rifle fire helping to break it up. Strong points were constructed and manned by our men[9] during the night, and our patrols were also pushed out. Rations were got up after dark, and a good hot meal heartened all ranks.

It had been deemed advisable for some reason shortly after the battle started to move Battalion Headquarters from the position first chosen to a different locality. The result, unfortunately, was that touch was lost with the front line for some time during a critical period of the battle, thus throwing an additional responsibility on the fighting officers.

Just at daybreak next morning (27th) the Germans formed up for another counter-attack, but were cut to pieces by our barrage, and suffered very heavy losses. Their stretcher-bearers were busy all day. Meanwhile 2nd-Lieut. Hyett's platoon (No. 9) took over portion of the red line.

*Another Counter-attack Repulsed.*

*Enemy Barrages.* The enemy put up three artillery barrages during the 27th, at 11 a.m., 6 p.m., and 10 p.m. respectively. The barrage at 6 p.m. was very severe, particularly on the 15th Battalion on our right, and everything portended a counter-attack on that unit. A characteristic message was sent down our line from mouth to mouth from Capt. Jacka: "If the Hun attacks the 15th, we shall hop out and meet the blighters. Advise the 15th." The attack, however, did not develop. The Battalion put in a third day (28th) in the line before it was relieved. The enemy put down a heavy barrage on our front line and supports on the 28th, but did not attack. His appetite for counter-attacks had apparently been whetted. 2nd-Lieut. L. H. Gill (No. 5 Platoon) was killed just before the relief, whilst 2nd-Lieut. F. G. Hyett was severely wounded earlier in the day. About 8 p.m. the 14th was relieved by the 45th Battalion, after a very gruelling time in the line. The exigencies of the battle had imposed a heavy strain on all ranks, and taxed to the utmost the energies of the combatants. Nevertheless all were justly proud of the splendid record put up by the Battalion, and of a success more brilliant than any previously achieved by the 14th in the whole of its long and chequered career. The intrepidity and élan of its attack had been equalled by the indomitable firmness of its defence. The pill

*Battalion's Splendid Record.*

---

[9] Sgt. Allan McDonald and Cpl. A. C. Hutton showed tenacity and resolution in charge of advance posts, whilst Cpl. R. L. McKenry and his section dealt effectively during the advance with a nest of enemy snipers.

boxes had been promptly and effectively dealt with, and had proved unable to hold back the onslaught of the 4th Brigade. Our front line, pelted by hostile missiles of every calibre for days, had never wavered, and all the enemy's counter-attacks, gallantly launched, had been smashed to fragments with tremendous hostile losses. The battle was a fitting climax to a succession of outstanding battalion achievements. As in 1916, so in 1917 the work of the 14th at Stormy Trench, Bullecourt, Messines, and Polygon Wood had throughout been a great record, and one that could be looked back upon with pride. The present engagement was an outstanding triumph for Capt. Jacka. His personal achievements **Capt. Jacka's** in previous battles had been the admiration **Record.** of his countrymen, but at Polygon Wood, when the opportunity came, he displayed in addition a power of leadership, a grasp of tactics, and a military intuition that many had not given him credit for. It is impossible to over-estimate the value of his services during those three days in the line. He carried the left wing of the Battalion forward with a magnificent dash to the second objective, and there took practical control of the unit, and was thereafter the guiding spirit of the storm of battle. His reckless valour, his excellent judgment, his skilful tactics, his prompt anticipation of the enemy's movements, and the force and vigour of his battle strokes gained the admiration of all ranks, and inspired everyone with the greatest confidence. Throughout the whole engagement he was an ubiquitous and fearless figure, the very incarnation of a great fighting soldier and a born leader of men. No more fearless or gallant soldier took part in the Great War.

Another officer who was very prominent and whose work was of a high order was Lieut. J. H. Johnson, the popular and courageous Intelligence Officer. He went for-
**Others** ward with the Battalion, taking an active part
**Prominent.** in directing the attack, and visited the front line on several occasions. He appears to have been the only officer from Battalion Headquarters at the front line during the engagement. Capt. Mitchell, Lieuts. Ramsay Wood, N. C. Aldridge, and other officers displayed marked courage, and put in much solid and conscientious work. It is difficult to speak too appreciatively of the work of the Battalion's staunch N.C.O.'s and other ranks during those three trying days: it was, as ever, solid, courageous, and unostentatious. A word of praise, too, must
**13th Battalion's** be accorded to our comrades of the 13th Bat-
**Work.** talion, in reserve, whose duties were arduous, and casualties severe, but who nevertheless

worked effectively and untiringly for their comrades in the front line.

After relief the 14th marched to the canal area, and next day (29th) to Winnipeg Camp—a number of wooden huts with galvanised roofs. A further move was made on the 30th by motor to Steenvorde, and the usual training recommenced. The popular padre (Major F. W. Rolland) had arranged as usual an entertainment supper for the combatants, after coming out of the line—a relaxation that was much appreciated by all ranks.

*Relief.*
*Post Battle Entertainment.*

The Regimental Aid Post was located in a pill box alongside Battalion Headquarters during the engagement, but, owing to the non-receipt by the company commanders of a message sent by the R.M.O. as to its locality, few of the 14th wounded were passed to it, most of them going to, and being treated at, the R.A.P. of the 15th Battalion. Owing to the heavy and continuous enemy barrages, the duties of the stretcher-bearers proved exceptionally dangerous, with consequent heavy casualties. They, however, worked unceasingly, with their usual gallantry. Thirty-two stretcher-bearers took part in the engagement, and at its conclusion only seven of them were fit for duty, and the whole of the eight stretchers, and most of the equipment, had been destroyed by enemy action.[10] Outstanding work was done by the following stretcher-bearers, viz.:—Ptes. William Watson, John Thompson, Abraham Milner, Frank Lowe, James Cooper, E. W. Hibberd, Maurice Harrison, and Thomas Connors. Sgt. H.G. Richmond and Cpl. A. P. Whitelaw were prominent among the signallers for efficient work and courageous conduct. The runners, in addition to having frequently to carry despatches through heavy hostile barrages, were often targets for enemy machine-gunners and snipers. Among them mention must be made of Ptes. H. L. Parman, Stan Adams, E. Wilkinson, and Varney Bradley, who were ubiquitous as well as resourceful. Bradley, though wounded, crawled back to his company, and delivered a message.

*The Medical Personnel.*

*Signallers and Runners.*

The brilliant victory at Polygon Wood was not purchased without severe losses, not so much numerically, as in the quality of those killed. Whilst the exact figures are not available, the number of combatants appears to have been about 450; but, including Battalion Headquarters, and other non-

---

[10]Information supplied by Capt. Hugh Trumble, M.C., the R.M.O.

*The History of the 14th Battalion.* 247

combatants, about 500 14th men must have taken part in the engagement. The casualties—nearly all in-
**Casualties.** curred on the 26th—numbered 170, including three officers and 37 other ranks killed or died of wounds; four officers and 119 other ranks wounded, and seven other ranks missing. The death of
**Capt. Wanliss.** Capt. Wanliss[11] created a profound impression on all ranks. As he was the son of the author of this history, it is more fitting that his character should be recorded by his C.O.'s and his comrades in arms. The written opinions of some of them are set out in the appendix to this chapter.

Second-Lieut. Gill[12] had joined up with the 4th Reinforcements, and now sealed his long connection with the unit by death. The N.C.O.'s killed included Sgt.-
**N.C.O. Casualties.** Majors A. J. K. Ayre and Andrew Hutton,
**Sgt. A. Hutton** Sgt. "Winch" Williams, Cpls. D. Watson,
**Killed.** Frank Davis and Frank Hunter. A. J. K. Ayre was a nautical man from Essex (England), whilst Andrew Hutton was an original, and one of the Battalion's finest soldiers who had distinguished himself at Pozieres.[13] Had he been spared, he would probably have attained commission rank. Frank Hunter (Lewis gunner) was another fine soldier (5th Reinforcements) who fell alongside the second objective. Two of the very best stretcher-bearers were also among the killed, viz., Ptes. Thomas Connors (A Company) and "Darkie" Rowse (C Company). Rowse had been one of the six chosen to represent the 14th at the Duke of Connaught's inspection at Bailleul, after the battle of Messines. He was the only representative of C Company on that historic occasion.[14]

The wounded included 2nd-Lieuts. G. F. Wilson, Cyril George, W. C. Fulton and F. G. Hyett. The following N.C.O.'s were wounded, viz.:—Sgts. J. Blair,
**Wounded.** D. Drummond, W. R. Amor, W. L. Edmonstone and E. J. Horrocks, L/Sgt. M. M. Lewis and Cpls. J. Scarf, F. Johnston and L/Cpl. J. J. Moriarty. Among the wounded was Pte. J. V. Cook (No. 44), an original who had distinguished himself at Quinn's Post on

---

[11] Capt. Harold Boyd Wanliss, D.S.O., Orchardist, of Lorne (V.). Born at Ballarat (V.) on December 11, 1891. Dux of Ballarat College and winner of the college "Rhodes" medal; dux of his year at Hawkesbury Agricultural College (N.S.W.). K.I.A. September 26, 1917.

[12] 2nd-Lieut. Lloyd Hassell Gill, Bank Clerk, of Melbourne. K.I.A. September 28, 1917.

[13] Vide Chap. 21.

[14] Vide Chap. 30.

April 27, 1915, where his heroism was probably the means of saving his wounded officer's life.

**Decorations.** A large number of decorations were awarded to the N.C.O.'s and men for their fine work in the battle of September 26 to September 28, but there was not any 14th officer who received a decoration—not even Captain Jacka.

The following is a list of the decorations referred to:— D.C.M.—392, Sgt. Charles Thompson (Orbost, V.); 4185, L/Sgt. W. H. Fergus (Maryborough, V.). Bar to M.M.— 6122, Pte. William Watson (Orford, V.), stretcher-bearer (M.M. won at Bullecourt). M.M.—6829, Pte. Ernest Wilkinson (Kogarah, N.S.W.), runner; 7094, Pte. John Thompson (Glasgow, Scot.), stretcher-bearer; 3238, Pte. E. C. Saunders (Fitzroy, V.), stretcher-bearer; 4612, L/Cpl. R. Spearing (Camperdown, V.), Lewis gunner; 1734, Pte. Geo. Radnell (Tarnagulla, V.); 5407, Abraham Milner, stretcher-bearer; 5695, Pte. F. A. V. Lowe (Nth. Fitzroy), stretcher-bearer; 5688, L/Cpl. V. W. Lalor (Healesville, V.), Lewis gunner; 6858, Cpl. A. C. Hutton (Sydney, N.S.W.); 6139, L/Cpl. E. "Darkey" Harrison (Maffra, V.), observer; 5376, Sgt. W. H. Fletcher (Box Hill, V.); 6022, Cpl. T. H. French (Geelong, V.); 1559, Cpl. J. R. H. Franklin (Carnegie, V.); 3265, Pte. James Cooper (Hexham, V.); stretcher-bearer; 2792, Pte. Varney Bradley (Nottingham, Eng.), runner; 676, Cpl. H. A. "Sarto" Anderson (Collingwood, V.), scout.

## APPENDIX.

The following are extracts from letters received on the death of Capt. Harold B. Wanliss :—

Lieut. General Sir John Monash, G.C.M.G., K.C.B.—"An infantry leader who had few equals."

Lieut. Col. J. H. Peck, C.M.G., D.S.O.—"Many brave men—many good men have I met and spoken to and lived with and fought with in this war, but he was the king of them all."

Lieut. Col. J. M. A. Durrant, C.M.G., D.S.O.—"His greatness of character was a remarkable feature among many brave men. A splendid soldier—none braver—none more beloved by his men."

Lieut. Col. F. W. Rolland, M.C.—"The best man and the best soldier and the truest gentleman in our Brigade . . . . and unless I was blind, he would have been Australia's leader in days when she will sorely need one."

Major A. R. Cox.—"The finest officer the Battalion ever had."

Captain A. Jacka, V.C., M.C. and Bar.—"A hero and a man."

Pte. A. Downie.—"A man among men, and worshipped by us all."

Vide also an article by Mr. C. E. W. Bean (the Australian Official Historian of the War) published in "The Link"—Toc H. newspaper—of October 1, 1926.—"One who, in the estimate of many of his numerous friends, had been destined—had he lived—to be a great leader of his countrymen."

## CHAPTER XXXIII.

### PASSCHENDAELE.

### 1917—October 1 to November 15.

**Reorganisation.** After a severe battle like Polygon Wood, where numerous casualties were incurred, there was much reorganisation to be done and vacancies for officers and N.C.O.'s to be filled, consequently the Battalion Headquarters was for some days busy with that necessary detail work. Sgts. Steve De Arango (A Company), R. J. Garcia (B Company), W. E. Manie (C Company) and F. H. Boyes (D Company) were promoted to be 2nd-Lieuts. All (except Manie, who came with the 4th Reinforcements) were originals with excellent records.

**Appointments as Commissioned Officers.**

**March Towards Battle Area.** On October 8 preliminary move orders were issued preparatory to another tour of duty in the line, and on the 11th the Battalion marched to Halifax camp, whilst the 33 per cent. of the unit (not required in the line) marched to Caestre, living there in tents until it rejoined the Battalion. Next day a further march brought the 14th to Belgian battery corner, one N.C.O. and ten men from each company being detailed as a working party for the purpose of pumping water out of underground dugouts. On the 13th the unit finally moved, as divisional reserve, to the support line, a sunken road about a kilo. in rear of the front line, and situated not far from the site of the Battalion's activity in the recent battle of Polygon Wood. The march to the line was made in intense darkness, often through mud and slush nearly thigh deep, several men getting stuck and having to be pulled out by their comrades. The battalions to be relieved were the 45th and 48th, the latter a very fine West Australian unit which had fought alongside the 14th at Pozieres in August, 1916.

**Move to Support Lines.**

**Adverse Conditions en Route.**

**Battalion in Reserve Line.** The reserve line, in which the Battalion now found itself, was not a trench, but a series of shell holes partly filled with slush and water, and during the night it was as far as possible consolidated. In front was a swamp several hundred yards wide tenanted on its other side by the enemy. Daylight (14th) disclosed gruesome surroundings. The locality was strewn with the bodies of dead Australians of other units who had fallen in the disastrous battle of October 12, the railway cutting on the left in particular being thick with the bodies of men who had been cut down by machine gun fire. D Company held the left sector (its left flank being the Ypres Roulers railway), with C on the right, and A and B in support. The enemy's artillery was very active on the morning of the 14th, both on our front and support lines (pelting the latter with gas shells). There was also further intermittent shelling during the day. Patrols were sent out both on the left and the right. The Battalion suffered a severe loss during the day owing to a chance shell mortally wounding Warrant-Officer R. S. M. Pringle, one of its outstanding personalities. He died on the 16th.

*Gruesome Surroundings.*

*Apportionment of Companies.*

*Enemy Artillery Active.*

*R. S. M. Pringle Mortally Wounded.*

On the 15th the enemy's artillery was very active during the day, also sending over a heavy barrage of 5.9's and gas shells soon after dark, but fortunately the soft and swampy nature of the surroundings proved a blessing in disguise, for most of the shells landed in the bog which did not possess sufficient resisting power to explode the detonators. Men were beginning to complain of their feet, the conditions being ideal for trench feet. A patrol of A Company, under 2nd-Lieut. George Huse (a very active member of the unit), scouted as far as "Assyria" to get in touch with the enemy. Hostile artillery and aircraft were active during the day—in the air the enemy seemed to predominate. Patrols sent out by A and D Companies found no signs of the enemy, who was evidently relying principally on his artillery. An intense enemy bombardment of 5.9's from 4 to 6 p.m. might have resulted in the annihilation of our men, but the boggy soil again proved our salvation. October 16 was an unfortunate day for the N.C.O.'s of the Battalion, for on that date Sgts. Richmond and Kohlmann and Warrant-Officer R. S. M. Pringle died of wounds and Cpl. W. T. Primrose was killed. On the evening of that day the 14th was relieved by the 15th Battalion, and moved back to the railway dugouts. The casualties during this tour of duty in the line

*Further Intense Hostile Bombardments.*

*Sgts. Richmond and Kohlman Killed.*

*14th Relieved.*

*Casualties.*

were set out as 4 officers wounded, 14 other ranks killed, 73 wounded, 8 missing and 37 sick. The casualties entailed in holding the line were as a rule not comparable numerically to those suffered in making an active attack on the enemy's position. Sgt. J. F. McPherson,[1] of C Company,

*Sgt. J. F. McPherson.* whose work in the line was always excellent, was awarded the D.C.M. for his courage and fortitude on the 15th, when he was blown up and badly shaken by a shell, but refused to leave the front line. Cpl. A. Webber, of B Company, also distinguished himself on the same day, remaining on duty though wounded.

*The R.A.P.* The R.A.P. was located in the cellar of the soda water factory at Zonnebeke cross roads (the super-structure having been destroyed). Owing to the heavy shelling and swampy surroundings the stretcher-bearers had an arduous time, but

*Stretcher-bearers.* carried out their duties with their usaul courage and devotion. W. A. Read, A. H. Kerr, W. E. Watts and Maurice Harrison were specially mentioned for their fine work. The runners as usual were splendid, some of them also acting as guides

*Runners.* to carrying parties. Among them Ptes. H. D. E. Withers, E. Wilkinson, H. Parman, S. A. McGrice and A. W. Kirby were prominent. The 14th Battalion transport men could always be relied

*Transport.* upon to get supplies of ammunition and rations to the fighting men, who could not have cerried on without their assistance. The hostile barrages tried their courage and abilities as drivers on many occasions, but could not turn them back. Cpl. James Reid and Drivers E. A. Mattson, Benjamin Hardner (an original No. 62), and R. L. S. ("Dooley") Dobson were prominent among them during this tour of duty. The signallers were another body of men whose work often had to be carried on under heavy

*Signallers.* shell fire, and it was doubly important, for, in addition to keeping up communication with Headquarters, it saved runners risking their lives when the telephone wires were intact. Sgt. H. G. Richmond's work on the 16th was outstanding, though it cost him his life; whilst Ptes. W. J. Hodge and R. M. Norman showed conspicuous courage and devotion to duty. Linesman J. Clough was killed on the 16th. The decorations awarded during this tour of duty are set out at the end of this chapter. Although the fatal casualties from October 13 to 16 had

*Casualties.* not been numerous, nevertheless, as was often the case, the quality of some of those killed

---

[1] Lieut. J. F. McPherson, D.C.M., Shop Assistant, of Yarra Glen (V.).

made their loss a serious one for the Battalion. Warrant-Officer R. S. M. Pringle[2] (4th Reinforcements) was a man of fine appearance, and one of the best soldiers in the Battalion. He was a splendid N.C.O. on parade, and shone above all others as an instructor; in addition he was brilliant and tactful, and had won the confidence of all ranks. Sgt. H. G. Richmond[3] was the original signalling sgt. of the Battalion (Regimental No. 10). He had been a very prominent figure in the famous route march of the 4th Brigade through the streets of Melbourne on December 17, 1914. He had been invalided from the Peninsula in September, 1915, and was thereafter engaged in instructional work in England, rejoining the Battalion on June 21, 1917. Had he lived he was almost certain to have attained commissioned rank. His courage and devotion to duty on the day of his death were worthy of the finest traditions of the Battalion.

*R. S. M. Pringle.*

*Sgt. H. G. Richmond.*

Immediately on being relieved on the 16th the Battalion moved back to the railway dugouts, and on the following day had a well-earned rest. On the 18th the Battalion left the railway dugouts and moved again towards the line, occupying various locations on Westhoek ridge. It was evident that the men were to be employed on the detested fatigues. The ridge was fairly high; on one side could be seen the remains of Ypres, and on the other the endless bursting of enemy shells: a few isolated ones reached our lines, of which practically no notice were taken. Our own guns in response were incessantly belching forth their messengers of destruction. Everywhere was Flanders mud, which had by this time become a nightmare to all ranks. Two veteran C Company N.C.O.'s (both originals) received well-earned commissions at this time, viz., Sgts. F. T. Larter and Chas. Thompson. Sundry fatigues were carried out during the next few days, including much carrying and laying of duck boards. The main roads were strewn with dead horses and mules; the surviving animals (accustomed to the eternal din) took no notice of the proximity of bursting shells. The

*Another Tour of Duty.*

*Sgts. F. Larter and C. Thompson Receive Commissions.*

---

[2]Warrant Officer A. Pringle (No. 1807), of Glenferrie (V.), Ironmonger. Born at Hawthorn (V.) on May 28, 1897. D.W. October 16, 1917.

[3]Sgt. H. G. Richmond (No. 10), of Abbotsford (V.), Wood Machinist. D.W. October 16, 1917.

nights were now becoming frosty, and the prospect of a third tour in the line was not alluring, but on the 21st orders were received for the 14th to take over the line and relieve the 13th Battalion. The 14th left Westhoek ridge about 5 p.m., and its personnel, marching in single file over the new line of duck boards (placed there on the two previous days), with deep bogs on either side, reached the front line. The relief had not been completed without casualties. A march in daylight in sight of Fritz's observation balloons brought the inevitable enemy shelling, with the result that one heavy high explosive landed right on the duck board track, killing Capt. H. V. Walklate (O.C. of D Company) and Sgt. C. Currie, and wounding two men. Capt. Walklate was the tenth (and last) captain of the 14th killed during the war.[4] The line occupied was very close to the one occupied by the 14th from October 14 to 16. A, B and D Companies were in front with C in support. There was some heavy enemy shelling in the early part of the night with fortunately very few casualties. The 22nd was a quiet day. Patrols, however, were sent out, and some wiring done. The 23rd was another comparatively quiet day, and the 14th was relieved during the evening by the 8th Battalion, and all wended their way thankfully back to camp near Ypres. The casualties during this third period in the line had fortunately been very slight, and were set out as 6 killed (including one officer), 17 wounded and 17 evacuated sick. A feature of the Passchendaele operations was the deadly gas sent over by the enemy, the lethal effects of which were often only disclosed at a later date.

*14th Relieves the 13th Battalion.*

*Death of Capt. Walklate and Sgt. C. Currie.*

*Relief.*

*Casualties.*

The R.A.P. was again located in the soda water factory as on the previous tour of duty. Sgt. W. Coleman, Pte. R. E. Denham (stretcher-bearer), Cpl. Frank Harding (No. 61, an original), and Pte. H. Parman (runner) distinguished themselves during this tour of duty. Parman, though wounded on the 21st three times when carrying a message, struggled on and delivered it before being sent to the R.A.P. Few as were the fatal casualties, again some valuable lives were lost. Capt. Harold

*R.A.P.*

---

[4]The others were Capts. W. R. Hoggart, W. E. Groom, A. Gillison, C. E. Connelly, S. M. Hansen, R. W. Orr, F. B. Stanton, A. Williamson and H. B. Wanliss.

Walklate,[5] (14th Reinforcements), though a rigid disciplinarian, was popular among all ranks. He was a brave man and always keen for action. Sgt. C. Currie[6] was one of three brothers fighting in the ranks of D Company, two of whom became sergeants. Another man much missed was Pte. Bill Porter[7] (killed on the 21st), an original D Company man (No. 1284) and one of its finest stretcher-bearers: a quiet and unassuming man his ideal was Christianity, which he practised both in and out of the line. He was highly respected by his comrades. Twice wounded on the Peninsula, and again at Bullecourt, he ranks among those conscientious and unostentatious heroes whose life and death helped to form the traditions of the Battalion.

*Death of Stretcher bearer W. Porter.*

The 14th moved to Devonshire camp on the 24th by bus, being rejoined by the 33 per cent. of the unit from Caestre. On the 27th a further move was made to Predifin, in the immediate vicinity of Fontaine-les-Boulans. Here the unit was among old friends, and inquiries from them were numerous as to the fate of many who fell at Polygon Wood and Paschendaele. Nearly three weesk were spent here, only light training being carried on. The locality was far from the front, and the temporary release from the eternal strain of war acted as a tonic on all ranks.

*Move to Predifin.*

It may be fairly claimed that the work of the Australians in the third battle of Ypres. and the staggering blows they struck their opponents had been outstanding, without in any way disparaging the fine work of the British and French troops who participated in the prolonged battle. Their losses,[8] however, had been appalling. This campaign, comparatively short as it was, had been the bloodiest of the many bloody campaigns in which the Australians participated during the Great War, whilst the hardships endured—everlasting mud, bitter cold, almost continual rain and waterlogged trenches—had tried the nerve and strength of all ranks to the utmost.

*Outstanding Work of Australians.*

---

[5]Captain Harold Vernon Walklate, of Malvern (V.), Accountant. Born Launceston (Tas.), July 20, 1884. K.I.A. October 21, 1917.

[6]No. 2350, Sgt. Charles Currie, of Footscray (V.), Labourer. K.I.A. October 21, 1917.

[7]No. 1284, Pte. William Porter, of Tylden (V.), Student. K.I.A. October 21, 1917.

[8]The Australian casualties from September 20 to end of October, 1917, averaged nearly 1000 per day.

**Unification of Australian Command.**

An incident worthy of record is that on November 15, the 3rd A.I.F. Division was transferred to the 1st Anzac Corps, and for the first time all the Australian Divisions in France came at length under one command.

**Decorations.**

The following is a list of the decorations awarded to the 14th during October, 1917:—

M.C.—Lieut. J. H. Johnson (Beeac, V.), intelligence officer (temporarily attached to 4th Brigade Headquarters). D.C.M.—No. 3391, Sgt. J. F. McPherson (Yarra Glen, V.). Bar to M.M.—No. 6829, Pte. Ernest Wilkinson (Kogarah, N.S.W.), runner (M.M. won at Zonnebeke (Polygon Wood), September 26, 1917). M.M.—No. 61, Cpl. Frank J. W. Harding (Footscray, V.); No. 5080, Pte. R. E. Denham (Geachville, V.), stretcher-bearer; No. 2464, Sgt. William Coleman (Sth. Preston, V.); No. 3803, Pte. W. J. Hodge (Caulfield, V.), linesman; No. 3450, Pte. H. Parman (Preston, V.), runner; No. 1656, Pte. R. M. Norman (St. Kilda, V.), linesman; No. 1952, Pte. Maurice Harrison (Euroa, V.), stretcher-bearer; No. 10, Sgt. H. G. Richmond (Abbotsford, V.), pioneer sergeant; No. 2040, Pte. D. E. Withers (Moyston, V.), runner; No. 283, Cpl. Albert Webber (Devon, England). Medaille Militaire—No. 771, Pte. James Reid (Philip Island, V.), transport.

## CHAPTER XXXIV

### THE LAST WAR WINTER.

1917-1918—November 16 to February 28.

On November 16 information was received that the 4th Brigade—after so many disappointments—was to get its frequently promised and long-overdue three months' rest, and that in furtherance thereof it was to move to Abbeville, near the mouth of the Somme, a reserve area almost on the sea coast.

*March North for Winter Quarters.* The Brigade accordingly left the Fruges sector on the 16th, and commenced its march North, a journey which lasted seven days, and was carried out in easy stages. Many localities of great historical interest were passed en route, among others the battlefields of Agincourt (A.D., 1415), with its soldiers' cemetery, and Crecy (A.D., 1346), where the famous Black Prince won his spurs, mediaeval battles fought between the English and French. It was from the mouth of the Somme that William the Conqueror with his army of freebooters sailed for the conquest of England (A.D., 1066). Few Australians had been in any of these localities before, consequently the local charges for refreshments or meals were reasonable, and not the extortionate demands that our men had frequently to submit to where they were well known.

*Historical Battlefields en Route.*

*Brigade Reaches Fressenneviele.* The Brigade's destination, Fressenneviele, was reached on November 24. The weather had been generally fine, but the cold was increasing, and darkness setting in early. As the whole winter was expected to be spent in the locality everyone proceeded to make themselves as comfortable as possible, and to get ready to prepare for a thorough course of systematic training which continual service in the line had rendered difficult for the Brigade to carry out previously.

*Germans Break Through at Cambrai.* Meanwhile towards the end of November the Germans broke the British line at Cambrai, and on December 3 orders were received for the Brigade to be prepared for an early move.

## The History of the 14th Battalion. 257

**4th Brigade Ordered to Meet It.**
Next day preliminary move orders were issued, and all realised that after a short spell of ten days they were again to be hurled into the furnace of battle. A train journey to Peronne was followed by a march over slippery frozen roads to Moislains, the horses and mules suffering severely on the journey. By this time, fortunately, the fighting at Cambrai had died down, and instead of being thrown into the line the 4th Brigade was in consequence only used as a reserve. The personnel was put on the usual fatigues, varied by tactical exercises and training. On December 20 another

**Templeux-la-Fosse.**
march over frozen roads brought the 14th to Templeux-la-Fosse, where a stay of three weeks was made. Here Christmas was spent —the last during the war. The locality was bleak, desolate and snow-covered, but, nevertheless, enjoyment reigned supreme for one day. The morning of the

**Xmas, 1917.**
25th was ushered in by Christmas carols, whilst the brigade pierrots provided an excellent entertainment, "Cinderella Up-to-date." The thoughts of all turned that day to the land they loved, and which many were destined never to see again. The Christmas dinner, in addition to the ordinary rations, was supplemented by gifts from the Australian Comforts Fund. The last week of the year was uneventful, and was spent in the same locality.

It will be advisable here to give a brief resume of the Battalion's doings during that trying year 1917. The French winter of 1916-17 was extraordinarily severe,

**Resume of Battalion's Record in 1917.**
and many of the Battalion were evacuated sick. The 14th, however, under the virile leadership of Col. Peck, attained in the early part of 1917 its high water mark of discipline and efficiency. The engagement at Stormy Trench, in which C Company acted in support of an attack made by the 13th Battalion, resulted in heavy losses, including the death of Capt. Stewart Hansen, O.C. of C Company, an original, and one of the unit's finest officers. The German retreat in March heartened all ranks, portending to many sanguine individuals the immediate end of the war. The disastrous battle of Bullecourt on April 11, however, resulted in what was doubtless the worst experience that the 4th Brigade had during the war. It was set a practically impossible task, and in spite of an heroic exhibition of gallantry, was cut to ribbons, and almost annihilated. Approximately the fatal casualties of the 14th in that engagement comprised twenty-five per cent. of the officers and fifteen per cent. of the other ranks who lost their

lives with the unit during the war. In spite of this holocaust the Brigade was subsequently put into the line on the Messines front on no less than three separate occasions during the summer, in the first of which Capts. Jones and Jacka did outstanding work. In spite of absolute exhaustion, caused by continual front line service and endless fatigues, the Brigade was again hurled into the battle of Polygon Wood on September 26, where the 14th gained great glory, and fought the most successful battle of its career up to that time, but at the cost of some very valuable lives. Two other tours of duty in the line near Passchendaele in October completed an extremely arduous year, with heavy attendant casualties, which included 17 officers killed, among whom were six captains. Major Margolin commanded the unit during the summer, and Lieut.-Col. Smith took charge in September. A march of seven days by the 4th Brigade in November towards the sea coast for a long promised three months' rest resulted in a short spell there of but ten days, when the Brigade was rushed down to Peronne, and then marched north to help stem a German break through at Cambrai. Here it remained till the end of the year.

The heavy fighting, with the necessary arduous preparatory work, the hated fatigues when out of the line, and the absolute want of rest during the year had worn the Brigade out. Merit and keenness in military life too often simply makes a unit, as well as an individual, a target for unceasing calls for unlimited effort. The career of the 14th during 1917 had been chequered though glorious—it had done, humanly speaking, all that any unit could be expected to do. Its record at Stormy Trench, Bullecourt, Messines and Polygon Wood had been superb, and its fighting reputation if possible had been enhanced. The muzzling effects of the newspaper censorship, however existent during the war, largely camouflaged the brilliant incidents of its career, and prevented the people of its home State from realising its great record. The war at the end of 1917 seemed as if it were to be interminable. Its prolongation was a matter of comparative indifference to the personnel habituated to the base camps, or behind the line, but many fighting officers and men at this time never expected to see Australia again.

*Battalion's Fine Record During 1917.*

### 1918.

The advent of 1918 found the Battalion still at Templeux-la-Fosse. The forenoon of New Year's Day was devoted to a brigade tactical exercise, which was a great success, whilst the afternoon was filled in with organised games. The Battalion strength was set out on January 2 as 49 officers and 730 other ranks—an enormous proportion of officers. The next few days were occupied with the usual training and fatigues, but as the enemy in the neighbourhood remained quiescent the services of the 4th Brigade as a fighting unit were not required, and orders were received for it to move north, return to its own corps, and take over the reserve sector near Hollebeke then held by the 63rd British Division.

**4th Brigade Rejoins Its Own Corps.**

The 4th Division had now been attached for some weeks to a British corps, and all were glad at the prospect of returning to their own Australian corps again. The 14th entrained at Peronne for Baillieul, which was reached on the 11th after a long journey. Next day a route march brought the unit to the vicinity of La Clytte. On the 20th the 4th Brigade relieved the 12th A.I.F. Brigade in the front line, the 14th being the reserve battalion at Tournai camp, where a few days were spent in training and fatigues.

**14th at Tournai Camp.**

**In Front Line.**

On the night of January 29-30 the Battalion relieved the 15th in the front line, C and D Companies taking over the right and left sectors respectively, with B in support, and A in reserve. Battalion Headquarters was located in Fusilier Wood. As usual in the Ypres salient the ground was very boggy, making communication difficult. The situation was quiet, working parties improving communications, and wiring parties working in front of the forward posts. On this sector were a number of outposts pushed out in front of the line in the form of a screen. These outposts, which were a feature of front line operations on the western theatre of war, consisted of miniature strongpoints, manned by from half a dozen to twenty men under an officer or N.C.O., and were scattered over No Man's Land, an occasional one sometimes as far as half a mile from our line. The duty of the garrisons was observation: they were the eyes of the unit, and in case of a German attack they had to warn the front line, delay the enemy and, if necessary, fight to the last. Sometimes a garrison was unrelieved for days, and during that time necessarily cut off from its own unit. The loneliness and danger of the work, especially at night, were nerve racking. Occasionally a daring battalion officer would find his way to these outposts in the darkness, and such visits were very cheering to the lonely garrisons. On

**Outpost Surprised.**
the 31st, under cover of a thick fog, the Germans rushed one of these outposts (Post C.3 Potsdam group) in daylight and captured by surprise the two occupants, Cpl. E. E. Frost[1] (No. 989, an original D Company man) and L/Cpl. Jeffries.

**Enemy's Violent and Prolonged Gas Bombardment.**
Apart from the above incident the enemy showed little enterprise except in one direction, which, however, proved disastrous to the Battalion, viz., in a prolonged gas bombardment. The unit was altogether in the line a week, and the night after its arrival Battalion Headquarters and the reserve and support company were bombarded by gas shells for fourteen consecutive hours. Unlike the usual gas barrage of short duration, this bombardment was steady and very prolonged. There were six or seven similar bombardments during this tour of duty, each lasting a considerable time. The weather was cold and frosty, and there was not sufficient sunshine to enable the gas to get away. The result was that dugouts, support and communication trenches were reeking with it. Battalion Headquarters and A Company being located on low-lying ground bore the brunt of the attack, while the two advanced companies being on higher ground were comparatively immune.

**Pioneer Sgt. O. G. McAllan Killed.**
One gas shell landing among the pioneers killed the pioneer sergeant O. G. McAllan (No. 1022), an original.

**Heavy Evacuations.**
As a result of the gas bombardments 17 officers and upwards of 250 men were evacuated, in addition to a large number evacuated sick from climatic and other reasons. The gas was of the ordinary mustard variety, and caused some of the evacuated to be returned to Australia. The great majority, however, returned after a comparatively brief absence to the unit. Among those evacuated was the Battalion's C.O., Lieut.-Col. W. J. Smith, who left the Battalion after it came out of the line. He did not return to the unit. He was a professional soldier prior to the war, and was a man

---

[1]His captors informed Frost that they were anxious to capture one of our men (i.e., Capt. Jacka), who spent his nights patrolling No Man's Land single handed. Frost informed them who their anticipated victim was, and indicated that the job might not only be unpleasant, but probably decidedly dangerous.

[2]No. 1022, Sgt. Oswald George McAllan. Carpenter, of Albert Park (V.). D.W. February 1, 1918.

of easy-going temperament. Capt. W. R. Wadsworth assumed temporary command of the Battalion.

Every crisis in the history of the Battalion had the effect of bringing some men into prominence. The enemy gas shelling did not form an exception. A battalion officer found several men at daybreak one morning coughing and evidently badly gassed. "Why don't you report to the R.M.O.," he queried; "it means a Blighty[3] for you." "Well," retorted a gassed sergeant,[4] "so many have gone that if we report there will not be enough men left to do the fatigue work—the outposts will starve, and that means that the Battalion for the first time will not be able to do its proper time in the line. It will be recalled." Every night, accordingly, till the relief came, these broken men reeled into the darkness, staggering along slippery tracks, carrying enormous loads so that the men in the front line should not lack anything. Some had to be rescued from drowning in shell holes—the fate of many marked "missing" during the war. The work was done solely for the honour of the Battalion, in the dead of night, and without any hope of official recognition. This incident is a striking tribute to that intense unit pride and feeling of comradeship which were such outstanding features in the A.I.F., and without a realisation of which its record cannot be appreciated or understood.

*Heroism of Suffering Men.*

On February 5 the 14th was relieved by the 45th Battalion, and moved back a few miles to La Clytte. A short spell out of the line enabled everyone to get a bath and clean underclothing—luxuries always appreciated after the dirt and vermin so often inseparable from the trenches. Numerous working parties were supplied, and the remainder of the Battalion engaged in general and specialist training. Major C. M. Johnston assumed command of the Battalion on the 14th; he was a staff officer, and for some time had been Brigade Major of the 4th Brigade. Lieut. J. H. Johnson, the unit's capable and popular intelligence officer resumed regimental duties from Brigade Headquarters on the 16th. On the night of February 20-21, the 4th Brigade took over another tour of duty in the line, relieving the 12th Brigade, and the 14th found itself again at Tournai camp. Some work was put in here on the corps line defences, for

*Major C. M. Johnston Assumes Command of the 14th.*

---

[3] Blighty, i.e., British leave.

[4] The author regrets that he is unable to supply the name of the sergeant. This incident (one of the finest in the history of the unit) was communicated by the Battalion padre, Lieut-Col. F. W. Rolland, M.C.

**Return of Capt. Reg. Jones.** General Headquarters was anticipating a German attack on a big scale. On the 25th Capt. Reg. Jones rejoined the unit. The return of that experienced and intrepid veteran was welcomed by all ranks. A German deserter having given information that a German attack was to be made on the Brigade's front on the 28th, the 14th moved out in battle formations, and took positions in rear of the 13th. The expected attack, however, did not eventuate, and after a four-mile march through the rain in the dark, and a stand to for some hours in the cold of a French winter, a tired, wet and weary crowd of men returned at daybreak next morning to their camp. This typical incident occurred on the last day of the last winter of the war.

**A Resultless Night March.**

The winters in France were usually distinguished by numerous evacuations for sickness owing to the severity of climatic conditions. . They were also noted as a rule for few battle casualties, the weather usually preventing active operations on either side. During the winter of 1917-18 the 4th Brigade had been engaged in a quiet sector, and though the 14th had suffered many evacuations through gas, the whole Brigade had fortunately been specially immune from battle casualties since October, 1917.

**Immunity from Battle Casualties During Winter.**

## CHAPTER XXXV.

### HEBUTERNE.

1918—March 1 to April 24.

*Unit Finally Leaves Ypres Salient.*
*Arrival at Neuve Eglise.*

March 1 was the last day spent by the 4th Brigade in the ill-omened Ypres salient, so full of evil memories, and where so many of its dead lay buried. The Brigade was relieved by the 3rd Brigade during the day, and on the 2nd the 14th arrived at Tournai camp (Neuve Eglise). The 4th Division was now in reserve, and three uneventful and pleasant weeks were spent by the 14th in its new camp. Much of the soldiers' comfort at the front (where nearly all their time is spent out of doors) depends on the weather, which fortunately at this time was exceptionally fine. In addition to the usual training and fatigues, football, boxing, and other sporting events were now in full swing. Football as ever where Australians congregate, was an absorbing topic of conversation, and considerable sums of money changed hands on the results. On the football field there was absolute equality, for all ranks (officers, N.C.O.'s and men) stripped together, and as football is so universally played in Australia, it may be an open question whether the team work in action which was such a marked characteristic of the A.I.F. did not owe much of its excellence to the adaptation of the team work practised on the football field prior to the war. At all events it is indisputable that the levelling influence of all branches of sport had much to do with that spirit of comradeship between officers and men which was so marked a feature of the A.I.F.

*Fine Weather.*
*Football.*

*Levelling Influence of Sport.*

On the 10th after a church parade medals and ribbons were distributed by General Birdwood to the 4th Brigade recipients. This ceremony was succeeded by a march past of all the units including transport. On the 13th a demonstration of rapid wiring was given by all units in the Brigade,

*Major Crowther Takes Command of the 14th.* — that of the 14th being specially commended. On the 15th Major H. A. Crowther,[1] D.S.O., assumed command of the Battalion. Major Johnston, D.S.O., taking over the duties of senior major. On the same date Capt. Reg. Jones finally evacuated the 14th for return to Australia. It would be difficult to estimate the value of his services to the Battalion. The 14th, like every unit, had its share of incompetents, but there passed through its ranks three or four officers unsurpassed by any in the A.I.F. Reg. Jones was one of them. It was intended at this time that the 4th Brigade should shortly take over the line in the Gapaard sector, where it had spent part of the summer of 1917. Owing to the imminence of an enemy's attack on a grand scale on the British front, large parties were supplied by the Brigade to wire and consolidate positions in the vicinity. Heavy shelling taking place round Neuve Eglise causing casualties the 14th was

*2nd Platoon Wins Brigade Rifle Competition.* — moved back to Bulford camp. On the 24th an open rifle competition for the best platoon in the 4th Brigade resulted in a handsome win for the 14th, which was represented by No. 2 Platoon (A Company), admirably trained and ably commanded by Lieut. Victor E. Hall (killed in action a few days later).

Meanwhile the tactical position on the Western front was now approaching a crisis, and perhaps the greatest battle in history was about to be initiated. By the

*German Achievements in the East.* — end of 1917 Germany had disposed of all her Eastern adversaries. Servia and Roumania had been prostrated, while the Eastern colossus (Russia) lay gasping, disabled and incapable of further effort. On the previous October, too, Italy had been struck a smashing blow, and there only remained the Western

*German Effort to End the War.* — front on which Germany had determined to concentrate all her attention and resources in a gigantic effort to bring the war to a close.

*Attack on British 3rd and 5th Armies.* — **During** the winter an enormous German army had been collected, admirably trained, and on March 21 launched against the British 3rd and 5th Armies on a front of upwards of 60 miles. The British troops fought with a valour that it would be difficult to surpass, but they were hopelessly outnumbered, continually outflanked and pushed

---

[1] Major Crowther was the Battalion's seventh C O The previous C.O.'s were Lieut.-Cols. Courtney, Dare, Peck, Major Margolin, Lieut.-Col. Smith and Major Johnston.

## The History of the 14th Battalion.

**Its Success.**
back. Days of fighting, followed by nights of marching, with little food and less sleep had been succeeded by absolute exhaustion among all ranks. Though disheartened and disorganised they were, however, in the great majority of cases not demoralised, but the whole front was fluid, and in retreat, and the German torrent, though often checked and sometimes hurled back, was moving inexorably onward. Territory recovered from them earlier in the war by months of strenuous effort and enormous casualties was passing again into their hands daily. The British territorial gains of nearly two years had been lost in a week.

The Australians who were in the far North had not been involved in the initial struggle, but were drawn into its closing stages, and the 4th Brigade, so often selected

**4th Brigade the First A.I.F. Brigade to Meet Enemy.**
for any particularly difficult task, seems to have been the first A.I.F. Brigade thrown into the breach, and brought into contact with the enemy. News had already drifted through to the Brigade of the disaster to the British troops down South, but there was a complete lack of definite information. However, orders were received to be prepared to move, and after an early breakfast at 3.30 a.m. on the 25th and a march through some fields the 14th

**Battalion Leaves Belgium.**
embussed² at 8 a.m. on a glorious morning for an unknown destination in the South. The long line of busses carrying the 4th Brigade was an imposing sight, the traffic on the road being enormous. Belgium was soon left behind, and all day the route lay

**Its Journey South.**
through pretty villages and sleepy towns. It was now spring and the country looked at its best. Estaires, Merville, St. Venant, Lillers, St. Pol were passed in succession, and then

**Reaches Bavincourt.**
the route turned south-easterly, via Maizieres, Avesnes to Bavincourt (which was reached about 6.30 p.m.) and where the 14th rested for the night.

A quiet night was succeeded by a day of doubt and excitement. Rumours of all sorts were rife, and knowledge of the enemy's movements uncertain, though it was recognised that they were not far off. Consequently, the morning was spent by all ranks getting ready for action. Orders were issued and countermanded, finally culminating in information

---

²The embussing strength of the Battalion at this time was 24 officers and 577 other ranks.

(subsequently proved to be incorrect) that the enemy had broken through at Hebuterne, and that the task allotted to the 4th Brigade was to recapture that village, and fill up a dangerous gap existing on the 3rd British Army front. After dinner the C.O. made a short address, stating that they were about to meet the enemy, that the 14th never retreated, and that all ranks would have to stand their ground at whatever cost. At 2 p.m. the Battalion moved to the Brigade rendezvous at the windmill near Bienvillers-aux-Bois, the Brigade having meanwhile been attached to the 62nd British Division.³ En route crowds of French refugees were met rushing back panic stricken from the neighbouring villages, bringing their belongings with them. Whole families could be seen (some comprising old women of four score to children barely able to walk), some leading cows and horses, others dragging perambulators or carts laden with household goods.⁴ Mixed up with them was the debris of the retreating army, all moving in the same direction, i.e., to the rear. Staff officers could be seen in motor cars, army transport and innumerable Tommies on foot, the latter exhausted and in some cases hungry, many of them telling terrible stories of the dangers our men were about to face, while others remarked pessimistically, "A lot of good these few Australians will do." The whole scene was memorable. Seldom have troops marched to meet a triumphant and overwhelming enemy under more disheartening and depressing conditions. Our men, however, were full of confidence, their lack of imagination and iron nerve standing them in good stead in this crisis. They felt certain of their ability to deal with Fritz in open warfare whatever his numbers, and their optimism prevented them considering the possibility of defeat.

A touching tribute to their value as fighting men was shown by many of the French refugee peasants whom our men passed en route from the North. When they realised that the long line of motors represented the vanguard of Birdwood's iron sided veterans advancing rapidly to the rescue, they broke into loud cries, "Les Australiens! Vivent

---

³The 62nd Division was a Yorkshire unit. It was the Division that had been adjacent to the 4th and 12th A.I.F. Brigade when the latter made their disastrous attack on Bullecourt on April 11, 1917.

⁴Macaulay's "Horatius," verses 13 to 15, contains a vivid description of civilian refugees retreating before an advancing army, and though the scene portrayed represents conditions upwards of 2400 years ago, it depicts practically what occurred in France in 1918.

les Australiens! Vous les tiendrez!" (you will stop them), and forthwith many of them discontinued their retreat, and carted their furniture back to their homes.

Now that the enemy were ascertained to be in the locality, no time was lost in accordance with Australian custom, in immediately assuming the offensive. Just after dark on the 26th an attack was launched by the 4th Brigade (16th Battalion on the right, 13th in the centre, 15th on the left, and 14th in reserve near the Crucifix), and Hebuterne was occupied before daylight. The night was quiet but very cold. Daylight brought heavy enemy shelling against both Hebuterne and Gommecourt, which increased in severity during the day, whilst our artillery support was as yet almost negligible. An attack by the enemy on the 27th south of Hebuterne towards Sailly was caught in enfilade by the 13th and 15th Battalions, and cut to pieces, the enemy suffering very severely. Most of the day was spent, however, by both combatants in endeavouring to obtain more definite information about each other's movements. Reconnoitring and liaison patrols pushed out by the 14th ascertained that only a handful of British troops lay between the left of our Brigade and the 62nd Division north of Rossignol Wood. An advance was made by the 14th to meet this contingency and endeavour to fill the gap. D Company was ordered to connect up with the left of the 15th Battalion, whilst the three remaining companies, with Battalion Headquarters, moved out protected by a screen of Scouts to occupy the ridge north-east of Hebuterne. The latter movement (a difficult and delicate nocturnal one, conducted under most adverse conditions) was undoubtedly one of the neatest operations ever carried out by the 14th. Notwithstanding the very poor visibility, and the fact that the ground crossed was hampered by old and very heavy wire entanglements and had not been patrolled, most efficient liaison existed between the various platoons, while each and all were in constant touch throughout with the C.O. who led the movement, accompanied by the I.O. and the L.G.O. This position was successfully occupied before midnight. A few isolated posts of British machine gunners were in front still holding out, some of whom joined up with our men. Orders were then received for a further advance to occupy some old German 1916 trenches to the east, and to extend the Brigade left to that point before daylight. This, too, was successfully accomplished without serious opposition, save in the case of one sentry group which was smartly and completely mopped up

*Capture of Hebuterne.*

*Advance of the 14th.*

by a party of B Company under Lieut. R. J. Garcia.[5] Daylight found the Battalion well established, and in touch with the 15th Battalion on the right, but with the left flank "in the air," and all attempts to find the British troops on the left unavailing. However, the front of Gommecourt was secured, and the Battalion's left flank strengthened.

*Its Success.*

On the morning of the 28th the 4th Brigade had already been in contact with the enemy for about thirty-six hours, and the result had been eminently satisfactory. The six days' continuous advance of the Germans had already been brought to a summary and abrupt conclusion. Hebuterne was now ours, though the quarries and cemetery to the south of it were still occupied by the enemy, while our men were dug in among some of the old 1916 trenches south and east of the village. Active patrolling during the day finally located the enemy in strength in Rossignol Wood. A daring daylight patrol carried out by Cpl. W. J. Harding resulted in obtaining valuable information, as well as securing a wounded prisoner, rescuing a wounded British soldier and capturing two enemy machine guns. Lieut. Victor Hall (A Company), accompanied by his batman, Pte. P. T. O'Dowd, made a daring capture of an enemy sentry, by working up a sap, and bringing him back almost under the eyes of his comrades. Two or three half-hearted thrusts by the enemy to find our strength provided most satisfactory targets for our Lewis gunners and riflemen who took an appreciable toll of them all day. At night a strong enemy patrol of thirty or forty men wandered on to the crest occupied by our troops, and being seen in the moonlight were fired upon with apparent effect. Meanwhile a comprehensive system of communication had been early established, and throughout maintained by the Battalion signalling officer (Lieut. J. Craven, D.C.M.).

*March 28.*

*Patrol by Cpl. Harding.*

*Lieut. Hall Captures an Enemy Sentry.*

On the 29th the enemy continued to offer excellent targets for our snipers and Lewis gunners, and, in fact, became threateningly active. The right flank of the British troops to the north was at last definitely located as the result of a daring daylight

*March 29.*

---

[5]Jack Garcia was one of the characters of the 14th and a man of iron nerve. A leading officer of the unit going through the front line one night during the above operations heard voices and sounds of excitement in No Man's Land. He was informed that Lieuts. Garcia and Schutz were there. Upon going over and making inquiries he was informed by Garcia that Schutz had just found his fifth "brother."

**The I.O. Locates British Troops.** patrol, carried out by the Battalion Intelligence Officer (Lieut. J. H. Johnson, M.C.) under the direct observation of the enemy. As the closest British post was near Rossignol Wood, steps were taken to fill the gap between it and our flank. At 3 p.m. a strong enemy concentration was observed in front of A Company, and Lieut. Hall was ordered to engage them and anticipate their attack. A reconnaisance in force disclosed the Germans in great numbers, and a subsequent advance by our men in greater strength met Fritz coming towards them. A brisk bomb fight followed, resulting in several casualties, including Hall, who was killed while setting a splendid example to his platoon. Sgt. George Bullen[6], an original A Company man immediately took command, and led the party with energy. Our bomb supply soon ran out, and Pte. P. D. Hamilton (a runner) was prominent carrying up bombs under heavy enemy fire. The seriousness of the position, however, was somewhat relieved by the initiative of Pte. Patrick Brennan,[7] who, with his Lewis gun put one enemy machine gun out of action, kept down the fire of another, and swept the enemy's trench with bullets. Finally a block was established by our men 150 yards ahead of our original line. Considerable casualties had been inflicted on the enemy.

**A Bomb Fight.**

**2nd-Lieut Victor Hall Killed.**

It was now evident that the enemy was meditating an offensive operation, the scale of which it was almost impossible to estimate. Repeated bombing raids by our men, however, assisted by Stoke mortars, successfully spoilt whatever serious offensive intentions our opponents had in mind. In the afternoon C Company, with a very light artillery support, and an insufficient Stoke barrage, went over on the left flank of the 15th and 16th Battalions to occupy some old trenches on the further side of the hill. The enemy was found in great strength, and owing to our imperfect artillery support it was found impossible to push the advance to a satisfactory conclusion. Cpl. Ray Jeffers[8] was prominent in this engagement, and carried back two wounded C Company sergeants under heavy enemy machine gun fire. Capt. Wadsworth (O.C. of C Company) was wounded in the head, and Lieut. Appleton took command of the Company.

**Advance of C Company.**

**Capt. Wadsworth Wounded.**

---

[6]Sgt. George Bullen (No. 38), Farm-hand (England). He was one of the participants in A Company's raid of July 2, 1916. Vide Chap. 18.

[7]Pte. Patrick Brennan (No. 5344), Labourer, of Tatong (V.).

[8]Sgt. Raymond Alva Jeffers (No. 6290), Farmer, of Cora Lynn (V.).

*Hebuterne.*

March 30.
March 31.
C Company
Captures Trenches.

The policy of nibbling forward behind strong patrols still continued and proceeded satisfactorily, finally culminating in the successful occupation by C Company with little opposition on the night of the 31st of the ridge attacked by it on the 29th. The captured trenches which were consolidated and made secure gave a splendid view of the enemy's position for several miles. The German transport could be seen moving about behind their lines, and at a later date when our heavy artillery came into action, its effect could be seen on the German columns—a sight seldom seen by the infantry in France. The tactical position now began to stabilise. The Germans did not make any attempt to advance, whilst the British troops were now finally in touch with our left flank.

Casualties for
Five Days.

The total casualties of the Battalion for the five days in the line (to the end of March) were three officers and fifty-two other ranks, by no means excessive considering the tactical results achieved, and the casualties inflicted by our men on the enemy.

Battalion
Relieved.

B Company's
Activities.

The Battalion, less B Company (Lieut. W. P. Boland, M.C.), was relieved on April 2 by the 8th Lincolns, and moved back into support. B Company meanwhile held the crest to the east of Hebuterne. On the 5th at 5.30 a.m. the British Brigade on its left, heavily supported by tanks, made an only partially successful attack on Rossignol Wood. B Company co-operated with it, and captured two enemy machine guns, destroyed four others, and earned considerable commendation for its fire and bomb support. B Company was relieved by A Company on the night of the 5th, its personnel being by that time absolutely exhausted, having been ten days in the line under trying and adverse conditions. Two heavy but unsuccessful attacks were made by the enemy on the 16th Battalion to the south of Hebuterne on the 5th. C Company of the 14th was moved up in support of the 16th, but its assistance was not required. An uneventful period followed, and on the 8th the 14th relieved the 16th in the front line, having the 13th on the left, and the 2nd Aucklands (New Zealanders) on the right. Settled trench warfare then began to develop, and the wet weather continuing the trenches became full of mud, necessitating an excessive amount of labour to drain and clean them. Several artillery barrages were put down by the

Attacks on
16th Battalion.

Trenches
Waterlogged.

enemy, which, however, were not followed up by infantry attacks. Our men did some extremely effective sniping in conjunction with a British battery during this tour of duty. The Battalion was relieved by the 16th on April 13 and moved back into reserve, where it was subsequently visited and addressed in commendatory terms on its fine work in the line by the G.O.C. of the 37th British Division. After a three days spell the Battalion on the 16th again moved forward and dug in in support. Considerable reinforcements joined the unit about this time, which, together with the arrival of some seasoned veterans rejoining from hospitals and schools, helped to fill up its depleted ranks. Finally on the 24th the New Zealanders relieved the 14th in support, and the unit embussed at midnight and proceeded south to Allonville, the actual embussment of the Battalion, completed in less than fifteen minutes on a wet and dark night, being a striking proof of its efficiency.

*Arrival of Reinforcements.*

*Battalion Leaves Hebuterne and Arrives at Allonville.*

The 4th Brigade had now finally left Hebuterne, after a series of operations extending over a month, which had enhanced even its reputation. It is worthy of note that this was the second occasion within four months when crises had arisen necessitating the detachment of the Brigade from its own corps, and its temporary connection with British Divisions. In the present instance the Brigade had been attached and transferred to several British Divisions in succession without relief, the Corps Commander frankly stating that he was afraid to let the defence of Hebuterne out of its hands. The Brigade was specially thanked by the Corps Commander for its work, whilst the G.O.C. of the 4th Division (A.I.F.) considered the Hebuterne operations "one of the best things done by the Brigade in France." Its activities had certainly abruptly stopped the German advance in that quarter, and it must be admitted that this success was largely due to sheer bluff. Our personnel from its first contact with the enemy on the night of March 26 showed so much confidence, attacked with such fierce energy, and handled the enemy so roughly that our numerical weakness was doubtless not realised by our opponents, though our lack of artillery support must have been apparent to them. The conditions, too, had been most trying—the bitter weather, the water-logged trenches, the **want of sleep, and the importance of the issues**

*4th Brigade's Success.*

*Commendations Earned.*

*Enemy's Advance Stopped.*

*Trying Conditions.*

## Hebuterne.

at stake imposed a tremendous strain on the vitality of all ranks. Fortunately biscuit and bully beef had been plentiful, and the rum issue fairly liberal, though the bread ration had been exceptionally scanty. One source of satisfaction to the whole unit had been that the new C.O. had shown himself a man of capacity, and capable of effectually dealing with a difficult and delicate situation.

Good work had been done by Capt. Wadsworth, Lieuts. N. C. Aldridge, W. P. Boland, Harry Schutze, Jack Garcia, and other officers, but the outstanding pair at Hebuterne were probably the popular, ubiquitous and courageous "Johnno" (Lieut. J. H. Johnson), whose intelligence work was, as always, invaluable; and young Hall,[9] whose inspiring leadership and gallant death were worthy of the Battalion's finest traditions. The other ranks netted no less than four D.C.M.'s,[10] and eleven M.M.'s, during the Hebuterne operations. Sgt. George Bullen, an Original, of A Co., with long service, amongst others won the D.C.M., whilst among the M.M.'s were the reliable signallers Will Rutherford and Rupert Gubby, the keen and daring scout C. E. F. (Rudolph) Feckner, and the energetic Charley Platt, of the 5th Platoon. The fatal casualties included Temporary-Sgt. G. A. H. Murray,[11] a veteran of the 1st Reinforcements, who had been wounded on the Peninsula on April 27, 1915, on the first occasion that the 14th went into action, and Cpl. R. Spearing, M.M.[12] (D Co.), whose gallant conduct at Polygon Wood had gained a recoration. The wounded included Stretcher-bearer W. Rattan and Pte. P. T. O'Dowd, each of A Co., and both wounded for the third time, Sgts. M. R. Johnson, W. Mooring, and P.

*Prominent Officers.*

*Prominent Other Ranks.*

*Fatal Casualties.*

*Other Ranks Wounded.*

---

[9]2nd-Lieut. Victor Ernest Hall, of the 13th Reinforcements (O.C. of No. 2 Platoon), Clerk, of Ivanhoe (V.). Born Chewton (V.), September 4, 1894. K.I.A. March 29, 1918.

[10]It is worthy of note that at Bullecourt where the Battalion's fatal casualties were nearly ten times as numerous as at Hebuterne, only one D.C.M. was allotted to the 14th. A successful operation was always followed by numerous decorations, while awards were always sparingly given after an unsuccessful operation, no matter what gallantry was displayed by the personnel.

[11]Temporary Sgt. G. A. H. Murray, No. 1379, Farm-hand, of Warracknabeal (V.). Born Warracknabeal. He transferred to the 4th Divisional Salvage Company on January 10, 1917, and rejoined the 14th on October 16, 1917. K.I.A. March 30, 1918.

[12]Cpl. R. Spearing, M.M. (No. 4612), Labourer, of Camperdown (V.). Born Camperdown. K.I.A. March 28, 1918. Vide Chap. 32.

Harris, and the following Originals:—Cpl. F. J. Harding (A Co., No. 61), and Ptes. E. W. McMahon (No. 626), and N. McKenzie (No. 625).

**Decorations.** The following is a list of the decorations awarded in respect of the Hebuterne operations:—Bar to M.C.[13]—Lieut. J. H. Johnson, M.C. (Beeac, V.), Intelligence Officer. M.C.—Lieut. N. C. ("Joe") Aldridge (Hawthorn, V.), A Co., 18th Reinforcements; Lieut. H. J. A. Schutz (Albert Park, V.), B Co., an Original, No. 778. D.C.M.—L/Cpl. Patrick Brennan, No. 5344 (Tatong, V.), Lewis gunner, A Co.; Sgt. George Bullen, No. 38 (Surrey, Eng.), A Co.; Sgt. T. H. French, No. 6022 (Geelong, V.), B Co.; C.S.M. Wm. Coleman, No. 2464 (South Preston, V.), B Co. M.M.—L/Sgt. Raymond Alva Jeffers, No. 6290 (Cora Lynn, V.), C Co.; Pte. P. F. O'Dowd, No. 7055 (Windsor, V.), A Co., bomber; Pte. W. M. Nolan, No. 1685 (Ballarat, V.), B Co., stretcher-bearer; Pte. F. Dennison, No. 1932 (England), stretcher-bearer; Pte. R. V. Gubby, No. 1861 (Rutherglen, V.), signaller; Pte. W. H. Rutherford, No. 2635 (East Malvern, V.), signaller; Pte. W. Marriott, No. 3543 (Burton-on-Trent, Eng.), D Co., bomber; Cpl. W. J. Harding, No. 3342 (Costerfield, V.), D Co.; Pte. P. D. Hamilton, No. 5110 (Abbotsford, V.), A Co., runner; L/Cpl. C. F. E. Feckner, No. 6021 (Willow Grove, V.), scout; L/Cpl. C. H. Platt, No. 7066 (Bacchus Marsh, V.), B Co., 5th Platoon.

---

[13]Bar to M.C. Other officers who won the Bar to the M.C. were Capt. Albert Jacka, V.C., and Lieuts. N. C. Aldridge and W. P. Boland.

## CHAPTER XXXVI.

### VILLERS-BRETONNEUX.[1]

1918—April 25 to May 26.

The 14th arrived at Allonville (a village situated a few miles north-east of Amiens) about 3 a.m. on Anzac Day, 1918, after a night journey through Authie, Thievres, Marieux, and Rubempre. Anzac Day had been duly celebrated by the unit in 1916 by aquatic sports in the Suez Canal, and again at Ribemont in 1917 by brigade sports; but the exigencies of service prevented any formal celebrations in 1918. The 4th Brigade was now rejoining its old comrades of the 4th Division, from whom there had been a temporary separation during the continuance of the Hebuterne operations. It was now back again in the Somme area, both the locality and inhabitants being well known to our men through the campaign of 1916, carried out in the neighbourhood. The fly in the ointment, however, was the fact that the Australians found themselves, after nearly two years of almost unparalleled efforts and sacrifices, back again in the vicinity from where they had commenced their first big offensive. The war had to be recommenced.

*Arrival at Allonville.*

*Previous Anzac Day Celebrations.*

*4th Brigade Rejoins other Brigades of 4th Division.*

*Again in the Somme Area.*

However, the first two or three days were spent by the

---

[1] Villers-Bretonneux has a special significance for Victorians, owing to the fact that Melbourne "adopted" it on July 14, 1920. The Victorian public subscribed towards the renovation of the wrecked township the sum of three million two hundred thousand francs (at the then ruling rate of exchange, £57,142/17/3). £12,500 (part of this sum) was voted from the Victorian Education Department's War Relief Fund, towards the erection of a school at Villers-Bretonneux, and in addition a quantity of Australian timber was sent by the department to panel the school assembly hall. The foundation stone of the school was laid on June 16, 1923, by Mrs. McWhae (wife of the then Victorian Agent-General) in the presence of several representative Victorian and French notables.—(Information supplied to the author by the Victorian Education Department.)

unit in idyllic conditions—greatly enjoyed after the arduous work in the north—under canvas in the beautiful Forest de Mai, with improved weather, and surrounded by trees bursting into bloom, and many coloured spring flowers.

**Pleasant Conditions.**

The prime tactical objective of the great German push in March, 1918, had been the capture of Amiens, an important city, and a position strategically only less important than Paris. The key to Amiens was Villers-Bretonneux (hereinafter called Villers), a small town situated on a hill about nine miles distant from it, and the possession of which dominated that important city. On April 24 the Germans with a great effort hustled the overfought and exhausted British troops out of Villers, but an immediate and brilliant counter-attack, delivered the same night by the keen and eager Australians (13th and 15th Brigades) recovered the township, which never again fell into German hands. The defence of Amiens—the safety pin of the Western Front—was henceforward practically placed in Australian keeping, and as another immediate attack on Villers by the enemy was considered probable, the 4th Brigade was ordered to relieve the exhausted 15th Brigade (one of the two which had captured the township), and take its part in the defence of that important key position.

**Villers-Bretonneux the Key to Amiens.**

**Captured by Germans.**

**Recaptured by Australians, and Held by Them.**

Accordingly, after an all too short spell in the forest adjoining Allonville, the Battalion moved into bivouac north of Bussy, and on the 28th relieved the 58th Battalion in the line north of Villers, having the 13th Battalion on the right, and the 55th on the left, with the 15th in support. The relief was effected with only three casualties. Our companies were then distributed as follows:—D, right forward; A, left forward; C, support; and B, reserve. The relief was completed before midnight. The night was extremely dark, and the position obscure, the front line in places being in close proximity to the strongly entrenched enemy, and the trenches taken over were far from perfect, some being enfiladed by enemy artillery and machine-gun fire, the previous occupants not having had time to properly consolidate after their victorious attack.

**14th in the Line.**

However, by next night gaps had been covered, posts sited and consolidated by our men, and proper touch gained with the flanking units. The ground had just recently been fought over, and daylight disclosed a lot of German equip-

**Consolidation of Trenches.**

ment, most of their packs being filled with wool and cotton taken from the mills at Villers. The artillery on both sides was extremely active, and an attempt to establish a Battalion Headquarters forward was frustrated by enemy shell fire. Little of importance occurred during the next two or three days, but a reference must be made to a tragic little incident which took place on the 30th—one inseparable from trench life on the Western Front, and of which two C Company men were the victims. Some of that company's Lewis gunners became short of panniers for their guns, and *Sgt. Pulford and Pte. Donaldson's Misfortune.* Sgt. Frank Pulford[2] and Pte. D. Donaldson[3] set out on a dark night with the intention of salvaging some. They did not return, and a thorough search for them proved ineffective, their disappearance being as mysterious as that of Cpl. Frost and L/Cpl. Jeffries on January 31, 1918.[4] Months later the mystery was elucidated. They had missed their way in the dark, and wandered on to the wire of a German outpost, where they were fired on by a machine gun at close range, with the result that Donaldson was killed, and Pulford wounded and captured. Both were splendid soldiers, and their disappearance was a great loss to C Company. Frank Pulford and his brother, J. H. Pulford, had both been wounded at the Battle of Bullecourt, in April, 1917. On *C.S.M. R. Scanlon Wins D.C.M.* the same day C.S.M. Roger Scanlon, an Original of D Company, and one of the most capable N.C.O.'s in the unit, won the D.C.M. *Casualties for April.* by going out under heavy enemy fire, dressing the wounds, and carrying back to safety a wounded officer. The casualties for April were very light, considering the results achieved, viz., eight killed or died of wounds, and nineteen wounded.

The advent of May brought increased activity in the Villers sector. The enemy still retained possession of the Monument and Hangard Wood, to the south of the village, and our High Command was meditating an attack upon them. According to the plan adopted, the 14th was to co-operate with this attack by advancing its line about 300 yards east of the road running north-east of Villers. On May 1, after dark,

---

[2]Sgt. Frank Pulford, No. 5437 (17th Reinforcements), miner, of Murrindindi, V.

[3]Pte. D. Donaldson, No. 2420, loco. fireman, of Adelaide (S.A.). Originally in 10th Battalion, A.I.F. Transferred to 14th Battalion on May 8, 1917. K.I.A. April 30, 1918. Aged at death 18 years and 9 months.

[4]Vide Chap. 34.

**Relief of Front Line Companies.** the support and reserve companies relieved those in the front line. The relief was completed by 11 p.m. without casualties, the disposition of the companies then being: C forward right, B forward left, D support, and A reserve. Next day a fine sun brought out the aircraft on both sides, with the result that there was considerable air fighting overhead. In the evening, according to programme, the Battalion advanced and dug in on its new objective with complete success and few casualties. The new line consisted of a series of the usual platoon posts, with forward listening groups and flanking Lewis guns. The forward guns of the celebrated 4th Machine Gun Company moved in with us, and established on the new line. The operation was not carried through without casualties, which, though not numerous, comprised some very valuable lives. Platoon-Sgt. Harry Brown,[5] an Original of B Company, was killed by a stray bullet during the relief, and Lieut. Frank Larter (O.C. of No. 11 Platoon, and an Original of C Company) was very severely wounded by a troublesome German sniper in front of C Company. The Battalion suffered a further loss that night—one of the severest in its history—in the death of the gallant and popular Intelligence Officer, Lieut. J. H. Johnson, M.C. and Bar, who was without exception one of the finest and most capable officers in the A.I.F. Accompanied by Scout Fechner, Johnson joined Capt. Blainey, who was inspecting C Company outposts, in company with C.S.M. Raymond Hare, and Pte. Harry Parman (C Company runner). The little party had just left Post No. 12 (Cleary's), which was astride a small road, and adjoining a German outpost only about 50 yards distant, when the trouble occurred. The night was very dark, and the little party got astray, with the result that it was opened on at short range by a German machine gun, which killed Johnson. Efforts to recover his body[6] and papers proved unsuccessful, and in one of them L/Sgt. H. R. Scott (C Company) and L/Cpl. Percy Aspinall were both wounded, the latter mortally. Scott, disregarding his own injuries, dragged back his wounded com-

**Battalion Advances to New Objective.**

**Death of Platoon-Sgt. H. Brown.**

**Lieut. Larter Wounded.**

**Death of Lieut. J. H. Johnson, I.O.**

**Account of His Death.**

**Attempts to Recover His Body.**

---

[5]Sgt. Henry Russell Brown, No. 172, diamond driller, of St. Kilda and Malvern (V.). Born at Ballarat (V.). K.I.A. May 3, 1918.

[6]Vide the recovery of Lieut. Garner's body by Lieut. Rule, chapter 31.

rade, until, becoming weak, he went for assistance, refusing to have his own wounds dressed until his sorely stricken comrade had been rescued. Aspinall, though little more than a lad, was one of the gamest men in C Company.

The morning of the 3rd found the Battalion firmly established in its new position, with telephones and visual lines of communication complete. Meanwhile the attack on the Monument, though most gallantly made by the 48th Battalion, failed, our artillery preparation (as so often during the war) being totally inadequate for the task involved. On the 4th the area north of Villers was heavily shelled by the enemy, causing three casualties among the Battalion cooks, besides damaging the cookers. Another of the few Originals still with the Battalion, viz., Pte. D. L. Morrison (No. 352), was killed this day by the same German sniper who had wounded Lieut. Larter. The 14th was relieved on the night of the 4th by the 15th Battalion, and moved back into support, the casualties during the tour amounting to three officers and sixty other ranks.

*Pte. D. L. Morrison Killed.*

*Relief of 14th.*

*Goes into Support.*

*Casualties During Tour.*

During the few days spent in support, the Battalion was camped in a little narrow valley about five hundred yards north of Villers. That township was being gradually turned into a miniature Gibraltar, and fortified with wire entanglements, strong points, and mines, so strongly, indeed, that the general wish was that Fritz would attempt to capture it. The Germans during their very brief occupancy of the township had drunk vast quantities of wine, and had pillaged it thoroughly, and after their expulsion were gradually blowing it to pieces. Most of the slate shingles of the roofs of the houses had been dislodged by shell fire, which gave Villers a stricken appearance. A pillaged town has always the same attraction for a soldier that a shipwreck has for a seasider. Our men were detailed as working parties up and down the reserve line, and when their work for the day was completed they used to drift into Villers, examine what was to be seen, souvenir among the wrecked houses, and enjoy themselves generally. A great deal of machinery and wool were sent back by the Brigade to the French mission, but much ownerless food and clothing were annexed and utilised by our men, some of whom enjoyed the comforts of civilisation again, and instead of sleeping in verminous surroundings, filled up their dugouts with luxuries in the shape of linen sheets, snow-white blankets, and kapok

*Pillage and Destruction of Villers-Bretonneux.*

mattresses. Many, too, got rid of their dirty "chatty"[7] underclothing, putting in its place clean fresh garments, many of them not intended for the use of the male sex.

**Gaiety of 14th Men.** A great deal of lighthearted gaiety, too, was indulged in; for example, "afternoon teas" were got up, and a crowd would gather round a piano in the open, one playing, and the rest singing lustily, all adorned in various objects of civilian attire—belltopper hats, evening dress, and ladies' finery. The French sentries and troops in the vicinity extracted a great deal of amusement watching the antics of their mercurial allies.

Meanwhile Higher Authorities were anxious and somewhat apprehensive during this period, and continually advised the 14th of enemy attacks which failed to materialise, but there was little of incident save some severe shelling of support and reserve areas. Such desultory shelling was almost invariably innocuous, but occasionally it claimed a victim, and on the 5th a shell killed C.S.M. J. J. Myers, an A **Death of C.S.M. Jack Myers.** Company Original (No. 619). He had just left his dugout, but returned for his gas helmet, when an enemy shell made a direct hit, blowing him to pieces. He had had a strong presentiment[8] of his approaching death.

The 4th Brigade was relieved on the 9th by the 12th Brigade, but owing to the reduced numbers of the latter the 14th remained behind in support, astride the **14th in Support.** railway just to the east of Villers, with two companies supporting the 13th Brigade on the right, and two companies the 12th Brigade on the left. Our men got into a series of dugouts excavated out of the railway embankment, while the officers were quartered in the roadway under the railway bridge. The road adjacent to our trenches was frequently shelled by the enemy, whose planes used to fly

---

[7]"Chatty," i.e., lousy. Vermin were inseparable from the trenches, and are one of the many curses of war.

[8]Several other well authenticated cases of fulfilled presentiments on the part of 14th men are on record. Among others might be mentioned:—
Pte. A. Wilkinson (No. 931), on the Peninsula, K.I.A. **Presentiments of Death.** April 30, 1915; Sgt. "Curly" Croft (No. 46), D.W. July 8, 1916; 2nd-Lieut. Lloyd Gill, K.I.A. September 28, 1917; and Sgt. Sarto" Anderson, M.M. (No. 676), the cool and daring sergeant of the Scouts, K.I.A. September 18, 1918—all of whom had presentiments immediately prior to their deaths. All of the above were exceptionally brave men, little prone to give way to unnecessary apprehensions.—(Information supplied by Raymond Hare, Fred Anderson, Jock Gifford, and other ex-members of the Battalion.)

overhead and fire at our men with little result, though Platoon-Sgt. Charles Durham[9] (No. 6 Platoon) was killed by a stray shell on the 13th. Little of incident occurred until the 4th Brigade relieved the 13th Brigade in the line on the night of May 13-14. The 14th went into the line on the right flank of its own Brigade. It now faced the Monument (south of Villers), with D Company right forward, A left forward, C right support, B left support. This disposition made the 14th (D Company in particular) the right unit of the British Army on the Western Front, with the 5th Battalion of the 2nd Zouave Regiment on our right. The 14th had now been fighting almost two years in France, and had had a varied experience of French civilians; but at Villers it found itself for the first time alongside French troops comprising the Colonial Moroccan Division. Australians always fraternise well with strangers, and the entente cordiale was soon happily cemented. The "Poste Internationale," established on the extreme left of the French, and the extreme right of the British Army, was jointly tenanted by a handful of French and 14th Battalion men. Several 14th men in this post enjoyed the unique experience of being the last man on the right flank of the British Army on the whole Western Front. The Zouaves liked our men, but disliked their habit of exposing themselves during daylight, as calculated to draw enemy fire. The French were far less particular about sanitation and cleanliness in the trenches than our men.

*4th Brigade Relieves the 13th.*

*14th Battalion the Right Unit of Whole British Army.*

*"Poste Internationale."*

About 3 p.m. on the 14th our artillery opened, in the full view of our men, a tremendous bombardment on the enemy in Monument Wood. It is alleged that about 5000 gas shells were poured into the diminutive wood in about a quarter of an hour, with the consequent result that it became simply a mass of flames, brickdust and gas. Enemy stretcher-bearers were at work the whole afternoon carrying out their wounded. The German garrison must have been composed of brave men, for this exposed post, contiguous to our position, was held by the enemy with the utmost tenacity for three months. That evening a hare-brained attempt was made by two 14th officers to plant a French flag on an aero-

*Bombardment of Monument Wood.*

---

[9] Sgt. Charles James Durham, No. 2810, clerk, of Coburg (V.). Born at Coburg. K.I.A. May 13, 1918. Aged 25 at death.

## The History of the 14th Battalion. 281

plane that had fallen upon the German side of No Man's Land. Fortunately there were not any casualties arising out of this escapade.

Early on the 15th the enemy opened a mustard gas bombardment of D Company, resulting in the evacuation of three officers and thirty other ranks. Incidentally it terminated Capt. Jacka's connection with the 14th for the remainder of the war, for his skin being broken enabled the gas to get into some of his old wounds, resulting in two operations and a long spell in hospital. Jacka[10] was probably the greatest fighting soldier that Australia sent to the war, and his exploits greatly increased the prestige of the unit. His contempt for death frequently led him to take risks that few men cared to face, but he was always a brainy fighter, and, contrary to the popular impression, the intrepidity of his character was tempered by the soundness of his judgment. It would be idle to pretend that the evacuations of **Captains** Reg. Jones[11] and Bert Jacka, and the death of Lieut. J. H. Johnson, did not seriously and appreciably weaken the Battalion.[12] They were practically irreplaceable, belonging to that rare class of officer (scarce in any service) whose personality acts as a tonic and inspiration to his subordinates, doubling their value and efficiency as soldiers.

*Capt. Jacka's Career with the Battalion Terminated.*

*His Great War Record.*

When the shelling ceased a party of our men commenced to fill in the shell holes, and sprinkle lime about to obviate the effects of the gas. Whilst engaged in this duty Pte. Bill Dawe,[13] a well known D Company character, was sniped and mortally wounded. Most front line Australians engaged in the war had little personal hatred of the enemy, but Dawe—a grim hard bushman, very difficult to

*Pte. Dawe Mortally Wounded.*

---

[10]It is a curious fact that though short men were rare in the A.I.F., the Australian V.C.'s were nearly all rather below medium height. Jacka was not an exception to this rule. His personal description on enlistment was as follows:—Height, 5 ft. 6½ in.; chest measurement, 34½/36½ inches; complexion fair, eyes blue, and hair brown. He was born in the Geelong district on January 10, 1893.

[11]Capt. R. W. Jones (Essendon, V.), M.C., M.M. (finally evacuated the 14th Battalion on March 15, 1918, for return to Australia.

[12]The 13th Battalion was also unfortunate at Villers in regard to its officers. Capt. "Doss" Wallach was killed, and Capt. Bone severely wounded on May 1, while Capt. Henderson was mortally wounded the same night. All were excellent officers.

[13]Pte. William Dawe, No. 6997, labourer, of Codrington (V.). Aged 41 years. Born at Codrington. D.W. May 20, 1918.

discipline, but a fierce fighter—was in deadly earnest, and carried into his fighting a dour hatred of the enemy. D Company, weakened by the bombardment, was relieved by C Company, which took over the gassed area.

**14th Relieved.** The 14th was relieved on the night of the 18th by the 15th Battalion, and moved back to support, and on the night of the 20th was again relieved by the 43rd Battalion, and moved back to Blangy Tronville, a tiny village on the banks of the Somme, about midway between Villers and Amiens. Daylight next morning found nearly everyone in the Battalion swimming in the Somme—a relaxation much enjoyed after the long spell in the trenches. Summer was now approaching, and the weather was growing appreciably warmer. At this time a particularly virulent form of "P.U.O."[14]

**Influenza Epidemic.** made its appearance, and was responsible for a good many evacuations. On the 22nd the 4th Brigade was relieved by the 9th Brigade,

**In Reserve at Allonville.** and the 14th went into Allonville, where a few days were spent in reorganisation, re-equipment, and training, with some relaxation in the way of football and cricket.

On Sunday the 26th a full church parade of the 4th Brigade was held, after which General Birdwood presented medals and ribbons for the last time, taking

**Gen. Birdwood Leaves A.I.F.** the opportunity to say farewell to the Brigade on relinquishing command of the Australian Corps to take over command of the Fifth British Army, taking with him as Chief of Staff Major-General C. B. B. White, the brilliant Australian to whom the A.I.F. owed so much in the Peninsula Campaign. General Birdwood had been in command of the Australians for three and a half years. His successor was Lieut.-General

**Gen. Monash Takes Command of Australian Corps.** Monash, the original Brigadier of the 4th Brigade, who proved a most efficient corps commander, and was an outstanding personality in peace as well as in war. It was only fitting that the A.I.F., after the prominent part it had taken in the war, should at length be commanded by one of its own Generals.

Special reference must be made to two of the unit's best known personalities who fell at Villers, viz., Lieut. J. H.

---

[14]"P.U.O.," i.e., pyaemia, of unknown origin. This was the precursor of the influenza epidemic which swept the world after the war in 1918/1919, claiming millions of victims.—Supplied by Capt. Hugh Trumble, the Battalion R.M.O.

**Character of Lieut. J. H. Johnson and C.S.M. Jack Myers.**

Johnson,[15] M.C. and Bar, and C.S.M. J. J. Myers.[16] M.M. Johnson was the Battalion Intelligence Officer, and his work in that department—involving great personal risk, and requiring high courage—has seldom been equalled. He had all the instincts of the true soldier, and must take his place as one of the very finest officers who was ever connected with the Battalion. He was also a gentleman—gallant, unselfish, truthful, and full of generous impulses. Few men during the long and chequered history of the Battalion were more mourned by all ranks. Myers at the time of his death was C.S.M. of A Company. An Original, he was twice wounded on the Peninsula, and again twice in France. One of the bravest in a Battalion of brave men, he was one of the unit's six representatives comprised in that little band of 4th Brigade heroes present at the Duke of Connaught's inspection at Bailleul on June 27, 1917.[17] Neat in appearance, clean living, intelligent, and extremely popular, he was a shining example of what a soldier could and should be. His loss, too, was greatly felt. Among the privates who fell at Villers was Pte. R. N. Nash,[18] killed on May 3, aged 17 years and 1 month—one of the youngest where so many were young. He had retired from the Australian Navy to join up in the A.I.F.

**Decorations Awarded.**

The following is a list of the decorations awarded in respect of the above operations. It is noteworthy that three of the five recipients were Originals, and another a first reinforcement. M.C.—Capt. W. R. M. Beamond (Geelong, V.), D Company, an Original, No. 551. D.C.M.—C.S.M. Roger Scanlon, M.M. (Sebastopol, V.), D Company, an Original, No. 528. M.M.—Sgt. H. R. Scott, No. 6357 (Fitzroy, V.), C Company, 20th Reinforcements; Driver Alex. Eric Mattson, No. 1384 (Mentone, V.), Transport, 1st Reinforcements; Driver Benjamin Hardner, No. 62 (Oakleigh, V.), Transport, an Original.

---

[15]Lieut. J. H. Johnson, M.C. and Bar (known as "Johnno"), of Beeac and Colac (V.). Born at Colac (V.) on April 19, 1888. K.I.A. May 2, 1918.

[16]C.S.M. J. J. Myers, No. 619, clerk, of Daylesford and Bendigo (V.). Born at Marong, near Bendigo (V.). K.I.A. May 5, 1918. Aged 21 years and 8 months.

[17]Vide Chapter 30.

[18]Pte. R. N. Nash, born April 7, 1901. Served in the Royal Australian Navy. Transferred to 14th Battalion on April 17, 1918. K.I.A. May 3, 1918.

## CHAPTER XXXVII.

### THE HOLOCAUST AT ALLONVILLE.

1918—May 27 to May 31.

    The comparatively restful days at Allonville came to an abrupt close towards the end of May. Divisional orders were received by Brigade on the 29th, that the Fourth should relieve the 14th Brigade in the front line on the night of May 31-June 1, and consequently during the 30th everybody was busy packing and getting ready for the line, choosing what to take and what to leave behind.

*Orders to Move.*

*Preparations for Departure.*

    Billets had previously been allotted to the 14th on a farm[1] of which, unfortunately, it was not permitted to remain long as sole occupant, for it had also subsequently been turned into a motor park for lorries of the 3rd Division of the A.I.F., which were ranged outside some barns in which many of our men were housed. Colonel Crowther, fearing enemy bombing, and realising that congestion meant casualties, had moved one company into Allonville Wood, and another to a distant part of the village, thus minimising the risk.

*14th Billeted on a Farm.*

*Third Division Lorries Parked on Farm.*

*Removal of B and D Companies to Other Part of Village.*

*A Company's Barn.*

    On the night of May 30-31, A Company was billeted in a huge barn, one side of which (facing a large number of motor and transport waggons) was open, whilst the opposite side contained large sliding doors, which were closed. At one end of the barn was a great mass of straw packed high, while at the end opposite was a

---

[1] This farm was alleged to belong to Hennessy, the well-known brandy distiller, who owned much property in France.

brick wall about two feet high, supporting wooden beams, which in turn supported a slate roof. The men slept in rows across the floor of the barn, the rows being parallel to the brick wall; a few, however, slept on the straw at the other end. A portion of the barn, partitioned off, was occupied by the Quartermaster's personnel and some of the Battalion transport drivers. About two chains away an adjoining two-storey brick building with a slate roof was occupied by C Company, the pipe and brass bands, the pioneers, signallers, and the 4th Division "smart set" Pierrot troupe.[2] The two barns that night thus contained upwards of one-half of the personnel of the unit, whilst the officers of the Battalion were camped under canvas in an adjacent wood about a quarter of a mile away.

*C Company's Barn.*

The night was very clear, and enemy planes in the vicinity were active, as they frequently were after dark. During the night bombs were dropped in the neighbourhood, and some of our men watched hostile planes endeavouring to get away from our searchlights. Pay had only recently been distributed to the men, with the consequent result that many were engaged during the evening enjoying the fruits of their expenditure. There was much hilarity and gaiety, both vocal and otherwise, before all finally got to sleep. The billets were situated about nine or ten miles from the front line, and though the possibility of being bombed was recognised, all felt as secure from artillery fire as if billeted in London or Paris.

*Enemy Planes in Locality.*

*Farm 10 Miles from Front Line.*

About 12.30 a.m. on the morning of the 31st, the enemy sent some shells into Allonville, and about the third or fourth of them (an H.V. shell from a gun of large calibre) crashed into the barn tenanted by A Company's personnel, dislodging one of the supporting beams, and, exploding in the building, causing two sections of the barn, together with the roof, to collapse, and fall upon the sleeping and crowded men, with terrible results. The falling timber and the flying slates inflicted awful wounds, disembowelling some, smashing others to pulp, and cutting off arms and legs as if they had been paper. There were some marvellous escapes: men in some

*Enemy Shell Explodes in A Company's Barn.*

*Collapse of Portion of the Building.*

*Shocking Carnage.*

---

[2] Picture 484 in the 12th volume of the Australian official history of the war, shows the "smart set" troupe in the barn at Allonville. Cpl. George Castles, a brother of the singers Amy and Dolly Castles, was a prominent member in this troupe.

instances with mortally or severely wounded comrades on either side escaped without a scratch. Darkness, too, added to the horror of the scene, and the moral effect was very severe, as all had gone to rest in fancied security, to be awakened by a chaos of death and destruction. The air was full of powder and dust, and on all sides rose the cry for stretcher-bearers, and the groans of mortally stricken men. All realised that some terrible calamity had occurred, but darkness prevented realisation of its cause, effect, or extent. Some of the survivors were temporarily stunned by the suddenness and magnitude of the disaster; some hurriedly left the building, while others of cooler nerve and a higher sense of duty worked like Trojans pulling the piled-up timber away to rescue the injured. The news soon spread, and officers and others hurried to the scene of the disaster. Lanterns and electric torches were procured, with the aid of which the victims were sought for, got out, and hurried to the dressing station for treatment, the transport men in charge of the motor lorries lending willing aid. One result of the explosion of the shell had been to cut a piece clean out of the barn, causing it to look from the outside like two buildings with about thirty feet between them. Those who had slept on the straw escaped without injury; that portion had remained intact. Australians rarely fail in a crisis, and the grim horrors of the tragedy were illuminated by many flashes of heroism among the victims, of which three examples will suffice. Pte. "Dick" Radnell, M.M.,[3] with a smashed limb, and mortally wounded, was carried out of the barn singing. He died next day. Another man with both legs severed above the knee, on being proffered assistance, said, "I am all right; get the badly wounded boys out." One of the staunchest and most sterling men in A Company was Cpl. Harry Reynolds,[4] a man upwards of forty years of age, who lost an arm in the disaster. As he was lying wounded on the stretcher one of his mates gave him a cigarette, whilst another offered to light a match

---

[3]Pte. David George Radnell, M.M. (No. 1734, 4th Reinforcements), of Tarnagulla (Vic.). Born at Tarnagulla in August, 1896, known as "Dick" Radnell. He won the M.M. by his intrepidity at Polygon Wood (vide Chapter 32).

[4]Cpl. Henry Robert Reynolds (No. 2773, 8th Reinforcements), of Oakleigh (Vic.), miner. Born at Stawell (V.) in February, 1875. The above

for him. "No," was the determined response of the veteran, whose sufferings had failed to quench his indomitable spirit, "I have to use one arm in the future, and I will start now," and he lit the match himself. Harry Reynolds was one of the undecorated heroes of the 14th Battalion. The casualties caused by this shell were set out officially as thirteen killed and fifty-six wounded, but many of the wounded subsequently died as the result of their injuries. It is difficult to conceive of one shell causing more casualties, and among the various A.I.F. records achieved by the 14th during the war may be the melancholy distinction of being the recipient of the most destructive shell[5] ever hurled by the enemy at the A.I.F. It rendered about one-half of A Company hors-de-combat. Among the killed were Cpl. Patrick Brennan,[6] the brilliant Lewis gunner who had just been awarded the D.C.M.; Ptes. Harry Delora,[7] L. Best, J. H. Dunn, and A. R. Anderson (all four being originally 2nd Reinforcements of the 29th Battalion who had joined up with the 14th in Egypt); Al Evans (A Company stretcher-bearer), and Driver J. C. Mills.[8] The wounded included L/Cpls. J. Andrews, E. P. Duxbury, and George Brookes.

It was a night of horrors, and the nocturnal troubles of the Battalion were not yet over. The crash of the shell and the cry for stretcher-bearers in A Company's barn had had the effect of waking many of the occupants in the adjoining shed. Most of them immediately got up, and started dressing for the purpose of rendering assistance to their comrades of A Company, speculating meanwhile as to what had actually

---

incident was communicated to the author by Pte. Alf. Cameron (No. 6978), who was also wounded at the same time. On one occasion Reynolds was in charge of the riflemen at an outpost. Among the occupants were some new hands who were "windy," and wanted to know which was the nearest way back. Reynolds heard them, and said significantly: "Here we stop. I would like to see the first man who tries to get back; he would not get far." There was no further talk about getting back.

[5]Two other very destructive shells of which the Fourth A.I.F. Division had experience were, firstly, one which landed at the battle of Bullecourt at the junction of the 14th and 16th Battalions, immediately prior to the advance, causing approximately about 40 casualties (vide Chapter 28 of this history); and secondly, one which landed among 48th Battalion men at Pozieres, killing 26 and wounding 16 (vide Padre Devine's history of the 48th Battalion, i.e., "The Story of a Battalion," p. 42).

[6]Cpl. Patrick Brennan, vide list of decorations in Chapter 35.

[7]Pte. H. Delora had been Capt. Wanliss's batman, and was in action with that officer when he fell at Polygon Wood on September 26, 1917.

[8]Driver J. C. Mills was the third of three brothers who lost their lives fighting in the ranks of the A.I.F. (communicated by his mother).

occurred. When so engaged a dull boom was heard in the direction of the enemy. There was a pause of a few seconds, all waiting in expectation of the inevitable explosion. The
tension was succeeded by a blinding flash, followed by a terrific roar, and the building started to collapse.

**Shell Strikes C Company's Barn.**

The German artillery from a long range on a dark night had within five minutes scored another marvellous and probably unexpected success. The shell ploughed through the roof of the barn, thence through the top storey floor, where the Headquarters details (including the brass band, pipe band, pioneers, and signallers) were sleeping, and exploded when it reached the ground floor, fortunately in an unoccupied stall. Portion of the top floor and roof collapsed, burying the brass band, pioneers, and signallers. The brass band suffered severely, two of its members being killed and several wounded, whilst the band instruments were badly smashed.

**17 Casualties.**

L/Cpl. Hughie Kent, a veteran signaller (an Original), was also killed, together with two of the scouts, whilst the wounded included the pioneer Sgt. Les Shelton. The pipe band, "the Smart Set" troupe (on the ground floor) and C Company personnel almost wholly escaped injury, the portion of the barn tenanted by them remaining more or less intact. The casualties officially credited to the second shell were set out as five killed and twelve wounded. The scene was a repetition of what had occurred in A Company's shed, except that the casualties were less numerous, and the moral effect less severe, because the previous disaster had aroused most from their sleep, and the propinquity of danger was therefore to some extent recognised. Still the last shell, coming immediately on the heels of its predecessor, accentuated the midnight horrors, and the survivors of both barns were badly rattled. The shelling stopped as abruptly as it had begun, and after the wounded had received attention and been forwarded to the dressing station, the survivors from the two sheds sought shelter and repose in the vicinity, some making their way to adjacent quarries, others to the village, and some to the neighbouring woods. The dead were buried in the cemetery at Allonville, and a cross erected over their grave. The horrors of that night had been rarely surpassed in the history of the unit.

**Wounded Attended to.**

**Survivors Seek Shelter.**

**Dead Buried in Allonville.**

The 14th was to have left Allonville at 6 a.m. on the 31st, but owing to the disaster it was unable to leave before

**Clean Up of Equipment.**

10 a.m. Prior to marching out a general clean-up of equipment belonging to the casualties had to be made. This was despatched to ordnance, with the exception of a few rounds of small arms ammunition, which were neatly stacked in the open, it being impossible for the already overloaded troops to carry the extra rounds. It was also impossible in the short time available to clear up the debris caused by the shelling. This trifling, and, under the circumstances, unavoidable incident provided the local Town Major with a complaint duly reported to Divisional Headquarters, that the area had not been cleaned up by the 14th. Divisional Headquarters, instead of dismissing the complaint as frivolous and trivial, forwarded it to Brigade, whence it was despatched to the C.O., then in the front line, for a report.

**Town Major's Action.**

The badly battered Battalion had to take over front line duties forthwith, and it was a sad body of men who marched off from Allonville on the morning of May 31. Almost everyone in the Battalion had lost friends—and friendship cemented on the battlefield is a tie of an infinitely stronger character than it is in peace time—and the tragic effects of the disaster took days to work off. Decorations were not awarded to any 14th men in connection with the incident.

The origin of the disaster will perhaps never be known. Attempts were made to attribute it to the operation of spies, but the German flying men had complete observation, and doubtless noted and probably reported the parking of the motor lorries in the immediate vicinity of the quarters of the sleeping men—a combination presenting a most tempting target. Some think that the shooting was purely accidental,[9] and that the fatal shells were either "shorts," fired at the chateau housing Divisional Headquarters, or were merely discharged on the chance endeavour to explode some of the ammunition dumps in the locality. Whether our misfortune was the result of accident or design on the part of the enemy, the success of the two shells out of the very few fired was undoubtedly a piece of unparalleled good fortune for our

**Cause of the Disaster.**

---

[9]There are some grounds for this theory owing to the few shells fired —perhaps a couple of dozen—and the abrupt way the firing ceased. Had the enemy any suspicion or even hope of the success actually achieved, the area would have been deluged with shells to increase the confusion and disaster.

## The Holocaust at Allonville.

**Summary.**

opponents. This grievous disaster and its results may be briefly summarised thus: It was one of the most dramatic and unique incidents in the history of the A.I.F.; the first shell may be an A.I.F. record in the matter of casualties; the resulting damage as far as its incidents were concerned, and the class of wounds inflicted resembled rather those accruing from a railway smash on a passenger train during a dark night, than the normal result arising from the explosion of shells; the total casualties from both shells were 86, of whom approximately four-fifths (i.e., 69) were suffered by A Company, and about one-third (i.e., 29) were fatal; the behaviour of a large number of the men under the trying and unexpected ordeal was magnificent, and quite in accord with the highest traditions of the Battalion, and within 24 hours of the disaster the personnel of the unit was again manning front line trenches.

As the incident was so unique a departure has been made in this instance from the usual practice, and a list of the twenty-nine men killed or mortally wounded on that fatal night is appended herewith:—

### Fatal Casualties.

Fatal Casualties Caused by the First Shell.[10]—2152, Pte. T. Brinkworth, station manager, Wiltshire (Eng.), from 4th Anzac L.H., K.I.A. 31/5/1918; 1734, Pte. G. D. Radnell, M.M., labourer, Tarnagulla (V.), 4th Reinforcements, D.W. 1/6/1918; 1805, Pte. H. W. Delora, driver, Prahran (V.), from 29th Battalion, D.W., 13/6/1918; 6221, Pte. C. Ballis, coach painter, Carlton (V.), 20th Reinforcements, K.I.A. 31/5/1918; 4760, Pte. S. E. Beverley, labourer, Essex (Eng.), from 29th Battalion, K.I.A. 31/5/1918; 2240, Pte. R. Delany, labourer, Cundare (V.), from 4th L.H., K.I.A. 31/5/1918; 5764, Pte. L. A. Downey, labourer, Thornton (V.), 18th Reinforcements, K.I.A. 31/5/1918; 1872, Pte. J. H. Dunn, labourer, Trentham (V.), from 29th Battalion, K.I.A. 31/5/1918; 266, Pte. L. Hustler, labourer, Penshurst (V.), from 1st Anzac L.H., K.I.A. 31/5/1918; 1383, L/Cpl. R. Mann, ship's cook, South Shields (Eng.), 1st Reinforcements, K.I.A. 31/5/1918; 55a, Pte. N. McLeod, labourer, Condah (V.), from 2nd Anzac L.H., K.I.A. 31/5/1918; 5757, Pte. G. Ray, teamster, Footscray

---

[10]When a casualty joined the 14th from other units, such units are referred to, but when joining the 14th in the first instance, the number of the reinforcements is set out. V. stands for Victoria. K.I.A. means killed in action, and D.W., died of wounds. One of the fatal casualties inserted in the first list should have been included in the second, but numerous inquiries have failed to locate this casualty.

14th Battalion Men at China Wall, Belgium
(Australian War Museum Official Photo.)

## The History of the 14th Battalion.

(V.), from 6th Battalion, K.I.A. 31/5/1918; 7588, Pte. G. W. Powell, fitter, Fitzroy (V.), 25th Reinforcements, K.I.A. 31/5/1918; 2730, Pte. A. T. Riley, driver, Elsternwick (V.), from 6th Battalion, K.I.A. 31/5/1918; 5344, Cpl. P. Brennan, D.C.M., labourer, Benalla (V.), 17th Reinforcements, D.W. 31/5/1918; 231, Pte. A. Green, labourer, Hattah (V.), from 1st Anzac L.H., D.W. 31/5/1918; 7522, Pte. C. E. Leigh, butcher, Dandenong (V.), 25th Reinforcements, D.W. 31/5/1918; 7080, Pte. A. E. Smith, boot clicker, Carlton (V.), 23rd Reinforcements, D.W. 31/5/1918; 1865, Pte. L. Best, driver, Belgrave (V.), from 29th Battalion, D.W. 4/6/1918; 5682a, Pte. A. M. Evans, clerk, Coburg (V.), from 6th Battalion, D.W. 31/5/1918; 4877, Pte. G. V. Reddish, ledger-keeper, Brunswick (V.), from 29th Battalion, D.W., 31/5/1918; 3442, Pte. F. Newbold, grazier, North Melbourne (V.), 11th Reinforcements, D.W. 8/6/1918; 2491, Driver J. C. Mills, butcher, Fitzroy (V.), 7th Reinforcements, D.W. 31/5/1918; 1668a, Pte. A. R. Anderson, contractor, Nhill (V.), from 29th Battalion, K.I.A. 31/5/1918; 6612, Pte. L. E. J. Witcombe, labourer, Winchelsea (V.), 21st Reinforcements, D.W. 31/5/1918.

Fatal Casualties Caused by the Second Shell.—7342, Pte. B. G. Englert, painter, Drummoyne (N.S.W.), 24th Reinforcements, K.I.A. 31/5/1918; 602, L/Cpl. H. A. G. Kent, student, Melbourne (V.), Original 14th, K.I.A. 31/5/1918; 6126, Pte. R. Madigan, packer, Chewton (V.), from Pioneers, K.I.A. 31/5/1918; 7606, Pte. W. Wootton, labourer, Rockhampton (Q.), from 15th Battalion, K.I.A. 31/5/1918.

## CHAPTER XXXVIII.

### THE BATTALION'S SECOND RAID, AND OTHER MATTERS.

1918—June 1 to June 25.

**Battalion leaves Allonville.**

**The 4th Relieves the 14th Brigade.**

**Disposition of 4th Brigade.**

The Battalion left Allonville about 10 a.m. on May 31, reaching Daours about noon, and, crossing the Somme, camped until dusk, for the taking over of the front line was always done under cover of darkness. About 11 p.m. the guides (who had previously reconnoitred the ground) led the respective companies into position. The locality in which the Battalion now found itself was a short distance north of Villers, near Corbie, and here the 4th Brigade relieved the 14th Brigade, which had previously held the line there. The 4th Brigade's disposition in the new sector was as follows:—14th Battalion on the right, 16th in the centre, 15th on the left, and 13th in reserve.

**Disposition of 14th Battalion Companies.**

**Description of Terrain.**

**Battalion Activities.**

The various companies of the 14th Battalion were arranged as follows:—C Company, right forward; B, left forward; A, support; and D, reserve. The 14th was posted on the side of a hill facing the enemy, who was also posted on the side of a hill facing us, while between the two hills lay a valley bisected by a sunken road. Vaire Wood, which was just inside the enemy's line, had been strongly fortified. A large portion of No Man's Land had been cultivated and sown prior to the big German push in the previous March, with the result that a portion of the crop was still standing. Small listening posts were immediately established in front of each of our platoons, and the platoons supplied patrols, the members of which, after consumption of their hot rations, went out nightly and patrolled the sunken road, returning before daybreak. Meanwhile, working parties from A and

D Companies were busy working in the front line and connecting up the various posts. Before our vacation of the sector, connection was effected both between flanks and rear.

The Germans facing us here, fortunately, belonged to a second-rate division, and were very peaceably inclined. Indeed, they did not hit back at the aggressive attentions of our men, who, of course, became more venturesome when that fact became realised. Our artillery barrages were very severe, several being usually put down nightly over the enemy lines. Altogether, our opponents had a most uncomfortable time. Subsequently, it was ascertained that they were under the impression that they were facing coloured troops. Their "heads," of course, knew differently, and were aware of the propinquity of Australians, but did not disclose the information.[1]

One morning, two German 'planes came over our front lines, causing considerable annoyance. A little later, one of our cumbrous old observation machines came crawling along and attracted their attention. Thinking it was easy prey the hostile machines made a dash for it, with the result that one was sent crashing to earth, where it burst into flames, and the second promptly retired. Every morning at daybreak this machine could be seen by our men flying over to the German lines and dropping bombs. Its two occupants were nicknamed "Sergeant" and "Corporal."

*Destruction of German 'Plane.*

The German Army was still actively aggressive, and at this period their headquarters launched a vigorous and very successful attack on the French near Rheims, capturing a great number of prisoners and stores, and gaining a considerable accession of territory. Our "heads" were anticipating a German attack on our front at any time, with the result that the 4th Brigade personnel was kept anxious and alert, but determined to show the enemy in the event of an attack being made what class of troops he would have to deal with. The attack, however, did not materialise. Summer was now coming on apace, succeeding a dry spring. The Somme Valley, where the 14th was stationed, was a blaze of colour; cornflowers, poppies and daisies making a wonderful combination with the emerald green of the crops—a startling and pleasant change from the dismal French winters of which the A.I.F. had such unpleasant memories. Attractive sur-

*German Attack Expected.*

*Summer Conditions in Somme Valley.*

---

[1] Perhaps the reason was an unintentional compliment to the prowess of the A.I.F.

roundings and enjoyable weather always had a beneficial result on the spirits of the men.

An amusing incident occurred on the night of June 7-8, on one of C Company's posts. No. 9 Platoon was on our right flank, connecting up there with a Battalion of the 3rd A.I.F. Division. One of their patrols, coming in from No Man's Land about 1.45 a.m., evidently lost its way, and ran into one of our listening posts. Their corporal in charge promptly challenged, but they were evidently not taking any chances, for before an answer could be returned by our men, they opened fire on us with rifles and grenades, to be met with seven rounds from our Lewis gun. Mutual and prompt recognition appears to have followed through the good Australian curses that were plentiful on both sides. The only tangible result (outside the wastage of ammunition, and many lurid explosions of profanity) was that two of our men were wounded. There was many a laugh over the incident afterwards.

**Collision Between Two A.I.F. Patrols.**

Another incident of a more tragic nature—to the enemy—occurred on the early morning of the 10th, this time on B Company's front (No. 5 Platoon), on the left. Our Headquarters, having reason to suspect that there had been some alteration in the enemy's personnel on our front, had been calling out for identification, and for some nights vain efforts had been made by our patrols to trap and capture an enemy. Just before daybreak, and after the last of B Company's patrols had returned, four men were plainly observed walking leisurely along in front of our wire, evidently seeking a passage through. They wore greatcoats, and little notice was taken of them, as our wiring and trench-mortar parties were often out near the wire. Having found an opening, the party filed through, and the leader (a corporal), on reaching our parapet, was challenged. Simultaneously he was recognised as a German, and apparently being too bewildered to surrender, was promptly shot dead. A second later, a bomb was thrown at his comrades, wounding one in the foot. The three survivors (one of whom could speak fairly good English) then surrendered, and it was ascertained that they had lost their bearings and wandered into our lines by mistake. They were new soldiers, and it was their first time

**German Patrol Walks into Our Lines.**

---

[2] The author is indebted to Lieut. Rule's diary for this incident—a diary on which he has drawn largely for information in this chapter.

in the line.³ It was understood that Headquarters obtained the necessary identification from the prisoners.

In spite of a large amount of indirect enemy machine gun fire put over our lines at night, there was fortunately very few resulting casualties. The number of casualties necessarily caused by enemy action is occasionally added to by the result of accidents. On the 10th, Pte. Patsy Quinn, of C Company, a mere youth, but who had seen much service in France, lost his life by picking up a cocked rifle and dropping the butt on the ground. It went off, and he was killed instantaneously. He was a courageous and irresponsible lad, the terror of the two-up schools, which (such was his luck) he almost invariably cleared out.

**Pte. Quinn Accidentally Killed.**

There was a certain amount of a complaint colloquially known as "dog fever" rampant at this time, which put up the temperature for two or three days, made the victim feel very sick, and then left. The Germans also suffered badly from it. It was one of the many ailments (incidental to climatic and other causes) which the 4th Brigade had to face in its long and varied career. A very welcome innovation during this tour of duty were hot showers, which were available at Corbie, in the vicinity of the line, and which were enjoyed by various platoons in turn. The Town Major of Corbie at this time was Lieut. Appleton, of C Company, 14th Battalion.

**Prevalence of "Dog Fever."**

**Hot Showers at Corbie.**

One day the C.O. was called to a conference, and on his return it was ascertained that a raid on the enemy's trenches was to be forthwith undertaken by the Battalion. The raid was to be a twofold one: one to be made by three parties of the 14th on Vaire Wood, and another the same night by two parties of the 16th, on the adjacent Pear Trench. The prime object of the two raids (outside the usual stereotyped reasons of identification and destruction) was to prepare the way for the Battle of Hamel, fought over the same ground about three weeks later. Raids always entail preparation (e.g., officers and men have to be selected, No Man's Land patrolled, artillery, trench mortar, and machine gun co-operation provided for), so that two or three

**Raid at Vaire Wood Ordered.**

---

³This incident was communicated by Cpl. Chas. Smith, of No. 5 Platoon, who was an eye-witness.

days were absorbed making the necessary preliminary arrangements. The personnel of the 14th raiders consisted of three separate parties, each comprising one officer, five N.C.O.'s, and twenty-four men selected from B, C and D Companies[4] respectively, or a grand total of ninety men. The officers were chosen by arrangement;[5] the other ranks were volunteers. The following comprised the officers and most of the N.C.O.'s who participated:—

*Selection of Raiders.*

The "left party" (B Company personnel: O.C., Lieut. Harold ("Darkey") Thompson; Platoon Sgt. A. S. ("Dolly") Smith; Sgt. W. H. Fletcher, M.M.; Cpl. Lewis R. Jones (brother of Capt. Reg Jones); Cpl. Chas. Smith; and L/Cpl. S. A. ("Titch") Foster.

*Personnel of Raiders.*

"Centre Party" (C Company personnel): O.C., Lt. Ramsay Wood; Platoon Sgt. E. ("Darky") Harrison, M.M.; Cpl. E. E. Bishop; L/Cpl. John Craig; L/Cpl. A. C. Kilby.

"Right Party" (D Company personnel): O.C., Lt. A. R. Bruford; Platoon Sgt. H. R. W. ("Andy") Anderson; Cpl. H. H. Lewis; Cpl. H. C. Goddard; and Cpl. W. J. Harding, M.M.

To meet possible eventualities, an officer and ten men with a Lewis gun were placed in support at the J.O.T. of each party. The three O.C.'s in charge of the raid were all capable and energetic officers, and they were supported by a fine body of N.C.O.'s. The preliminary work had been thoroughly and efficiently done; all were keen and eager, and, barring anything unforeseen happening, everything pointed to a successful issue.

The night selected (June 15) was bright moonlight, and some time before "zero" (11.30 p.m.) the three parties crept out past our wire and arrived at their respective J.O.T.'s without any casualties. Here they remained waiting for the opening of our barrage—always a trying time. It opened punctually at "zero" hour, but it was observed

*Reach J.O.T. Without Casualties.*

---

[4] A Company was probably omitted on account of the heavy casualties recently suffered by it at Allonville. In any case, A Company had a raid altogether on its own account on July 2, 1916 (vide Chapter 18).

[5] The O.C. of C's party of raiders was chosen as follows: It was arranged among the Company officers that whoever picked the two of hearts out of four cards should be allotted to the position. Major Wadsworth (O.C. of C Company) held the cards, while Lieuts. Cleary, Wood, Rule, and Bain were to draw, in that order. Wood drew the two of hearts.—(Lieut. Rule's diary.)

**Barrage Opens.**

**Attack by Left Party (B Co.)**

with some concern that some of our shells were falling short, endangering the lives of some of our men.⁶ Dealing with the adventures of the several parties in detail, the left party, which had a long way to go, had barely started on the heels of the barrage when a flare from an enemy listening post just ahead showed up the raiders. Lieut. Thompson, seeing that they were observed, took his men forward across the sunken road "at the trail" in extended order. Some of the occupants of the enemy listening posts in front of our advance, bolting back to their trenches, provided excellent targets for our men. Passing the listening posts, the bodies of several of the enemy (victims of our artillery and rifle fire) could be seen lying in grotesque attitudes. After a considerable advance, our men made a concerted rush, and found themselves up against the enemy's uncut wire. Our opponents were in force behind the wire, and there was neither the time nor the means of hacking a way through it. A brisk interchange of bombs and rifle fire with the enemy then took place. The enemy's hand bombs continually burst among our men—who had spread out and avoided bunching together—happily with little effect. Presently the retiring signal (coloured lights) was given from the rear and our men slowly retired to our lines. They had captured a machine gun and brought back two prisoners, besides accounting for several of the enemy. Our losses had been infinitesimal, and did not include any fatal casualties.

**Its Result.**

The centre party pushed on after the barrage, practically without opposition from the enemy, who retired before its advance. Swinging somewhat to the right, the objective was reached, and found vacated, but showing signs of recent occupation. One German found wandering about was captured, and one large dugout (apparently a Company Headquarters) was accidentally set on fire by the usual premonitory bomb, the result being that the inmates (if any) were killed and possibly valuable documents destroyed. Numerous small dugouts were also dealt with. On receiving the retiring signal the party returned, but Lieut. Ramsay Wood, between Vaire Wood and our wire, called the roll, and ascertained

**Attack by Centre Party (C Co.)**

---

⁶The 16th Battalion men had the same experience in their raid on the same night, and unfortunately suffered several casualties from our artillery.

**Sgt. "Darky" Harrison Mortally Wounded.**

that the Platoon Sgt. ("Darky" Harrison) was missing. It was an unwritten law in the A.I.F. never to desert a comrade in distress, and back into the danger zone rushed Wood, accompanied by two of his section leaders—Cpls. Bishop and Craig. Wood was lamed by some wire en route, but the N.C.O.'s, after some difficulty, discovered Harrison lying at the side of a dugout mortally wounded, and unconscious. He had evidently been humanely endeavouring to induce the garrison to surrender without bloodshed, and paid the penalty with his life. He was speedily avenged. Some Mills bombs hurled down the dugout among the occupants put it out of the power of any one of them to repeat such conduct again. Bishop then carried the dying sergeant back to our lines.

**Attack of Right Party.**

The right party had the shortest distance to reach its objective. Marching through crop, it reached its J.O.T. near the Quarry Crossing. Advancing from there on the heels of the barrage, some uncut light wire was easily crossed in single file, and, swinging to the left, an enemy's unoccupied continuation trench was encountered. Enemy machine gun fire opened on the party, but owing to the excellent file kept by the men, under the guidance of their section N.C.O.'s, there were not any resulting casualties. No. 15 Platoon (on the left) first struck enemy resistance. A concerted rush was made for Vaire Wood (just ahead) and some of the enemy retiring were here captured. Just inside Vaire Wood, the centre party—which had attacked the wood from a different angle—was met. By arrangement, the right party then undertook the clearing out of the top dugouts on the road, and investigations led to the discovery of the spot where the enemy's flares were stored. Whilst collecting material for their destruction, a German stick bomb ex-

**Sgt. Anderson Mortally Wounded.**

ploded, blowing off both Sgt. Anderson's hands, wounding him mortally, and also wounding Pte. Deler. Anderson, disregarding his sufferings, crawled out across a machine-gun-fire swept road to two stretcher-bearers and a volunteer, who had come to his assistance. He was rescued almost under the nose of the machine gun. L/Cpl. W. O'Dowd—who had been sent back to our lines in charge of two prisoners—was found dead in the crop, apparently killed by machine-gun fire. The two prisoners escaped. The retirement of the party was troubled by an enemy machine gun from the southern flank, which had apparently been pushed up through the barrage. There were nine casualties in the right party, viz.: One killed, one died of wounds, and seven wounded, whilst it accounted for about a dozen enemy killed (six identification tabs were brought back), in addition to nine prisoners (not including two who escaped after capture). Among the wounded was Pte. H. J. Deler (eleven wound-marks on his body), who had shown marked courage, and Pte. H. G. Stewart, of the 13th Platoon. Stewart came over with the 25th Reinforcements—the last reinforcements which left Australia to join the 14th—and his name and number (No. 7608) were the last on the 25th Reinforcement roll.

**Our Casualties.** The grand total of casualties for the three parties was three killed or died of wounds, and ten wounded—a total that might have been far heavier but for capable leadership and the war experience of all hands. The fatal casualties of the enemy on a conservative estimate must have been from two dozen to thirty, in addition to their wounded, prisoners captured, and the material damage inflicted by our men.[7]

**Congratulations Received on Raid.** The whole operation went off exactly as planned, and was a highly satisfactory piece of work, reflecting credit on all concerned. It was made, too, by men who had had a very long spell in the line, and were more or less worn out for lack of relief. It proved an exhibition of vitality that seems to have rattled the enemy, whose resistance was not as strenuous as it might have been. Congratulations on the result of the raid were received from, respectively, Corps, Division, and Brigade. The list of decorations awarded in connection with the operation appears at the end of the chapter.

**Harrison's Burial and Character.** Next day "Darky" Harrison[8] was buried in the clay pit cemetery, alongside his mate, Patsy Quinn. He was held in high esteem by his comrades, and nearly all the raiders attended his funeral. It is no exaggeration to say that he was one of the gamest lads who crossed the seas, and, in addition to his military qualifications, he had a

---

[7] There were subsequent rumours of bayonet fighting on our part, but careful enquiry by the author among the survivors of the three parties has convinced him that the bayonet was never used in the engagement—for lethal purposes, at any rate.

[8] No. 6139, L/Sgt. Edward ("Darky") Harrison, M.M., labourer, of Maffra (Vic.).

sense of humour and that touch of the comic in his character which made him popular with all ranks.

Sgt. H. R. W. Anderson,[9] of the right party, who was mortally wounded, also stood in the front rank, both as a soldier and a man, and was a reliable, cool and competent N.C.O. Men like Harrison and Anderson were very difficult to replace; raiders were always the cream of the Battalion and their losses cannot be calculated on a purely numerical basis.[10]

*Sgt. H. R. W. Anderson.*

On the night of the day after the raid (June 16), the 14th was relieved by the 13th Battalion, and marched into support near Fouilloy. B Company had just completed fifteen days in the front line trenches, winding up with participation in a raid—a record that must have been rare in the A.I.F. The dugouts in support were built into the side of a hill, and were very comfortable and well timbered, but had the disadvantage of being under direct artillery fire from the enemy, and when the German gunners had no other suitable occupation, they occasionally directed their unwelcome attentions on our trenches. Once they caught a fatigue party just going out to dig trenches, and some casualties resulted. About ten days were spent here and a lot of fatigue work near the line carried out. The weather was fine, and the enemy generally quiet, so that conditions were not unpleasant. The casualties were fortunately few, consisting of five killed and five wounded. Among the former, however was Sgt. Fred Banyard,[11] of B Company (1st Reinforcements) killed by a chance shell—a brave, conscientious and popular soldier who had been connected with the unit practically from its initiation. Wounded in the Battalion's first engagement, and also on several subsequent occasions, he had a

*14th Marches Into Support.*

*B Company's Long Spell in Front Line.*

*Sgt. Fred Banyard (B Co.) Killed.*

---

[9]No. 1503, Sgt. H. R. W. Anderson, clerk, of St. Kilda (Vic.) Born at Hawthorn (Vic.).

[10]Although the 14th were not in action after September, 1918, the following officers and N.C.O.'s who participated in the raid were killed in action between the raid and that time. Left party: Lieut. Harold Thompson, Sgt. "Dolly" Smith, and Cpl. L. R. Jones. Centre party: Lieut. Ramsay Wood. Right party: The three section leaders, Cpls. H. H. Lewis, H. C. Goddard, and W. J. Harding—an eloquent but melancholy tribute to the work of the Battalion during the last three months of its fighting career.

[11]No. 1330, A/Sgt. Frederick Joseph Banyard, farm hand, of London, England. K.I.A. 20th June, 1918.

long and honourable connection with the unit. He had been well educated, and his influence in the Battalion was always for good.

Another link with the past was broken by the final departure from the 14th of Capt. Blainey, evacuated sick. He had been a British N.C.O. sent with others to Australia for training purposes, and as an Original did good initiatory work in connection with the formation of the Battalion, which was considerably smartened up by his efforts and of which he was the first R.S.M. He was also for some time machine gun officer on the Peninsula. In France, however, he saw little front line service, and it is questionable whether his military ideals in the orderly room were suited to the Australian temperament. He was one of the first N.C.O.'s appointed to commissioned rank in the unit.

*Capt. Blainey Evacuated Sick.*

The following is a list of the decorations awarded in connection with the above tour of duty[12]:—M.C.—Lieut. Harold William Thompson (North Melbourne), Lieut. Alexander Romilly Bruford (Hawthorn, Vic.). Bar to M.M.—5376, Sgt. W. H. Fletcher (Box Hill, Vic.) M.M.—293a, Sgt. Albert Scott Smith (Clifton Hill, Vic.); 141, Cpl. Llewellyn Roland Jones (Essendon, Vic.); 1503, L/Sgt. Herbert Robert William Anderson (St. Kilda, Vic.); 6871, Pte. George Wm. L. Rofe (Sydney, N.S.W.).

*Decorations.*

---

[12]As the war progressed, decorations were more lavishly distributed. In the Battalion's raid in 1916, where the fighting was desperate and the casualties nearly four times as numerous as the raid on Vaire Wood, only three decorations were granted, as against seven in the Vaire Wood raid.

## CHAPTER XXXIX.

### THE BATTLE OF HAMEL.

1918—June 26 to July 30.

On the evening of June 26, the 13th Brigade relieved the 4th Brigade, less the 14th Battalion—A and C Companies of which remained in support, whilst B and D Companies marched to reserve in the Aubigny line near Daours. Fatigue parties were formed at night to dig trenches, but during the day, time was often available for a swim in the Somme or for hot showers and a change of underclothing at the Divisional baths, which added greatly to the comfort, self-respect, and health of the participants. The short stay in this spot, pleasant though it was, was not wholly free from misfortune, for on one occasion, several men were wounded by a shell burst. One amusing incident in this sector was the vagaries of a battery of field artillery, which developed a habit of pulling up near our lines at night, unlimbering, using up their shells on the enemy, and then limbering up and off—leaving the infantry to bear the return punishment, if any.

*Hot Showers at Divisional Baths.*

*Vagaries of a Battery of Field Artillery.*

Meanwhile Lieut.-Gen. Monash, ever since he had taken over the command of the Australian Army Corps, had determined on the capture of Hamel, and the elimination of that salient from the British front. His plans for its capture having been approved by the Army Commander, he set to work to make the necessary preparations. His plans included an extensive use of tanks, and for several days detachments of officers and men destined for the battle were taken by 'bus to Vaux—a little village north-west of Amiens —to take part in tank demonstrations. The failure of the tanks at Bullecourt had left a very bad impression of them on the personnel of the 4th Brigade, but all noted with satisfac-

*Capture of Hamel Determined on by General Monash.*

*Tanks to be Utilised.*

*14th Men Take Part in Tank Demonstrations.*

tion the greatly improved mechanism of the new Mark 5 tanks, and the higher morale of the crews. Dislike and mistrust began to be replaced by confidence. Another incident that attracted notice at this time was the great accumulation of camouflaged artillery in the rear. The "Aussies" were quick at drawing deductions, and had seen too many preliminary preparations for engagements not to realise that the Brigade was about to participate in another of its apparently never-ending battles. The great majority of all ranks had, however, by this time, become fatalists, and the news was accepted without relish, but as part of the game.

Events now moved rapidly, and on July 1st Brigade orders for the engagement were issued, by which it was ascertained that the 16th Battalion was to capture Vaire and Hamel Woods, whilst the 15th was to attack on the north, and the 13th on the south of the 16th. The role allotted to the 14th was to act as reserve, and subsequently as support, Battalion. It had to move up behind the three sister Battalions with the stores and supplies to a point 500 yards behind the Brigade's final objective, dump them there, and then to proceed to dig in in support near the artillery halt line. The Battalion in addition had to supply one platoon to construct one of the three strong-posts to be constructed in the support line. It will be noted that the heat and burden of the day was to be borne in this battle by the sister Battalions of the Brigade; the work of the 14th, though useful and essential, was subordinate.

**Brigade Orders for Engagement Issued.**

**14th to be Reserve Battalion.**

The 6th Brigade (Victorian) was ordered to attack with two Battalions on the right, and the 11th Brigade with two Battalions on the left, of the 4th Brigade. A novelty in the battle was the participation in it of United States troops—the first occasion on which they fought alongside Australians. Five of their companies were allotted to the 4th Brigade for the battle—two to the 16th, and one respectively to the 13th, 14th, and 15th Battalions. They belonged to the 131st United States Infantry Regiment of the 33rd American Division, and were recruited from the State of Illinois. One company joined the 14th on July 1, and was broken up and allotted to our various companies. Our men quickly fraternised with the newcomers, with whom they had much in common. It was their first time in the line, and they were

**6th and 11th Brigades also to Participate.**

**United States Troops Join 4th Brigade for Battle.**

visibly pleased that their initial fighting experience was to be gained alongside our men, on whom their presence also had a most stimulating effect. Instead of the grim, set faces usually noticeable immediately prior to battle, our men were all smiles and laughter, and determined to show the newcomers what Australians were capable of on the battlefield. In addition to the Americans, tankmen, artillery and engineer liaison officers were attached to the 4th Brigade for the engagement.

After the issue of Brigade orders, a strenuous time was spent by all completing the essential preparatory work for the battle. Plans and orders were given out; conference followed conference—conferences of senior officers being followed by conferences with junior officers, N.C.O.'s and men—until all thoroughly understood their parts. Every man was allotted 220 rounds of ammunition, together with Mills bombs and iron rations. Effective counter-battery work was arranged for, and armour-piercing bullets were distributed for use in the event of German tanks putting in an appearance. The intention was to surprise the enemy, consequently there was not to be any preliminary bombardment advertising the battle, which was to be opened by a barrage and supported by sixty tanks.[1] Ammunition also was to be dropped in the front line for our men from aeroplanes.[2] Every contingency was provided for, and nothing was left to chance, with the result that everyone instinctively recognised the excellence of the staff work, and confidence reigned supreme. All were convinced of the success of the venture. The date of the engagement was fixed for July 4, out of compliment to our American Allies (being the anniversary of the Declaration of their Independence).

**Preparations for Battle.**

**Conferences.**

**Enemy to be Surprised.**

**Sixty Tanks to Participate.**

On July 2, B and D Companies moved up from the Aubigny line, and that night our platoons got their material

---

[1] At Bullecourt, where the Australian forces were relatively about the same strength as at Hamel, they were supported by only twelve tanks, mechanically much inferior to the Mark 5 tanks employed at Hamel. At Bullecourt, the result of the battle depended wholly on the success of the tanks.

[2] This device would have been invaluable if carried out at Bullecourt, where the ammunition ran out, leaving our men practically defenceless.

**Final Preparations.**

**Withdrawal of Americans Attached to 14th.**

ready to pick up on the following night. Final preparations were made on the 3rd, aerial photos of the terrain being distributed, iron rations issued, and watches synchronised. Something in the nature of a bombshell was dropped on the unit that evening through orders being received by the Americans—just on the eve of battle—to withdraw. The order was decidedly unpalatable to the Americans themselves, who were loud in their expressions of disgust, and made many pointed observations, prior to their departure, upon the mental attitude of those who swayed their destinies. Our men equally regretted their departure. Their companies attached to the 16th were also withdrawn, but the companies attached to the 13th and 15th respectively remained, took part in the battle, and acquitted themselves most creditably.

"Zero" hour for the opening of the battle was fixed at 3.10 a.m., when there was light enough to see about 20 yards.

**"Zero" 3.10 a.m.**

The night was calm and soft. Two hours before "zero," companies moved through specially cut gaps in the wire, and an hour before "zero" were in position without a hitch, every man with his load waiting for the opening of the barrage. Fortunately, the enemy had not any inkling of the storm silently gathering in his front, and his artillery remained quiescent at this critical time, when our front line might have been cut to pieces. The Battalion "over the top" strength was set out as 23 officers and 409 other ranks. Com-

**Disposition of 14th Companies.**

panies were disposed from right to left as follows:—C Company (Capt. W. R. Wadsworth, M.C.); A Company (Capt. N. Wilson) supporting the 13th Battalion; B Company (Lieut. W. Jacka), supporting the left of the 16th Battalion; D Company (Capt. W. R. Beamond, M.C.), supporting the right of the 15th Battalion. Battalion Headquarters was established at Pioneer Observation Post.

At 3.10 a.m. precisely, in the semi-twilight of the early morn, our barrage opened.[3] For miles every gun burst out simultaneously. The air was full of the tumult

**Our Barrage Opens.**

of high explosives, and the whole of the enemy's lines seemed one mass of fire and flame. Overhead, like gigantic war birds, were aeroplanes; just behind the barrage waddled the tanks,

---

[3] There was the usual percentage of "shorts," which caused several casualties in the 4th Brigade, especially in the 15th Battalion.

and behind them the long lines of the grim Australian infantry. A ground mist facilitated our operations, and added to the enemy's troubles. In answer to his S.O.S. signals, his artillery opened, and, under the circumstances, put up a creditable display, but it was too late, for our men were mostly already in his lines.

*Advance Facilitated by Ground Mist.*

The 14th men, loaded with wire and equipment, and moving forward rapidly, closely followed the leading waves of the attack. Dealing with the advance of the various companies in rotation, C Company on the right advanced in artillery formation, being held up for a short time by some barbed wire just as our barrage opened. A few casualties were suffered in the advance from some of our "shorts" prior to dumping their material. Advancing from there to their objective, they started digging in the new support line. Daylight was now breaking, and from a gap in front which had not been closed by the leading Battalions, a group of Germans opened fire on our men, but finally put up the white flag. Lieuts. Rule and Wood, with five others, thereupon advanced to take them prisoners, and were not far distant from them when they opened fire again. Pte. Dave Floyd was here mortally wounded by one of our "shorts," and Cpl. Stan Cochrane fell dead with a bullet in his brain a moment later. The white flag reprobates fled up the trench when our men got near them, and then Ramsay Wood fell dead with a bullet through his temple. Only three of the little party were now left, so Rule went back and sent forward Sgt. "Red" Campbell and six men with rifle bombs, which enabled the post to be held. He also brought up and posted two machine guns, which swept his unprotected flank. Unwittingly, the little party had now cut off no fewer than forty Germans, who finally surrendered. In addition to the above haul, C Company captured twelve other prisoners and one heavy trench mortar.

*C Company's Advance.*

*Death of Cpl. Cochrane and Pte. Floyd.*

*Lieut. Ramsay Wood Killed.*

*Forty Germans Captured.*

On the left of C Company, A Company went over, established the dumps, and proceeded with little trouble to the new support line with its left on the central strong point, and its right in touch with C Company. Owing to the troops of the front line Battalions having been drawn to the

*A Company's Advance.*

left flank (where greater resistance had been experienced), there was a gap in front of A Company, where the enemy was giving trouble. Two platoons under Lieut. S. J. J. Garton, D.C.M., and 2nd-Lieut. G. F. Davies were sent forward to occupy it, which they did with considerable success. Several casualties were inflicted on the enemy, 22 prisoners taken, and three trench mortars captured; the latter were turned against the enemy in Accroche Wood, facing our front line. Cigars and hot coffee (soon sampled) were found in a dugout. The two platoons then dug in on the front line, and remained there until relieved by a platoon of the 16th Battalion, when they returned to the support line and dug in there.

*Two Platoons Occupy Gap.*

*Twenty-two Prisoners Captured.*

Meanwhile No. 2 Platoon of A Company (O.C., Lieut. Tom Griffith)—a virile platoon badly cut up at Allonville on the previous May 31—had been detailed for a special piece of work, viz., to establish a strongpost on which the alignment of the new support line would largely depend. Attached thereto for the engagement were two Vickers machine guns and one light trench mortar. A start had barely been made from Pioneer Switch when the veteran Sgt. W. T. Fisher was killed. On the side of the road near the quarries some prisoners were taken, and a few of the enemy who would not come out of their dugouts were killed. Skirting the south of Vaire Wood, more prisoners were taken from a shell-hole in the south-east corner. Past the wood, the advance proceeded north-easterly, and a German officer and six men were intercepted and sent back. Advantage was taken, during the wait on the artillery halt line, to bomb a dugout, where two more prisoners were taken. A further advance took the platoon to its objective, where consolidation was commenced, but Griffith, noting that the front line troops consolidating were not linked upon the right, took his platoon forward about seventy yards and dug the strong point in a new position. Later, the platoon was relieved by the 16th Battalion.

*Advance of No. 2 Platoon to Establish Strong Post.*

*Sgt. W. F. Fisher Killed.*

*Strong Point Established.*

B Company advanced north of the wood, following in close support of the 16th Battalion, with the right platoon on Huns' Walk. Little opposition was met with, our artillery having played havoc with the enemy, whose dead bodies could be seen everywhere. After giving some assistance

*Advance of B Company.*

in the mopping up of Hamel Wood, loads were dumped, and digging in was then proceeded with—the right of the Company abutting on the central strong post. D Company, marching behind the 15th Battalion, also had an easy passage, save in the vicinity of Pear Trench, where oné of our artillery "shorts" wiped out a Lewis gun team. After establishing their dump and commencing the line in prolongation of B Company, it was found that the party detailed from the 15th Battalion to construct the left strong post had met with heavy casualties, rendering the digging of the post impossible. D Company, however, established a satisfactory line, and captured 15 prisoners.

*Advance of D Company.*

Prior to the battle, the Signallers laid a telephone wire from Battalion Headquarters to the jumping-off trench. From this point a forward party,[4] comprised of ten signallers and two runners, in charge of Cpl. W. H. Rutherford, M.M., was detailed to move forward with the attacking waves between the two woods, and establish a forward centre by laying a direct line from there to Battalion Headquarters. Advancing behind the 16th Battalion, the party established and maintained communication with Battalion Headquarters during the advance, until the line was broken by shell-fire after passing the enemy front line. A party of about a dozen Germans (young soldiers) was encountered en route, but surrendered after a brief bomb fight. There was not any further opposition, but some dugouts were mopped up during the advance, and the party, pushing on with the gear, succeeded in establishing a forward post close to the support line. Telephonic and visual communication to Battalion Headquarters and all companies was speedily established, and maintained until the close of the operations.[5] Owing to the telephone lines being laid down over open country, they had to be continually patrolled both by day and by night, and when they were broken, messages had to be got through by the runners, who were kept busy.

*Advance of Forward Party of Signallers.*

*Telephonic and Visual Communication Established.*

---

[4]The party consisted (among others) of C. A. Crapper and W. J. Wilson (both wounded), Norman Ingamells, W. H. Brunt and G. B. Fielden. The runners were John Inglis and Jas. McCormick.

[5]This was one of the first occasions in which all communication was centred in the forward post, lines being laid from the post to the various companies. The original system had been to have four lines—one from each company—to Battalion Headquarters, thus quadrupling the communications. The new system was adopted in future battles.

**Work of Medical Personnel.**
The medical personnel and the R.M.O. (Capt. H. C. Trumble), following close on the heels of the 16th Battalion, were well established on the ledges, and at work ten minutes after "zero," and before the assaulting troops had dealt with the enemy first line. This regimental aid post administered to a great proportion of the wounded of the Brigade, and did excellent work till relieved on the evening of July 6. In addition to the aid post, Chaplain-Major Rolland established a rest centre within one hour of the capture of the enemy's front line, and good work, too, was done there, assisting the wounded with drinks of hot cocoa and coffee.

**Chaplain Rolland's Rest Centre.**

All objectives had been captured in ninety minutes, and then began the work of consolidation, i.e., the necessary labour to protect and retain the newly-acquired territory. It was just daylight; our barrage was to continue for another half-hour, and as the tanks and aeroplanes retired, the infantry would then be left to its own resources. Time was not to be lost, for safety could only be secured by vigorous digging, and everyone working with the greatest energy soon made the trenches comparatively safe. Some enemy artillery and machine gun fire was experienced during consolidation, but it did not become intense till late in the day, when it was realised that our attack was not to be pushed further. The trenches, deep and narrow, formed a very difficult target, and, unless a shell fell right between their lips and among the occupants, no harm resulted. Consequently, though there was a considerable strain imposed on all ranks, there were few casualties. B and D Companies were relieved by the 49th Battalion on the 5th, whilst A and C Companies were relieved on the following day, and all moved back into reserve well pleased with the result of the action. The decorations awarded appear at the end of this chapter. So excellent had been the Corps Staff work[6] that the battle may be said to have been won before it began, due to the care with which every contingency was provided for, the effect of surprise on the enemy, and the excellent collaboration of all arms. Only one battle in France up to date in the varied experience of the

**Work of Consolidation.**

**Relief.**

**Excellence of Corps Staff Work.**

---

[6] So impressed was G.H.Q. with the efficiency of the staff work at Hamel that it published and distributed to the British Army a narrative of the battle, with an official commentary on the reasons of its success.

A.I.F. was comparable to it for higher staff work efficiency, viz., Messines. Again the 4th Brigade, with the assistance of a Brigade on each flank, had dealt the enemy a staggering blow; the fruits of victory were prolific, whilst our casualties were comparatively slight. The long-coveted woods opposite our line were now permanently ours, and the groundwork was laid for the great battle of August 8. The work of the tanks had been excellent, whilst our aeroplanes dropped ammunition for our men during the battle.

*Enemy Dealt Staggering Blow.*

The casualties of the 14th were slight, comprising one officer killed (Lieut. Ramsay Wood, No. 9 Platoon), one officer wounded (Lieut. Stan. Booley, No. 12 Platoon), four other ranks killed, and forty-nine wounded[7] (some mortally). Ramsay Wood[8] was an intrepid officer in the line, and had only recently commanded C Company's personnel in the Vaire Wood raid. Sgt. W. T. Fisher[9] (A Company), another fatal casualty, was a quiet, unassuming man who had won his position through merit. He had been gas sergeant during 1917. Cpl. Stan Cochrane[10] had been wounded at Stormy Trench, whilst Pte. Dave Floyd[11] was a C Company Original who had seen much service.

*Casualties.*

One result of the Battle of Hamel was the arrival in the Amiens area, on July 7, of Monsieur Clemenceau, the grand old man of France, who came specially from Paris to thank the Australians for their victory. Speaking in English, he said (among other things): "We knew you would fight a real fight, but we did not know from the very beginning you would astonish the whole continent with your valour."

*Clemenceau Thanks Australians.*

The 14th remained for a few days after Hamel near Daours, being employed mostly on fatigues. On the 11th, a

---

[7]C.S.M. Bob Stanley and Sgt. Fred Dawes, two originals of C Company, had been wounded a few days prior to the battle.

[8]Lieut. Ramsay Wood, journalist, of Carlisle (England). K.I.A. July 4, 1918.

[9]No. 1709, Sgt. W. T. Fisher, carpenter, of Camperdown (Vic.), originally one of the 2nd Reinforcements of 29th Battalion, A.I.F. K.I.A. July 4, 1918. A brother of Sgt. Fisher—Pte. L. Fisher, farmer, of Camperdown (Vic.)—was a member of the 14th Battalion, and died in Caulfield Military Hospital on February 7, 1920.

[10]No. 5762, Cpl. Harry Stanley Cochrane, farmer, of Powong (Gippsland, Vic.). K.I.A. July 4, 1918.

[11]No. 317, Pte. David William Floyd, butcher, of Wangaratta (Vic.). D.W. July 4, 1918.

**March to Querrieu.**

march brought the Battalion to dugouts near Querrieu, so far behind the line as to be immune from the enemy's fire. The spell here —after the strain and anxiety of the previous six weeks—was one of the most enjoyable in the history of the unit—a flash of sunlight amid the sombre realities of war.

**Pleasant Conditions.**

The weather was excellent, duties were light, and spare hours were filled in largely by sport of every description—swimming, cricket, and athletics of every kind. The nights, too, provided their quota of enjoyment, concerts being plentiful. A welcome innovation was leave to Abbeville per motor-lorry. Each day, a selected few from each Company, usually in charge of a sergeant, were allowed to make the trip, a day's leave being granted for that purpose. About eight hours were taken up with the double trip, there and back, and the return journey in the dark, with all lights out, was borne with good humour on account of the enjoyment that had preceded it.

**Prevalence of Sport.**

**Leave to Abbeville.**

On the 18th the Battalion adjutant was robbed of thirty-two thousand francs, representing the Battalion pay. The wallet containing the money was taken out of the assistant adjutant's dugout; the wallet was afterwards found empty in a barn at Querrieu, but the thief or thieves were never discovered. The robbery had the effect of postponing the pay for a few days, and lessening the amount available for betting on some interesting sporting events immediately following the robbery.

**Battalion Pay Stolen.**

Saturday, July 20, 1918, will long be remembered as one of the red letter days of the 4th Brigade, for on it was held in the park attached to the Querrieu Chateau, perhaps the most successful sports gathering in its history. Each Battalion of the famous Brigade marched in column of fours to the entrance gates of the chateau in the bright morning sunlight, preceded by its band playing martial airs. Soon some thousands were gathered in the grounds, and found their way into the adjoining park. The arrangements for the sports were a triumph of organisation. Tin hats and rifles were discarded for felt hats and canes. Several side shows were in evidence, and many fancy costumes could be seen, including "diggers" dressed up as ladies in Parisian costumes. A certain number of privates were allowed to act as bookmakers, whilst a tote was run by a 15th Battalion officer, for Australians must back financially their opinion on sporting events.

**Brigade Sports at Querrieu.**

Among the visitors were Generals Monash and Birdwood. The arrival of the band of the 132nd United States Infantry Regiment, which played selections during the afternoon, was greeted with tumultuous applause. Proceedings opened at 10.30 a.m., the forenoon being devoted to aquatic, and the afternoon to athletic contests. The competitors were stimulated by the knowledge that the honour of their units was involved in the contests, and their efforts were increased by the torrents of encouragement and advice hurled at them by their comrades. The keenness accordingly imported into the events was tremendous. The air was rent by the shouts of the barrackers, who had a day of unrestrained hilarity. The Brigade Cup (allotted to the unit scoring most points in the competition) was won by the 4th Machine Gun Company[12] —a win that was both popular and highly creditable, considering the numerical weakness of the successful unit. The 14th had its share of wins, among them being the officers' 100 yards championship (Capt. Fred Anderson), and the mile walking championship (Lieut. George Huse). Amidst all the excitement, the cause of charity was not forgotten; 2,500 francs were collected and handed in to the treasurer of the Prisoners of War Fund.

The proceedings terminated at night by a concert given by the United States Engineers to a very large gathering in front of the Querrieu Chateau. It was the end of a perfect day, and all then dispersed— most lighter in pocket, all lighter in heart. The war was temporarily forgotten, and all day the air had been filled with the sound of jests, laughter, shouts and music. Seldom in the whole course of the war was there gathered together on any of the fronts a happier or more carefree or jovial body of men than those clustered round the Querrieu Chateau grounds on July 20, 1918.[13]

Two days later (Monday, 22nd) there was a divisional race meeting at Allonville. It was alleged by some to have

---

[12] The 4th Machine Gun Company was a famous unit (vide Capt. C. E. W. Bean—"Australian Official History of the War," Vol. 2, p. 662: "The magnificent machine gun sections of the 4th Brigade . . . . possibly the finest unit that ever existed in the A.I.F.").

[13] An excellent account of the above sports gathering, written by Cpl. Jack Moriarty (No. 12 Platoon) a few days before his death in action, has enabled the author to set out the above facts at some length.

**Divisional Race Meeting at Allonville.**

been one of the greatest sporting events held during the war. In addition to the 4th Division men, British, American and French troops swarmed into the village. The 14th lads entrained on a light railway and were taken to the racecourse. The races were a great success, but marred by an unfortunate incident—two officers losing their lives in the first race. At the conclusion of the day, some Australian airmen carried out some flying stunts of a harebrained character before returning to their aerodrome.

On the 24th a march was made via Allonville to trenches to go through a gas demonstration. The next few days till the 30th were taken up with training preparatory to another move to the front line to participate in the great battle of August 8.

On the 26th, the 14th won the Brigade cricket competition by defeating the 4th Field Ambulance in the grand final match by an innings and 28 runs. Prior thereto, the 14th had won four out of five matches played earlier in the month, beating the 13th and 15th Battalions, the 4th Pioneers, and Brigade.

**Decorations.**

The following decorations were awarded during the above tour of duty:—M.C.: Capt. Hugh C. Trumble (Brighton, Vic.), R.M.O.; Lieut. G. Forrest Davies (South Yarra, Vic.). D.C.M.: No. 5995, R.S.M. Leslie Collins (Brunswick, Vic.). Bar to M.M.: No. 2635, Cpl. W. H. Rutherford (East Malvern, Vic.), Headquarters signaller. M.M.: No. 2833, L/Cpl. Norman Ingamells (Strathbogie, Vic.), Headquarters signaller; No. 4574, Pte. Patrick McMahon (Camperdown, Vic.), stretcherbearer; No. 294, Cpl. E. E. Bishop (East Brunswick, Vic.); No. 6046, L/Cpl. A. C. Kilby (Drysdale, Vic.); No. 2559, Sgt. Dennis Curry[14] (Footscray, Vic.); No. 7040, L/Cpl. Andrew McDonald (Hamilton, Vic.), Lewis gunner; No. 5131, Pte. William Johnson (Footscray, Vic.); No. 2869, Pte. Harry Twining (Maribyrnong, Vic.), company runner; No. 1336, Cpl. J. E. Barker (Heathcote, Vic.); No. 5557, L/Cpl. Wm. Allwood (Dennington, Vic.).

---

[14]Sgt. Curry had two brothers—one a sergeant and one a private—in D Company, 14th Battalion. The former (Sgt. C. Curry, No. 2350) was killed in action on October 22, 1917, by the same shell which killed Capt. Walklate.

## CHAPTER XL.

### THE BATTLE OF AMIENS.

#### 1918—July 31 to August 20.

**Battalion Leaves Querrieu.**

**Relieves the French.**

The Battalion, much refreshed by the pleasant fortnight spent near Querrieu, left that village on the last day of July, about 6 a.m., and marched via Daours to a wood near Villers Bretonneux, where it remained till about 9 p.m. preparatory to going into the front line. The unit to be relieved was a French one, being the 1st Battalion of the 3rd Zouaves. The relief—carried out as usual under cover of darkness—was a practical and tragic illustration of the difficulty of dealing with troops speaking a different language. One platoon of D Company, mistaken by the Frenchmen for Germans, was received with a shower of bombs, resulting in the death of Cpl. H. H. Lewis[1] and the wounding of L/Cpl. B. A. T. Jones. The position taken over was situated near the Monument, the scene of sanguinary fighting earlier in the year. No. 5 Platoon took over what was known as International Post.[2] Some of the trenches required considerable work on our part to make them clean and habitable. The locality contained numerous dead bodies of various nationalities, which the French had neglected to bury. Our stay here was short and comparatively uneventful, in spite of some activity on the part of the enemy's artillery. On August 4 a hostile shell got a direct hit on a dugout tenanted by Pte. Chas. Ekenberg, of No. 5 Platoon, killing him instantly.

**Death of Cpl. H. H. Lewis.**

**No. 5 Platoon Takes Over International Post.**

---

[1] Cpl. Herbert Harold Lewis (No. 5404), labourer, of Donald (Vic.). Lewis had been prominent in the Battalion raid of June 15, 1918. B. Kapunda (S. Aus.). K.I.A. August 1, 1918.

[2] International Post, or "Poste Internationale." Vide Chapter 36; also vide "Australian War Photographs," page 48.

**4th Brigade Relieved.**
On the night of August 4-5 the 4th Brigade was relieved, and the 14th marched via Hamelet to Vaire-sous-Corbie, arriving about 5 a.m. Billets were obtained in the town.

On the 6th the enemy launched a heavy offensive[3] on the British troops north of the Somme, driving them back upwards of half a mile. For the purpose of camouflaging that attack, some tremendous shelling was directed on our area, causing 45 casualties in the Brigade.[4] The 15th Battalion suffered most severely, its I.O. being killed, adjutant severely wounded, and Col. McSharry mortally wounded. McSharry was one of the most popular and intrepid officers in the A.I.F., and his loss was a serious one for the Brigade.

**Offensive Against Adjacent British Troops.**

**C.O. of 15th Battalion Mortally Wounded.**

The A.I.F. was now on the eve of the greatest battle in its history—one that will be remembered as long as military history is read. Only a fraction, however, of the story can be told here. General Monash had greatly impressed his own Army Commander (General Rawlinson) and G.H.Q. by his brilliant handling of all arms at the Battle of Hamel in July. Since that engagement he had persistently pressed for an offensive on a large scale designed to give the enemy a staggering blow. His suggestions were favorably received, and a major offensive operation to be directed by the Fourth Army against the enemy's Somme salient was finally arranged to be carried out on August 8—the third anniversary of the disastrous battle of Sari Bair, on the Gallipoli Peninsula.

**Great Battle Arranged.**

The battle was to be delivered by the Fourth Army on a front of nearly twelve miles.[5] The centre of the battle was allotted to the Australian Corps, which was supported on the left (i.e., north of the Somme River) by the British Third Corps, and on the right by the Canadian Corps. The Australian front comprised about four miles. The plans included the same collaboration of all arms that was so distinctive and successful in the Hamel battle, and the depth of territory

**To be Carried Out by 4th Army, comprising British 3rd Corps, Australian Corps and Canadian Corps.**

---

[3] This was carried out by a Wurtemberg Division. The Wurtembergers were among the best troops in the German army. It was Wurtembergers who fought the 4th Brigade so stoutly at Bullecourt.

[4] Though the 14th did not suffer any fatal casualties in this bombardment, Cpl. W. H. Rutherford, M.M., and Ptes. W. H. Brunt and Tim Corboy (all of the Battalion Signallers) were wounded and evacuated.

[5] In addition to the above, the French carried on the battle to the south another four or five miles.

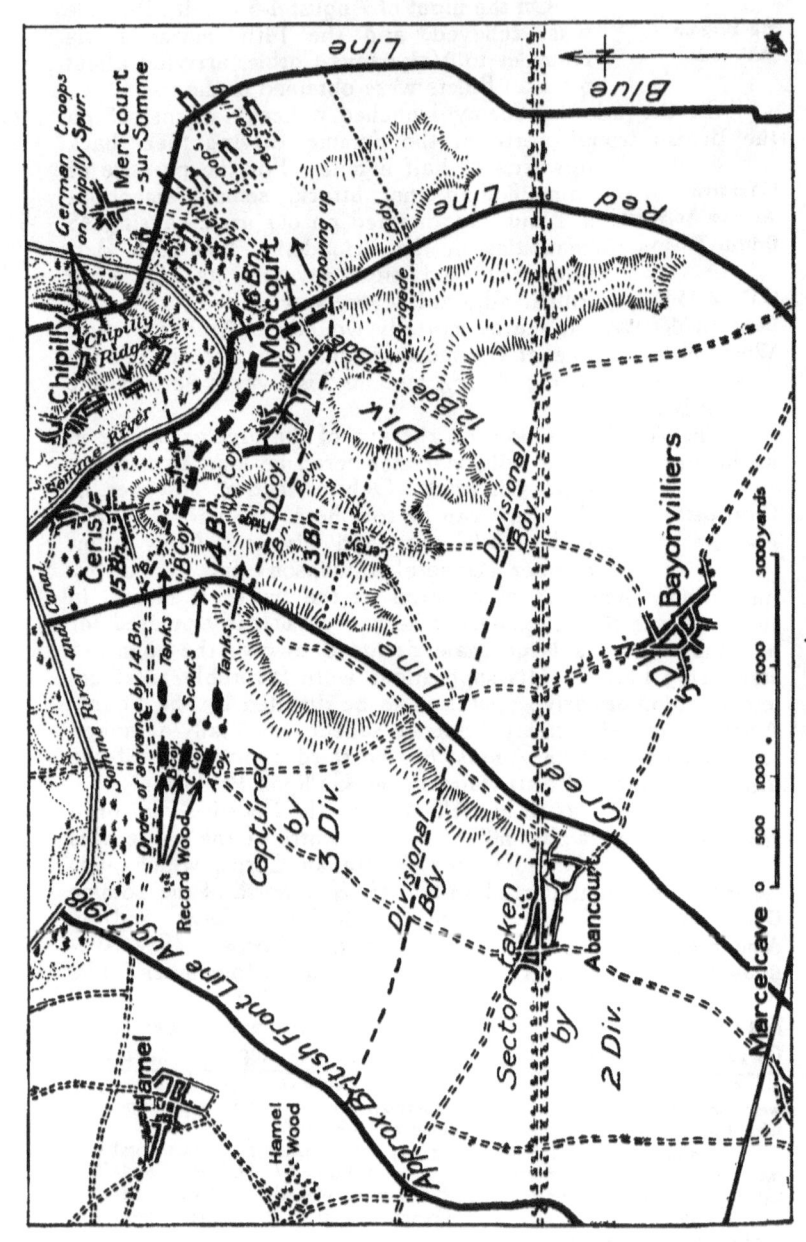

THE BATTLE OF AMIENS.

*The History of the 14th Battalion.* 317

**Australian Front Comprises Four Miles.**

**Surprise of Enemy Paramount Object of Attack.**

to be penetrated exceeded anything attempted on the British front in France in previous engagements, the intention being to capture the enemy's artillery, and not to stop short at a limited objective, and permit the hostile artillery to shorten its range, and pulverise the assaulting troops in their captured objectives, as had been the method adopted in countless prior engagements. All preliminary arrangements were made with great secrecy, the paramount object being to effect a surprise of the enemy.

**Three Objectives Allotted to the Australians.**

There were three successive objectives allotted for capture on the Australian front, known respectively as the green, red, and blue lines. The 2nd and 3rd Divisions were given the task of capturing the green line, whilst the 5th and 4th Divisions, passing through them, were to attack, capture, and consolidate the red and blue lines.

**4th Brigade Allotted Second and Third Objectives.**
**13th, 14th and 15th Battalions Second Objective.**
**16th Battalion Third Objective.**
**Brigade Area Two Miles Deep.**

The role allotted to the 4th Brigade was, four hours after "zero," i.e., 8.20 a.m., to pass through the green line after its capture by the Third Division, in the following order:—13th Battalion on the right, 14th in the centre, and 15th on the left; then to capture and consolidate the red line, whilst the 16th Battalion, passing through the red line, was to capture and consolidate the blue line. The area to be dealt with by the Brigade had a frontage of about 1000 yards by a depth of about two miles, with three obvious enemy's centres of resistance, viz.: The Cerisy Spur, the village of Morcourt (the capture of which was allotted to the 14th), and the red line spur. An obvious source of danger was that all objectives allotted to the Brigade were dominated by the Chipilly Spur across the River Somme, and at the outset of the battle, held by the enemy. Its capture, however, was an objective for the British troops north of the Somme, and definite assurances were given (as far as assurances can be definite in battle) that it would be captured prior to the personnel of the 4th Brigade passing it on the way to their objectives.

**Picturesque Scenery.**

The ground to be fought over, comprising ridges crowned by waving crops, flanked by the Somme Valley, dotted with foliage, and dominated by the Chipilly Ridge, formed a striking picture of scenic beauty.

The day before the battle, an inspiring message promulgated by the Corps Commander to all the troops, set out that the engagement of next day was to be the most important battle ever fought by the A.I.F., and calling on all ranks to do their utmost.

*Inspiring Message from General Monash.*

The Battalion was organised to attack on a three company front as follows:—Right, A Company (Capt. Norman Wilson); Centre, C Company (Capt. Fred Anderson, M.M.)[6]; Left, B Company (Capt. Cole), with D Company (Capt. Norman Harris) in close support to right and centre. A and C were ordered to proceed direct to the red line and consolidate; D to move up in support, mop up Morcourt, and become support company at the final objective; while B, conforming to the flank of the 15th Battalion and the bend of the river, was to clean up the steep bank south-east of Cerisy, and when the situation on the north was clear, move up to be battalion reserve. Battalion Headquarters and the R.A.P. were to be mobile, till the capture of Morcourt, and then to be established there. Attached to the Battalion for the operation were No. 6 Section, 8th Tank Battalion, one section 38th A.F.A., two guns of the 24th M.G. Company, two guns of the A.L.T.M. Battery, and one section of the 13th Light Horse. In addition to the above, four supply tanks were allotted to the Brigade, and one N.C.O.—Cpl. C. E. Booker (No. 3352)—and three privates, i.e., H. O. Atherton (No. 6955), W. G. W. McDonnell (No. 3419), and H. E. Fitzpatrick (No. 2380) from C Company, 14th, were detailed as a fatigue party to assist them in the carriage of stores and ammunition.

*Battalion Attacks on Three Company Front.*

*Duties of Companies.*

*Outside Arms Attached to Battalion.*

All were impressed with the excellence of the Corps staff work, and the elaborate care with which every detail had been worked out. Every officer, N.C.O., and man knew where to go and what to do. There was every confidence in the result—still the great depth of the enemy's territory to be captured, and the numerical weakness of the battle-worn Australian battalions, gave cause for anxiety. All

*Excellence of Corps Staff Work.*

---

[6]Capts. Anderson and Harris (then non-commissioned officers) had been specially prominent in A Company's trench raid on July 2, 1916 (vide Chap. 18). Capts. Wilson, Anderson and Harris were all A Company originals.

thinking soldiers realised the great issues involved in the coming conflict.

On the 7th, "iron" rations, six Mills and four egg bombs, together with 220 rounds of S.A.A., were issued to each man. This load proved heavy enough next day. The last pre-battle meal was served about midnight, and shortly after a movement was made to the first forming up position, about 1000 yards in rear of the front line, there to await "zero" hour, i.e., 4.20 a.m. Companies moved out in the following order:— A, C, B, D, and Headquarters. Guides were provided who knew the way, and men were posted at intervals to set right any unit that went astray. The night was mild, calm, and perfectly quiet—eminently suited for the massing of troops and pushing up of guns and tanks. The enemy was quiescent, and apparently unaware of the concentrated storm of destruction that was silently but inexorably gathering on his front—i.e., the flower of the young manhood of Australia and Canada, as formidable a body of fighting men as the modern world has seen. On arrival at the first forming up position in the wheatfields behind Hamel. the 14th men waited in suspense for "zero" hour.

*Movement to First F.U.P.*

*Arrival at First F.U.P.*

Punctually at 4.20 a.m. our barrage came down with a fearful crash, which sounded like the concentration of a score of tropical thunderstorms. Its appalling noise and tumult simply baffles description. In addition to its volume, its direction had been ably planned, with the result that its counter-battery work was strikingly effective. The enemy's artillery was smothered, and its response was so feeble during the crisis of the battle that the quick military intuition of the Australians immediately realised that their opponents had been out-generalled and surprised. The moral value of that knowledge during the progress of the engagement it is difficult to estimate. The barrage had the immediate effect of galvanising into activity scores of thousands of our men, who had been patiently awaiting its advent. and it was the signal for a great forward movement among all troops allotted to the capture of the green line.

*Our Barrage Opens.*

*Effective Counter-Battery Work.*

At 5.50 a.m. the 4th Brigade got ready to carry out its part of the programme. Meanwhile a dense fog had arisen, rendering both control and direction difficult, all landmarks being completely extinguished. The 13th Battalion on our right started to advance slightly before schedule time, and A Company of the 14th immediately advanced to conform; then all the companies went forward. After a difficult and anxious journey through the fog[7] the Battalion arrived at 7 a.m. at the second forming up position. Here a short stay was made for the purposes of reorganisation and to pick up the bearings. The tanks then went through the infantry, and were placed in position, one to each of the three leading companies. At 7.20 a.m., with tanks as advanced guard, followed by a screen of scouts, the three forward companies (A, C, B, from right to left), moved forward, accompanied by machine guns and trench mortars. Large numbers of prisoners captured by the 3rd Division had been met going towards the rear, and it was ascertained that the green line had been captured. A stirring incident about this time, which created a great impression, was the trotting through the advancing infantry of a battery of field artillery, which went into action alongside of them. Such incidents had been seen in army manœuvres in Egypt, but it was an absolute novelty as far as practical warfare in France was concerned. The material results arising therefrom may not have been great, but the moral result was pronounced, and the effect on the infantry most stimulating. The fog was now clearing, and on approaching the Gailly road, the Battalion was steadied for final reorganisation prior to going into action, and the companies opened out into artillery formation. So far the advance had been practically without casualties, but during the next half-mile our men were continually harassed by the short shooting of a British howitzer of a very large calibre, whose shots were falling nearly a mile short of its target. Battalion Headquarters personnel[8] was the recipient of many favours

*Appearance of Fog.*

*Advance of Battalion.*

*Arrival at Second F.U.P.*

*Appearance of Tanks.*

*Battery of Field Artillery Passes Through Infantry.*

*Short Shooting of British Howitzer Causes Trouble.*

---

[7] Some map bearings previously taken by Lieut. W. C. Fulton. of A Company, of a road located during the fog proved of considerable assistance during this advance.

[8] It has been facetiously suggested by one of the 14th Company officers in the engagement that the howitzer shelling of Headquarters details may have been due to the fact that the extremely well fed appearance of some members of the party had erroneously caused some forward observing officer to imagine that they were a party of Germans in retreat. It can be imagined accordingly from this suggestion that there was much humorous rivalry between Headquarters and the Company officers.

from this howitzer, its first missile narrowly missing the C.O., and shortly after the R.M.O. (Capt. Hugh Trumble, M.C.) was wounded, and some of the ambulance men killed.[9] A further advance brought the Battalion to the crest on one of the ridges running at right angles to the Somme, and its forward slope disclosed the 3rd Division consolidating on the green line. Some mutual chaff took place between the representatives of the two Divisions, and then, shortly before schedule time (i.e., 8.20 a.m.) the 14th went into action.

In front was a valley, and on the opposite side of it Cerisy Ridge, tenanted by the enemy. As the infantry reached the crest of the ridge, it came into **Battalion Attacks** the enemy's vision, and consequently under **Cerisy Ridge.** machine-gun fire and sniping, which grew hotter and hotter as the advance progressed. It developed into a series of short dashes forward, as men rushed from shell-hole to shell-hole. There was little cover, and casualties began to increase. Lieut. **Lieut. Appleton** Appleton (O.C. No. 10 Platoon) was killed; **Killed.** Lieut. Schutz (No. 9 Platoon) severely wounded; the gifted Cpl. Jack Moriarty (No. **Cpl. Moriarty** 12 Platoon) killed; and the veteran Cpl. E. E. **Killed.** Bishop (No. 9 Platoon) wounded. Capt. Norman Harris (O.C. of D Company) was **Cpl. Lamprell** wounded (Lieut. Roxburgh, of No. 14 Pla- **Killed.** toon, forthwith taking charge of D Company), whilst Cpl. Harry Lamprell (No. 14 Platoon) one of the finest soldiers and best Lewis gunners in the Battalion, was killed. Some of the entrenchments whence the enemy fire was coming could be seen, and although some of our Lewis gunners engaged them, their fire had little noticeable effect across the valley, and for a short time there was almost a hold-up. Meanwhile, however, our tanks **Good Work by** had gone ahead and reached the enemy's **Tanks.** ridge and their machine-gunners could be seen running out with their hands up in token of surrender. The enemy's fire then ceased, and our onward march was resumed. In the valley between the ridges was a battery of German guns, deserted by **Battery of** the gunners, who had probably bolted into **German Guns** dugouts to escape from the tanks. When our **Captured.** men reached Cerisy Ridge numerous captured machine guns and their crews were found. This attack of the tanks seemed to break up the morale of

---

[9]Extract from Chaplain Rolland's diary.

**Capture of Cerisy Ridge.**

the Germans, who that day showed little desire to fight except at long range. Thereafter there was comparatively little direct resistance. By 8.50 a.m. Cerisy Ridge was in our hands.

Meanwhile A Company, favoured by the lay of the ground, emerged from the enemy's fire on Cerisy Ridge without casualties, and moved forward with little opposition in touch with the 13th Battalion on the right, but with its left flank in the air. On reaching the ridge overlooking Morcourt, swarms of Germans escaping from our advance could be seen bolting along the low ground near the banks of the Somme. A hurried conference was then held by the A Company officers, as to the possibility of capturing Morcourt unassisted with A Company's attenuated personnel. It was decided to take the risk and storm the village—a thoroughly characteristic Australian decision.[10] Accordingly, ten men, each under Lieuts. Fulton and Crellin, flanked the village, whilst the residue, under Captains Wilson and Aldridge, stormed it from the south, entering by the main road, headed by the tank with machine guns and six-pounders in rapid action. No. 2 Platoon was the first to effect an entry, Cpl. H. C. Clements and Pte. Joe Marmo being prominent in the advance. The Germans put up a fight in the first instance, but were quickly demoralised by the dash and impetuosity of our men, and the village and all it contained was soon ours.

**Capture of Morcourt by A Company.**

The capture had been achieved practically without casualties on our part, the brilliant and clever handling of the tank having been of the greatest moral and material assistance. It is indeed difficult to over-estimate the value of the support extended by the tanks to the infantry in this engagement. The German regimental commander escaped in a motor car, but two of his staff officers who attempted to follow his example on horseback were shot by Pte. Joe Marmo[11] and killed. Two hundred and seventy-five prisoners and several guns were captured here,

**Pte. Marmo Kills Two German Officers.**

---

[10] The Australian character revels in taking risks, and does so in all directions—e.g., financial, political, matrimonial, sport and adventure.

[11] Pte. Joseph John Marmo (No. 5161), of Footscray, Vic., labourer. one of the "staff officers" shot, may have been a canteen sergeant. At all events, he had a sugar bag over his shoulders containing 4000 marks (normally £200). This incident was communicated by Cpl. Clements, who saw the happening and helped to count the money.

14th Battalion Men under Cover of Two Captured Shelters at Battle of Polygon Wood

(Australian War Museum Official Photo.)

"Smart Set" Concert Party in Barn at Allonville on May 31, 1918.

(Australian War Museum Official Photo.)

## The History of the 14th Battalion.

**Large Capture of Prisoners.** besides much material. In addition, many fugitives bolting over open country provided excellent targets, of which our men took full advantage. Altogether, it was a splendid piece of work by A Company, numbering less than 70 men,[12] and a fitting climax to the career of that grand old company. Our heavy artillery was still playing on the western end of the village, and whilst the A Company men were waiting for it to lift before resuming their advance, the enforced leisure was profitably employed in routing prisoners out of their dugouts, and **Many Souvenirs Annexed.** in "souveniring," i.e., acquiring the spoils of war. The souvenirs obtained here both in number and in value exceeded anything of which the 14th men had had experience.[18]

Meanwhile the other three companies were now approaching Morcourt—the 5th Platoon[14] (B Company) advancing on the extreme left of the Battalion. When not far from the village, its O.C. (Lieut. Harold Thompson), accompanied by Cpl. Chas. Smith (acting as platoon sergeant) crossed the road on the left flank of the Battalion, and, climbing a steep bank, found themselves overlooking the Somme River. Between them and the river, and distant about a quarter of a mile, was a party of about two dozen Germans. After some hesitation, some of them, in response to Thompson's **Death of Lieut. Harold Thompson, the Last 14th Officer Killed in the War.** signals, put up their hands in token of surrender. A few moments later, however, Thompson, who was about to go forward to take them prisoners, fell with a bullet through his temple, which shattered his skull. He died next day, and was the 41st (and last) officer of the 14th to lose his life in the war. The rest of the platoon, heavily laden, struggled up the embankment immediately after, and took in the situation at a glance. The two Lewis-gun teams (one in charge of L/Cpl. Dave Larkin), and the rest of the platoon concentrated their fire on the miscreants

---

[12]Capt. Wilson. O.C., of A Company, writes that he took only 65 men into action.

[13]One N.C.O. of A Company, as his share of the Morcourt spoil, obtained 22 watches. 6 revolvers. 5 safety razors. the best pair of field glasses he ever saw, and a regimental barber's outfit (which alone subsequently realised 100 francs).

[14]This was the platoon which, under Lieut. Jacka's leadership. did such magnificent work on Pozieres Ridge on August 7, 1916 (vide Chap. 21).

responsible for his death, who were all killed, wounded, or scattered.[15]

The tide of success was now flowing strongly in our favour, the final objective being close at hand, and victory seemingly assured, when there occurred one of those unexpected and dramatic crises which so often affect the fortune of war, and sometimes nullify the best of plans. The complete success of the role allotted to the 4th Brigade in the battle was dependent upon the capture before 8.20 a.m. of the Chipilly Ridge (which dominated our objectives) by the adjacent British Corps fighting on our left flank north of the Somme. The "Tommies" across the river, though partially successful, failed to capture the most important objective allotted to them, with the result that the German garrison, having repulsed them, swung round their artillery and machine-guns, and commenced heavily enfilading our companies at short range over open sights.[16] The enemy had ideal conditions for causing us damage, including complete observation, a dominant position, and prepared trenches. One by one all the tanks attached to the Battalion—save the one with A Company—were put out of action by direct hits, and considerable casualties caused to our infantry, though far less than, under the circumstances, might have been expected. Our attached artillery went smartly into action against the ridge, and machine-guns were pushed down towards the river to engage the enemy's batteries, which in one or two instances could be seen loading and firing. Though their batteries and machine-guns were too well posted to be effectively dealt with from our side of the river, some diversion of their fire was caused by the above efforts.

*Failure of 3rd Corps.*

*4th Brigade Enfiladed from Chipilly Ridge.*

*Destruction of Tanks.*

Some inevitable initial confusion and uneasiness naturally resulted from this unexpected development, but the C.O. was

---

[15] This incident was communicated by Cpl. Chas. Smith (No. 1679), a veteran who had seen much service, and who by a curious coincidence had taken an active part in the battles of August 8, 1915, August 7, 1916, and August 8, 1918. He appears to have been the only member of the platoon who fought in both the last two engagements. He is the author of the poem "Withdrawn," appearing at the end of Chapter 13 of this history.

[16] This was not by any means the first occasion in which the 4th Brigade had suffered through the failure of troops on its left flank. By an extraordinary coincidence, exactly three years before (August 8, 1915), and almost at the same hour, the failure of the Suvla Bay force to support the attack of the 4th Brigade resulted in the loss of the battle and extremely heavy casualties in the Brigade. (Vide Chap. 10.)

cool and resourceful, and the war-hardened veterans of the 4th Brigade—inured to all war's emergencies—quickly adapted themselves to the contingencies arising from this unexpected exhibition of the enemy's vitality. Cover was temporarily sought by some in the sunken road, and after a short hold-up, it was decided by the C.O. to leave B Company in touch with the 15th Battalion, and responsible for the river, whilst C and D Companies, despite the fire, were to push over the ridge and enter Morcourt from the north and west.

C Company accordingly moved down the sunken road into Morcourt, except the 9th Platoon (under Platoon Sgt. A. A. Johnston) which moved into the marshy land near the river bank. The rest of the Company moved through the main street, and then formed up on the outskirts of the village. Meanwhile A Company, after the capture of Morcourt, and as soon as our artillery had lifted its fire from the western corner of the village, advanced towards the red line ridge about 400 yards in front, from which machine-gun fire and snipers' activities were causing some concern. The position, however, was speedily captured by two platoons ably handled by Capt. Aldridge, M.C.; the manner in which the attacking party took advantage of the scanty cover was a fine exhibition of skill and war cunning. The capture of the red line ridge was facilitated by the direct co-operation of two platoons of C Company (Nos. 11 and 12, O.C.'s, Lieuts. Jordan and Cleary respectively), which swung round to help A Company, whilst a Lewis gun, pushed forward by the 10th Platoon, took the enemy opposing A Company in flank. This threat to their rear caused the rapid retreat of the Germans under heavy rifle and Lewis gun fire from A and C Companies, whose personnel took full advantage of the excellent targets made by the retreating enemy. Many of them were driven into dugouts by our fire, and were later captured. Pte. Wm. Miles (11th Platoon) showed great initiative here, pushing forward his Lewis gun and driving a large party of the enemy to cover, and keeping them in their dugouts until a tank went forward and captured them.

*Capture of the "Red Line" by A and C Companies.*

A and C Companies' men started digging in on the red line when they were caught by enfilade fire from a battery on Chipilly Ridge, which caused several casualties in a few minutes, necessitating a temporary withdrawal to a sunken road nearby. Meanwhile, that staunch soldier, Sgt. Ray Jeffers, M.M. (10th Platoon)—who had been busy with his platoon clearing the low ground near the river—took a Lewis gun to the river bank and engaged the battery, which created a diversion in our favour, though his gun crew was severely handled in the encounter. About this time the 16th Battalion, to whom had been allotted the capture of the blue line (the most difficult task of the Brigade that day) went through our ranks, and its appearance had the effect of drawing most of the fire from the Chipilly Spur, and thereby easing the position of the 14th, and enabling the digging in on the red line to be proceeded with. By 10.30 a.m.—a little over two hours after passing the green line—the red line had been reached by both the 13th and 14th Battalions. The "mopping up"[17] of Morcourt was the task of D Company, and the work was thoroughly done. Many more prisoners were captured there, for the village was a perfect warren of dugouts. After a short period in support, D Company took over, from portion of the 13th Battalion, of part of the red line on our right, as some companies of that unit had been required to assist the 16th Battalion in the blue line. When the situation settled down, B Company moved through Morcourt in small parties, and took up a position beyond it, acting as support company to the Battalion. At midnight the 15th Battalion, which had been relieved by the 1st Battalion, moved up into support of the 14th just outside of Morcourt, and the 1st A.I.F. Brigade established an outpost line along the southern bank of the Somme, westward from Morcourt. The crisis caused by the enemy's enfilade fire had been neutralised by our men taking advantage of the folds in the ground, and other cover, whilst his frontal resistance had been broken down by skilful enveloping tactics. All of the objectives of the 4th Brigade had been captured, except a small pocket adjacent to the river in the third objective, which was dominated by the Chipilly Spur. This spur was finally captured on the afternoon of the 9th by the British 3rd Corps, assisted by American troops, some of our men having a fine panoramic view of the engagement across the river. During the next couple of days the enemy brought up some guns and shelled Morcourt fairly heavily, whilst his 'planes were very active both by day and night. On the night of

*16th Battalion Passes Through 14th.*

*D Company Mops Up Morcourt.*

*Final Battle Arrangements.*

*Final Capture of Chipilly Spur.*

*4th Brigade Relieved.*

---

[17]"Mopping up," i.e., the clearing of dug-outs and fortified posts which the enemy continues to hold after the initial waves of an attack have passed them.

*The History of the 14th Battalion.* 327

4th Reaches Sailly-Laurette.
August 10-11, the Brigade was relieved, and the 14th reached Sailly-Laurette (a village on the northern bank of the Somme, not far from Hamel), all being in great spirits on account of the wonderful success achieved in the recent battle.

After the R.M.O. had been wounded and the ambulance sergeant killed, as has been related, Chaplain-Major Rolland took temporary charge of the medical personnel, hurrying them along towards the front and establishing an R.A.P. in a sunken road. This was subsequently transferred to Morcourt after its capture by our men, and another R.M.O. was forwarded by Brigade Headquarters, who took charge of the R.A.P. German prisoners were utilised to assist in the evacuation of the wounded. Two stretcher-bearers (L/Cpl. W. J. Earll and Pte. W. Blake) received decorations.

Medical Personnel in Battle.

The wounding of three of the Headquarters signallers on August 6[18] left the section shorthanded, with the result that the remaining linesmen had a nerve-racking time during the engagement in their efforts to mend the numerous breaks in the wires. The inimitable signalling sergeant, Chas. Clarke, was very prominent, and displayed an absolute disregard for his personal safety, whilst running and maintaining lines over bare ground swept by field guns and machine-gun fire. He was awarded the D.C.M.—his second decoration. The veteran linesmen—Ptes. Herbert Morrison and Fred Notting —co-operated with Clark in his arduous duties. Cpl. Lawrence Webb, in charge of A Company signallers, also did sterling work.

Work of Battalion Signallers.

The Lewis gunners were prominent in this engagement, and with the Scouts were usually the first to draw the enemy's fire. Cpl. V. W. Lalor[19] did splendid work covering the advance of his platoon (No. 10), and on three separate occasions neutralised the fire of enemy machine guns. L/Cpl. Wm. Croker engaged and silenced an enemy machine gun which was raking his platoon. L/Cpl. Wm. Wilson and Pte. W. J. Fitzpatrick did outstanding work in the 14th Platoon.[20] The

Prominent Wor': of Lewis Gunners.

---

[18]Vide footnote 4 of this chapter.
[19]Cpl. U. W. Lalor, M.M., of Healesville (Vic.), labourer. He had won the M.M. at the battle of Polygon Wood on September 26, 1917.
[20]Communicated by Sgt. W. H. Boyes, D.C.M., M.M. (Platoon Sgt.). He states:—"Wilson (No. 7333), a late comer from New South Wales (Lockhart), was as dashing a fellow when things were doing as one could wish to see. Fitzpatrick (No. 1175) was the original bugler of the Battalion," and incidentally one of the youngest soldiers who ever joined up in the ranks of the 14th.

latter took charge of Lamprell's gun team when that N.C.O. was killed. The names of other prominent Lewis gunners receiving decorations appear at the end of this chapter.

All ranks had contributed to the success of the day, though as in every battle there were two or three individual instances in which there was failure to do all that was expected. The C.O. (Lieut.-Col. H. A. Crowther, D.S.O.) throughout displayed both capacity and courage, whilst the I.O. (Lieut. Thomas M. Grant) was a prominent as well as ubiquitous figure. The fruits of the victory accruing to the 14th were: 400 prisoners, six guns, 93 machine guns, a regimental headquarters, a wireless station, signalling exchange, horses, transport, quantities of ammunition, medical stores, engineers' dumps, and quartermasters' stores. The brilliant victory was cheaply purchased, our casualties being: One officer (Lieut. F. W. Appleton, Croix de Guerre) killed, one (Lieut. H. W. Thompson, M.C.) died of wounds, and four wounded, viz., Lieut. H. C. A. Schutze, M.C., severely, T/Capt. N. C. Harris, and Capt. H. C. Trumble, R.M.O., M.C., and Capt. C. R. T. Cole, both slightly. Among the other ranks, 17 were killed, five died of wounds, and 52 were wounded, being a grand total of six officers and 74 other ranks.

*Captures by the Battalion.*

*Casualties.*

Fred Appleton had been wounded both at Pozieres and Bullecourt, and shortly before his death had been Town Major of Corbie, where he salvaged many thousands of pounds worth of property on behalf of the French inhabitants. Harold Thompson was an Original, who had seen much service. His impulsive courage had brought on the Battalion's first patrol fight in France (in June, 1916), when he was wounded.[21] He had only recently won the M.C. The fatal casualties among the other ranks included the following:—Cpl. Jack Moriarty,[22] a gifted soldier of high ideals, whose death was a great loss to the Battalion; L/Cpl. Harry Lamprell, M.M., a sterling soldier who had been D Company's representative at the Duke of Connaught's inspection[23] at Bailleul in June, 1917—he won his decoration on the

*References to Prominent Casualties.*

---
[21] Vide Chapter 17.
[22] Cpl. J. J. Moriarty (No. 7285), of Ashburton, New Zealand, architect. The author has had the privilege of perusing Moriarty's war diary, forwarded by his fiancee from America, and has been much impressed by the nobility of his character and his fine spiritual nature. His influence on the Battalion was always for good. He had a presentiment of his death. Vide footnote 8 of Chapter 36.
[23] Vide Chapter 30.

bloodstained field of Bullecourt; Sgts. Bert ("Dolly") Smith, M.M.[24] (B Company), and Archie Waddell[24]; Cpls. H. C. Goddard[24] (D Company) and G. A. Heron[24] (B Company) and Signaller N. Jenkins (B Company)—all well-known soldiers.

As far as the Australians were concerned, the battle was a picnic compared to many of their previous experiences in France. A feature of the engagement was the poor fight put up by the Germans, and in most cases their speedy surrender when our men got to close quarters. This appears to have been due to their intuitive knowledge that in this battle at least they had been surprised and out-generalled. The ease with which the battle was gained seems to have distracted attention from the high quality of the controlling leadership, with its consequent marvellous results. It was the greatest defeat which the German army had suffered since the battle of Jena, upwards of 100 years before. It was also the decisive battle of the greatest war in history, and the greatest victory of the Allies in France. It first caused the enemy to stagger; subsequent battles were merely designed to prevent the recovery of his footing. The material gains were immense,[25] but the moral gains even greater. It broke Ludendorff's morale,[26] and, when the leader of a great army loses his nerve, dry rot invariably spreads rapidly among all ranks. Indirectly it caused the abdication of the Hohenzollerns, who had ruled Prussia for over 500 years, and the collapse of the German Empire. It will always rank as one of the great battles of history, and in it Australian prowess and Australian leadership

**Australian Casualties Small.**

**The Greatest Allied Victory in France.**

**Immense Results.**

---

[24] Sgt. A. S. Smith, of Clifton Hill (Vic.), won his M.M. on June 15, 1918. L/Sgt. A. J. D. Waddell, of Beechworth (Vic.), had been long with the unit, whilst Cpl. H. C. Goddard, of Ballarat (Vic.), had been prominent in the Battalion raid of June 15, 1918. Cpl. G. A. Heron, of Newport (Vic.), had done good work in front of Villers Bretonneux in May, 1918.

[25] The Australians alone captured in this battle 8000 prisoners, the Canadians 5000 and the British 2400. In addition to the captures by the 4th Army, the French farther south captured 3000. These figures are taken from Montgomery's "Story of the 4th Army," the author having had access to the official figures of all the combatants.

**Prisoners Captured.**

[26] This is clearly proved by a perusal of Ludendorff's memoirs.

played a most prominent part. The battle
tactics employed by the Australian Corps on
that day were the conception of John Monash
(the 4th Brigade's original Brigadier), and it
was largely at his instigation that the battle
was fought. Much of the credit for the battle
and its wonderful results must therefore be credited to him.
Australian battle prowess became famous from the first day
the A.I.F. landed on the Peninsula. Australian higher leadership, in the few instances when given a free hand, showed
itself equal to the very best produced by the Allies during the
war.

*General Monash Responsible Largely for Victory.*

The Battalion put in but a brief stay at Sailly-Laurette,
where the glorious weather—reminiscent of Australia—was
much appreciated. Rest and reorganisation were both indulged in, but a long spell could not be expected, as the
Higher Command had decided that Fritz was not to be allowed
to recover from the recent smashing blow of August 8.
Accordingly, the 4th Brigade received orders
to relieve the 3rd Brigade, which was in the
line near Lihons. A march on the 13th
brought the Battalion to the neighbourhood of
Harbonnieres, and on the night of the 15th
(after the usual preliminaries) the relief was
complete—the Battalion having the 13th on its right, and the
23rd of the 6th A.I.F. Brigade on its left. We were now in
the old French system of trenches of 1916.
"Peaceful penetration" was the watchword
here, and in pursuance thereof, the Brigade
next day pushed forward about 500 yards
through some old communication trenches, and established
itself in another trench system, whilst on the following day
another advance of about the same distance was made, the
6th Brigade on our left also moving forward to conform. The
advances were made practically without opposition, the enemy
confining his attentions to long-range shelling from his strongly
reinforced artillery (which sometimes reached almost barrage
intensity) and to aircraft work.

*4th Brigade Relieves 3rd Brigade Near Lihons.*

*"Peaceful Penetration."*

On the night of the 18th, the 6th Australian Brigade was
relieved by the 32nd British Division, the 2nd Manchester
Regiment of that Division being posted on our
left. That regiment was composed largely
of raw soldiers, many were boys who had
little war experience. The enemy (well informed as usual) took advantage of the relief
of the seasoned troops formerly stationed there to make a

*2nd Manchesters Raided by Germans.*

cleverly executed and successful raid in broad daylight, under cover of a heavy barrage, on the 2nd Manchesters, killing and wounding a considerable number, and taking several prisoners. The operation appears to have been carried out by some of the enemy's best troops. Their attempts to exploit the initial success, however, were foiled by the foresight, courage, and initiative of Platoon Sgt. W. H. Boyes (14th Platoon), who, on learning of the critical situation on his left, put Sgt. W. H. Fergus in charge of the platoon, and single-handed and on his own initiative, took charge of and rallied the disorganised "Tommies," and twice led about a dozen of them against the triumphant enemy, shooting three of the most prominent Germans himself. When the enemy, strongly reinforced, swarmed back against his little party, Boyes, kneeling by a sandbag, held them practically single-handed at bay, playing on them with rifle-grenades. Cpl. W. J. Harding, M.M.[27] (14th Platoon), who accompanied Boyes in the first instance, had been sent back by the latter for more bombs, but was killed during the operation. Lieut. Bruford and Cpl. Wm. Goodsell (14th Platoon) subsequently joined Boyes and co-operated with him in the defence. The three of them and a handful of "Tommies" were cut off by a "box barrage" from all outside assistance. Just as the Germans were finally repulsed, Boyes and one of the "Tommies" were severely wounded by the barrage. It was feared by some that the former would lose his sight. Boyes received the D.C.M. in recognition of his splendid piece of work, and had the unique experience, as far as the 14th was concerned, of winning two decorations within eleven days.[28] Cpl. Wm. Goodsell received the M.M. for his active participation, and Lieut. G. T. Trewheela, who was O.C. of D Company (Lieut. Roxburgh having been injured a few days previously) received the M.C.

*Sgt. Boyes Goes to Their Assistance.*

*Cpl. Harding Killed.*

*Boyes Severely Wounded.*

Directly after the raid, and at frequent intervals during the remainder of the day, our front line was subjected to terrific bombardments by the enemy "minenwerfers" (i.e., trench-mortars). Sgt. David Drummond, M.M. (14th Platoon) was wounded in one of them (for the fourth time) and had to be evacuated. The 14th Platoon suffered severely

---

[27]Cpl. W. J. Harding (No. 3342), of Costerfield (Vic.), labourer, was a sterling soldier who had specially proved his worth and won a decoration at Hebuterne on March 28, 1918.

during this tour of duty—Cpl. J. G. Horne and Pte. J. G. Taylor (among others) being wounded, in addition to the several casualties already referred to. It is worthy of note that the 14th Platoon, which started its war career in France on July 3, 1916, by a sterling exhibition of soldierly conduct in resisting the only German trench raid on the 14th, should have practically closed its war account by another brilliant effort in resisting a German raid on the troops on our flank. L/Cpl. Adam Currie[29] (12th Platoon), a veteran long connected with the Battalion and who had won the M.M. only a few days prior to his death, was also mortally wounded, dying on August 20.

**Death of L/Cpl. Adam Currie.**

On the night of August 20 the 16th Battalion relieved the 14th in the front line, the relief being completed about 10.30 p.m. The 14th then went into support near Harbonnieres. A list of decorations won during this tour of duty is set out below. It is worthy of note that Wilson, Trewheela, Mew, McLennan, and Fitzpatrick, all mentioned therein, were Originals. Owing to the great historical importance of the Battle of Amiens, a list of the Battalion killed and wounded is also appended.

**The Battalion Relieved.**

**Decorations.**

M.C.—Capt. C. R. T. Cole (Malvern, Vic.), B Company; Capt. Norman Wilson (Auburn, Vic.), A Company; Lieut. Thomas M. Grant (Hampton, Vic.), Intelligence Officer; Lieut. G. T. Trewheela (Geelong, Vic.), D Company. D.C.M.—No. 6290, L/Sgt. Raymond A. Jeffers, M.M. (Cora Lynne, Vic.); No. 1512, A/Sgt. Chas. J. Clarke, M.M. (St. Mary's, Tas.); No. 742, C.Q.M.S. T. J. Mew (Carlton, Vic.); No. 1672, Sgt. W. H. Boyes, M.M. (Lardner, Vic.). Bar to M.M.—No. 5688, Cpl. V. W. Lalor, M.M. (Healesville, Vic.). M.M.— No. 7111, Pte. H. L. Thompson (Derry, Ireland); No. 5330, L/Sgt. J. W. Baker (Donald, Vic.), No. 6804, L/Cpl. Wm. Crocker; No. 5112, Pte. Norman Harris (Windsor, Vic.); No. 59, Sgt. A. B. McLennan (Armadale, Vic.); No. 5161, Pte. J. J.

---

[28] The author is not aware whether this is also a 4th Brigade or even an A.I.r. record.

[29] L/Cpl. Adam Currie (No. 2357), labourer, of Falkirk, Scotland. Adam Currie, who was a Schotchman, must not be confused with the three Currie brothers of D Company, two of whom became sergeants, and another of whom won the M.M. at Hamel (vide footnote 14 to Chap. 39). The author has been informed that Adam Currie was the last member of the Battalion to be wounded on the Peninsula. The statement may be correct, but the author has been unable to verify it.

Marmo (Footscray, Vic.); No. 6923, Sgt. W. R. Bell (Surrey Hills, Vic.); No. 5994, Cpl. H. C. Clements (North Fitzroy, Vic.); No. 5149, Cpl. Alex. Lee (Weerite, Vic.); No. 6614, Cpl. L. A. Webb (Hawthorn, Vic.); No. 1672, Sgt. W. H. Boyes (Lardner, Vic.); No. 2373, L/Cpl. W. J. Earll (Cavendish, Vic.); No. 4143, Pte. Wm. Blake (Collingwood, Vic.); No. 3761, L/Cpl. S. A. Foster; No. 2357, L/Cpl. Adam Currie (Falkirk, Scotland); No. 1175, Pte. W. J. Fitzpatrick (Bendigo, Vic.); No. 1808, Cpl. George Robb (Kew, Vic.); No. 6735, Cpl. Wm. Goodsell (Campsie, N.S.W.).

## CASUALTIES AT THE BATTLE OF AMIENS.

Killed and Died of Wounds.—Lieut. F. W. Appleton, Croix-de-Guerre (C Company), K.I.A. August 8, 1918; Lieut. H. W. Thompson, M.C. (B Company), D.W. August 9, 1918; No. 6998, Pte. C. J. Donoghue, D.W. August 8, 1918; No. 7604, Pte. V. W. Norman, D.W. August 8, 1918; No. 5729, L/Cpl. T. Richardson, D.W. August 8, 1918; No. 7436, Pte. H. W. Adams, K.I.A. August 8, 1918; No. 2333, Pte. A. Aitken (C Company), K.I.A. August 8, 1918; No. 7444, Pte. C. C. Bell, K.I.A. August 8, 1918; No 6977, Pte. A. Cameron (A Company), K.I.A. August 8, 1918; No. 7231, Pte. J. A. Dix, K.I.A. August 8, 1918; No. 7014, Pte. S. G. Garner (C Company), K.I.A. August 8, 1918; No. 7021, Pte. J. F. Harvey (B Company), K.I.A. August 8, 1918; No. 4344, Cpl. G. A. Heron (B Company), K.I.A. August 8, 1918; No. 5683, Pte. W. T. Hopley (B Company), K.I.A. August 8, 1918; No. 5398, Pte. N. McD. Jenkins (B Company), signaller, K.I.A. August 8, 1918; No. 5398a, Pte. H. J. Lamprell, M.M. (D Company), K.I.A. August 8, 1918; No. 7285, Cpl. J. J. Moriarty (C Company), K.I.A. August 8, 1918; No. 2914, Sgt. A. S. Smith, M.M. (B Company), K.I.A. August 8, 1918; No. 2433, Pte. R. C. Thomas, K.I.A. August 8, 1918; No. 2450, L/Sgt. A. J. D. Waddell (B Company), K.I.A. August 8, 1918; No. 5999, L/Cpl. John Craig, D.W. August 9, 1918; No. 1628, Pte. H. Thornton, D.W. August 10, 1918; No. 5097a, Pte. R. Grist (C Company), K.I.A. August 8, 1918; No. 1945, Cpl. H. C. Goddard (D Company), K.I.A. August 8, 1918.

Wounded.[30]—Capt. H. C. Trumble, M.C.; Capt. C. R. T. Cole; T/Capt. N. C. Harris; Lieut. H. C. A. Schutze; No. 459, Pte. C. Hawkins; No. 830, Pte. R. S. Callander; No. 8592, Pte. G. J. Gaster; No. 2178, L/Cpl. L. Moore; No. 2640, Pte. G. S. Smith; No. 3857, Pte. A. R. Larter; No. 4933, Pte. J. Twyford,

---

[30]The list of wounded, though apparently lacking two names, is as nearly correct as the author has been able to ascertain.

No. 5377, Pte. I. Griffiths; No. 7113, Pte. G. H. Rowe; No. 7275, Pte. A. H. Liersch; No. 7442, Pte. J. Campbell; No. 7495, Pte. C. Gale; No. 7511, Pte. M. J. Callaghan; No. 7528, Pte. A. P. Larsen; No. 7538, Pte. A. T. Nichols; No. 7540, Pte. J. O'Callaghan; Pte. 7559, Pte. M. W. W. Byrne; No. 7560, Pte. C. H. T. Lord; No. 7569, Pte. L. Taylor; No. 2838, Pte. S. Abell (2nd occasion); No. 2932, Pte. C. A. E. Gilbert (2nd occasion); No. 3539, L/Cpl. J. R. Wood (2nd occasion); No. 3815, L/Cpl. J. Howell (2nd occasion); No. 4130, Pte. A. A. Birtles (2nd occasion); No. 761, Pte. C. Osborne (2nd occasion); No. 4260, L/Sgt. K. McKenzie (2nd occasion); No. 4300, L/Cpl. A. Roberts (2nd occasion); No. 6106, L/Cpl. F. Thomas (2nd occasion); No. 6539, L/Cpl. P. A. Leach (2nd occasion); No. 6597, Pte. S. C. Stearman (2nd occasion); No. 6807, Pte. M. Rowbottom (2nd occasion); No. 6983, Pte. A. J. Connor (2nd occasion); No. 7180, Pte. E. A. Wilcock (2nd occasion); No. 7265, Pte. C. G. James (2nd occasion); No. 7319, Pte. W. B. Sherrard (2nd occasion); No. 375, Pte. L. J. P. Smith (3rd occasion); No. 1247, Pte. J. Maxwell (3rd occasion); No. 2385, Cpl. S. J. Gaul (3rd occasion); No. 2896, Pte. W. E. Watts (3rd occasion); No. 3291, Pte. G. H. Collins (3rd occasion); No. 4248, Pte. J. A. Matthews (3rd occasion); No. 4579, Pte. H. G. O'Brien (3rd occasion); No. 5699, Pte. A. M. Mackie (3rd occasion); No. 5737, Pte. G. A. Seal (3rd occasion); No. 5761, L/Cpl. W. D. Cochrane (3rd occasion); No. 7000, Pte. L. A. Dunk (3rd occasion); No. 7038, Pte. E. E. Ladner (3rd occasion); No. 4432, Pte. A. C. C. Baker (4th occasion); No. 294, Cpl. E. E. Bishop (2nd occasion); No. 2831, Pte. W. A. E. Clarke (3rd occasion).

## CHAPTER XLI.

### THE BATTLE OF THE HINDENBURG OUTPOST LINE.*

1918—August 21 to November 11.

After its retirement from the Harbonnieres area, the Battalion remained about a fortnight at Cardonnette, near Allonville, reorganising and refitting after recent operations. During this respite, the men were better clothed than they had been for a considerable time.

**Battalion Reorganisation.**

Meanwhile, stirring events were taking place at the front. The Battle of Amiens had been the turning point of the war, leading to a gradual enemy retirement along the whole front. The German army was at length showing signs of exhaustion and loss of morale under the continuous blows that were being showered upon it. Its retreat was generally covered by the machine gunners (the flower of its army) between whom and the Australians, who were very prominent in the Allied advance, developed many Homeric contests. Upwards of one-third of the V.C.'s won by the A.I.F. during the war were gained during its last three months of warfare, mostly by the successful rushing and wiping out of enemy machine-gun nests. The retirement of the enemy was hastened by the fall of Peronne, brought about by some exceptionally brilliant work by the 2nd and 5th A.I.F. Divisions. During this period, the 4th Division was moved from its "rest billets" for the purpose of relieving the 5th A.I.F. Division, whose strenuous and successful efforts had merited a well-earned rest.

**Gardual Retirement of German Army.**

**Covered by Its Machine Gunners.**

**The 4th Relieves the 5th Division.**

The 4th Division was then thrown into the breach, the pursuit of the enemy being taken up by the 13th Brigade, with

---
*Known by the British as the Battle of Epéhy.

## The Battle of Hindenburg Outpost Line

the 12th Brigade in support and the 4th Brigade in reserve (the 14th Battalion being the reserve Battalion of the 4th Brigade). In accordance with these arrangements, the 14th embussed on September 8, travelling easterly to the river bank at Biaches, near Peronne. Everywhere signs of the hasty German retreat were visible in the shape of blown-up bridges, and captured and abandoned guns, the sight of which naturally stimulated the ardour of our men. Some casualties were suffered at Biaches from "booby traps." Surplus gear having been dumped here, the 4th Brigade moved forward in fighting order through Peronne, over roads rendered difficult by inclement weather, in addition to enemy destruction. On the 12th, after the usual reconnaissances, the Battalion was allotted a most comfortable camp in the old aerodrome near Estrees. A formation of the enemy's bombing Gothas running into our searchlights were here attacked from above by our planes, and many of them set on fire and brought down in the vicinity of the camp. Their exploding rockets and bombs as they collapsed made a brilliant display of fireworks. The stay here, however, was short, for the stiffening of the enemy's resistance indicated an intention on his part to make a determined stand in the old British defence line of March, 1918, with its intricate system of trenches and wire easily adapted to his own use.

*Battalion Reaches Biaches.*

*Signs of German Retreat.*

*Camp Near Estrees.*

The generally favourable military outlook had resulted in the determination of G.H.Q. to launch an attack upon the tremendously strong line of enemy outposts in front of the Hindenburg line, and this, combined with the intention of the enemy to make a resolute stand there, brought about the inevitable collision which was to terminate the 4th Brigade's active participation in the war. The plan arranged was an attack on the 4th British Army front by several divisions, with the 1st and 4th A.I.F. Divisions in the centre —the former on the left and the latter on the right. The attack of the 4th Division was to be delivered by the 4th and 12th Brigades, fighting side by side from left to right. The 4th Brigade orders provided for the capture, by the 16th Battalion, of the village of Le Verguier, perched on a slight hill. The 13th and 15th Battalions, passing respectively on the right and left of that village, were then to capture the brown line. The 16th Battalion, after mopping up Le Verguier, was thereupon to

*Attack on Hindenburg Outpost Line Decided On.*

*1st and 4th A.I.F. Divisions to Participate.*

*Plan of Battle.*

advance and occupy the brown line, thereby enabling the 13th and 15th Battalions, by means of a further advance, to capture the red line. The role allotted to the 14th Battalion—probably the most difficult of all—was to pass through the red line, and exploit the success of the 13th and 15th, with a view of establishing itself on the blue line, in so doing extending and covering the other two Battalions' front. The British Army had now fought its way back to where the great German assault of March 21, 1918, had started. The brown line took in the old British line of resistance of that date, whilst the taking of the red line involved the capture of the old British outpost line. The blue line included 1800 yards of the old enemy outpost line, immensely strong, and now heavily garrisoned and flanked by the two perhaps most strongly fortified points on the famous Hindenburg line—Bellicourt and Bellenglise. It consisted of front and support trench with communication trenches, prepared blocks, and deep dug-outs, giving covering fire from machine-guns from front to rear, as well as in enfilade.

*The 14th to be Exploiting Battalion.*

The 4th Brigade attack was to be supported by a heavy creeping barrage, which, however, was available only to the red line, and the 14th was warned only to expect the support of the heavies and its own attached batteries. A heavy machine-gun barrage was certainly provided for, but tanks were very scarce, and limited to the first objective, though some "dummy tanks" were improvised to draw the enemy's fire. All Australian Battalions at this time were very weak numerically, continuous warfare and heavy casualties having reduced them to mere shadows. The "over-the-top" strength of the 14th was only 360, with a rifle strength of about 300. All available men of the A.I.F. had been recently sent to the front—many of them having been dug out of safe and comfortable billets which they had held for years.

*Numerical Weakness of Battalion.*

The line of advance was easterly, the ground to be fought over consisting for the most part of open grassed country, comprising several ridges and gullies at right angles to the line of advance. The attenuated companies of the 14th were called upon to capture 1800 yards of the strongest enemy

*Description of Terrain.*

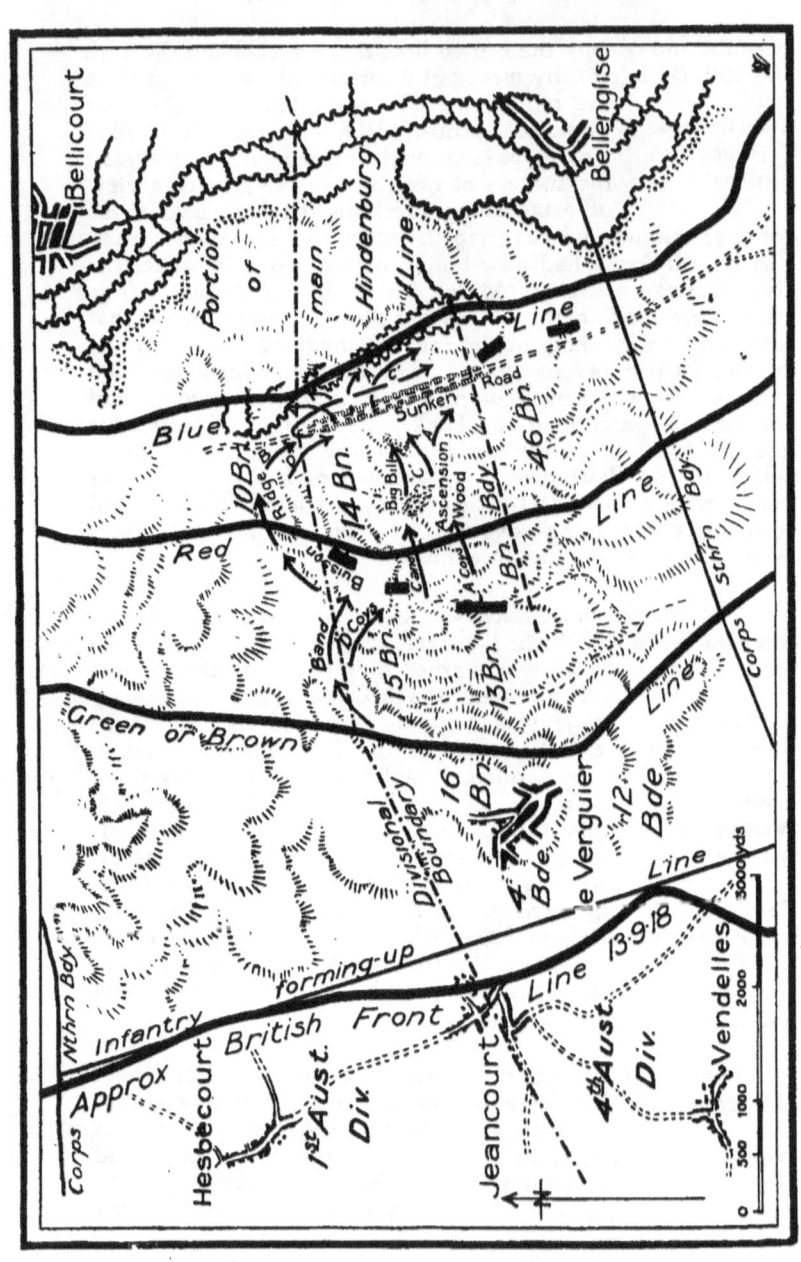

THE BATTLE OF THE HINDENBURG OUTPOST LINE.

## The History of the 14th Battalion.

**14th to Attack Over Open Country without Artillery Barrage and Without Tanks.**

outpost line in France, advancing over the open without tanks and without an artillery barrage. Those who had been through Bullecourt, and knew the enormous strength of the Hindenburg line, realised the immensity of the allotted task. Seldom was the Battalion, in the whole of its long and chequered career, faced with a tougher proposition. It looked like attempting the impossible.

The 4th Brigade moved forward on the night of September 16-17, and relieved the left portion of the 13th Brigade, whilst the 12th Brigade relieved the right. The 13th Brigade then took up its position in reserve. Mobile batteries, trench mortars, and Vickers guns were placed under direct control of battalion commanders, and all preparations for the forthcoming battle were completed. Heavy rain fell that night, soaking everything and everyone, but with true Australian philosophy the men made a joke of their discomfort. The loss of sleep, however, entailed thereby put an extra physical strain on them during the subsequent operations. It was decided to attack with two companies in front and the other two in support. Battalion dispositions were as follows:—Front—Right, C Company (Major W. R. Wadsworth, M.C.); left, B Company (Capt. Joe Mackay); Support—Right, A Company (Lieut. N. C. Aldridge, M.C.); left, D Company (Lieut. Eugene Chubb).

**4th Relieves 13th Brigade.**

**Heavy Pre-Battle Rain.**

**Disposition of Companies.**

The dawn of the 18th was heralded by another night of rain, soaking the already weary waiting troops in their trenches near Vendelles, and again interfering with their rest. "Zero" hour was fixed for 5.20 a.m., and on that precise moment the whole countryside was lit up with one stupendous flash of light. Our barrage had opened, and the splendid battalions of the 4th Brigade were let loose on their last battle in the great war. The 14th was not to advance till 7 a.m., and at daylight the transport came up and gave our men a hot breakfast. Meanwhile, the 16th had captured Le Verguier according to plan, followed by the 13th and 15th in close support. These two latter units, shaking into formation behind the brown line, followed the barrage down into the slope of the gully and found themselves under heavy machine-gun fire from the opposite slope.

**Barrage Opens.**

**Hot Breakfast.**

**Capture of Le Verguier by the 16th Battalion.**

During this advance, a brilliant piece of work by Sgt. Gerald Sexton, of the 13th, added another V.C. to those gained by the 4th Brigade in the war.

*Sgt. Sexton, of 13th, Wins V.C.*

Some severe fighting was undergone by both Battalions in reaching their objectives, and, owing to the exhaustion of all ranks through the heavy going, and their great expenditure of ammunition against semi-concealed posts, they were too exhausted at first to consolidate, and could not bring to bear the overhead supporting fire on the Hindenburg outpost line so much counted on by the 14th.

A little before 7 a.m. our companies formed up in artillery formation and moved off. The mud underfoot made very heavy going, and, as each man's load consisted of a pick and shovel, 220 rounds of ammunition, three bombs, and, in some cases, machine-guns and panniers, whilst in addition, few had had any sleep during the previous 48 hours, the exhaustion of all ranks can be imagined. Externally wet, the men were steaming inside their clothes. At 9 a.m. the forming-up position was reached—a road running across the ground captured by the 13th and 15th—with only half-a-dozen casualties, and platoons were shaken out, whilst the Battalion settled down in attack formation to await the capture of the red line. The 15th Battalion men, digging in the locality, made no effort to hide their misgivings about the difficulties of our part of the battle.[1] At 9.25 a.m. the companies moved forward in good order, and a few minutes later our barrage died away, but not before some short-shelling on its part on our extreme left compelled our left companies (B and D) to go round the area shelled, by deviating into and behind the 10th Battalion, which was attacking on our left flank. Uncertainty arose among our men on recovering their position as to the boundary between the Divisions, and bunching occurred. Scarcely had the Battalion passed the red line (about 9.40 a.m.) and topped the ridge opposite Buisson Ridge, than the objective, as well as the copses in front, vomited innumerable machine-gun bullets from camouflaged positions. B and D Companies on the left suffered considerable casualties, and found difficulty in dealing with these nests, before the daring and skilful work of the Lewis gun teams and

*14th Companies Move Off.*

*Exhaustion of All Ranks.*

*F.U.P. Reached.*

*Battalion Passes Red Line.*

---

[1] Vide Lieut. Rule's diary.

*The History of the 14th Battalion.* 341

**B and D Companies Charge.** individual snipers, of the advanced as well as support Company—both drawn into the free fight — enabled superiority of fire to be obtained, for the whole line to dash down the exposed forward slope and to obtain the partial protection of the reverse slope of Buisson Ridge. This dash yielded some

**Resulting Captures.** booty in the shape of field guns, trench mortars, and a considerable crop of machine-guns, but the ascent of Buisson Ridge was attained only with more casualties, and, on the crest, the terrible machine-gun fire for the second time brought the advance to a halt.

Meanwhile, C and A Companies on the right were having a similar experience. Their advance to Ascension Wood

**Advance of C and A Companies.** showed the Australian infantry at its best, little bodies of men, singly or in pairs, dashing forward amidst the bullet-swept slopes, dropping to ground for cover, and then making another dash forward with that skill and cunning which probably distinguished Australian troops beyond all others in the war. It was only the paucity of our numbers which prevented heavy casualties. Ascension

**Ascension Wood Captured.** Wood was reached and cleared, the Germans bolting when our men got to close quarters.

The direction on the right of the Battalion was from Ascension Wood to Big Bill, thence on to the sunken road, and thence to the objective. An attempt to push out of the left hand-corner of Ascension Wood by the 11th Platoon (O.C., Lieut. Ted Rule), supported by No. 2 Platoon (O.C., Lieut. Tom Griffith), was met with such a stream of enemy lead as rendered advance impossible. Direct advance being thus barred, a successful effort was made by the two platoons to reach a copse on the left, known as Big Bill, but on attempting to debouch, such a torrent of bullets swept the crest as again brought matters to a standstill. Subsequently

**Sunken Road Reached on Right.** the right flank of C and A Company reached the sunken road, close to the German line, but barred by masses of impenetrable barbed wire, which could not be dealt with without that artillery support which was lacking. Later, Rule's and Griffith's platoons joined up here. The Germans turned some trench mortars on our trenches in the sunken road, but fortunately their missiles fell a little short.

Meanwhile, touch had been maintained on the left with the 10th Battalion, and on the right with the 46th, but owing to the poverty of our numbers, personal, though not visual, connection had been lost between our two left and our two right companies. At 11 a.m. the position was as follows:—B Company, with the right of the 10th Battalion was hung up on the crest of Buisson Ridge, reinforced by the D Company Lewis guns, with the remainder of D Company lying close up in support. C and A Companies were lying along the sunken road. Enemy machine-guns were extremely numerous and active from behind his wire, and his artillery was shelling the woods and gullies in front of the red line. Reconnaissances undertaken about this time showed it possible to work along behind the crest into the 10th Battalion area (that Battalion having managed to reach the front line of the Hindenburg outpost line), enter behind there, and block and bomb down the enemy trench. Accordingly, under a covering fire from D Company, B Company was withdrawn into the valley, worked along behind the crest, and, by 12.30 p.m., was established and bombing down towards C and A Companies in the sunken road. By a similar route D Company and Rule's 11th Platoon from C Company, also got successfully in, and a determined effort—helped by the attached 41st Battery—was made to clear an entrance for C and A Companies. Straight sections of trench, cunningly blocked and heavily enfiladed, prevented further progress, and, after severe casualties,[2] counter-blocks were formed, and it was decided to postpone further movement till after dark, when our numerical weakness could be camouflaged. All ranks, too, were thoroughly exhausted, for movement in the sticky glutinous mud of the old trenches encumbered with dead was most trying, whilst the supply of bombs necessary for such warfare had run short. Conditions were eminently favourable for an enemy counter-attack, but, fortunately, it was not attempted, the threatening and aggressive attitude of our men throughout having imposed upon the enemy. The Battalion, sadly reduced in numbers, had established itself on the lip of the system it had set out to capture, and by sheer bluff it clung to its gains.

Our men in the sunken road remained quiet till night, many of them playing cards to while away the time.[3] The

---

[2]Almost the whole of the 11th Platoon except one man was wounded by a volley of stick bombs hurled into them at close quarters (vide Lieut. Rule's diary).

[3]Communicated by Cpl. H. C. Clements.

enemy, who appeared to be somewhat rattled, kept up an incessant fire, which did not draw any response from our men. During the afternoon, some of our wounded were carried 2000 yards to the R.A.P. in the rear.

After dark, leaving the great part of the front deliberately uncovered, the two right Companies (A and C) were disengaged, marched right across the enemy's front, and entered the trench on the enemy's vulnerable point on the left sector, silently filing to their places for the final assault. The move was most audacious, but desperate situations require desperate remedies, and the manœuvre proved eminently successful. Colonel Crowther ordered Major Wadsworth, who had been very active all day, to organise the assault and put Lieut. Rule in charge of C Company.

*A and C Companies March Across Enemy's Front.*

*Major Wadsworth Organises Assault.*

"Zero" hour was fixed at 11 p.m. The 46th Battalion[4] —the exploiting Battalion of the 12th Brigade co-operating on our right flank—had also been held up, and was to participate in our night attack. The assault of the 14th was planned as follows:—

*Plan of Night Assault.*

A Company was to bomb the enemy's front line to the right (i.e., south) to get in touch with the 46th Battalion; C Company was to hop over from his front line, capture his support line, and bomb along it to the right parallel to A Company; B Company was to hop over with C Company, get into his support line, and bomb to the left to get into touch with the 10th Battalion; D Company was to be held in reserve. Bombs, and a hot meal for the men, were brought up. Shortly before 11 p.m. heavy rain fell, soaking everyone.

Our artillery opened at 11 p.m., but as far as the 14th was concerned, its support was practically nil. Five minutes later, our men "hopped the bags," advancing into what appeared certain death, for the enemy, firing phosphorous tracer bullets from numerous machine-guns, skimmed our trenches with innumerable balls of fire—the air appeared alive with them. It seemed at first as if our companies were doomed to

*Battalion's Night Attack.*

---

[4]Mr. F. M. Cutlack ("Australians—Their Final Campaign") points out:—"There was a fine piece of romance about this night attack. The 46th Battalion is the pup of the 14th, from which it was formed in Egypt. . . . . The two Battalions, the old dog and the younger one, drove home that last attack with splendid spirit, and won all they went for." The 46th carried the same colours as the 14th, though under a different formation.

destruction, but some very courageous work on the part of some of our Lewis gunners, and a few shots from a Stokes gun in our trenches, had the effect of compelling the hostile machine-gunners to keep their heads down, with the result that they began firing too high, and their bullets started passing overhead.

This short preliminary work was followed by a furious charge by our men, yelling like fiends, and headed by the C Company bombers—a picked body of men, ably and most courageously led by Sgt. "Lofty" Bauchop. It was the 14th Battalion's last charge in the war. Our numerical weakness—the Battalion trench strength was now only a little over 200—was not evidently realised by the enemy in the darkness, and before our men reached his support trench, the machine-gunners' morale went "snap," and they fled incontinently, some toward the canal in the rear, while others bolted down the trench and were captured by the 46th Battalion, for whom our bombers acted as a military ferret. "It was the lightning stroke and not the weight of it which smashed the enemy in this splendid assault."[5] Some opposition was put up by one enemy regiment fresh in, but our charge was not to be denied, and drastic treatment of dugouts and pockets speedily broke down the enemy's resistance and morale. By 11.30 p.m.—half-an-hour after "zero"—practically his whole line was in our hands, though odd saps were cleared out till about daylight. Heavy casualties had been inflicted on the enemy.

*14th Battalion's Last Charge.*

*Capture of All Objectives and Retreat of Enemy.*

Daylight disclosed that we had captured the enemy's most dominating position, comprising an easily convertible trench system along the crest, the support and front line being immediately reversed by us. About a mile and a half in front lay the famous Hindenburg main line—which had held up the Allied armies in 1917—and between our men and it lay the canal. Wonderful targets were observed—guns, motor cars, and lorries all in plain view—but our artillery was not available, and only long range rifle fire, mostly ineffective, could be used. The Battalion was faced with the problem of holding 1800 yards of trench with 200 men, exhausted by heavy fighting over most difficult and muddy

*Enemy's Most Dominant Position Captured.*

---

[5]Quotations from Mr. Cutlack's book, page 307, referring to the above described charge.

ground, and who had now passed a third night without sleep; the eyes of many were becoming bloodshot. Every preparation was made to resist an enemy counter-attack, which, fortunately, did not eventuate. Later in the day, a company of the 15th Battalion was offered in support, and gratefully accepted.

On the night of the 19-20th, outposts were pushed out for an average distance of 300 yards to cover the wiring of a new line by a company of the 4th Pioneers. **Outposts Pushed Out.** At dawn the enemy shelled us unmercifully for about half-an-hour, and, though inflicting few casualties, one shell caused the death of the **Death of Sgt. "Lofty" Bauchop and Sgt.-Major A. A. Johnstone.** hero of the 14th Battalion's last charge—Sgt. "Lofty" Bauchop[6] was mortally wounded. Idolised by his comrades, there was many a moist eye as he was carried to a dugout to die. Sgt.-Mjr. A. A. Johnstone[7] (also of C Company)—one of the finest lads in the Battalion—was mortally wounded about the same time. He winked at his comrades when too weak to speak, and died after lingering a couple of hours.[8] A victory purchased by the death of such men is never cheap.

On the night of the 20th/21st, the left half of our line was taken over by the 15th Battalion, and the right half by the 13th Battalion. The relief was completed before midnight, and the 14th, absolutely worn out, retired **14th Retires into Support. Rest Billets at Hengest.** into support. The Brigade subsequently moved by road to Tincourt and Brie, whence it embussed for rest billets at Hengest. The long-looked-for rest, so frequently promised during the previous sixteen months, but which had never eventuated, became a reality at last.

Credit must be given to the signal personnel for admirable communication under more than usual difficulty. The report centre went forward with the companies and **Work of the Signallers.** established in Big Bill, to which, despite heavy fire, the signal section maintained almost unbroken communication, and further, took a wire to the C.O. of the firing line. The Company Signallers connected their respective wires with the latter. The Assist-

---

[6]Sgt. L. R. Bauchop, clerk, of Williamstown (Vic.). Born Greta, Vic. Age at death, 24. K.I.A. September 20, 1918.
[7]Sgt. A. A. Johnstone, accountant, of Melbourne (Vic.). Age at death, 23 years 9 months. D.W. September 20, 1918.
[8]Details of Bauchop's and Johnstone's deaths taken from Lieut. Rule's diary.

ant Signalling Officer (Lieut. W. C. Thomas) and Signaller C. A. Crapper were wounded.

All the Company Commanders appear to have shown efficiency and judgment, whilst some of the platoon officers[9] displayed exceptional initiative, but it was essentially a soldiers' battle—a battle of sections—the whole of the attack, however, being co-ordinated by the universal desire to move forward according to plan. As a result of the operations, the Battalion took 75 prisoners, eleven guns, four heavy trench mortars, upwards of eighty light and heavy machine-guns, two messenger dogs, two anti-tank rifles, and the usual assortment of shells, ammunition, telephones and military gear, besides inflicting heavy casualties on the enemy.

*Battalion's Captures of Prisoners and Material.*

Our casualties were 101,[10] including three officers wounded (Lieuts. Les. Ebbot, Syd. Garton, and W. C. Thomas), and 21 other ranks killed or died of wounds—certainly a large proportion of the Battalion's fighting strength, but relatively small considering the difficulties surmounted, casualties inflicted, and wonderful results achieved. The fatal casualties included no less than five sergeants—a striking tribute to their gallant leadership. They were: L. R. Bauchop, A. A. Johnstone, and H. B. Clark,[11] of C Company, and B. V. Almond[12] and C. C. Serjeant,[13] of B Company. Almond was an Original who had been in charge of the Battalion records in Egypt and Rouen. "Snowy" Clark and C. C. Serjeant were veterans who had seen much service with the Battalion.

*Our Casualties.*

*Five Sergeants Killed.*

---

[9]The platoon commanders in the battle of September 18 comprised the following subalterns:—A Company: Syd. Garton, Tom Griffith and W. R. Crellin. B Company: H. B. Jackson, D. H. L. Hawkins and G. H. Clarendon Hyde. C Company: Ted Rule, Les. Ebbott and J. W. Jordan. D Company: A. R. Bruford, E. G. Chamberlain and A. P. Stone.

[10]Capt. Aldridge reports A Company casualties as 27 (6 killed out of a fighting strength of 72). B Company's casualties were 30 (6 killed). The casualties of the other companies are not set out.

[11]L/Sgt. H. B. Clark, carpenter, of Ballarat (Vic.). Born Sebastopol (Vic.) on August 20, 1895. D.W. October 7, 1918.

[12]S/Sgt. B. V. Almond, journalist, of Geelong (Vic.). Born Sydney (N.S.W.). K.I.A. September 18, 1918.

[13]Sgt. C. C. Serjeant, law clerk, of Burnley (Vic.). K.I.A. September 18, 1918.

## The History of the 14th Battalion. 347

**Death of Cpl. "Sarto" Anderson.**
Another N.C.O. whose loss was greatly felt was Cpl. "Sarto" Anderson, M.M.,[14] the cool and resolute N.C.O. in charge of the Battalion Scouts. An Original (No. 676), his military career had been a succession of daring achievements, and he fell near Big Bill heroically attempting, single-handed, to capture a German machine-gun nest. Cpl. Lew Jones, M.M. (B Company), a brother of Capt. Reg. Jones, was another N.C.O. who lost his life in this battle. There was not anything more pathetic in this engagement than the fate of those who, facing innumerable dangers for years, laid down their lives as the Battalion was finally entering the harbour of safety—a few hours before its last shot was fired.

**Some Battalion Wounded.**
Among the wounded were Sgts. W. R. M. Bell, H. R. M. Scott (5th occasion) and W. L. Edmondstone (4th occasion), all of C Company; Sgt. A. E. Allen, Cpl. H. P. Curwen, and Signaller Crapper (3rd occasion); the latter was a nephew of Sgt. Crapper, whose successful efforts to find water on the Peninsula have been described in a previous chapter. One of the outstanding personalities of the engagement was Stretcher-bearer John L. Schmit,[15] who, though severely wounded in the hand at the outset of the attack, nevertheless showed throughout most untiring devotion to his comrades under heavy and accurate enemy fire.

Several decorations were awarded to the surviving combatants. Major Wadsworth was awarded the D.S.O., Lieut. "Joe" Aldridge a bar to his M.C., and Lieuts. Rule and Griffith the M.C. Among the other ranks, Sgt. Charlie Clark (signaller) received a bar to his M.M. (third decoration), Cpl. V. W. Lalor, the D.C.M. (third decoration), L/Cpl. Charlie Platt bar to M.M. (2nd decoration), and the veteran Sgt. D. W. Blackburn the M.M. A complete list of decorations awarded appears at the end of this chapter.

**Decorations.**

The battle was not only the last, but also one of the most successful of the battles[16] in which the 1st and 4th Divisions

---

[14]Cpl. Hugh Alexander Anderson, labourer, of Collingwood (Vic.). K.I.A. September 18, 1918. Details of his death were communicated by Sgt. Charlie Clarke, D.C.M., M.M. and Bar, who buried him next day.

[15]Pte. John Lawrence Schmit, blacksmith, of Kew (Vic.).

[16]Lieut.-General Sir John Monash ("Australian Victories in France in 1918") states in reference to this battle:—"The 1st Division attacked with a total strength of 2854 infantry. They suffered only 490 casualties. . . . They captured 1700 prisoners. . . . The 4th Division had a total assaulting strength of 3048 of all ranks, of whom 532 became casualties. Their captures of live prisoners amounted to 2543."

had participated, and with it the long and varied career of the 14th had terminated in a blaze of glory.[17] Its personnel could look back on a past, chequered indeed, but highly creditable, and one that reflected honor not only on themselves, but on their native land. The price paid, however, had been a heavy one, some of Australia's noblest sons giving their lives freely to found those traditions which will always be associated with the 14th Battalion and the splendid State which gave it birth.

*End of Battalion's War Career.*

*Great Traditions Founded.*

The Battalion remained at Hengest till November 14, engaged in training and recreation. During this period, several members of the Battalion with the longest service took their departure to Australia on leave. Many Australian officers and N.C.O.'s were loaned about this time to the United States forces to give them the one essential in which they were lacking—war experience. On November 1, the 4th Brigade, at the invitation of the local residents, and accompanied by them, marched to the adjoining British cemetery, where flowers were placed on the graves. Meanwhile, fighting had been going on with the military position of Germany becoming steadily worse. Finally the Kaiser fled to Holland, and on November 11 the Armistice was signed, and this war-ridden planet knew peace once more. The news caused great excitement all over the world, and was a matter of intense relief to the war-weary combatants of all nationalities.

*Flight of Kaiser.*

*Armistice Signed.*

On November 21, Major W. L. Arrell (49th Battalion) took over command of the 14th, Lieut.-Col. H. A. Crowther, D.S.O., leaving for Australia next day. The retiring C.O. had proved a capable and energetic officer, whose regime had been eminently successful. During the winter in Belgium, efforts were made, by means of classes of instruction, to fit the men for a return to civilian life. During the spring, drafts made their way to England, en route for Australia. Australia was reached, usually by the Capetown and Durban route, and, as the steamers were generally comfortable, and the food good,

*Lieut.-Col. Crowther Leaves Battalion for Australia.*

---

[17]The author is indebted for details in the above engagement, in addition to contributions from some company and platoon commanders, to the lucid account of Col. Crowther, Lieut. Rule's valuable diary, and Lieut. Bruford's able narrative essay, from which some excerpts have been taken verbatim.

with the prospect of Australia near at hand, good fellowship generally prevailed. Some had contracted marriages in the old land, and returned in "family boats" with wives and children. On the anniversary of Anzac Day the Australian Divisions marched through London with fixed bayonets. Australia gave her soldier sons a splendid welcome, Capt. Jacka, V.C., receiving probably the most enthusiastic reception accorded to any returned member of the A.I.F.

*March Through London on Anzac Day.*

*Australia's Reception to Her Soldier Sons.*

This chapter will close with a brief recapitulation of the Battalion's doings in 1918. That year opened without any signs of the end of the war, and with the Battalion stationed at Templeux-la-Fosse. A few days later, the 4th Brigade moved north, the weather then prevailing preventing active operations on a large scale on either side. A heavy enemy gas bombardment resulted in the evacuation of nearly 300 officers and men, including the C.O. (Lieut.-Col. Smith), who did not return to the unit. Major C. M. Johnston assumed command of the Battalion in February, and Major H. A. Crowther on March 15.

*Resume of Battalion's Record in 1918.*

On March 21, the Germans launched their tremendous attack on the British Third and Fifth Armies, crumpling them up and pushing them back nearly 40 miles. The Australians were rushed down from the north in an attempt to stem the torrent. The 4th Brigade was taken to the scene of action in 'buses, and, after being separated from the remaining two Brigades of the 4th Division, was sent in to fill a dangerous gap which had arisen on the Third Army front near Hebuterne. It appears in this campaign to have been the first Australian Brigade to have met the enemy, and, after a prompt seizure of Hebuterne, it brought the German advance in that quarter to a summary conclusion. The work of the 4th Brigade in this sector was worthy of its high reputation, and, after a very strenuous and exhausting time (being attached to no fewer than four British Divisions in succession without relief), it finally rejoined the other Brigade of the 4th Division near Villers Brettoneux. At the end of April the 14th went into the line, and during the operations here, it was at one time the extreme right unit of the whole British Army on the western front. An enemy gas bombardment about this time terminated Capt. Jacka's connection with the 14th.

On May 22 the 4th Brigade was relieved, and the 14th went into billets at Allonville for a few days. On the night of May 30-31, when our men were resting here in fancied security far behind the front line, the enemy landed two heavy shells on two sheds tenanted respectively by A and C Companies. The buildings were completely wrecked, the debris falling upon the sleeping men with terrible results. A Company's shed in particular was turned into a perfect shambles, and yielded nearly 70 casualties. This was perhaps the most destructive shell ever hurled into the ranks of the A.I.F. The 14th left Allonville on May 31, and marched to the vicinity of Corbie. On June 15, B, C, and D Companies carried out a successful and cheaply purchased trench raid on the enemy opposite us at Vaire Wood. Trophies and prisoners were secured. It was the Battalion's second trench raid in France. Next day the unit was relieved and moved into support near Fouilloy.

On July 4 the 14th participated in the very successful battle of Hamel, in which heavy casualties were inflicted on the enemy. Subsequent to that engagement, a most enjoyable time was spent at Querrieu, some very successful sports meetings being held in the vicinity. On August 8, at the Battle of Amiens, the A.I.F. fought the greatest and most successful engagement in its history. The 4th Brigade, owing to the failure of troops on its flank, was confronted with perhaps the most difficult A.I.F. task in the battle, but it faced its responsibilities in fine style under most adverse conditions. The work of the 14th this day was brilliant, for with only 80 casualties it captured 400 prisoners and a large amount of material. A few days spent at Sailly Laurette subsequent to the battle was followed by another turn in the line in the neighbourhood of Harbonnieres. Then followed a fortnight's reorganisation near Allonville, and finally, on September 18, the 14th closed its battle career by a brilliant engagement, in which it captured the immensely strong line of outposts in front of the Hindenburg line—an action which was not only a tactical success, but of considerable strategic importance, and which gained the encomiums of historians,[18] who have described that day's fighting. The fighting career of the 14th terminated here, and it is unnecessary to follow its fortunes further. A list of decorations won in this tour of duty is set out below. Other decorations granted subsequently will appear later.

D.S.O.—Major W. R. Wadsworth, M.C. (Castlemaine, Vic.), C Company. Bar to M.C.—Lieut. N. C. Aldridge,

---

[18] Among others, Major-General Sir Archibald Montgomery, "The Story of the 4th Army," and Mr. F. M. Cutlack, the Australian historian.

**Decorations.** M.C. (Hamilton, Vic.), A Company. M.C.—Lieut. T. H. Griffith (Abbotsford, Vic.), A Company; Lieut. E. J. Rule, M.M. (Cobar, N.S.W.), C Company. D.C.M. — No. 7316, Pte. J. L. Schmit (Kew, Vic.), A Company, stretcher-bearer; No 2435, C.Q.M.S. Wm. F. P. Ryan (Laanecoorie, Vic.), acting C.S.M., B Company; No. 5688, Cpl. V. W. Lalor, M.M. and bar (Healesville, Vic.), C Company, Lewis gunner; No. 3255, C.Q.M.S. A. J. Beaton (Fitzroy, Vic.), C Company. Bar to M.M.—No. 1578, L/Sgt. Chas. J. Clarke, D.C.M. and M.M. (St. Mary's, Tas.), Headquarters signaller; No. 7066, L/Cpl. Chas. H. Platt, M.M. (Bacchus Marsh, Vic.), B Company. M.M.—No. 1798, Pte. Jack O'Brien (Mildura, Vic.), C Company; No. 4543, Cpl. J. P. Lumsden (Koroit, Vic.), B Company; No. 3328, Cpl. James Grieves (Ballan, Vic.), A Company; No. 7605, Pte. W. T. Serjeant (West Brunswick, Vic.), B Company, Lewis gunner; No. 7602, Pte. Cyril Metcalf (West Melbourne, Vic.), B Company; No. 416, Sgt. D. W. Blackburn (Camperdown, Vic.), A Company, Lewis gunner; No. 3252, Cpl. C. E. Booker (Port Melbourne, Vic.), C Company, bomber; No. 2342a, Pte. F. G. Notting (England), Headquarters signaller; No. 6773, Cpl. H. G. Lovejoy (Penshurst, N.S.W.), D Company; No. 5466, Sgt. H. J. Somerville (Port Fairy, Vic.), B Company; No. 799, Pte. F. H. Voce (Coleraine, Vic.), C Company; No. 7587, Pte. P. P. Butterworth (Mittagong, N.S.W.), C Company, bomber; No. 4650, Pte. G. A. Dietrich (Mirboo, Vic.), A Company. Medaille Militaire.—No. 6961, L/Cpl. C. R. F. Beard (Essendon, Vic.), B Company.

## CHAPTER XLII

### REFLECTIONS AND CONCLUSIONS.

The relative position and merits to be assigned to the 14th Battalion among the 60 infantry units of the A.I.F. will have to be decided by history. There were, however, times —under competent battalion leadership—when its efficiency and battle discipline were seldom equalled. It certainly put up some remarkable A.I.F. records. Its ranks contained the winner of the first V.C., the first chaplain killed in action, the first Anzac to be buried in Great Britain, and the first subaltern to win the D.S.O. These are indisputable, and its ranks are also believed to have contained the youngest A.I.F. captain and sergeant[1] respectively. When Colonel Dare became C.O. of the 14th, he was Australia's youngest C.O. Sgt. Wm. Boyes (14th Platoon) won two decorations within eleven days, whilst C.S.M. W. P. Boland appears to have been the first warrant officer to be awarded the M.C. Pte. H. J. Gibb,[2] who was killed in action on June 7, 1918, at the age of 63 years, must have attained old age's high water mark among Australia's valiant dead. The brothers Moore (twins) of the 3rd Platoon, were killed on the same day at Bois Grenier in July, 1916, whilst on May 31, 1918, the 14th was the recipient of probably the deadliest shell which ever landed in the ranks of the A.I.F.[3]

*Marginal notes:* Some Battalion Exploits and Records.

---

[1] Sgt. Wm. Groves, of Sebastopol (Vic.). Taken prisoner at the Battle of Bullecourt, April 11, 1917.

[2] Pte. Henry Gibb, of Tumut (N.S.W.), grazier. Born near Penshurst (Vic.). Fought with the British South African forces in Mashonaland in 1896 and was twice wounded. Also fought in the South African war as sergeant in the 2nd Regiment of N.S.W. Mounted Rifles. Enlisted in the A.I.F. on July 31, 1916.

[3] A paragraph containing these details and supplied by the author appeared in the Sydney "Bulletin" of April 19, 1923.

## The History of the 14th Battalion.

**Changes in Command.**

The 14th laboured throughout its career under one decided disadvantage, there being no less than eight successive C.O.'s placed in command, with the consequent result that continuity of administration was much interfered with.

**Internal Organisation of Battalion.**

Every Battalion was a self-contained community, and the best type of man was always glad to get back to it after a temporary absence. The efforts of the fighting men had to be supplemented by much internal organisation, to which some reference must be made. The R.M.O. and his staff looked after the wounded, and attended to sanitation matters. The Chaplain (inter alia) attended to spiritual affairs and corresponded with the relatives of those who made the supreme sacrifice. The staff of cooks had the important duty of providing the meals, whilst the bootmaker sergeant (No. 1354, Sgt. J. E. Elliott) and his assistants were responsible for keeping in order the soldiers' boots, on which the continual route marching made sad havoc. The regimental tailor (No. 4651, Pte. Ray Fisher), as can be understood, was kept fully employed. A useful institution was the regimental post office (under the charge of Cpl. Annear), where mails and parcels were received and despatched—the men's letters being censored by the officers. A very important establishment was the quartermaster's store, where rations and equipment were allotted. The executive work of the unit was transacted in the orderly room, which was also its court of justice, as well as the holder of its records. The personnel of the Battalion comprised sports organisers, concert artists, and physical training instructors. The unit also had its cricket and football teams, debating society, and band, so that it did, or should have, satisfied the athletic, intellectual, and aesthetic aspirations of all ranks.

**Some Battalion Identities.**

The patriotism of the Australian people was strikingly exemplified by the rush to the colours, which attracted not only men of all classes, but men of all ages. The ranks of the 14th contained not only mere lads like Graham or Fitzpatrick, but old men like "Dad" Brotchie (who was the father of nine children when he enlisted); Barney Clarke and H. J. Gibb (who had sons fighting in the A.I.F.); "Dad" O'Shea, Harry Reynolds, and many others. Some of the old men were extraordinarily keen, and made excellent soldiers.

The efforts on behalf of the troops by outside organisations, such as the Red Cross and Salvation Army, tended to lighten the burden of military life, whilst a special debt of gratitude must be extended to workers of the 14th Battalion Comforts Fund, consisting mainly of the mothers and sisters of the 14th men. Branches of this organisation were formed in Melbourne, Ballarat and Geelong. The work of those noble women was unceasing throughout the war, and it would be difficult to exaggerate the happiness conferred by the result of their labour on the fortunate recipients.

*Co-operation of Outside Organisations.*

*14th Battalion Comforts Fund.*

Prior to closing this final chapter, it is but fitting that a brief reference should be made to the A.I.F., of which the 14th Battalion was but a unit. One of its most distinguishing traits among all the armies engaged in the war was that it was composed purely of volunteers, who were a comparative handful surrounded by millions of conscripts. The consequent result was that its representatives were throughout dominated by an exceptionally high sense of duty and patriotism. A finer body of young men than those comprising the A.I.F. has perhaps never crossed the seas. It represented, during the greatest cataclysm in history, the concentrated hopes, ambitions, aspirations and efforts of a young and virile nation. Its personnel, in short, was the finest human material of a continent, and, prior to the outbreak of hostilities, it was comprised almost entirely of civilians, without any knowledge or thought of war. When the war terminated fifty-one months later, these raw civilians had established a reputation as fighting men that has been rarely equalled. It would be absolutely incorrect, as well as bad taste, to say that the Anzacs won the war, but it would not, perhaps, be an exaggeration to say that, when they gained battle experience, they were the finest soldiers on either side who took part in the greatest war in history. Little opportunity was accorded to them to prove their qualities of higher leadership, but the Anzac retirement from the Peninsula, and the Battle of Amiens, are outstanding proofs of the excellence of their staff work. Whilst it must

*The A.I.F.*

*Some of Its Traits.*

*Fine Quality of Its Personnel.*

*Represented the Hopes of Australia.*

*Composed of Civilians.*

*Reputation as Fighting Men.*

*Staff Work.*

**War an Abomination.**

be admitted that war is an abomination, and those statesmen who bring it about heedlessly or needlessly with the stroke of a pen incur a frightful responsibility, nevertheless the young men of all nations who flocked to the colours were not responsible for the criminal folly of those who, in 1914, precipitated this gigantic horror.

**Soldiers Not Responsible for Its Origin.**

**Destruction of Flower of Australian Manhood.**

**Exploits of Anzacs an Australian Epic and a Beacon Light for Australia's Future.**

The great results achieved by the Anzacs on the battlefield were purchased at a fearful price. The flower of Australian manhood perished, and not only have we to mourn the fallen, but also those who would have been their sons. The future, however, will do them justice, and their exploits will always be Australia's great epic, whilst her war heroes will be her national heroes, when her politicians and millionaires are forgotten. Their victories won, their hardships endured, their heroism displayed, have set a standard for all time, and will ever be a beacon light illuminating the future of Australia, and glistening and sparkling in her honour through the dullness of centuries.

**Necessity for National Ideals. The Standard Set by Australia's Dead Worthy of Emulation.**

A nation never achieves true greatness unless it is permeated by high national ideals, and if future generations of Australians seriously endeavour to emulate the generous aspirations and intense patriotism of those who died so willingly and so freely for her sake, then the future of our glorious heritage is secure for all time, and our heroic dead will not have died in vain.

"LORD GOD OF HOSTS, BE WITH US YET,
LEST WE FORGET! LEST WE FORGET!"[4]

---

[4] Quotation from Rudyard Kipling.

# APPENDICES

## APPENDIX A.

The following Roll of Honour comprises the Battalion dead as contained in the official list to the end of February, 1919. The list comprises 41 officers and 1008 other ranks, or a grand total of 1049. The battle casualties have been increased by a handful who died as a result of disease, injury, or accident. Sixteen officers and 387 other ranks died at Gallipoli or Egypt, and 25 officers and 621 other ranks as the result of operations in France and Belgium. The heaviest casualties were incurred on August 8, 1915, and at Hill 60 on the Peninsula, and at Pozieres and Bullecourt, in France.

It is worthy of note that, in almost every action in the war in which the 4th Brigade was engaged, it attacked—it rarely fought a defensive action. In addition to the regimental number, rank, name, nature and date of casualty, the list of dead has been arranged in chronological order, together with the locality to which the deceased belonged. This has been done for the purpose of future identification. The question of domicile is always difficult, and the rule almost invariably adopted has been as follows:—(1) In the case of married men, to fill in the locality with which the deceased was specially identified, or, failing that, to set them out as belonging to the addresses in which their respective wives lived; and (2) in the case of single men, failing any special locality with which identified, the addresses of their next of kin. In some cases, where the deceased have been identified with two localities, both are set out.

Abbreviations used are as follows:—K.I.A. (killed in action), D.W. (died of wounds), D.I. (died of illness), D.Inj. (died of injury), and D.A. (died from accident).

# Roll of Honour

"*On Fame's eternal camping-ground,*
*Their silent tents are spread,*
*And Glory guards with solemn round*
*The bivouac of the dead.*"
—Theodore O'Hara (1820-1867).

### GALLIPOLI AND EGYPT.
### 1915.

#### OFFICERS.

Rank and Name:      Belonged to:      Nature of Casualty:      Date:

Capt. W. R. Hoggart, Geelong and Brighton (V.)—K.I.A.—27th April, 1915.
Lieut. J. B. Rutland, Canterbury (V.)—K.I.A.—1st May, 1915.
Lieut. A. H. Curwen-Walker, Ballarat (V.)—D.W.—3rd May, 1915.
Lieut. Q. R. Smith, Outtrim and Essendon (V.)—D.W.—3rd May, 1915.
Lieut. H. B. Skertchly, Kew (V.)—D.I.—15th May, 1915.
Lieut. W. H. Hamilton, Ballarat (V.)—K.I.A.—19th May, 1915.
Capt. W. E. Groom, Brighton (V.)—K.I.A.—7th August, 1915.
Lieut. T. N. W. Hill, Sandringham (V.)—K.I.A.—8th August, 1915.
2nd/Lieut. J. H. Matthews, Ararat (V.)—K.I.A.—8th August, 1915.
Lieut. K. Curlewis, Malvern (V.)—K.I.A.—8th August, 1915.
Lieut. R. Warren, Brunswick (V.)—K.I.A.—8th August, 1915.
Lieut. H. R. Harris, Maryborough (V.)—K.I.A.—8th August, 1915.
2nd/Lieut. F. Duffield, Footscray (V.) and Lancashire (Eng.)—K.I.A.—21st August, 1915.
Lieut. K. G. W. Crabbe, St. Kilda (V.)—K.I.A.—21st August, 1915.
Capt. Rev. A. Gillison, E. St. Kilda (V.)—D.W.—22nd August, 1915.
Capt. C. E. Connelly, Bendigo and Hampton (V.)—K.I.A.—27th August, 1915.

#### OTHER RANKS.

1212, Pte. J. C. Hooke, Melbourne (V.) and London (Eng.)—D.I.—7th March, 1915.
1292, Pte. J. W. McDougall, Tarwin (V.)—D.I.—26th March, 1915.
1258, Sgt. A. Sutcliffe, Mildura (V.)—D.I.—30th March, 1915.

## The History of the 14th Battalion. 359

902, Sgt. W. P. Murphy, Warracknabeal (V.), and Norwich (Eng.)—K.I.A.—26th April, 1915.

1223, Pte. W. Booth, Coburg (V.) and Cheshire (Eng.)—K.I.A.—26th April, 1915.

904, Cpl. H. McLaren, Willow Grove and Moe (V.)—K.I.A.—27th April, 1915.

105, Pte. R. J. Oliver, Wonthaggi and Clunes (V.)—K.I.A.—27th April, 1915.

1358, Pte. E. J. Jeal, Charlton (V.) and Kent (Eng.)—K.I.A.—27th April, 1915.

40, Cpl. J. Butterworth, Tongala (V.) and Lancashire (Eng.)—K.I.A.—27th April, 1915.

135, L/Cpl. J. W. Thompson, N. Carlton (V.)—K.I.A.—27th April, 1915.

150, Pte. D. Wren, Sydney (N.S.W.) and Liverpool (Eng.)—K.I.A.—27th April, 1915.

57. Pte. C. Gist, Ballarat (V.)—K.I.A.—27th April, 1915.

609, Cpl. M. F. Macoboy, Bendigo (V.)—K.I.A.—27th April, 1915.

1375, Pte. A. H. Love, Coburg (V.)—K.I.A.—27th April, 1915.

1338, Pte. A. E. Bolger, Frankston (V.)—K.I.A.—27th April, 1915.

675, Pte. C. Chisholm, Sydney (N.S.W.) and London (Eng.)—K.I.A.—27th April, 1915.

583, Pte. D. H. Findlay, Echuca (V.)—K.I.A.—27th April, 1915.

579, Pte. R. B. Earll, Woohlpooer (V.)—K.I.A.—27th April, 1915.

1399, Pte. T. S. Ross, Bracknell (Tas.)—K.I.A.—27th April, 1915.

757, Sgt. F. McDermott, Albert Park (V.)—K.I.A.—27th April, 1915.

218, L/Cpl. J. A. Harding, Dubbo (N.S.W.)—K.I.A.—27th April, 1915.

1275, Pte. D. Lee, Colac (V.), and London (Eng.)—K.I.A.—27th April, 1915.

792, Pte. W. G. M. Theobald, Londrigan (V.), and Cambridge (Eng.)—K.I.A.—27th April, 1915.

1278, Pte. H. Wilson, Exeter (Eng.)—K.I.A.—27th April, 1915.

207, Pte. L. Hyde, Bendigo (V.)—K.I.A.—27th April, 1915.

206, Pte. H. Honeychurch, Bright and Wandiligong (V.)—K.I.A.—27th April, 1915.

187, Pte. A. Elmslie, Wanyaratta and Benalla (V.)—K.I.A.—27th April, 1915.

748, Pte. S. Mars, Geelong (V.)—K.I.A.—27th April, 1915.

219, Cpl. A. C. Howat, S. Melbourne (V.)—K.I.A.—27th April, 1915.

777, Pte. S. H. Smith, Mildura (V.)—K.I.A.—27th April, 1915.

354, Pte. J. R. McLean, Broken Hill (N.S.W.) and Auckland (N.Z.)—K.I.A.—27th April, 1915.

515, L/Cpl. W. Wilson, Lyonville (V.)—K.I.A.—27th April, 1915.

437, L/Cpl. W. J. Doyle, Richmond (V.)—K.I.A.—27th April, 1915.

1607, Pte. T. Jamieson, St. Arnaud (V.)—K.I.A.—27th April, 1915.

189, Pte. G. C. English, Preston (V.)—K.I.A.—27th April, 1915.

383, Pte. G. F. H. Smith, Ararat (V.)—K.I.A.—28th April, 1915.

## The Roll of Honour.

1249, Pte. J. J. Henkel, South Melbourne (V.)—K.I.A.—28th April, 1915.
483, Sgt. R. Newton, Werribee (V.)—K.I.A.—28th April, 1915.
192, Pte. P. Fraher, Fitzroy (V.)—K.I.A.—28th April, 1915.
1655, Pte. G. B. Dyer, Brunswick (V.)—K.I.A.—28th April, 1915.
248, Pte. E. Partridge, Clifton Hill and Fitzroy (V.)—D.W.—28th April, 1915.
959, Cpl. R. H. Burton, Richmond (V.)—K.I.A.—29th April, 1915.
1049, L/Sgt. P. Smith, Northcote (V.)—D.W.—29th April, 1915.
33, Cpl. J. Bowen, Moonee Ponds (V.)—D.W.—29th April, 1915.
153, L/Cpl. R. E. Young, Avenel (V.)—D.W.—29th April, 1915.
1273, Pte. A. Stephens, Raywood (V.)—K.I.A.—25/30th April, 1915.
1137, Pte. J. Donohue, Geelong (V.)—D.W.—29th April, 1915.
1017, Pte. P. Mattingly, Geelong West (V.)—D.W.—29th April, 1915.
666, Bugler J. Trevan, Ballarat (V.)—D.W.—29th April, 1915.
1014, Pte. G. B. Lewis, Sale (V.)—K.I.A.—29th April, 1915.
1034, Pte. A. G. Pettigrew, Shepparton and Congupna Road (V.)—K.I.A.—29th April, 1915.
1163, Pte. O. F. Dean, Bendigo (V.)—K.I.A.—29th April, 1915.
43, Pte. W. Cohen, Fitzroy (V.)—D.W.—30th April, 1915.
575, Pte. G. E. Davis, North Melbourne (V.)—D.W.—30th April, 1915.
387, Bugler F. L. Sheldon, Bendigo (V.)—K.I.A.—30th April, 1915.
412, Pte. C. Dodds, Cobden and Scott's Creek (V.)—K.I.A.—30th April, 1915.
372, Pte. A. R. Rackstraw, Port Welshpool (V.)—K.I.A.—30th April, 1915.
931, Pte. A. Wilkinson, S. Melbourne (V.) and Manchester (Eng.)—K.I.A.—30th April, 1915.
973, Pte. F. Davies, Craigie (V.)—D.W.—30th April, 1915.
58, Pte. C. G. Greenham, Wando Vale (V.)—D.W.—1st May, 1915.
884, Sgt. F. H. Kewley, Ballarat East (V.)—K.I.A.—1st May, 1915.
1197, Sgt. T. L. Barratt, Golden Square (V.)—K.I.A.—1st May, 1915.
818, L/Cpl. R. C. Bazin, Devenish (V.)—K.I.A.—1st May, 1915.
373, Pte. N. P. Rooney, Ringwood (V.)—K.I.A.—1st May, 1915.
362, L/Cpl. F. M. Neal, Tara (Q.)—K.I.A.—1st May, 1915.
319, Pte. W. W. Fraser, Footscray (V.)—K.I.A.—1st May, 1915.
862, Pte. F. G. Gorman, Warragul (V.)—K.I.A.—1st May, 1915.
370, Pte. L. Richards, Boolarra (V.) and London (Eng.)—K.I.A.—1st May, 1915.
331, Pte. H. V. Jordan, Wonthaggi (V.)—K.I.A.—1st May, 1915.
390, Pte. G. Tippett, Glenrowan (V.)—K.I.A.—1st May, 1915.
1328, Pte. G. H. Allen, South Melbourne (V.)—K.I.A.—1st May, 1915.
1520, Pte. A. Delaney, Otford (N.S.W.)—K.I.A.—1st May, 1915.
831, Pte. H. Currie, Swan Hill (V.)—K.I.A.—1st May, 1915.
1360, Pte. J. Hislop, Fitzroy (V.) and Glasgow (Scotland)—K.I.A.—1st May, 1915.
1251, Pte. P. Williams, Flemington (V.)—D.W.—2nd May, 1915.

## The History of the 14th Battalion. 361

632, L/Cpl. W. H. O'Bree, Orange (N.S.W.)—K.I.A.—2nd May, 1915.
92, Pte. J. McNab, Burnie (Tas.)—K.I.A.—2nd May, 1915.
683, Pte. W. A. Brown, Hamilton (Tas.)—K.I.A.—2nd May, 1915.
1130, Pte. H. W. A. Baker, Seymour (V.)—K.I.A.—2nd May, 1915.
1305, Pte. C. Thewlis, Euroa (V.)—K.I.A.—2nd May, 1915.
1326, Pte. A. Abernethy, Maffra (V.)—K.I.A.—2nd May, 1915.
274, Pte. R. M. Thornton, Woomelang (V.)—K.I.A.—2nd May, 1915.
1013, Pte. N. S. Layton, Richmond (V.)—K.I.A.—2nd May, 1915.
1178, Pte. W. H. C. Leeson, Garfield (V.)—K.I.A.—2nd May, 1915.
649, Pte. E. H. Spencer, Bendigo (V.)—K.I.A.—3rd May, 1915.
1350, Pte. J. H. Feetam, Burnley (V.)—K.I.A.—3rd May, 1915.
741, Pte. H. A. Mew, Carlton (V.)—K.I.A.—3rd May, 1915.
1122, Sgt. G. W. Smith, St. Kilda (V.)—K.I.A.—4th May, 1915.
85, Pte. S. M. McDermott, Albert Park (V.)—D.W.—5th May, 1915.
445, Pte. W. B. Fletcher, Traralgon (V.)—K.I.A.—5th May, 1915.
1483, Pte. M. J. Kelly, Epping (V.)—K.I.A.—5th May, 1915.
524, L/Cpl. T. Ritchie, Mysia (V.)—K.I.A.—5th May, 1915.
514, Pte. J. W. Woods, Moonee Ponds (V.)—K.I.A.—6th May, 1915.
1073, Pte. S. J. Stratham, Korumburra (V.)—K.I.A.—6th May, 1915.
95, L/Sgt. J. A. Mahoney, Hawthorn (V.)—K.I.A.—7th May, 1915.
1413, L/Cpl. B. G. Stillwell, Melbourne (V.) and Liverpool (Eng.)—D.I.—7th May, 1915.
1682, Pte. J. Gartshore, Dumbarton (Scotland) and Prahran (V.)—D.I.—8th May, 1915.
1462, Pte. W. H. Waters, Hamilton (V.)—D.W.—8th May, 1915.
1053, Pte. G. W. Steele, Geelong (V.)—D.W.—8th May, 1915.
1371, Pte. R. Irwin, W. Melbourne (V.)—D.W.—9th May, 1915.
1616, Pte. E. Leslie, Melbourne (V.) and London (Eng.)—K.I.A.—10th May, 1915.
397, Pte. G. Turnbull, Inverleithen (Scotland)—K.I.A.—12th May, 1915.
303, Pte. R. Cowan, Clunes (V.)—D.W.—13th May, 1915.
586, Pte. H. S. Geyer, Bendigo (V.)—D.W.—13th May, 1915.
1003, Pte. C. Hicks, Mernda (V.)—D.W.—14th May, 1915.
158, Pte. H. C. Abbey, N. Fitzroy and Yarraville (V.)—D.W.—19th May, 1915.
1423, Pte. A. Walker, Kyabram (V.) and London (Eng.)—K.I.A.—19th May, 1915.
702, Pte. W. A. Day, Kyabram (V.)—K.I.A.—19th May, 1915.
1108, L/Cpl. R. Sayers, Wonthaggi (V.)—K.I.A.—19th May, 1915.
174, Pte. H. D. Cole, Brighton (V.)—K.I.A.—19th May, 1915.
247, Pte. R. F. Osborn, Woomelang (V.)—K.I.A.—19th May, 1915.
1579, Pte. D. Clement, Brighton (V.) and Ayrshire (Scotland)—K.I.A.—19th May, 1915.
530, Pte. R. L. Angus, Benalla (V.)—K.I.A.—19th May, 1915.
1416, Pte. J. Tyler, Richmond (V.)—K.I.A.—19th May, 1915.
560, Pte. F. S. Binns, Footscray (V.)—K.I.A.—19th May, 1915.

1683, Pte. W. V. Mow. Nevertire and Lithgow (N.S.W.)—K.I.A.—19th May, 1915.
612, Pte. H. J. Mullen,* Mitiamo (V.)—D.W.—19th May, 1915.
1052, Pte. H. Simmons, South Yarra (V.)—K.I.A.—20th May, 1915.
68, Pte. H. J. Hickey, Deniliquin (N.S.W.)—K.I.A.—23rd May, 1915.
887, L/Cpl. T. E. Kitchener, Mallala (S.A.)—D.W.—24th May, 1915.
1689, Pte. C. A. Lindrea, St. Kilda (V.)—K.I.A.—24th May, 1915.
1394, Pte. G. Philip, Kensington (V.)—K.I.A.—24th May, 1915.
1332, Pte. J. W. Briggs, Donald (V.) and Grantham (Eng.)—D.A.—24th May, 1915.
1433, Cpl. G. P. Scott, Echuca (V.)—K.I.A.—24th May, 1915.
1230, Pte. H. H. Jarman (correct name, Jerman), Ipswich (Eng.)—K.I.A.— 26th May, 1915.
328, L/Cpl. A. Harrison, Geelong and Albert Park (V.)—D.W.—27th May, 1915.
661, Pte. L. J. Smith, Ballarat West (V.)—K.I.A.—27th May, 1915.
1156, Pte. W. R. Earl, Wedderburn (V.)—K.I.A.—28th May, 1915.
1573, Pte. D. Blythen, Ballarat East (V.)—D.W.—29th May, 1915.
225, Cpl. J. F. Johnson, West Richmond (V.)—K.I.A.—29th May, 1915.
911, Pte. R. L. P. Oldham, Mildura (V.)—K.I.A.—29th May, 1915.
1672, Pte. N. Clark, S. Melbourne (V.)—K.I.A.—30th May, 1915
745, Pte. W. Milne, Albury (N.S.W.) and Aberdeenshire (Scotland)— D.W.—1st June, 1915.
558, Pte. T. A. Beaudoin, Dunolly (V.)—D.I.—4th June, 1915.
1095, Pte. R. T. Muirson, Williamstown (V.)—K.I.A.—5th June, 1915.
177, Pte. R. A. Caldwell, Albany (W.A.)—K.I.A.—6th June, 1915.
1507, Pte. N. S. Block, Ballarat (V.)—D.W.—8th June, 1915.
506, Pte. S. Wilson (correct name, H. D. Holtum), Zeehan (Tas.)—D.W. —9th June, 1915.
554, L/Sgt. E. A. Benson, E. Malvern (V.)—D.I.—10th June, 1915.
1426, Pte. H. Woodroff, London (Eng.)—D.I.—19th June, 1915.
1664, Pte. J. R. Owen, Melbourne (V.) and Liverpool (Eng.)—D.W.—20th June, 1915.
282, Pte. C. W. Williams, Numurkah (V.)—D.I.—28th June, 1915.
134, Pte. V. F. Thompson, Richmond (V.)—D.W.—9th July, 1915.
2236, C.S.M. D. MacArthur, Narrabi (N.S.W.)—D.I.—13th July, 1915.
879, Pte. J. T. Inman, Swan Hill (V.)—D.W.—26th July, 1915.
1919, Pte. V. P. Cahill, Colac (V.)—D.W.—29th July, 1915.
618, Pte. W. Middlebrook, Kernot (V.)—D.W.—29th July, 1915.
1770, Pte. H. Kent, Fitzroy (V.)—D.I.—31st July, 1915.
1948, Pte. H. L. Grey, Tarnagulla (V.)—D.W.—2nd August, 1915.
2121, Pte. H. Caley, Ballarat (V.)—K.I.A.—6/7th August, 1915.
940, Dvr. L. Williams, Stawell (V.)—K.I.A.—7th August, 1915.
368, Pte. G. W. Preston, Ararat (V.)—K.I.A.—7th August, 1915.

---

* Pte. H. J. Mullen was the first Anzac to die and be buried in the United Kingdom.

## The History of the 14th Battalion. 363

1640, Pte. F. Williams, Skipton (V.)—K.I.A.—7th August, 1915.
1670, Pte. A. F. Boden, Footscray (V.)—K.I.A.—7th August, 1915.
2070, Pte. N. J. Veal, Bendigo (V.)..K.I.A.—7th August, 1915.
1829, Pte. L. L. Williams, N. Carlton (V.)—K.I.A.—7th August, 1915.
337, L/Cpl. E. G. Kneale, Armadale (V.)—K.I.A.—7th August, 1915.
1931, Pte. F. S. Davison, Melbourne (V.)—D.W.—7th August, 1915.
1517, Pte. T. Chettle, Munro (V.)—K.I.A.—7th August, 1915.
1290, Pte. J. Leydin, Carlton (V.)—K.I.A.—7th August, 1915.
256, Pte. J. T. Reece, Windsor (V.).—K.I.A.—8th August, 1915.
196, Pte. R. Greenfield, London (Eng.)—K.I.A.—8th August, 1915.
744, Pte. J. Malcolm, Scotland—K.I.A.—8th August, 1915.
893, Bugler W. J. P. Morgan, Euroa (V.)—K.I.A.—8th August, 1915.
908, Pte. D. McArthur, Ararat (V.)—K.I.A.—8th August, 1915.
473, L/Cpl. G. L. Murphy, Bendigo (V.)—K.I.A.—8th August, 1915.
1551, Pte. G. Garnett, Ascot Vale (V.)—K.I.A.—8th August, 1915.
1392, Pte. M. Maxwell, Maffra (V.)—K.I.A.—8th August, 1915.
2169, Pte. N. P. Kennelly, Stratford (V.)—K.I.A.—8th August, 1915.
1922, Sgt. H. D. Chippendale, E. Brunswick (V.)—K.I.A.—8th August, 1915.
1217, Pte. A. Simpson, Balranald (N.S.W.)—K.I.A.—8th August, 1915.
1047, Pte. H. J. Schmidt, London (Eng.)—K.I.A.—8th August, 1915.
1991, Pte. J. S. Owen, Camberwell (V.)—K.I.A.—8th August, 1915.
399, Cpl. C. Wells, St. Kilda (V.)—K.I.A.—8th August, 1915.
1114, L/Cpl. D. T. Allan, Williamstown (V.)—K.I.A.—8th August, 1915.
1400, Pte. H. W. Rasdell, Lexton (V.)—K.I.A.—8th August, 1915.
1297, Pte. T. W. Cameron, Fitzroy (V.)—K.I.A.—8th August, 1915.
1164, Pte. V. L. Lees, S. Melbourne (V.)—K.I.A.—8th August, 1915.
963, Pte. F. Canning, Creswick (V.)—K.I.A.—8th August, 1915.
180, Pte. B. Callaghan, N. Melbourne (V.)—K.I.A.—8th August, 1915.
278, Pte. J. Wight, Ballarat (V.)—K.I.A.—8th August, 1915.
2171, Pte. H. R. Lee, Penshurst (V.)—K.I.A.—8th August, 1915.
254, Pte. J. E. Phillips, Walhalla (V.)—K.I.A.—8th August, 1915.
402, Cpl. E. R. Whitteron, Kew (V.)—K.I.A.—8th August, 1915.
446, L/Cpl. W. Goble, Glasgow (Scot.)—K.I.A.—8th August, 1915.
395, Pte. H. Twyford, Somerville (V.)—K.I.A.—8th August, 1915.
340, Pte. W. J. Kelsall, Oakleigh (V.)—K.I.A.—8th August, 1915.
245, Pte. W. S. Naismith, N. Melbourne (V.)—K.I.A.—8th August, 1915.
325, Pte. W. A. Garton, Cavendish (V.)—K.I.A.—8th August, 1915.
1911, Pte. W. Bebbington, S. Melbourne (V.)—K.I.A.—8th August, 1915.
2197, Pte. A. J. Parsons, Keilambete E. (V.)—K.I.A.—8th August, 1915.
2009, Pte. A. T. H. Seymour, Northcote (V.)—K.I.A.—8th August, 1915.
1522, Pte. J. Winters (correct name, E. C. Logan), Kalgoorlie (W.A.), and Flemington (N.S.W.)—K.I.A.—8th August, 1915.
2219, Pte. H. Truscott, Abbotsford (V.)—K.I.A.—8th August, 1915.
531, Pte. N. W. Folks, Bonnie Doon (V.)—K.I.A.—8th August, 1915.
2032, Pte. R. Webb, Port Melbourne (V.) and Lancashire (Eng.)—K.I.A.—8th August, 1915.

## 364  The Roll of Honour.

692, Pte. J. H. Cartwright, Korumburra (V.)—K.I.A.—8th August, 1915.
2231, Pte. P. A. Young, Richmond and Maldon (V.)—K.I.A.—8th August, 1915.
505, Pte. W. E. Warnes, Cranbourne (V.)—D.W.—8th August, 1915.
453, Cpl. T. F. Hope, Sunbury and Queenscliff (V.)—K.I.A.—8th August, 1915.
501, Sgt. E. Twose, Glen Thompson and Burnley (V.)—K.I.A.—8th August, 1915.
518, Pte. J. Wills, Port Melbourne (V.)—K.I.A.—8th August, 1915.
1537, Pte. H. Baxter, Rothesay, Bute (Scot.) and Mildura (V.)—K.I.A.—8th August, 1915.
1540, Pte. T. V. Johnstone, Eurack (V.)—K.I.A.—8th August, 1915.
883, Pte. F. W. Janes, Coburg (V.)—K.I.A.—8th August, 1915.
1434, Cpl. G. W. Greengrass, Footscray and Yarraville (V.)—K.I.A.—8th August, 1915.
1569, Pte. O. A. Batch, E. Richmond (V.)—K.I.A.—8th August, 1915.
1401, Pte. R. M. Ryan, Heathcote (V.)—K.I.A.—8th August, 1915.
494, Pte. A. E. Sheehan, Macarthur and Hamilton (V.)—K.I.A.—8th August, 1915.
1226, Pte. L. W. Miller, Eaglehawk (V.)—K.I.A.—8th August, 1915.
1752, Pte. W. J. Hegarty, Abbotsford (V.)—K.I.A.—8th August, 1915.
2015, Pte. N. T. E. Somers, Mornington (V.)—K.I.A.—8th August, 1915.
2031, Pte. F. Wassell, Surrey Hills (V.)—K.I.A.—8th August, 1915.
357, Pte. C. McKenzie, Chillingollah (V.)—K.I.A.—8th August, 1915.
1051, Cpl. A. Smith, Yarrawonga (V.)—K.I.A.—8th August, 1915.
839, A/Cpl. A. Cubitt, Abbotsford (V.)—K.I.A.—8th August, 1915.
1727, Pte. A. Spence, Maxfield and Leicester (Eng.)—K.I.A.—8th August, 1915.
2212, Pte. J. H. Short, Lancefield (V.)—K.I.A.—8th August, 1915.
975, Pte. A. B. De Broughe, Deniliquin (N.S.W.)—K.I.A.—8th August, 1915.
1502, Pte. J. Booley, Ouyen and Nyah (V.)—K.I.A.—8th August, 1915.
1516, Pte. G. L. Twight, Northcote (V.)—K.I.A.—8th August, 1915.
1343, Pte. T. W. Dray, Moonee Ponds (V.) and Gravesend (Eng.)—K.I.A.—8th August, 1915.
1757, Pte. F. G. Hudson, Melbourne (V.) and Durham (Eng.)—K.I.A.—8th August, 1915.
1788, Pte. W. R. McKay, Rutherglen (V.)—K.I.A.—8th August, 1915.
1227, Pte. F. M. Slater, Croydon (V.) and Manchester (Eng.)—K.I.A.—8th August, 1915.
1950, Pte. W. Hammond, Melbourne (V.) and Liverpool (Eng.)—K.I.A.—8th August, 1915.
2250, Pte. A. S. Atridge, Wandiligong (V.)—K.I.A.—8th August, 1915.
1997, Sgt. W. M. Quirke, Coburg (V.)—K.I.A.—8th August, 1915.
1916, Pte. J. J. Bray, Donald (V.)—K.I.A.—8th August, 1915.
1849, Pte. J. McNamara, Bendigo (V.)—K.I.A.—8th August, 1915.

## The History of the 14th Battalion. 365

1051, Pte. A. Smith, Yarrawonga (V.)—K.I.A.—8th August, 1915.
2120, Pte. W. Bowley, Auburn (V.)—K.I.A.—8th August, 1915.
1928, Pte. F. E. Davis, St. Kilda (V.)—K.I.A.—8th August, 1915.
2198, Pte. F. E. Pearce, Brim (V.) and Kent (Eng.)—K.I.A.—8th August, 1915.
1012, Pte. P. B. Laker, Dingley (V.) and Sussex (Eng.)—K.I.A.—8th August, 1915.
1008, Pte. J. Keenan, Rochester (V.)—K.I.A.—8th August, 1915.
1023, Pte. W. A. McColl, Bamganie (V.)—K.I.A.—8th August, 1915.
1028, Pte. C. McPherson, Albert Park (V.)—K.I.A.—8th August, 1915.
1037, Pte. F. H. Pither, Mildura (V.)—K.I.A.—8th August, 1915.
1958, Pte. J. R. Holloway, Barnawartha (V.)—K.I.A.—8th August, 1915.
1740, Pte. J. M. Fitzpatrick (served as Joseph Cook), South Yarra (V.) —K.I.A.—8th August, 1915.
492, Pte. S. W. Smith, London (Eng.)—K.I.A.—8th August, 1915.
1418, L/Cpl. E. Taylor, Corowa (N.S.W.)—K.I.A.—8th August, 1915.
2039, Pte. H. Wise, Carnegie (V.)—K.I.A.—8th August, 1915.
1211, Cpl. E. White, Melbourne (V.)—K.I.A.—8th August, 1915.
2042, Pte. T. Younger, Banyena (V.)—K.I.A.—8th August, 1915.
1389, Pte. G. Morrison, Invergordon (Scot.) and Bendigo (V.)—K.I.A.— 8th August, 1915.
1299, Pte. W. J. McAlpine, Trentham (V.)—K.I.A.—8th August, 1915.
1975, Pte. T. Makin, Korumburra (V.)—K.I.A.—8th August, 1915.
1167, Cpl. W. D. Minogue, Maylands (W.A.)—K.I.A.—8th August, 1915.
1431, Sgt. W. McAllister, Lithgow (N.S.W.) and Glasgow (Scotland)— K.I.A.—8th August, 1915.
1294, L/Cpl. F. J. Negro, Richmond (V.)—K.I.A.—8th August, 1915.
2257, Pte. W. H. Elliott, Clifton Hill (V.)—K.I.A.—8th August, 1915.
2213, Pte. V. A. Silva, Dunolly (V.)—K.I.A.—8th August, 1915.
1544, Pte. W. Welsh, Lascelles (V.)—K.I.A.—8th August, 1915.
1422, Pte. J. L. Walsh, Amphitheatre (V.)—D.W.—8th August, 1915.
568, Pte. J. G. Dupuy, Wedderburn (V.)—K.I.A.—8th August, 1915.
1356, Pte. A. E. Fawkner, S. Melbourne (V.)—K.I.A.—9th August, 1915.
1786, Pte. C. McJarrow, Moranding (V.) and Girvan (Scot.)—D.W.—10th August, 1915.
1402, Pte. V. Rowles, Cardiff (Wales)—D.W.—10th August, 1915.
507, Pte. J. B. Wheelaghan, Sydney (N.S.W.) and Leith (Scot.)—D.W. —10th August, 1915.
593, Cpl. F. Hewitt, Wedderburn (V.)—K.I.A.—10th August, 1915.
1946, Pte. F. W. Greenwood, Morwell (V.)—D.W.—11th August, 1915.
1369, Pte. L. Hutchinson, Mount Barker (S.A.)—D.W.—11th August, 1915.
1775, Pte. J. Leyden, E. Brunswick (V.)—D.W. whilst P.W.—11th August, 1915.
1974, Pte. J. Lampard, Balmoral (V.)—D.W.—12th August, 1915.
1664, Pte. S. C. Williams, Los Angeles, California (U.S.A.)—D.W.—12th August, 1915.

## The Roll of Honour.

1856, L/Cpl. P. J. Brewer, Terang (V.)—D.W.—12th August, 1915.
774, Cpl. C. J. Robinson, Thornton (V.)—D.W.—13th August, 1915.
1072, Pte. A. H. Lewis, Hamilton (V.)—D.W.—13th August, 1915.
1903, Pte. E. F. T. Anderson, Dunluce (V.)—D.W.—14th August, 1915.
1188, Pte. E. Meadows, E. Melbourne (V.)—D.W.—14th August, 1915.
29, Pte. R. J. J. Bethel, Moorina (Tas.)—K.I.A.—14th August, 1915.
1830, Pte. J. Woodhouse, Spotswood (V.) and Birmingham (Eng.)—D.W.—15th August, 1915.
1540a, Pte. C. Eldridge, N. Carlton (V.)—D.W.—18th August, 1915.
1177, Pte. B. Wood, Prahran (V.)—D.W.—19th August, 1915.
160, Pte. J. P. Aldous, Northcote (V.)—K.I.A.—19th August, 1915.
126, Pte. S. S. Smith, Sussex (Eng.)—K.I.A.—19th August, 1915.
1754, Pte. C. Harris, Caulfield (V.)—D.W.—20th August, 1915.
1471, Pte. M. Halligan, Bendigo (V.) and Dublin (Ire.)—K.I.A.—20th August, 1915.
367, L/Cpl. J. T. O'Bryan, Mildura (V.)—K.I.A.—20th August, 1915.
2183, Pte. F. E. Mehegan, Preston (V.)—K.I.A.—20th August, 1915.
2194, Pte. R. E. O'Shannassy, Ballarat (V.)—K.I.A.—20th August, 1915.
2019, L/Cpl. C. Stabell, Williamstown (V.)—K.I.A.—20th August, 1915.
1600, Pte. J. A. Hoare, Donald (V.)—D.W.—20th August, 1915.
2137, Pte. L. H. Edmunds, Windsor (V.)—K.I.A.—20th August, 1915.
1361, Pte. W. Hartland, Creswick (V.)—K.I.A.—20th August, 1915.
1767, Pte. C. B. James, Bruthen (V.)—K.I.A.—20th August, 1915.
48, Pte. T. Conroy, E. Brunswick (V.)—K.I.A.—20th August, 1915.
1054, Pte. A. E. Stevenson, Albury (N.S.W.) and Wodonga (V.)—K.I.A.—20th August, 1915.
2141, Pte. S. Fenwick, Carlton (V.)—K.I.A.—20th August, 1915.
1790, Pte. R. J. P. McDonagh, Warrnambool (V.) and Dublin (Ireland)—K.I.A.—20th August, 1915.
438, Pte. C. C. T. Douglas, Hamilton (V.)—K.I.A.—21st August, 1915.
2046, Pte. P. Miller, Footscray (V.)—K.I.A.—21st August, 1915.
2155, Pte. W. Hales, Ballarat (V.)—K.I.A.—21st August, 1915.
668, Pte. G. C. Veel, Bendigo (V.)—K.I.A.—21st August, 1915.
1386, Pte. John Lynch, Gloucestershire (Eng.) and Melbourne (V.)—K.I.A.—21st August, 1915.
1710a, Pte. T. Foley, Dimboola (V.)—K.I.A.—21st August, 1915.
222, Pte. A. R. Jones, Ballarat (V.)—K.I.A.—21st August, 1915.
2103, Pte. W. W. Anderson, Footscray (V.)—K.I.A.—21st August, 1915.
141, Pte. J. W. Verswyvelt, Chelsea (V.)—K.I.A.—21st August, 1915.
2128, Pte. C. P. Chapman, Dunolly (V.) and Peterboro (Eng.)—K.I.A.—21st August, 1915.
616, Pte. A. T. Marsh, Ballarat (V.)—K.I.A.—21st August, 1915.
1172, Pte. H. G. Smith, Wedderburn (V.) and Northamptonshire (Eng.)—K.I.A.—21st August, 1915.
1356, Pte. E. R. Gibson, Kerang (V.) and Durham (Eng.)—K.I.A.—21st August, 1915.

1968, Pte. P. Killen, Fitzroy (V.)—K.I.A.—21st August, 1915.
2253, Pte. H. Neilson, Lancashire (Eng.)—K.I.A.—21st August, 1915.
1444, Pte. Arthur Aitken,* St. Kilda (V.) and Glasgow (Scotland)—K.I.A. 21st August, 1915.
2188, Pte. W. Malady, Fitzroy (V.)—K.I.A.—21st August, 1915.
1240, Cpl. W. R. N. Skilton, Williamstown (V.)—K.I.A.—21st August, 1915.
1789, Pte. W. Marshall, Essendon (V.)—K.I.A.—21st August, 1915.
1940, Pte. A. Garner, Trawalla (V.)—K.I.A.—21st August, 1915.
2029, Pte. L. G. A. Wallis, Hawthorn (V.)—K.I.A.—21st August, 1915.
1962, Pte. H. L. Johns, Mathoura (N.S.W.)—K.I.A.—21st August, 1915.
1153, Pte. W. S. Dewell, Melbourne (V.) and London (Eng.)—K.I.A.—21st August, 1915.
1608, Pte. A. Richardson, Hamilton (V.)—D.W.—21st August, 1915.
662, Sgt. A. T. Swift, Moonee Ponds (V.)—K.I.A.—21st August, 1915.
1538, Pte. W. Dummett, Northcote (V.)—D.I.—21st August, 1915.
1972, Pte. V. G. Lewis, Hawthorn (V.)—D.W.—22nd August, 1915.
2119, Pte. R. S. Briant, Bournemouth (Eng.) and Richmond (V.)—K.I.A.—22nd August, 1915.
600, L/Cpl. A. Johnston, Euroa (V.)—D.W.—22nd August, 1915.
1759, Pte. H. A. Hungerford, Petersham (N.S.W.)—D.W.—24th August, 1915.
1377, Pte. D. Laredo, St. Kilda (V.)—D.W.—24th August, 1915.
1993, Pte. H. J. Partridge, Melbourne (V.) and Taunton (Eng.)—D.W.—25th August, 1915.
2105, Pte. E. B. Armstrong, Barham (N.S.W.)—K.I.A.—25th August, 1915.
2162, Pte. A. G. Ison, Euroa (V.)—K.I.A.—25th August, 1915.
2211, Pte. C. R. Sharp, Colac (V.)—K.I.A.—25th August, 1915.
1365, Pte. T. Higginbottom, Melbourne (V.), and Salford (Eng.)—K.I.A.—25th August, 1915.
2058, Pte. J. J. Galvin, Hay (N.S.W.)—D.W.—25th August, 1915.
398, Pte. J. A. Wiseman, Dunluce (V.)—K.I.A.—26th August, 1915.
808, Pte. A. L. Ansell, Collingwood (V.)—K.I.A.—26th August, 1915.
1851, Pte. B. Rattray, Benalla (V.)—K.I.A.—26th August, 1915.
1002, Cpl. J. Hart, Mildura (V.)—K.I.A.—26th August, 1915.
1722, Pte. C. H. Chandler, Rutherglen (V.)—K.I.A.—27th August, 1915.
1099, Sgt. T. C. Stokan, Malvern (V.)—K.I.A.—27th August, 1915.
1750, Pte. E. W. Gilchrist, Moonee Ponds (V.)—K.I.A.—27th August, 1915.
1669, Pte. R. G. Davey, Ballarat (V.)—K.I.A.—27th August, 1915.
1714, Pte. W. Brewster, Box Hill (V.)—K.I.A.—27th August, 1915.
1912, Pte. W. J. Beaton, Euroa (V.)—K.I.A.—27th August, 1915.
1939, Pte. F. Franklin, Heywood (V.)—K.I.A.—27th August, 1915.
1981, Pte. H. R. Morris, Elmhurst (V.)—K.I.A.—27th August, 1915.

---

* There were two men named "Aitken" with the single initial "A." in the 14th Battalion. Both were killed. The other, Albert Aitken, was killed on 8th August, 1918.

## 368   The Roll of Honour.

2260, Pte. C. W. Gilroy, Melbourne (V.) and Newcastle-on-Tyne (Eng.)—K.I.A.—27th August, 1915.

1904, L/Cpl. N. Baker, Bridgewater (V.) and Margate (Eng.)—K.I.A.—27th August, 1915.

1938, Pte. H. Francis (correct name, H. F. White), Alexandria (N.S.W.)—K.I.A.—27th August, 1915.

190, Pte. A. E. Freeman, Bendigo and Windsor (V.)—K.I.A.—27th August, 1915.

1676, Pte. S. Griffiths, Lancashire (Eng.)—K.I.A.—27th August, 1915.

333, Pte. J. Kelly, Trentham (V.)—K.I.A.—27th August, 1915.

1480, Pte. C. R. Jenkins, W. Melbourne (V.)—K.I.A.—27th August, 1915.

2102, Pte. T. H. Aldridge, Kensington (V.)—D.W.—28th August, 1915.

1305, Pte. P. D. Annear, Elsternwick (V.)—D.W.—28th August, 1915.

1372, Sgt. A. L. Jack, Christchurch (N.Z.) and N. Melbourne (V.)—K.I.A.—28th August, 1915.

320, Cpl. H. Fegan, Bendigo (V.)—D.W.—28th August, 1915.

449, Sgt. L. L. Grant, Allansford (V.), and Stirlingshire (Scotland)—D.W.—28th August, 1915.

2110, Pte. B. Battilana, Dunolly (V.)—D.W.—28th August, 1915.

53, Pte. A. E. Freestone, Ballarat (V.)—K.I.A.—28th August, 1915.

561, Pte. T. Coleman, Melbourne (V.) and Isle of Wight (Eng.)—K.I.A.—28th August, 1915.

1475, Pte. J. McCabe, Leith (Scotland)—K.I.A.—28th August, 1915.

371, Pte. W. Russell, Richmond (V.) and Clackmannanshire (Scotland)—K.I.A.—28th August, 1915.

1604, Pte. J. Paterson, Melbourne (V.)—K.I.A.—29th August, 1915.

1375, Pte. W. B. Jenkins, Kyabram (V.)—D.I.—29th August, 1915.

2045, Pte. L. Poulett-Harris, Windsor (V.)—K.I.A.—29th August, 1915.

224, Pte. H. Jennings, Norfolk (Eng.) and Albert Park (V.)—D.W.—30th August, 1915.

148, Sgt. W. E. Williams, Barrakie (V.) and Llandudro (Wales)—D.W.—31st August, 1915.

2002, Pte. D. Robertson, Moyston (V.)—D.W.—4th September, 1915.

2216, Cpl. G. A. Stewart, Mount Duneed (V.)—D.W.—5th Sept., 1915.

652, Pte. L. H. H. Sames, London (Eng.) and Banyena (V.)—D.W.—7th September, 1915.

1452, Pte. L. G. Curnow, Bendigo (V.)—D.I.—8th September, 1915.

966, Cpl. G. R. Clapham, Sale (V.)—K.I.A.—13th September, 1915.

2189, Pte. W. B. Miller, Arcadia (V.)—D.W.—14th September, 1915.

59, Pte. D. J. Griffin, Crowlands (V.)—D.W.—16th September, 1915.

969, Sgt. C. Crapper, Tandara (V.)—D.I.—27th September, 1915.

1698, Pte. F. McKenzie, Berringa (V.)—D.I.—30th September, 1915.

1343, Pte. C. H. Coleman, Newport (V.)—K.I.A.—1st November, 1915.

1372, Pte. R. J. Kerr, Camperdown (V.)—D.W.—7th November, 1915.

234, Pte. J. Moss, London (Eng.)—D.W.—19th November, 1915.

## The History of the 14th Battalion.

580, Pte. R. A. Earey, Lascelles (V.) and Stratford (Eng.)—D.I.—22nd November, 1915.
1367, Pte. J. P. Hennessy, N. Melbourne (V.)—D.W. (P.W.)—4th December, 1915.
2345, Pte. R. C. Bennett, Birchip (V.)—D.W.—17th December, 1915.

1916.
1603, Cpl. W. Hancock, Melbourne (V.) and Kent (Eng.)—D.I.—8th January, 1916.
1560, Sgt. L. R. T. Gilbert, Hawthorn (V.)—D.W.—20th January, 1916.
1524, Pte. R. Thomas, Morwell (V.)—D.I.—30th January, 1916.
510, Pte. J. Winterbourne, Dingee (V.) and Essex (Eng.)—D. Inj.—6th February, 1916.
1411, Cpl. C. M. Stevens, Bathurst (N.S.W.)—D.I.—22nd February, 1916.
2451, L/Cpl. J. T. Weir, Prahran (V.)—D.I.—15th April, 1916.
3369, Pte. A. E. Jarvis, Sebastopol (V.)—D.I.—15th May, 1916.
4731, Pte. G. D. Baker, Sth. Yarra (V.)—D.I.—16th May, 1916.
5253, Pte. T. H. Backus, Footscray (V.)—D.I.—26th May, 1916.
1424, Pte. E. R. Wilson, Fitzroy and Brunswick (V.)—D.I. (P.W.)—30th May, 1916.


### FRANCE.—1916 to 1918.

#### OFFICERS.

1916.
2nd-Lieut. R. D. Julian, Geelong (V.)—K.I.A.—2nd July, 1916.
2nd-Lieut. H. S. Dobbie, M.C., Footscray (V).—D.W.—7th August, 1916.
2nd-Lieut. A. R. Dean, M.C., Sydney (N.S.W.)—D.W.—2nd December, 1916.

1917.
Capt. S. M. Hansen, M.C., Williamstown (V.)—D.W.—7th February, 1917.
Lieut. G. W. McQueen, Hamilton (V.)—K.I.A.—29th March, 1917.
Capt. R. W. Orr, Footscray (V.)—K.I.A.—11th April, 1917.
Capt. F. B. Stanton, Melbourne (V.)—K.I.A.—11th April, 1917.
Capt. A. Williamson, Toongabbie (V.)—K.I.A.—11th April, 1917.
Lieut. F. H. Dadson, Cairns (Q.)—K.I.A.—11th April, 1917
2nd-Lieut. S. B. Thompson, St. Kilda (V.)—K.I.A.—11th April, 1917.
2nd-Lieut. L. H. Mullett, Malvern (V.)—K.I.A.—11th April, 1917.
2nd-Lieut. M. O'Donnell, Gisborne (V.)—K.I.A.—11th April, 1917.
Lieut. H. R. McKinley, Hawthorn (V.)—D.W.—11th April, 1917.
Lieut. N. A. Kent, M.S.M., Narre Warren (V.)—D.W.—12th April, 1917.
2nd-Lieut. A. J. Harris, Echuca (V.)—D.W.—12th April, 1917
2nd-Lieut. V. G. Garner, Talbot (V.)—K.I.A.—8th August, 1917.

370    The Roll of Honour.

Lieut. T. H. Templeton, Yea (V.)—K.I.A.—24th September, 1917.
Capt. H. B. Wanliss, D.S.O., Ballarat and Lorne (V.)—K.I.A.—26th September, 1917.
2nd-Lieut. L. H. Gill, Elwood (V.)—K.I.A.—28th September, 1917.
Capt. H. V. Walklate, Malvern (V.)—K.I.A.—22nd October, 1917.

1918.

2nd-Lieut. V. E. Hall, Ivanhoe (V.)—K.I.A.—29th March, 1918.
Lieut. J. H. Johnson, M.C. and Bar, Colac (V.)—K.I.A.—2nd May, 1918.
Lieut. R. Wood, Melbourne (V.) and Carlisle (Eng.)—K.I.A.—4th July, 1918.
Lieut. F. W. Appleton, Croix de Guerre, St. Kilda (V.)—K.I.A.—8th August, 1918.
Lieut. H. W. Thompson, M.C., N. Melbourne (V.)—D.W.—9th August, 1918.

## OTHER RANKS.

1916.

3455, Pte. B. Pring, Ballarat (V.)—D.W.—29th June, 1916.
517, Pte. R. Wellwood, Warracknabeal (V.)—K.I.A.—30th June, 1916.
3808, Pte. G. W. Holland, Shepparton (V.)—K.I.A.—1st July, 1916.
4192, Pte. W. H. Fletcher, Cobden (V.)—K.I.A.—1st July, 1916.
1889, Pte. J. Beggs, Elmhurst (V.)—K.I.A.—2nd July, 1916.
1929, Pte. L. Davis, Carlton (V.)—K.I.A.—2nd July, 1916.
3033, Pte. T. Brocklebank, Lancashire (Eng.) and Swan Hill (V.)—K.I.A.—2nd July, 1916.
3458, Pte. J. R. Pender, Geelong (V.)—K.I.A.—2nd July, 1916.
4256, Pte. I. T. Moore, Ballarat (V.)—K.I.A.—3rd July, 1916.
4257, Pte. C. L. Moore, Ballarat (V.)—K.I.A.—3rd July, 1916.
3482, Pte. C. E. O. Rich, Geelong (V.)—K.I.A.—3rd July, 1916
1580, Pte. J. Meehan, Rutherglen (V.)—K.I.A.—3rd July, 1916.
3100, Pte. H. G. Nicholas, London (Eng.)—K.I.A.—3rd July, 1916.
4147, Pte. E. J. Brownfield, Ballarat E. (V.)—K.I.A.—3rd July, 1916.
4174, Pte. H. Drummond, Sebastopol (V.)—K.I.A.—3rd July, 1916.
1340, Pte. W. H. Botsford, Richmond (V.)—D.W.—3rd July, 1916.
2633, Pte. A. E. Robinson, Coburg (V.)—D.W.—3rd July, 1916.
3306, Pte. B. Duffy, Whittlesea (V.)—K.I.A.—3rd July, 1916.
3023, Pte. J. T. R. Easton, Kensington (V.)—D.W.—4th July, 1916.
2561, Sgt. W. H. Pearce, Pearcedale (V.)—D.W.—4th July, 1916.
3122, Pte. W. O'Shea, Fitzroy (V.)—D.W.—4th July, 1916.
4341, Pte. J. A. C. Snow, Warracknabeal (V.)—D.W.—5th July, 1916.
316, Sgt. B. O. Edmonstone, Ararat (V.)—D.W.—5th July, 1916.
46, Sgt. H. H. Croft, Elmhurst (V.)—D.W.—8th July, 1916.
3516, Pte. A. Vincent, Richmond (V.)—K.I.A.—9th July, 1916.

## The History of the 14th Battalion. 371

4426, Pte. A. Albert, Jung (V)—K.I.A.—7th August, 1916.
223, Cpl. R. A. Jones, Wrexham (Wales) and Melbourne (V.)—K.I.A.—7th August, 1916.
5159, Pte. J. V. Murphy, Carlton (V.)—K.I.A.—7th August, 1916.
2687, Pte. E. J. Holland, Flemington (V.)—K.I.A.—7th August, 1916.
1767, Pte. R. A. Lamb, Morwell (V.)—K.I.A.—7th August, 1916.
3762, Pte. G. A. Fowles, Marungi (V.)—K.I.A.—7th August, 1916.
2037, L/Cpl. E. Williamson, Surrey Hills (V.)—K.I.A.—7th August, 1916.
1315, Pte. L. Boag, S. Melbourne (V.)—K.I.A.—7th August, 1916.
5106, Pte. J. Grayland, Macarthur (V.)—K.I.A.—7th August, 1916.
761, L/Cpl. W. McKissack, Metcalfe (V.)—K.I.A.—7th August, 1916.
4315, Pte. F. Snibson, Ararat (V.)—K.I.A.—7th August, 1916.
2025, Pte. C. C. J. Taylor, Carlton (V.)—K.I.A.—7th August, 1916.
4466, Pte. J. W. Connolly, Warrnambool (V.)—K.I.A.—7th August, 1916.
2332, Pte. W. J. Bennett, Southend-on-Sea (Eng.) and Kinnabulla (V.)—K.I.A.—7th August, 1916.
2458, Pte. L. L. Handley, Lacey West (V.)—K.I.A.—7th August, 1916.
736, Sgt. H. Lewis, Port Melbourne (V.)—K.I.A.—7th August, 1916.
4533, Pte. R. P. Laurie, Diamond Creek (V.)—K.I.A.—7th August, 1916.
3092, Pte. L. W. McKay, Moonee Ponds (V.)—K.I.A.—7th August, 1916.
5347, Pte. C. Buckler, Wangaratta (V.)—K.I.A.—7th August, 1916.
4312, Pte. A. Smithson, Clunes (V.)—K.I.A.—7th August, 1916.
4171, L/Cpl. R. H. S. Dean, Ballarat (V.)—K.I.A.—7th August, 1916.
3751, Pte. J. A. Finlay, S. Melbourne (V.)—K.I.A.—7th August, 1916.
1326, Pte. H. L. Carroll, Ballarat (V.)—K.I.A.—8th August, 1916.
1512, Pte. P. Smith, S. Melbourne (V.)—K.I.A—8th August, 1916.
4288, Pte. E. N. Pinney, Ballarat (V.)—K.I.A.—8th August, 1916.
4477, Pte. F. H. Edwards, Footscray (V.)—K.I.A.—8th August, 1916.
1174, Bugler F. S. Evans, Bendigo (V.)—K.I.A.—8th August, 1916.
5047, Pte. J. A. Buller, Warburton (V.)—K.I.A.—8th August, 1916.
2053, Pte. G. S. Booth, S. Melbourne (V.)—K.I.A.—8th August, 1916.
4433, Pte. C. W. Baker, Warrnambool (V.)—K.I.A.—8th August, 1916.
5219, Pte. W. J. Sharp, Fitzroy (V.)—K.I.A.—8th August, 1916.
3101, Pte. H. Neale, W. Footscray (V.)—K.I.A.—8th August, 1916.
4189, Pte. A. L. Featherston, Ballarat East (V.)—K.I.A.—8th August, 1916.
1134, Pte. G. Smith, Tarnagulla (V.)—K.I.A.—8th August, 1916.
2481, Pte. C. S. Barnes, Middle Park (V.)—K.I.A.—8th August, 1916.
2896a, Pte. H. H. Barnes, Middle Park (V.)—K.I.A.—8th August, 1916.
5471, Pte. R. J. Taylor, Malvern (V.)—K.I.A.—8th August, 1916.
3976, Pte. A. Ellis, Garvoc (V.)—K.I.A.—8th August, 1916.
1058, Pte. J. McG. Stewart, Mirboo N. (V.)—K.I.A.—8th August, 1916.
2934, Pte. H. Le Blanc, Northcote (V.)—K.I.A.—8th August, 1916.
3436, Pte. G. M. Mayne, Port Melbourne (V.)—K.I.A.—8th August, 1916.
3497, Pte. C. C. Smith, Chelsea (V.)—K.I.A.—8th August, 1916.
4630, Pte. G. A. Webb, Purdeet (V.)—D.W.—9th August, 1916.
3064, Pte. H. McNeill, Mildura (V.) and Argyllshire (Scot.)—K.I.A.—9th August, 1916.

## The Roll of Honour.

1844, Pte. A. W. Brown, N. Melbourne (V.)—K.I.A.—9th August, 1916.
1891, Pte. T. A. Blanchard, Warracknabeal (V.)—K.I.A.—9th Aug,. 1916.
2787, L/Cpl. H. J. Armstrong, Carlton (V.)—K.I.A.—9th August, 1916.
5345, Pte. W. Brown, Geelong (V.)—K.I.A.—9th August, 1916.
4502, Pte. G. C. Griffith, Albury (N.S.W.)—D.W.—9th August, 1916.
2386, Pte. F. W. Gilbert, Chirrup (V.)—K.I.A.—9th August, 1916.
1732, Pte. R. Gregory, Eaglehawk (V.)—D.W.—10th August, 1916.
3446, Pte. T. M. O'Connell, Massachusetts (U.S.A.)—K.I.A.—10th August, 1916.
4896, Pte. J. G. O'Halloran, Smeaton (V.)—K.I.A.—10th August, 1916.
3122, Pte. N. A. Pearce, Surrey Hills (V.)—K.I.A.—10th August, 1916.
312, Pte. C. P. Degner, Richmond (V.)—K.I.A.—10th August, 1916.
734, Pte. G. T. Lampard, Balmoral (V.)—K.I.A.—10th August, 1916.
4207, Pte. W. E. Hartshorne, Williamstown (V.)—K.I.A.—10th August, 1916.
2848, Pte. E. W. Mayer, Melbourne (V.)—K.I.A.—10th August, 1916.
3473, Pte. F. R. Russell, Bacchus Marsh (V.)—K.I.A.—10th August, 1916.
5165, Pte. A. McKay, Avenel (V.)—K.I.A.—10th August, 1916.
2214, Pte. H. Skerritt, Dublin (Ire.)—D.W.—11th August, 1916.
3475, Pte. W. J. Rodwell, St. Kilda (V.)—K.I.A.—11th August, 1916.
1329, Pte. R. Anderson, Melbourne (V.) and Oldham (Eng.)—K.I.A.—11th August, 1916.
2841, Pte. W. McWilliam, Riddell's Creek (V.)—K.I.A.—11th Aug., 1916.
1920, Pte. L. Calvert, M. Brighton (V.)—K.I.A.—11th August, 1916.
1441, Sgt. A. T. Pearce (served as John Pearce), Trawalla (V.)—K.I.A.—11th August, 1916.
1743, L/Cpl. J. A. Gilbert, St. Leonards (V.)—K.I.A.—11th August, 1916.
366, Dvr. I. J. O'Malley, Richmond (V.)—D.W.—11th August, 1916.
4286, Pte. L. R. Pattenden, Melbourne (V.)—D.W.—12th August, 1916.
3880, Pte. W. Roberts, Locksley (V.)—K.I.A.—12th August, 1916.
3797, Pte. F. T. Hayle, Ararat (V.)—K.I.A.—12th August, 1916
1725, L/Cpl. B. Carloss, Terang (V.)—D.W.—12th August, 1916.
2803, Pte. J. Copeland, Darnum (V.)—K.I.A.—12th August, 1916.
175, Pte. H. Campbell, Footscray (V.)—K.I.A.—12th August, 1916.
4219, Pte. W. Hunt, Mount Egerton (V.)—K.I.A.—12th August, 1916.
2743, Pte. F. W. Malcolmson, Collingwood (V.)—K.I.A.—12th August, 1916.
4296, Pte. W. C. Rashleigh, Ballarat (V.)—D.W.—12th August, 1916.
165, Pte. J. H. Bolton, Brunswick (V.)—D.W.—12th August, 1916.
2766, Cpl. F. G. Coleman, S. Melbourne (V.)—D.W.—13th August, 1916.
677, Dvr. J. L. Archibald, Smeaton (V.)—D.W.—13th August, 1916.
3496, Cpl. F. Smith, Strathewen (V.) and Birmingham (Eng.)—K.I.A.—13th August, 1916.
3366, L/Cpl W. I. F. Issell, Korumburra (V.)—K.I.A.—13th August, 1916.
3267, Pte. C. N. Coe, Williamstown (V.)—D.W.—14th August, 1916.
1405, Pte. B. Schroeder, Warragul (V.)—D.W.—16th August, 1916.

## The History of the 14th Battalion. 373

2568, Pte. D. R. Colley, Drouin (V.)—D.W.—17th August, 1916.
4240, Pte. H. Lynch, Trafalgar (V.)—D.W.—17th August, 1916.
5100, Pte. J. T. Good, Oakleigh (V.)—D.W.—24th August, 1916.
5465, Pte. R. W. Snowdon, Melbourne (V.) and London (Eng.)—K.I.A.—
   27th August, 1916.
2853, Pte. F. Short, Glenferrie (V.)—K.I.A.—28th August, 1916.
3425, Pte. H. P. Morris, Brighton (V.)—K.I.A.—28th August, 1916.
4808, Pte. J. F. Gleeson, Warrnambool (V.)—K.I.A.—28th August, 1916.
3807, Pte. C. S. Holland, Shepparton (V.)—D.W.—28th August, 1916.
3422, Pte. C. Matthew, S. Richmond (V.)—K.I.A.—28th August, 1916.
5190, Pte. A. N. Platt, Yarra Junction (V.)—K.I.A.—28th August, 1916.
3395, Pte. N. J. McLeod, S. Melbourne (V.)—D.W.—29th August, 1916.
5423, Pte. H. H. A. Nielsen, Creighton (V.) and Copenhagen (Denmark)—
   K.I.A.—29th August, 1916.
2423, Pte. J. C. Ronald, Middle Park (V.)—K.I.A.—29th August, 1916.
5358, Pte. S. Coutts, Daylesford (V.)—K.I.A.—29th August, 1916.
2494, L/Cpl. C. C. Sharp, Hawthorn (V.)—K.I.A.—29th August, 1916.
3019, Pte. A. Barklay, Richmond (V.)—K.I.A.—29th August, 1916.
1532, Pte. D. E. Docwra, Hertford (V.)—K.I.A.—29th August, 1916.
4984, Pte. G. V. Osborne, Ballarat (V.)—K.I.A.—29th August, 1916.
4184, Pte. O. W. Eason, Scotsburn (V.)—K.I.A.—29th August, 1916.
3357, Pte. H. Herring, Newport (V.)—K.I.A.—29th August, 1916
3333, Pte. V. Graham, S. Melbourne (V.)—K.I.A.—29th August, 1916.
5373, Pte. T. R. Fenner, Dunach (V.)—K.I.A.—29th August, 1916.
5409, L/Cpl. S. R. McCarthy, Bairnsdale (V.)—K.I.A.—29th August, 1916.
3239, Pte. B. S. Bent, S. Melbourne (V.)—D.W.—31st August, 1916.
3363, Pte. G. Hamilton, Narracan (V.)—D.W.—31st August, 1916.
4839, Pte. E. E. Jennings, Woodstock (V.) and Stratford (Eng.)—D.W.—
   31st August, 1916.
3312, Pte. A. R. Dodemaide, M.M., Mildura (V.)—D.W.—13th Sept., 1916.
4857, Pte. H. R. D. Lee, Clunes (V.)—K.I.A.—25th September, 1916
 53, Pte. P. Pigot, Mt. Gambier (S.A.)—K.I.A.—1st October, 1916.
2367, Pte. J. Duggan, Sunbury (V.)—K.I.A.—2nd October, 1916.
5365, Pte. A. Draper, Hexham (V.)—K.I.A.—16th October, 1916.
 374, Sgt. G. A. Ross, D.C.M., St. Arnaud (V.)—K.I.A.—16th Oct., 1916.
5503, Pte. P. J. Hill, Rutherglen (V.)—K.I.A.—16th October, 1916.
3360, T/Cpl. Ivan H. Harrison, Donald (V.)—K.I.A.—16th Nov., 1916.
5464, Pte. R. B. Wharton, Warburton (V.)—K.I.A.—28th November, 1916.
5466, Pte. W. Williams, Neerim (V.)—K.I.A.—28th November, 1916.
 766, Pte. J. Pattie, Ballarat North (V.)—K.I.A.—28th November, 1916.
4537, Pte. A. A. G. Litolff, Melbourne (V.)—K.I.A.—1st December, 1916.
4590, Pte. W. S. Pooley, Melbourne (V.) and Ipswich (Eng.)—K.I.A.—
   1st December, 1916
1158, L/Cpl. A. Jarvis, Kent (Eng.)—K.I.A.—3rd December, 1916.
6063, Pte. P. A. Makeham, Korumburra (V.)—K.I.A.—3rd December, 1916.
1414, Pte. H. J. Stephens, S. Melbourne (V.)—K.I.A.—3rd December, 1916.

1269, Pte. T. J. Murphy, Footscray (V.)—K.I.A.—4th December, 1916.
5985, Pte. D. Colquhoun, Warrenheip (V.)—K.I.A.—4th December, 1916.
4197, Pte. M. J. Gavin, Ballarat E. (V.)—D.W.—16th December, 1916.
2124, Pte. B. Calcutt, Williamstown (V.)—D.I.—18th December, 1916.
5378, Pte. T. Griffiths, Cardiff (Wales) and Newmarket (V.)—D.I.—20th December, 1916.

### 1917.

1748, Pte. P. A. Giddens, Kew (V.)—D.I.—1st January, 1917.
1547, Pte. M. W. Costigan, N. Fitzroy (V.)—K.I.A.—11th January, 1917.
6973, Cpl. D. J. Burgess, Kilmore (V.)—D.I.—19th January, 1917.
6028, Pte. H. R. Gibbons, Geelong (V.)—K.I.A.—26th January, 1917.
5430, Pte. C. H. Rawlings, Melbourne (V.)—K.I.A.—26th January, 1917.
5705, Pte. H. C. Morris, Coburg (V.)—D.W.—27th January, 1917.
6572, Pte. A. A. Patchett, Collingwood (V.)—K.I.A.—27th January, 1917.
5129, Cpl. J. W. Jackson, M.M., Numurkah (V.)—K.I.A.—28th Jan., 1917.
6118, Pte. I. A. Williams, Geelong (V.)—K.I.A.—29th January, 1917.
5361, Pte. R. S. Davis, Oakleigh (V.)—K.I.A.—29th January, 1917.
5981, Pte. N. Burn, Geelong (V.)—D.W.—1st February, 1917.
5229, Pte. H. V. Thomas, Waratah (Tas.)—K.I.A.—2nd February, 1917.
1490, Pte. F. May, Footscray (V.)—K.I.A.—3rd February, 1917.
2577, Pte. T. C. Coulter, Glenrowan (V.)—D.W.—5th February, 1917.
5201, Pte. T. Ryan, Casterton (V.)—D.W.—5th February, 1917.
6520, Pte. A. R. Hitchins, Richmond (V.)—K.I.A.—5th February, 1917.
6295, Pte. P. G. L. King, Cobram (V.)—K.I.A.—5th February, 1917.
5415, L/Cpl. J. Mattison, East Lothian (Scotland) and Warrnambool (V.) —K.I.A.—5th February, 1917.
1643, Pte. A. D. McAskil, Coburg (V.)—K.I.A.—5th February, 1917.
109, Cpl. H. Perry, Deer Park (V.)—K.I.A.—5th February, 1917.
3127, Pte. L. Robins, Bendigo (V.)—K.I.A.—5th February, 1917.
5462, Pte. J. J. Smith, Richmond (V.)—K.I.A.—5th February, 1917.
1194, Pte. M. Scott, Moulamein (N.S.W.)—K.I.A.—5th February, 1917.
5646, Pte. R. Archer, Bairnsdale (V.)—K.I.A.—5th February, 1917.
5652, Pte. H. Callan, St. Kilda (V.)—K.I.A.—5th February, 1917.
5656, Pte. C. H. Carson, Cressy (V.) and Leicester (Eng.)—K.I.A.—5th February, 1917.
5655, Pte. G. H. Cheesman, Brighton (V.)—K.I.A.—5th February, 1917.
6023, Pte. E. J. Folwell, Black Rock (V.)—K.I.A.—5th February, 1917.
401, Pte. L. A. Wallace, Melbourne (V.) and Woolwich (Eng.)—K.I.A. —5th February, 1917.
1504, L/Cpl. G. Richie, Hamilton (V.)—K.I.A.—5th February, 1917.
1729, Pte. H. F. Dunn, W. Brunswick (V.)—D.W.—6th February, 1917.
769, L/Sgt. G. Ryan, Horsham (V.)—D.A.—6th February, 1917.
5463, Pte. A. Walton, Lancashire (Eng.)—D.W.—6th February, 1917.
6642, L/Cpl. D. Hearfield, St. Kilda (V.)—D.W.—7th February, 1917.
5739, Pte. T. G. Tope, Brighton (V.)—D.W.—9th February, 1917.

## The History of the 14th Battalion. 375

6559, Pte. S. R. Mulcahy, N. Melbourne (V.)—D.W.—11th February, 1917.
4872, Pte. R. J. Murray, Koroit (V.)—D.W.—11th February, 1917.
3073, Pte. T. F. Moore, N. Melbourne (V.)—K.I.A.—11th February, 1917.
6057, Pte. M. D. McRae, Culcairn (N.S.W.)—K.I.A.—11th February, 1917.
6147, Pte. L. Melbourne, Brighton (V.)—D.W.—12th February, 1917.
5986, Pte. H. Bebbington, Geelong (V.)—D.W.—16th February, 1917.
876, L/Cpl. H. J. Hassett, Hobart (Tas.)—D.W.—17th February, 1917.
3372, Pte. R. Kelly, Brunswick (V.)—D.W.—4th March, 1917.
6254, Pte. J. F. Donavan, Yarraville (V.)—D.W.—25th March, 1917.
1425, Pte. T. Young, Richmond (V.)—K.I.A.—29th March, 1917.
2878, Pte. T. A. Thorn, Northcote (V.)—K.I.A.—29th March, 1917.
8, Cpl. W. W. Goodwin, M.M.—Caulfield (V.)—K.I.A.—29th March, 1917.
1937, Cpl. L. I. Foster, Geelong (V.)—K.I.A.—7th April, 1917.
5653, Pte. A. S. Collins, N. Fitzroy (V.)—K.I.A.—7th April, 1917
6238, Pte A. D. Claridge, Macarthur (V.)—K.I.A.—7th April, 1917.
3229, Sgt. A. G. Ansett, Clifton (V.)—K.I.A.—7th April, 1917.
726, Pte. W. Isbel, Ararat (V.)—K.I.A.—11th April, 1917.
4237, Pte. A. C. Kilpatrick, Mont Albert (V.)—K.I.A.—11th April, 1917.
6472, Pte. W. J. Birthisel, Gre Gre (V.)—K.I.A.—11th April, 1917.
1797, L/Cpl. F. L. Bell, Armidale (N.S.W.)—K.I.A.—11th April, 1917
5326, Pte. D. Allan, Largs (Scotland)—K.I.A.—11th April, 1917.
4596, Pte. A. O. Roach, St. Kilda (V.)—K.I.A.—11th April, 1917.
382, Cpl. C. B. Smith, Cambridge (Eng.)—K.I.A.—11th April, 1917.
6083, Pte. C. Rutter, Terang (V.)—K.I.A.—11th April, 1917.
1995, Cpl. C. B. Postlewaite, M.M., Canover (V.)—K.I.A.—11th April, 1917.
6091, Pte. T. G. J. Riley, Caramut (V.)—K.I.A.—11th April, 1917.
5258, Pte. P. H. Noseda, E. Prahran (V.)—K.I.A.—11th April, 1917.
4255, Cpl. C. F. Miller, Stawell (V.)—K.I.A.—11th April, 1917
1707, Pte. N. J. Whelan, Nar-Nar-Goon (V.)—K.I.A.—11th April, 1917.
2411, Pte. W. L. Lovell, Hamilton (V.)—K.I.A.—11th April, 1917.
6547, Pte. J. McCormick, Fitzroy (V.)—K.I.A.—11th April, 1917.
3388, L/Sgt. J. McRae, D.C.M., Bairnsdale (V.)—K.I.A.—11th April, 1917.
4243, Pte. A. E. Lester, Jeparit (V.)—K.I.A—11th April, 1917
6480, Pte. A. J. Blackman, N. Fitzroy (V.)—K.I.A.—11th April, 1917.
5343, Pte. A. J. Bowman, Yarpturk (V.)—K.I.A.—11th April, 1917
2054, L/Cpl. N. K. Buckman, Ballarat E. (V.)—K.I.A.—11th April, 1917.
5350, Pte. N. Carson, Stonyford (V.)—K.I.A.—11th April, 1917.
4205, Pte. J. Gross, Mt. Pleasant (V.)—K.I.A.—11th April, 1917.
2393, Pte. R. E. Hardy, E. Brunswick (V.)—K.I.A.—11th April, 1917.
2395, Cpl. W. A. Hart, Canterbury (V.)—K.I.A.—11th April, 1917.
4222, Pte. E. J. Irwin, Belfast (Ireland)—K.I.A.—11th April, 1917.
605, Pte. T. E. Johnstone, Brighton (V.)—11th April, 1917.
4528, Pte. T. Kirby, E. Brunswick (V.)—K.I.A.—11th April, 1917.
5449, Pte. E. R. Read, Camperdown (V.)—K.I.A.—11th April, 1917.

## The Roll of Honour.

5730, Pte. W. Reid, Glasgow (Scotland)—K.I.A.—11th April, 1917.
3543, Sgt. C. F. Ross, Bendigo (V.)—K.I.A.—11th April, 1917.
6087, Pte. P. E. Ross, Deniliquin (N.S.W.)—K.I.A.—11th April, 1917.
2007, Sgt. A. E. Schultz, Richmond (V.)—K.I.A—11th April, 1917
384, Pte. J. Stewart, Wallacedale (V.)—K.I.A.—11th April, 1917.
5740, Pte. R. H. Thompson, Sale (V.)—K.I.A.—11th April, 1917.
4490, Pte. E. Fraher, N. Fitzroy (V.)—K.I.A.—11th April, 1917.
4338, Pte. D. K. Wallis, Middle Park (V.)—K.I.A.—11th April, 1917.
3419, Pte. C. Morris, Bendigo (V.)—K.I.A.—11th April, 1917.
5163, Pte. J. S. McCarty, Warrnambool (V.)—K.I.A.—11th April, 1917.
6502, Pte. T. R. Eason, Footscray (V.)—K.I.A.—11th April, 1917.
79, Sgt. L. R. Jones, Essendon (V.)—K.I.A.—11th April, 1917.
4645, Pte W. Castle, Carlisle (Eng.)—K.I.A.—11th April, 1917.
2028, Sgt. A. Urie, D.C.M., Glasgow (Scotland)—K.I.A.—11th April, 1917.
5328, Pte. D. C. R. Black, Chelsea (V.)—K.I.A.—11th April, 1917.
6470, Pte. R. Beattie, Moreland (V.)—K.I.A.—11th April, 1917.
5337, Pte. P. C. Bird, Neerim (V.)—K.I.A.—11th April, 1917.
6003, Pte. C. W. Clifford, Terang (V.)—K.I.A.—11th April, 1917.
4431, Pte. R. C. Baillie, Warrnambool (V.)—K.I.A.—11th April, 1917.
6457, Pte. F. D. Archer, Kensington (V.)—K.I.A.—11th April, 1917.
6214, Pte. A. A. Andrews, Balranald (N.S.W.)—K.I.A.—11th April, 1917
817, Sgt. R. H. Berry, Elsternwick (V.)—K.I.A.—11th April, 1917.
815, Cpl. W. Bickford, Bendigo (V.)—K.I.A.—11th April, 1917.
6465, Pte. G. Abbott, Newmarket (V.)—K.I.A.—11th April, 1917.
923, L/Cpl. D. J. Cavanagh, Yarrawonga (V.)—K.I.A.—11th April, 1917.
5067, Pte. J. B. Cleary, Sunshine (V.)—K.I.A.—11th April, 1917.
5996, Pte. S. G. Challis, Connewarre (V.)—K.I.A.—11th April, 1917.
3247, Pte. A. Burrows, Manchester (Eng.)—K.I.A.—11th April, 1917.
6481, Pte. G. B. Brodie, Romsey (V.)—K.I.A.—11th April, 1917.
5989, Pte. C. C. Bourdon, Nhill (V.)—K.I.A.—11th April, 1917.
6225, L/Cpl. A. B. Bott, Brunswick (V.)—K.I.A.—11th April, 1917.
162, Sgt. R. S. Blamey, Albert Park (V.)—K.I.A.—11th April, 1917.
6269, Pte. E. W. Graf, Zurich (Switzerland)—K.I.A.—11th April, 1917.
4178, Pte. A. G. Dudley, Corindhap (V.)—K.I.A.—11th April, 1917.
3469, Sgt. J. L. G. Ridge, Boat Harbor (Tas.)—K.I.A.—11th April, 1917.
3263, Pte. D. R. Cramond, Preston (V.)—K.I.A.—11th April, 1917
590, L/Sgt A. S. Glen, Walpeup (V.)—K.I.A.—11th April, 1917.
2391, L/Cpl. H. J. Gillies, Balmoral (V.)—K.I.A.—11th April, 1917.
5675, Pte. M. N. Green, Brighton (V.)—K.I.A.—11th April, 1917.
3329, L/Cpl. D. L. Greer, Clifton Hill (V.)—K.I.A.—11th April, 1917.
5380, L/Cpl. P. E. Green, Moonambel (V.)—K.I.A.—11th April, 1917.
2604, Pte. R. M. S. Hammerberg, Port Melbourne (V.)—K.I.A.—11th April, 1917.
6030, Pte. R. L. Higgs, Broken Hill (N.S.W.)—K.I.A.—11th April, 1917.
4523, Pte. G. A. Johnstone, Terang (V.)—K.I.A.—11th April, 1917.
4223, Pte. J. F. Irvine, Yarra Glen (V.)—K.I.A.—11th April, 1917.

## The History of the 14th Battalion. 377

6039, Pte J. J. Jago, Warrnambool (V.)—K.I.A.—11th April, 1917.
5687, Pte. V. J. Kennedy, Yarraville (V.)—K.I.A.—11th April, 1917.
6300, Pte. W. R. Lambert, Mildura (V.)—K.I.A.—11th April, 1917.
4214, Pte. F. W. Harris, Ballarat (V.)—K.I.A.—11th April, 1917.
4234, Pte. A. J. Kannan, Surrey Hills (V.)—K.I.A.—11th April, 1917.
1970, L/Cpl. G. J. Le Brun, Darlimurla (V.)—K.I.A.—11th April, 1917.
1166, Cpl. P. W. Lewis, Port Melbourne (V.)—K.I.A.—11th April, 1917.
2738, Pte R. Lilley, Daylesford (V.)—K.I.A.—11th April, 1917.
6048, Pte. J. Luke, Terang (V.)—K.I.A.—11th April, 1917.
6303, L/Cpl. J. Long, Preston (V.)—K.I.A.—11th April, 1917.
4546, Pte. H. G. Manson, Warrnambool (V.)—K.I.A.—11th April, 1917.
6623, Pte. O. McCarthy, Bairnsdale (V.)—K.I.A.—11th April, 1917.
1826, Pte. W. Mayne, Sth. Yarra (V.)—K.I.A.—11th April, 1917.
4247, Pte. A. Markham, Flemington (V.)—K.I.A.—11th April, 1917.
2186, L/Cpl. J. McDonald, Maindample (V.)—K.I.A.—11th April, 1917.
3402, Sgt. R. N. S. McDonald, Yarraville (V.)—K.I.A.—11th April, 1917.
5710, Pte. W. McGowan, Wee Wee Rup (V.)—K.I.A.—11th April, 1917.
3396, Pte. A. McKissock, Ascot Vale (V.)—K.I.A.—11th April, 1917.
6059, Pte. W. J. S. McLachlan, Geelong (V.)—K.I.A.—11th April, 1917.
4163, Pte. D. Craig, Steiglitz (V.)—K.I.A.—11th April, 1917.
1925, L/Cpl. W. F. Conole, Cope Cope (V.)—K.I.A.—11th April, 1917.
6239, Pte. L. H. Cutler, Carlton (V.)—K.I.A.—11th April, 1917.
1933, L/Cpl. J. Dickinson, Kew (V.)—K.I.A.—11th April, 1917.
3357, Pte. T. J. Edwards, Tasmania—K.I.A.—11th April, 1917.
3494a, Pte. P. H. Giffard, Wail (V.) and Newcastle-on-Tyne (Eng.)—K.I.A. —11th April, 1917.
4258, Pte. K. N. McNamee, M.M., Ballarat (V.)—K.I.A.—11th April, 1917.
6396, Pte. G. McPherson, Sunbury (V.)—K.I.A.—11th April, 1917.
6317, Pte. W. D. Mehegan, Brunswick (V.)—K.I.A.—11th April, 1917.
3415, Pte. D. Menzies, Yarraville (V.)—K.I.A.—11th April, 1917.
6068, Pte. F. Mills, Colac (V.) and Lancashire (Eng.)—K.I.A.—11th April, 1917.
2181, Cpl. J. H. Moir, Swift's Creek (V.)—K.I.A.—11th April, 1917.
6072, Pte. G. P. Needham, Willow Grove (V.)—K.I.A.—11th April, 1917.
6073, Pte. J. Neighbour, Beech Forest (V.)—K.I.A.—11th April, 1917.
5714, L/Cpl. A. E. Nelson, Mansfield (V.)—K.I.A.—11th April, 1917.
6074, Pte. L. F. Neville, Geelong (V.)—K.I.A.—11th April, 1917.
2923, Sgt. W. J. Orr, St. Arnaud (V.)—K.I.A.—11th April, 1917.
6338, Pte. G. S. Phillips, Kensington (V.)—K.I.A.—11th April, 1917.
5425a, L/Cpl. J. H. Porter, Port Melbourne (V.)—K.I.A.—11th April, 1917.
5724, Pte. H. Pateman, Quambatook (V.) and Hertford (Eng.)—K.I.A.— 11th April, 1917.
1705, Pte. W. G. Duff, Williamstown (V.)—K.I.A.—11th April, 1917.
5725, Pte. D. A. Quinton, Echuca (V.)—K.I.A.—11th April, 1917.
3294, L/Sgt. R. H. Catterson, Hamilton (V.)—K.I.A.—11th April, 1917.
4328, Pte. G. H. Wearn, Ballarat E. (V.)—K.I.A.—11th April, 1917.

## The Roll of Honour.

8027, Pte. H. Berg, Trentham (V.)—K.I.A.—11th April, 1917.
2919, L/Cpl. W. T. V. Young, St. Arnaud (V.)—K.I.A.—11th April, 1917.
5468a, Pte. L. J. Yorke, Footscray (V.)—K.I.A.—11th April, 1917.
3537, Pte. R. J. Wilson, Williamstown (V.)—K.I.A.—11th April, 1917.
5476, Pte. E. R. Wade, Port Fairy (V.)—K.I.A.—11th April, 1917.
5461, Pte. A. S. Twigg, Pyramid Hill (V.)—K.I.A.—11th April, 1917.
6108, Pte. H. G. Townsend, Geelong (V.)—K.I.A.—11th April, 1917.
6112, Pte. B. P. Thomas, Mt. Gambier (S.A.)—K.I.A.—11th April, 1917.
2026, Pte. C. H. Steele, Port Fairy (V.)—K.I.A.—11th April, 1917.
2434, Cpl H. Storer, Carapooe West (V.)—K.I.A.—11th April, 1917.
4137, Pte. E. Blake, Bowenvale (V.)—K.I.A.—11th April, 1917.
5426, Pte. C. D. Parker, Camperdown (V.)—K.I.A.—11th April, 1917.
6271, Pte. A. W. Gemmell, Cobden (V.)—D.W.—12th April, 1917.
805, Cpl. A. L. Whitfield, Creswick (V.)—D.W.—12th April, 1917.
6012, Pte. R. A. Douglass, Geelong (V.)—D.W.—12th April, 1917.
4156, L/Cpl. L. Coward, Ballarat (V.)—D.W.—12th April, 1917.
5452, Pte. H. H. Rogers, Warrnambool (V.)—D.W.—12th April, 1917.
6101, Pte. M. J. Sheedy, Fish Creek (V.)—D.W.—12th April, 1917.
5498, Cpl. R. Jones, Bendigo (V.)—D.W.—12th April, 1917.
4348, Sgt. F. Collins, Yackandandah (V.)—D.W.—12th April, 1917.
90, Sgt. A. McLellan, Outtrim (V.)—D.W.—14th April, 1917.
2756, Pte. W. Guest, Bendigo (V.)—D.W.—15th April, 1917.
2460, Pte. G. R. Grimmond, Wahgunyah (V.)—D.W.—15th April, 1917.
3767, Cpl. J. Hogan, Dunolly (V.)—D.W.—15th April, 1917.
6328, Pte. J. A. McNay, Burnley (V.)—D.W.—16th April, 1917.
6371, Pte. C. V. Waller, Preston (V.)—D.W.—17th April, 1917.
5778, Pte. J. F. Rowe, Daylesford (V.)—D.W.—18th April, 1917.
1984, L/Cpl. A. G. McArthur, Sea Lake (V.)—D.W.—21st April, 1917.
6649 Pte. C. H. Harvey, Carlton (V.)—D.W., P.W.—24th April, 1917.
3303, L/Cpl. J. Dickson, Williamstown (V.)—D.W.—29th April, 1917.
6310, Pte. H. M. L. McGregor, Armadale (V.)—D.W.—2nd May, 1917.
1983, Pte. M. Murphy, Canterbury (V.)—D.W.—8th May, 1917.
6538, Pte. E. W. Law, Malvern (V.)—D.W.—10th May, 1917.
4812, L/Cpl. R. C. Garratt, Ivanhoe (V.)—K.I.A.—11th May, 1917.
6071, Pte. A. V. Muller, Ballarat (V.)—D.W.—2nd June, 1917.
5441, Pte. M. Rollins, Curlewis (V.)—K.I.A.—10th June, 1917.
1598, L/Cpl. S. A. Markham, M.M. and Bar, Riddell's Creek (V.)—K.I.A.
—11th June, 1917.
5758, Pte. D. P. Bourke, Lang Lang (V.)—K.I.A.—11th June, 1917.
6884, Pte. G. J. Ferguson, Caramut (V.)—K.I.A.—12th June, 1917.
6492, Pte. T. Dunne, Wellington (N.Z.)—D.W.—13th June, 1917.
2606, Sgt. C. S. Hall, Vermont (V.)—D.I.—22nd June, 1917.
6719, Pte. C. Carr, Sydney (N.S.W.) and Hawke's Bay (N.Z.)—D.W.—
5th July, 1917.
4458, Pte. J. Checkley, Inverloch (V.)—K.I.A.—5th July, 1917.
1228, Cpl. R. E. Antill, London (Eng.) and Windsor (V.)—K.I.A.—5th
July, 1917.

## The History of the 14th Battalion. 379

539, Pte. W. R. Colwyn-Stevens, London (Eng.) and Warracknabeal (V.) —K.I.A.—6th July, 1917.
4552, Pte. G. H. Moore, Woolsthorpe (V.)—K.I.A.—9th July, 1917.
757, Pte. M. V. Barry, Northcote (V.)—K.I.A.—9th July, 1917.
5717, Pte. C. B. O'Meara, Colac (V.)—K.I.A.—10th July, 1917.
2430, Pte. S. Bee, Auburn (V.)—D.W.—10th July, 1917.
6846, Pte. W. E. Coulter, Bathurst (N.S.W.)—D.I.—8th August, 1917.
5719, Cpl. A. E. Oakley, Box Hill (V.)—K.I.A.—10th August, 1917.
2754, L/Cpl. R. Y. Smith, McKinnon (V.)—K.I.A.—10th August, 1917.
2670, Pte. E. Guest, Bendigo (V.)—K.I.A.—10th August, 1917.
7099, Pte. A. Washington, Mansfield (V.)—K.I.A.—10th August, 1917.
5382, Pte. T. Hale, Bothwell (Tas.)—D.W.—10th August, 1917.
5768, Pte. O. Keast, Maryborough (V.)—K.I.A.—11th August, 1917.
7054, Pte. W. J. O'Brien, Benalla (V.)—K.I.A.—11th August, 1917.
430, Pte. E. Carrick, Tungamah (V.)—D.W.—11th August, 1917.
1801, Pte. T. E. Clifford, Fitzroy (V.)—D.W.—12th August, 1917.
3341, Pte. S. A. Gaskell, Footscray (V.)—D.W.—17th August, 1917.
6042, Pte. T. Jackson, Terang (V.) and Staffordshire (Eng.)—D.W.—20th August, 1917.
6984, Pte. C. W. Cook, S. Melbourne (V.)—K.I.A.—23rd August, 1917.
7015, Pte. V. C. Gaudion, Footscray (V.)—K.I.A.—23rd August, 1917.
5408, Pte. F. A. Mackay, Strangways (V.)—D.W.—29th August, 1917.
6766, Pte. L. A. Lee, Holbrook (N.S.W.)—D.W.—9th September, 1917.
1803, L/Cpl. J. W. Carey, North Carlton (V.)—D.A.—14th Sept., 1917.
6789, Pte. J. K. Mackenzie, Urana (N.S.W.)—D.W.—25th September, 1917.
4628, Cpl. D. Watson, Melbourne and Warrnambool (V.)—K.I.A.—25th September, 1917.
5402, Pte. W. H. McPherson,* Geelong (V.)—K.I.A.—25th Sept., 1917.
3533, Sgt. W. E. Williams, Brunswick (V.)—K.I.A.—26th September, 1917.
1184, Sgt. A. C. Hutton, S. Melbourne (V.)—K.I.A.—26th September, 1917.
1960, Cpl. F. C. E. Hunter, Geelong (V.)—K.I.A.—26th September, 1917.
5354, L/Cpl. J. F. Cleary, Echuca (V.)—K.I.A.—26th September, 1917.
6971, Pte. D. Brown, Tallygaroopna (V.)—K.I.A.—26th September, 1917.
6506, Pte. P. Fabian, Footscray (V.)—K.I.A.—26th September, 1917.
6049, Pte. J. T. Lennox, Camperdown (V.)—K.I.A.—26th September, 1917.
7035, L/Cpl. D. T. J. Kearney, Geelong (V.)—K.I.A.—26th Sept., 1917.
7030, Pte. W. H. Hutchinson, Nathalia (V.)—K.I.A.—26th September, 1917.
6085, Pte. P. Rowe, Geelong (V.)—K.I.A.—26th September, 1917.
7343, Pte. W. J. Enright, Deloraine (Tas.)—K.I.A.—26th September, 1917.

---

* The dates allotted to the Polygon Wood casualties in this list are unreliable. The battle lasted three days (26th to 28th September). The total fatal casualties, including D.W. and some casualties incurred on the 24th and 25th, were 3 officers and 37 other ranks. Almost all of these were incurred on the 26th. The lists, however, allot numerous casualties to the 27th and 28th which should have been credited to the 26th. The author has corrected some palpable mistakes, from the evidence of combatants, but many had to remain uncorrected from want of reliable evidence.

380   *The Roll of Honour.*

2551, Sgt. A. J. K. Ayre, Yarraville (V.) and Essex (Eng.)—K.I.A.—26th September, 1917.
1686, Pte. J. Watkins, Richmond (V.)—K.I.A.—26th September, 1917.
7012, Pte. W. Gallagher, Footscray (V.)—K.I.A.—27th September, 1917.
2705, Pte. J. C. Mayberry, Bendigo (V.)—D.W.—27th September, 1917.
4954, Cpl. F. Davis, Ballarat E. (V.)—K.I.A.—27th September, 1917.
6551, Pte. G. L. McCallum, Apsley (V.)—D.W.—27th September, 1917.
5341, L/Cpl. F. Boyd, Pomborneit (V.)—K.I.A.—27th September, 1917.
7020, Pte. S. O. Harris, Metcalfe (V.)—K.I.A.—27th September, 1917.
7277, Pte. P. J. Lyford, Carlton (V.)—K.I.A.—27th September, 1917.
7075, Pte. W. J. Robinson, Merrigum (V.)—K.I.A.—27th September, 1917.
7243, Pte. J. J. Gorrie, E. Brunswick (V.)—K.I.A.—27th September, 1917.
2005, Pte. W. Rowse, M.M., Emmaville (N.S.W.)—K.I.A.—27th September, 1917.
3976, Pte. C. Burns, Geelong (V.)—K.I.A.—28th September, 1917.
5433, Pte. E. Pizer, Geelong (V.)—K.I.A.—28th September, 1917.
6004, Pte. J. Casey, Noorat (V.)—K.I.A.—28th September, 1917.
7305, Pte. A. E. Phipps, Wynyard (Tas.)—K.I.A.—28th September, 1917.
3056, Pte. J. S. Coull, Footscray (V.)—D.W.—28th September, 1917.
7207, Pte. F. W. Brock, Lancefield (V.)—K.I.A.—28th September, 1917.
6857, Pte. J. Davis, London (Eng.)—K.I.A.—28th September, 1917.
1809, Pte. H. G. S. Ellis, Broken Hill (N.S.W.)—D.W.—28th Sept., 1917.
1271, Pte. R. Swale, Inglewood (V.)—D.W.—29th September, 1917.
2363, Pte. T. Connors, Northcote (V.)—D.W.—29th September, 1917.
6051, L/Cpl. A. E. Little, Geelong (V.)—D.W.—30th September, 1917.
5706, Pte. H. Moore, Daylesford (V.)—K.I.A.—10th October, 1917.
1461, L/Cpl. E. J. Davis, M.M., Goorambat (V.)—K.I.A.—13th Oct., 1917.
2352, Pte. J. Clough, Portarlington (V.)—K.I.A.—15th October, 1917.
7376, Pte. A. H. Rhodes, Kensington (V.)—K.I.A.—15th October, 1917.
6711, Pte. R. W. Croker, Newcastle (N.S.W.)—K.I.A.—15th October, 1917.
6017, Pte. J. B. Edwards, Hawkesdale (V.)—K.I.A.—15th October, 1917.
5777, Pte. L. J. Powell, Kyneton (V.)—K.I.A.—15th October, 1917.
2554, Sgt. M. F. W. Kohlmann, Camberwell (V.)—D.W.—16th Oct., 1917.
10, Sgt. H. G. Richmond, M.M., Abbotsford (V.)—D.W.—16th October, 1917.
1807, W.O. A. Pringle, Glenferrie (V.)—D.W.—16th October, 1917.
7004, Pte. E. R. Edwards, Daylesford (V.)—K.I.A.—16th October, 1917.
6125, Cpl. W. T. Primrose, Boolara (V.)—K.I.A.—16th October, 1917.
6340, Pte. T. H. H. Riley, Albert Park (V.)—K.I.A.—16th October, 1917.
5475, Pte. H. S. Viccars, Geelong (V.)—K.I.A.—16th October, 1917.
6755, Pte. E. W. Hubbard, Koorawatha (N.S.W.) and Leicestershire (Eng.)—K.I.A.—16th October, 1917.
1694, Cpl. E. C. Gleed, Melbourne (V.) and London (Eng.)—K.I.A.—16th October, 1917.
5053, Pte. C. Brown, Killarney (V.)—K.I.A.—16th October, 1917.
5449a, Pte. J. H. Spooner, Kyneton (V.)—K.I.A.—16th October, 1917.

## The History of the 14th Battalion. 381

4621, Pte. J. S. Tillotson, Carlton (V.)—K.I.A.—16th October, 1917.
2886, T/Cpl. A. R. Turner, Ararat (V.)—K.I.A.—16th October, 1917.
1284, Cpl. W. E. W. Porter, M.M., Terang (V.)—K.I.A.—21st Oct., 1917.
2350, Sgt. C. Curry, Footscray (V.)—K.I.A.—21st October, 1917.
1409, Pte. J. G. Murphy, Bendigo (V.)—K.I.A.—22nd October, 1917.
7087, Pte. P. Sperling, Tongala (V.)—K.I.A.—22nd October, 1917.
2013, Pte. J. H. Smith, Elmore (V.)—K.I.A.—22nd October, 1917.
7117, Pte. L. J. James, Geelong (V.)—K.I.A.—22nd October, 1917.
6990, Pte. J. Crockett, N. Fitzroy (V.)—K.I.A.—22nd October, 1917.
4906, Pte. J. Purcell, Tourello (V.)—D.I.—3rd November, 1917.
1836, Pte. R. Fuzzard, Tatura (V.)—D.W.—4th November, 1917.
7036, Pte. J. O'N. Kelly, Clifton Hill (V.)—D.W.—5th November, 1917.
213, Pte. A. McK. Hepburn, Newport (V.)—D.I.—12th November, 1917.

1918.

5218, Pte. C. Spencer, Alphington (V.)—K.I.A.—31st January, 1918.
1022, Sgt. O. G. McAllan, Albert Park (V.)—D.W.—1st February, 1918.
6981, Pte. H. B. Challinor, Melbourne (V.) and Cheshire (Eng.)—D.W.—5th February, 1918.
6356, Pte. A. Streeter, Ascot Vale (V.)—D.W.—7th February, 1918.
6715, Pte. R. C. Chew, Young (N.S.W.)—D.W.—10th March, 1918.
1708, Sgt. E. P. Riley, Irrewillipi (V.)—D.I.—22nd March, 1918.
1646, Pte. T. McGuane, Coburg (V.)—D.I.—24th March, 1918.
7196, Pte. R. S. Baird, Lismore (V.)—K.I.A.—24th March, 1918.
2292, Pte. D. Kirby, Carlton (V.)—D.W.—24th March, 1918.
4612, Cpl. R. Spearing, M.M.—Camperdown (V.)—D.W.—28th March, 1918.
7309, Pte. E. B. Revill, Colac (V.)—K.I.A.—29th March, 1918.
676, Pte. G. L. Hughes, Blyth (S.A.)—K.I.A.—29th March, 1918.
1793, Pte. A. W. Yeatman, Elliminyt (V.)—D.W.—29th March, 1918.
677, Pte. L. A. Lambson, Adelaide (S.A.) and London (Eng.)—D.W.—30th March, 1918.
1379, T/Sgt. G. A. H. Murray, Warracknabeal (V.)—K.I.A.—30th March, 1918.
6081, Pte. T. Pollock, Dixie (V.)—K.I.A.—30th March, 1918.
4919, Pte. J. W. Smilie, Richmond (V.)—K.I.A.—30th March, 1918.
7455, Pte. D. A. Teasdale, Rupanyup (V.)—K.I.A.—30th March, 1918.
7332, Pte. E. C. E. Williams, Brunswick (V.)—K.I.A.—30th March, 1918.
3302, Pte. L. Dunn, Richmond (V.)—D.W.—30th March, 1918.
6111, Pte. A. J. Toogood, Warrnambool (V.)—D.W.—7th April, 1918.
4834, Pte. W. H. Johnston, Liverpool (Eng.)—K.I.A.—11th April, 1918.
5447, Pte. A. Simmonds, Hawksburn (V.)—K.I.A.—11th April, 1918.
3488, Pte. T. P. Williams, Dunkeld (V.)—D.W.—18th April, 1918.
2420, Pte. D. Donaldson, Adelaide (S.A.)—K.I.A.—30th April, 1918.
1616, Pte. H. McGill, Belgrave (V.)—K.I.A.—30th April, 1918.
4284, Pte. W. H. Pettavel, Budgerie (V.)—K.I.A.—30th April, 1918.
7019, Pte. J. P. Harrington, Moama (N.S.W.)—K.I.A.—30th April, 1918.

382   *The Roll of Honour.*

6740, Pte. R. E. A. Hall, Grenfell (N.S.W.)—K.I.A.—1st May, 1918.
172, Sgt. H. R. Brown, Malvern (V.)—K.I.A.—3rd May, 1918.
3448, Pte. R. N. Nash, Prahran (V.)—K.I.A.—3rd May, 1918.
6099, Pte. F. J. Skjellerup, Colac (V.)—K.I.A.—3rd May, 1918.
352, L/Cpl. D. L. Morrison, Irymple (V.) and Glasgow (Scotland)—K.I.A. —4th May, 1918.
5660, L/Cpl. P. Aspinall, Echuca (V.)—D.W.—5th May, 1918.
619, C.S.M. J. J. Myers, M.M.—Bendigo (V.)—K.I.A.—5th May, 1918.
2237, Pte. J. T. Gill, Elsternwick (V.)—D.W.—7th May, 1918.
2810, Sgt. C. J. Durham, Coburg (V.)—K.I.A.—13th May, 1918.
5188, Pte. F. H. Porter, M.M., Benalla (V.)—D.W.—14th May, 1918.
4190, L/Cpl. D. J. Ferguson, Morrisons (V.)—K.I.A.—15th May, 1918.
5429, Pte. J. Paisley, Camperdown (V.)—K.I.A.—15th May, 1918.
7083, Pte. J. F. Smith, Ensay (V.) and Portsmouth (Eng.)—D.W.—17th May, 1918.
2683, Pte. W. E. Hadler, Illabarook (V.)—K.I.A.—18th May, 1918.
4591, Pte. J. M. Picken, Casterton (V.)—K.I.A.—18th May, 1918.
6997, Pte. W. Dawe, Codrington (V.)—D.W.—20th May, 1918.
6771, Pte. J. O. Lugton, Wagga Wagga (N.S.W.)—D.W.—28th May, 1918.
2152, Pte. T. Brinkworth, Brisbane (Q.) and Wiltshire (Eng.)—K.I.A.—31st May, 1918.
7342, Pte. B. G. Englert, Drummoyne (N.S.W.)—K.I.A.—31st May, 1918.
6221, Pte. C. Ballis, Warrnambool (V.)—K.I.A.—31st May, 1918.
4760, Cpl. S. E. Beverley, Ballangeich (V.) and Essex (Eng.)—K.I.A.—31st May, 1918.
2240, Pte. R. Delaney, Nirranda (V.)—K.I.A.—31st May, 1918.
5764, Pte. L. A. Downey, Thornton (V.)—K.I.A.—31st May, 1918.
1872, L/Cpl. J. H. Dunn, Trentham (V.)—K.I.A.—31st May, 1918.
266, Pte. L. Hustler, Penshurst (V.)—K.I.A.—31st May, 1918.
602, L/Cpl. H. A. G. Kent, Malvern (V.) and Bournemouth (Eng.)—K.I.A.—31st May, 1918.
6126, Pte. R. Madigan, Chewton (V.)—K.I.A.—31st May, 1918.
1383, L/Cpl. R. Mann, South Shields (Eng.) and Melbourne (V.)—K.I.A. —31st May, 1918.
7606, Pte. W. Wootton, Rockhampton (Q.)—K.I.A.—31st May, 1918.
55a, Pte. N. McLeod, Condah (V.)—K.I.A.—31st May, 1918.
7588, Pte. G. W. Powell, Fitzroy (V.)—K.I.A.—31st May, 1918.
5757, Pte. G. Ray, Mansfield (V.)—K.I.A.—31st May, 1918.
2750, Pte. A. T. Riley, Elsternwick (V.)—K.I.A.—31st May, 1918.
5344, Cpl. P. Brennan, D.C.M., Benalla (V.)—D.W.—31st May, 1918.
231, Pte. A. V. Green, Birchip (V.)—D.W.—31st May, 1918.
7522, Pte. C. E. Leigh, Dandenong (V.)—D.W.—31st May, 1918.
7080, Pte. A. E. Smith, Carlton (V.)—D.W.—31st May, 1918.
5682a, Pte. A. M. Evans, Coburg (V.)—D.W.—31st May, 1918.
4877, Pte. G. V. Reddish, Albert Park (V.)—D.W.—31st May, 1918.

## The History of the 14th Battalion. 383

1668a, Pte. A. R. Anderson, Nhill (V.)—K.I.A.—31st May, 1918.
2491, Dvr. G. C. Mills, Bruthen (V.)—D.W.—31st May, 1918.
6612, Pte. L. E. J. Witcombe, Winchelsea (V.)—D.W.—31st May, 1918.
1734, Pte. G. D. Radnell, M.M., Tarnagulla (V.)—D.W.—1st June, 1918.
1868, Pte. L. Best, Belgrave (V.)—D.W.—4th June, 1918.
6733, Pte. H. J. Gibb, Tumut (N.S.W.)—K.I.A.—7th June, 1918.
6734, Pte. R. Gulliksen, Pyrmont (N.S.W.)—K.I.A.—7th June, 1918.
3442, Pte. F. R. Newbold, Richmond (V.)—D.W.—8th June, 1918.
5429a, Pte. J. P. Quinn, Brunswick (V.)—D.A.—9th June, 1918.
1805, Pte. H. W. Delora, Prahran (V.)—D.W.—13th June, 1918.
6318, Cpl. F. Mears, South Yarra (V.)—K.I.A.—15th June, 1918.
6139, L/Sgt. E. Harrison, M.M., Maffra (V.)—K.I.A.—16th June, 1918.
6330, L/Cpl. W. O'Dowd, Wangerrip (V.)—K.I.A.—16th June, 1918.
1503, Sgt. H. R. W. Anderson, M.M., St. Kilda (V.)—D.W.—16th June, 1918.
5384, Pte. A. Hawkins, Seymour (V.)—K.I.A.—18th June, 1918.
7071, L/Cpl. W. A. Read, Clifton Hill (V.)—K.I.A.—18th June, 1918.
1330, A/Sgt. F. J. Banyard, London (Eng.)—K.I.A.—20th June, 1918.
2318, Pte. W. A. Harding, Brunswick (V.)—K.I.A.—20th June, 1918.
2875, Pte. T. Taynton. St. Arnaud (V.)—K.I.A.—20th June, 1918.
5694, Pte. H. Lawry, Echuca (V.)—D.W.—22nd June, 1918.
4506, Pte. W. R. Hancock, Northcote (V.)—D.W.—22nd June, 1918.
6331, Pte. A. E. O'Shea, Richmond (V.)—D.W.—4th July, 1918.
6859, Pte. L. H. Hawksbee, Mittagong (N.S.W.) and London (Eng.)—D.W.—4th July, 1918.
1709, Sgt. W. T. Fisher, Camperdown (V.)—K.I.A.—4th July, 1918.
5394, Pte. W. L. Hughes, Collingwood (V.)—K.I.A.—4th July, 1918.
317, Pte D. W. Floyd, Wangaratta (V.)—K.I.A.—4th July, 1918.
5762, Cpl. H. S. Cochrane, Poowong (V.)—K.I.A.—4th July, 1918.
2626, Pte. C. E. Thomas, St. Kilda (V.)—K.I.A.—5th July, 1918
5747, Pte. F. D. Ward, Bacchus Marsh (V.)—D.W.—15th July, 1918.
5404, Cpl. H. H. Lewis, Donald (V.)—K.I.A.—1st August, 1918.
7484, Pte. C. G. Ekenberg, Gaffe (Sweden)—K.I.A.—4th August, 1918.
6998, Pte. C. J. Donoghue, Echuca (V.)—D.W.—8th August, 1918.
7604, Pte. V. W. Norman, Colac (V.)—D.W.—8th August, 1918.
5729, L/Cpl. T. Richardson, Footscray (V.)—D.W.—8th August, 1918.
7436, Pte. H. W. Adams, Moonee Ponds (V.)—K.I.A.—8th August, 1918.
2333, Pte. A. Aitken, Sale (V.)—K.I.A.—8th August, 1918.
7444, Pte. C. C. Bell, Fairfield Park (V.)—K.I.A.—8th August, 1918.
6977, Pte. A. Cameron, Melton (V.)—K.I.A.—8th August, 1918.
7231, Pte. J. A. Dix, Sale (V.)—K.I.A.—8th August, 1918.
7014, Pte. S. G. Garner, Kamarooka (V.) and Surrey (Eng.)—K.I.A.—8th August, 1918.
7021, Pte. J. F. Harvey, Murrurundi (N.S.W.)—K.I.A.—8th August, 1918.
4344, Cpl. G. A. Heron, Newport (V.)—K.I.A.—8th August, 1918.
5683, Pte. W. T. Hopley, N. Carlton (V.)—K.I.A.—8th August, 1918.

384          *The Roll of Honour.*

5398, Pte. N. McD. Jenkins, Grasmere (V.)—K.I.A.—8th August, 1918.
5398a, Pte. H. J. Lamprell, M.M., Wonthaggi (V.)—K.I.A.—8th Aug., 1918.
7285, Cpl. J. J. Moriarty, Melbourne (V.) and Ashburton (N.Z.)—K.I.A.—8th August, 1918.
293a, Sgt. A. S. Smith, M.M., Clifton Hill (V.)—K.I.A.—8th August, 1918.
2433, Pte. R. C. Thomas, St. Kilda (V.)—K.I.A.—8th August, 1918.
2450, L/Sgt. A. J. D. Waddell, Beechworth (V.)—K.I.A.—8th August, 1918.
5097a, Pte. J. R. Grist, Skipton (V.)—K.I.A.—8th August, 1918.
1945, Cpl. C. H. D. Goddard, Ballarat (V.)—K.I.A.—8th August, 1918.
5999, L/Cpl. J. Craig, Melbourne (V.) and Antrim (Ireland)—D.W.—9th August, 1918.
1642, Pte. H. Thornton, Goornong (V.)—D.W.—10th August, 1918.
6134, Pte. L. J. P. Casey, Geelong (V.)—K.I.A.—16th August, 1918.
2894a, Pte. G. R. Lancaster, Essendon (V.)—K.I.A.—18th August, 1918
6517, Pte. W. Humphries, Northcote (V.)—D.W.—18th August, 1918.
3342, Cpl. W. J. Harding, M.M., Toorborac (V.)—K.I.A.—20th Aug., 1918.
3571, Pte. A. Sherlock, Piggoreet (V.)—K.I.A.—20th August, 1918.
7181, Pte. J. Smith, South Yarra (V.)—D.W.—21st August, 1918.
2357, L/Cpl. A. Currie, M.M., Edinburgh (Scotland) and Melbourne (V.)—D.W.—23rd August, 1918.
2640, Pte. G. S. Smith, Collingwood (V.)—D.W.—5th September, 1918.
1509, Pte. A. G. Spendlove, Geelong (V.)—D.I.—15th September, 1918.
1116, S/Sgt. B. V. Almond, Geelong (V.)—K.I.A.—18th September, 1918.
676, Cpl. H. A. Anderson, M.M., Collingwood (V.)—K.I.A.—18th September, 1918.
1812, Pte. A. A. Fletcher, Collingwood (V.)—K.I.A.—18th September, 1918.
7489, Pte. J. H. Foster, Melbourne (V.) and Birmingham (Eng.)—K.I.A.—18th September, 1918.
7023, Pte. G. N. Hein, Kyneton (V.)—K.I.A.—18th September, 1918.
7518, Pte. C. F. James, Omeo (V.)—K.I.A.—18th September, 1918.
141, Cpl. L. R. Jones, M.M., Essendon (V.)—K.I.A.—18th Sept., 1918.
7073, Cpl. A. E. Ristrom, Rushworth (V.)—K.I.A.—18th September, 1918.
2429, Sgt. C. C. Serjeant, Burnley (V.)—K.I.A.—18th September, 1918.
2643, Pte. H. F. S. Skidmore, Footscray (V.)—K.I.A.—18th Sept., 1918.
4309, Pte. A. W. Smith, Sebastopol (V.)—K.I.A.—18th September, 1918.
737, Pte. J. Smith, Port Melbourne (V.)—K.I.A.—18th September, 1918.
7006, L/Cpl. M. L. Evans, S. Melbourne (V.)—K.I.A.—18th Sept., 1918.
4365, Pte. J. Bracken, Richmond (V.)—K.I.A.—19th September, 1918.
7451, Pte. P. Brady, Ararat (V.)—K.I.A.—19th September, 1918.
151, Pte. H. J. Wright, Essendon (V.)—K.I.A.—19th September, 1918.
7578, Pte. J. Witt, Bairnsdale (V.)—D.W.—19th September, 1918.
6999, Pte. H. J. Douglas, Melbourne (V.)—D.W.—20th September, 1918.
7448, Sgt. L. R. Bauchop, Williamstown (V.)—K.I.A.—20th Sept., 1918.
2402, Sgt. A. A. Johnstone, Clifton Hill (V.)—D.W.—20th September, 1918.
6550, Pte. J. A. McMillan, Lauriston (V.)—D. while P.W.—25th September, 1918.

## The History of the 14th Battalion.

3270, Sgt. H. B. Clark, Sebastopol (V.)—D.W.—7th October, 1918.
1952, Pte. M. Harrison, M.M., Euroa (V.)—D.I.—22nd October, 1918.
145, Pte. E. S. Wearne, Brighton (V.)—D.I.—31st October, 1918.
1339, L/Cpl. C. F. Bromfield, Childers (V.)—D.I.—7th November, 1918.
2580, Cpl. M. J. Doyle, Yarrawonga (V.)—D.I.—24th November, 1918.
6016a, Pte. F. W. Fay, Ballarat (V.)—D.I.—28th November, 1918.
688, Pte. W. R. W. West, Brighton (S.A.)—D.I.—3rd December, 1918.
5423, Pte. J. N. Pell, Kyabram (V.)—D.I.—3rd December, 1918.
5765, Pte. J. J. Francis, Glengarry (V.)—D.I.—30th December, 1918.

1919.

7284, Pte. D. McDougall, Lakes Entrance (V.)—D.I.—31st January, 1919.
6994, Pte. R. Davies, Richmond (V.)—D.Inj.—14th February, 1919.
84, Pte. W. Lovett, Port Melbourne (V.)—D.I.—25th February, 1919.

## APPENDIX B.

### DECORATIONS AND MENTIONED IN DESPATCHES.

It may be said briefly that, the longer the war lasted, the more freely were decorations distributed. At Gallipoli they were few and far between; in 1918 they were distributed with considerable freedom. It is worthy of note that some who performed eminent services for the Battalion failed to receive decorations. Among them may be mentioned Chaplain Capt. Gillison, Capt. Loughran (R.M.O.), Capt. "Lofty" Williamson, and Lieut.-Col. Crowther. One paramount distinction accruing to the 14th was, that one of its number secured the first Victoria Cross awarded to an Australian in the Great War.

The distinctions earned by member of the unit were 251. Three decorations each were gained by four 14th Battalion men, viz.: Capt. Albert Jacka (Wedderburn, V.), the O.C. of D Company; Lieut. Chas. Thompson (Orbost, V.), C Company, and Intelligence Officer; Sgt. Chas. J. Clarke (Tasmania), signaller; and Cpl. V. W. Lalor (Healesville, V.), Lewis gunner of No. 10 Platoon (C Company).

The names of the recipients are arranged in alphabetical order, with the rank at the time of the award. Those who are deceased are marked with an asterisk.

#### Victoria Cross (V.C.)
Lance-Corporal Albert Jacka.

#### Companion of the Order of the Bath (C.B.)
Lieut.-Colonel Richard Edmond Courtney.*

#### Distinguished Service Order (D.S.O.)
Lieut.-Colonel C. M. M. Dare (Gallipoli)
Lieut.-Colonel J. H. Peck* (afterward, when on 5th Div. Headquarters, awarded C.M.G.)
Major Robert Rankine (Gallipoli)
Major W. R. Wadsworth (M.C.)
Lieut. H. B. Wanliss*

#### Military Cross (M.C.)

Capt. N. C. Aldridge (awarded bar to M.C.)
Capt. W. R. M. Beamond
Capt. A. R. Blainey
C.S.M. W. P. Boland (awarded bar to M.C.)
Lieut. A. R. Bruford
Capt C. R. T. Cole
Lieut. George Cooper (Gallipoli)
Lieut. G. F. Davies
Lieut. A. R. Dean*
Lieut. H. S. Dobbie*

## The History of the 14th Battalion.

**Military Cross—Continued.**

Lieut. T. M. Grant
Lieut. T. H. Griffith
Capt. S. M. Hansen*
Lieut. Albert Jacka, V.C. (awarded bar to M.C.)
Lieut. J. H. Johnson* (awarded bar to M.C.)
Capt. R. W. Jones, M.M.
Capt. J. A. Mitchell

Major (Chaplain) F. W. Rolland
Lieut. E. J. Rule, M.M.
Lieut. H. J. A. Schutz
Lieut. H. W. Thompson*
Lieut. G. T. Trewheela
Capt. H. C. Trumble
Capt. W. R. Wadsworth
Capt. N. Wilson

### Bar to Military Cross.

Capt. N. C. Aldridge
Lieut. W. P. Boland

Capt. Albert Jacka, V.C.
Lieut. J. H. Johnson*

### Distinguished Conduct Medal (D.C.M.)

3255, T/C.Q.M.S. A. J. Beaton
1672, Sgt. W. H. Boyes, M.M.
5344 Cpl. Patrick Brennan*
38, Sgt. Geo. Bullen
1578, Cpl. C. J. Clarke, M.M.
2464, C.S.M. W. Coleman, M.M.
5995, R.S.M. Leslie Collins
4185, Cpl. W. H. Fergus
6022, Cpl. T. H. French, M.M.
197, Sgt. R. J. Garcia
6290, Sgt. R. A. Jeffers, M.M.
5688, Cpl. V. W. Lalor, M.M. and Bar
3409, Sgt. C. H. Mayer

742, C.Q.M.S. T. J. Mew*
3391, Sgt. J. F. McPherson
3388, L/Sgt. John McRae*
1542, Sgt. M. J. O'Brien (Gallipoli)
374, Sgt. G. A. Ross*
2433, C.Q.M.S. W. F. P. Ryan
528, L/Cpl. Roger Scanlon M.M.
7316, Pte. J. L. Schmit
269, Sgt. J. S. Stewart
392, Sgt. Chas. Thompson, M.M. and Bar
2028, Sgt. Archibald Urie*

### Military Medal (M.M.)

3226, T/Q.M.S. A. J. A'Court (A.A.M.C., attached to 14th Battalion)
3228, Pte. Chas. Alexander
5557, Cpl. Wm. Allwood
2784, Pte. Wm. Amor
545, Sgt. Fredk. Anderson
676, Cpl. H. A. Anderson*
1503, L/Sgt. H. R. W. Anderson*
5330, Cpl. W. J. Baker
1336, Cpl. J. E. Barker

14, Sgt. N. Bear
6923, Sgt. W. R. Bell
6704, Sgt. W. Berry
294, Cpl. E. E. Bishop
416, Sgt. D. W. Blackburn
4143, Pte. Wm. Blake
3252, Cpl. C. E. Booker
1672, Sgt. W. H. Boyes
2792, Pte. V. Bradley
7387, Pte. P. P. Butterworth
2769, Sgt. C. J. M. Campbell

## Military Medal—Continued.

1363, Cpl. Thos. Carberry (A.A.M.C., attached to 14th Battalion)
2734, Pte. J. G. Casson
1578, L/Cpl. C. J. Clarke
5994, Cpl. H. C. Clements
840, Pte. Wm. A. Cox
2464, Sgt. Wm. Coleman
3265, Driver James Cooper
6804, Pte. Wm. Crocker
2357, L/Cpl. Adam Currie*
2589, Sgt. Denis Curry
2579, Sgt. F. W. Dalitz
1461, Pte. E. J. Davis*
1700, L/Cpl. J. M. Deacon
5080, Driver R. E. G. Denham
1932, Pte. Fredk. Dennison
4650, L/Cpl. G. A. Dietrich
5312, Pte. A. R. Dodemaide*
4172, Sgt. David Drummond
2373, L/Cpl. W. J. Earll
442, Pte. R. W. C. Eddy
6011, Pte. Rudolph Fechner
1175, Pte. W. J. Fitzpatrick
5376, Sgt. W. H. Fletcher
3761, L/Cpl. S. A. Foster
1559, Cpl. J. R. H. Franklin
6022, Cpl. T. H. French
197, Sgt. R. J. Garcia, D.C.M.
994, Pte. W. A. Gill
4200, Sgt. F. A. Goode
6735, Cpl. Wm. Goodsell
8, Cpl. W. W. Goodwin*
4203, Pte. Alfred Gray
3328, Cpl. James Grieves
1861, Pte. R. V. Gubby
5110, Pte. P. D. Hamilton
61, Cpl. F. J. W. Harding*
3342, Cpl. W. J. Harding*
62, Driver B. Hardner
5112, Pte. Norman Harris
6139, L/Cpl. Edward Harrison*
1952, Pte. Maurice Harrison*
7257, Pte. H. L. Herlitz
717, Sgt. E. P. Hill (Gallipoli)
3803, Pte. W. J. Hodge
3811, Sgt. A. A. Hore
2607, Pte. T. V. Hughes
1692, Cpl. P. G. Hume
6858, Cpl. A. C. Hutton
2833, L/Cpl. H. N. Ingamells
1321, Pte. John Inglis
5129, Pte. W. J. Jackson*
6290, L/Sgt. R. A. Jeffers
5131, Pte. Wm. Johnson
141, Cpl. L. R. Jones*
80, Cpl. R. W. Jones (Gallipoli)
6046, Cpl. A. C. Kilby
3377, Pte. E. L. Kohls
5638, Cpl. V. W. Lalor
5398, Pte. H. J. Lamprell*
5149, Cpl. Alex. Lee
4534, Pte. John Lee
6775, Cpl. H. G. Lovejoy
6052, Pte. G. K. Lovekin
5695, Pte. F. A. V. Lowe
4543, Cpl. J. P. Lumsden
1598, Pte. S. A. Markham*
5161, Pte. J. J. Marmo
3543, Pte. Wm. Marriott
1384, Pte. A. E. Mattison
7602, Pte. C. Metcalf
5407, Pte. Abraham Milner
3424, L/Cpl. Percy F. Muir
619, Cpl. J. J. Myers*
4889, L/Cpl. J. McCormick
7048, L/Cpl. A. McDonald
59, Sgt. A. B. McLennan
4574, Pte. P. McMahon
4258, Pte. K. N. McNamee*
1685, Driver Wm. Nolan
1656, Pte. R. M. Norman
2342, Pte. F. G. Notting
1798, Pte. J. O'Brien
7055, Pte. P. F. O'Dowd
3450, Pte. H. L. Parman
487, L/Cpl. B. H. Perry
7066, L/Cpl. Chas. H. Platt
1284, L/Cpl. W. E. W. Porter*
1995, Cpl. C. B. Postlethwaite*

## The History of the 14th Battalion.

**Military Medal**—Continued.

1734, Pte. G. D. Radnell*
10, Sgt. H. G. Richmond*
1808, Cpl. George Robb
6871, Pte. G. W. L. Rofe
2005, Pte. Wallace Rowse*
2636, Sgt. E. J. Rule
2635, Pte. W. H. Rutherford
3258, Pte. E. C. Saunders
528, C.S.M. Roger Scanlon,
6357, Cpl. H. R. Scott
7605, Pte. W. T. Serjeant
293, Sgt. A. S. Smith*
5466, Sgt. H. J. Somerville
4615, Cpl. R. Spearing*
922, Sgt. Robert Stanley

1512, Driver J. P. Taylor
392, Cpl. Chas. Thompson
714, Pte. H. L. Thompson
7094, Pte. John Thomson
2889, Pte. H. Twining
799, Pte. F. H. Voce
6122, Pte. Wm. Watson
6614, Cpl. L. A. Webb
283, Cpl. Albert Webber
6829, Pte. Ernest Wilkinson
4331, Pte. G. A. Willison
2040, Pte. H. D. E. Withers
1307, Pte. N. T. Wynne (Gallipoli)

### Bar to Military Medal

1578, Cpl. C. J. Clarke, D.C.M.
5376, Sgt. W. H. Fletcher
5638, Cpl. V. W. Lalor
1598, L/Cpl. S. A. Markham*
7066, L/Cpl. Chas. H. Platt

2635, Cpl. W. H. Rutherford
392, Sgt. Chas. Thompson
6122, Pte. Wm. Watson
6829, L/Cpl. Ernest Wilkinson

### Meritorious Service Medal (M.S.M.)

952, Sgt. C. A. Bruckner
4229, C.Q.M.S. T. J. Jenkins*
1009, C.Q.M.S. N. A. Kent*
751, Sgt. C. L. S. Marshall

3421, L/Cpl. J. A. Merrill
914, Cpl. F. L. Russell
2557, Sgt. B. O. W. Timms

### Mentioned in Despatches (M.I.D.)

Capt. N. C. Aldridge
Lieut. F. W. Appleton*
5333, Cpl. Daniel Baxter
2nd-Lieut. W. R. M. Beamond
Lieut. F. H. Boyes
2769, C.S.M. C. J. M. Campbell
Lieut. G. H. Clarendon-Hyde
1363, Cpl. Thos. Carberry
Lieut. George Cooper
Lieut.-Col. R. E. Courtney*
Lieut.-Col. C. M. M. Dare (twice)

49, C.S.M. Stephen De Arango
Lieut. R. J. Garcia
Chaplain Capt. Gillison*
Lieut. O. C. D. Gower
1202, Sgt. A. J. Harris*
Capt. P. J. Hayes
Q.M. and Hon. Capt. R. E. Hayes
1304, L/Cpl. Geo. Huse
4229, L/Sgt. T. J. Jenkins*
Lieut. J. H. Johnson* (twice)
H/Capt. and Q.M. W. G. Laver

## Appendices.

**Mentioned in Despatches**—Continued.

3573, Pte. J. P. Nesbitt
1542, Sgt. M. J. O'Brien
526, Sgt. Wm. Oram
Lieut.-Col. J. H. Peck*
Major R. Rankine

Sgt. F. C. W. Symonds
Major W. R. Wadsworth
Lieut. H. B. Wanliss*
Lieut. Ramsay Wood*

### Order of the British Empire (O.B.E.)

Lieut.-Col. T. H. Steel

### FOREIGN DECORATIONS.

#### Croix de Guerre.

5970, Pte. S. W. Adams
Lieut. F. W. Appleton*

Major A. R. Cox
3490, Sgt. George Shields

#### Medaille Militaire.

6961, Pte. C. R. F. Beard
771, Cpl. James Reid

201, C.Q.M S. A. L. Guppy

### SUMMARY.

| | |
|---|---:|
| V.C. | 1 |
| C.B. | 1 |
| D.S.O. | 5 |
| M.C. | 25 |
| D.C.M. | 24 |
| M.M. | 136 |
| M.S.M. | 7 |
| O.B.E. | 1 |
| Foreign | 7 |
| **Bars** | |
| M.C. | 4 |
| M.M. | 9 |
| | 220 |
| Mentioned in Despatches | 31 |
| Total | 251 |

## APPENDIX C.

### A.I.F. AND 4th BRIGADE CASUALTIES.

The total number of enlistments in the A.I.F. during the war was 416,809, whilst embarkations from Australia totalled 331,781. The deaths incurred numbered 59,038 (considerably more than one per cent. of the then population of the continent), whilst the total casualties were set out as 225,855.

The 4th Brigade suffered the heaviest losses incurred by any Australian Brigade in the Gallipoli campaign, the 15th Battalion casualties being by far the heaviest of any A.I.F. unit there. In France, the 7th Brigade suffered most severely, the 25th Battalion incurring the heaviest unit losses.

The following list (according to official figures) comprises the total battle casualties of the four infantry units of the 4th Brigade in the Gallipoli campaign and in France and Belgium:—

| Unit. | Gallipoli Casualties. | France and Belgium Casualties. |
|---|---|---|
| 13th Battalion | 785 | 2,694 |
| 14th Battalion | 737 | 2,690 |
| 15th Battalion | 1,095 | 2,554 |
| 16th Battalion | 834 | 2,633 |
| | 3,451 | 10,571 |

Grand Total for the Brigade during the war:—14,022.

## APPENDIX D.

The following war statistics of the British Empire are interesting. They are taken from the Australian Encyclopædia, but founded on official figures. The high percentage of Australian and New Zealand casualties are noteworthy.

| Country. | Troops Raised. | Troops Sent Overseas. | Total Casualties. | Killed, Died, Missing. | Percentage of Casualties to Numbers Engaged. |
|---|---|---|---|---|---|
| United Kingdom | 5,704,416 | 5,000,000 | 2,626,743 | 1,010,001 | 52¼ |
| Canada | 628,964 | 411,834 | 210,151 | 60,425 | 51 |
| Australia | 416,809 | 330,000 | 226,073 | 59,285 | 68½ |
| New Zealand | 105,629 | 99,822 | 57,887 | 16,483 | 58 |
| South Africa | 228,907 | 228,907* | 18,718 | 7,274 | 8¼ |
| Newfoundland | 11,922 | 11,922 | 3,509 | 1,195 | 30 |
| India | 1,401,350 | 953,374 | 104,684 | 43,695 | 11 |

\* Includes 92,837 coloured troops used for labour and transport. South Africa was a theatre of war.

## APPENDIX E.

### SOME A.I.F. STATISTICS.

A.I.F. embarkations from Australia by religions:—

| | |
|---|---:|
| Church of England | 162,774 |
| Presbyterian | 49,631 |
| Roman Catholic | 63,705 |
| Methodist | 33,706 |
| Jews | 1,214 |
| Other Denominations | 20,751 |
| | 331,781 |

Embarkation from Australia according to places of birth:—

| | |
|---|---:|
| Victoria | 92,553 |
| New South Wales | 88,250 |
| Queensland | 28,253 |
| South Australia | 27,761 |
| Western Australia | 8,042 |
| Tasmania | 13,104 |
| United Kingdom | 64,221 |
| New Zealand | 4,214 |
| Other British Countries | 2,246 |
| Foreign Countries | 3,137 |
| | 331,781 |

Enlistments in the A.I.F., according to States, to 1st September, 1918:—

| | |
|---|---:|
| New South Wales | 161,821 |
| Victoria | 111,305 |
| Queensland | 57,084 |
| South Australia | 34,566 |
| Western Australia | 32,028 |
| Tasmania | 15,262 |
| | 412,066 |

### DECORATIONS.

A grand total of 3879 British decorations was awarded to A.I.F. officers and nurses, to 30th June, 1919, and 12,935 to other A.I.F. ranks. These included 63 V.C.'s, 610 D.S.O.'s, 2355 M.C.'s, 1756 D.C.M.'s, and 9449 M.M.'s. Foreign decorations numbering 258 were awarded A.I.F. officers and nurses, and 578 to other A.I.F. ranks.

## APPENDIX F.

### BATTLE HONOURS.

The following are the 14th Battalion Battle Honours, as approved by His Majesty the King in March, 1927:—

LANDING AT ANZAC
Anzac
Defence of Anzac
Suvla
SARI BAIR
Gallipoli 1915
Egypt 1915-16
France and Flanders 1916-18.
Somme 1916, 1918
POZIERES
BULLECOURT
MESSINES 1917
YPRES 1917
Menin Road
POLYGON WOOD
Passchendaele
Arras 1918
Ancre 1918
HAMEL
AMIENS
Albert 1918
HINDENBURG LINE
Epehy.

All infantry battalions throughout the Empire are entitled to not more than ten battle honours on their regimental colours.

Those in block letters have been emblazoned on the regimental colours of the 14th Battalion, Australian Military Forces, as custodians of the traditions of the 14th Battalion, A.I.F.

## APPENDIX G.

### BROTHERS KILLED.

The following is a list of brothers who lost their lives fighting in the ranks of the Battalion, or died as the result of injuries or disease incurred on war service. The list does not profess to be complete, as, in some cases of possible brothers, essential information has been lacking.

757, Sgt. C. McDermott—K.I.A.—27th April, 1915.
85, Pte. S. McDermott—D.W.—5th May, 1915.
741, Pte. H. A. Mew—K.I.A.—3rd May, 1915.
742, C.Q.M.S. J. T. Mew,[1] D.C.M.—Died.
1974, Pte. J. Lampard—D.W.—10th August, 1915.
734, Pte. G. T. Lampard—K.I.A.—10th August, 1916.
3808, Pte. G. W. Holland—K.I.A.—1st July, 1916
3807, Pte. C. S. Holland—D.W.—28th August, 1916.
4256, Pte. C. Moore } twins { —K.I.A.—3rd July, 1916.
4257, Pte. I. Moore            —K.I.A.—3rd July, 1916.
756, Sgt. H. Lewis—K.I.A.—7th August, 1916.
1166, Pte. P. W. Lewis—K.I.A.—11th April, 1917.
79, Sgt. R. L. Jones—K.I.A.—11th April, 1917.
141, Cpl. L. R. Jones, M.M.—K.I.A.—18th Sept., 1918.
4247, Pte. A. Markham—K.I.A.—11th April, 1917.
1598, L/Cpl. S. A. Markham, M.M. and Bar—K.I.A.—11th June, 1917.
1709, Sgt. W. T. Fisher—K.I.A.—4th July, 1918.
1711, Pte. L. Fisher[2]—D.I.—7th February, 1920.
2481, Pte. C. S. Barnes—K.I.A.—8th August, 1916.
2896a, Pte. H. H. Barnes—K.I.A.—8th August, 1916.

---

[1] Date of death of T. J. Mew unknown.
[2] Pte. Fisher died in Caulfield Military Hospital as the result of war service.

396          *Appendices.*

## APPENDIX H.

### DETAILS.

The following is a list of the personnel contained in certain battalion details (at the outset of the campaign in France), taken from Chaplain Cope's records. The stretcher-bearers, who are fully dealt with in Chapter XIV., have not been included.

#### Machine-Gun Section.

336, Sgt. A. King; 416, Sgt. D. W. Blackburn; 1376, Cpl. J. H. Laidlaw; 1228, L/Cpl. R. E. Antill; 2054, L/Cpl. N. K. Buckman; 1256, L/Cpl. Chas. Farnbach; 109, L/Cpl. H. Perry; 4439, Pte. A. R. Barrett; 422, Pte. F. Brash; 2583, Pte. A. W. Day; 3303, Pte. Jas. Dickson; 3315, Pte. Wm. Eckhardt; 2381, Pte. H. G. E. Finger; 3768, Pte. P. Gabell; 2931, Pte. H. J. Gillies; 2606, Pte. C. S. Hall; 1723, Pte. C. J. Harris; 650, Pte. A. Hollywood; 3811, Pte. A. A. Hore; 1960, Pte. F. C. E. Hunter; 2945, Pte. S. F. Jorgensen; 3844, Pte. C. G. McKenzie; 2663, Pte. A. Murphy; 3444, Pte. W. T. C. Nicholl; 301, Pte. H. Pike; 658, Pte. W. A. Smith; 2883, Pte. G. A. Trewhitt; 2655, Pte. R. Wheeler.

#### Pioneers.

1022, Sgt. O. G. McAllan; 943, Cpl. R. Andrews; 577, L/Cpl. J. T. P. Edwards; 2566, Pte. P. C. S. Bland; 964, Pte. J. Clark; 943, Pte. C. McD. Crowl; 440, Pte. G. H. Dickinson; 2374, Pte. W. G. D. Edgar; 1706, Pte. W. Shaw; 2473, Pte. L. Shelton; 273, Pte. E. Townsend.

#### Signallers.

14, Sgt. N. J. Bear; 8, Cpl. W. W. Goodwin; 1151, L/Cpl. B. Brodal; 1878, L/Cpl. C. J. Clarke; 2392, L/Cpl. C. H. Ditterich; 578, L/Cpl. W. S. Evans; 4347, Pte. P. J. Borthwick; 2352, Pte. J. Clough; 1744, Pte. J. W. Gaw; 2589, Pte. M. H. Griffith; 4344, Pte. N. A. Groening; 2355, Pte. J. T. Gifford; 3318, Pte. G. B. Fielden; 2444, Pte. R. B. Hallett; 2635, Pte. W. H. Rutherford; 2754, Pte. R. Y. Smith; 2447, Pte. A. W. Thiel; 994, Pte. W. A. Gill; 1652, Pte. F. L. Ruggles.

#### A.M.C. Details.

1363, Cpl. T. Carberry; 3226, Pte. A. J. a'Court; 3232, Pte. W. H. Bruckner; 3334, Pte. A. H. A. Giroud; 3345, Pte. H. E. Hasselbach.

## APPENDIX I.

### THE 14th BATTALION A.M.F.

The 14th Battalion, Australian Military Forces, has, since the war, been allied to the Prince of Wales' Own West Yorkshire Regiment of the British Army; to the Waikato Regiment of Hamilton, New Zealand; and to the Royal Montreal Regiment of Westmount, Canada.

## APPENDIX I.

### RATIONS IN FRANCE.

By No. 1679, Cpl. Chas. Smith, 5th Platoon, B Company, 14th Battalion.

On active service, rations are divided into three classes: Wet, dry, and iron rations. Wet rations consist of tea, stew, fried or boiled bacon, porridge, boiled rice, pork and beans, and such like. Dry rations comprised (per man): ¼ loaf of bread, ⅛ tin (¼ lb.) jam, and a small piece of cheese, the latter every alternate day. Biscuits were also generally available in unlimited quantities. Iron rations were simply "bully" beef and biscuits; they were always on issue immediately before going into action, and the "diggers" simply helped themselves. A pound tin of beef was carried, with sufficient biscuits to last 48 hours. The iron ration was only to be consumed in case of emergency, and was always carried on the person. Indeed, it was regarded as of equal importance to the equipment of a soldier as was his field dressing or identity disc.

When out of the line, rations were issued thus: Dry rations every day about 4 p.m. Each Company Quartermaster-Sergeant took three or four men to the Battalion Q.M.'s store, and drew his company's rations, obtaining, beforehand, the ration strength from the company clerk. The C.Q.M.S. then divided the rations into four platoon lots, including signallers, etc., and issued them to platoon sergeants. The latter in turn issued them to section commanders, who finally passed the rations on to the men under them. Wet rations were not issued by platoons when a company was out of the line. The Orderly Corporal for the company took a small ration party of men to the cook-house, drew the meal (including generally two or three dixies of tea each meal per company) and supervised its distribution. The men lined up in a queue, and two or three lance-corporals portioned out the tea and stew with their own mess-tins. Fried bacon was usually issued (with tea) for breakfast; and stew (made with fresh meat) for lunch, or midday meal. "Tea and tea," as the "diggers" said, was issued at tea time. For this meal, the dry rations (bread and jam) were in evidence.

Comforts Fund money was sometimes available to each company, and was spent to the best advantage. Oatmeal was occasionally an official issue, therefore, when the unit was out of the line and billeted near a farmhouse (as was generally the case), the officer entrusted with his company's share of the fund asked the orderly corporal to arrange with the French householder to supply sufficient milk on certain mornings for the company's need. Porridge and milk made an acceptable dish for tired troops on cold mornings. Again, potatoes and onions were purchased as "extras" for the midday stew, and were likewise welcomed. Whilst in the Messines sector, the men of the 14th (in common with those of other units) enjoyed many meals of stew with turnips, the latter being gathered from the fields vacated by the retreating Germans.

When in the line, however, many difficulties had to be faced. It was essential that the troops should be fed with hot food, and ration parties had, therefore, to be employed to carry it from the cook-house to the trenches. Both tea and stew were made in similar containers—known as dixies. As a rule, two men could handle a dixie fairly comfortably—one at each handle. Another type of container was tried for stew (one that fitted over the back), but the unfortunate carrier generally had his tunic ruined by hot stew cascading over him. This type was only tried experimentally, and was soon withdrawn. Naturally, ration parties were often shelled (especially if they had to cross open country) and on many occasions front line troops waited in vain for their hot meals. It was often a mystery where the rations disappeared. Speaking generally, though, everything that was humanly possible was done to get hot food to the trenches, as it was recognised that an army fought as well as marched on its stomach.

Breakfast in the line was generally at 10 or 11 p.m., and hot stew (normally the midday meal) about 2 or 3 a.m. Most "diggers" partook of dry rations at midday, washed down with a drink from the water-bottle. "Tommy" cookers were a welcome innovation toward the latter part of the war, and were extensively used. They were provided by the Comforts Fund. This cooker consisted of two small tins, the bottom one containing congealed (this may not be the correct term) methylated spirit, the top tin serving as a tray to support the mess-tin. Tins of sweetened coffee and cocoa were also supplied in a semi-liquid form, ready for use. Passable rissoles have been made with grated "bully beef" and bread, over a "Tommy" cooker, and many an appetising hot drink have they been the means of providing in the trenches.

Orderly corporals were not appointed in the line, for there the platoon sergeants took charge when the rations arrived, and issued them direct. Dry rations were treated similarly. Wet and dry rations were sent up at night by the company Q.M. sergeant, who drew them in the rear from the battalion Q.M. sergeant. Company cooks' supplies (fresh meat, bacon, vegetables, etc.), were drawn direct by the cooks from the battalion Q.M. store, so that the orderly corporal never saw them till issued. The latter was responsible for every man in the company getting his proper share of rations. "McConochy's rations" and "pork and beans" (both tinned) were sometimes issued in lieu of bacon for breakfast, the former being probably the best ration on issue. It was certainly the most popular. It was an agreeably seasoned stew, and each tin contained sufficient for two men. Pork and beans, though not as good, were yet enjoyable, and always provided a delightful change.

# INDEX

Abbeville—page 311.
Abernethy, Pte. A.—38.
Abdel-Rahman Bair—54, 60, 62.
Accroche Wood—307.
A'Court, L/Cpl. A. J.—206, 212.
Adams, Major J.—7, 21, 72, 73, 74.
Adams, Pte. S.—246.
Aden—11.
Agar, Pte. W.—48, 87.
Aghyl Dere—55, 74.
Agincourt—256.
Albany—10.
Albert—133.
Alberta Camp—163.
Aldridge, Capt. N. C.—165, 179, 242, 245, 272, 273, 322, 325, 339, 347.
Alexander, Pte. C.—206.
Alexandria—11, 12, 15, 51, 80, 96.
Allan, L/Cpl. D. T.—64.
Allen, Sgt. A. E.—347.
Allonville—271, 274, 282, 284, 288, 292.
Almond, S/Sgt. B. V.—346.
Alston, Q.M.S. V.—26.
American Troops—303, 305, 312, 348.
Amiens—275.
Amor, Pte. W. R.—205, 211, 247.
Anderson, Cpl. H. A.—222, 223, 242, 248, 279, 347.
Anderson, A. R.—287.
Anderson, Capt. F.—120, 123, 143, 146, 153, 279, 312, 318.
Anderson, Sgt. H. R. W.—296, 298, 300.
Andrews, L/Cpl. J.—287.
Andrews, Sgt. R.—149.
Annear, Pte. P. D.—73.
Annear, Cpl.—353.
Angus, Pte. R.—45.
Ansett, Sgt. A. G.—156, 187.
Antill, Cpl. R. E.—226.
Anzac Day—95.
Appleton, Lieut.—130, 140, 149, 199, 269, 295, 321, 328.
Arles—105.
Armentieres—108, 172.
Armistice—46.
Armstrong, L/Cpl. H. J.—145.
Arras—188.
Arrell, Major W. L.—348.
Aspinall, L/Cpl. P.—277.
Atherton, Pte. H. O.—318.
Australian Imperial Force (A Tribute)—354.
A.I.F. First Member Buried in Great Britain—38.
Australian Physique—14.
Avignon—105.

## Index

Ayre, Sgt. A. J. K.—174, 242, 247.
Baby 700—36, 67.
Bailey, Sgt. G.—149.
Bailey, Sgt. J.—180.
Baillieul—130, 223, 259.
Bain, Lieut. L.—179.
Bain, Pte. L. W.—147.
Baker, Pte. H. W. A.—38.
Baker, L/Cpl. N.—73.
Baldock, Capt. N. C. W.—12, 21.
Ball, Lieut. L. E.—37.
Bamford, L/Cpl. J.—205.
Banyard, A/Sgt. F. J.—149, 300, 301.
Bapaume—134, 184.
Barker, Pte. F.—203.
Barratt, Sgt. T. L.—36.
Bauchop, Sgt. L. R.—344, 345, 346.
Bavincourt—265.
Bazen, L/Cpl. R. C.—36.
Beamond, Capt. W. R. M.—130, 143, 149, 283, 305.
Bear, Lieut. N. J.—89, 222, 223.
Beardsley, L/Cpl. A. A.—87.
Beck, Sgt. C. H. (48th Battalion)—139.
Belgian Battery Corner—249.
Bell, Sgt. W. R. M.—347.
Bernafray Wood—166.
Berry, Sgt. R. H.—64, 210.
Best, Pte. L.—287.
Beugnatre—185, 207.
Biaches—336.
Bickley, Pte. J. F.—43, 149.
Big Bill—341.
Binns, Pte. F. S.—45.
Birdwood, General Sir Wm.—16, 79, 123, 146, 162, 213, 215, 263, 266, 282, 312.
Bishop, Cpl. E. E.—296, 298, 321.
Black, Major P. (16th Battalion)—209, 210.
Blackburn, Sgt. D. W.—149, 195, 347.
Blainey, Capt. A. R.—46, 49, 75, 76, 88, 157, 170, 231, 235, 277, 301.
Blair, Sgt. J. C.—119, 238, 247.
Blamey, Sgt. R. S.—210.
Bland, Sgt. P. C.—230.
Blauen Molen—222.
Bloody Angle—26.
Boden, Pte. A. F.—64.
Bois Grenier—108, 112, 148.
Boland, Lieut. W. P.—203, 211, 214, 270, 272, 352.
Booker, Cpl. C. E.—318.
Booley, Lieut. S.—156, 310.
Booth, Lieut. N. G.—46.
Bott, L/Cpl. A.—182, 210.
Bowell, Pte. F. H. G.—203.
Bowen, Cpl.—23.
Boyes, Lieut. F. H.—91, 125, 157, 249.
**Boyes, Sgt. W. H.**—110, 127, 129, 327, 331, 352.
Boyle, Capt. H. N.—21, 30, 34, 37, 42, 45, 47, 51, 64, 91.
**Bradley, Pte. V.**—246, 248.

Bradley, Lieut. (16th Battalion)—191, 192.
Brand, Brig.-General C. H.—131, 196, 234.
Brennan, Cpl. P.—269, 287.
Brewer, L/Cpl. P. J.—64.
Bridges, Major-General W. T.—31, 40.
Broadmeadows Camp—3, 5, 9, 81, 83.
Brodal, L/Cpl. B.—123, 129.
Bronson, L/Sgt. M.—26, 168.
Brotchie, Sgt. J. A.—148, 240, 353.
Brown, Sgt. H. R.—277.
Brown, Pte. H. N.—63.
Brown, Pte. W. A.—38.
Bruford, Lieut. A. R.—296, 331, 346.
Brunt, Pte. W. H.—308.
Bullecourt, Battle of—188, 217.
Bullen, Sgt. G.—269, 272, 273.
Burial Parties—26.
Burnt Farm—109.
Burns, Pte. H.—185.
Burton, Cpl. R. H.—23.
Butterworth, Cpl. J.—23.
Caestre—165, 236, 249.
Cairo—12, 13.
Calway, Pte, F.—128.
Campbell, Pte. H.—145.
Campbell, Sgt.—306.
Campbell, Pte. J.—226.
Canadian Tunnelling Company—163.
Candas—130.
Canteen—148.
Carberry, Cpl. T.—206, 211.
Carroll, Pte. H. L.—139.
Cartledge, Pte. M.—205.
Casson, Pte. J. J.—203, 212.
Catterson, Sgt. R. H.—210.
Cerisy Spur—317, 321.
Chamberlain, Lieut. E. C.—346.
Cheyne, Sgt. J. B.—149.
China Wall—238.
Chippendale, Sgt. H. D.—64.
Chisholm, Cpl. C.—23.
Christian, Judge G. L. (Richmond, Va., U.S.A.)—88.
Chubb, Lieut. E. R.—214, 339.
Clarke, C. J.—149, 347.
Clarendon Hyde, Lieut. G.—209, 346.
Clark, Capt. G. H.—47, 74, 89, 94.
Clark, Sgt. H. B.—346.
Cleary, Lieut. E. A.—277, 325.
Clement, Pte. D.—45.
Clements, Cpl. H. C.—322, 342.
Clifford, Pte. T. Y. E.—229.
Clough, Pte. J.—251.
Cochrane, Cpl. S.—306, 310.
Cole, Capt. C. R. T.—95, 318.
Cole, Pte. H. D.—45.
Coleman, Pte. C. H.—24, 78.
Coleman, C.S.M. W.—253.

Cohen, Pte. W.—24.
Collins, W.O. F.—210.
Colwyn-Stevens, Pte. W. R.—226.
Combes, Capt. B.—5, 37, 38, 47.
Connors, Pte. T.—229, 246, 247.
Connelly, Capt. C. E.—12, 29, 73.
Conscription Vote—164.
Constantinople—16, 41, 53, 58, 79.
Cook, Pte. A. T.—25, 247.
Cooper, Capt. G.—40, 61, 73, 74, 90, 91.
Cooper, Pte. J.—246, 248.
Cope, Capt. J. L. (see 14th Battalion).
Courtney, Lieut.-Col. R. E.—3, 19, 48, 81, 90.
Courtney's Post—20, 27, 47, 48, 49, 82.
Couttie, Lieut. V. J. G.—47, 51, 72.
Cox, Lieut.-General Sir H. B.—53, 62, 94, 131, 151, 162, 171, 216.
Cox, Major A. R.—19, 27, 66, 91, 112, 132, 143, 152, 164, 214, 227, 248.
Cox, Major C. R. M.—15, 126, 152.
Cox, Pte. W. A.—157.
Cowan, Pte. R.—31.
Coward, L/Cpl.—210.
Crabbe, Lieut. K.—19, 26, 27, 42, 43, 52, 57, 69, 72.
Craig, L/Cpl. J.—296, 298.
Crapper, Sgt. C.—66, 85.
Crapper, Pte. C. A.—308, 346, 347.
Craven, Capt. J.—132, 186, 205, 268.
Crellin, Lieut. W. R.—322, 346.
Crete—101.
Cricket—313.
Croft, Sgt. H.—103, 119, 121, 172, 279.
Croker, L/Cpl. W.—327.
Crowther, Lieut.-Col. H. A.—264, 272, 284, 295, 325, 328, 343, 348.
Cubitt, L/Cpl. A.—64.
Curlewis, Lieut. K.—62, 63.
Currie, L/Cpl. A.—332.
Currie, Pte. H.—36.
Curry, Sgt. C.—252, 254, 313.
Curwen, Cpl. H. P.—347.
Curwen-Walker, Lieut. A. H.—36.
Dadson, Lieut. F. H.—27, 47, 72, 198, 210.
Dalitz, Sgt. A. C.—156, 210.
Dalitz, Sgt. F. W.—212.
Daours—292, 302.
Dare, Lieut.-Col. C. M. M.—3, 47, 53, 60, 62, 69, 74, 75, 90, 96, 112, 135, 155, 168, 352.
Davies, Lieut. G. F.—307.
Davies, Pte. A.—120.
Davis, Pte. E. J.—212.
Davis, Cpl. F.—247.
Davison, Cpl. E. R.—64.
Dawe, Pte. W.—281.
Dawes, Sgt. F. A.—149, 229, 310.
Day, Pte. W. A.—45.
Deacon, Pte. J. M.—211.
Dean, Lieut. A. R.—95, 104, 157, 173.
Dean, L/Cpl. P. H. S.—141, 144, 153.
De Arango, Lieut.—43, 118, 119, 157, 249.

Deconinck—221.
Decorations—
    On Peninsula—27, 90.
    Jacka's V.C.—42.
    In France—122, 149, 157, 211, 212, 223, 248, 255, 273, 301, 313, 346, 350, 351, Appendix B.
Delaney, Pte. A.—36.
Deler, Pte. H. J.—298, 299.
Delora, Pte. H.—287.
Denham, Pte. R. E.—253.
Denholm, Pte. C.—87.
Devereau, Pte. W.—127.
Dobbie, Lieut. H. S.—95, 137, 149, 172, 179.
Dobson, Driver R. L. S.—251.
Docwra, Pte. D. E.—156.
Dodemaide, Pte. A. R.—147, 149, 156.
Dods, Pte. C.—35.
Dolan, Driver P.—91.
Donaldson, Pte. D.—276.
Dowell, Pte. T. H.—63.
Downes, Pte. R. M.—129.
Downie, Pte. A.—248.
Doyle, L/Cpl. W. J.—23.
Drummond, Sgt. D.—149, 222, 223, 247, 331.
Duffield, Lieut. F.—62, 69, 72.
Duffy, Pte. B.—127.
Duke of Connaught's Inspection—223, 247.
Dunn, Pte. J. H.—287.
Dunworth, Capt. D. (15th Battalion)—138, 201, 202.
Durham, Sgt. C. J.—280.
Durrant, Lieut.-Col. J. M. A.—175, 179, 187, 248.
Durrant's Post—74, 78, 82.
Duntroon College Trainees—7.
Duxbury, Pte. E. P.—287.
Duxbury, Sgt. J. C.—222.
Earll, Pte. R. B.—24.
Ebbot, Lieut. L. H.—143, 144, 149, 346.
Edmonds, Lieut. E. J. L.—165, 179, 210.
Edmonstone, Sgt. B.—70, 128, 172.
Edmonstone, Sgt. W. L.—247, 347.
Ekenberg, Pte. C.—314.
Elliott, Sgt. J. E.—353.
Elmslie, Pte. A.—31.
English, Pte. G. C.—
Estaminets—181.
Evans, Pte. A.—287.
Feckner, Pte. C. E. F.—272, 277.
Feetam, Pte. H. J.—38.
Fegan, Cpl. H.—73.
Fergus, Sgt. W. H.—242, 248, 330.
Fethers, Major N. D.—92, 96, 168.
Field, Pte. J. W.—91.
Field, Sgt. W. V.—144.
Fielden, Pte. G. V.—308.

"Fighting Thirteenth" Quoted—187.
Finger, Pte. H.—178, 205.
Finlay, Pte. J. A.—139.
Fisher, Pte. L.—310.
Fisher, L/Cpl. L. J.—156.
Fisher, Pte. R.—353.
Fisher, Sgt. W. T.—143, 307, 310, Appendix G.
Fitzpatrick, Pte. H.—139.
Fitzpatrick, Pte. H. E.—318, 353.
Fitzpatrick, Pte. W. J.—327.
Flers—174.
Fletcher, Major W. M. A. (see 14th Battalion).
Fletcher, Sgt. W. H.—248, 295.
Floyd, Pte. D.—306, 310.
Football—263.
Fort Rompu—112.
Foster, L/Cpl. S. A.—296.
Fontaine-les-Boulans—234, 235.
Fourteenth Battalion—
    Aid Posts—205, 222, 246, 251, 253, 327.
    Band—9, 88.
    Bombers—52, 131, 145, 344.
    Casualties—31, 39, 45, 63, 90, 121, 128, 141, 148, 149, 153, 179, 210, 222, 227, 231, 347, 250, 251, 253, 270, 272, 276, 290, 299, 300.
    Chaplains—
        Cope, Capt. J. L.—79.
        Gillison, Capt. A.—5, 18, 19, 26, 38, 55, 71, 72, 82.
        Rolland, Lieut.-Col. F. W.—163, 182, 206, 246, 248, 309, 327.
    Colours—5.
    Colour Patches—14.
    Comforts Fund—354.
    Cooks—89, 145, 207, 226, 278.
    Education Scheme—183.
    Epitome of Events, 1914-1915—81, 82, 83.
    Epitome of Events, 1916—171, 172, 173.
    Epitome of Events, 1917—257, 258.
    Epitome of Events, 1918—349, 350.
    First Death—14.
    First Member K.I.A., Gallipoli—20.
    First Member K.I.A., France—109.
    Headquarters 3, 22, 41, 134, 152, 195, 201, 207, 222, 225, 244, 276, 305.
    Internal Organisation—353.
    Last Charge—344.
    Lewis Gunners—176, 204, 229.
    Mascot—24.
    Medical Officers—
        Fletcher, Major W. M. A.—168, 206, 222, 236.
        Loughran, Capt. H. G.—19, 31, 38, 48, 55, 59, 71, 72, 73, 75, 76, 86.
        Trumble, Capt. H.—235, 309, 321, 328.
        Winn, Capt. R. C.—78, 128, 147, 168.
    March Regimental—9, 88, 185.
    Marches, Route—6, 13, 81, 95.
    Machine Gun Section—29, 49, 55, 65, 79, 88.

Officers—7, 96, 97, 183, 184, 195, 228, 239.
Non-Commissioned Officers, Reputation of—98, 99, 100, 157.
Pioneers—69, 230.
Raids—Chapters 18, 19, 38.
Reinforcements

| | | | | | |
|---|---|---|---|---|---|
| 2nd | 19 | 9th | 95 | 13th | **95** |
| 3rd | 39 | 10th | 95 | 17th | **131** |
| 6th | 52 | 11th | 95 | 22nd | **214** |
| 7th | 76 | 12th | 95 | 23rd | **214** |
| 8th | 79 | | | | |

Signallers—58, 89, 205, 220, 246, 251.
Sports—4, 184, 227, 235.
Strength—53, 75, 76, 79, 83, 227, 259, 304, 337.
Stretcher-Bearers—19, 31, 79, 87, 147, 206, 246.
Unit Pride—48, 235, 261.
Fourth Brigade Machine Gun Company—62, 94, 115, 195, 240, 276, 312.

Foxcroft, Pte. H.—63.
Fraser, Pte. D. H.—87, 147.
Francis, Sgt. A. L.—129, 194.
Franklin, Cpl. J. R. H.—248.
French, Cpl. P. H.—91, 242, 248.
French Troops—280, 314.
Frost, Cpl. E. E.—149, 260, 276.
Fruges—256.
Fuhrmann, Major P. C. W.—15, 79, 132, 137, 140, 152, 218, 233.
Fulton, Pte. E.—110.
Fulton, Lieut. W. C.—214, 247, 320, 322.
Gaba Tepe—16, 18, 22.
Gapaard—221.
Garcia, Lieut. L.—214.
Garcia, Lieut. R. J.—90, 122, 163, 224, 249, 268, 272.
Garford, Pte. R.—147.
Garner, Lieut. V. G.—24, 220, 229, 238.
Garton, Lieut. S. J. J.—149, 214, 307, 346.
George, 2nd Lieut. C.—247.
Gibb, Pte. H. J.—352.
Gifford, L/Cpl. J. T.—205, 279.
Gill, Lieut. L. H.—214, 244, 247, 279.
Gill, Pte. W. A.—89, 149.
Gillison, Chaplain (see 14th Battalion).
Giles, Capt. C. L.—62, 75, 76.
Giroud, Pte. A. H. A.—206.
Goble, L/Cpl. W.—64.
Goddard, Cpl. H. C.—296, 329.
Godley, Major-General Sir A. J.—13, 19, 55, 76, 112, 130, 222.
Goode, Sgt. F. A.—156, 222, 223, 229.
Goodsell, Cpl. W.—331.
Goodwin, Cpl. W. W.—157, 186.
Gorman, Pte. F. G.—36.
Gough, General—191.
Gower, Lieut. O.—199, 210.
Graham, Pte. E. J.—156.

Graham, Capt. R. W.—73.
Grant, Sgt. L. L.—73.
Grant, Lieut. T. M.—328.
Gray, Pte. A.—145, 149.
Greengrass, Cpl. G. W.—64.
Greene, L/Cpl. P. E.—210.
Greenham, Pte. C. G.—24.
Grieves, L/Cpl. J.—215.
Griffith, Lieut. T. G.—214, 307, 341, 347.
Groom, Capt. W. E.—47, 51, 59, 63, 64.
Groves, Sgt. W. C.—211, 352.
Guest, Pte. E.—229.
Gubby, Pte. R. V.—205, 272.
Guppy, Sgt. L.—90, 211.
Hamel—295, 302.
Hamilton, General Sir I.—16, 53, 68, 79.
Hamilton, Sgt. D. J.—91.
Hamilton, P. D.—269.
Hamilton, Lieut. W. H.—5, 42, 44, 45, 82.
Hale, Pte. T.—229.
Hall, Lieut. V. E.—264, 268, 269, 272.
Hanby, Capt. J. G. T.—21, 23, 25.
Hangard Wood—276.
Hansen, Capt. S. M.—40, 47, 74, 75, 76, 132, 144, 152, 153, 155, 157, 166, 176, 177, 179, 180, 238, 257.
Haig, Field Marshal Sir D.—209.
Hardner, Driver B.—283.
Harding, Cpl. J. A.—31.
Harding, Cpl. W. J.—268, 296, 331.
Harding, Cpl. F. J.—91, 258, 272, 296.
Hare, C.S.M. R.—91, 277, 279.
Harris, Lieut. A. J.—87, 88, 128, 147, 157, 210.
Harris, Lieut. H. R.—37, 63.
Harris, Sgt. P.—180.
Harris, Capt. N. C.—62, 119, 120, 223, 318, 321, 328.
Harrison, Sgt. E.—248, 296, 298, 299.
Harrison, Sgt. G. F.—156, 229.
Harrison, Pte. M.—246, 251.
Hart, Cpl. J.—73.
Hartigan, Pte. W.—72.
Harvey, Lieut. A. T.—95, 113, 118.
Hassett, L/Cpl. H. J.—180.
Hastian, 2nd Lieut. A. E.—75.
Havis, Pte. H.—50, 91.
Hawkins, Lieut. D. H. L.—214, 346.
Hayes, Capt. P. J.—105, 153.
Hayes, Capt. R. E.—181, 199, 209.
Hebuterne—266, 267, 268.
Heliopolis—12, 15.
Hengest—344.
Hennessy, Pte. J. P.—63.
Henry, Capt. A.—12, 16, 51, 62, 164.
Henshall, Pte. S.—87, 147.
Hepburn, Sgt. A. M.—149.
Heron, Cpl. G. A.—329.
Hewitt, Cpl. F.—64.
Hibberd, Pte. E. W.—246.

Hill, Lieut. E. P.—69, 90, 214, 220.
Hill, Lieut. T. N. W.—63.
Hill 60—68, 82.
Hindenburg, Field Marshall—184.
Hindenburg Line—187, 189, 207.
Hislop, Pte. J.—36.
Hodge, Pte. W. J.—251.
Hodges, Pte. R. W.—147.
Hoggart, Capt. W. R.—12, 23, 82.
Holland, Pte. C. S.—156. Appendix G.
Holmes, Major-General W.—171, 226.
Holmes, Pte. H. R.—26.
Honeychurch, Pte. H.—31.
Hook, Pte.—14, 89.
Hope, Cpl. T. F.—64.
Hore, Sgt. A. A.—205, 212.
Horne, Cpl. W. J.—128.
Horne, Cpl. J. G.—332.
Horrocks, Sgt. E. J.—247.
Hospital Ships—19, 52.
Howard, Cpl. W. D.—43, 211.
Hudson, Cpl. J. B.—25, 87.
Hughes, Pte. T. V.—147, 149, 180.
Hume, Cpl. P. G.—180.
Hunter, Cpl. F.—247.
Huse, Lieut. G.—87, 121, 250, 312.
Hutton, Sgt. A. C.—91, 125, 143, 242, 247.
Hutton, Cpl.—244, 248.
Hutton, Capt. C. R.—35, 51, 64.
Hyde, Pte. L.—31.
Hyett, Lieut. F. G.—244, 247.
Imbros Island—50, 51, 78.
"Incinerator Kate"—182.
Indian Units—52, 55, 60.
Inflamingerie Farm—109.
Ingamells, Pte. N.—308.
Inglis, Pte. J.—308.
Isbel, Pte. W.—4, 91, 210.
Jack, Sgt. A. L.—73.
Jacka, Capt. A.—39, 42, 43, 44, 82, 90, 95, 97, 109, 137, 139, 140, 141, 142, 149, 168, 172, 186, 188, 191, 192, 196, 208, 210, 211, 220, 221, 223, 224, 227, 228, 242, 243, 244, 245, 248, 260, 281, 349.
Jacka, Capt. W.—147, 305.
Jackson, Lieut. H. B.—346.
Jackson, Cpl. W. J.—156, 157, 174.
Jenkins, Pte. N.—329.
Jenkins, Cpl. J. T.—205.
Jeffers, 2nd Lieut. R. A.—269, 325.
Jeffries, L/Cpl. C.—260, 276.
Jennings, Pte. R.—226.
Johnson, Cpl. J. F.—31.
Johnson, Lieut. J. H. (The I.O.)—214, 222, 227, 245, 255, 261, 269, 272, 273, 277, 283.
Johnson, L/Sgt. M. R.—272.
Johnston, Lieut.-Col. C. M.—261, 264.
Johnstone, Sgt.-Major A. A.—325, 345, 346.

Johnston, Cpl. F.—247.
Johnston, L/Cpl. A.—71.
Jones, Capt. R. W.—26, 39, 66, 90, 91, 95, 97, 110, 163, 181, 186, 220, 221, 223, 224, 227, 230, 262, 264.
Jones, Sgt. R.—24, 210, Appendix G.
Jones, Cpl. L. R.—296, 347, Appendix G.
Jones, L/Cpl. B. A. T.—314.
Jordan, Lieut. J. W.—325, 346.
Julian, Lieut. (52nd Battalion)—206.
Julian, Lieut. R. D.—95, 113, 119, 172.

Kaiser, Wilhelm—1, 2, 348.
Kearney, Pte. D.—241.
Kent, Lieut. N.—204, 210.
Kent, L/Cpl. H.—288.
Kerr, Pte. A. H.—251.
Kerr, Cpl. C. E.—63.
Kewley, Sgt. F. H.—36.
Kilby, L/Cpl. A. C.—296.
King, Lieut. A.—214.
Kirby, Pte. A. W.—251.
King, Lieut. A.—214.
Kirby, Pte. A. W.—251.
Kitchener, Earl—78, 103.
Kneale, L/Cpl. E. G.—64.
Kohlmann, Sgt. M.—250.
Kohls, Pte. E. L.—154, 157, 180.
Koja Chemen Tepe—53, 60, 82.

La Clytte—163, 259, 261.
La Houssoie—110.
Laker, L/Cpl. P. B.—64.
Laloe, Lieut.—47, 51.
Lalor, Cpl. V. W.—248, 327, 347.
Lamprell, Cpl. H. J.—203, 211, 224, 321, 328.
Laredo, Pte. D.—91.
Larkin, L/Cpl. D.—323.
Larsen, Pte. J. T.—37.
Larter, Lieut. F. T.—252, 277.
Laver, Capt. W. G.—76.
Lawson, Pte. R. C.—38.
Lee, Pte. D.—31.
Lee, Pte. H.—147.
Leeson, Pte. W. H. C.—38.
Le Brun, L/Cpl. J. B.—210.
Le Fevre, Lieut. L. J.—229.
Lemnos Island—15, 76, 80, 81.
Les Laumes—105.
Le Verguier—336, 339.
Lewis, Cpl. H. H.—296, 314.
Lewis, Cpl. J.—39, 66, 91.
Lewis, Sgt. H.—141, 149, Appendix G.
Lewis, Pte. P. W.—210, Appendix G.
Lewis, Sgt. M. M.—247.
Lowe, Pte. F.—246.
Loughead, 2nd Lieut. T. H.—144.
Loughran, Capt. (see 14th Battalion).
Lovekin, Pte. G. K.—211.

Luke, Pte. E. L. (19th Battalion)—129.
Luscombe, Capt. L. H.—51, 62, 64.
Lyons—105.
Lyons, Pte. J. H. (Bugler)—27.
Lyon, Lieut. W. J. G.—210.

Macdermid, Capt. D. R.—26, 47, 57, 62, 69, 75, 76, 132, 164, 208, 219, 223.
Macoboy, Cpl. M. F.—23.
Macon—105.
Mackay, Capt. J.—95, 104, 125, 127, 163, 339.
Mahoney, Sgt. J. A.—27, 39.
Malcomson, Pte. W. F.—145.
Malta—101.
Mametz—174, 213.
Manders, Pte. P.—87, 185.
Manie, Lieut. W. E.—249.
Margolin, Major E. L.—30, 219, 233.
Markham, L/Cpl. S. A.—147, 149, 206, 211, 223, Appendix G.
Markham, Pte. A.—210, 223, Appendix G.
Marmo, Pte. J.—322.
Marseilles—96, 103, 104.
Masterton, Pte. J.—63.
Mathers, Pte. J. (15th Battalion)—63.
Matthews, Lieut. J. H.—47.
Mattinson, L/Cpl. J.—180.
Mattson, Driver E. A.—251, 283.
Mayer, Sgt. C. H.—199, 211.
Mayne, Pte. W.—154.
Mediterranean Sea—101.
Menin Road—238.
Meredith, Pte. J. C.—147.
Messines—218.
Mew, Pte. H. A.—38, Appendix G.
Michie, L/Cpl. G.—38, 87, 91.
Miles, Pte. W.—325.
Miller, Pte. F. G.—139.
Millis, Lieut. J.—130, 149.
Miller, Pte. A.—246, 248.
Mitchell, Capt. J. A.—165, 199, 211, 245.
Mitchell, L/Cpl. J. H. (19th Battalion)—129.
Mills, Driver J. C.—287.
Moascar—92, 171.
Moir, Cpl. J. H.—210.
Monash, Lieut.-General Sir John—3, 6, 52, 61, 112, 130, 131, 187, 248, 282, 302, 312, 315, 330.
Moore, Pte. C.—128, 352, Appendix G.
Moore, Pte. I.—128, 352, Appendix G.
Monument Wood—276, 280.
Morcourt—322, 325, 326.
Morehouse, Lieut. L. J.—51, 64, 94.
Moriarty, Cpl. J. J.—247, 321, 328.
Morrison, Pte. D. L.—278.
Morrison, Pte. H.—327.
Mortimer, Sgt. D.—137, 138, 140, 149.
Mow, Pte. W. V.—45.
Mudros—16, 18, 80, 81.

Muir, L/Cpl. P.—178, 180.
Mullen, Pte. H. J.—38.
Mullett, Lieut. L. H.—181, 200.
Munro, General Sir Chas.—78.
Murray, Sgt. G. A. H.—272.
Murray, Lieut.-Col. H. (13th Battalion)—178, 179, 201, 202, 209, 210, 223.
Murphy, Sgt. W. P.—20.
Myers, C.S.M. J. J.—91, 124, 154, 156, 157, 224, 279, 283.

McAllan, Sgt. O. G.—230, 260.
McAllister, Sgt. W.—64.
McCallum, Lieut. P.—176, 199, 211.
McCormick, Pte. J.—308.
McDonald, Sgt. A.—182, 244.
McDonald, Sgt. R. N. S.—210.
McDonald, Pte. W. G. W.—318.
McDermott, Pte. S.—24, Appendix G.
McDermott, Sgt. C.—24, Appendix G.
McGill, Capt. (19th Battalion)—109.
McGrice, Pte. S. A.—251.
McKenry, Cpl. R. L.—244.
McKenzie, Lieut. N.—125, 185, 192.
McKenzie, Pte. N.—273.
McKinley, Lieut. H. R.—141, 196.
McKissack, L/Cpl. W. M.—141.
McKissock, Pte. A.—147.
McLaren, Cpl. H.—31.
McLellan, Sgt.—91, 207.
McMaster, Pte. E. J.—25.
McMahon, Pte. E. W.—273.
McNamee, Pte. K. N.—157, 210.
McNab, Pte. J.—38.
McNally, Pte. J.—44.
McPherson, Lieut. J. F.—156, 251.
McQueen, Lieut. G. W.—69, 186, 210.
McRae, Sgt. J.—149, 210.
McSharry, Lieut.-Col. T/P. (15th Battalion)—187, 315.
McQuiggan, Lieut. A. J.—199, 211.

Nash, Pte. R.—283.
Neal, L/Sgt. R. R.—149.
Neale, Lieut. J. A.—64.
Neuve Eglise—223, 225, 227, 229, 232, 264.
New Zealand Engineers—26.
New Zealand Forces—68, 72, 85, 219, 225, 270.
Neyland, Sgt. N.—63.
Night March—55, 57.
Noreuil—193, 207.
Notting, Pte. F.—327.
Nowotna, Pte.—89.
Nurses—76, 159, 161.
Oakley, Cpl. A.—229.
O'Bree, L/Cpl. W. H.—38.
O'Brien, Sgt. M.—89, 90.
O'Brien, Sgt. J. T.—110, 156.
O'Bryan, L/Cpl. J. T.—72.
O'Connor, Pte. P.—63.

O'Donnell, Lieut M.—200.
O'Dowd, Pte. P. T.—268, 272.
O'Dowd, L/Cpl. W.—298.
O'Hara, Theodore—Cited Appendix A.
O'Keefe, Pte. T.—147.
Oram, Sgt. W.—125, 156, 157.
**Orpwood, Pte. G. W.—89.**
Orr, Capt. R. W.—76, 132, 142, 197.
Orr, Cpl. W. J.—156, 210.
Osborne, Pte. G.—156.
O'Shea, Pte. W.—128, 353.
Outposts—259.

Paris—106.
Parman, Pte. H. L.—246, 251, 253, 277.
Pascoe, Pte. L. H.—91.
Patterson, Pte. W. G., "Tug"—185, 211.
Patten, Pte.—206.
Pearce, Sgt. J.—123, 145, 149.
Pearce, Sgt. W. H.—110, 128, 145, 172.
Peck, Lieut.-Col. J. H.—168, 170, 173, 175, 181, 183, 187, 192, 194, 202, 205, 207, 208, 214, 216, 218, 248.
Pellett, Sgt. C. E.—91, 205.
Peronne—335.
Perry, Cpl. B. H.—211.
Perry, Cpl. H.—177, 180.
Phillips, Pte. R.—87.
Picketts' Charge at Gettysburg—208.
Pigott, Pte. P.—163.
Pitts, Pte. "Baldy"—89.
Platt, Sgt. C.—273, 347.
Ploegsteert—225, 226.
Plumer, General—216, 235.
Poliness, Pte. F. E.—43.
Pope, Colonel H.—21, 30, 37, 60, 62.
Porter, Pte. W.—91, 206, 212, 254.
Poste Internationale—280.
Pozieres—134.
Presentiments of Death—278.
Primrose, Cpl. W. T.—250.
Prince of Wales—95.
Pring, Pte. A.—109.
Pringle, R.S.M. A.—250, 252.
Pulford, Sgt. F.—276.

Queant—191.
Querrieu—311.
Quinn, Major H. (15th Battalion)—48.
Quinn, Lieut. G.—153.
Quinn, Pte. P.—295.
Quinn's Post—21, 22, 40, 46, 82.
Quirk, Lieut. J.—38.
Quirke, Sgt. W. M.—64.

Rackstraw, Pte. A. R.—35.
Radnell, Pte. G. D.—156, 242, 248, 286.
Rankine, Lieut.-Col. R.—12, 21, 27, 41, 53, 61, 90.
Rations—Appendix J.
**Rattan, Pte. W.—272.**

Read, Pte. W. A.—251.
Reid, Sir George—38.
Reid, Cpl. J.—251.
Rennie, Pte. A. J.—25.
Reserve Gully—49, 50, 51, 54, 66, 82.
Reynolds, Cpl. H. R.—286, 287, 353.
Reynolds, Sgt. J. B.—24.
Ribemont—165, 168, 170, 174, 181, 184, 213, 215.
Richardson, Capt. D. L. K.—75, 76, 164, 174.
Richmond, Sgt. H. G.—89, 246, 250, 251, 252.
Richthofen, Baron von—186.
Ridge, Sgt. L.—210.
Reincourt—196, 200, 201, 202, 203.
Ritchie, L/Cpl. G.—180.
Robinson, Pte. A. E.—127.
Roderick, Lieut. J. B.—95, 113.
Rogers, Lieut. J. S.—95, 125.
Rolland, Lieut.-Col. F. W. (see 14th Battalion).
Rollins, Pte. M.—220.
Ronald, Pte. J. C.—156.
Rose, Sgt. T. A.—125, 142.
Rose, Capt. J. M. (N.Z. Force)—62.
Ross, Sgt. C. F.—119, 120, 210.
Ross, Sgt. G. A.—157, 164.
Ross, L/Cpl. F. S.—229.
Rowse, Pte. W.—206, 212, 224, 247.
Roxburgh, Lieut. R. O.—321, 331.
Rule, Lieut. E. J.—109, 153, 156, 157, 214, 229, 277, 341, 343, 346, 347.
Rutherford, Cpl. W. H.—272, 308.
Rutland, Lieut. J. B.—36, 88.
Ryan, Sgt. G.—141.
Ryan, Cpl. F. P.—121.

Sailly Laurette—327, 330.
Sanders, Lieut. R. E.—47, 51, 163.
Sari Bair—52, 53.
Saunders, Pte. E. C.—248.
Sausage Valley—135.
Sayers, L/Cpl. R.—45.
Scanlon, Lieut. R.—110, 129, 157, 227, 276,. 283.
Scarf, Cpl. J.—247.
Schmit, Pte. J. L.—347.
Schultz, Sgt. A. E.—210.
Schutz, Lieut. H. J.—214, 272, 273, 321, 328.
Scott, Sgt. H. R.—277, 283, 347.
Seaborne, Pte. R.—206.
Serjeant, Sgt. C. C.—346.
Sheldon, Pte. F. L. (Bugler)—35.
Shelton, Sgt. L.—288.
Showers, Pte. B.—109.
Shrapnel Gully—20, 49.
Smith, Cpl. A. S.—180, 296, 329.
Smith, Capt. B. T.—95.
Smith, Cpl. C.—84, 156, 295, 296, 323, 324.
Smith, Lieut.-Col. W. J.—233, 260.
Smith, Cpl. F.—141.
Smith, Lieut. Q. R.—39.

## The History of the 14th Battalion. 415

Smith, Cpl. W. A.—156.
Snipers (Enemy)—26, 35, 40, 47, 48, 59, 82, 130, 221.
Snuggs, L/Cpl. J.—206.
Spearing, Cpl. R.—242, 248, 272.
Stach, Sgt. H. F.—187.
Stanley, C.S.M. R.—149, 310.
Stanton, Capt. F. B.—181, 191.
Steel, Lieut.-Col. T. H.—12, 21, 29, 40.
Steele's Post—20, 29.
Stephens, Pte. A. A.—127.
Stephens, L/Cpl. R. A.—210.
Stewart, Pte. H. G.—299.
Stewart, Sgt. S.—152, 154, 156, 157, 173.
Stewart, Pte. J.—210.
Stokan, Sgt. T. C.—73.
Stone, Lieut. A. P.—346.
Stormy Trench—175.
Straughair, Pte. J. T.—37.
Stringer, Pte. W. H.—63.
Subalterns, Carnage Among—28, 233.
"Suwanne River" (March), see 14th Battalion Regimental March.
Sutcliffe, Sgt. A.—15, 89.
Swift, Sgt. A. T.—71, 72.
Symonds, Lieut. F. C. W.—79, 92.

Tanks—208, 302, 318.
Taylor, L/Cpl. E.—64.
Taylor, Pte. J. G.—332.
Taylor, Pte. C. C. J.—139.
Tel-el-Kebir—92, 94, 95, 172.
Templeton, Lieut. T. H.—238.
Thomas, Lieut. W. C.—346.
Thomas, Sgt. S.—210.
Thompson, Major D.—233.
Thompson, Lieut. C.—203, 211, 248, 252.
Thompson, Lieut. H. W.—109, 144, 296, 297, 323, 328.
Thompson, L/Cpl. J. W.—23.
Thompson, Pte. J.—246, 248.
Thompson, Lieut. L. B.—147.
Thompson, Lieut. S. B.—147, 149, 163, 200.
Thorn, Pte. F. A.—186.
"Times History of the War" Cited—86.
Transports :—
    Abassia—76.
    Ceramic—10.
    California—15.
    Hazel—80.
    Hereford—96.
    Itonus—16
    Osmanieh—78.
    Seang Choon—15, 17, 19, 40, 81.
    Transylvania—96, 172.
    Ulysses—9, 10, 11, 81.
Trench Feet—167.
Trench Mortars—196, 199.
Trewheela, Lieut. G.—214, 331.
Trevan, Pte. J.—26.
Trickey, L/Cpl. R. L.—156.
"Triumph" Warship (Torpedoed)—47.
Trumble, Capt. H. (see 14th Battalion).
Turner, Sgt. J:—141.
Twose, Sgt. E.—64.

Tyler, Pte. J.—45.
Urie, Sgt. A.—110, 127, 156, 199, 210.
Vaire Wood—292, 295.
Veel, Pte. G. C.—70, 91, 203.
Vernall, Sgt. H.—64.
Verswyvelt, Pte. J. W.—26, 72.
Vincent, Pte. A.—130.
Villers Bretonneux—275, 278, 292.
Waddell, L/Sgt. A. J. D.—329.
Wadsworth, Major W. R.—95, 96, 104, 202, 203, 209, 211, 228, 269, 272, 305, 339, 343, 347.
Walker, Pte. A.—45.
Walker, Lieut. M. R.—95.
Walklate, Capt. H. V.—252, 254.
Wallach, Capt. N. (13th Battalion)—281.
Wanliss, Capt. H. B.—95, 113, 119, 122, 163, 170, 186, 231, 242, 247, 248 (see also "the Adjutant"—192, 193, 205, 208, 222, 227).
Warburton, S/Major, F. H.—65.
Warloy—131, 151.
Warren, Lieut. R.—35, 51, 59, 62, 63, 64.
Watson, Cpl. D.—238, 247.
Watson, Pte. W.—206, 212, 246, 248.
Watts, Pte. W. E.—251.
Webb, Cpl. L.—327.
Webber, Cpl. A.—251.
Wheeler, Cpl. J. G.—156.
White, Lieut.-General, C. B. B.—282.
Whitelaw, Cpl. A. P.—246.
Whitteron, Cpl. E. R.—64.
Wilkinson, Pte. E.—246, 248, 251.
Williams, Sgt. W. E.—242, 247.
Williams, Pte. W. J. C.—139.
Willison, Pte. G. A.—142, 149.
Williamson, Capt. A.—95, 125, 166, 176, 178, 200, 210, 238.
Wilson, Lieut. G. F.—123, 242, 247.
Wilson, Capt. N.—95, 176, 186, 305, 318, 322, 323.
Wilson, Pte. W. J.—308.
Wilson, L/Cpl. W.—327.
Winn, Capt. R. C. (see 14th Battalion).
Withers, Pte. H. D. E.—251.
"Withdrawn," Poem—83, 84.
Wood, Lieut. R.—245, 296, 297, 298, 306, 310.
Wounded :—
    Heroism of—19, 86.      At Gallipoli—91.
    Care of—158 to 161.      At Battle of Amiens—333, 334.
Wright, Capt. F. H.—12, 19, 23, 27.
Wright, L/Cpl. F. L.—110, 129, 142, 149, 211.
Wurtemburg Division—315.
Wynne, Pte. N. T.—50, 90, 149.
Young, Major H. N.—3, 75, 76.
Young, L/Cpl. R. E.—23.
Young, Pte. T.—186.
Ypres—252, 263.
"Zealandia," Battleship—80.

www.ingramcontent.com/pod-product-compliance
Lightning Source LLC
Chambersburg PA
CBHW022006300426
44117CB00005B/61